"Readers will find clear guides to basic information. . . . Editorial introductions to the various sections clarify and summarise the material. Each chapter ends with extensive lists of references and further reading. A glossary of linguistic terms, reflection 'the terms as used by the authors,' is included. As with all the Blackwell Companions, the presentation of this substantial volume is of the highest standard."
Reference Reviews

"Anyone with even a passing interest in the history of the language, whether an old-fashioned description of Middle English morphology or an au courant discussion of global Englishes, will be glad to have [this] *Companion* on the shelf."
Times Literary Supplement

This comprehensive picture of English and its history is a must for scholars. Highly recommended.
E. L. Battistella, Southern Oregon University

Blackwell Companions to Literature and Culture

This series offers comprehensive, newly written surveys of key periods and movements and certain major authors, in English literary culture and history. Extensive volumes provide new perspectives and positions on contexts and on canonical and post-canonical texts, orientating the beginning student in new fields of study and providing the experienced undergraduate and new graduate with current and new directions, as pioneered and developed by leading scholars in the field.

A COMPANION TO

THE *H*ISTORY
OF THE *E*NGLISH
*L*ANGUAGE

EDITED BY

HARUKO MOMMA AND MICHAEL MATTO

WILEY-BLACKWELL
A John Wiley & Sons, Ltd., Publication

This paperback edition first published 2011
© 2011 Blackwell Publishing Ltd

Edition history: Blackwell Publishing Ltd (hardback, 2008)

Blackwell Publishing was acquired by John Wiley & Sons in February 2007. Blackwell's publishing program has been merged with Wiley's global Scientific, Technical, and Medical business to form Wiley-Blackwell.

Registered Office
John Wiley & Sons Ltd, The Atrium, Southern Gate, Chichester, West Sussex, PO19 8SQ, United Kingdom

Editorial Offices
350 Main Street, Malden, MA 02148-5020, USA

9600 Garsington Road, Oxford, OX4 2DQ, UK

The Atrium, Southern Gate, Chichester, West Sussex, PO19 8SQ, UK

For details of our global editorial offices, for customer services, and for information about how to apply for permission to reuse the copyright material in this book please see our website at www.wiley.com/wiley-blackwell.

The right of Haruko Momma and Michael Matto to be identified as the editors of the editorial material in this work has been asserted in accordance with the UK Copyright, Designs and Patents Act 1988.

Wiley also publishes its books in a variety of electronic formats. Some content that appears in print may not be available in electronic books.

Designations used by companies to distinguish their products are often claimed as trademarks. All brand names and product names used in this book are trade names, service marks, trademarks or registered trademarks of their respective owners. The publisher is not associated with any product or vendor mentioned in this book. This publication is designed to provide accurate and authoritative information in regard to the subject matter covered. It is sold on the understanding that the publisher is not engaged in rendering professional services. If professional advice or other expert assistance is required, the services of a competent professional should be sought.

Library of Congress Cataloging-in-Publication Data
A companion to the history of the English language / edited by Haruko Momma and Michael Matto.
   p. cm. — (Blackwell companions to literature and culture)
     Includes bibliographical references and index.
     Hardback ISBN 978-1-4051-2992-3 (alk. paper); Paperback ISBN 978-0-470-65793-5
1. English language — History.   I. Momma, H.   II. Matto, Michael.
PE1072.C56 2008
420.9 — dc22
A catalogue record for this book is available from the British Library.

This book is published in the following electronic formats: ePDFs 9781444302868; Wiley Online Library 9781444302851; ePub 9781444395655

Set in 11 on 13pt Garamond 3 by Toppan Best-set Premedia Limited
Printed and bound in Singapore by Fabulous Printers Pte Ltd

1   2011

Contents

List of Figures

Notes on Contributors

Richard W. Bailey is the Fred Newton Scott Collegiate Professor of English Language and Literature at the University of Michigan. He is the author of many books, including *Nineteenth-Century English* (1996), and the editor of *Milestones in the History of English in America: Papers by Allen Walker Read* (2002).

Philip Baldi is Professor of Linguistics and Classics at Penn State University. He is the author of *The Foundations of Latin* (2002) and editor of *Linguistic Change and Reconstruction Methodology* (1990) and has also published numerous articles on various subjects, including Indo-European linguistics and morphology.

Robert Bayley is Professor of Linguistics at the University of California, Davis. He is the author of *Sociolinguistic Variation in American Sign Language* (with C. Lucas and C. Valli) (2001) and *Language as Cultural Practice: Mexicanos en el Norte* (with S. R. Schecter) (2002), and editor of *Language Socialization in Bilingual and Multilingual Societies* (with S. R. Schecter) (2003).

Allan Bell is Professor of Language and Communication and Director of the Centre for Communication Research at Auckland University of Technology. He has led a dual career combining academic research with journalism and communications consultancy, and authored several books on language and media discourse, including *The Language of News Media* (1991). He is co-founder and co-editor of the *Journal of Sociolinguistics*.

Mary Blockley is Professor of English at the University of Texas at Austin. Her publications include "Cædmon's Conjunction: *Cædmon's Hymm* 7a Revisited," *Speculum* (1998) and *Aspects of Old English Poetic Syntax: Where Clauses Begin* (2001). She is preparing the third edition of the late C. M. Millward's *A Biography of the English Language*.

Charlotte Brewer is Fellow of Hertford College, Oxford, and Lecturer at Oxford University. Her publications include *Editing Piers Plowman: The Evolution of the Text* (1996) and *The Oxford English Dictionary: Treasure House of the Language* (2007).

Thomas Cable is Professor of English and Jane Weinert Blumberg Chair at the University of Texas at Austin. He is the author of *The English Alliterative Tradition* (1991), *The Union of Words and Music in Medieval Poetry* (with R. A. Baltzer and J. I. Wimsatt), and *A History of the English Language*, 5th edn. (with A. C. Baugh) (2002).

Deborah Cameron is Rupert Murdoch Professor of Language and Communication at Oxford University. She is the author of *On Language and Sexual Politics* (2006) and *Verbal Hygiene* (1995), and the editor of *The Feminist Critique of Language: A Reader* (1990, 1998).

Tony Crowley is Hartley Burr Alexander Chair in the Humanities at Scripps College and Visiting Professor in the Institue of Irish Studies at the University of Liverpool. He is the author of *Language in History: Theories and Texts* (1996), *Standard English and the Politics of Language* (2003), and *Wars of Words: The Politics of Language in Ireland, 1537–2004* (2005).

Anne Curzan is Associate Professor of English at the University of Michigan. Her publications include *Gender Shifts in the History of English* (2003), *Studies in the History of the English Language II: Unfolding Conversations* (editor, with K. Emmons) (2004), and *How English Works: A Linguistic Introduction* (with M. Adams) (2006).

Terence Patrick Dolan is a Professor of English in the School of English and Drama at University College Dublin. He is the compiler and editor of the *Dictionary of Hiberno-English: The Irish Use of English* (1998, 2004, repr. 2006) and Director of the UCD hiberno-english.com website.

Daniel Donoghue is John P. Marquand Professor of English at Harvard University. He is the author of *Old English Literature: A Short Introduction* (2004) and *Style in Old English Poetry* (1987) and the editor of *Beowulf: A Verse Translation* (trans. Seamus Heaney) (2002), and *The Year's Work in Old English Studies* (2000–present).

John Edwards is Professor of Psychology at St. Francis Xavier University. His books include *Language and Disadvantage* (1989), *Multilingualism* (1994), and *Language in Canada* (editor) (1998). He is also editor of *Journal of Multilingual and Multicultural Development* and the book series *Multilingual Matters*.

Eugene Chen Eoyang is Chair Professor of Humanities and Head of the English Department at Lingnan University and Professor Emeritus of Comparative Literature

and of East Asian Languages and Cultures at Indiana University. He is the author of *The Transparent Eye: Translation, Chinese Literature, and Comparative Poetics* (1993), *The Coat of Many Colors* (1995), *"Borrowed Plumage": Polemical Essays on Translation* (2003), and *Two-Way Mirrors: Cross-Cultural Studies in Glocalization* (in press).

Olga Fischer is Professor of English Linguistics and Linguistics of the Germanic Languages at the University of Amsterdam. She is the author of *The Syntax of Early English* (with A. van Kemenade, W. Koopman, and W. van der Wurff) (2000) and *Morphosyntactic Change: Functional and Formal Perspectives* (in press).

Robert D. Fulk is Class of 1964 Chancellors' Professor of English at Indiana University. His publications include *A History of Old English Meter* (1992), *A History of Old English Literature* (with C. M. Cain and R. S. Anderson) (2002), and the forthcoming revised edition of Frederick Klaeber's *Beowulf and the Fight at Finnsburg* (with R. E. Bjork and J. D. Niles).

Dirk Geeraerts is Professor of Linguistics at the University of Leuven. His publications include *The Structure of Lexical Variation* (1994), *Diachronic Prototype Semantics: A Contribution to Historical Lexicology* (1997), and *Words and Other Wonders: Papers on Lexical and Semantic Topics* (2006). He founded the journal *Cognitive Linguistics* and is co-editor (with Hubert Cuyckens) of the *Handbook of Cognitive Linguistics* (forthcoming).

Br. Andrew Gonzalez FSC (d. 2006) was President Emeritus and Professor of Languages and Literature at De La Salle University, Manila and Secretary of the Department of Education, Culture and Sports of the Philippines. His publications include *Language and Nationalism: The Philippine Experience Thus Far* (1980).

Mechthild Gretsch is Professor of English Philology at Universität Göttingen. She is the author of *The Intellectual Foundations of the English Benedictine Reform* (1999, 2006) and *Aelfric and the Cult of Saints in Late Anglo-Saxon England* (2005).

Reinhard R. K. Hartmann is Honorary University Fellow at the University of Exeter and Honorary Professor of Lexicography at the University of Birmingham. He is the author of *Dictionary of Lexicography* (with G. James) (1998) and *Teaching and Researching Lexicography* (2001) and the editor of *Lexicography: Critical Concepts*, 3 vols. (2003).

David L. Hoover is Professor of English at New York University. He is the author of *A New Theory of Old English Meter* (1985), *Language and Style in The Inheritors* (1999), and *Approaches to Corpus Stylistics: The Corpus, the Computer, and the Study of Literature* (with J. Culpeper and B. Louw) (2007).

Jonathan Hope is Reader in the Department of English Studies at the University of Strathclyde. His publications include *The Authorship of Shakespeare's Plays: A Socio-Linguistic Study* (1994) and *Shakespeare's Grammar* (2003).

Geoffrey Hughes was an Honorary Research Associate at Harvard University, is Emeritus Professor of the History of the English Language at the University of the Witwatersrand (Johannesburg), and Honorary Research Associate at the University of Cape Town. His recent publications include *A History of English Words* (2000) and *Swearing: An Encyclopedia* (2006).

Werner Hüllen is Professor Emeritus of English Linguistics at the University of Duisburg-Essen. He is the author of *English Dictionaries, 800–1700: The Topical Tradition* (1999, 2006), *Werner Hüllen: Collected Papers on the History of Linguistic Ideas* (ed. M. M. Isermann) (2002), and *A History of Roget's Thesaurus: Origins, Development and Design* (2004, 2006).

Gavin Jones is Associate Professor of English at Stanford University. He is the author of *Strange Talk: The Politics of Dialect Literature in Gilded Age America* (1999) and has published articles on George W. Cable, Theodore Dreiser, W. E. B. DuBois, Sylvester Judd, Paule Marshall, and Herman Melville.

Braj B. Kachru is Center for Advanced Study Professor of Linguistics, and Jubilee Professor of Liberal Arts and Sciences Emeritus, at the University of Illinois at Urbana-Champaign. His recent publications include *Asian Englishes: Beyond the Cannon* (2005), *The Handbook of World Englishes* (with Y. Kachru and C. L. Nelson) (2006), and *World Englishes: Critical Concepts in Linguistics* (with K. Bolton) (2006).

Tabish Khair is Associate Professor of English at the University of Aarhus. He is the author of *Babu Fictions: Alienation in Contemporary Indian English Novels* (2001), and co-editor of *Unhinging Hinglish: The Languages and Politics of Fiction from the Indian Subcontinent* (2001) and *Other Routes: 1500 Years of African and Asian Travel Writing* (2005). Khair is also a novelist and poet; his most recent novel is *Filming: A Love Story* (2007).

John N. King is Distinguished University Professor and also Humanities Distinguished Professor of English and of Religious Studies at the Ohio State University. His publications include *Voices of the English Reformation: A Sourcebook* (2004) and *Foxe's Book of Martyrs and Early Modern Print Culture* (2006). He is editor of *Reformation* and co-editor of *Literature and History*.

Lucia Kornexl is Professor of English Historical Linguistics and Medieval English Literature at the University of Rostock. Her publications include a commented edition of the *Regularis Concordia* and its Old English gloss (1994). She is the editor of *Book-*

marks from the Past: Studies in Early English Language and Literature in Honour of Helmut Gneuss (with U. Lenker) (2003) and co-editor of *Anglia*.

Robin Tolmach Lakoff is Professor of Linguistics at the University of California, Berkeley. Her publications include *Talking Power: The Politics of Language in Our Lives* (1990), *The Language War* (2000), *Language and Woman's Place: Texts and Commentaries, Revised and Expanded Edition* (editor, with M. Bucholtz) (2004), and *Broadening the Horizon of Linguistic Politeness* (with I. Sachiko) (2005).

Seth Lerer is Professor of English and Comparative Literature and Avalon Professor in the Humanities at Stanford University. His most recent books include *Error and the Academic Self: The Scholarly Imagination, Medieval to Modern* (2002) and *Inventing English: A Portable History of the Language* (2007).

Marion Löffler is a Research Fellow at the Centre for Advanced Welsh and Celtic Studies at the University of Wales. Her publications include *Englisch und Kymrisch in Wales. Geschichte der Sprachsituation und Sprachpolitik* (1997) and *A Book of Mad Celts: John Wickens and the Celtic Congress of Caernarfon 1904* (2000), as well as numerous articles on Welsh language, history, and sociolinguistics.

J. Derrick McClure is Senior Lecturer in English at the University of Aberdeen. He is the author of *Scots and Its Literature* (1995), *Why Scots Matters* (1988, revd. 1997), *Language, Poetry and Nationhood* (2000), and *Doric: The Dialect of North-East Scotland* (2002), and the editor of the annual journal *Scottish Language*.

Carey McIntosh is Professor Emeritus of English at Hofstra University. He is the author of *The Choice of Life: Samuel Johnson and the World of Fiction* (1973), *Common and Courtly Language: The Stylistics of Social Class in Eighteenth-Century England* (1986), and *The Evolution of English Prose, 1700–1800: Style, Politeness, and Print Culture* (1998).

Adam N. McKeown is Assistant Professor of English at Adelphi University. He has published articles on visual rhetoric in early modern England, and is the co-creator of Sterling's *The Young Reader's Shakespeare* series. His book *English Mercuries: Elizabethan Soldier Poets* is forthcoming.

Michael Matto is Assistant Professor of English and Director of Writing Programs at Adelphi University. He has published essays on Old English literature and HEL, and is guest-editor (with Haruko Momma) of a special issue on HEL pedagogy and research for *Studies in Medieval and Renaissance Teaching* (2007). He is currently editing (with Greg Delanty) a collection of new translations of Old English poems (forthcoming in 2009).

Alamin M. Mazrui is Professor of Africana Studies at Rutgers University. He is the author of *The Power of Babel: Language and Governance in the African Experience* (with A. A. Mazrui) (1998), *Debating the African Condition: Ali Mazrui and His Critics* (with W. Mutunga) (2004), and *English in Africa After the Cold War* (2004).

Laurent Milesi is Senior Lecturer in the School of English, Communication and Philosophy at Cardiff University. He is the editor of *James Joyce and the Difference of Language* (2003) and translator of Jaques Derrida's *H. C. for Life, That Is to Say . . .* (with S. Herbrechter) (2006).

Robert McColl Millar is Lecturer in Linguistics at the University of Aberdeen. He is the author of *System Collapse, System Rebirth: The Demonstrative Systems of English 900–1350 and the Birth of the Definite Article* (2000) and *Language, Nation and Power* (2005).

Donka Minkova is Professor of English at the University of California, Los Angeles. She is most recently the author of *English Words: History and Structure* (with R. Stockwell) (2001), *Alliteration and Sound Change in Early English* (2003), and co-editor of *Studies in the History of the English Language: A Millennial Perspective* (with R. Stockwell) (2002).

Haruko Momma is Associate Professor of English at New York University. She is the author of *The Composition of Old English Poetry* (1997) and *From Philology to English Studies: Language and Culture in the Nineteenth Century* (forthcoming in 2009), as well as essays on Anglo-Saxon literature, historical linguistics, and philology. She guest-edited with Michael Matto a special issue on HEL pedagogy and research for *Studies in Medieval and Renaissance Teaching* (2007).

Salikoko S. Mufwene is Frank J. McLoraine Distinguished Service Professor in the Department of Linguistics at the University of Chicago. His publications include *The Evolution of Languages* (2001), *Créoles, écologie sociale, evolution linguistique* (2005), and *Polymorphous Linguistics: Jim McCawley's Legacy* (with E. Francis and R. S. Wheeler) (2005). He is also the series editor of the *Cambridge Approaches to Language Contact*.

Lynda Mugglestone is Professor of History of English at the University of Oxford. She is the author of *Lexicography and the OED: Pioneers in the Untrodden Forest* (2002), *Talking Proper: The Rise of Accent as Social Symbol* (2003), and *Lost for Words: The Hidden History of the Oxford English Dictionary* (2005), and the editor of *The Oxford History of English* (2006).

Terttu Nevalainen is Professor of English at the University of Helsinki and Director of the Research Unit for Variation, Contacts and Change in English (VARIENG),

National Centre of Excellence (Finland). Her publications include *Historical Sociolinguistics: Language Change in Tudor and Stuart England* (with H. Raumolin-Brunberg) (2003) and *An Introduction to Early Modern English* (2006).

Pam Peters is Professor and Deputy Head of the Department of Linguistics at Macquarie University and Director of the Dictionary Research Center. Her publications include *The Cambridge Australian English Style Guide* (1995) and *The Cambridge Guide to English Usage* (2004).

John F. Plummer is Professor of English at Vanderbilt University. He is the author of *Vox Feminae: Studies in Medieval Woman's Songs* (1981) and the editor of *The Summoner's Tale: A Variorum Edition of the Works of Geoffrey Chaucer*, Vol. 2 (1995) and *"Seyd In Forme and Reverence": Essays on Chaucer and Chaucerians In Memory of Emerson Brown, Jr.* (with T. L. Burton) (2005).

Noel Polk is Professor of English at Mississippi State University. He is the author of *Eudora Welty: A Bibliography of Her Work* (1993), *Children of the Dark House: Text and Context in Faulkner* (1996), and *Outside the Southern Myth* (1997). He is the editor of the *Mississippi Quarterly* and of "The Corrected Text" editions of William Faulkner's novels.

Mary Poovey is Professor of English and founder of the Institute for the History of the Production of Knowledge at New York University. Her publications include *Making a Social Body: British Cultural Formation, 1830–1864* (1995), *A History of the Modern Fact: Problems of Knowledge in the Sciences of Wealth and Society* (1998), and *The Financial System in Nineteenth-Century Britain* (2003).

Fred C. Robinson is Douglas Tracy Smith Emeritus Professor of English at Yale University. He is the author of *The Tomb of Beowulf and other Essays* (1993), *The Editing of Old English* (1994), and *A Guide to Old English*, 7th edn. (with B. Mitchell) (2006), and editor of *Beowulf: An Edition with Relevant Shorter Texts* (with B. Mitchell and L. Webster) (1998).

Geoffrey Russom is Professor of English at Brown University. He is the author of *Old English Meter and Linguistic Theory* (1987) and *Beowulf and Old Germanic Metre* (1998). He has also published several articles on the linguistic history of English, the multicultural backgrounds of *Beowulf*, and preliterate verse traditions.

David Simpson is Professor of English at the University of California, Davis. He is author of numerous books on Romanticism, literary theory, and cultural studies, including *The Politics of American English, 1776–1850* (1986), *Situatedness; or Why we Keep Saying Where We're Coming From* (2002), and *9/11: The Culture of Commemoration* (2006).

Jeremy J. Smith is Professor of English Philology and Head of the Department of English Language at Glasgow University. His publications include *An Historical Study of English: Function, Form and Change* (1996), *Essentials of Early English* (1999), and *An Introduction to Middle English* (with S. Horobin) (2002).

Philippa K. Smith is Projects Manager at the Centre for Communication Research at Auckland University of Technology. She has presented papers at international conferences on identity construction in broadcasting and is writing a book chapter on discourse research methodologies. She is a co-author of "Television Violence in New Zealand: A Study of Programming and Policy in International Context" (2003).

Mary Soliday is Associate Professor of English at the City College of New York. She is the author of *The Politics of Remediation: Institutional and Student Needs in Higher Education* (2002) and many articles on teaching college composition and rhetoric.

Kamal Sridhar is Associate Professor of Linguistics at the State University of New York, Stony Brook. Her publications include *English in Indian Bilingualism* (1989), as well as several articles on the English language in India, and languages in the Indian Diaspora in the US.

Robert P. Stockwell is Professor Emeritus of Linguistics at the University of California, Los Angeles. His recent publications include *English Words: History and Structure* (with D. Minkova) (2001). He is the co-editor of *Studies in the History of the English Language: A Millennial Perspective* (with D. Minkova) (2002).

Justine Tally is Professor of American Literature at the Universidad de La Laguna. She is author of *Paradise Reconsidered: Toni Morrison's (Hi)stories and Truths* (1999) and *The Story of Jazz: Toni Morrison's Dialogic Imagination*, and editor of *The Cambridge Companion to Toni Morrison* (forthcoming).

Thorlac Turville-Petre is Professor of Medieval English Literature at the University of Nottingham. His publications include *A Book of Middle English* (2004), *The Piers Plowman Electronic Archive, British Library Add. MS 35287 (M)* (2005), and *Reading Middle English Literature* (2007).

Donald Winford is Professor of Linguistics at the Ohio State University. He is the author of *Predication in Caribbean English Creole* (Creole Language Library Vol. 10) (1993) and *An Introduction to Contact Linguistics* (2002), as well as several recent articles on creoles and vernaculars.

Walt Wolfram is William C. Friday Distinguished Professor of English at North Carolina State University. His publications include *Dialect Change and Maintenance on the Outer Banks* (1999), *Language Variation in the School and Community* (1999), *The*

Development of African American English (with E. Thomas) (2002), *American English: Dialects and Variation*, 2nd edn. (2006), and *Dialects in Schools and Communities* (2007).

Mary B. Zeigler is Associate Professor of English Language and Linguistics at Georgia State University. Her publications include "Theorizing the Postcoloniality of African American English" (2002), "'Fixin(g) to': A Grammaticalized Form in Southern American English" (2002), and "Don' Be Callin Me Outta My Name: Language Variation and Linguistic Difference" (2004).

Acknowledgments

The history of the English language (HEL) is arguably the most complex subject being taught in English programs today. HEL was among the first courses to be offered at the college level when English became a discipline in the mid- to late nineteenth century. In its 150-year history, HEL has developed its methodology by adapting new material from the rapidly growing fields of linguistics and English studies, while simultaneously drawing inspiration from such allied disciplines as sociology, psychology, anthropology, and history. The history of HEL studies also coincides with the time during which English increased its influence and became one of the most widely used languages in the world. Because of the complexity of the subject and the vastness of its material, the editing of this volume took us to many shores, both known and unknown, where we were so fortunate as to meet many people who gave us support and inspiration. At Blackwell we owe our thanks to Emma Bennett, Hannah Morrell, Rosemary Bird, Karen Wilson, Jenny Phillips, and Astrid Wind for their warm support, patience, and professionalism. We would also like to thank Andrew McNeillie for suggesting the project at its beginning stage and Dan Donoghue for making our involvement possible. We would like to express our sense of gratitude to Carlos J. Manuel, who gave us linguistic advice on the Glossary and the Notes on Phonetic Symbols and Orthography, and to our copy-editor Benedick Turner, whose steadiness and quiet encouragement helped us remain anchored in the last stretch of editing. We are also indebted to friends and colleagues who gave us suggestions and encouragement at various stages: Mark Atherton, Catherine A. M. Clarke, Heide Estes, Kathleen Fitzpatrick, Jennifer Fleischner, Elaine Freedgood, Ernest Gilman, John Guillory, Gayle Insler, John Maynard, Chris Mayo, and Martha Rust. Our special thanks go to Fred C. Robinson for his generosity, and to Adam McKeown for his remarkable selflessness as a friend and colleague. To Lahney Preston-Matto, who was there from the very beginning and helped make this collaboration possible, we can only continue to say thank you.

The production of this volume was aided by the generous support of the Stein Fund from the Department of English, New York University, and a grant from the Dean of the College of Arts and Sciences at Adelphi University.

The editors and publisher gratefully acknowledge the permission granted to reproduce the copyright material in this book. We thank Oxford University Press for allowing us to use (with slight modification) "Prologue: 1776" from David Simpson's *The Politics of American English, 1776–1850* (Oxford University Press [1986]: pp. 19–28, 261) as our chapter 25. The University of Mississippi graciously gave permission to reprint parts of Noel Polk's *Children of the Dark House* (1996) in our chapter 47. Sage Publications Ltd generously allowed us to incorporate parts of Eugene Eoyang's "Teaching English as Culture: Paradigm Shifts in Postcolonial Discourse" (originally published in *Diogenes* Vol. 50, No. 2 [2003]: pp. 3–16) in our chapter 53. All other copyright materials (tables, maps, and other images) are identified where used. Every effort has been made to trace copyright holders and to obtain their permission for the use of copyright material. The publisher apologizes for any attribution errors or omissions and would be grateful if notified of any corrections that should be incorporated in future reprints or editions of this book.

Finally, we would like to dedicate this volume to Seizo Kasai and the late Julian Boyd, our undergraduate teachers through whose guidance we were introduced to the world of HEL and developed our love of language, history, and English.

Note on Phonetic Symbols and Orthography

Though the study of the history of the English language does not require an extensive linguistic background, it is helpful to know some typographic conventions of linguistic analysis and some letters and abbreviations no longer found in current orthography.

Phonetic Transcription

Brackets

Readers will note three kind of brackets placed around letters and other symbols in these essays: angle brackets <t>, slashes /t/, and square brackets [t].

<t>   angle brackets indicate *graphemes*: how a sound is represented in written form.

/t/   slashes indicate *phonemes*: the smallest meaningfully distinct sound within a language.

[t], [tʰ]   square brackets indicate *phonetic transcription*: the exact description of a spoken sound.

While phonemics and phonetics are often virtually identical in practice, very precise phonetic transcription offers more phonological detail. For example, the phoneme /t/ in *top* and *stop* is spelled with the grapheme <t> and for most speakers represents essentially the same sound, but the <t> in *top* is aspirated (i.e., accompanied by a puff of breath) and so signified by the superscript ʰ in phonetic transcription [tʰ], while the <t> in *stop* is not aspirated [t].

Phonetic alphabet

The desire among linguists for a systematic method for transcribing the spoken sounds of languages was realized with the creation of the International Phonetic Alphabet (IPA) in 1888 by the International Phonetic Association. Designed to represent the

discrete sounds of all the world's languages within one set of symbols, the IPA allows linguists to transcribe spoken sounds consistently.

The IPA provides symbols for far more sounds than any individual language uses, so the symbols are not always intuitive for speakers of a given language. Variations on the IPA have therefore been developed, often for use in dictionaries, but also for scholarly use. One set of such variants, though not codified by any official organization, is known informally as the Americanist Phonetic Alphabet (APA), with symbols based primarily on English spelling. Also, differences in transcription systems sometimes reflect differing underlying phonetic theories. For instance, the English sounds represented by the letters <y> and <w> in the words *yet* and *wet* might be categorized as kinds of consonants (as IPA does) or as glides or semi-vowels (as APA generally does).

The editors of this volume have decided to allow each contributor his or her choice of transcription system, thus symbols from both the IPA and the APA appear in this book. This results in some small inconsistencies across essays using different systems. To clarify for readers, we offer the following charts to outline the correspondences.

Consonants

The chart below contains all the consonant sounds discussed in the book, most of which are standard in English pronunciations throughout the world. Some (/φ, ß, x, ɤ, χ/) were important in the earlier history of the language, but are no longer in wide use. Two symbols in one cell represent variants from APA (left) and IPA (right) as used in this book.

		LABIAL		DENTAL			PALATO-VELAR			GLOTTAL
		Labial	Labio-dental	Dental	Alveolar	Alveo-palatal	Palatal	Velar	Uvular	
Stops (Plosives)	voiceless	p			t			k		
	voiced	b			d			g		
Fricatives	voiceless	φ	f	θ	s	š/ʃ	ç	x	χ	h
	voiced	ß	v	ð	z	ž/ʒ		ɤ		
Affricates	voiceless					č/tʃ				
	voiced					ǰ/dʒ				
Nasals		m			n			ŋ		
Approximants (Liquids)	rhotic				r					
	lateral				l					
Approximants (Glides, Semi-Vowels)	voiced						y/j			
	voiceless labialized							hw/ʍ		
	voiced labialized							w		

Superscript symbols

ʰ   aspiration: indicates that the sound is accompanied by a puff of breath.
ʷ   labialized: indicates that the sound is accompanied by a rounding of the lips.

Compare the /k/ aspirated in *kit* [kʰɪt], unaspirated in *skit* [skɪt], and labialized in *quit* [kʷɪt].

Consonant sounds of modern English illustrated

/p/	pit	/f/	fan	/š/, /ʃ/	sure	/m/	mine	/y/, /j/	yet
/b/	bit	/v/	van	/ž/, /ʒ/	azure	/n/	nine	/hw/, /ʍ/	whet
/t/	tip	/θ/	thigh	/č/, /tʃ/	char	/ŋ/	sing	/w/	wet
/d/	dip	/ð/	thy	/ǰ/, /dʒ/	jar	/r/	rat		
/k/	cot	/s/	sue	/ç/	huge	/l/	let		
/g/	got	/z/	zoo	/h/	hot				

The following fricative consonant sounds are not generally found in modern American or British RP pronunciation, but are important to the history of English.

/φ/   voiceless like /f/, but with lips together as if pronouncing /p/
/ß/   voiced like /v/, but with lips together as if pronouncing /b/
/x/   unvoiced like /ç/ but slightly further back, as if pronouncing /g/
/χ/   slightly further back than /x/, but not so far as /h/
/ɣ/   like /x/, but voiced

Vowels

The various schemas and symbols for representing vowel systems are difficult to reconcile with one another. While most vowel schemas attempt to reproduce the biological manner of articulation, they employ different terminologies. For instance, IPA describes the openness of the mouth (with "close – mid – open,") while APA instead indicates the level of the tongue (with "high – mid – low").

Like the consonant chart, the schematic below represents only the sounds discussed in this book. One should imagine the graph represents a mouth facing left, and the symbols mark places of articulation. Three of the sounds are given two symbols, which represent transcription variants from APA (left) and IPA (right): ü/y, ö/ʏ, and ö/ø. Note that the vowel phoneme /y/ (from IPA) is different from the consonant or glide phoneme /y/ (from APA), though they use the same symbol. Symbols to the left and right of bullet points represent unrounded and rounded variants, respectively (rounded sounds are pronounced with the lips pulled into a circle and slightly protruding).

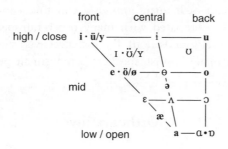

Long and short vowels

: indicates a long vowel, which is held longer than its short counterpart, but is otherwise articulated in the same place. Compare the long vowel of *sea* [si:] with the short vowel of *seat* [sit]. Length can also be indicated by a doubling of the phonetic symbol: /sii/ versus /sit/.

Vowel sounds of modern English

Examples are from standard American pronunciation.

/i/	bee	/ə/	bud	/u/	boo
/ɪ/	bid	/ʌ/	bug	/ʊ/	book
/e/	bade			/o/	boat
/ɛ/	bed			/ɔ/	bought
/æ/	bad			/ɑ/	body

The following vowel sounds are not generally distinguished in modern American or British Received Pronunciation, but are important to the history of vowels in English.

/ü/, /y/	like /i/, but rounded (like the French *du*)
/ö/, /ʏ/	like /ɪ/, but rounded
/ö/, /ø/	like /e/, but rounded
/ɵ/	like /ə/, but slightly higher
/ɨ/	like /ɵ/, but slightly higher (e.g., the unstressed first syllable of *begin*)
/a/	like /æ/, but slightly lower
/ɒ/	like /ɑ/, but rounded

Diphthongs

Many of the vowels of English are pronounced as a movement from one vowel to another; these are called diphthongs. The three most commonly pronounced diphthongs in English can be heard in the standard American pronunciations of *boy* /bɔɪ/,

buy /baɪ/ and *bough* /baʊ/; each unambiguously contains a movement between two vowel sounds. However, compared with many other European languages, modern English has few pure vowel sounds at all. For instance, even the /e/ of *bade* has a slight glide from /e/ to /ɪ/ for many English speakers, a movement perhaps more noticeable in the word *bane* or *bay*.

Orthography

Handwriting and typographic conventions change over time and vary among languages. Some of the essays in this collection make use of unfamiliar orthography when quoting from period sources or languages other than English. The following notes may be of use:

<3> is called *yogh*, and is related orthographically to <g>. Yogh was used in the Middle English period to represent a variety of related velar sounds, including /y/ and /x/.

<7> is the so-called "Tironian *et*" used in medieval manuscripts as an abbreviation for *and*, much as modern printers use <&>.

<þ> is called *thorn* and was used to represent either /θ/ or /ð/ in Old and Middle English. It was virtually interchangeable with <ð>.

<ð> is called *eth* and was used to represent either /θ/ or /ð/ in Old and Middle English. The grapheme <ð> thus does not always carry the same sound as the voiced fricative /ð/. It was virtually interchangeable with <þ>.

<v> and <u> were used either interchangeably or in the reverse of modern convention in medieval and early modern English. Often, <v> is used at the beginning of a word, <u> in the middle. In other texts, <v> might regularly represent the vowel, and <u> the consonant.

A Timeline for HEL

The following timeline will help readers contextualize the historical events discussed in this volume. While this list emphasizes topics covered by the contributors (as noted), it also includes other important events.

>1000 BCE	Indo-European languages spread throughout Europe and southern Asia, some already attested in writing for hundreds of years. (Baldi)
ca. 1000–1 BCE	Gradual sound shifts (Grimm's Law) take place in Germanic languages. (Fulk)
55–54 BCE	Julius Caesar invades Britain.
43 CE	Romans under Claudius conquer Britain; the "Roman Britain" period begins.
ca. 50–100	Scandinavian Runic inscriptions are produced, which remain the oldest attestations of a Germanic language. (Baldi)
ca. 98	Roman historian Cornelius Tacitus writes *Germania*. (Fulk)
ca. 350	Bishop Wulfila translates the Bible into Gothic, an East Germanic language. (Baldi)
410	Roman troops withdraw from Britain as Visigoths sack Rome; the "Roman Britain" period ends.
449	According to tradition, Anglo-Saxons (Angles, Saxons, Jutes) begin invasion and settlement of Britain, bringing their West Germanic dialects to the island.
597	Pope Gregory sends Augustine to Kent where he converts King Æthelberht and 10,000 other Anglo-Saxons to Christianity. (Donoghue)
793–ca. 900	Vikings (Danes, Norwegians, Swedes) raid England periodically and establish settlements.
878	King Alfred's victory over Guthrum's Danish army at Edington paves the way for the creation of the Kingdom of the Anglo-Saxons. (Gretsch; Donoghue)
886	King Alfred and Guthrum sign a treaty establishing the "Danelaw" north and east of London, heavily settled by the Norse-speaking vikings. (Donoghue)
890s	King Alfred translates Pope Gregory's *Regula pastoralis* into English. (Gretsch)

ca. 900	Bede's *Ecclesiastical History* is translated from Latin into Old English. (Donoghue)
ca. 975–1025	The four great manuscripts containing Old English poetry (Exeter Book, Junius Manuscript, Vercelli Book, and *Beowulf* Manuscript) are compiled, though many of the texts they contain were likely composed over the previous 300 years.
993–5	Aelfric composes his Latin–Old English *Glossary*. (Hüllen)
1066	William the Conqueror leads the Norman conquest of England, solidifying French as the language of the nobility. (Turville-Petre)
1171	Henry II leads the Cambro-Norman invasion of Ireland, bringing French and English speakers to the island. (Dolan)
1204	King John of England loses Normandy to France. (Turville-Petre)
ca. 1245	Walter of Bibbesworth compiles his *Tretiz de Langage* to improve the French of English-speaking landowners. (Hüllen; Turville-Petre)
1282	Wales is conquered by King Edward I of England. (Löffler)
1348–50	The Black Plague kills about one-third of the English population.
1362	Statute of Pleading requires English be spoken in law courts. (Plummer)
1366	Statutes of Kilkenny outlaw (among other Irish customs) speaking Irish by Englishmen in Ireland. (Dolan)
1370–1400	Chaucer writes his major works. (Plummer)
1380s	John Wycliffe and his followers illegally translate the Latin Vulgate Bible into English. (Nevalainen)
1380–1450	Chancery standard written English is developed. (Lerer)
ca. 1450	Johannes Guttenburg establishes the printing press in Germany.
1476	William Caxton sets up the first printing press in England. (Nevalainen; King)
1492	Christopher Columbus explores the Caribbean and Central America.
1497	Italian navigator John Cabot explores Newfoundland.
1500–1650	Great Vowel Shift takes place. (Lerer; Stockwell & Minkova)
1525	William Tyndale prints an English translation of the New Testament. (King; Nevalainen)
1534	The first complete English translation of the Bible from the original Greek and Hebrew is produced. (Nevalainen)
1536 and 1543	Acts of Union (Laws in Wales Acts) annex Wales to England. (Löffler)

1542	Crown of Ireland Act makes the English king also the Irish king.
1558–1603	Queen Elizabeth I reigns.
ca. 1575–1600	English becomes an important trade language in West Africa. (Mazrui)
1580s–1612	Shakespeare composes his plays. (McKeown)
1583–1607	British attempt unsuccessfully to establish colonies in America.
1588	The Bible is translated into Welsh. (Löffler)
1589	George Puttenham publishes his *Art of English Poesy* (King; Matto)
1600	British East India Company receives its charter, facilitating economic expansion into India. (Sridhar)
1600s	Atlantic slave trade begins, bringing Africans to America. (Zeigler)
1603	Union of the Crowns: James VI of Scotland becomes James I of England and Scotland, accelerating the Anglicization of Scots-English. (Nevalainen)
1604	Robert Cawdrey compiles *A Table Alphabeticall*, the first monolingual English dictionary (Brewer; Nevalainen; Crowley)
1607	The Virginia Company of London successfully establishes a colony in America at Jamestown, Virginia.
1610	British establish fishing outposts in Newfoundland.
1611	The King James Bible is published. (Nevalainen)
1620	Pilgrims establish a colony at Plymouth Rock.
1623–ca. 1660	British establish colonies throughout Caribbean.
1642–51	English Civil Wars are ongoing. (McIntosh)
1660	The Restoration: Charles II returns to the throne. (Nevalainen)
1663	The Royal Society is founded. (McIntosh; Matto)
1689	British establish the three administrative districts of Bengal, Bombay (now Mumbai), and Madras (now Chennai) on the Indian subcontinent. (Sridhar)
1694	French publish a national dictionary. (Brewer)
1695	The Licensing Act expires, giving anyone the freedom to publish without government permission. (McIntosh)
1707	Acts of Union unite governments of England and Scotland, creating the Kingdom of Great Britain.
1712	Jonathan Swift writes his "Proposal for Correcting, Improving and Ascertaining the English Tongue." (Matto & Momma; McIntosh; Bailey)
1755	Samuel Johnson's *Dictionary of the English Language* is published. (Brewer)
	French-speaking Acadians are expelled from Canada by British, settle in Louisiana and are called Cajuns.

1773	British establish a Governor Generalship in India. (Sridhar)
1776	Thomas Jefferson drafts American Declaration of Independence. (Simpson)
1780s	British begin to settle in Australia. (Peters)
1783	Treaty of Paris recognizes an independent United States of America; Noah Webster's "blue-back" spelling book is published. (Brewer)
1786	William Jones suggests a common root for Sanskrit, Greek, and Latin, promoting comparative linguistics and Indo-European studies. (McIntosh)
1787	English speakers of African origin are repatriated to Africa in Freetown, Sierra Leone. (Mazrui)
1789–99	The French Revolution takes place. (Poovey)
1795	Lindley Murray's *English Grammar* is published. (Curzan)
1800	Act of Union unites governments of Ireland and Great Britain, creating the Kingdom of Great Britain and Ireland and requiring that Irish politicians speak English in British government. (Dolan)
1803	The Louisiana Purchase allows US to expand westward.
1811–18	Jane Austen's novels are published. (Poovey)
1819	The British government passes the Six Acts, aimed to suppress the publication of radical newspapers. (Poovey)
1820	Freed English-speaking slaves repatriated from America to the newly created West African nation of Liberia. (Mazrui)
1828	Noah Webster's *Dictionary of American English* is published. (Brewer; Simpson)
1831	A system of Primary School Education is introduced in Ireland, with English as the medium of instruction. (Dolan)
1835	Lord Macaulay's Minute initiates the introduction of English language education into South Asia. (Sridhar)
1836	The phrase "standard English" first appears in a philological sketch on the history of the language in the *Quarterly Review*. (Crowley)
1837–1901	Queen Victoria reigns.
1840s	British begin to settle in New Zealand. (Peters)
1845–9	Many monoglot Irish speakers die as a result of the Great Famine in Ireland. (Dolan)
1852	*Roget's Thesaurus* is first published. (Hüllen)
1858	Act for the Better Government of India results in the British governing India directly. (Sridhar)
1859	*Proposal for the Publication of a New English Dictionary* initiates work on what will be the *Oxford English Dictionary*. (Crowley)

1873	Harvard University introduces the first American college program in English composition for native speakers. (Soliday, Matto)
1898	Americans take over control of the Philippines from Spain, beginning America's colonial period. (Gonzalez)
1914–39	James Joyce's major works are published. (Milesi)
1922	Ratification of the Anglo-Irish Treaty recognizes an independent Irish Free State, which will become the Republic of Ireland.
1925	The Phelps-Stokes Commission recommends teaching both English and native languages in Africa. (Mazrui)
1926–62	William Faulkner's major works are published. (Polk)
1928	*Oxford English Dictionary* is completed. (Brewer)
1946	The Philippines achieve independence from the United States.
1947	India achieves independence from Britain; Pakistan splits from India. (Sridhar)
1953	English made a compulsory subject in national examinations in elementary schools throughout Anglophone Africa. (Mazrui)
1957–68	Most of Britain's African colonies achieve independence.
1967	The Official Languages Act makes English and Hindi India's two official languages (Sridhar)
	Tanzania launches a "Swahilization" program. (Mazrui)
1970–	Toni Morrison's major works are published. (Tally)
1975–	Salman Rushdie's major works are published. (Khair)
1979	Lawsuit (*Martin Luther King Jr Elementary School Children vs. Ann Arbor School District Board*) sets precedent for requiring teachers to study AAVE. (Ziegler)
	Urdu replaces English as the language of instruction in schools in Pakistan. (Sridhar)
1991	Helsinki corpus of English words from the Old English period through 1720 is completed. (Curzan)
1993	Welsh Language Act makes Welsh an official language in Wales alongside English. (Löffler)
1996–7	The "Ebonics" debates begin in Oakland, California. (Zeigler; Jones)
1998	The Good Friday Agreement grants "parity of esteem" to the Irish language and to Ulster Scots (Ullans) in Northern Ireland. (Dolan)

Part I
Introduction

1

History, English, Language: Studying HEL Today

Michael Matto and Haruko Momma

This *Companion to the History of the English Language* represents a somewhat unusual entry in the Blackwell Companions to Literature and Culture series, for this is not fundamentally a book about literature. We nevertheless expect our edition will complement the study of English-based literature and culture in a productive way, especially given the tendency since the middle of the last century for students of English studies to focus on criticism of modern literature, contemporary theory, and cultural phenomena. Our aim is to offer those working with literary and cultural material a fuller perspective on language, one that enhances their interests in the light of the history of the English language (HEL) as it has been researched and studied for more than a century. To this end, the current volume reflects contemporary concerns with colonialism and post-colonialism, race and gender, imperialism and globalization, and Anglophone cultures and literatures, but approaches these contemporary issues from a historical perspective with special attention paid to the role played by language. In this introduction we will contextualize HEL studies in today's world so that we may create a framework within which to read the 58 essays that follow.

In 1712, Jonathan Swift, the satirist and author of *Gulliver's Travels*, wrote his "Proposal for Correcting, Improving, and Ascertaining the English Tongue," in which he entreated the Earl of Oxford to establish a national "Society" to arbitrate and limit changes in the English language. In his proposal, Swift condemned change as the bane of any language, insisting that linguistic change is "infallibly for the worse" and arguing that "it is better a Language should not be wholly perfect, than it should be perpetually changing" (Swift 1907: 15). Swift's anxiety over linguistic instability and his longing to rescue his language from decline and corruption ironically came after a thousand years of radical change to the language of the Anglo-Saxons had produced the English he recognized as his own. We, like Swift, commonly perceive our own language to have reached the pinnacle of its development, and we often resist change even if we are aware of the evolutionary history that led to its current state. But as evolutionary biologist Stephen Jay Gould reminded us, we often imagine the

evolutionary process to be a teleological development towards some perfected end when in fact evolution is by definition an ongoing process whose perpetual state is change. HEL as a subject is the study of an evolutionary process in Gould's strict sense: it is not the story of the "perfection" of the language, but rather of its ongoing metamorphosis within changing environments. At any moment the language represents at once the culmination of past changes and the starting place for future evolution.

The environmental factors that cause change in language are also themselves affected by language in a kind of feedback loop; HEL as it is currently studied therefore concerns itself with politics, economics, culture, technology, religion – any area of human experience in which language plays a role. In next chapter, Thomas Cable traces the "history of the history of the English language," so we will not attempt here what he has already so expertly accomplished. But to underscore one point, we would emphasize that the subject of HEL now engages the environmental situatedness of language more deeply than ever before. As Cable makes clear, this was not always so: the history of HEL moves gradually from the study of language alone to the study of language in culture in general. The present collection reflects HEL's new, broader scope without abandoning its focus on language. It may therefore be useful to reconsider the three fundamental concepts that define HEL: English, Language and History.

English: Nation and Tongue

Swift was not alone in calling for an English "Society" or "Academy" of language; many late seventeenth-century and eighteenth-century British political writers recognized that the language of the expanding Empire was becoming important enough to warrant an attempt to control its future. Swift saw a cautionary tale in the history of Latin: after spreading throughout the Roman Empire, Latin declined in elegance, admitted foreign words and syntactic constructions, and splintered into a number of regional dialects that would become the Romance languages. Thus the source of his claim that change is "infallibly for the worse": for Swift, this process represented the death spiral of a perfect language.

Swift seems to have thought of all languages in terms of states and their subjects. He used the phrase "the Roman Language" as often as the proper noun "Latin," and regularly wrote "our language" and "our words" when referring to English. Such usage suggests that when he wrote "the French tongue" or "the English language," Swift was defining these languages through the identities of their speakers rather than through the languages' inherent characteristics. Nevertheless, Swift recognized, through his analogy with the Roman Empire, that political expansion would lead to an increase in the number of English speakers around the world, thus complicating his notion of "our" English language. Today, in our post-colonial world, an easy equation of nationality and language is impossible. Obviously many more native English speakers live outside England and Great Britain than within, and beyond Anglophone

nations, best estimates suggest there are currently some three times as many ESL speakers and learners in the world as native speakers. The Englishes used throughout the world today — whether called dialects, creoles, or varieties of "broken" English — belie the notion that *English* can any longer imply primarily "the language of England," other than in a purely historical sense.

While a study of HEL must, of course, trace English's beginnings to that small island off the northwest corner of the European mainland, the term *English* has ranged far away from its ancestral home. To continue Swift's analogy with Latin, since at some point Gallic Latin became Old French, we might ask when the English of, say, Jamaica will have earned its own moniker, and should no longer be called "English" at all. But such a question reinscribes Swift's equation of language and sovereign state — Jamaican English is not English only to the extent that it is not the English of England. We may soon find we need a terminology similar to "Romance Languages" to accommodate the Englishes born in the wake of British expansion: the "English language *family*" perhaps, as David Crystal among others has suggested. With such a formulation, Swift's fear of language decay and death becomes a celebration of generation and proliferation; as one language spreads and evolves to become many, it lives on more abundantly than it could have otherwise. In such a case, change might be seen as "infallibly for the better."

Language: Monolingualism, Register, and Genre

As Cable's chapter demonstrates, the history of the English language is an academic subject that has regularly been taught at the university level for more than one hundred years. HEL has customarily been offered in English programs. This seems like a logical choice at first, because most English departments confer degrees in English "language" and "literature." For students who engage in English studies at English-speaking institutions, however, the "language" part of the degree they work towards may seem somewhat redundant. After all, don't they know English already? Indeed, English programs today probably attract students who hope to apply their competence in their native language to the study of literature. This invisibility of language in literary studies is a relatively recent phenomenon, however. Historically speaking, the practice of coupling "language" and "literature" for an academic study of English goes back to the nineteenth century when the discipline of modern-language studies was developed within the paradigm of the new philology, which placed emphasis on the historicity of the vernaculars. Prior to modern philology, the literary education of the West had long concerned the study of Latin (and Greek), for which the mastering of grammar was a prerequisite for the study of rhetoric. In the long history of liberal arts education, therefore, monolingualism is more an exception than the norm.

Today HEL provides students of English with an opportunity to develop a new perspective on the language. When given a text written in pre-Chaucerian Middle

English or Gullah, for instance, we must approach the language not as an instrument for study but as an object of study itself. Texts written in either of these varieties of English require careful analysis, because the language, though called English, is distant and unfamiliar. Moreover, the scale of linguistic unfamiliarity is not necessarily in proportion to the historical or geographical distance of the texts. In reading Shakespeare, for instance, we often find poetic passages more accessible than some of the prose passages, even though the average English speaker in Shakespeare's time would have found it the other way around. This discrepancy derives in part from our privileging of the elevated style of Shakespearean sonnets or soliloquies over the plainer style of his prose which often represented the informal or colloquial speech of lower classes. But the discrepancy also derives from the conservative nature of literary language itself. In comparison, spoken language is so mutable that the colloquialism of one generation is often incomprehensible to the next.

Just as playwrights and novelists would choose different registers for different characters, ordinary people are likely to speak more than one "language" in their daily life even if they belong to a small or secluded community. This important point is made by M. M. Bakhtin with an example of a rural laborer in Russia:

> Thus an illiterate peasant, miles away from any urban center, naively immersed in an unmoving and for him unshakable everyday world, nevertheless lived in several language systems: he prayed to God in one language (Church Slavonic), sang songs in another, spoke to his family in a third and, when he began to dictate petitions to the local authorities through a scribe, he tried speaking yet a fourth language (the official-literate language, "paper" language). All these are *different languages*, even from the point of view of abstract socio-dialectological markers. (Bakhtin 1981: 295–6)

The key to understanding Bakhtin's claim that one's existence in society is fundamentally multilingual lies in the multivalence of language itself. When used as an uncountable noun, the word *language* refers to verbal communication in general. As a countable noun, a language comprises a specific variety of speech used in one or more countries, regions, or communities of people with a distinct group identity. Strictly speaking, *language* in the second sense is not a linguistic entity, because a language as such is formally indistinguishable from a dialect, and one can be separated from the other only through socio-political factors. The word *language* has yet another meaning in a phrase like "paper language," or "literary language." The word *language* used in this sense constitutes a cultural entity that functions at the level of discourse, register, or genre.

HEL has traditionally dealt with diverse genres, many of which are excluded from the narrow definition of literature: governmental documents, familial letters, religious or scientific treatises, conduct books, advertisements, to name a few. By becoming familiar with genetically diverse texts, we realize that each genre has a history of its own. Some, like advertisements, change their form and format as fast as material culture and media technology, whereas others, like the epistle and the homily, have

sustained a certain formality that cuts across the boundaries of periods or states. Cookbooks comprise yet another case. The following passage comes from a fifteenth-century recipe for *sauce galentyne*:

> Take faire crustez of broun brede, stepe þem in vinegre, and put þer-to poudre canel [i.e. cinnamon powder], and let it stepe þer-wyþ til it be broun; and þanne drawe it þurwe a straynour .ij. tymes or .iij., and þanne put þerto poudre piper and salte: and let it be sumwhat stondynge, and not to þynne, and serue forth. (Austin 1964: 108–9)

This culinary instruction has a tone and a contour that are familiar to anyone who has used modern cookbooks: it consists of a series of imperatives followed by the names of ingredients, methods of preparation, and desired outcomes including how the product should be consumed. We recognize a similar pattern in the following passage, this time taken from an Old English medical book:

> Wið hwostan: nim huniges tear and merces sæd and diles sæd; cnuca þa sæd smale, mæng ðicce wið ðone tear, and pipera swiðe; nim ðry sticcan fulle on nihtnihstig.

> [For cough: Take honey droppings and marche seed and dill seed. Pound the seeds small, mix into the droppings to thickness, and pepper well. Take three spoonfuls after the night's fast.] (Grattan & Singer 1952: 100–1)

The examples from Old and Middle English demonstrate that the genre of recipe writing has not undergone major change at the discourse level. They are also the reminder that some of the linguistic characteristics of English have remained unchanged for more than a thousand years.

History: Two Models

What does "history" mean when applied to a language? One commonly invoked model distinguishes an "internal" or linguistic history of English from an "external" or cultural history. As Cable makes clear, the study of language in the nineteenth and early twentieth centuries was almost exclusively philological. Sound shifts, developments in vocabulary, and syntactic changes were of primary interest, while historical events were at best secondary. Throughout the twentieth century, scholars became more interested in the relationship between language and history. In 1935, the first edition of Albert Baugh's famous textbook promised "a proper balance" between internal and external history (Baugh & Cable 2002: v). Still, as the term "external" implies, cultural and political history remained outside language itself. The latter part of the twentieth century saw the publication of new textbooks (e.g., Gerry Knowles' *A Cultural History of the English Language* in 1979, and Dick Leith's *A Social History of English* in 1983) that foregrounded what had been called the external history. In such books, external history was transformed into a "sociolinguistic profile" of a

language (Leith 1997: 8), with emphasis on the social function of language rather than on its grammar, phonology, syntax, etc.

Today, the usefulness of "internal" and "external" as defining conceptions within HEL may have run its course. Above we referred to a "feedback loop" running between language and its "environment"; these terms seem salient to us because they acknowledge that a language makes up part of the environment it inhabits. Language is recognized simultaneously as an agent of history and as a product. For example, the rate of linguistic change did slow following the time of Swift and other prescriptivists. But can we really identify a simple cause-and-effect relationship? Their efforts would likely have been impossible without the earlier invention of print media and would have been unnecessary if England had not entered the nascent global economy. The argument can be made that the printing press itself created the prescriptivists' attitude. In fact, the language may well have regularized even without their efforts, because the market forces were driving the use of the press. Ironically, the printing technology that made the "fixing" of English necessary and possible would later facilitate its global spread, which has, in turn, led to the current period of radical linguistic change. The history of the English language abounds with such cyclical developments, effects becoming causes.

While the division between internal and external history is being blurred, a second model of history, the chronological development of language, still holds sway. The tripartite history of Old, Middle, and Modern English defines two historical moments as central to English's development: the Norman Invasion of 1066, and the rise of the Tudor Dynasty and the Protestant Reformation. These events are traditional dividing lines for good reason – they do in fact represent moments when language, politics, religion, and economics underwent radical transformations. But the model defined by these terms is linear, tracing a straight-line trajectory for a well-defined, unitary language, thus denying a full history to the offshoots, the non-standard dialects, the conservative backwaters, or the avant-garde neologisms of a given historical period. But even if we grant that the "standard" language has until recently had enough momentum to pull along most variants in its wake, such a single straight-line trajectory is insufficient to capture the current global spread and multidimensional changes in the world's Englishes. It may be time to consider the "Old–Middle–Modern" triptych as complete, and to seek new models for representing English in the world today as well as for the processes that led to it.

Recent schematic models of English in today's world include Braj Kachru's "Concentric Circles" model which emphasizes the larger and ever-growing number of non-native speakers over time (see WORLD ENGLISH IN WORLD CONTEXTS). Somewhat different is Tom McArthur's "Circle of World English" with a hypothetical World Standard English at its hub, and increasingly local variants, including those in Anglophone countries, radiating outward. McArthur's arrangement radically decentralizes British and American Standard English, projecting a future of English in the world uncontrolled by British or American hegemony. We cannot offer here a unified image that captures all aspects of the history of English; the result would of necessity be a

schematic chimera of chronological lines, branching trees, holistic circles, interactive networks, and evolutionary processes. Such a chimera cannot be easily imagined, but we anticipate that the essays in this collection will illuminate individually for students the many possible approaches to the study of HEL that, taken together, provide more than a single model or historical emphasis might do.

How to Use this Book

The current collection is intended as a *Companion* to the history of the English language rather than a comprehensive textbook. The chapters are written to stand alone so that readers may dip into them at will. Readers might also use the extensive cross-referencing among the chapters as well as the recommended further reading to develop a fuller picture of a given topic. We have provided below a list of available HEL textbooks with brief annotations. Some of the textbooks, including Pyles/Algeo and Baugh/Cable, have accompanying workbooks.

HEL Textbooks

Baugh, A. C. & Cable, T. (2002). *A History of the English Language*. 5th edn. London: Routledge. [Offers a narrative explanation of linguistic evolution in relation to social and political changes in Britain and America]

Crystal, D. (2003). *The Cambridge Encyclopedia of the English Language*. 2nd edn. Cambridge: Cambridge University Press. [Arranges historical and contemporary material by theme; offers abundant visual aids]

Culpepper, J. (2005). *History of English*. 2nd edn. Routledge Language Workbooks Series. New York: Routledge. [Focuses on student-friendly linguistic analyses of language change; includes exercises and "discussion points"]

Fennell, B. A. (2001). *A History of English: A Sociolinguistic Approach*. Oxford: Blackwell. [Provides a linguistic history informed by issues like multilingualism and creolization]

Gelderen, E. van. (2006). *A History of the English Language*. Philadelphia: John Benjamins. [Gives a detailed introduction to linguistic topics and historical principles]

Knowles, G. (1997). *A Cultural History of the English Language*. London: Arnold. [Introduces the development of English from socio-cultural perspectives; offers a useful bibliography]

Lass, R. (1987). *The Shape of English: Structure and History*. London: Dent. [Provides a linguistic approach; plus a detailed chapter on dialects]

Leith, D. (1997). *A Social History of English*. 2nd edn. New York: Routledge. [Narrates linguistic history through socio-political issues like standardization and language imposition]

McCrum, R., MacNeil, R., & Cran, W. (2002). *The Story of English*. 3rd. edn. London: Faber. [Emphasizes cultural varieties of English; originally compiled as a companion to a BBC television series]

Millward, C. M. (1996). *A Biography of the English Language*. 2nd. edn. Fort Worth: Harcourt Brace. [Gives a succinct, all-around treatment from Indo-European to creoles]

Pyles, T. & Algeo, J. (2005). *The Origins and Development of the English Language*. 5th edn. Fort Worth: Harcourt Brace. [Offers a user-friendly introduction to linguistic history; with additional chapters on word studies]

Schmitt, N. & Marsden, R. (2006). *Why is English Like That? Historical Answers to Hard ELT Questions*. Ann Arbor: University of Michigan Press. [Summarizes HEL topics for English language teachers; comes with "Classroom Activities"]

Strang, B. M. H. (1989). *A History of English*. New York: Routledge. [Details the facts of linguistic history; arranged backwards chronologically]

Svartvik, J. & Leech, G. (2006). *English: One Tongue, Many Voices*. New York: Palgrave. [Emphasizes the "global" period and modern language issues, with a shorter overview of Old, Middle, and Early Modern periods]

REFERENCES AND FURTHER READING

Austin, T. (ed.) (1888 [1964]). *Two Fifteenth-Century Cookery-books*. Early English Text Society, o.s. 91. Oxford: Oxford University Press.

Bakhtin, M. M. (1981). Discourse in the novel. In M. Holquist (ed.), *The Dialogic Imagination: Four Essays* (pp. 259–422). Trans. C. Emerson and M. Holquist. Austin: University of Texas Press.

Crystal, D. (1998). Moving towards an English family of languages? In *Folia Anglistica* (Festschrift for Olga S. Akhmanova) (pp. 84–95). Moscow: Moscow State University Press.

Gould, S. J. (1996). *Full House: The Spread of Excellence from Plato to Darwin*. New York: Harmony.

Grattan, J. H. G. & Singer, C. (1952). *Anglo-Saxon Magic and Medicine: Illustrated Specially from the Semi-Pagan Text 'Lacnunga'*. Oxford: Oxford University Press.

Knowles, G. (1979). *A Cultural History of the English Language*. London: Arnold.

Leith, D. (1983). *A Social History of English*. 1st edn. New York: Routledge.

McArthur, T. (1998). *The English Languages*. Cambridge: Cambridge University Press.

Swift, J. (1907). Proposal for correcting, improving, and ascertaining the English tongue. In T. Scott (ed.), *The Prose Works of Jonathan Swift*, Vol. 11 (pp. 1–21). London: George Bell.

2
History of the History of the English Language: How Has the Subject Been Studied?

Thomas Cable

The earliest single-volume, narrative histories of the English language came late in a period of remarkable linguistic progress. These were Victorian and Edwardian distillations of scholarly traditions that flourished throughout the nineteenth century. The discoveries in comparative and historical linguistics by Rasmus Rask, Jacob Grimm, Franz Bopp, and other philologists in Continental Europe provided the foundations of the study as early as 1818. In England the Philological Society's sponsorship of a *New English Dictionary*, beginning in the middle of the century, and the textual support for that project by the Early English Text Society, displayed the English language on a scale beyond the reach of eighteenth-century writers. Samuel Johnson's 1755 *Dictionary of the English Language* included a perfunctory "History of the English Language," but his history was simply a selection of older texts available to him and a thin connecting thread.

Three-quarters of a century later Noah Webster's understanding of the history of the English language was even less adequate than Johnson's. Accepting the scriptural account of the dispersion, the folk hero of American lexicography ignored the discoveries that were transforming historical linguistics in Europe. The basis of Webster's etymologizing in his 1828 *American Dictionary of the English Language* has been described as "simple fantasy" (Sledd & Kolb 1955: 197). Inevitably, however, advances in historical linguistics had their effect on dictionaries and histories. Gneuss (1996) names Latham (1841 and its later editions) as a main precursor to modern histories of the English language, especially because Latham was better informed than most British and American philologists about advances in Germany. Other early treatments include Bosworth (1836), Marsh (1862), and two three-volume historical grammars in German, Koch (1863–9) and Mätzner (1860–5).

With Lounsbury (1879) the history of the English language acquired a shape that can be compared with textbooks of the next hundred years. During the three decades after Lounsbury several similar surveys appeared: Emerson (1894), Bradley (1904), Jespersen (1905), Wyld (1906), and Smith (1912). From the perspective of the

twenty-first century, one might expect these early histories to have had a lack of his-torical materials for analysis within a modern linguistic framework. A look at the textbooks shows that almost the opposite is the case: the wealth of discoveries during the nineteenth century posed a challenge of selection, organization, and presentation. The first histories of the English language focused on one aspect or another, often with the lament that much was omitted and usually with an ideological bias that helped shape the choices.

The most obvious division was between the "internal" history – sounds, inflections, vocabulary – and the "external" history – the political, social, and intellectual forces that determined the development of the language at different periods. Within the internal history decisions had to be made about balancing the treatments of phonol-ogy, morphology, and lexicon. Lounsbury (1879) divided his book into Part I, General History (the internal history from the Roman Conquest up to the spread of English "over a large share of the habitable globe") and Part II, History of Inflections (specifi-cally nouns, adjectives, pronouns, and verbs). Lounsbury offered no treatment of phonology except to the extent that umlaut and other processes were relevant to declensions and conjugations. As he acknowledged, the division of his history into two parts, "involved in a few instances the necessity of going over the same ground" (pp. v–vi).

An interesting feature of Lounsbury's treatment was the division of the periods of the language. For the earliest stage, many Victorian philologists saw the English language as beginning with what we now call "Middle English." The choice between the terms "Anglo-Saxon" and "Old English" was more than stylistic, because "Anglo-Saxon" emphasized the continuation of the language of the Continent. By this view "English" began after the Norman Conquest of 1066, and what we now call "Early Middle English" was called "Old English." Lounsbury's divisions identified Anglo-Saxon (from the middle of the fifth century to 1150), Early English (1150–1350), Middle English (1350–1550), and Modern English (from the middle of the sixteenth century to the present). Within Early English, he posited Semi-Saxon (1150–1250) and Old English (1250–1350). It is ironic that the Anglo-Saxons themselves called their language *Englisc*. By the second edition of his book (1894), Lounsbury had to spend a page of the preface defending his usage.

In explicit contrast with approaches such as Lounsbury's, Emerson (1894), fifteen years later, chose to give prominent attention to two aspects: the phonology and the "native element." He called the earliest stage by the name now used, "Old English." The focus on Old and Middle English aligned Emerson with the historian E. A. Freeman and his work of 1867–79, to which Emerson expressed indebtedness. It was Freeman's contention that the Norman Conquest was an aberration in the develop-ment of English culture but one that the English people had absorbed and recovered from. Thus, "Old English" was a charged term and a part of strong sentiments of the Victorian period, as traced by recent works such as Frantzen (1990) and Frantzen and Niles (1997). As Emerson put it, his own treatment emphasized the native element, because "many studies of the English language seem to give undue prominence to the

foreign element. . . . Such an incorrect impression results mainly from a wrong conception of the Norman conquest and of its effect upon the English language" (p. vii).

Like Lounsbury, Emerson treated the external history separately, then repeated the chronology for the internal history. Because Emerson covered vocabulary and sounds as well as inflections, aspects of the chronology were repeated three times. This kind of division by topics was typical of the histories during the decades before and after the turn of the century. It was only in the 1930s that phonology, morphology, and lexicon were treated in a single chapter for a particular stage of the language, preceded in the same chapter by an external overview of the cultural conditions. There are advantages and disadvantages for each format.

Bradley (1904) explicitly limited the scope of his book by excluding phonology almost completely and referring readers to other works for "changes in their chronological sequence" (p. 10). As might be expected from an editor of the *New English Dictionary*, Bradley focused on word-formation and changes of meaning. Jespersen (1905) acknowledged his indebtedness to the *NED* and displayed English word-formation and borrowings even more richly than Bradley. Like Bradley he had little to say about phonology, though not for lack of interest or expertise. Four years later in his synchronic grammar "on historical principles," Jespersen (1909: I.231–2) had a significant influence on phonological description by giving a name to "the Great Vowel Shift" and introducing the familiar diagram of changes in the long vowels between Chaucer and Shakespeare. (See PHONOLOGY: SEGMENTAL HISTORIES.)

Wyld (1906) and (1914) drew heavily on monumental studies in Germany to trace the sounds of English in staggering detail. Although both books are valuable as reference works, it is hard to imagine their use in British or American classrooms, then or now. Wyld has nothing to say about American English or indeed British varieties other than RP (Received Pronunciation). This is no surprise for a scholar who expresses a primary indebtedness to Henry Sweet, the philologist and phonetician who in turn was the model for George Bernard Shaw's Henry Higgins in *Pygmalion*. Bailey (1991) has a compelling account of Wyld's views on contemporary usage of the early twentieth century. (See BRITISH ENGLISH SINCE 1830 and CLASS, ETHNICITY AND THE FORMATION OF "STANDARD ENGLISH.")

Baugh (1935) established a format that has proved enduring – a chapter more or less on all aspects of the language in each major period. It is a format that has been adopted by most textbooks since, with modifications in the strict chronological sequence depending on the interests and expertise of the author. For Baugh, the modification was especially in the Middle English period, where he devoted two chapters to the external history of the Norman Conquest and the reestablishment of English. Otherwise, the progression, after an introductory chapter, was a chapter on Indo-European, two chapters on Old English, a chapter on the internal history of Middle English, one on the Renaissance, one on the late seventeenth and eighteenth centuries, and one on the nineteenth century to the present. A final chapter on "The

English Language in America" is approximately in its chronological order, although the English settlement of the American continent and the colonial history, of course, reach back to periods already treated in British English.

Pyles (1964) used much the same format with a core of chapters for the major periods in the center of the book, preceded and followed by chapters on topics of special interest to the author – two chapters on letters and sounds after the introductory chapter and three chapters on words after the six chronological chapters. John Algeo kept this format as co-author in subsequent editions, and he added a workbook, a feature that went a long way toward solving the main problem that had vexed one-volume histories from the beginning – how to include all the material.

Another way of getting at the instruction in linguistics that is necessary for the history of any language was used successfully by Strang (1970). By beginning with Modern English and working back, her history reviewed the most accessible stage of the language at the same time that it introduced phonetics.

As for the later stages, current histories are much fuller than Edwardian histories and not simply because another century has passed. Even in 1900 the English language in America had a history that could have been explored but was not; and English as a world language was ignored until the mid-twentieth century. The incorporation of these subjects is partly a story of an increasingly liberal attitude toward language and its users. The study of American English was greatly facilitated by Krapp (1925). Within Britain itself, varieties other than RP were hardly mentioned in the early histories: English in Scotland, Wales, and Ireland, Cockney, and the rural dialects of England had to wait until the 1920s.

Advances in linguistic theory during the twentieth century had varying effects on the traditional histories. The "phonemics" of structural linguistics between the 1930s and 1950s caused little disruption in the way sounds were presented. In fact, a vaguely phonemic transcription was easily adaptable as a "broad" transcription, and if anything it made life easier. In a textbook designed for an undergraduate course, it was simpler to make phonemic distinctions than to try to justify the exact phonetic values of, say, the configuration of sounds in the Great Vowel Shift at a certain moment.

Generative-transformational grammar was another story. The complexity of the constantly changing theory required, in effect, a separate course to cover even the basics, but neither the curriculum nor the economics of book publishing allowed adequate treatment of a "generative" approach to the history. Such syntheses as McLaughlin (1970), with pages of deep structure trees, as deep structure was conceived at the time, have been abandoned.

Instead, the emphasis of the past four decades has been on social varieties following William Labov's pioneering studies, and on national and areal varieties around the world. The most thoroughly studied variety of American English within a sociolinguistic approach has been African American Vernacular English. (See MIGRATION AND MOTIVATION IN THE DEVELOPMENT OF AFRICAN AMERICAN VERNACULAR ENGLISH; see also LATINO VARIETIES OF ENGLISH.)

As late as 1970 one of the few guides to English as a world language was Partridge and Clark (1951), despite sources such as dictionaries of Australian, Indian, and South African English going back to the turn of the century: Morris (1898), Yule, Burnell, and Crooke (1903), and Pettman (1913). During the past thirty years, a wealth of information has been published on English in individual countries along with dictionaries in the *OED* tradition. Anthologies such as Bailey and Görlach (1983) have made summaries and overviews available for classroom use. English as a world language, including English pidgins and creoles, has become an essential component of the history of the English language, and some universities offer a separate course in the subject. (See CREOLES AND PIDGINS; WORLD ENGLISH IN WORLD CONTEXTS.)

A final development in both research and teaching is the use of the computer in "corpus linguistics." The digitalized retrieval of tagged data is widely familiar to scholars and students in commercial products such as the online *OED* and the Chadwyck-Healey literature databases. Several universities in North America and Europe currently sponsor projects that focus either on a broad sweep of the English language or on a particular period. Between the *Helsinki Corpus of English Texts* and *A Representative Corpus of Historical English Registers* (*ARCHER*), the language can be displayed from its earliest records to the present. The *Helsinki Corpus* collects texts from Cædmon to the beginning of the eighteenth century, while *ARCHER* (supported by the University of Northern Arizona and the University of Southern California) goes from the mid-seventeenth century to 1990. The University of Toronto provided one of the first electronic resources in the database for the *Dictionary of Old English* (in progress); the University of Michigan has combined its materials for the *Middle English Dictionary* with other archives into the *Middle English Compendium;* and both Oxford University and the University of Virginia publish Middle English texts in digital form. The University of Edinburgh, which supported the invaluable *Linguistic Atlas of Late Mediaeval English* in four volumes (McIntosh, Samuels, & Benskin 1986) is currently sponsoring the *Corpus of Early Middle English Tagged Texts and Maps.* For a comprehensive survey of resources in corpus linguistics, see Rissanen (2000). (See also CORPUS-BASED LINGUISTIC APPROACHES TO THE HISTORY OF ENGLISH.) An excellent example of the insights that can come from the use of the computer for historical English linguistics is Nevalainen (2000), which combines the new technology with both old topics (the spread of the *–es* present tense ending) and current topics (gender and language) to show developments that had not been noticed.

A casual observer might imagine that 200 years of modern scholarship on 1,300 years of the recorded language would have covered the story adequately and that only incremental revisions remain. Yet the subject continues to expand in fructifying ways, and interacting developments contribute to the vitality of the field: the recognition that cultural biases often narrowed the scope of earlier inquiry; the incorporation of global varieties of English; the continuing changes in the language from year to year; and the use of computer technology in reinterpreting aspects of the English language from its origins to the present.

REFERENCES AND FURTHER READING

Bailey, R. W. (1991). *Images of English: A Cultural History of the Language.* Ann Arbor: University of Michigan Press.

Bailey, R. W. & Görlach, M. (eds.) (1983). *English as a World Language.* Ann Arbor: University of Michigan Press.

Baugh, A. C. (1957 [1935]). *A History of the English Language.* 2nd edn. New York: Appleton-Century-Crofts. Co-authored with Thomas Cable (1978–2002). 3rd–5th edns. Englewood Cliffs, NJ: Prentice-Hall.

Bosworth, J. (1848 [1836]). *The Origin of the Germanic and Scandinavian Languages and Nations.* 2nd edn. London: Longman, Rees, Orme, Brown, and Green.

Bradley, H. (1967 [1904]). *The Making of English.* Revd. edn. B. Evans and S. Potter (eds.). New York: Walker.

Crystal, D. (2004). *The Stories of English.* Woodstock, NY: Overlook Press.

Emerson, O. F. (1894). *The History of the English Language.* New York: Macmillan.

Frantzen, A. J. (1990). *Desire for Origins: New Language, Old English, and Teaching the Tradition.* New Brunswick, NJ: Rutgers University Press.

Frantzen, A. J. & Niles, J. D. (eds.) (1997). *Anglo-Saxonism and the Construction of Social Identity.* Gainesville: University Press of Florida.

Gneuss, H. (1996). *English Language Scholarship: A Survey and Bibliography from the Beginnings to the End of the Nineteenth Century.* Binghamton, NY: Medieval and Renaissance Texts & Studies.

Grimm, J. (1822–37 [1819]). *Deutsche Grammatik.* 4 vols. 2nd edn. Göttingen: Dieterichsche.

Jespersen, O. (1982 [1905]). *Growth and Structure of the English Language* 10th edn. London: Harcourt.

Jespersen, O. (1909.) *A Modern English Grammar on Historical Principles.* 7 vols. London: Allen & Unwin.

Kachru, B. B. (ed.) (1982). *The Other Tongue: English Across Cultures.* Urbana: University of Illinois Press.

Kennedy, A. G. (1927). *Bibliography of Writings on the English Language.* Cambridge, MA, and New Haven, CT: Harvard University Press and Yale University Press.

Koch, K. F. (1863–9). *Historische Grammatik der englischen Sprache.* 3 vols. Weimar: H. Böhlau.

Krapp, G. P. (1909). *Modern English, Its Growth and Present Use.* New York: Scribner's.

Krapp, G. P. (1925). *The English Language in America.* 2 vols. New York: Century.

Kurath, H., Kuhn, S. M., Reidy, J., and Lewis, R. E. (eds.) (1952–2001). *Middle English Dictionary.* Ann Arbor: University of Michigan Press.

Labov, W. (1966). *The Social Stratification of English in New York City.* Washington, DC: Center for Applied Linguistics.

Labov, W., Ash, S., & Boberg, C. (2006). *The Atlas of North American English: Phonetics, Phonology, and Sound Change: A Multimedia Reference Tool.* Berlin: Mouton de Gruyter.

Latham, R. G. (1862 [1841]). *The English Language.* 5th edn. London: Taylor, Walton, and Maberly.

Lounsbury, T. R. (1894 [1879]). *A History of the English Language.* 2nd edn. New York: Holt.

McIntosh, A., Samuels, M. L., & Benskin, M. (1986). *A Linguistic Atlas of Late Mediaeval English.* 4 vols. Aberdeen: Aberdeen University Press.

McKnight, G. H. (1928). *Modern English in the Making.* New York: Appleton.

McLaughlin, J. C. (1970). *Aspects of the History of English.* New York: Holt, Rinehart and Winston.

Marsh, G. P. (1885 [1862]). *Lectures on the English Language.* Revd. edn. New York: Scribner's.

Mätzner, E. (1880–5 [1860–5]). *Englische Grammatik.* 3 vols. 3rd edn. Berlin: Weidmann.

Matthews, D. (2000). *The Invention of Middle English: An Anthology of Primary Sources.* Turnhout: Brepols.

Millward, C. M. (1996 [1989]). *A Biography of the English Language.* 2nd edn. New York: Harcourt.

Morris, E. E. (1898). *Austral English: A Dictionary of Australian Words, Phrases and Usages.* London: Macmillan.

Nevalainen, T. (2000). Gender differences in the evolution of Standard English: evidence from

the Corpus of Early English Correspondence. *Journal of English Linguistics*, 28, 38–59.

Partridge, E. & Clark, J. W. (1951). *British and American English since 1900, with Contributions on English in Canada, South Africa, Australia, New Zealand and India.* London: Dakers.

Pettman, C. (1913). *Africanderisms.* London: Longmans, Green.

Pyles, T. (1964). *The Origins and Development of the English Language.* New York: Harcourt, Brace & World. Co-authored with John Algeo (1971–2004). 2nd–5th edns. New York: Thomson Heinle.

Rissanen, M. (2000). The world of English historical corpora: from Cædmon to the computer age. *Journal of English Linguistics*, 28, 7–20.

Sledd, J. H. & Kolb, G. J. (1955). *Dr. Johnson's Dictionary: Essays in the Biography of a Book.* Chicago: University of Chicago Press.

Smith, L. P. (1912). *The English Language.* London: Williams and Norgate.

Strang, B. M. H. (1970). *A History of English.* London: Methuen.

Wyld, H. C. (1906). *The Historical Study of the Mother Tongue.* London: Murray.

Wyld, H. C. (1927 [1914]). *A Short History of English.* 3rd edn. London: Murray.

Yule, H. & Burnell, A. C. (1903 [1886]). *Hobson-Jobson: A Glossary of Colloquial Anglo-Indian Words and Phrases.* 2nd edn. William Crooke. London: Murray.

3

Essential Linguistics

Mary Blockley

How much linguistics is necessary in a History of the English Language course for a literature student? How much should a student of literature know about language studies? I take these questions as an invitation to think about the minimal amount of linguistics needed to convey change in English over at least the last thousand years. I chose not to focus on the outcomes of the four or so main stages of English that provide the organizing principle of most overviews. For one thing, the number of necessary topics and amount of detail vary dramatically with the centuries that an instructor chooses to cover, whether starting from Proto-Indo-European or no earlier than Early Modern English. N. F. Blake (1996) and Dick Leith (1997) have gone to some effort to avoid using those periodizing terms, probably because of the assumptions that go along with such metaphors, recasting the ever-renewable life of a language as the stages of a single human life.

My approach in this overview is rather to direct attention to a few disparate linguistic objects of various sizes, from the phoneme to the sentence, and a few terms for the linguistic descriptions that are claimed to affect such objects. Some, such as fronting, repeat themselves over the centuries, but as significant are other concepts, like phonemic length, that are almost inaccessible to those who know only Present-Day English.

These topics are therefore "essential" not so much in representing core concepts of linguistics as a science, but rather in the paramedic sense of indispensable – whether or not these perceived units and processes turn out to be central to the history of English, you cannot describe the set of language changes that encompass English without knowledge of and reference to them. That so many of them remain or have become controversial is part of the terror for novice lecturers, who find contradictory dicta everywhere they turn, and part of the continuing attraction they have as topics for research. The selection here is therefore relentlessly practical. A grasp of the issues involved with any of these topics is the crucial bridge into understanding the more demanding books. I hope that even those who find this cross-training teasingly

minimalist may consider these and other combinations that raise questions of definition. Such questions lead us across disciplines, theoretical orientations, and subperiods of English.

Palatalization

In Modern English, palatalization can be heard more easily than seen. In normal rapid speech an alveolar consonant under the influence of a following glide becomes an affricate, so that in the phrase "without you," a "yew" becomes a "chew." This word-boundary palatalization underlies jokes like "What do you call a cheese that is not yours? Nacho cheese." The life-or-death *shibboleth* (Judges 12:6) can be paralleled millennia later within English (*OED*, s. v palatalization). Present-day Anglists can probably nonetheless live without mastering the articulation of *Das Palatalgesetz*, though Prokosh (1939) cites the Law of Palatals as evidence for an East/West Indo-European language divide abbreviated in their development from the common root for "a hundred": *satem* (sibilant, palatalized) and *kentum* (velar). Though the satem/ kentum distinction is now discredited as a simplification, it represents a moment in the history of the language sciences that is worth re-examining in the context of developments in areal linguistics (Collinge 1985). To the extent that *i*-umlaut is characterizable as a palatalization (Sievers & Brunner 1965: §95), it is a mark of the West in smaller linguistic areas, such as fifth-century West Germanic. Later, it may give us the Middle English innovation *she*, the American Dialect Society's "word of the millennium." Palatalization is uncontroversial as a medieval isogloss. Unpalatalized Scandinavian loanwords in northern Middle English supplanted certain words with consonants palatalized in Old English; for example, *give* has replaced the *yife* used by Chaucer. Other Scandinavian words developed a different meaning in the company of the palatalized Old English cognate; hence, *skirt* and *scuffle* alongside *shirt* and *shuffle*. Loanwords from French reveal their dialectical origins in that those from Norman French, like *catch*, show less palatalization than do those from Central French, which gave *chase*. Within Early Modern English as now, the spelling of Latinate terminations in words like *station*, *musician*, and *immediate* does not indicate palatalization, and these word-medial consonants were indeed only gradually palatalized, with allophonic variation in their pronunciation.

Allophones

A simple but widely distributed current allophonic variation is the pronunciation of *often* either with silent *t* or as "off ten." Another example is the strong form of *the*, with the high vowel generally appearing pre-vocalically as in "the odds," but alternating with the usual schwa vowel. Though the term *allophone* first appears as late on the linguistic scene as 1957 (Whorf), the idea that some vocal sounds are best thought

of as forming sets within a language or an idiolect; that, for a given place, time, and speaker a variety of sounds register simply as variants on a single phoneme is surely one of the first insights of phonetic description. From this one, many emerge. Descriptive HEL's business is often the coronation of a former allophone as a next-stage phoneme, as with, to name but one, the /v/ that emerges in ME from the allophone of fricative *f* in OE, so that *vat* became a distinct word alongside *fat*. The smaller range of allophonic variation within English itself is of course a staple of introductory description, such as the glide that only marks dialectical differences in the pronunciation of *news* as rhyming either with *views* or with *lose*. The glide is also allophonic in a number of Latinate words like *accurate*, though phonemic in differentiating *beauty* and *booty*. This fundamental insight about how sounds group and split inspires theorizing into linguistic areas where its application is less certain. For example, Lass (1997: 57) proposes "allophonic spelling" – the idea that spelling variation even within the wilder reaches of Middle English varies within a set.

Regularized DO

Auxiliary *do* began in the mid-sixteenth century with a semantically empty auxiliary that emerged fairly suddenly from the west and was used freely but became narrowed over the course of the next hundred and fifty years to expressions involving negation or interrogation, and ultimately required in those expressions in the absence of other light verbs. Hamlet's statement that "the lady doth protest too much" exemplifies the non-emphatic affirmative declarative *do* that vanished first. The motivation for this *doth* may have been the difficulty of either "protesteth" or of the new inflection in "protests." The remaining required *do* that characterizes Present-Day English, when suppressed under exceptional circumstances, produces an archaic effect. Courts of law preserve "What say you?" though the standard language requires "What do you say?" and while Kennedy famously commanded "Ask not what your country can do for you," we expect "Don't ask." Gabriella Mazzon (2004: 75–81) in summarizing the interaction of negation with the new sentence structures of Early Modern English notes that *do* rises first in prose and is adapted early by women writers. Even the so-called difficult verbs, those that seem to resist the auxiliary with the old negative adverb patterns such as *say not* and *doubt not*, though salient to us, do not vary significantly from the *do not go* pattern that prevailed (Nurmi 1999). Shakespeare lagged behind his exact contemporary Marlowe and others in embracing the new auxiliary for the positions it now has in the standard language: forming negative clauses and questions (Hope 1994). A piece of external history that has now to be taken into consideration is comparison with the auxiliary in sister languages with which English remained in contact. Notably, in German a parallel sixteenth-century development in *tun*, seen in the casual language use of bilingual travelers and guides for merchants, never found more of a foothold in the printed language (Langer 2001).

Stress Shift

The shift of word stress to the initial syllable in Germanic languages has contributed to the orthographic untidiness of English paradigms, leaving its traces in the voicing of medial fricatives that account for the *was/were, seethe/sodden, lost/lorn* contrasts. With the exception of a few suffixes like *–eer* and *–ee*, the trend since Early Modern English, sometimes detectable from meter, is for any loanword to shift its stress forward. Yet in Present-Day English, even disyllabic words are not always predictable. In contrast to *debit* and an increasing number of *re-* verbs like *recap* "recapitulate," even some nouns (*demand* and *result*) resist initial stress. Changes in lexicographic pronunciations reveal patterns of antepenultimate stress for polysyllables, sometimes supporting transparency (Bauer 1994: 95–103), as when the silent *n* of *autumn* resurfaces in *autumnal*.

Grammaticalization

As "the change whereby lexical items and constructions come in certain linguistic contexts to serve grammatical functions, and once grammaticalized, continue to develop new grammatical functions" (Traugott & Hopper 2003: xv), grammaticalization accounts for much historical syntactic variation. Examples include adverbs like *indeed* and *really* and all the modal auxiliaries of English, such as *will*, which began life as main verbs. Grammaticalized items cross part-of-speech boundaries and even create parts of speech out of reduced phrases or words; grammaticalization theory has revived the study of the role of adverbials, a part of speech neglected by early formal linguistics, even though "no other Teutonic language has developed to the same degree the faculty of expressing so much by a single adverb as English" (Western 1905: 97).

Phonemic Length

Phonemic length, a distinction wholly lost in Present-Day English, is perhaps the most difficult of these topics in that the evidence is correspondingly difficult to grasp for those who know only Present-Day English. Phonemic length is nonetheless important for what it indicates about spelling conventions that underspecify the quantity of vowels in medieval texts and yet provide more if not always adequate specification of consonants. The loss of phonemic length raises questions of how and why a wide-ranging set of contrasts disappears so completely, and why digraph spellings did not generally emerge for long vowels. The contrast that separated *īs* "ice" and *is* "is," *āc* "oak" and *ac* "but," and *gōd* "good" and *god* "God," indicates that phonemic length was a living force in OE.

Complementation

Complementation is the syntactic art of making clauses bigger to make them smaller, that is, to convert them from wholes into parts of larger wholes. For example, the conjunction "because" in "The king died because the queen died" makes the second clause grammatically dependent on the first. In this instance it also makes the implied temporal order of events explicit and contrary to the order of the clauses themselves. To work without conjunctions, complementation requires that some left-edge boundary be apparent, some marker for the subordinate clause that acts as a noun. Sometimes, as in the next example, a complement even acts as a modifier of a noun that is understood from context alone. In "I can serve *whoever's next*," the indefinite relative "whoever" does this, but a clause boundary is somehow clear to speakers for whom "I can serve *who's next*" is its equivalent. Intonational contours or punctuation occasionally disambiguate structures, but complement status can be difficult to diagnose. Gender differences in the use of sentential complement clauses in spoken and written Present-Day English has a yet-to-be-explored link with the preposed, left-handed complement clauses in earlier prose, including Old English. Mondorf (2004: 87–100) indicates that the fronted adverbial complement clause, such as "when the queen died, the king died," is more characteristic of men than women.

Diphthongization

"The most prominent feature of our present English is its tendency towards diphthongization," wrote Henry Sweet. A diphthong is two vowels doing the phonemic work of one; for example the /aɪ/ of *I*. Diphthongization raises questions that have endured longer than any answer to them. Are the seven new ME diphthongs proper assimilations of vowels with the subsequent semivowels of OE /w/, /j/, and /v/, as seen in *sew* and *gray*? What are we to make of Present-Day English's retention of /ɔɪ/ as a diphthong borrowed from French, when the usual tendency is to assimilate loans to native norms of realization; that is, why do we have a diphthong in *joy* but not in *fruit*? What makes [əi], the centralized but unrounded EMnE diphthong that preceded [aɪ], so difficult and foreign-sounding for students of Shakespearian English (Crystal 2006: 115)?

"You was" Declared Ungrammatical Though Not Plural

The loss of "thou" meant that "you" had to cover singular as well as plural second-person reference, and second-person verbs had already lost the distinction of number. A sentence like "you was there" embodies an obsolete innovation that jabs the prescriptive nervous system of many English speakers. The singular "you was" is distinct

from dialects with the loss of "were" in all persons. Anecdotal evidence doesn't always bother to distinguish these two causes of "you was," and both seem condemned in a letter reporting the mathematician John Nash reproaching the grammar of his twelve-year-old illegitimate son and namesake to his sister Martha Nash Legge, May 1, 1966: "all John David had to do was let a 'you was' slip out and Nash would be all over him" (Nasar 1998: 315). The acceptability of "you was" as a distinctive singular is noted in Jespersen, and in Algeo and Pyles (2005: 186), who give examples from the prose of John Adams as well as Samuel Johnson and hail the result as the rare victory of a mere schoolmaster over educated use. Tellingly, the eighteenth-century grammarian Robert Lowth criticizes the "enormous Solecism" without having the courage to admit the singular "you were" into his paradigms, resorting instead to the *thou* form that he acknowledged to be "disus'd" (Lowth 1762: 51–3). It is less well known that "you was" persists beyond the eighteenth century. McWhorter (2001: 229–31) notes it in the otherwise style-conscious letters of a self-educated man in the 1830s. As late as 1892, the readers of Richard Grant White, a nineteenth-century equivalent of the *New York Times*'s language maven, were answered that "*you was* has the support of eminent example" (White 1892: 446), though White himself preferred the plural form of the verb with the plural form of the pronoun.

Raising and Fronting

Vowels are notoriously underspecified in writing systems. With the evidence for raising and fronting, like that for palatalization, we end with changes that proceed audibly but invisibly, sometimes leaving no trace in orthography. The terms "raising" and "fronting" also leave surprisingly little trace in introductory linguistics textbooks, though scholarship in historical phonology continues to use them (Lutz 2005). When one English speaker's "Adam" sounds like "Edam" to another, we can say that the first speaker's vowel has raised, relative to the phonetic boundaries of the auditor's phonemic [æ]. Similarly, fronting is relative. Fronting often correlates with the loss of lip rounding of vowels. One of the clearest breaks with continental Germanic appears in the early OE fronting of the mid low [a] to [æ], still heard, after the raising and diphthongization caused by the Great Vowel Shift, in the *day/Tag* contrast between English and German. In the US, Northern Cities fronting (Labov 1991) of the lax mid-back vowel to [æ] means that inner-city Detroit "blocks" sounds to other Americans like "blacks." Is fronting easier to detect than backing? Stockwell and Minkova (2001: 100) provide an intriguing generalization about the direction of assimilation.

There you have it. These ten linguistic ideas surface in any phase of description that goes above the level of the lexical word or plunges below the surface of standardized spelling's imperfect record of sound. Unlike the pages of the texts that are the basis for evidence of change, they are abstract, and like any scientific abstraction they are subject to revision or even retirement by ideas with more to offer.

References and Further Reading

Algeo, J. & Pyles, H. (2005). *Origins and Development of the English Language*. 5th edn. Boston: Thomson/Wadsworth.

Bauer, L. (1994). *Watching English Change*. New York: Cambridge University Press.

Blake, N. F. (1996). *A History of the English Language*. New York: New York University Press.

Collinge, N. E. (1985). *The Laws of Indo-European*. Philadelphia: John Benjamins.

Crystal, D. (2006). *Pronouncing Shakespeare*. New York: Cambridge University Press.

Ellegård, A. (1953). *The Auxiliary 'Do': The Establishment and Regularizaton of its Use in English*. Stockholm: Almqvist and Wiksell.

Hope, J. (1994). *Authorship of Shakespeare's Plays*. Cambridge: Cambridge University Press.

Jespersen, O. (1942). *Modern English Grammar*. London: George Allen and Unwin.

Labov, W. P. (1991). The three dialects of English. In P. Eckert (ed.), *Quantitative Analyses of Sound Change* (pp. 1–44). New York: Academic Press.

Ladefoged, P. (2006). *A Course in Phonetics*. 5th edn. Boston: Thompson/Wadsworth.

Langer, N. (2001). *Linguistic Purism in Action: How Auxiliary Tun was Stigmatized in Early New High German*. Berlin: Walter de Gruyter.

Lass, R. (1997). *Historical Linguistics and Language Change*. New York: Cambridge University Press.

Leith, D. (1997). *A Social History of English*. 2nd edn. New York: Routledge and Kegan Paul.

Lowth, R. (1762). *Short Introduction to English Grammar*. London.

Lutz, A. (2005). The first push. *Linguistic Inquiry*, 32, 405–37.

McWhorter, J. (2001). *Power of Babel: A Natural History of Language*. New York: Times Books, Henry Holt.

Mazzon, G. (2004). *A History of English Negation*. New York: Pearson Longman.

Mondorf, B. (2004). *Gender Differences in English Syntax*. Linguistische Arbeiten 491. Tübingen: Max Niemeyer.

Nasar, S. (1998). *A Beautiful Mind*. New York: Simon and Schuster.

Nurmi, A. (1999). *A Social History of Periphrastic DO*. Helsinki: Mémoires de la Société Néophlologique de Helsinki LVI.

Prokosh, E. (1939). *A Comparative Germanic Grammar*. Philadelphia: Linguistic Society of America.

Sievers, E. & Bruner, K. (1965). *Altenglische Grammatik*. 3rd auflage. Tübingen: Max Niemeyer.

Stockwell, R. & Minkova, D. (2001). *English Words*. New York: Cambridge University Press.

Traugott, E. (2006). Historical expressions of modality. In W. Frawley (ed.), *The Expression of Modality* (pp. 107–39). New York: De Gruyter.

Traugott, E. & Dasher, R. B. (2002). *Regularity in Semantic Change*. New York: Cambridge University Press.

Traugott, E. & Hopper, P. (2003). *Grammaticalization*. 2nd edn. New York: Cambridge University Press.

Western, A. (1905). Some remarks on the use of English adverbs. *Englische Studien*, 36, 75–99.

White, R. G. (1892). *Every-Day English*. Boston: Houghton, Mifflin.

Whorf, B. L. (1957). *Language, Thought, and Reality*. Boston: MIT Press.

Part II
Linguistic Survey

Introduction

The following five essays focus on the transformation of English in a number of linguistic criteria: patterns of speech sounds (phonology, by Donka Minkova and Robert Stockwell), inflectional endings and other grammatical components (morphology, by Robert McColl Millar), word order and sentence structure (syntax, by Olga Fischer), vocabulary and word formation (lexicology, by Geoffrey Hughes), and verse form (prosody, by Geoffrey Russom). In its history, the English language has gone through such major changes that Old English often seems closer to German than to modern English: the prepositional phrase "with the poor child," for instance, is *"mid þæm earman cilde"* in Old English and *"mit dem armen Kind"* in German. Here the definite article and the adjective have grammatical endings in both Old English (*þæm*, *earman*) and German (*dem*, *armen*), each denoting number (singular), case (dative), and grammatical gender (neuter). In modern English, neither *the* nor *poor* is declined under any syntactic circumstances.

The diachronic study of English requires a synthesis of observations made in individual subfields of linguistics. To take an intersection between morphology and phonology for an example, the simplification of grammatical endings is interconnected with the weakening of unaccented syllables in the Middle English period. As shown above, the Old English prepositional phrase *"mid þæm earman cilde"* contains distinct grammatical endings, *-æm*, *-an*, and *-e*. These inflections became "leveled" or phonologically undistinguished in the Middle English period (e.g. from *-an* to *-en* to *-e*). By the beginning of the early modern period, even the leveled ending *-e* was dropped entirely. Such a morphological simplification, in turn, may have influenced syntax. The prepositional phrase *"mid þæm earman cilde"* represents common word order in Old English (as in modern English), with a preposition (*mid*) preceding the noun phrase it governs, an adjective (*earman*) preceding the noun it modifies, and a demonstrative pronoun (*þæm*) preceding the rest of the noun phrase with which it agrees. Because of its rich morphology, however, Old English accommodated other word order as well: a preposition might follow the noun phrase, or an adjective might follow the noun. In fact, an Old English poet might have said *"cilde þæm earman"* (without the preposition *mid*) to mean 'with the poor child.' With the leveling and eventual loss of grammatical endings in Middle English, many such syntactic variations became unavailable to poets and everyone else.

The diachronic change of English is closely associated with the changes in its social and political environment. The rise of the phoneme /v/ in Middle English (from the status as an allophone of /f/ in Old English) was accelerated by the borrowing of Romance words that begin with the *v*-sound, like *voice* and *virtue*. The English lexicon may be compared to an archeological site where the culture and power relations of the past are preserved in different strata or layers. To take the concept of poverty, the native adjective *(e)arm* became obsolete by the mid-thirteenth century, presumably because its semantic domain was taken over by *poor*, an Anglo-Norman loanword first

attested in the earlier part of the same century. The English vocabulary of poverty was subsequently enriched by loanwords from more prestigious languages: *privation* from French (mid-14th c.), *destitute* from Latin (late 14th c.), and *penury* from classical Latin (15th c.), to name but a few. As for prosody, Old English poetry consistently employed alliterative meter, a traditional verse form common to all early Germanic poetry. In later medieval periods, English poets used continental verse forms such as regular rhymes and syllable-based prosody, although alliteration continued to be used in many poems as it kept adapting, with remarkable resilience, to the ever-changing phonology and morphology of Middle English. The alliterative tradition lasted until the early sixteenth century when the native prosody finally became incompatible with the language because of the systematic loss of the final -*e*.

Haruko Momma

4
Phonology: Segmental Histories

Donka Minkova and Robert Stockwell

The Stressed Vowels in Old English

Evidence for the vowel system of Old English (OE) is of two types: the systematic orthography developed at Winchester in the late tenth century, and the study of the sound changes which lead up to the Winchester usage and which to some extent enlighten us about the graphemic regularities and anomalies found there. We depart from nineteenth- and twentieth-century interpretations of the orthographic evidence that over-value the assumption that the orthography is entirely phonemic and that vowel symbols should be read in strict accord with their values in Latin. Instead we present a compromise view which gives greater weight to evidence from sound change. However, at all times we cite also the orthographic paradigm which Anglo-Saxonists have generally endorsed.

The earliest records of Old English (the *Corpus, Épinal,* and *Erfurt Glossaries,* 8–9th c.) require us to posit a simple six-vowel system, all six vowels occurring as both long and short. Peripherality (relative closeness to the edge of the vowel space) as an additional feature of long and short vowels is redundant: the long vowel is always peripheral, and the short vowel is always non-peripheral. If we discount peripherality, we are left with an (idealized) familiar vowel triangle (figure 4.1).

These six vowels provide the launch pad for a survey of the English vowel system from earliest times. Two more vowels played almost no continuing role in English – the rounded front vowels [ö(:)] and [ü(:)]. Early OE had the three back-gliding diphthongs [iw], [ew], and [æw], but it had none of the front-gliding diphthongs that are so prominent in Present-Day English (PDE), namely [ey], [ay], [oy], as in *bait, bite, void.* The system found in "classical" Old English is essentially the same, plus one maverick [ü(:)], usually spelled <y>, to be explained below. The back-gliding diphthongs change into in-gliding (V-w → V-ə) and eventually into long vowels which merge with the pre-existing long vowels. The result is the system in figure 4.2, where the late OE mergers are circled.

Figure 4.1   Idealized vowel triangle for early Old English

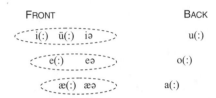

Figure 4.2   Vowel triangle for late Old English

The OE scribes did not distinguish between short and long vowels; the insertion of macrons over etymologically long vowels in printed texts is a modern editorial convenience.

The so-called "short diphthongs" have not appeared in our summary to this point. These are the vowels spelled <ea, eo, io> when followed by [-rC, -lC, -h] and [-w], the last with a back vowel in the following syllable. They are etymologically short, they count as short in the prosody, and they merge with simple short vowels later. They have attracted a great deal of scholarly controversy, and no fully satisfactory solution to the problem exists; they require special treatment. Some examples are <earm> 'arm', <healf> 'half', <heofon> 'heaven', <nieht> 'night'. Since contrasting sets of "short" and normal bimoraic diphthongs are typologically unattested, we treat them as simple short vowels. Thus, for the pronunciation of the exotic "short diph-thongs," since in all instances they soon merge again with the vowels that they sprang from, we recommend the corresponding short vowels: *earm* is [ærm], *heofon* is [hɛvən], *nieht* is [nɪht].

That leaves the high front rounded [ü:] vowel, spelled <y>. The only source for this vowel in OE was the process known as "I-Mutation" (ca. 6–7th c.). It is a right-to-left (regressive) assimilation: back vowels, both long and short, became front, and low front vowels were raised, when an inflectional or a derivational suffix beginning with [-i, -y] was added to the root. All back vowels, short and long, underwent muta-tion; among the front vowels only [æ(:)] was mutated, and the first element of diph-thongs was raised to a high front vowel [i:]. The changes are shown in figure 4.3; the dashed line indicates the direction of the sound change from early OE to late OE and ME.

Both the long and the short vowels were subject to I-Mutation. The change created stem alternations such as FULL-FILL, FOOT-FEET, MAN-MEN:

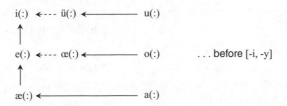

Figure 4.3 Effects of i-mutation

OE *full* 'full', adj. – *fyllan*, v. < *full + *yan* 'to make full, to fill'
OE *fōt* 'foot', sg. – *fēt*, < *fōt-iz 'feet', pl.
OE *mann* 'man', sg. – *menn*, pl. < *mann + *iz*- 'men', pl.

In late OE times the vowels represented by <y> generally merged with [i]. Another option was a retraction back to [ʊ/uː], spelled <u>; this type of spelling was retained, mostly in the Southwest Midlands, until the fourteenth century. A third option, which involves both unrounding and lowering to [ɛ/eː], spelled <e>, is associated with the dialect area south of London (Kentish). This results in some unexpected dialect forms surfacing in PDE: *bury* [bɛri] < OE *byrgan* [büryən] is a dialectal hybrid – the spelling is Southwestern, the pronunciation, from Kentish. Other examples are *merry-mirth* < OE *myrie*, *busy* < OE *bysig*.

Transition to Middle English

Simplifying somewhat, three types of sound changes took place after 1150–1200 which had the effect of massively reorganizing the system. They were:

* Long vowels tended to move upwards in the vowel space.
* All OE diphthongs became monophthongs, and new diphthongs arose.
* Vowel length came to be almost completely predictable.

The quality of the *short vowels* remained stable, except for the mergers shown and exemplified in figure 4.4.

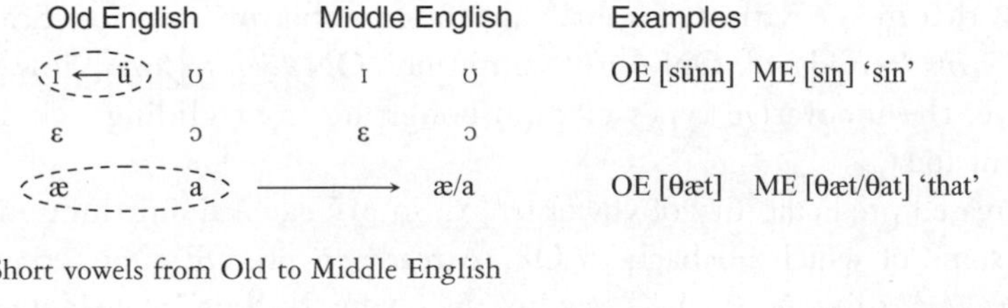

Old English		Middle English		Examples
ɪ ← ü ʊ		ɪ ʊ		OE [sünn] ME [sɪn] 'sin'
ɛ ɔ		ɛ ɔ		
æ a	→	æ/a		OE [θæt] ME [θæt/θat] 'that'

Figure 4.4 Short vowels from Old to Middle English

The *long vowels* were also generally stable. The changes in that subsystem are shown in figure 4.5.

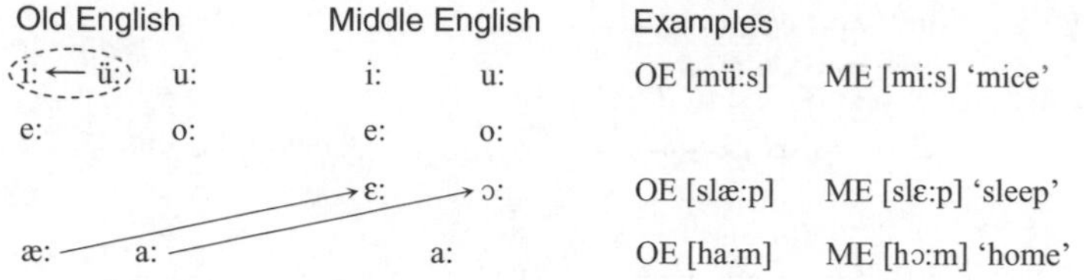

Old English		Middle English		Examples	
(iː ← üː)	uː	iː	uː	OE [müːs]	ME [miːs] 'mice'
eː	oː	eː	oː		
		→ εː	→ ɔː	OE [slæːp]	ME [slɛːp] 'sleep'
æː ——— aː ———			aː	OE [haːm]	ME [hɔːm] 'home'

Figure 4.5   Long vowels from Old to Middle English

Note that the long and short vowels are mismatched in terms of vowel height. As we will see below, this affects the outcome of quantitative changes, e.g., when /eː/ shortens, for any reason, the new vowel is not [ɛ] but [ɪ], as in OE/EME *selig* [seːlig] → *silly*, OE/EME *redels* [reːdəls] → ME/PDE *riddle*. When the short high vowels are lengthened, they emerge as [eː] and [oː], as in *wicu* > ME [weːk] 'week', *wudu* > ME [woːd] 'wood'. The long low front vowel [æː] was raised to [ɛː]; words that had been spelled with <æ> came to be spelled with <*ea, ee*>. Even before Chaucer's time there were two kinds of "long *e*": "close long *e*" [eː], and "open long *e*" [ɛː]. They were consistently spelled alike, generally <*ee*>, but they were clearly different since they do not rhyme freely with each other in Chaucer's verse.

The monophthongization of all OE diphthongs in ME was noted above. The formation of new diphthongs came about in two ways: by reanalysis (resyllabification) of the post-vocalic [y, w] as the coda of the syllabic nucleus on its left, whereas it had previously been the onset of the syllable on its right; or by epenthesis of a glide before a velar fricative [h]:

V + [y, w] → Vi/Vu	OE dæg [dæy]	ME [dai] 'day'
	OE cnāwan [knaːwən]	ME [knɔu(ə)n] 'know'
V (front) + [h] → Vi	OE ehta [ɛhtə]	ME [eiht(ə)] 'eight'
V (back) + [h] → Vu	OE bōhte [bɔhtə]	ME [bɔuht(ə)] 'bought'

Although referred to as "new," these diphthongs are rooted in the phonology of late OE. They are the result of co-articulatory changes occurring when a vowel and a following [y, w], or the voiceless fricative [h], come in contact within the same syllable. The vocalization of [y, w] is an easy step – these sounds are on the borderline between vowels and consonants. When they are no longer consonantal, they produce diphthongs that merge with the diphthongs found in borrowings from Scandinavian, as in ON *hreinn* 'rein(deer)', ON *heill*, 'salutation', ON *lágr* > [loːw] 'low, flame'. As noted above, the innovative types of diphthongs are front-gliding – it is the type predominant today.

The increased predictability of vowel length in ME came about through a series of processes, some of which go back to OE. Already in pre-OE times, the vowels in *lexical monosyllables* like *hwa* 'who', *swa* 'so', *hwi* 'why' became long (if they were not already). This accounts for the constraint against lexical monosyllables ending in short vowels, to this day.

Open Syllable Lengthening (OSL) is the most famous of the quantitative changes in ME. It affects the short vowels in "open" syllables, mostly in disyllabic words ending in schwa (Minkova 1982):

OE *talu*	[talu] 'tale'	ME *tale*	[taːl(ə)]
OE *nosu*	[nɔzu] 'nose'	ME *nose*	[nɔːz(ə)]
OE *stelan*	[stɛlən] 'steal'	ME *stel(e)*	[stɛːl(ə)]

OSL came about for two main reasons: compensation for the loss of final schwa and a general linguistic preference for stressed syllables to be heavy. The first, and stressed, syllable in OE *talu* 'tale', *nosu* 'nose', is open and light and eligible for lengthening; the first syllable of OE *strengþu* 'strength', *heorte* 'heart', is closed and heavy and therefore ineligible for lengthening. The domain of the compensatory process is the entire word: the vowel in the stressed syllable gains weight as the weak final vowel is omitted. The majority of words that underwent OSL are of that type: they start as disyllabic in OE and end up as monosyllables with a long vowel.

Pre-consonantal (-CC(C)) Shortening: in late OE-early ME (with some residual effects today), two post-vocalic consonants commonly caused shortening of the stem vowel. This explains the verb-form alternations in, e.g., *keep-kept*, *mean-meant*, *lose-lost*, where the long vowels of the stem were shortened in front of the cluster created by adding a dental consonant to form the preterite. A similar shortening occurs occasionally if three consonants follow the stem in a derived environment, e.g., *Christmas* (<Christ-mass).

Trisyllabic Shortening affects the stem vowel if the derived word has two syllables to the right of the stem. The bulk of examples are Latinate words, with the short vowel already in place when the words were borrowed, as in *abound-abundance*, *vine-vinegar*, *vain-vanity* and several hundred more.

Transition to Early Modern English and PDE

This section will only address processes which tended to change the quality of vowels. The first one is R-lowering: a common sound change, neutralizing the quality of the vowels in stressed syllables with [r + C] in the coda: *clerk, work, nurse, first*. The lowering is most consistent with the short vowels, but it can affect the long vowels too, producing pairs such as *bear* vs. *year*, *tear* (v). vs. *tear* (n)., *floor* vs. *boor*.

The Great English Vowel Shift

If one has looked even casually at the long vowels of words in Spanish, Italian, French, or Classical Latin, it is clear that they differ from English in a systematic way: where Romance has [i(ː)] for a vowel spelled <i>, English has [ay] (unless the word was borrowed long after the vowel shift was completed, as in *machine*).

The traditional picture of these events that took place in the south of England between 1200 and 1600 was represented by Otto Jespersen (1909: 232), who named it the "Great Vowel Shift" (figure 4.6).

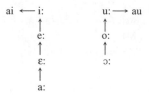

Figure 4.6   Traditional picture of the Great Vowel Shift

This says that each lower vowel moves up to the next higher position, and the highest vowel becomes a diphthong. Jespersen dates the change to around 1450.

A quite non-traditional picture, the one for which we argue, following Stockwell (2002), is shown in figure 4.7.

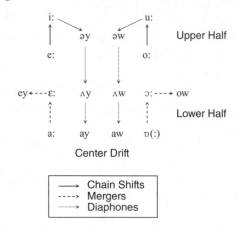

Figure 4.7   Revised picture of the Great Vowel Shift

In our representation, mergers are shown with dashed arrows and *diaphones* (allophones which are non-contrastive by virtue of their distribution across dialects) are shown with dotted arrows, whereas true chain shifts are shown with solid arrows.

The most conspicuous part of the vowel shift, which we call the "center drift," is not a chain at all. "Center drift" is the diphthongization, centralizing, and lowering (in either order, chronologically) of [iː] and [uː] to some variant of [ay] and [aw]. In contrast, the defining feature of sound changes which are arranged in a chain is this: any two adjacent contrastive entities – any two links in the chain – must move in lockstep, without merger. They always maintain their distance and their functional contrast. In these famous vowel-shift instances of drifting down the center, nothing is ever displaced, no merger occurs, and no phonological change has occurred. All the variants, top to bottom, coexist. They are non-contrastive in all dialects and all accents.

We know that in childhood all speakers build their own grammars. When it comes to learning language, everyone is an island. From that point of view, when people are still immature and haven't traveled much or mixed in wider social circles, [əy] and [əw] (Canadian or Virginia pronunciations) may not immediately be perceived as allophonically related to [ay] and [aw] at all. As we expand our linguistic horizons and talk with Australians and Cockneys and Canadians and Virginians and Philadelphians, these dialect variants become functionally single phonemes and "Canadian raisings" are hardly noticed by the rest of us because they are increasingly familiar diaphones of [ay] and [aw].

The upper half of the vowel shift was completed by about 1550. The lower half was still taking place (Lass 1999: 95–8) into the eighteenth century. And the center drift continues (to different degrees in different dialects) to this day.

By Shakespeare's time the language he spoke would have been (except for some lexical items) almost fully intelligible to a twenty-first-century speaker of English – probably easier for an American than for an RP speaker or a Yorkshireman or a Scot, just because American English is retrograde in many accentual features, especially the post-vocalic [-r] (see below). Dialectal differences continue, of course, especially after the explosion of new varieties of English that went with the adventurers and settlers who took the language around the world.

Unstressed vowels

The vowels in unstressed syllables had started to lose distinctiveness in Proto-Germanic, when stress began to fall on the first (root) syllable. By the time of the OE texts the inherited long vowels in unstressed syllables had been shortened. The set of unstressed vowels around the ninth century was limited to [e, a, o]. Orthographic interchangeability of the unstressed vowels in late OE suggests that some kind of schwa [ə], most commonly spelled <e>, was already in place before the Norman Conquest. Word-medially, vowel reduction is attested in widespread syncope and epenthesis of word-internal <-e->, thus <myc(e)le> 'much', <heof(e)nes> 'of heaven'. In the following two hundred years <-e> became the default spelling for post-tonic final vowels: <bane> 'killer' (OE <bana>), <deme> 'judge' (OE <dema>), <nose> 'nose' (OE <nosu>).

The process of vowel reduction culminated in the complete loss of schwa in ME, especially word-finally. Except for [-i] in the suffix <-y> (<OE –*ig*), all uncovered vowels in final unstressed syllables in native words were lost during ME: OE <hwæte>, ME <whet(e)> 'wheat'; OE <(to) scipe>, ME <(to) ship>. Schwa loss is amply attested in the earliest ME syllable-counting verse texts, *The Owl and the Nightingale* and *The Ormulum*: e.g., *bitæch(e) icc, bliss(e) inoh*, where the parenthesized <-e>'s are elided. Metrical and orthographic evidence shows loss of final vowels in trisyllabic words: *almes(se), lover(e), loved(e)*. Apocope of final <-e> also occurred early in words likely to occupy prosodically weak positions: pronouns, conjunctions, auxiliaries.

Parallel to schwa loss in open final syllables was the reduction and eventual syncope of schwa in the inflectional suffixes: <-e(n), -es, -eth, -ed>. The process was blocked in stems whose final consonants would create phonotactic incompatibilities: [-s, -z, -š, -ž, -č, -ǰ] for the <-es> suffix and [t, d] for the <ed> suffix; this gives rise to the PDE patterns *rates* vs. *aces*, *faked* vs. *lauded*. The rate of syncope is considerably higher before vowels and weak <h>, and stems ending in a sonorant (*berth* < *bereth*, *comth* < *cometh*) are more prone to undergo the change early.

Consonants

Compared to the complexity of the vocalic developments, the consonantal changes in English have been less dramatic, and the evidential bases for their reconstruction are less controversial. The major differences between the consonantal system of OE and the PDE consonantal system are:

- Simplification of long consonants
- Phonemicization of the voiced fricatives [v, ð, z]
- Vocalization or loss of [ɣ], [x], [ç] and distributional restrictions on [h]
- Loss of [-r] in some varieties of English
- Simplification of the consonant clusters [kn-], [gn-], [wr-], [-mb], [-ng]

The system that we take to be the input for these changes is shown in table 4.1.

The table shows only the short consonants. From West Germanic, OE had inherited geminate consonants: *pytt* 'pit', *tellan* 'to tell', *cuppa* 'cup'. Historically, consonant gemination was restricted to stems in which the vowel was short; that restriction holds for OE too. By the tenth century the geminates began to be simplified in

Table 4.1 The consonants of Old English

	Labial	Labio-dental	Dental	Alveolar	Palato-alveolar	Palatal	Velar
Voiceless Stops	p		t				k
Voiced Stops	b		d				g
Voiceless Fricatives		f	θ	s	š		h
Voiced Fricatives							
Affricates					č, ǰ		
Nasals	m		n				
Liquids				r, l			
Approximants	w					y	

unstressed medial syllables: OE <gyldenne> 'golden' > ME <gyldene>. Word-final geminates were simplified in early ME. Consonant degemination started in the northern dialects where the loss of final <-e> was more advanced. The commonly posited preservation of geminates in disyllabic forms in the south until the end of the fourteenth century (Chaucer's *knobbe, wynne, calle, happe*), is deceptive: the final vowels there were already provably unstable, so the forms would not have been disyllabic. The system disallowed final geminates; therefore these forms would have been pronounced with simple consonants every time the schwa was dropped. We assume the orthographic doubling of consonants in late ME simply marked the preceding vowel as short, a practice initiated by Orm at the end of the twelfth century.

Fricative voicing

"Fricative voicing" refers to the lenition of the fricatives [f, θ, s] to [v, ð, z] in OE. The only other voiced fricative in OE was [ɤ]; it had been phonemic in early OE, but by the second half of the tenth century it had become a positional allophone of [g]; it is therefore excluded from this set.

The voicing contrast in the pairs [f-v], [θ-ð], and [s-z] in OE was allophonic: voicing/lenition occurred if the consonant was the onset of an unstressed syllable. In all other environments the fricatives were voiceless (figure 4.8).

The voicing is also morphologically conditioned. For voicing to occur, the fricative must not be the initial consonant of the root, so in OE *gefara* 'travel companion', *asyndran* 'separate', *beþencan* 'bethink, consider' were not subject to voicing. The consonants of the fricative-initial adjectival suffixes *-fæst, -feald, -full, -sum* were not affected by voicing, suggesting that these suffixes maintained root-like properties; their affiliation with roots is confirmed by their ability to fill a metrical ictus in verse. The verbal suffix *-sian*, however, is treated like an inflection and its initial consonant is voiced, as in OE *clænsian* 'to make clean'. The OE voicing of fricatives root-finally before a vowel-initial grammatical suffix accounts for PDE alternations of the type found in *lose-lost, leave-left, nose-nostril, thrive-thrift, staff-staves, calf-calves, dwarf-dwarves, wife-wives, woof-weave, glass-glaze, brass-brazen* (originally 'made of brass'), *cloth-clothe, mouth* (n.) – *mouth* (v.), *wreath-wreathing*.

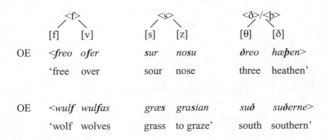

Figure 4.8 Allophonic voicing contrast in Old English fricatives

In ME the clear-cut complementary distribution of the voiceless and voiced fricatives was put in jeopardy. Intense lexical borrowing in Middle English obscured the inherited restriction on voiced fricatives at the left edge of the root. A search of headwords and forms in <va-, vo-, vi-, ve-> in the *MED* yields more than 800 borrowed items, including common words like *voice, vomit, void, virtue*; this would have been a leading factor for establishing an [f]-[v] contrast initially. About 45 words with initial [z] were also borrowed in ME, but for the [s]-[z] contrast in initial position the most important evidence would have been dialectal: the initial fricatives in native words had been voiced already in OE in the dialectal areas south of the Thames, and especially Kent, where we find spellings such as <vaire> 'fair', <vo> 'foe', and large numbers of spellings like <zong> 'song', <zalt> 'salt', <zwo> 'so'. While words beginning with [ð] were not borrowed, lenition of [θ] to [ð] in all dialects in late ME occurred in weakly stressed words as in *the, this, then, thus, there, them*.

In word-final position the phonemicization of the voicing contrast was driven by the loss of the unstressed vowels which had previously provided the context for voicing, e.g., before final schwa loss, <knave> 'knave' would have [-v] and <bathe> 'bathe' would have [ð] in word-final position. Similarly, the voicing contrast would be preserved in pairs such as <wif> 'wife' and <wif(e)s> 'of the wife', even after the schwa was lost and the fricative was adjacent to an obstruent. The degemination of the earlier voiceless [-ff-, -ss-, -θθ-] in word-medial position depleted further the input evidence for complementary distribution. By the end of ME such evidence was completely lost and the consonantal system of the language with respect to the labiodental, dental, and alveolar fricatives had reached its modern state, i.e., [f, v, θ, ð, s, z] were independent phonemes, contrasting in all positions: *vine-fine, silver-sulphur, sieve-if, zeal-seal, visor-nicer, laze-lace, either-ether*.

As noted above, in OE the voiced velar fricative [ɣ] was an allophone of [g]; it appeared medially between back vowels. In that position [ɣ] underwent further lenition and developed into the approximant [w] in ME, e.g., OE [laɣu] > ME [law(ə)] 'law'. The preservation of the original [g] in later borrowings from Old Norse results in etymological doublets (table 4.2).

Table 4.2 Etymological doublets

Old English	Middle English	Loanword
dragan 'to draw'	draw(en)	drag (1440) < ON draga
sagu 'saying'	saw(e)	saga (1709) < ON saga

The historical instability of {h}

Another set of changes targets the velar fricative [h]. In OE it could appear freely initially, finally, and in consonantal clusters: <hu> 'how', <heah> 'high', <mihtig> 'mighty', <hring> 'ring', <hlot> 'lot'. Although the evidence for its allophonic

realizations – [x] after a back vowel and [ç] after a front vowel – is inconclusive (Lass 1994: 74–5), its ME developments support the reconstruction of [x, ç] in the respective environments. The history of this consonant is one of progressive weakening and loss, reversed only comparatively recently under the influence of orthography.

The loss of [h-] in word-initial consonant clusters was already under way in the eleventh century. By the middle of the thirteenth century [hl-, hr-, hn-] had become [l-, r-, n-]:

OE <hlot>   ME <lot>
OE <hræfn>   ME <raven>
OE <hnecca>   ME <neck>

The simplification of [hw-] to [(h)w-] started around the same time in ME.

In intervocalic position [-h-] had been lost in early OE, but it was preserved in geminates: <cohhetan> 'to cough', <hlæhhan> 'to laugh'. After the loss of geminate consonants in ME, the [h] in this position formed the basis of new diphthongs in [-w] and [-y]. In word-final position and before [-t] the fricative [h] was also unstable. Beginning in the fourteenth century that instability resulted either in lenition, taking the consonants through the stage of being an approximant into a glide, or in fortition, strengthening the [h] to [f]. The vocalization of [h] occurs both after front and back vowels, while the change of [h] to [f] can only occur after back vowels, suggesting that the input consonant for that change was the velar allophone [x] whose fortition was most likely perceptually driven (figure 4.9).

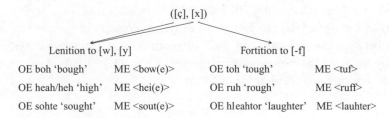

Figure 4.9   Lenition and fortition of [ç] and [x]

In word-initial position before vowels the realization of [h-] in ME depends on regional, prosodic, and etymological factors. Broadly speaking, in the north [h-] maintained its consonantal nature, while in the south evidence for early h-dropping is plentiful. Weakly stressed words (pronouns, auxiliaries) were more likely to undergo h-loss. The etymology of a word was also of consequence: Late Latin had started losing [h-]; the change had affected French prior to the massive introduction of Romance words into ME. Words like *heir, arbor* came into English without [h-], though cognates borrowed later may preserve it: *heir* (1275) – *heredity* (1540), *able* (1325) – *habilitation* (1612), *arbor* (1300) – *herbarium* (1700), *hour* (1225) – *horologic* (1665), *honor* (1200), but *honorarium* (1658) with or without [h-] in British English.

In seventeenth- and eighteenth-century England [h]-lessness was stigmatized. The spelling of many borrowed words kept initial <h-> as new classical words flooded the language, and words in *hept(a)-*, *hex(a)-*, *hypo-*, *hydro-*, *hyper-*, *hetero-* kept the initial aspirate. By the end of the eighteenth century only a random set of frequently used borrowed items spelled with <h-> allowed [h]-less pronunciation. Today *heir, honest,* and *hour* and their cognates are the sole surviving instances of a once widespread phonetic weakening and loss.

Loss of {r} in some varieties of English

The exact phonetic nature of the consonant [r] in OE is still debated. It could have been an initial coronal trill, developing into a retroflex approximant with glide-like properties in coda position in late ME, when the first written evidence of weakening and loss of [r] begins to appear (Lass 1999: 114–16). There is good evidence that [-r]-loss was preceded by the development of an epenthetic schwa-glide between the nuclear vowel and [-r]: <mier(e)> 'mire' <lyerni > 'to learn', <dierth(e)> 'famine'. Before [-s], the early loss of [r] is reflected in the spelling: *bust < burst, ass < arse, cuss* (US, first recorded 1775) < *curse*. By the end of the eighteenth century, [r]-lessness was spreading in England, though it was not generalized in southern England (and parts of the US East Coast) until the early nineteenth century.

Other consonantal changes

Until about 1500, the digraphs <wr-, kn-, gn-> represented real consonant clusters, as attested in fourteenth-century alliterative verse matching of, e.g., *writ* to *wonder,* *gnaw* to *God,* *knight* to *kiss*. The loss of the initial consonants in the clusters occurred gradually between the sixteenth and the eighteenth century (Minkova 2003: 330–40, 365–8); by the time the process was completed in the spoken language, the written form of the clusters was fossilized (table 4.3).

Table 4.3   Fossilized consonant clusters

ME	post-1700	Examples
writ [wr-]	[r-]	*wrath, wretch, wrong*
gnaw [gn-]	[n-]	gnash, gnarly, gnome, gnu
knight [kn-]	[n-]	knack, knit, know, knee

The assimilation of the second consonants to the preceding ones in [-mb] and [-mn] in final position is just cluster simplification. In the case of [-mb] the process started in Middle English, resulting in scribal uncertainty as to the value of <-mb> and <-m>; some "inverse" spellings began to appear, in which the <-b> was inserted unetymologically (table 4.4).

Table 4.4   Cluster simplification and some unetymological "inverse" spellings

OE	ME	Examples (all [-m])
<lamb> [-mb]	<lamb> [-m]	lamb, -combe 'valley', climb, succumb
<lim> [-m]	<limb> [-m]	crumb, numb, thumb

The rejection of the [-mb] cluster word-finally in native words led to the simplification of the cluster in borrowed words: *tomb* (1225), *bomb* (1588), *rhomb* (1575), *hecatomb* (1598), *aplomb* (1828), have lost the final [-b] present in the source. Note, however, that if the cluster straddles two syllables: *tomboy, rhomboid, limber*, the identity of both consonants is preserved.

The cluster <-mn> in word-final position appears only in non-native words: *autumn, column, condemn, damn, hymn, solemn*. The phonetic trigger of the simplification is perceptual difficulty if they are tautosyllabic. However, the second consonant can be "restored" if a vowel-initial suffix is added: *autum-nal, hym-nal, solem-nity*.

A special case of historical cluster simplification affects the cluster <-ng> in word-final position. Until the sixteenth century [ŋ] was an allophone of [n] before velar stops. In the seventeenth century the velar nasal and the velar stop [-ŋg] developed into a single phoneme [-ŋ] in word-final position. It is a "defectively distributed" phoneme: the sound is distinctive only in coda position. The acoustic closeness of [-ŋ] and [n] leads to frequent substitution of [-ŋ] by [-n] in the morpheme <-ing>.

Finally, a note on inventory enrichment: the voiced palatal fricative [-ž] was not part of the Old or Middle English phonemic systems, though the allophone [ž] could appear in borrowed words where [z] was followed by a palatal glide ([zy] → [ž]): *division, treasure, usual, Parisian*. The full integration of [ž] occurred gradually after the seventeenth century when new French borrowings introduced the sound in initial and final position: *gendarme, Giselle, Zhivago, beige, rouge, espionage*, etc.). Thus, [ž] is the latest addition to the inventory of English consonants. The development of a single fricative [ž] out of a sequence of an alveolar consonant plus a palatal glide (*division, treasure, usual*) is part of a more general pattern of palatalization and affrication of alveolar stops and fricatives when followed by [-y]:

[-sy-]	→	[š]:	*mission, sugar, passion*
[-zy-]	→	[ž]:	*occasion, derision, measure*
[-ty-]	→	[č]:	*mature, mutual, rapture*
[-dy-]	→	[ǰ]:	*soldier, verdure, procedure*

The same process continues in PDE across word boundaries within a larger prosodic domain: *this year, unless you* with [š], *as you say, as yet* with [ž], *got + you* (*gotcha*), *not yet* with [č], *had you, did you* with [ǰ].

References and Further Reading

Jespersen, O. (1909). *A Modern English Grammar on Historical Principles, Vol. 1: Sounds and Spellings*. London: George Allen and Unwin.

Lass, R. (1994). *Old English: A Historical Linguistic Companion*. Cambridge: Cambridge University Press.

Lass, R. (1999). Phonology and morphology. In R. Lass (ed.), *The Cambridge History of the English Language, Vol. 2: 1476–1776* (pp. 56–186). Cambridge: Cambridge University Press.

MED: The Electronic Middle English Dictionary. www.//ets.umdl.umich.edu/m/med.

Minkova, D. (1982). The environment for Middle English open syllable lengthening, *Folia Linguistica Historica*, 3 (1), 29–58.

Minkova, D. (1991). *The History of Final Vowels in English*. Berlin: Mouton de Gruyter.

Minkova, D. (2003). *Alliteration and Sound Change in Early English*. Cambridge: Cambridge University Press.

Stockwell, R. (2002). How much shifting actually occurred in the historical English vowel shift? In D. Minkova and R. Stockwell (eds.), *Studies in the History of the English Language: A Millennial Perspective* (pp. 267–282). Berlin: Mouton de Gruyter.

5
History of English Morphology

Robert McColl Millar

When non-specialists think of linguistic change, this is often envisaged in terms of alterations in word meaning, or the replacement of some words by others. But whilst it would be wrong to downplay the importance of semantic and lexical change to our understanding of language change, this is only part of a much broader pattern. Changes to the morphology of a language – the ways that meaning and function are represented by how a word is constructed – are central to our understanding of the manner in which a language as a whole changes.

In order to illustrate this, this essay will discuss morphological change in English, concentrating, due to space considerations, and in the interest of clarity, on changes in the noun phrase inflectional morphology. Even this limited introduction should demonstrate that morphological change has had profound effects upon what *type* of language English is.

Linguistic Typology

Linguists categorize languages not only according to genetic relationship, but also according to *type*: unrelated languages can be similar in their phonological, morphological, and syntactic structures. A number of types are recognized; but the typological distinction which has particular relevance for the history of English inflectional morphology is that between *synthetic* and *analytic* language types.

A purely *synthetic* language describes the function of a phrase within a clause only according to form. Thus, in Finnish, *nuori tyttö* means 'young girl' in a sentence equivalent to **The young girl** *saw the film*, while *nuorelta tytöltä* means 'young girl' in a sentence equivalent to *The beautiful music was coming* **from the young girl**. In Modern English, this distinction is made by position in the sentence and through the use of a preposition; in Finnish, however, it is supplied using inflectional morphemes on both adjective and noun. In highly synthetic languages, element order is flexible

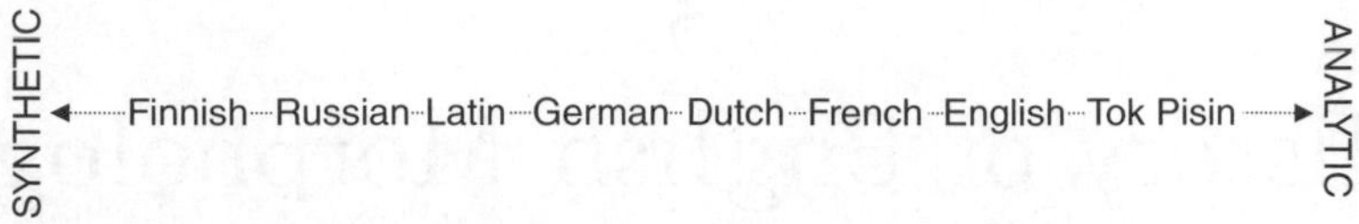

Figure 5.1 Synthetic–analytic language continuum

because denotative meaning is represented by word form rather than position in the clause.

At the other end of the scale, context alone reveals the relationship between clause elements in a purely *analytic* language. A language of this type must employ a rigid element order system. Many creole languages demonstrate a highly analytic typology. For instance, Tok Pisin, an English-based creole, does not generally express even plurality through inflections, so that *man* can be either singular or plural, depending on the context (Holm 1989: II.529–41). Present-Day English is not as analytic as Tok Pisin; it is not rich in inflectional morphology, however. The position of Present-Day English on a typological continuum is seen in figure 5.1.

Old English, however, would fall in between Latin and German. This essay will give some idea of how this change in type occurred in English.

Noun Phrase Morphology in Indo-European

In proto-Indo-European, seven grammatical cases were used to represent function through inflections: the *nominative* case, largely employed when a phrase represented the subject; the *accusative* case, largely triggered when a phrase represented the direct object; the *dative* case, largely used when a phrase represented something which is being given, often the indirect object; the *ablative* case, representing where something has been brought from; the *locative* case, referring to the place where someone or something is; the *genitive* case, largely associated with the expression of possession; and the *vocative* case, used when someone or, occasionally, something is being called by someone. These cases were marked on nouns, pronouns, and adjectives (Fortson 2004: ch. 4). Although some cases have been retained by many contemporary Indo-European languages, a general *drift* (Sapir 1921: 144) towards the simplification of case-marking has occurred in most. This is particularly true for languages originating in central and western Europe.

Nouns, pronouns, and adjectives were also marked for number. This means of distinction has, of course, survived into Present-Day English, with nouns and pronouns, although not adjectives, still normally marked for singular and plural. In proto-Indo-European, however, these word classes were all potentially marked for singular (one being or item), dual (two beings or items), and plural (more than two beings or items). Dual marking has not survived well in the Indo-European languages as a

whole. Indeed, by the time English began to be written, dual number was only marked for first and second person pronouns.

Elements of the noun phrase were also marked for grammatical gender, according to a tripartite division, termed *masculine*, *feminine*, and *neuter*. These classes did not always coincide with natural sex associations, so that, in Old English, words which had obvious female denotation, such as *wifmann* and *wif*, 'woman', were members of the masculine and neuter gender-classes, respectively. Grammatical gender has survived fairly well in the modern Indo-European languages, although "simplifying" from three genders to two is widespread, as seen, albeit in different ways, in many modern Germanic and Romance languages. Some modern Indo-European languages, such as Bengali and Afrikaans, do not preserve grammatical gender; nor does Modern English.

Beyond these broad means of "corralling" the nouns, the Indo-European languages also had smaller noun-classes, often termed *declensions*, membership of which appears to have been dependent upon the phonology of a word. Although declined following the same criteria – gender, case, number – the formal expression of these was often strikingly different from declension to declension. Similar declension forms were also present for the adjective. Each case, number, and gender "cell" was represented with a separate inflectional morpheme.

Whilst some of these features have been maintained by many Indo-European languages, very few retain absolute formal distinctiveness for the paradigms of all declensions, in all cases, with all genders, in all numbers. Instead, even in the most synthetic of the daughter languages, *syncretism*, the "falling together" of two or more originally separate forms representing separate categories, has taken place. Indeed, even the earliest recorded Indo-European languages have already passed through some, albeit limited, syncretism of this type (for instance, Sanskrit, as discussed by Fortson 2004: 193–4). (See also ENGLISH AS AN INDO-EUROPEAN LANGUAGE.)

Noun Phrase Morphology in the Germanic Languages

In the first recorded Germanic languages, five cases are given expression: the nominative, accusative, dative, genitive, and instrumental (Prokosch 1939). The instrumental, which replaced (or developed from) the ablative (and possibly also the locative), should express the means or instrument by which an action takes place. Those examples which we have of this case in the early Germanic languages do not bear this out entirely (Mitchell 1985: 3–8); indeed, ascertaining why this case is triggered rather than the dative is often difficult. The case went through syncretism with the dative very early, leaving only a few "fossilized" usages, such as Modern English *the more, the merrier*, where *the* is descended from a demonstrative in the instrumental (Small 1926, 1930).

A further feature of the Germanic noun phrase is the distinction between "strong" and "weak" adjectives, which survives in all Germanic languages except English and

Afrikaans. In Modern German, 'the poor man' is *der arme Mann*, while 'a poor man' is *ein armer Mann*. Case, gender, and number are identical for these forms; what distinguishes them is the level of case and gender information necessary to express concord between adjective and noun. In the first example, the determiner *der* tells us that the noun is a member of the masculine gender-class in the nominative case. Because this functional information is so explicit, there is no need for the "weak" adjective to carry this level of information. With the second example, however, the indefinite article *ein*, while carrying some grammatical information (for instance, the noun cannot be feminine), is not as explicit or thorough in its presentation of this information. The "strong" adjective form, *armer*, carries more grammatical information, therefore, informing us that the noun modified is masculine. Old English also made this distinction, the "strong" equivalent being *se earm mann*, the weak, *sum earma mann*.

All of these distinctions survived into Old English. With the exception of noun and pronoun plurality, however, practically nothing has come down to us. What happened?

The Old English Noun Phrase

Noun declensions

In Old English, a number of noun declensions existed, to which we can only give a cursory examination. Generally, they can be divided into two sets: the *strong* and the *weak* nouns (these terms refer to the level of case, gender, and number distinctive inflectional morphology shown). A typical "weak" masculine noun is *nama*, 'name' (table 5.1).

Very similar paradigms are found for feminine and neuter nouns. The lack of distinction between cases, genders, and numbers is significant.

With the strong nouns, however, a great deal more case, gender, and number distinction is possible, although there are similarities which bind the declensions together. One of the central of these is the *a*-declension (table 5.2), where *stān* 'stone' is masculine, while *word* 'word' and *scip* 'ship' are neuter.

Word represents the "ancestors" of the *zero* plurals of which a small number survive into Modern English, such as *sheep* and *fish*.

Table 5.1   Weak declension: *nama* 'name'

Case	Singular	Plural
Nominative	nama	naman
Accusative	naman	naman
Dative	naman	namum
Genitive	naman	namena

Table 5.2   The *a*-declension: *stan* 'stone', *word* 'word', and *scip* 'ship'

Case	Singular	Plural
Nominative	stān, word, scip	stānas, word, scipu(-o)
Accusative	stān, word, scip	stānas, word, scipu(-o)
Dative	stāne, worde, scipe	stānum, wordum, scipum
Genitive	stānes, wordes, scipes	stāna, worda, scipa

Table 5.3   The *ō*-declension: *ār* 'grace' and *giefu* 'gift'

Case	Singular	Plural
Nominative	ār, giefu	āra(-e), giefa(-e)
Accusative	āre, giefe	āra(-e), giefa(-e)
Dative	āre, giefe	āra(-ena), giefa(-ena)
Genitive	āre, giefe	ārum, giefum

Table 5.4   The *u*-declension: *sunu* 'son', *feld* 'field', *duru* 'door', and *hand* 'hand'

Case	Singular	Plural
Nominative	sunu, feld, duru, hand	suna, felda, dura, handa
Accusative	sunu, feld, duru, hand	suna, felda, dura, handa
Dative	suna, felda, dura, handa	sunum, feldum, durum, handum
Genitive	suna, felda, dura, handa	suna, felda, dura, handa

The feminine equivalent to this large class is the *ō*-declension, represented in table 5.3 by *ār* 'grace' and *giefu* 'gift'.

While there are many dissimilarities between the two declensions, there are, in, for instance, the dative plural forms, case-distinctive forms which transcend gender and declension. This is also true for the *u*-declension, represented here by *sunu* 'son', *feld* 'field', *duru* 'door', and *hand* 'hand', where the first two nouns are masculine, the last two feminine (table 5.4).

The other strong declensions are essentially variants on these themes, with the exception of those which show at least part of their functional material through alternation of vowels (table 5.5), where *mann* 'man' is masculine and *bōc* 'book' feminine.

As can be seen even in this non-exhaustive discussion, much syncretism already existed between cases: often the nominative and accusative forms are the same; at other times, the dative and genitive forms are identical; plurality is not always marked in all contexts. There is also some gender form syncretism, often between masculine and neuter, but also between masculine and feminine.

Table 5.5   Other strong declensions: *mann* 'man' and *bōc* 'book'

Case	Singular	Plural
Nominative	mann, bōc	menn, bēc
Accusative	mann, bōc	menn, bēc
Dative	menn, bēc	manna, bōca
Genitive	mannes, bēc	mannum, bōcum

Table 5.6   Declension of strong adjectives: *blind* 'blind'

Case	Masculine	Neuter	Feminine	Plural (m/n/f)
Nominative	blind	blind	blind	Blinde / blind(e) / blinde(-a)
Accusative	blindne	blind	blinde	Blinde / blind(e) / blinde(-a)
Dative	blindum	blindum	blindre	blindum
Instrumental	blinde	blinde	blindre	n/a
Genitive	blindes	blindes	blindre	blindra

Table 5.7   Declension of weak adjectives: *blind* 'blind'

Case	Masculine	Neuter	Feminine	Plural
Nominative	blinda	blinde	blinde	blindan
Accusative	blindan	blinde	blindan	blindan
Dative	blindan	blindan	blindan	blindum
Instrumental	blindan	blindan	blindan	n/a
Genitive	blindan	blindan	blindan	blindra(-ena)

The adjective

Simplifying somewhat, in Old English the strong adjective declension, represented here by *blind* 'blind', had the following forms, depending on case, gender, and number (table 5.6).

In the weak declension (table 5.7), there was already considerable case, gender, and number syncretism, as well as (with the dative plural in particular) syncretism between strong and weak paradigms.

The demonstratives

Also connected to the expression of function through form in Old English are the demonstrative pronouns. Two demonstrative paradigms existed: the simple demonstratives (table 5.8) and the compound demonstratives (table 5.9).

Table 5.8 Simple demonstratives

Case	Masculine	Feminine	Neuter	Plural
Nominative	sē	sēo	þæt	þā
Accusative	þone	þā	þæt	þā
Dative	þæm	þǣre	þæm	þǣm
Genitive	þæs	þǣre	þæs	þāra
Instrumental	þȳ, þon		þȳ, þon	

Table 5.9 Compound demonstratives

Case	Masculine	Feminine	Neuter	Plural
Nominative	þes	þēos	þis	þās
Accusative	þisne	þās	þis	þās
Dative	þis(s)um	þisse	þis(s)um	þis(s)um
Genitive	þis(s)es	þisse	þis(s)es	þāra
Instrumental	þȳs, þīs		þȳs, þīs	

Whilst to native speakers of English the use of a definite article is natural, indeed necessary, there are a great many languages which do not have such a discrete form. It does not appear to have been an Indo-European feature; a number of Indo-European languages, such as Russian, do not have an equivalent. Although article function existed in Old English, there was no separate article form. Instead, article function was carried by the simple demonstrative pronoun paradigm, as it still is in German. The creation of a discrete definite article was the product of the changes the morphology of the noun phrase went through in late Old English and early Middle English (Millar 2000).

The Old English system

Let us look at a short piece of "classical" Old English:

Vercelli Homily 5 (tenth century)
Her segð þis halige godspel be þære hean medomnesse þisse halgan tide þe nu onweard is, 7 us lǣreð þætte we þas halgan tiid gedefelice 7 clǣnlice weorðien, Godes naman to lofe 7 to wuldre . . .

"Here this holy gospel tells about the high dignity of this holy season which is now upon us, and teaches us that we should make this holy season worthy with dignity and purity, for the praise and glory of God's name . . ."

This is obviously English, but an English based upon grammatical and morphological precepts we no longer have. Element order, for instance, is more variable, with the

Subject–Verb–Object order so necessary for comprehension in Modern English not so obvious, even in this brief passage. The use of each noun, adjective, and demonstrative form is predicated upon the relationship between case, gender, number, and (with the adjectives) level of grammatical information carried by the determiner. Thus, in the phrase *be þære hean medomnesse þisse halgan tide*, the form of þære tells us that the following noun is dative, when taken in combination with *be*, which triggers that case; *hean* is a weak adjective, because *þære* carries sufficient case and gender information for concord between elements to be expressed, while *medomnesse*, by the use of –*e*, announces itself not to be in the nominative or accusative case. *þisse* is the compound demonstrative form for either genitive or dative case with feminine nouns; the former case can be seen to be the one intended as this noun phrase is subordinate to the prepositional phrase. *Halgan*, again, is a weak adjective, because of the level of function information carried by the demonstrative; *tide* uses –*e* to mark (at least to some extent) case.

That we have to go into such complexity to parse a brief and essentially simple phrase is primarily due to our having to learn Old English as if it were a foreign language; to native speakers, these distinctions would have been natural and would have aided them (unconsciously) to follow the meaning of what was being said.

The Breakdown of Gender and Case Systems

Even in early Old English, the inherited system was beginning to "fray round the edges," with considerable syncretism apparent. This process, of originally distinct forms gradually being "worn down," is particularly common with endings, since there is a tendency for such morphemes to be unstressed. This is also apparent with noun declensions. In the more conservative dialects of Old English, the vowels in the endings ,<-a>, <-o>, and <-u> were probably distinct. By the early Middle English period, however, there is considerable evidence suggesting that they have fallen together as /ə/ generally spelled <-e>.

In northern England, this loss of distinctiveness developed, from an early period, into what Samuels (1989a) termed "phonetic attrition": the ongoing loss of almost all case-, number-, gender-, and declension-sensitive endings (Blakeley 1948–9). Tracing these developments from northern to southern England from the tenth to thirteenth centuries, Jones (1988) argues that these "mistakes" were actually part of an attempt to shore up one part of the inherited system – marking function by form – by sacrificing another – grammatical gender. Instead of having a system where forms and endings were normally associated both with gender and case (table 5.10), a reinterpretation took place, with – in theory at least – only one form being associated with one function in one number (table 5.11 – in the table I have retained the traditional case names, despite the fact that this subsystem was used to denote function, not case).

This "simplification" cannot explain how the loss of case forms also came about, however.

Table 5.10 Forms associated with gender, number, and case

Case	Masculine	Feminine	Neuter	Plural
Nominative	se/þe	seo/þeo	þæt	þa
Accusative	-ne	þa	þæt	þa
Dative	-m	-re	-um	-m
Genitive	-s	-re	-s	-ra

Table 5.11 Forms associated with number and case only

Case	Singular	Plural
Nominative	þe	þa
Accusative	-ne	þa
Dative	-m/n	-m/n
Genitive	-s	-ra

The problem appears to have been that, as part of the same process which broke down gender reference, many originally distinct forms in the same paradigms began to fall together. Thus, with the simple demonstratives, accusative masculine *þone* and dative masculine and neuter *þæm* coalesced as *þVn* (where *V* stands for any vowel), due to the loss of *–e*, in particular, at least originally, before a vowel, as seen in

Vices and Virtues (Kent; late thirteenth century) 13/30–1
ȝewiss hafð godd forworpen *ðan* ilche man

"indeed God has cast out that very man"

where we would expect accusative *þVne*, but also elsewhere, as in

Peterborough Chronicle First Continuation (southeast midlands; early twelfth century) 1123/41
he sæde *þone* king þet hit wæs togeanes riht

"he told the king that it was against the right way [of doing things]"

where a dative form would have been expected in Old English, combined with the considerable confusion between nasal consonants possible in English (for instance, Old English *hænep* becoming Modern English *hemp*) (Minkova 1991). I have termed these developments "ambiguity in ending" (Millar 1995, 2000).

An analogous phenomenon can be found with the compound demonstratives, where the originally distinct forms *þes* (nominative masculine), *þeos* (nominative feminine), *þis* (nominative and accusative neuter), and *þas* (accusative feminine) began to be confused, before falling together as *þis* or *þes* (in unstressed contexts, probably both

/θəs/, the ancestor of modern *this*. Some evidence for this can be found in the variation within a single text of the demonstratives realized with the feminine noun *miht*, whether this be the descendant of the "correct" form:

> **Vices and Virtues** 29/ 32–4
> Ðies ilke haliʒe mihte . . . makeð him unwurð
>
> "this same holy power makes them unworthy"

a descendant of the historical masculine form,

> **Vices and Virtues** 105/ 9
> Ðes ilche hali mihte iusticia
>
> "this same holy power justice"

or the neuter,

> **Vices and Virtues** 25/ 10–1
> Ðis hali mihte . . . is an soþ almihti godd
>
> "this holy power is one true almighty God"

I have termed this development "ambiguity in form" (Millar 1995, 2000).

These processes did not work independently, moreover. With the simple demonstratives, ambiguity in ending between –*ne* and –*m* was exacerbated by ambiguity in form between *þe* (nominative masculine), *þeo* (nominative feminine) (these <þ> forms, originating in the north of England in the late Old English period, gradually replaced the <s> forms, due probably to analogy with the rest of the paradigm, in all but the most conservative dialects), and *þa* (accusative feminine); with the compound demonstratives, the ambiguity in form was matched by ambiguity in ending between *þisne* (accusative masculine) and *þissum* (dative masculine and neuter).

These ambiguities imperilled the inherited system: neither case-marking nor gender-marking could be maintained; the functional categories which underlay them were rendered unworkable and, eventually, meaningless, as with the "mistakes" made by a number of Middle English authors attempting either to copy Old English texts (see, for instance, Franzen 1991; Millar & Nicholls 1997) or to make their texts appear older than they actually are (Stanley 1988).

If this breakdown was dangerous for the distinctive demonstrative paradigms, the results were devastating for the noun declensions, where gender and case information expressed through form was not always transparent in "classical" Old English. Whilst the more conservative dialects in southern English maintained final –*e* on nouns (as well as adjectives) until the end of the fourteenth century, this survival was vestigial, "fossilized," rather than information-carrying (Samuels 1989b).

In all dialects of English, grammatical gender and case could no longer be marked for demonstrative pronouns, adjectives, or nouns by the end of the fourteenth century.

A number of exceptions to this general tendency exist. In the first place, possession in English can still be expressed through what are apparently noun endings, for instance *the king's daughter* where <'s> is the descendant of the Old English masculine and neuter genitive ending *–es*. It should be noted, however, that the modern use of <'s> is different from its ancestor. In Old (and Middle) English, a phrase such as *the king of Norway's daughter* would have been impossible, the closest "correct" phrase being *the king's daughter of Norway*. By being placed at the end of the phrase, rather than with the head noun, <'s> reveals itself as a possessive marker instead of a genitive noun ending (Janda 1980).

It should also be noted that some function marking is retained for some personal pronouns (for instance, *she* in relation to *her*) and relative pronouns. Nevertheless, not all pronouns show this (for example, *you*); the distinction between *who* and *whom* is one which, for most native speakers, has been learned at school rather than directly in speech from parents and peers.

The Partial Breakdown of Noun Declensions and Plurality

For the nouns, declension distinctions were largely, although not fully, leveled, with a general drift from the weak declension to the strong. Within the strong declensions, loss of gender distinctions meant that nouns in other declensions moved towards what had been the masculine *a*-class, with the proviso that the pronunciation of the descendant of *–as* was affected by the context: thus the plural markers in *maps*, *tabs*, and *horses* are pronounced differently, but derive from the same source. "Irregular" plurals, such as those realized through a change in root vowel, where *–r* is used as a plural marker, or where there is no overt plural marker, have generally also moved to the *–s* declension.

These processes are by no means complete, however. The "mutation" plurals, such as *men*, are still quite common, even if the plural of *book* is *books* rather than the expected **beek*. There are still a few *–en* plurals found in Standard English, such as *oxen*. Zero plurals, such as *fish* or *sheep*, are still normal. The only *–r* plural remaining in the Standard is *children*. This form actually has the remnants of three kinds of plural marking. In Old English, the plural of *cild* was *cild*. Since this marking quickly became opaque, the *–er* plural was added (this form is retained in some dialects). Because *–er* ceased being analyzed as a plural marker, *-(e)n* was added.

There is dialectal evidence for more survival. Many English speakers would refer to *twenty pound* rather than *pounds*, for instance. In Scots, the plural for *ee*, 'eye', is *een*, and in the dialect of northeast Scotland, the plural of *brou*, 'brow', is *breer*, and for *cou*, 'cow', *kye* (although analogical plurals such as *brous* and *cous* are also found, particularly with younger speakers) (Beal 1997).

A counter-indicative development is that Modern English has also borrowed plural morphology from other, "classical" languages, such as Latin, *foci* (< *focus*), Greek, *stadia* (< *stadium*), and Hebrew, *cherubim* (< *cherub*). The artificial, somewhat contrived, nature

of these forms can be seen in the way that native plurals, such as *stadiums* or *cherubs*, are also common (for a discussion of why these plural forms are not well maintained in Modern English, see Millar 2005: 68).

Moves away from the overt expression of plurality can be found in other elements of the noun phrase. No number distinctions survived into Modern English for the adjectives, for instance.

With the demonstrative pronouns, similar processes can be seen at work, although the eventual results were variable. With the simple demonstratives, the nominative and accusative plural form *þa* was, in many dialects in Middle English, in danger of falling together with either of the remaining singular forms from the same paradigm, *the* or *that*. Possibly due to Scandinavian influence in the north of England (Millar 2000), *the* became associated solely with the article function previously incorporated within functions connected to the simple demonstrative paradigm as a whole. *That*, on the other hand, originally associated only with neuter nouns in nominative and accusative, became the sole singular distal demonstrative form.

While *the* was not distinguished for plural, most dialects maintained such a distinction for *that* (although northern Scots makes no such distinction) (McRae 2000). The natural southern descendant of *þa* – *tho* – was still the most common plural form in Chaucer's works. But while this form – in its northern realization, *thae* – is still found in Scots dialects, *tho* was replaced (probably because of confusion with *though*, recently imported from northern dialects) (Samuels 1989c) in the course of the fifteenth century by *those*, an apparently "artificial" form created by the combination of *tho* and the "regular" plural form *–es*.

A similar "protection" for plurality can be found with the compound demonstratives. For while *this* became, eventually, the sole proximal form in the singular, and indeed is still used in the plural in the traditional dialects of northern Scotland, the southern midland ancestor of Standard English adopted an "artificial" plural *these*, formed in the same way as *those*. Other dialects continued to use other plural forms, so that in my dialect (West Central Scots), the plural of *this* is traditionally *thir*, probably borrowed from Norse.

Conclusion

Because of the exigencies of space, I have been forced to concentrate only on noun phrase morphology. Even so, a great deal of the history of English is encapsulated in this limited survey, and many of its characteristics are shared by, for instance, the development of verb morphology, as discussed by Brinton (1988), Stein (1990), and Krygier (1994). What we can see is a relatively rapid typological shift from synthetic to analytic, accompanied by a considerable "simplification" of the inflectional morphology which rendered much of what had structured English previously redundant. These changes, spreading over time from northern to southern England, had considerable influence upon all other levels of the grammar of English – from phonology, in

the loss of long consonants due to the loss of noun endings, through to the rather rigid element order patterns now necessary.

REFERENCES AND FURTHER READING

Beal, J. (1997). Syntax and morphology. In C. Jones (ed.), *The Edinburgh History of the Scots Language* (pp. 335–77). Edinburgh: Edinburgh University Press.

Blakeley, L. (1948–9). Accusative-dative syncretism in the *Lindisfarne Gospels*. *English and Germanic Studies*, 1, 6–31.

Brinton, L. J. (1988). *The Development of English Aspectual Systems: Aspectualizers and Post-verbal Particles*. Cambridge: Cambridge University Press.

Campbell, A. (1959). *Old English Grammar*. Oxford: Clarendon Press.

Faiss, K. (1992). *English Historical Morphology and Word-formation: Loss versus Enrichment*. Trier: Wissenschaftlicher.

Fortson, B. W., IV (2004). *Indo-European Language and Culture: An Introduction*. Oxford: Blackwell.

Franzen, C. (1991). *The Tremulous Hand of Worcester*. Oxford: Clarendon Press.

Holm, J. (1989). *Pidgins and Creoles*. 2 vols. Cambridge: Cambridge University Press.

Janda, R. D. (1980). On the decline of declensional systems: the overall loss of Old English nominal case inflections and the Middle English reanalysis of *-ES* as *HIS*. In E. C. Traugott, R. Labrum, & S. Shepherd (eds.), *Papers from the 4th International Conference on Historical Linguistics* (pp. 243–52). Amsterdam: John Benjamins.

Jones, C. (1988). *Grammatical Gender in English 950–1250*. London: Croom Helm.

Krygier, M. (1994). *The Disintegration of the Strong Verb System*. Frankfurt: Peter Lang.

McRae, S. M. (2000). The demonstrative pronouns in the North-East: an introductory discussion. *Scottish Language*, 19, 66–82.

Millar, R. M. (1994). Ambiguity in function. Old English *þæt* and the demonstrative systems of Laȝamon's *Brut. Neuphilologische Mitteilungen*, 95, 415–32.

Millar, R. M. (1995). Ambiguity in ending and form. "Reinterpretation" in the demonstrative systems of Laȝamon's *Brut. Neuphilologische Mitteilungen*, 96, 145–68.

Millar, R. M. (2000). *System Collapse System Rebirth*. Oxford: Peter Lang.

Millar, R. M. (2005). *Language, Nation and Power*. Basingstoke: Palgrave Macmillan

Millar, R. M. & Nicholls, A. (1997). Ælfric's *De Initio Creaturae* and London, British Library, Cotton Vespasian A.xxii: omission, retention and innovation. In P. E. Szarmach & J. T. Rosenthal (eds.), *The Preservation and Transmission of Anglo-Saxon Culture* (pp. 431–63). Kalamazoo: Medieval Institute Publications.

Minkova, D. (1991). *The History of Final Vowels in English: The Sound of Muting*. Berlin: Mouton de Gruyter.

Mitchell, B. (1985). *Old English Syntax*. 2 vols. Oxford: Clarendon Press.

Prokosch, E. (1939). *A Comparative Germanic Grammar*. Philadelphia: Linguistic Society of America.

Samuels, M. L. (1989a). Chaucerian final "-e." In J. J. Smith (ed.), *The English of Chaucer and his Contemporaries* (pp. 7–12). Aberdeen: Aberdeen University Press.

Samuels, M. L. (1989b). The Great Scandinavian Belt. In M. Laing (ed.), *Middle English Dialectology: Essays on some Principles and Problems* (pp. 106–15). Aberdeen: Aberdeen University Press.

Samuels, M. L. (1989c). Some applications of Middle English dialectology. In M. Laing (ed.), *Middle English Dialectology: Essays on some Principles and Problems* (pp. 64–80). Aberdeen: Aberdeen University Press.

Sapir, E. (1921). *Language: An Introduction to the Study of Speech*. New York: Harcourt, Brace and World.

Small, G. W. (1926). Syntax of THE with the comparative. *Modern Language Notes*, 41, 300–13.

Small, G. W. (1930). The Syntax of THE and Old English ÞON MA ÞE. *Publications of the Modern Languages Association*, 45, 368–91.

Stanley, E. G. (1988). Karl Luick's "Man schrieb wie man sprach" and English historical philology. In D. Kastovsky & G. Bauer (eds.), *Luick Revisited* (pp. 311–34). Tübingen: Narr.

Stein, D. (1990). *The Semantics of Syntactic Change: Aspects of the Evolution of* Do *in English*. Trends in Linguistics Studies and Monographs 47. New York: Mouton de Gruyter.

Welna, J. (1996). *English Historical Morphology*. Warsaw: Wydawnictwa Uniwersytetu Warszawskiego.

6
History of English Syntax

Olga Fischer

In the course of its history English has changed considerably from the point of view of its spelling, its phonology, morphology, and lexicon. As far as syntax is concerned, it can be said that, overall, English in its earliest stages was a heavily inflected language, much like modern German, with a relatively free word order, and that a rapid loss of inflexions brought about by both internal factors and external ones made it into what it is today: a highly analytic language with a strict word order. (For such internal factors as phonological weakening of inflexions followed by loss, see PHONOLOGY: SEGMENTAL HISTORIES and HISTORY OF ENGLISH MORPHOLOGY; for such external factors as intense contact with other languages during the Viking and Norman invasions, see EARLY OLD ENGLISH and EARLY MIDDLE ENGLISH.) Changes in all these areas can easily be spotted when one compares an Old English [OE] text with a Present-Day English [PDE] gloss:

> *Ferdon we þa forþ be þære ea ofre. þa wæs seo eahtoþe tid dæges. þa cwoman we*
> Traveled we then forth by the river's bank. Then [it] was the eighth hour day's. Then came we
> *to sumre byrig. Seo burg wæs on midre þære ea in anum eglande getimbrod. Wæs seo*
> to some town. That town was in the middle of-the-river on an island built. Was the
> *burg mid þy hreode and treowcynne þe on þære ea ofre weox, and we ær bi writon and*
> town with the reed and tree-kind that on the river's bank grew, and we before about wrote and
> *sægdon, a-sett and geworht.*
> told, set-up and built.
>   (From *Alexander's Letter to Aristotle*, a tenth-century ms.)

A PDE speaker, not familiar with OE, would not be able to understand the OE text by itself, but the literal gloss, although perhaps somewhat awkward, is comprehensible, showing that the changes in syntax offer less of a problem than the changes on the other levels. Concerning those other levels, changes in spelling are the least troublesome, mainly restricted to the loss of some unfamiliar letters such as þ and æ, and the use of such spellings as <o> for <u> in 'some' (*sumre*) and <y> for <g> in 'days'

(*dæges*) introduced by French scribes in the Middle English [ME] period (cf. Barber 1993: 151–3). More problematic are the sounds that have changed and inflectional endings that have disappeared. Sound change makes *eahtope* and *hreode* almost unrecognizable from their modern counterparts 'eighth' and 'reed', and the presence of inflectional morphology (expressing case, gender, and number) makes the determiner *the* look like a number of rather different words altogether, appearing sometimes as *þære*, sometimes as *seo* or *þy*. Similarly, both *burg* and *byrig* are used for the same noun. Most notable perhaps are the lexical and semantic changes. Some words have totally disappeared and been replaced by Scandinavian or French loanwords, e.g., *ofre* has become *bank* (from Old Norse), *ea* has turned into *river* (from Old French), and *geworht* (now only used in set expressions like 'over*wrought*' and '*wrought* iron') has been replaced by *built*, another English verb. Changes in meaning are clear from the way *tid* 'tide' is used (for which we now use *hour* (from French) or *time*) – it has been narrowed down to a particular kind of time, namely that of ebb and flood – while *weox* 'waxed' has been reduced to the 'growing' of the phases of the moon, or restricted to poetic or humorous diction (at the same time losing the vowel change characteristic of the past tense of strong verbs, becoming weak instead).

Even though the changes in syntax present less of a problem to the uninitiated reader, this does not mean that they have not occurred. They are more difficult to pinpoint as "change," however, because the particular element orders found in this text sometimes are still possible in present-day discourse for stylistic and/or emphatic purposes. Thus the inversion of subject and finite verb found in *Pa cwoman we* 'then came we', is still possible today after some initial elements, e.g., after *only* (*Only yesterday **did I** discover . . .*), in set expressions like *White, **said he**, is my favorite color*, and in poetic or religious language. Similarly, we can still put a direct object or prepositional phrase in front of the main verb (resulting in SOV order, which is considered the basic word order for OE), as in *þe on þære ea ofre weox* 'that on the river's bank grew', provided it is used emphatically or contrastively. Alternatively, SVO order – the normal PDE order – was also regularly found in OE in main clauses due to what is called the Verb-second rule; and it occurred in subordinate clauses when the object was particularly long or heavy.

Thus, as far as syntax is concerned, it is not so much a concrete replacement (as on the level of morpho-phonology or the lexicon) that constitutes a change; rather it involves a change in the relative frequency of a particular element order, an extension of a structure, or a restriction of a certain order or structure to a particular context or register. (Only rarely do we see the introduction of a completely new structure.) For instance, the structure *on þære ea ofre* 'on the river's bank' with *þære ea* in the genitive, is still a possible construction in PDE (though there has been a change in structure in that in OE both the noun and the determiner (or pronoun) bear genitive case, while in PDE the -'s is a clitic that appears only once, after the complete NP), but it now sounds a little formal or poetic; in spoken language normally the *of*-phrase would be used. In some cases, as here, a compound structure, *river bank*, would also be a possibility. The *of*-structure replaced most OE genitives, except in the case of animate

possessors (cf. Rosenbach 2002); e.g., we can still say *John's looks have considerably improved*, while *He didn't like the house's look* sounds awkward. Partitive, descriptive, and objective genitives now normally take the *of*-phrase: OE *an pund goldes* has become *a pound of gold*, *mæres lifes man* has turned into *a man of glorious life/conduct*, *þæs landes sceawunge* into *the surveying of the land*, respectively. These examples also show that the position of the genitive has changed from pre- and post-noun, to pre-noun only. This is related to the reanalysis of the possessive genitive into a determiner, but the loss of postnominal position for adjective phrases around the same time and the development of fixed word order have also had a bearing on this (cf. Rosenbach 2002; Fischer 2006). Note, however, that in both types of replacement, compound or *of*-structure, the construction was already available. Hence the construction itself is not new, but it has been extended to new uses. Such extensions may occur by the mere force of analogy, which is an important principle in all human (and animal) learning (cf. Holyoak & Thagard 1995; Fischer 2007), or by the fact that a linguistic gap, caused by other changes, has to be filled.

Change in syntax is less visible because it deals with abstract structures rather than concrete elements (i.e., it looks at the *position* that a particular grammatical *category* expressing a particular *function* takes); it is not concerned with *actual* sounds or words. When we describe phonological, morphological, or lexical-semantic change, our task is relatively easy in that we may compare concrete, phonetically expressed, items; variants that are related in form and/or meaning as used in their particular contexts. The case is rather different for syntax. When we compare two syntactic constructions from two different periods, we have to establish first that there *is* some diachronic relation between them, even when the structures look superficially the same. In other words, whereas it is relatively easy to establish a link between *hreode* and *reed*, and even between *seo* and *the*, it is much harder to know whether an SOV order in OE has the same function as an SOV order today.

It will not be possible to discuss in this short space all the syntactic shifts and innovations that English has undergone between the OE period and today. Table 6.1 gives an indication of the main changes. A description and possible explanations for most of these can be conveniently found in Fischer and van der Wurff (2006), from which the table has been adapted, and in much greater detail in Jespersen (1913–40) and Hogg (1992–2001). Visser (1963–73), Denison (1993), and Allen (1995) provide useful information on changes in the verbal system, word order, and case system. Fischer et al. (2000) provide a succinct description of the syntactic characteristics of the OE and ME periods, while for the individual periods, Mitchell (1985), Mustanoja (1960), Barber (1997), and Beal (2004) are very useful.

Here I will concentrate on one or two changes that will elucidate the kind of factors that play a role in syntactic change. In almost all cases of change there is interplay between external and internal factors. Some external factors, such as language contact, have already been mentioned above. Also very important in the development of most established languages is the rise of a written standard and the influence of this standardization on the spoken language (see LATE MIDDLE ENGLISH; BRITISH ENGLISH IN

Table 6.1 Main syntactic changes in the history of English

Changes in:	Old English	Middle English	Modern English
Nouns/NPs:			
case forms	most case forms intact	most case forms lost	all case forms lost
genitive case	genitive case still has various functions + is attached to the bare (pro)noun	genitive case restricted to subjective/possessive function, with *of*-phrase used elsewhere	genitive case ending becomes a clitic that follows the entire NP
Determiner system:	articles present in embryo form, system developing	articles used for presentational and referential functions	extended to use in predicative and generic contexts
Adjectives/APs:			
position	both pre- and post-nominal with a functional distinction	mainly prenominal, French adjectives may be postnominal	prenominal with some lexical exceptions
form/function	strong/weak forms, functionally distinct	remnants of strong/weak forms; not functional	one, inflectionless, form only
as head	fully operative	reduced; introduction of prop-word *one* becomes possible	restricted to generic reference and idioms
'stacking' of adjectival correlative clause	not possible	new relatives: *that, (the) which, whose, whom*; zero object relative possible	regular *who* introduced as relative referring to people, *which* becomes restricted to inanimates
	form of relative: *se, se þe, þe*; zero subject relative possible		
Aspect-system:			
use of perfect	embryonic	more frequent; in competition with 'past'	perfect and 'past' grammaticalized in different functions
form of perfect	use of auxiliaries *be/have* (past participle sometimes declined)	both *be/have*, but *have* becoming more frequent	*have* becomes the rule in the nineteenth century
form and function of progressive	*be+-ende* (*-ende*); no clear aspectual function	*be+-ing* (*-ende* lost), infrequent, becoming more aspectual	frequent; becomes fully grammaticalized as aspect in the nineteenth century
Tense-system:			
present tense form	used for present tense, progressive aspect, future 'tense'	used for present tense and progressive (future with *will/shall* develops)	becomes restricted to 'timeless' and 'reporting' uses

past tense form	used for past tense, (past)perfect, and past progressive	still used for past progressive and perfect; new: the modal past tense	restricted in function through the grammaticalization of perfect and progressive
Mood-system: *expressed by*	subjunctive inflexions, modal verbs, epistemic adjectives and adverbs	mainly modal verbs (and development quasi-modals); past tense used modally	*idem* and development of new modal expressions
category of core modals	verbs (with exception features)	verbs (with exception features)	auxiliaries (with some verbal features)
Voice-system: *passive form*	*weorðan/beon* + (inflected) past participle	*be/have been* + uninflected past participle	*idem*; new *get* passive
indirect passive	absent	developing	(fully) present
Prepos. passive	absent	developing	(fully) present
Passive infinitive	only after modal verbs	after full verbs, with some nouns and adjectives	*idem*
Negative-system:	*ne* + verb + other negator (e.g.: *na(wi)ht*)	*(ne)* + verb + *not*; *not* + verb	auxiliary + *not* + verb; (verb + *not*)
Interrog. system:	inversion: VS	inversion: V/Aux S	Aux SV
DO *as operator:*	absent	infrequent, not grammaticalized	becoming fully grammaticalized
Subject: *position filled*	some omission possible outside coordinate clauses; dummy subjects not compulsory	omission rare outside coordinate clauses; dummy subjects become the norm	omission highly marked stylistically; dummy subjects obligatory
subject-clauses	absent	occurs with *that*-clauses and infinitival clauses	new type: *for* NP *to* V clauses
subjectless/impersonal constructions	common; experiencer role usually in the dative	subject position becomes obligatorily filled by *it* or by the original dative	extinct (some lexicalized expressions, such as *methinks*)
position with respect to V	both S(...)V and VS	S(...)V; VS becomes restricted to *yes/no* questions	only S(adv)V; VS > Aux SV

Table 6.1 *Continued*

Changes in:	Old English	Middle English	Modern English
Object:			
object-clauses	mainly finite *þæt*-clause, also zero/*to*-infinitive	stark increase in infinitival clauses, mainly with *to*	introduction of accusative with infinitive and *for* NP *to* V clauses
position with respect to V	VO and OV	VO; OV becomes restricted	VO everywhere
position IO-DO	both orders; pronominal IO-DO preferred	nominal IO-DO the norm, introduction of : DO *for/to* IO	IO/DO with full NPs; pronominal DO/IO predominates
Clitic pronouns:	syntactic clitics, i.e., pronouns occupy special positions in clause	clitics disappearing	clitics absent
Adverbs:			
position	fairly free	more restricted	further restricted
adverb-clauses	use of correlatives + different word orders in main and subord. clause	distinct conjunctions; word order mainly SVO in both clauses	all word order SVO (exc. some conditional clauses have VS)
Phrasal verbs:	position of particle: both pre- and postverbal	great increase; position particle: postverbal	*idem*
Preposition stranding:	only with pronouns, (inc. R-pronouns: *þær etc.*) and relative *þe*	no longer with pronouns, but new with prep. passives, interrogatives and other relative clauses	no longer after R-pronouns (*there* etc.) except in fixed expressions (*therefore*)

THE LONG EIGHTEENTH CENTURY; CLASS, ETHNICITY, AND THE FORMATION OF "STANDARD ENGLISH"). Standardization has led towards the elimination of variants, and an increase in structures of subordination, introduced by clear subordinating markers. Important internal factors are changes on the phonological and morphological levels, which may lead to fixation of word order (as noted above), and the force of analogy. Each linguistic element consists of a particular phonetic form, which is linked, usually by convention, to a semantic signification; this is true for single words or morphemes but also for larger and more abstract structures. Each time we use a form or structure we use it with its attached meaning in a particular context. Since these contexts are never exactly the same, we may extend the use of these forms to other situations, which seem to us similar. For instance, we may use concrete terms belonging to one semantic field to describe abstract activities that convey a similar meaning or effect, as in *He grasped the truth*, which is derived analogically (via metaphor) from expressions such as *He grasped her arm*. Similarly, a structure such as *He fell into a chair* or *He brought them back* may be analogically extended to other verbs such as *collapse* or *walk*, creating new subcategorization frames for these verbs: *He collapsed into a chair*/*He walked them back* (cf. Hampe & Schönefeld 2003).

A process known as grammaticalization is also mostly internal in character, and is a frequent phenomenon in morphosyntactic change. It is driven by both analogical and metonymic forces, and also shows features characteristic of phonetic and semantic change. Many developments in English, such as the rise of modal auxiliaries and the operator *do*, the emergence of a periphrastic perfect and progressive, and the rise of a determiner system, have been interpreted as processes of grammaticalization. Other examples are the adverbial ending *-ly* (which developed from the noun *lic* 'body'), the infinitival marker *to* (the particle *to* expressing direction), and the development of modal *have to* (from the possessive verb *have*). Discussion of these cases in relation to grammaticalization can be found in Fischer et al. (2000) and Fischer (2000, 2006). Whether this is an independent process or not remains a matter of some dispute (cf. Campbell 2001 versus Hopper & Traugott 2003), but what characterizes it is the development of a lexical item or, more often, a combination of lexical items, into a grammatical/functional element, whereby its content – for reasons of frequency and economy – becomes gradually reduced both phonetically and semantically (e.g., the directional concrete expression '*is going* [somewhere] *to*+infinitive' develops into a mere future marker, '*gonna*+infinitive'). When the item increases in frequency, it begins to push out rivals within its paradigm (i.e., semantically similar items that could fill the same slot in the clause), and becomes more and more restricted as to position (cf. Lehmann 1995). (See CORPUS-BASED LINGUISTIC APPROACHES TO THE HISTORY OF ENGLISH.)

I will illustrate some of the problems connected with syntactic change and the causes or mechanisms involved in it, with an example. If we are interested, for instance, in the history of infinitival complements in English, and wish to find out whether there have been changes there in structure or not, we could begin by comparing clauses from different periods containing exactly the same concrete items in a

similar context. This might rule out changes on other levels, enabling us to have a "purer" look at any syntactic change that may have occurred. Unfortunately, such clauses are rare. But even if we could find instances such as OE *Ic seah hie gan* against ME *I saugh hire goon*, and PDE *I saw her go*, where each clause element seems to be a perfect cognate of the elements in the other two periods, and where element order is also the same on the surface, we still do not know whether the underlying *structure* is also the same. It is quite possible that the construction was reanalyzed in the course of time: that a new generation of speakers ascribed a different abstract structure to it because of changes taking place elsewhere in the language, influencing the form of their grammar. Such a reanalysis of surface structure happened for instance with OE *an nædder*, which at some point in ME became analyzed as *an adder* rather than *a nadder*. We can deduce the new structure from the fact that speakers at that time began to produce *the adder* instead of *the nadder*. The reanalysis took place not because of some phonological change in *nadder*, but due to a change in the overall grammatical system involving the development of a new determiner category. This new category developed via the grammaticalization of the numeral *ān* 'one' into the indefinite article *a(n)* whereby the vowel was reduced and the <n> gradually lost before consonants (showing both phonetic and semantic reduction, cf. above). *A(n)nadder* thus offered two possible options because the first element could be interpreted as both *a* and *an* (in ME [n] and [nn] were no longer phonemically distinctive, cf. PHONOLOGY: SEGMENTAL HISTORIES).

An example of reanalysis of an infinitival construction can be found in the development that takes place in the so-called *for NP to V*-construction. Structures such as (1),

(1)   When I realized it might be used in evidence against me, I asked *for it to be finger-printed* (Online *OED*, s.v. 'finger')

did not occur in OE, with *for* used as a complementizer rather than a preposition. In OE and ME, *for* immediately before an NP could only be interpreted benefactively (i.e., with the *for* NP functioning as an argument of the main clause predicate), as in (2):

(2)   a ... it were bettre *for yow to lese* so muchel good of youre owene ...
       (Chaucer *CT-Melibee* 3030)
       '.... it would be better for you to lose so many possessions of your own'
       b Hit bycomeþ for clerkus crist for to seruen (*PiersPl.* Skeat 1886: 85)
       'It is befitting for clergymen to serve Christ'

Quite clearly a benefactive interpretation such as found in (2) is impossible in (1) because of the inanimate NP *it* which follows *for* (we need animate NPs to "benefit" from whatever is said in the predicate). In order to understand why *for NP to V* comes to be reanalyzed, from a structure such as (3) into one like (4),

(3)   [[predicate for NP] [to V]]
(4)   [predicate [for NP to V]]

– in other words, from an NP analyzed as a verbal argument in the main clause, to the same NP acting as a subject in the non-finite clause – we need to look at many different constructions with *for* that were in use at the time of the change, and also at other infinitival constructions that are close in form and/or meaning and therefore may have something to do with the change (by analogy). Thus, we must consider benefactive constructions such as (5), which show a bare dative NP rather than a prepositional NP:

(5)   now were it tyme *a lady to gon henne* (Chaucer, *T&C* BkIII, 630)
      'Now it would be time [i.e., it would be proper] for a lady to leave'

We must also consider the rise of a new infinitival marker *for to*, which begins to appear in early ME next to the *to*-infinitive. What looks likewise relevant, is the appearance at about the same time of constructions such as (6),

(6)   þa   lette he his cnihtes, dæies & nihtes/ æuere beon iwepned
                              (Layamon's Brut, Caligula ms 8155–56)
      then let   he his knights day and night   ever   be   weaponed
      'Then he let his knights always be armed, day and night'

which were replacing OE constructions found in (7),

(7)   seofon nihtum ær he gewite he *het his byrgene geopenian* (ÆCHom 11 108.556)
      seven nights before he departed he commanded his grave open [Infinitive]
      'Seven days before he passed away, he ordered his grave to be opened'

In both (6) and (7), there is an NP immediately in front of the infinitive (*crowne* and *byrgene,* respectively). In OE, an NP before an infinitive usually had an object function; in ME, however, this same NP came to be reanalyzed as a subject (with the concomitant change of the active infinitive into a passive one in (6)), due to the change in basic word order already referred to above.

A close investigation of the new structures found in (1) and (6) (cf. Fischer et al. 2000) shows that these new types can be related to the SOV>SVO change that was taking place around that time, and to the syncretism of dative and accusative case. In OE, the object of the verb tended to precede the verb in infinitival clauses; this preverbal position was further strengthened by a frequent parallel order in finite subordinate clauses. In ME, the word order of verb and object becomes increasingly fixed to VO in all types of clauses. At the same time, the subject becomes firmly established in a position immediately before the predicate. This had as a result that any NP positioned before a verb became, as it were, automatically interpreted in ME as subject, rather than object. It seems clear that for an explanation of developments such as these we must consider the analysis of surface structures within the larger framework of the grammatical system in which they operate.

The result of this change then was that a new infinitival structure arose containing a lexical subject, as represented for example in (4). It seems more than likely that the appearance of the construction in (6) also facilitated the appearance of the one in (1), or the other way around, since both are new types of infinitivals in ME. The new structural type may have been further reinforced by the influx of Latinate accusative and infinitive constructions in the late medieval period, as in *I believe* [*him to be innocent*], with which text writers (mainly clergymen and scholars) must have been familiar from their education in Latin. It seems likely, however, that this construction only became borrowed from Latin because there were native constructions available that were similar. In this respect it is interesting that modern German and Dutch, which kept basic SOV word order, did not take over the Latin constructions, even though the influence of Latin must have been equally strong. This also suggests that borrowing of syntax occurs less easily in language than the borrowing of other elements (lexis, idioms).

Another danger inherent in the comparison of syntactic structures, which is much less likely to occur in a diachronic comparison of phonological and morphological forms, is that there is a natural tendency to interpret an older construction very much from the point of view of the modern system (this concerns both form and function, e.g., see Lightfoot 1979: 34ff.). This happens especially when the form of the construction has remained more or less the same. I will briefly illustrate how older syntactic constructions may be misinterpreted because they are seen through the lens of the present-day grammar-system. The first example (again) involves the new infinitival development discussed above. The clause in (8) occurs in a late ME text:

(8)   God bade the rede See divide (c. 1390, Gower Confessio Amantis BkV: 1661)
      'God bade the Red Sea [to] divide'

This particular sentence is ambiguous because it could be interpreted according to the OE OV structure, i.e., with *See* as the object of *divide*, or as the new, late ME VO structure with *See* as the subject of *divide*, making the verb intransitive. Macauley, the editor of this text, indeed reads *divide* as intransitive, i.e., as a "modern" construction (as is clear from the entry of "divide" in his glossary), even though the OED indicates that the intransitive use of "divide" is found only from 1526 onwards. It is possible that the OED date is wrong here, of course, but what I want to emphasize is that the editor does not even consider the other, older interpretation, which was still current in Gower's time and hence more likely here in view of the OED evidence.

In the case of *divide*, the editor's misanalysis towards a modern construction is not so serious since the oversight is really one of timing and the sense of the clause remains more or less the same (this, indeed, must have made the later reinterpretation possible). Often a syntactic reanalysis takes place first in those positions where it does not disturb communication or where both meanings are possible but where by pragmatic inferencing from frequently occurring contextual situations, one interpretation may ultimately come to be preferred, which may at some later stage cause the construction to change

formally. Aitchison (2001: 99–100) notes that syntactic changes "nearly always steal in at a single, vulnerable point in the language," "in an almost underhand way . . . like a disease which can get a hold on a person before it is diagnosed."

In some cases, however, an editor's misinterpretation can be more serious. One such instance concerns the translation of the *be+to-infinitive* construction in OE (cf. Fischer 1991: 146–51). Editors often equate this construction to the modern one where *be+to-infinitive* expresses necessity, as in *Who is to go next?* ('Who must go next?'). In OE only a so-called passival infinitive was possible with *beon to* (i.e., an infinitive active in form but passive in meaning, as we still see in the relic structure *He is to blame*), which however carried all sorts of modal shades, and not necessarily one of necessity, as (9) illustrates:

(9) a . . . þæt hi   him geræddon hwæt him   be   ðam selost ðuhte oððe *to done   wære.*

     (LS 26 (MildredCockayne)72)

      . . . that they him advised   what them about that best   seemed or to do   were
      'that they would advise him what seemed best to them in this matter or what
      could/should/might be done'

     b þæt is to geþencanne þeoda gehwylcum, wisfæstum werum, hwæt seo wiht   sy

     (Riddles 41.8)

      that is to think of-people   for-each,   for-wise   men,   what this creature may-be
      'it is possible for each one of us, for wise men, to find out what   this creature might
      be'

These examples show how important it is for a correct analysis of historical syntactic structures to have a sense of the synchronic system of the language at the time in which the structure was used. Too strong a reliance on the present-day system of grammar of the language in question may result in the wrong analysis.

Thus, this one brief example from the history of English may show that after all, in spite of surface similarity, the structure of the clause *I saw her go* may well have changed: from OE [*Ic seah hie* [*gan*]] with *gan* dependent on the object *hie*, to modern [*I saw* [*her go*]] with *her* as the subject of the verb *go*. The example has also shown the influence of morphological loss on syntax, the analogical relation that exists with other infinitival structures, which may be a cause for reanalysis as well as analogical extension, and the role played by language contact.

References and Further Reading

Aitchison, J. (2001). *Language Change: Progress or Decay?* 3rd edn. Cambridge: Cambridge University Press.

Allen, C. (1995). *Case Marking and Reanalysis: Grammatical Relations from Old to Early Modern English*. Oxford: Oxford University Press.

Barber, C. (1993). *The English Language: A Historical Introduction*. Cambridge: Cambridge University Press.

Barber, C. (1997). *Early Modern English*. Edinburgh: Edinburgh University Press.

Beal, J. (2004). *English in Modern Times: 1700–1945*. Oxford: Oxford University Press.

Campbell, L. (ed.) (2001). *Grammaticalization: A Critical Assessment*. Special issue of *Language Sciences*, 23.2–3.

Denison, D. (1993). *English Historical Syntax*. London: Longman.

Fischer, O. (1991). The rise of the passive infinitive in English. In D. Kastovsky (ed.), *Historical English Syntax* (pp. 141–88). Berlin: Mouton de Gruyter.

Fischer, O. (2000). Grammaticalization: unidirectional, non-reversable? The case of *to* before the infinitive in English. In O. Fischer, A. Rosenbach, & D. Stein (eds.), *Pathways of Change – Grammaticalization in English* (pp. 149–69). Amsterdam: Benjamins.

Fischer, O. (2006). On the position of adjectives in Middle English. *English Language and Linguistics*, 10, 253–88.

Fischer, O. (2007). *Morphosyntactic Change: Functional and Formal Perspectives*. Oxford: Oxford University Press.

Fischer, O., van Kemenade, A., Koopman, W., & van der Wurff, W. (2000). *The Syntax of Early English*. Cambridge: Cambridge University Press.

Fischer, O. & van der Wurff, W. (2006). Syntax. In D. Denison & R. Hogg (eds.), *History of the English Language* (pp. 109–98). Cambridge: Cambridge University Press.

Hampe, B. & Schönefeld, D. (2003). Creative syntax: iconic principles within the symbolic. In W. G. Müller & O. Fischer (eds.), *From Sign to Signing: Iconicity in Language and Literature 3* (pp. 243–61). Amsterdam: Benjamins.

Hogg, R. (ed.) (1992–2001). *The Cambridge History of the English Language*. 6 Vols. Cambridge: Cambridge University Press.

Holyoak, K. J. & Thagard, P. (1995). *Mental Leaps: Analogy in Creative Thought*. Cambridge, MA: MIT Press.

Hopper, P. J. & Traugott, E. C. (2003 [1993]). *Grammaticalization*. 2nd edn. Cambridge: Cambridge University Press.

Jespersen, O. (1913–40). *A Modern English Grammar on Historical Principles*. Vols. 2–5. Copenhagen: Munksgaard.

Lehmann, C. (1995 [1982]). *Thoughts on Grammaticalization*. Munich: Lincom Europa.

Lightfoot, D. W. (1979). *Principles of Diachronic Syntax*. Cambridge: Cambridge University Press.

Mitchell, B. (1985). *Old English Syntax*. 2 vols. Oxford: Oxford University Press.

Mustanoja, T. F. (1960). *A Middle English Syntax*. Helsinki: Société Néophilologique.

Rosenbach, A. (2002). *Genitive Variation in English: Conceptual Factors in Synchronic and Diachronic Studies*. Topics in English Linguistics 42. Berlin: Mouton de Gruyter.

Visser, F. T. (1963–73). *An Historical Syntax of the English Language*. Vols. 1–3b. Leiden: E. J. Brill.

7

A History of the
English Lexicon

Geoffrey Hughes

Lexicon, like *lexis*, is usually defined as the totality of words, idioms, and expressions contained in a language. Whereas a dictionary, being alphabetical, will focus principally on the vocabulary, the lexicon or lexis of a language is better revealed by a thesaurus, which is conceptual and thematic, including synonyms, idiomatic phrases, and cultural references. *Lexicology*, a comparatively recent term, denotes the study of the structure of lexis, for example lexical concentrations or gaps, and the analysis of word-fields to reflect culture, values, authorial preferences, technological developments, and so on.

The distinctive feature of English lexis is that it is mixed, being made up of three main etymological components, which can be identified on an archeological model as the Germanic base, a Norman French stratum, and a classical superstructure, exemplified in Anglo-Saxon or Old English *word* and *word-hoard*, French *term*, Latin *vocabulary*, and Greek *lexicon* and *lexis*. This pattern of different *registers*, or words of broadly similar meaning which differ in connotation and contextual appropriateness, is apparent in word-fields of all kinds. In table 7.1, for each case the first term is common, the second is formal, and the third is technical. Such collocations of words can be replicated many times and endorse the point that in English there are few, if any, exact synonyms.

The structure of the vocabulary broadly reflects the complex history of the English people in various social dynamics of invasion, subservience, dominance, colonization, and expansion into global varieties. English itself was originally an invading language, brought by the Angles, Saxons, and Jutes from the fifth century. The aboriginal Celtic languages of Britain, those of the true natives, have been displaced by the tongues of successive waves of Roman, Anglo-Saxon, Norse, and Norman invaders. Just as the descendants of the Celts, namely the Scots, the Irish and especially the Welsh, were driven from central parts of the British Isles, so the vestigial survivors of Celtic words now occupy the periphery of the vocabulary. The ancestor of *Welsh* is Anglo-Saxon

Table 7.1   Three registers in English, by language of origin

Anglo-Saxon	Norman French	Latin/Greek
ask	question	interrogate
hearty	cordial	cardiac
holy	sacred	consecrated
go	depart	exit
guts	entrails	intestines

wealh, originally meaning a Celt, then a slave. (See also ENGLISH IN IRELAND; ENGLISH IN SCOTLAND; ENGLISH IN WALES.)

Not all of these invasions were of the same intensity, comprehensiveness, and character. Whereas the Roman visitation was colonial and comparatively temporary, the Norse was permanent, at the grassroots level but regionally concentrated in the Northeast, reflecting the boundary of the Danelaw according to the treaty of Wedmore drawn up in 878, intending to confine the Vikings to that area of England (see EARLY OLD ENGLISH). However, hundreds of basic words from Norse such as *husband*, *law*, *leg*, *skin*, *skull*, *sky*, *egg*, *call*, *take*, *ill*, *flat*, *ugly*, and *thing* have become part of the lexical core, which is mainly Germanic. By contrast, Norman-French was essentially the language of a conquering administering élite, establishing itself in words of authority like *court*, *crown*, *parliament*, *government*, *justice*, *state*, and *office*. Only the Anglo-Saxon invasion was comprehensive, both regionally and socially. Consequently it still represents the base, while the lexical contributions of the other invaders to the word-stock reflect different models of diversity and hierarchy. However, as we shall see, although words have origins, like people, they can become socially mobile.

After the Norman Conquest (1066) English was the language of the majority; in a dynamic typical of colonialism it ceased to be the official language of the land for three centuries, until 1362, when it eventually displaced Norman-French as the language of law and administration. By the fourteenth century England was a bilingually stratified nation and English was no longer a "pure" language, since many terms of power and prestige derived from the French overlords became assimilated. Latin, initially and for centuries the language of the Church and scholarship, was steadily displaced in these roles by English translations, becoming the basis of the language of law and, together with Greek, that of medicine and science (see EARLY MIDDLE ENGLISH). The invention of printing (ca. 1450) meant that the slow lexical transmission by word of mouth was accelerated by the swift proliferation of first editions (see EARLY MODERN ENGLISH PRINT CULTURE). From the sixteenth century England became a colonial power, the language absorbing exotic terms as a result of expansion, generating the modern mixed, cosmopolitan vocabulary (see Part VI: "English in History").

This model of the lexicon as an indicator of power relations is remarkably revealing, but it is achievable principally by lexicographical tools which became available

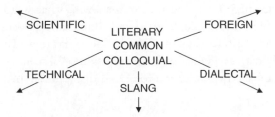

Figure 7.1   Murray's diagram of the structure of the English lexicon

only from the eighteenth century. The monumental *Oxford English Dictionary* or *OED* (1884–1928) was an astonishing historical reconstruction of the language in all its aspects, of which the lexical and semantic are the most relevant to this discussion. Naturally the work is principally dependent on written evidence, which has the advantage of being reliable, but cannot reflect the multiplicity of oral usage. The difference is apparent between the formal lexis of, say, Charles Dickens writing as a journalist or social commentator and the extraordinary range of idiolect (individual, often eccentric speech-forms) which he created as a novelist to convey character (see JOHNSON, WEBSTER, AND THE OED).

Despite this complex history, and "borrowings" which now comprise a heterogeneous lexicon of well over half a million words, the central core, those words "whose Anglicity is undisputed" in James Murray's famous description in the Preface of the *OED* (1887), still remains predominantly Anglo-Saxon in origin. Thus the basis of daily communication, the language of first resort and most emotion is still *help, life, death, love, laughter, food, drink, bread, wine, beer, sing, play, work, house, home, man, woman, child, earth, fire, water, sun, moon,* and *star.* Obviously with the coming of modern industrialization and rapidly expanding technology, there has been a corresponding lexical growth of technical terms, commonly formed on Latin and Greek roots. These include *transistor, nuclear, electronic, energy, computer,* and *molecule* (see BRITISH ENGLISH SINCE 1830). An illuminating but contrasting lexical model is supplied by Icelandic, since the inhospitable climate and terrain discouraged invasion, contributing to the purity and stability of the original language. In modern times these qualities have been maintained artificially by a policy of resisting borrowing and promoting native word-creation for new technological developments, generating *simi* for *telephone, sjonvarp* for *television,* and *tolva* for *computer.* While these word-formations seem quaint to us now, we should recall that Anglo-Saxon also used its own resources to the fullest extent: the native word for "astronomy" was *tungolcræft* (literally "star-craft"), that for "medicine" was *leechdom,* while *rimcræft* was the term for "mathematics." Compounding has been an essential mode of word-formation in English.

In his great Preface Murray set out in a simple diagram the lexical configuration of functional varieties (figure 7.1).

Although by definition the "Common" words are at the core, there is a fundamental hierarchy of usage, designated by the categories of "Literary," "Colloquial," and "Slang" arranged in descending order, with "Technical," "Scientific," "Foreign," and

"Dialectal" at various perimeters, with arrows showing that words are "in" the language to differing degrees. It is an original and illuminating document, but it too is set in time, being in various ways quintessentially Victorian. Today "literary" language is notoriously hard to define; so is "slang," while "obscene," a category ignored by Murray, has established itself after a long and disreputable history.

Literary Words

In Anglo-Saxon there were different vocabularies for poetry and prose, a distinction surprising to the modern age. Thus the *Anglo-Saxon Chronicle* writes sparely of the Viking invasions in terms of the local English *fyrd* and the invading *here*. However, *The Battle of Maldon* (the poem celebrating the local battle of 991) describes the Vikings poetically as *wæl-wulfas* ("slaughterous wolves") and *sæ-lida* ("pirates"). Although the poetic word-hoard was regarded as traditional, creative permutations by means of new compounds and *kennings* or compound metaphors were achievable on a great scale. Thus "sun" could be rendered as *woruldcandel*, "sea" as *hwælesweg* ("the way of the whale"), "ship" as *mere-hengest* ("sea-horse") and "body" as *banhus* ("bonehouse"). The lexis of the epic *Beowulf*, in common with other Anglo-Saxon poetry, is virtually pure Germanic. Despite the poem's martial content, *fyrd* is never used and *here* appears only three times in the poem's 3,182 lines, but forms the basis of no less than 14 compounds. Klaeber's fine edition marks words found only in poetry and those unique to the poem. Even the latter are surprisingly numerous, amounting to nearly 800 forms. Discussing the problems of translating *Beowulf* over half a century ago, J. R. R. Tolkien noted the great lexical concentration "of things with which Northern heroic verse was especially concerned – such as the sea, and ships, and especially men (warriors and sailors)" (1950: xxi). In the last category there are "at least ten virtual synonyms" and "the list can be extended to at least twenty-five items" because of the semantic overlap in heroic culture between terms for "man" and "warrior." Today, he noted, such synonymic richness cannot be achieved, even by including incongruous items such as *cove*, *individual*, *guy*, and *bloke*. Furthermore, virtually none of the rich original word-field has survived, in any sense. The generally elevated tone of the surviving Anglo-Saxon literature would seem to exclude the category of obscenity, an aspect explored by R. W. Burchfield (1985). The exception lies in certain riddles which definitely have a bawdy significance, but this is conveyed by metaphor and innuendo rather than by improper words (see further THE ANGLO-SAXON POETIC TRADITION).

Today the lexical distinction between prose and verse has largely fallen away, being apparent only in self-conscious poetic creations like *Bible-black* by Dylan Thomas or *fire-folk* by Gerard Manley Hopkins. Words such as *serpent*, *Stygian*, *steed*, *lambent*, *lucent*, *spectral*, *hue*, and *sepulchral* which would have been naturally used by Milton, are now literary and old-fashioned. There are virtually none which can still be designated "poetic."

The medieval notion of literary decorum was largely class-based, with different lexis regarded as appropriate to the aristocracy, the bourgeois, and the working class. The classic description is by John of Garland in the thirteenth century. Following the model of Virgil, society is divided into courtiers (*curiales*), citizens (*civiles*), and rustics (*rurales*), with matching narratives in serious, mixed, or low style and register. Thus the courtly fourteenth-century romance *Sir Gawain and the Green Knight* is largely in an elevated and sophisticated French-based register, while the contemporary religious satire *Piers Plowman* uses a mixed register, contrasting liturgical Latin with mundane idioms and coarse demotic speech: Gluttony "pissed in a potel a *paternoster* while" (Passus B, V 348). Chaucer largely subscribes to this social distinction, exploiting in the *Prologue to the Canterbury Tales* entirely different aspects of the lexicon, creating the oafish Miller exclusively out of a dense concentration of earthy Anglo-Saxon and Norse words (ll. 545–66), using a contrasting artificial array of French terms (ll. 118–62) to create the *grand dame* of the Church, the Prioress. Between these lexical extremes is the Knight, a balanced blend of Saxon solidity and French courtliness. However, the portraits of the Doctor, the Man of Law, and even the Merchant are dense with opaque technical vocabulary and arcane learning, presented as a clear anticipation of the lexical barrier of obfuscation which characterizes modern professional language (see Corson 1985).

In the varied tales of his ambitious frame narrative Chaucer is equally pointed, allocating an elevated chivalric romance to the Knight, a romantic Breton lay focusing on *gentillesse* or "nobility" to the social-climbing Franklin (a land baron), and coarse bedroom farces or *fabliaux* to the gross Miller and mean-spirited Reeve. However, the most piercing moments of comedy and irony are achieved by bizarre disjunctions of register, as when Absolon, the effeminate admirer of the adulterous Alison in the *Miller's Tale*, serenades her in the rarefied vein of the Song of Solomon while she is *in flagrante* with her student lover (ll. 3698–707). Chaucer's use of the "four-letter" words, now rather over-emphasized, is certainly daring, but judiciously managed: the pilgrim narrator stresses in advance that the Miller was a "cherl," as was the Reeve, warning the reader thus to expect sordid tales of "harlotrie" or smut. However, the outrageously unconventional, oft-married, and devastatingly frank Wife of Bath refers to her genitalia in an exuberant range of register: the coyly euphemistic Saxon *thinge*, the taboo but ambiguous *queynte*, the stylishly French *bele chose*, and pseudo-scholarly Latinism *quoniam*.

Although printing standardized the language grammatically, it also encouraged "borrowing" on an entirely new scale, mainly as a consequence of translation, as is demonstrated in the *Chronological English Dictionary* (*CED*) (1970) and graphically in Hughes (2000: 403–5). The *CED* rearranges the data of the *Shorter Oxford Dictionary* (1933) in the form of annals. These show a huge efflorescence of the vocabulary in the Renaissance period, the annual number of neologisms and new senses rising sharply from about fifty in the year 1500 to an astonishing peak of over 350 in 1600, followed by a period of diminished growth. (See, however, Algeo 1999: 63–5.) With the erosion of grammatically distinctive inflections, creative interventions through

grammatical "conversion" (e.g., from noun to verb) accelerated greatly. Extraordinary literary effects were achieved by both the juxtaposition of registers and by creative neologisms. Both are apparent in Shakespeare's evocation of Macbeth's horrified recognition that the royal blood on his hands will be ineradicable:

> This my hand will rather
> The multitudinous seas incarnadine,
> Making the green one red.
> (*Macbeth* 2.2.60–2)

Here the first and third lines are in the plain, simple, physical, and amoral register of a child, but the central line shows an escape from "the present horror" via the most recherché and poetic terms imaginable, notably the inspired neologism *incarnadine* and the archaic *multitudinous*. Both extremes avoid the fundamental key term of guilt, *blood*.

Although writing in a popular dramatic form, Shakespeare pre-eminently indulged in word-creation and extended the semantic range of words on an astonishing scale. Thus of the 250 new words and senses recorded in the *CED* for the year 1602, 43 out of 250 (17.2 per cent) are directly traceable to *Hamlet*, while for 1605 some 45 words out of 349 (12.8 per cent) are recorded in *Macbeth* and *King Lear*. It is an illuminating exercise to gather Shakespearean original uses in the compendious lexicon of the *OED*. The number of instances traceable to *Hamlet* then rises from 43 in the *CED* to over 150, and those in *Macbeth* from 27 to over 110. These come from all parts of the word-stock. Thus the outrage of Hamlet's father that he was murdered before making atonement for his sins is stressed by three extraordinary terms describing his vulnerable spiritual state: "unhouseled, disappointed unanealed" (1.5.77).

Although many Shakespearean neologisms are classically derived, they have become the commonest words in the language, including *accommodation, addiction, admirable, amazement, assassination, castigate, comply, compulsive, consign,* and *counterpart* under the letters "A" and "C" alone. Fuller details can be found in Hughes (2000: 181–2) and Garner (1987), who lists more than 600 Latinate neologisms. Some of these are, admittedly, nonce-words. A *nonce-word*, deriving from Anglo-Saxon *for þæm anes* ("for the once"), is strictly a word made up for a special context. These include deliberately artificial and slightly opaque words, such as *orgulous, immures, fraughtage,* and *corresponsive*, used in the Prologue to *Troilus & Cressida* to evoke the ponderous military Greek invasion. Others are made up on the spur of the dramatic moment, as when the illegitimate villain Edmund in *King Lear* dismisses astrological influence on his nature: "I should have been that I am had the *maidenliest* star in the firmament twinkled on my *bastardizing*" (1.2.148). Many are transparent, incorporating aspects of irony and revelations of dramatic character. Neologism became less fashionable in the eighteenth century, but is the hallmark of some later authors, such as Hopkins and especially James Joyce (see JOYCE'S ENGLISH).

One less expected and longstanding consequence of the correctness of print format was the modern notion of "language fit to print." Obscene language which Chaucer and his contemporaries had used with discretion in the old manuscript culture steadily disappeared, surfacing in *double-entendres* and "cant" or underground slang, the source of the earliest glossaries, such as Thomas Harman's *Caveat for Commen Cursetors* (1566). As the studies of Partridge (1947) and Williams (1997) have shown, Shakespeare's bawdy avoids the taboo "four-letter" words, substituting multitudes of sexual puns and innuendoes, extensions of basic words like *stand*, *foot*, *yard*, and *die*.

New Words, Taboo Words, and the Dictionary

The great volume of new classical borrowings created a market for the earliest "proper" dictionaries, such as Robert Cawdrey's slim and interestingly titled *A Table Alphabeticall of hard usuall English wordes* (1604). Its list of 2,560 items explains common words of classical origin which were "hard" or difficult for "unskilfull persons," namely those without a classical education. These "hard words" dictionaries clearly fulfilled a public service function, becoming quite fashionable in the seventeenth century, and included Henry Cockeram's *The English Dictionarie* (1623) and Thomas Blount's *Glossographia* (1656). Other works are covered in the standard history of the early dictionary by Starnes and Noyes (1946) (see also ENGLISH ONOMASIOLOGICAL DICTIONARIES AND THESAURI). These were the precursors of the more comprehensive dictionaries with which we are now familiar, the prototypes of which were the works of Nathaniel Bailey (1721, 1728, 1730) and pre-eminently Samuel Johnson (1755). Today we take dictionaries for granted as authoritative guides to usage. However, the genre is comparatively recent in the great time-span of the language, since all the major authors prior to the mid-eighteenth century (i.e., Chaucer, Shakespeare, Jonson, Milton, Dryden, Pope, Swift, and Fielding) managed without dictionaries. Interestingly, the original division between slang and "proper" dictionaries has continued right down to the present, with the great *Random House Historical Dictionary of American Slang* (ed. J. Lighter) still in production.

It is possible to demonstrate a shift in the lexical balance over time between the Germanic base and the classical superstructure. Frederick T. Wood undertook such an analysis some fifty years ago, generating the following table of percentages of native origin in major authors from ca. 1600 to ca. 1900:

Authorised Version – King James Bible (1611)	94%
Shakespeare (1564–1623)	90%
Milton (1608–74)	81%
Swift (1667–1745)	75%
Johnson (1709–84)	72%
Tennyson (1809–92)	88%

Wood found that contemporary authors such as Shaw, Galsworthy, T. S. Eliot, and Aldous Huxley ranged between 73 percent and 77 percent, and that his own personal correspondence rated 82 percent (1969: 47–8). These figures trace the change of diction from the simple core vocabulary used by the translators of the Authorised Version of the Bible (1611) to the more weighty and artificial latinization preferred in the eighteenth century. However, they also show the resilience of the Anglo-Saxon core. Although Dr. Johnson expressed a famous preference for "the wells of English undefiled" in the Preface to his Dictionary (1755), he himself was noted (some would say notorious) for his latinized vocabulary, apparent in such concentrations as his definition of *network* as "anything reticulated or decussated, at equal distances, with interstices between the intersections." Yet even this dense and opaque definition boils down to 50 percent Germanic and 50 percent Classical, showing that the essential grammatical "building blocks" of the language (which are Germanic) still make a high proportion of any utterance. Although criticized for this Classical preference (see Baugh 1959: 327–8), Johnson was not alone, as is shown in the texts of David Hume and especially Edward Gibbon, who in his masterpiece, *The Decline and Fall of the Roman Empire* (1765–87), thus described the sensual Empress Theodora: "the matchless excellence of her form . . . was degraded by the facility with which it was exposed to the public eye, and prostituted to licentious desire . . . her murmurs, her pleasures and her arts, must be veiled in the obscurity of a learned language" (chapter 30).

In this memorable phrase Gibbon was identifying Latin and Greek as prime sources of euphemism in English, a feature copiously apparent in such words as *excrement*, *flatulence*, *urinate*, *defecate*, *copulate*, *ejaculate*, *genitalia*, *perspire*, and *expire*. At a time when sexual terms were taboo, the lexicographer Nathaniel Bailey was bold enough to include *fuck* in his *Dictionarium Britannicum* (1730), but defined it opaquely as *subagitare foeminam*. His similar definition for *cunt*, namely *pudendum muliebre*, was to become traditional and abbreviated. These classicisms seem quaint now, but the mode is not extinct: the *Collins English Dictionary* (2003) defines *fart* in similar high register as "an emission of intestinal gas from the anus, especially an audible one." Originally, sexual terms like *consummation*, *seduce*, *erection*, *intercourse*, and *orgasm* were learned, opaque euphemisms, but have become common in recent decades through the increasing openness encouraged by the sexual revolution.

Historically, dictionaries were concerned over which kinds of words should be recorded and whether their policy should be prescriptive (indicating "correct" usage), proscriptive (indicating "incorrect" usage), or descriptive, i.e., simply recording usage. But whose usage? Dr. Johnson, in keeping with the tenets of his age, was strongly prescriptive and proscriptive. The *OED* aimed at a policy of inclusiveness, notably articulated by one of its founders, Dean Trench, that the work should have "all the words, good and bad." It was astonishingly comprehensive, recording the forms, pronunciations, and meanings of 424,825 words, but excluded *fuck*, *cunt*, *condom*, and a few other taboo terms, then regarded as legally obscene. Modern English dictionaries are generally free of such restraints.

However, the descriptive policy is not welcomed by all, as was shown in the critical furore which greeted the publication of *Webster's Third International* in 1961. Academic reviews were generally favorable, but those of journalists and literati were universally hostile. The ferocity of the controversy derived essentially from the perception that the dictionary had adopted a *laisser faire* policy in matters of usage, thereby abandoning its assumed role as arbiter and authority in setting the standard. Its numerous critics regarded *Webster III* as having kow-towed to the current "permissive" school of descriptive linguistics. In particular "slang labels were not used enough and were not applied consistently" (Morton 1994: 248). The texts of the main exchanges are collected in the casebook *Dictionaries and THAT Dictionary* (Sledd & Ebbitt 1962). By giving greater weight to oral usage than its predecessors, *Webster III* manifestly attracted hostility and criticism. By contrast, the praise accorded the *OED Supplement* (1972–86) derived both from maintaining the standards of the original, and from what the editor Robert Burchfield described as its notional standard of "British written English."

The notion of taboo has also changed. Sexual terms omitted in standard dictionaries from Bailey (1730) up to the 1960s are included in all major modern works, and are read and heard increasingly in the media and popular culture. However, racist terms and those referring to the disabled, previously used without embarrassment, have in the past three decades become genuinely taboo (i.e., unutterable) and euphemized by formulas such as "a person of color," "a member of a minority group," "physically challenged," and so on. Some dictionaries have even adopted a policy of the selective lexicographical expungement of racist terms, described as "Guralnikism" by R. W. Burchfield (1989: 100).

The acceptability of new words has varied according to the fashion of the time. Up to about World War I, "literary" language generally implied a lexis which was established, even perhaps slightly archaic. The exceptions tended to be authors writing in a dramatic framework, such as Chaucer, Shakespeare, Jonson, and Dickens. As a lexicographer and as a writer Johnson was hostile to the new fashion for French terms, which if allowed to continue unchecked, he averred, "will reduce us to babble a dialect of France." Isaac D'Israeli wrote in 1814 of "the vicious neologist, who debases the purity of English diction by affecting new words and phrases."

However, in the course of the past century, new words have become both fashionable and desirable, mainly through the rise of popular journalism and also the imperatives of Modernism in literature. Neologism does not consist only of evidently novel forms like *beatnik*, *blurb*, or *brunch*. As Hans Marchand shows (1969), there are many kinds of word-formation achieved by compounding, prefixes, suffixes, and so on. There is, however, a general difference in attitude between the more conservative British culture and the more innovative American attitude. This is epitomized by the regular American publication *Among the New Words*, which started in 1941. There is no equivalent British publication. The collection *Fifty Years Among the New Words* (Algeo 1991) contains about 7,000 headwords.

Neologisms are evidently becoming increasingly fashionable. Today dictionaries vie with each other in being "up to date," which in part means including the latest

vocabulary of technology and fashion. Thus *Collins English Dictionary* (2003) emphasizes these selling points: "Find out what the very latest buzz words mean" and "Keep up to date with hi-tech vocabulary." As with all innovations, the durability of neologisms is unpredictable. R. W. Burchfield noted in the third edition of Fowler's *Modern English Usage* (1996) that "the language tolerates the introduction of something of the order of 450 neologisms a year . . . but many fall by the wayside as time goes on."

Today, in a very competitive market, most standard dictionaries claim to be "the authority" on the English language, but avoid appearing overly prescriptive by including usage guides for controversial terms. The demand for dictionaries continues apace, so that they are now probably consulted more frequently than sacred texts. The first truly manageable short work was the *Concise Oxford Dictionary*, edited by Henry and Francis Fowler in 1911.

The lexicon has traditionally been regarded as a spontaneous reflector of social change. While political movements have generated some new terms and meanings, these were within a particular framework, such as the Communist uses of *bourgeois*, *class struggle*, and *proletariat*. The recent initiatives of Feminism and Political Correctness have shown that language is not only the bearer of normative notions, but can be used to raise consciousness in areas of prejudice and even to promote new agendas. These have been highlighted by coinages such as *herstory*, *lookism*, *phallocentric*, and *wimmin*, as well as many words ending in *–ism* and *–ist*. Other established terms, such as *challenged*, *Eurocentric*, *gay*, *homophobic*, *patriarchy*, and *person*, have been given new meanings, mainly relating to sexual and cultural politics.

The English lexicon retains its Anglo-Saxon core, but is increasingly cosmopolitan and polyglot. Many terms have been assimilated through cultural exchange and from the languages which Britain encountered as a colonial power. These include *algebra*, *anorak*, *apartheid*, *blarney*, *brogue*, *cash*, *caucus*, *cookie*, *disinformation*, *dogma*, *galore*, *intelligentsia*, *karma*, *ketchup*, *kow-tow*, *lexicon*, *mafia*, *nadir*, *oasis*, *pariah*, *pyjamas*, *robot*, *saga*, *sauna*, *schmaltz*, *silhouette*, *smuggle*, *tabby*, *taboo*, and *trek*. There are obviously many recherché or literary terms of foreign origin like *éclaircissement*, *hoi-polloi*, *schadenfreud*, *paparazzi*, and *sprezzatura*, as well as enormous numbers of new technical terms made up from ancient classical roots, such as *antibiotic*, *chlorophyll*, *cholesterol*, *dynamo*, *electron*, *geopolitical*, *psephology*, and *vitamin*. Celia Millward points out that these formations now outnumber "the total known vocabulary of classical Greek and Latin" (1989: 281). Some are alien, such as *chthononosology* and *sphygmomanometer*, and even bizarre, such as *pneumonoultramicroscopicsilicovolcanoconiosis*.

These words constitute a periphery. But what of the core? Today, with the use of modern corpora or bodies of data both written and spoken, it is possible to rate words in terms of their actual frequency. The *Longman Dictionary of Contemporary English* (*LDOCE*) (1995) highlights the 3,000 most common words in both oral and written usage and rates them accordingly. Thus *bad* is rated S1 and W1, meaning it is in the 1,000 most frequently used words, both spoken and written. Yet *bugger* is rated as only S2, in the 2,000 most frequently spoken words, while *zone* is W3, in the 3,000

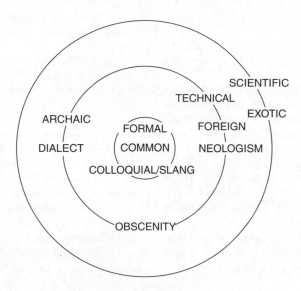

Figure 7.2 Update of Murray's diagram of the structure of the English lexicon

most frequently written words. Isolating those terms which are both S1 and W1 produces a core of some 600 words. This can be analyzed on the basis of various criteria, namely institutions, values, and etymology. Although the core is still predominantly Anglo-Saxon, there is a surprising number of social, organizational, and business terms, such as *class*, *company*, *competition*, *manager*, *management*, *society*, and *system*. The technical and materialist emphasis of modern society is shown in *environment*, *computer*, *energy*, *machine*, *product*, *production*, *programme*, and *science*. Significantly, none of the central religious and moral terms of the past, such as *heaven*, *hell*, *soul*, *false*, *foul*, *fair*, *honour*, *virtue*, *crime*, or *evil* occur in this core.

Updating Murray's diagram, the structure of the Modern English lexicon looks more like figure 7.2.

REFERENCES AND FURTHER READING

Algeo, J. (ed.) (1991). *Fifty Years Among the New Words*. Cambridge: Cambridge University Press.

Algeo, J. (1999). Vocabulary. In S. Romaine (ed.), *The Cambridge History of the English Language*, Vol. 4 (pp. 57–91). Cambridge: Cambridge University Press.

Baugh, A. C. (1959). *History of the English Language*. 2nd edn. London: Routledge & Kegan Paul.

Burchfield, R. W. (1985). An outline history of euphemisms in English. In D. J. Enright (ed.), *Fair of Speech* (pp. 13–31). Oxford: Oxford University Press.

Burchfield, R. W. (ed.) (1986). *The New Fowler's Modern English Usage*. Oxford: Clarendon Press.

Burchfield, R. W. (1989). The treatment of controversial vocabulary in the *Oxford English Dictionary* (pp. 83–108). In *Unlocking the English Language*. London: Faber.

Corson, D. (1985). *The Lexical Bar*. Oxford: Pergamon Press.

Finkenstaedt, T., Leisi, E., & Wolff, D. (eds.) (1970). *A Chronological English Dictionary*. Heidelberg: Carl Winter.

Garner, B. (1987). Shakespeare's Latinate neologisms. In V. Salmon & E. Burness (eds.), *A Reader in the Language of Shakespearean Drama* (pp. 207–28). Amsterdam: John Benjamin.

Hughes, G. (2000). *A History of English Words*. Oxford: Blackwell.

Klaeber, F. (1950). *Beowulf*. Boston: D. C. Heath.

Marchand, H. (1969). *The Categories and Types of Present-Day English Word-Formation*. Munich: Beck.

Millward, C. (1989). *A Biography of the English Language*. Fort Worth: Holt, Rinehart.

Morton, H. C. (1994). *The Story of Webster's Third: Philip Gove's Controversial Dictionary and its Critics*. Cambridge: Cambridge University Press.

Partridge, E. (1947). *Shakespeare's Bawdy*. London: Routledge & Kegan Paul.

Sledd, J. & Ebbit, W. (eds.) (1962). *Dictionaries and THAT Dictionary*. Chicago: Scott, Foresman.

Starnes, de Witt T. & Noyes, G. (1946). *The English Dictionary from Cawdrey to Johnson*. Chapel Hill: University of North Carolina Press.

Tolkien, J. R. R. (1950). Prefatory remarks. In C. L. Wrenn (ed.), *Beowulf and the Finnesburg Fragment: A Translation into Modern English Prose* (pp. viii–xli). London: George Allen & Unwin.

Williams, G. (1997). *A Glossary of Shakespeare's Sexual Language*. London: Athlone Press.

Wood, F. T. (1969). *An Outline History of the English Language*. London: Macmillan.

8

History of English Prosody

Geoffrey Russom

In literary usage, *prosody* is the art of versification; in linguistic usage, it is the study of sound patterning within the word, the phrase, and the sentence. As this dual usage suggests, metrics and linguistic prosody are closely allied fields (Kiparsky 1977). Representative Old, Middle, and Modern English meters can provide valuable information about English linguistic history.

Example (1) illustrates the most important features of Old English meter, which are also present in the cognate Old Norse and Continental Germanic meters (Sievers 1893; Russom 1998).

(1) Wedera leode   on **wang** stigon,
     sæ-wudu sældon.   Syrcean hrysedon,
     guþ-gewædo.
     'The people of the Weders descended to the shore,
     tied down the sea-wood [i.e., their boat]. Armor rattled,
     war-equipment.'

An Old English line consists of two half-lines bound by alliteration. The first half-line is called the a-verse; the second is called the b-verse. In standard editions, the a-verse and b-verse are spaced apart, as above. Each verse normally consists of a natural syntactic unit such as a small phrase or clause. Alliteration must occur in the first syllable with metrically significant stress, which may stand at the beginning of the verse (as with the stressed syllable of *Wedera*) or inside the verse (as with stressed *wang* after unstressed *on*). A second stressed word in the a-verse may share in the alliteration (as with *sældon*). Only one alliteration is permitted in the b-verse. (See THE ANGLO-SAXON POETIC TRADITION.)

Old English rules for alliteration differ from those of an otherwise similar Old Irish meter called *roscad* (Murphy 1961: 36–9):

(2)   Eo **Rossa**,   **roth ruir**thech,
      recht flatha,   **fuaimm** tuinne
      'Yew of Ross, wheel strong-running,
      power of a chieftain, sound of a wave.'

In roscad, the first stressed syllable of the b-verse normally alliterates with the last stressed syllable of the a-verse. The last stressed syllable of the b-verse may continue the line-internal alliteration and often alliterates with the first stressed syllable of the following line. In (2), *ruirthech* alliterates with *Rossa* and *roth* in its own line and with *recht* in the following line.

Comparison with the distinct yet similar roscad helps us understand Old English meter as a meter of a certain kind. Old Irish and Old English have predictable stress on word-initial syllables, and alliterative meters seem to arise naturally in languages with this kind of fixed stress (Minkova 2003: 82–3). In both roscad and Old English meter, matching of the first consonant before the vowel of a stressed syllable usually suffices for alliteration. In both meters, we also find essentially the same rules for special cases: (1) all stressed syllables that lack a prevocalic consonant alliterate with one another, as if they began with the same "zero consonant"; and (2) *sp-* alliterates only with *sp-*, *st-* only with *st-*, and *sk-* only with *sk-*. Roscad differs slightly in restricting *sm-* to alliteration with *sm-*.

Both roscad and Old English meter favor verses consisting of a two-word syntactic constituent (Russom 1998; Travis 1973). In roscad, this preference is obvious at a glance. In Old English meter, it becomes evident when we observe that syntactic constituents of two stressed words have strikingly elevated frequency in poetic texts. *The Battle of Brunanburh*, a 365-word heroic poem composed no earlier than 937 CE, contains 51 verse phrases of two stressed words. The *Cynewulf and Cyneheard* entry of the *Anglo-Saxon Chronicle*, a heroic prose narrative of 447 words in a manuscript dated to about 900 CE, contains only four prose phrases of two stressed words. In the prose narrative, stressed words are not often adjacent, and when they are adjacent, an unstressed word usually stands before them within the same phrase.

Differences between poetry and prose in Old English can be attributed in part to preservation of verse technique from the early Germanic period, when the finite verb stood after its governed object complement, as with *stigon* and *sældon* in (1). Languages with object-verb (OV) word order also place the governing word after its complement in other kinds of phrases (Lehmann 1994: 34; see also ENGLISH AS A GERMANIC LANGUAGE). In a consistent OV language, prepositions appear after their noun objects as postpositions, reversing the normal order of Modern English. In Germanic OV constructions, the phrase-initial complement had full stress and its phrase-final governor might have weak stress or no stress. Finite verbs had weak stress in phrase-final position. OV genitive-noun and adjective-noun constructions had a somewhat stronger stress on the phrase-final noun.

Of the five verse types identified by Sievers (table 8.1), OV structures readily yield three types, illustrated below by examples from *Beowulf*.

Table 8.1 Sievers' five types

Type	Sievers' notation	Word-foot notation
A	/ x | / x	Sx/Sx
B	x / | x /	x/Sxs
C	x / | / x	x/Ssx
D	/ | / \ x	S/Ssx
E	/ \ x | /	Ssx/S

(3) beaga bryttan   'rings' distributor' = 'distributor of rings'
(4) leof land-fruma   'beloved land-king' = 'beloved king of the land'
(5) Scede-landum in   'Swedish-lands in' = 'in Swedish lands'

Verse (3), a genitive-noun construction, represents type A, the most heavily used pattern, in which each "word foot" has the normative word pattern, a trochaic pattern created by a stressed root syllable and an unstressed inflection (Dresher & Lahiri 1991). The highly valued verse pattern of (3), more narrowly designated as type A1, establishes a norm of two stresses and four metrical positions. Verse (4), an adjective-noun construction with a stressed simplex word followed by a trisyllabic compound, represents type D. Verse (5), representing type E, has a trisyllabic compound followed by a postposition.

By the Old English period, some Germanic OV structures were being replaced by VO structures with unstressed phrase-initial words. These innovating VO structures could not be accommodated in types A1, D, or E, so additional types with an unstressed word foot in initial position were required. The most important additional types are represented below.

(6) þis / ellen-weorc   'this brave deed'   Type B
(7) mid / scip-herge   'with a ship-army'   Type C

In type B, the medial syllable of the compound is unstressed; in type C, the final syllable is unstressed.

This overview cannot provide full treatment of minor verse patterns, but a category of hypermetrical types should be mentioned. Examples below represent the most common hypermetrical types, which consist of an A1 verse preceded by additional linguistic material (before the double slash).

(8) æghwylc // oþrum trywe   'each true to others'
(9) swylce þær // Unferþ þyle   'also there Unferth the orator'

Examples like (8), with an alliterating word before the A1 pattern, appear only as a-verses. Examples like (9), with unstressed words before the A1 pattern, appear

primarily as b-verses. Hypermetrical verses appear in "runs" of two or more. Their complexity is mitigated by unusually strict adherence to metrical norms in the closing portion that corresponds to a normal verse. In (8) and (9), the closing portion, with two trochaic words, expresses the normative A1 pattern in the most direct way.

A word foot ideally occupied by a word may sometimes be occupied by a word group with a similar stress pattern. In the following examples, a single slash marks the boundary between feet.

(10)	on / **fleam** gewand	'in flight departed'	Type B
(11)	on / **deop** wæter	'in deep water'	Type C
(12)	**gid** / oft wrecen	'a song often sung'	Type D
(13)	**fif** nihta / **fyrst**	'five nights' time'	Type E

Another permissible deviation from two-word norms is addition of extrametrical unstressed words that create "long dips" of two or more adjacent unstressed syllables. Extrametrical words may be added quite freely before the second foot of a verse but must not occur "in anacrusis" before the first foot of type E. Although permitted in types A1 and D, anacrusis is not very common, and it is usually restricted to a single unstressed prefix.

In late Old English, the productivity of compounding began to decline, and a sharper decline followed in Middle English (Sauer 1992: 719). The first hundred lines of *Beowulf* contain 55 compounds. The first hundred alliterative lines of *Sir Gawain and the Green Knight* (SGGK), a paradigmatic example of Middle English versecraft, contain only six compounds. Declining employment of compounds obscured word-foot structure in types B, C, D, and E, which required a compound for their direct, two-word expressions. Employment of two-word verses was also restricted by increased use of extrametrical function words to replace grammatical endings. By the time of SGGK, two-word verses did not have elevated frequency and no longer served as metrical norms.

In Old English meter, as in other meters, adherence to metrical norms becomes stricter toward the end of a metrical unit (Bliss 1967; Hayes 1983). This principle of closure restricts deviation from norms in the second half of the alliterative line. During the late Old English period, complex verses most appropriate to the first half of the line increased in frequency, displacing less deviant verses to the second half. In *Beowulf*, the most direct expression of type A1, with two trochaic words, appears in the b-verse with a relative frequency of 65 percent. In *The Battle of Maldon*, composed no earlier than 991 CE, this frequency jumps to 96 percent. Since two-word verses of type A1 did not require compounds, they were easier for the *Maldon* poet to construct than two-word verses of other types. In *Beowulf*, two-word type A1 accounts for 14 percent of total verses; in *Maldon*, it still accounts for 11 percent of total verses and for 20 percent of b-verses. As the only surviving type with a viable two-word expression, type A1 provided highly valued closure in *Maldon*. The late Old English poet also used syntactic means to highlight the boundaries of increasingly complex lines.

Beowulf employs a "plurilinear" verse syntax in which sentences often begin with a b-verse and end with an a-verse. In *Maldon*, the sentence is aligned much more consistently with the line (Scragg 1981: 29, 53 n. 142).

Strict constraints on the Middle English b-verse were already strong tendencies in Old English b-verses of type A1. In the following examples, extrametrical words are in parentheses.

(14) **sun**nan / (ond) monan   'the sun and the moon'
(15) (ðurh-)**fon** ne / mihte   'could not pierce through'

In type A1, long dips created by extrametrical words normally appeared before the second foot, as in (14); and extrametrical anacruses before the first foot were normally prefixal, as in (15). Since most Old English prefixes were monosyllabic, most anacruses were monosyllabic. In general, then, verses with two trochaic feet allowed for free use of a long dip in only one location. This generalization includes hypermetrical b-verses, which allowed for free use of a long dip verse-initially but stayed closer to verse norms in the closing portion, as in (9). During the Middle English period, when the basic two-word verse structure was obscured by more frequent employment of extrametrical words, such words would be added by careful poets in the correct traditional locations, which could still be identified as expandable sites in a linear stress pattern. What remained perceptible would be the preference for two stresses, a trochaic word at the end of the line, and no more than one long dip per verse. Straightforward regularization of these tendencies yields the rules for the b-verse in SGGK, which require exactly two stresses, a verse-final trochee, and a single long dip (Cable 1991: 85–113; Duggan 1988; Russom 2004). Middle English poets continued to employ syntactic markers not only for line boundaries, as in *Maldon*, but also for verse boundaries. In *Beowulf*, the verse is usually a small subclausal phrase; in SGGK, the verse is often a complete clause with all the unstressed function words required by Middle English grammar. This change in verse syntax would have created the impression that a long dip was desirable as well as permissible.

The following pair of lines from SGGK illustrates the most important features of its meter:

(16) His lif liked him ly3t,   he louied þe lasse
      Auther to longe lye   or to longe sitte.
      'He liked his life (to be) active; he loved the less
      either to lie too long or to sit too long.'

The boundary between verses is marked in the first line of (16) by a syntactic boundary requiring punctuation. In the second line, the verses are parallel clauses. Line structure is highlighted by shared alliteration and also by differing tendencies in the opening and closing verses. The a-verse, with an average of five words, is normally longer than the b-verse, which has an average of four words. The a-verse usually has

two or three alliterations; the b-verse normally alliterates only on its first stress, as in Old English poetry. The b-verse must end with a trochaic constituent, which will not normally alliterate; the a-verse usually ends with a monosyllable or an alliterating trochee. A few lines have double alliteration in the b-verse, like the first line in (16); but this line maintains asymmetry in its a-verse with a third alliteration and a verse-final monosyllabic word. The b-verse has exactly two stresses; in the a-verse, stress count varies considerably. The b-verse must have one and only one long dip. The a-verse often has more than one long dip.

Trochaic words employed for closure in traditional poems were painstakingly cultivated by Middle English poets. In SGGK, etymologically trochaic words were still employed with precision line-finally at a time when scribes had begun to spell them as monosyllables, leaving out the final unstressed -*e* (Putter & Stokes 2000). Alliterative meter could not survive the systematic elimination of final -*e* in early Modern English, however. By the sixteenth century, the old verse form was breathing its last (Turville-Petre 1977: 122–3). The death of alliterative meter coincides with the rise to prominence of rhymed iambic pentameter, a very different verse form employing a single foot pattern with rising rhythm.

When we review the pertinent linguistic changes, it is easy to see why Modern English provided such fertile soil for rhymed iambic poetry. By the sixteenth century, trochaic words with grammatical inflections had largely been replaced by small phrases in which a stressed monosyllable was preceded by an unstressed grammatical word. This newly dominant linguistic unit had iambic stress. Iambic feet were ideally suited, of course, to prestigious French borrowings with iambic stress. In the old OV structures, a phrase-initial word with full stress provided the most prominent site for the sound echo called alliteration. In Modern English VO structures, the last stressed word of the phrase has the strongest stress, providing the most prominent site for the sound echo called rhyme.

Important features of iambic meter can be seen in the following excerpt from Shakespeare's sonnet 130 (lines 11–14). A single slash represents the boundary between iambic feet, and stressed syllables are in boldface.

(17) I **grant** / I **nev**- / er **saw** / a **god**- / dess **go**,
      My **mis**- / tress, when / she **walks**, / **treads** on / the **ground**.
      And **yet**, / by **Heav'n**, / I **think** / my **love** / as **rare**
      As **a**- / ny **she** / belied / with **false** / compare.

Since iambic pentameter employs a fixed, predictable verse pattern, it allows for frequent deviation from the norm, in part to avoid metrical banality (Kiparsky 1977). In (17), words with unstressed suffixes (*mistress, goddess*) create mismatches between word boundaries and foot boundaries, establishing a trochaic lexical counterpoint to the predominantly iambic movement. The second foot of the second line in (17) consists of two unstressed syllables. Such "pyrrhic" feet, which vary the iambic rhythm but do not go against it, occur frequently in the work of canonical poets. The trochaic

realization of the fourth foot (**treads** on) represents a less common type of deviation. Such reversals of iambic rhythm are normally preceded by a syntactic pause that diminishes the relative prominence of the displaced stress, giving the foot an acceptably pyrrhic character. In the last two lines of (17), which are also the last lines of the poem, iambic feet are realized more consistently as iambic words and phrases, illustrating the principle of closure as it applies to sonnet structure. Application of this principle on a smaller scale is illustrated by the final line, in which boundary mismatch is restricted to the opening foot and the closing foot is occupied by an iambic word.

Interesting problems of detail remain to be worked out, but it is already clear that English historical metrics and English historical linguistics have much to offer one another. Works listed below provide convenient entry to a variety of special topics and additional bibliography for those who would like to pursue interdisciplinary research in these fields.

REFERENCES AND FURTHER READING

Bliss, A. J. (1967). *The Metre of Beowulf.* Oxford: Blackwell.

Cable, T. (1991). *The English Alliterative Tradition.* Philadelphia: University of Pennsylvania Press.

Dresher, E. B. & Lahiri, A. (1991). The Germanic foot: metrical coherence in Old English. *Linguistic Inquiry*, 22, 251–86.

Duggan, H. N. (1988). Final -e and the rhythmic structure of the b-verse in Middle English alliterative poetry. *Modern Philology*, 86, 119–45.

Fulk, R. D. (1992). *A History of Old English Meter.* Philadelphia: University of Pennsylvania Press.

Hayes, B. (1983). A grid-based theory of English meter. *Linguistic Inquiry*, 14, 357–93.

Kiparsky, P. (1977). The rhythmic structure of English verse. *Linguistic Inquiry*, 8, 189–247.

Lehmann, W. P. (1994). *Gothic and the Reconstruction of Proto-Germanic.* In E. König & J. van der Auwera (eds.), *The Germanic Languages* (pp. 19–37). London: Routledge.

Minkova, D. (2003). *Alliteration and Sound Change in Early English.* Cambridge: Cambridge University Press.

Momma, H. (1997). *The Composition of Old English Poetry.* Cambridge: Cambridge University Press.

Murphy, G. (1961). *Early Irish Metrics.* Dublin: Royal Irish Academy.

Preminger, A., Brogan, T. V. F., et al. (1993). *The New Princeton Encyclopedia of Poetry and Poetics.* Princeton, NJ: Princeton University Press.

Putter, A. & Stokes, M. (2000). Spelling, grammar and metre in the works of the *Gawain*-poet. *Parergon*, 18, 77–95.

Russom, G. (1998). *Beowulf and Old Germanic Metre.* Cambridge: Cambridge University Press.

Russom, G. (2004). The evolution of Middle English alliterative verse. In A. Curzan & K. Emmons (eds.), *Studies in the History of the English Language II: Unfolding Conversations* (pp. 279–304). Berlin: Mouton de Gruyter.

Sauer, H. (1992). *Nominalkomposita im Frühmittelenglischen.* Tübingen: Niemeyer.

Scragg, D. G. (ed.) (1981). *The Battle of Maldon.* Manchester: Manchester University Press.

Sievers, E. (1893). *Altgermanische Metrik.* Halle: Niemeyer.

Travis, J. (1973). *Early Celtic Versecraft.* Ithaca, NY: Cornell University Press.

Turville-Petre, T. (1977). *The Alliterative Revival.* Cambridge: Brewer.

Part III
English Semantics and Lexicography

Introduction

Attempts by lexicographers to capture and give order to a language also affect its development. The three essays in Part III take up the abundance of glossaries, wordlists, dictionaries, and thesauri written to make sense of the semantic and lexical structure of English. In "Dictionaries Today" R. K. K. Hartmann offers an overview of the science of dictionary-making and of the challenges that face the modern lexicographer; Werner Hüllen's "English Onomasiological Dictionaries and Thesauri" provides a history of early attempts to order the lexicon; and Charlotte Brewer takes a closer look at the motivations behind three landmark modern English dictionaries in "Johnson, Webster, and the *Oxford English Dictionary*."

Dictionaries, Hüllen reminds us, have two primary semantic uses: to look up the meaning of an unknown word, or to find the right word to express an idea. The modern English speaker can choose from literally hundreds of dictionaries, from the smallest pocket speller to the heaviest unabridged tome, and the number will only swell as users turn increasingly to a growing number of electronic resources: spell-checkers, free online dictionaries, and user-created projects such as Wiktionary and the slang Urban Dictionary. Still, rarely do we feel the need to specify which diction-ary we cite; we instead refer simply to the authority of "the dictionary." But a dic-tionary's structure and purpose determine the user's experience of it, and so of their own language. In the face of this abundance of resources, Hartmann writes of the need for a "reference science" which would encompass "the study of all aspects of organizing data, information, and knowledge" with an eye toward both the end user and the lexicographer.

The desire to organize everything in God's creation in terms of language was strong early in English's history as well, especially during the Middle Ages. Hüllen explains that early dictionaries arranged on onomasiological principles – what today we gener-ally call thesauri – helped language learners find vocabulary while also functioning as ontological exercises for the compilers. But beginning in approximately the seven-teenth century, the need to define and codify the language not onomasiologically but semasiologically – that is, in an alphabetized wordlist with illustrated definitions – overwhelmed the earlier, more philosophical subject-based arrangements (see EARLY MODERN ENGLISH (1485–1660); CLASS, ETHNICITY, AND THE FORMATION OF "STAN-DARD ENGLISH"). Brewer in her essay explores the nationalist rivalries that inspired the three greatest alphabetical English dictionary projects: Johnson's desire to match the achievement of the *Academie Francaise*; Webster's mission to foster an American identity through an American language; and the *OED*'s aspiration to adopt the meth-odologies of the German philologists.

Though often produced out of nationalist pride, dictionaries in everyday use remain primarily tools for language users – readers, writers, speakers, and listeners. Paradoxi-cally, users need their language to be both flexible and stable, progressive and con-servative. Too much change too quickly or too much variation among speakers would

impede communication, while too much deference to dictionaries, style handbooks, and other prescriptive guides favored by language mavens would lead to a language unable to meet the needs of its users. This section therefore traces within the history of dictionaries – in their myriad forms – the story of the uneasy balance between the creative force of the mass of users and the conservative forces of codification.

Michael Matto

9
Dictionaries Today: What Can We Do With Them?

Reinhard R. K. Hartmann

Introduction

The 250th anniversary of the publication of Samuel Johnson's *Dictionary of the English Language* (*DEL*) is a convenient occasion (celebrated by McDermott & Moon 2005) to reflect on the nature and value of dictionaries. I want to use it as a starting point for a guided tour to introduce you to some of the most important places and personalities linked to the subject of English dictionaries, beginning with Samuel Johnson's and working towards the most important issue of all, whether and how dictionaries are useful today.

Setting the Scene

Does it make sense to start our tour by looking at the past? Are today's dictionaries not very different from those in Johnson's day? It might be worthwhile, at least, to compare the dictionaries of his time with those that we are used to nowadays.

What motivated Johnson to compile a dictionary for the English language was his valiant intention to "fix the language." (In the early eighteenth century English spelling and usage were so diverse that many literary figures worried about it, but by 1755 Johnson had to admit defeat on that score.) Tensions remained throughout his project between the conflicting aims of imposing an authoritative standard ("prescriptivism") and providing an accurate record of a living language ("descriptivism"), but he had to learn all this by trial and error. He and his assistants did much copying from other sources (plagiarism has always been a problem in dictionary-making), but there are also several changes of approach as he went along (e.g., reduction of encyclopedic and technical details) and innovations he tried that are still valid today (e.g., adding grammatical details such as phrasal verbs, refining labels for marking frequency, currency, and style, and exemplifying usage by putting in citations from selected authors).

While the *DEL* thus laid the foundations for the development of the so-called "general" dictionary, it also prepared the ground for the nineteenth-century preoccupation with the question of where English words have come from in the first place, leading to the plan for a dictionary "on historical principles" which James Murray turned into what later become known as the *Oxford English Dictionary* (*OED*). Such historical dictionaries in fact constitute a "hybrid" genre combining the provision of both general-lexical and etymological-historical information.

Two Basic Notions

One of the most basic distinctions for understanding language and communication – and the way dictionaries can help to improve both – is that between words and things. To use the word *genre* as an example, we can say that it stands for the thing it refers to; or, to put it slightly more technically, the lexical unit ("lexeme") *genre* expresses an object or idea ("denotatum") that encapsulates something like "type of work." The relationship between the spoken ("phonic") or written ("graphic") forms that we use for expressing the word, on the one hand, and the mental picture we have of the "notion" referred to, on the other, is what we call the sense or meaning of the word (see figure 9.1).

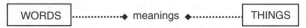

Figure 9.1   Two basic notions

Of course, in reality, it can often be much more complicated than this, as words can have variant forms (pronunciations or spellings), and their meaning(s) can vary depending on their relationships with the things they denote (e.g., concrete/abstract, general/technical, literal/metaphorical).

Dictionaries are designed to help their users find (at least) two basic types of facts. One is the linguistic background that is needed for understanding words, which involves information on syntagmatic/formal aspects (morphology, or the shape of words, and syntax, or the grammatical co-occurrence of words), paradigmatic/semantic aspects (sense, or meaning), and pragmatic aspects (contexts and levels of usage). Often dictionaries also include encyclopedic information. This involves explanations of onomastic facts such as personal or place names, cultural facts such as customs, ideological facts such as religious beliefs, commercial facts such as product names, scientific facts such as plant taxonomies, and very often the use of technical terminology. No wonder that often dictionaries are full of such details; many encyclopedias contain a dictionary or glossary section, and hybrid reference works ("encyclopedic dictionaries") offer both (many reference works such as handbooks, guides, manuals, catalogues, and atlases are not even called "dictionaries").

As an illustration, here is a typical dictionary entry for the word *genre* (taken from the *New Oxford Dictionary of English* [*NODE*] Pearsall 1998: 766):

genre /ˈʒɑnrə, ˈ(d)ʒɑnrə/ ▶ **noun** a category of artistic composition, as in music or literature, characterized by similarities in form, style, or subject matter. – ORIGIN early 19th cent.: French, literally 'a kind' (see GENDER).

Time for an exercise. You will have noticed that only one sense is indicated in this entry for the lexeme *genre*, by means of a definition (definition styles can vary, but here the traditional genus & differentia formula is used: "a category of artistic composition . . ."). Grammatical information is provided by stating the word class, i.e., "noun." Pragmatic information is absent (some usage label such as "special" or "technical," or a field label such as "lit.," might have been provided), and further encyclopedic elaboration is limited (to the mention of the fields "music or literature"). However, what happens if words have more than one sense? Supposing we were to follow up the cross-reference at the end of the entry on *genre* and look up that entry on *gender*, we would find a word with at least two meanings (so we may call it ambiguous or polysemous), and a distinction would have to be made, presumably, between its grammatical sense ("class of noun, such as masculine and feminine . . .") and its biological sense ("state of being male or female . . ."), the latter also being a synonym of *sex*. If we were to do this with words of even more senses (such as the noun *head* or the verb *turn* and their numerous collocations with other words, such as the prepositions *of* and *over*), this would have to be indicated in some way. How? And how are these different senses arranged in a typical dictionary entry? Are they numbered? Are they in alphabetical order, historical order, systematic order, frequency order? Or a mixture of these? (In *NODE*, the sense order starts with a "basic" meaning and then progresses to more "derived" ones, e.g., *head* 1. "upper part of (human) body . . . ," 2. "shape of head . . . ," 3. "front of something . . . ," 4. "person in charge . . . ," . . . 10. [Geology] "deposit of rock . . .").

Information on things other than meaning, such as pronunciation, grammar, and etymology, is also treated in entries of this kind of dictionary, but we can leave that until later. Meanwhile, perhaps I can induce some skepticism about a view that only allows for one basic type of dictionary. If there are so many different types of information, the range of reference works must surely be much wider now than in Johnson's time (spelling dictionaries and pronunciation dictionaries, dictionaries of idioms and quotations, dictionaries of synonyms and technical terms, etc.).

Three Levels of Reference

For now, let me introduce you to an old friend of mine, Tom McArthur, an expert on the "Englishes" around the world who has also contributed substantially to the dictionary field, first by compiling a learner's thesaurus, then by editing a companion to the English language, and most recently by working on a trilingual dictionary (English, Mandarin Chinese, and Cantonese). Some of his multifarious experience has benefited dictionary research, e.g., through a book of his which traces the history of reference works right back to the clay tablets in Ancient Mesopotamia.

Half-jokingly, he used to tell us that "information" is an all-pervasive phenomenon, manifold and hard to handle, but if we had the right reference works and reference skills, we could all progress up the pyramid to the level of "knowledge," and if we are really fortunate, eventually get to the top, to "wisdom." More seriously, we all agreed with him that an overarching and all-embracing "reference science" was the way forward, which would incorporate both traditional lexicography and the various contemporary electronic ways of processing information. Reference science can be defined, according to McArthur (1998), as "the study of all aspects of organizing data, information, and knowledge in any format whatever, for any purpose whatever, using any materials whatever" (p. 218), involving (1) *lexicography* (e.g., monolingual and bilingual dictionaries), (2) *encyclopedics* (e.g., manuals and atlases), and (3) *tabulations* (e.g., catalogues and directories). The benefit of such a wider view would be that we could talk of reference professionals producing reference works for the reference needs of users, who would have to acquire certain reference skills to become more proficient in accessing the information they are looking for.

Four Protagonists

So let us move on now to the typical players on the dictionary scene. They include, as we have seen, the compiler (lexicographer or dictionary maker), the user looking for information, the teacher (especially if the user is a learner), and the investigator (metalexicographer or dictionary researcher). The problem is that these four protagonists do not always interact with each other, so they do not know enough about each other's difficulties. Compilers have to make decisions about how comprehensive, how accurate, how innovative they want to be, they have to agree with their publishers what to put in and what to leave out, and usually they do not have enough space and time to manage everything they set out to do. Users get very little training (if any) on which dictionary to choose and how to get the best out of it, and reference skills accumulate slowly by learning from mistakes. In an educational context, teachers sometimes help their students not to get discouraged by dictionary problems, but this may not cover all the various possibilities. Investigators are supposed to look at the whole picture, but there are very few of them in even fewer dictionary research centers around the world, and they get little support from their academic colleagues, although at least there are now more publications and conferences (e.g., of the Dictionary Society of North America and EURALEX; see below for their websites) where they can report their findings (see figure 9.2).

The biggest problem they all face is that they do not communicate with each other directly, but via the "text" of the dictionary. (We have already seen above how packed with various kinds of information the entries in such reference works can be.) The protagonists are also not uniform, particularly if we see them as part of a crowd. For instance, the compiler can be part-time or full-time, freelance or employed, trained on a course or on the job, working on a general or a specialized reference work. The

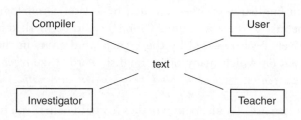

Figure 9.2 Four protagonists

user can be a school pupil or a university student, a general reader or a language learner, a lay person or an expert in a technical subject.

Five Information Categories

As we have seen, most dictionaries provide a combination of linguistic and encyclopedic information (which turns into knowledge, if the user can find and extract it out of the text). Concentrating on the linguistic-lexical rather than encyclopedic-technical content, the most basic information categories include:

1. *Meaning*, usually explained in the form of a definition (illustrated by specifying *genre* as "text type" or "type of work of art") or in the form of an example (one sentence from my own recent writing might qualify as a candidate: *New dictionary genres which are the result of "hybridization" . . . are appearing all the time . . .*), or – in bilingual dictionaries – in the form of a translation equivalent (e.g., German *Gattung*).
2. *Spelling*, based on the conventions of orthography that develop for languages with a literary tradition, sometimes giving variants, such as *filo* and *phyllo*, or *encyclopedia* and *encyclopaedia*.
3. *Pronunciation*, reflecting educated usage, but often with considerable variations between regional and social dialects (in a word like *genre*, "borrowed" from French, there may be additional problems).
4. *Synonyms*, or words of similar meaning (such as *genre* and *class*, or *gender* and *sex*), are usually separated from each other by the alphabetic order of the word-list in the general dictionary, but can be brought together through the thematic order used in a thesaurus. In one of the modern editions of *Roget's Thesaurus* (e.g., Davidson, 2004), these words would be treated under such notions as *class*, together with *category*, *sort*, *breed*, etc., or *painting*, together with *style*, *portrait*, *still life*, etc.
5. *Etymology*, or the origin of words, typically in a "historical dictionary" such as the *OED* where the whole history of the vocabulary would be traced, e.g., for each of three main senses of *gender* ("kind," "word class," and "sex"), the word's first

occurrence in English would be indicated by a date, chronological label and/or citation. The first of these meanings ("kind") could be marked as obsolete since it has effectively been replaced by the French word *genre*, in turn derived from the Latin *genus* on which many other English words (like *cognate, gene, generate, genesis, genitals, genius, gentle, kin, kind, king, malign,* and *nation*) are based.

Time for another exercise. Think about whether it would help if you had a more active vocabulary for discussing these information categories. Have you ever discussed them with anyone? Who? What are your own preferred information categories? Any (or none) of these five?

Six Lexicographic Structures

Practitioners and theoreticians have been trying for the last generation or two to clarify the complex and often compressed components of the dictionary, and the terminology that might be needed to refer to them. Six have been singled out for attention (e.g., in the *Dictionary of Lexicography* by Hartmann & James 2001):

1. *Megastructure* refers to the whole text of the dictionary, together with any front matter (such as a preface about the background of the dictionary or instructions on how to use it), back matter (such as lists of names or bibliographical references), and sometimes even middle matter (in the form of pictorial illustrations or usage guide panels).
2. *Macrostructure* is another convenient term for the word-list, typically arranged in either alphabetic or thematic order.
3. *Microstructure* refers to the entry and its components, with senses arranged in frequency, historical, or some other logical order.
4. *Mediostructure* is the name given to the system of cross-references that can take the user from one part of the dictionary (e.g., an entry) to another.
5. *Access structure* is the sum total of guide-posts that assist the user's search for information, e.g., alphabet markers at the top and/or side of each page, or a "menu" at the start of complex entries (such as the one given in the *Macmillan English Dictionary for Advanced Learners* (Rundell 2002) at *head*, which warns the user that there are ten senses of the word and therefore ten subsections in the entry on it).
6. *Distribution structure* is the relative positioning of lexical vs. encyclopedic information in a reference work, e.g., inside entries, in framed articles, or in the outside matter.

All this may be changing as a result of IT, of course, and new genres of (electronic) dictionaries have already been developed, such as multimedia encyclopedias and the Internet. Students may want to check whether and how these structures are presented in the dictionaries that are their own personal favorites.

Seven Reference Skills

Is there a best way of ensuring that the user can find the information sought? Seven steps in the "reference act" have been distinguished in the literature (Hartmann 2001: 91), starting at the bottom left of figure 9.3 (below) with the kind of activity the user is engaged in at the time (reading? writing? translating?); secondly, the realization that the problem may be caused by a particular word or phrase; thirdly, the selection of a particular dictionary to locate the problem word; then the consultation of (fourthly) the alphabetic word-list (external search), and fifthly the appropriate entry (internal search). Having found the relevant information, the user then has to (sixthly) extract and (seventhly) integrate it into the process that caused the look-up need in the first place.

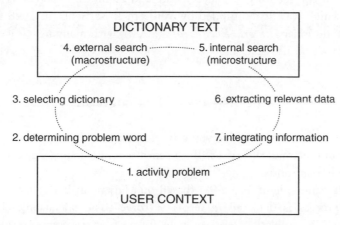

Figure 9.3 Seven reference skills

The so-called "user perspective" has recently come to the fore in dictionary research. However, many difficulties remain (check this against your own experience), e.g., what (in)formal instruction is provided in English classes? Which reference works are recommended by teachers and dictionary buying guides (such as the *Dictionary of Dictionaries and Eminent Encyclopedias* [Kabdebo & Armstrong 1997])? Which information is needed and most often looked up (and what kind of guidance is given)?

Eight Pioneering Dictionaries

What are the most significant dictionaries? This is a difficult question, and the answer depends on the various functions and purposes they are supposed to fulfill for particular user groups. The entire tradition of English lexicography is surveyed by Jonathon Green (1996), including Johnson's efforts to "codify" the language and the way his practice of giving examples in the form of citations was copied by others, notably Noah Webster in his *American Dictionary of the English Language* (1828).

Another dictionary that broke new ground was *Roget's Thesaurus* (1852), whose design features are described by Werner Hüllen (2004) (see also Chapter 10 on ENGLISH ONOMASIOLOGICAL DICTIONARIES AND THESAURI). Towards the end of the nineteenth century, James Murray et al. compiled the *Oxford English Dictionary*, which set new standards for historical and period dictionaries of English and other languages (see Winchester 2003).

Two pedagogically oriented dictionaries that initiated what was to become pedagogical lexicography were the *American College Dictionary* by Clarence Barnhart (1947), aimed at young native speakers, and the *Oxford Advanced Learner's Dictionary of Current English* by A. S. Hornby (1948), intended for foreign learners of English. The latest of five such British products, as described in Cowie (1999), is the *Macmillan English Dictionary for Advanced Learners* (ed. Michael Rundell 2002).

Bordering on the territory of encyclopedic and technical expertise is *The Reader's Encyclopedia*, which was first compiled by William Rose Benét in 1948 and, finally, the electronic dictionary *Encarta Encyclopedia* (2000), with many new features, including sound and visual illustrations.

Nine Aspects of Lexicography

To conclude our tour, let me give you a brief overview of the field of lexicography itself, both in practice and theory. I will concentrate on the main issues, some of which we have already confronted.

On the left-hand side of figure 9.4 (based on Hartmann 2003: I.2), the practical compilation process is depicted in terms of three basic operations: (1) recording linguistic usage, by collecting sources in the form of written texts (corpus evidence)

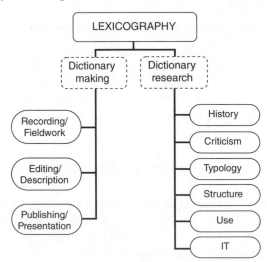

Figure 9.4 Nine Aspects of Lexicography (adapted from R. R. K. Hartmann (ed.) (2003) *Lexicography: Critical Concepts, Volume 1: Dictionaries, Compilers, Critics and Users*. New York: Routledge; "Directions of Dictionary Research," p. 2). Reprinted with permission

and/or spoken language (fieldwork); (2) editing the material into a format of structural elements that I presented above (notably alphabetic word-list and entries); (3) publishing the result in book or electronic form.

On the right of figure 9.4 are listed the six main branches of dictionary research, all contributing answers to the question "What can we do with dictionaries today?":

- Dictionary history can teach us how they have evolved, from period to period and from language to language, and how these traditions still affect them today.
- Dictionary criticism can help us to improve them, by realizing their limits (from excessive copying to extreme text compression) and utilizing new ideas and tools.
- Dictionary typology can help us to classify them into genres (some of which may be hybrids of subgenres).
- Dictionary structure can help us to understand them in terms of overall formats and design components.
- Dictionary use can help us to benefit from them, given sufficient direct observation of actual users in actual look-up situations, discovery of "user-friendly" features and provision of user training.
- Dictionary IT can help us to make them more easily available, by combining them, and by improving the potential benefits of corpus evidence.

Let us conclude with a quotation from Philip Gove, editor of *Webster's Third New International Dictionary of the English Language* (1961: 6a): "A dictionary opens the way to both formal learning and to the daily self-instruction that modern living requires."

Ten Exercises

Finally, students may want to pursue a number of topics further:

1. For one famous dictionary, the *OED*, and its maker(s), you will enjoy reading Simon Winchester's book (2003).
2. How dictionaries are made is described in the textbook by Sidney Landau (2001).
3. On how the user can get the best out of a dictionary, look at a workbook such as Jon Wright's (1998).
4. How lexicographic practice and theory interact is discussed in the textbook by R. R. K. Hartmann (2001).
5. How dictionaries fit into the context of English studies is illustrated by Howard Jackson (2002).
6. Information on how and where to find suitable reference works for various situations is provided in guides such as the *Dictionary of Dictionaries and Eminent Encyclopedias* (Kabdebo & Armstrong 1997).

7. How IT can help with lexicographic corpus work is demonstrated by Vincent Ooi (1998).
8. How dictionary use can be studied is shown by Yukio Tono (2001).
9. Journals, e.g., the *International Journal of Lexicography*.
10. Websites, e.g., *Dictionary Society of North America*: www.polyglot.lss.wisc. edu/dsna/.

REFERENCES AND FURTHER READING

Barnhart, C. L. (comp.) (1947). *American College Dictionary*. New York: Random House.

Benét, W. R. (comp.) (1948/1972/1987). *The Reader's Encyclopedia*. New York: T. Crowell/ Harper & Row.

Cowie, A. (1999). *English Dictionaries for Foreign Learners – A History*. Oxford: Clarendon Press.

Davidson, G. W. (ed.) (2004). *Roget's Thesaurus of English Words and Phrases*. London: Penguin.

Encarta Encyclopedia Deluxe. (2000). Redmond, WA: Microsoft.

Gove, P. B. (ed.) (1961). *Webster's Third New International Dictionary of the English Language*. Springfield, MA: G. & C. Merriam.

Green, J. (1996). *Chasing the Sun: Dictionary-Makers and the Dictionaries They Made*. London: Cape.

Hartmann, R. K. K. & James, G. (comps.) (2001). *Dictionary of Lexicography*. London: Routledge/ Taylor & Francis.

Hartmann, R. R. K. (2001). *Teaching and Researching Lexicography*. Applied Linguistics in Action Series. Harlow: Longman/Pearson Education.

Hartmann, R. R. K. (ed.) (2003). *Lexicography: Critical Concepts*. 3 vols. London: Routledge/ Taylor & Francis.

Hornby, A. S. (comp.) (1948). *Oxford Advanced Learner's Dictionary of Current English*. Oxford: Oxford University Press.

Hüllen, W. (2004). *A History of Roget's Thesaurus: Origins, Development, and Design*. Oxford: Oxford University Press.

Jackson, H. (2002). *Lexicography: An Introduction*. London: Routledge/Taylor & Francis.

Johnson, S. (comp.) (1755). *Dictionary of the English Language*. . . . London: W. Strachan et al.

Kabdebo, T. & Armstrong, N. (comps.) (1997). *Dictionary of Dictionaries and Eminent Encyclopedias*. London: Bowker-Saur.

Landau, S. (2001). *Dictionaries: The Art and Craft of Lexicography*, 2nd edn. Cambridge: Cambridge University Press.

McArthur, T. (1998). What then IS reference science? In T. McArthur, *Living Words: Language, Lexicography, and the Knowledge Revolution* (pp. 215–22). Exeter: University of Exeter Press.

McDermott, A. & Moon, R. (eds.) (2005). Johnson in context. Introduction to thematic issue of *International Journal of Lexicography*, 18: 2, 153–266.

Murray, J. (ed.) (1884–1928/1933). *Oxford English Dictionary*. Oxford: Clarendon Press.

Ooi, V. B. Y. (1998). *Computer Corpus Lexicography*. Edinburgh Textbooks in Empirical Linguistics. Edinburgh: Edinburgh University Press.

Pearsall, J. (ed.) (1998). *(The New) Oxford Dictionary of English*. Oxford: Clarendon Press.

Roget, P. M. (comp.) (1852). *Roget's Thesaurus of English Words and Phrases*. London: Longman.

Rundell, M. (ed.) (2002). *Macmillan English Dictionary for Advanced Learners*. London: Macmillan Education (& Bloomsbury).

Tono, Y. (2001). *Research on Dictionary Use in the Context of Foreign Language Learning: Focus on Reading Comprehension*. Lexicographica Series Maior 106. Tübingen: M. Niemeyer.

Webster, N. (comp.) (1828). *American Dictionary of the English Language*. New York: S. Converse.

Winchester, S. (2003). *The Meaning of Everything: The Story of the Oxford English Dictionary*. Oxford: Oxford University Press.

Wright, J. (1998). *Dictionaries*. Resource Books for Teachers. Oxford: Oxford University Press.

10
English Onomasiological Dictionaries and Thesauri

Werner Hüllen

Lexicographical Principles

Semasiological and onomasiological dictionaries

Dictionaries are consulted, *either* to identify the meaning(s) of a word, *or* to obtain information on its proper use in a text. The former (which is what concerns us here) can be done in two ways:

1. People encounter a word that they do not know. This means they do, in fact, know it in its phonetic and/or graphetic appearance, but not as a semantic entity. This can pertain to their own or to a foreign language, but is, of course, much more frequent in the latter case. They look the word up in an alphabetical dictionary which provides the word meaning(s).
2. People are looking for a word whose meaning they have in their mind, if not always precisely, and whose phonetic and/or graphetic expression they are looking for. This can pertain to their own as well as to a foreign language. They find the meaning in the ordering system of a topical dictionary that provides the word's phonetic and/or graphetic shape.

(1) is the way from the sign to the meaning, and pertains to listening and reading; it is the semasiological method. It is equivalent to the question: "What does this word mean?" (2) is the way from the meaning to the sign, and pertains to speaking and writing, it is the onomasiological method. It is equivalent to the question: "What is the name of this thing/concept?" The one is part of receptive, the other part of productive performance.

Obviously, both types of dictionaries are needed in comprehensive language use, but nevertheless semasiological dictionaries are in much greater demand; sometimes the term "dictionary" is even restricted to them. The alphabet is an unfailing and easy instrument of retrieval, although the techniques of meaning differentiation can cause

difficulties. The fact that homographs cannot be formally differentiated (e.g., *well* as an interjection and *well* as the name of a place with a water supply) is, however, hardly disturbing.

Admittedly, the onomasiological dictionary (also called *topical dictionary*) is rather difficult to handle. Its entries are ordered by semantic affinity on various hierarchical levels, and dictionary readers must command a conspectus of the whole before they can find an individual entry. As a rule, these dictionaries do not provide any comment on word use; they expect that readers can infer this from the surroundings in which a single lexeme occurs. This means that onomasiological dictionaries presuppose a more perfect command of the language than semasiological ones do.

Synonymy dictionaries and thesauri

Synonyms are understood to be words with almost identical meanings. To the extent that this identity prevails, they can replace each other. To the extent it does not, they must not be confused. (*Bravery*, for example, can mean general boldness; *courage* boldness in action.) The question of whether there are words with totally identical meanings has been discussed time and time again. Though there is some philosophical (semiotic) interest in this, the outcome of the question is of no practical importance. It is the language users who must decide in a given context whether two (or more) words – like *courage* and *bravery* – mean the same or something different. The context is the decisive parameter.

It is an axiom of semantics that *all* words of a language have some overlapping semantic areas with some other words, because this is a precondition for communication; a word totally without could not be defined and would, therefore, be communicatively dead. Of more common interest are such words as have only minimal semantic differences between them and are therefore prone to being confused. Particular dictionaries of synonyms are devoted to them. Their entries are organized as rows of words, either with or without explanations of their differences. These rows are, in the macrostructure of the whole dictionary, either organized semasiologically (i.e., with the headwords of these rows in alphabetical order, although the rows themselves belong, in the microstructure of each entry, to the same semantic area and therefore adhere to the onomasiological principle), or they are organized onomasiologically (i.e., even with the headwords arranged in a system of semantic affinity). They are usually called "thesauri." The most famous is *Roget's Thesaurus*, originally of 1852 (Davidson 2002).

The Onomasiological Tradition

Early glossaries and the technique of semantic clustering

In the *Petersborough Manuscript* (Bodleian Library MS Laud, 636), the *Anglo-Saxon Chronicle* starts with the sentence: "The island of Britain is eight hundred miles long

and two hundred broad; and here in this island are five languages: English and British and Welsh and Scottish and Pictish and Book-Language" (Swanton 2000: 3). The "book-language" is, of course, Latin. In England, as on the whole Western continent, it was the language of intellectual interaction and prestige, whereas the vernaculars, alive in its various dialects, served literature and common communication. Teaching and explaining Latin entailed that the relevant indigenous language was also explained as the means of understanding the foreign one. Along with this linguistic project went the endeavor to gather as much knowledge of the classical world as possible. Learning Latin was the best way of acquiring this knowledge, and acquiring knowledge was the best way of learning Latin (Fischer 1989).

It was in this interest that the idea (not the practice) of a thesaurus stood at the beginning of the lexicographical history of English. The linguistic and the encyclopedic strategies, working in tandem, influenced the relevant Latin-English and (later) English-Latin works between the eleventh and the seventeenth centuries, during which time the bilingual glossaries developed into the topical dictionary with its prototypical features. Of course, alphabetical glossaries and dictionaries were, in their own way, subservient to the same didactic purpose that later also included the learning and teaching of French and other foreign languages, respectively (Green 1997).

The first and best example is *Aelfric's Glossary* (Aelfric, ca. 955–1020; Wright & Wülcker 1884 [as "Anglo-Saxon Vocabulary, 11th century"]; Zupitza & Gneuss 1966), which was appended to his grammar, written around 993–5 (Hunt 1991). It has Latin lemmata glossed with Anglo-Saxon lexemes. Semantically, the entries of the glossary are ordered thus: 1. *God, heaven, earth, humankind*. 2.1 *Parts of the human body*; 2.2 *church offices*; 2.3 *family relations*; 2.4 *state offices including crafts and instruments as well as tools*; 2.5 *negative features of human character*; 2.6 *intellectual work*; 2.7 *diseases, afflictions, merits*. 2.8 *weather, universe*. 3. *Birds*. 4. *Fish*. 5. *Wild animals*. 6. *Herbs*. 7. *Trees*. 8.1 *Buildings (churches, monasteries), materials and objects used there*; 8.2 *war, castles, arms, valuable materials*; 8.3 *various*; 8.4 *human vices* (Hüllen 1999: 64; Starnes & Noyes 1991: 198; Gneuss 2002).

This order is proof of what can be called "all-inclusiveness" and "philosophical grounding." Almost everything is significant: the first position of God and the second of man, the human world with body, church community, family, state community, and various faculties; the kingdoms of nature. Some sections are more homogeneous than others; some are more and some less convincing. A postscriptum discloses that the author regrets not being able to write down all names he can think of – a clear indication of his wish to present the whole world, as he saw it and found it in preceding works (e.g., in Isidore of Seville's *Etymologiae*). The large domains of *Aelfric's Glossary* – God, humans as natural individuals and in society, nature, including edibles, and houses, including tools – will appear time and time again in later relevant works.

During the twelfth and early thirteenth centuries, several treatises on language learning were published which have flowing Latin texts with interlinear glosses in Anglo-Saxon and Norman-French (Adam of Petit Pont, fl. 1132–before 1159: *De*

utensilibus, between 1140 and 1150; Alexander Nequam, 1157–1217: *De utensilibus*, between 1175 and 1185; John of Garland, unknown dates: *Dictionarius*, 1122). They are less comprehensive in their topics, concentrating on the names of equipment for daily work in the house, garments, food production, farming, etc. In fact, they cannot be called glossaries or dictionaries proper, but they share with them the onomasiological technique of semantic clustering. They are glossaries in the guise of natural direct speech. As such they prove that the onomasiological principle is not something artificial, like the alphabet, but an outcome of cognitive linguistic behavior (Hunt 1991).

Arranging descriptive text or dialogue as if it were contextualized vocabulary with juxtaposed translations came to be an influential genre for teaching Latin and French to English-speaking learners. A noteworthy author of the thirteenth century is Walter of Bibbesworth (fl. between 1270 and 1283, *Tretiz de Langage* between 1240 and 1250). William Caxton (ca. 1420–92) adapted Flemish-French dialogues to create an English-French version (1483). Grammarians and teachers, like John Stanbridge (1463–1510, *Vocabula* 1496, *Vulgaria* 1508), William Horman (d. 1535, *Vulgaria* 1519), and Robert Whitynton (fl. 1519, *Vulgaria* 1520), published books with up to three thousand Latin sentences, often in aphoristic fashion, with their English equivalents, employing roughly the same order as had been introduced in the earlier glosses. Whitynton was the first to change the sequence of languages from Latin-English to English-Latin, which indicates a change in teaching techniques. Eminent printers like Wynkyn de Worde and Richard Pynson printed these books. Nearer to the prototypical dictionary form came so-called *nominales*, i.e., lists of Latin nouns and adjectives with their Middle English equivalents. The *Mayer Nominale* (Wright & Wülcker 1884: col. 673–744; Stein 1985: 53–65; Hüllen 1999: 68–77), for example, contains some 2,000 entries with seven Latin *capitula* headings and many subheadings. They create a panorama, in particular in the domains of the human world and the productive arts. Most significant for the time of origin is that the glossary does not now start with entries on God but with such concerning man. There were also *verbales* in existence (Stein 1985: 56–9; 1997: 130, 145–6), but the *nominales* were much more in the foreground.

Early onomasiological dictionaries

The first work to appear as an onomasiological dictionary in the full lexicographical sense is that of John Withals (fl. 1553), *A shorte Dictionarie for yonge begynners* (Withals 1553; Hüllen 1999: 168–201). There were 16 editions until 1634 with slightly different titles, the last one consisting of 464 pages. This testifies to the success the book had in teaching Latin. The all-inclusive tendency is shown by the topical macrostructure, which can be summarized thus: A *world*: A1 *universe*, A2 *elements*; B *the three elements of nature*: B1 *air*, B2 *water*, B3 *earth*; C *fire as the element of man*: C1 *crafts*, C2 *housing*, C3 *city*; D *Society*: D1 *law*, D2 *church*, D3 *family*; E *life and death*: E1 *human body* (*life*), E2 *war* (*death*), E3 *human senses*. The English lexemes precede the Latin ones.

On closer inspection, the various topical sections of the dictionary reveal one or several additional order(s) on a medium level that are dependent on the objective constraints of the topic. Lemmata pertaining to "house," for example, repeat in some clusters the order in which a house is built, from the foundations to the roof, or in which the rooms of a house can be inspected after entering by the door. Lemmata pertaining to "body" follow an inspection from head to foot. Such pragmatic ordering may be more or less strict and in almost every case have entries that (literally) seem out of place, but they always testify to the idea that the sequence of entries in topical dictionaries must make sense not only in the macrostructure but also on lower levels. Obviously the compilers expect that the ensuing semantic coherence is a help for retrieval.

In his preface, John Withals shows that he had clear ideas on the function of the topical arrangement of dictionary entries: "[Though the dictionary] leadeth not, as do the rest, by way of *Alphabet*, yet hath it *order*, and *method* both, and the fittest *order*, and the fittest method for yong beginners" (Hüllen 1999: 176).

During the second half of the sixteenth century, when Withals's dictionary flourished, onomasiological (topical) dictionaries enriched the English-speaking scene further in at least three ways:

1. They were a part of so-called dialogue books for the learning of a foreign language other than Latin, which extended all over Europe. In England, the best known were Claudius Holyband's *The French Littleton* (1566) and *The French Schoolmaister* (1573) (which put English into French) and John Florio's (?1553–1625) *His firste Fruites* (1578) and *Second Fruites* (1591) (which put Italian into English) (Rossebastriano 2000).
2. They were combined with alphabetical dictionaries, thus serving the receptive training as well as the productive training in language teaching. John Rider's *Bibliotheca Scholastica* (1562–1632, 1589), for example, had a topical English-Latin dictionary between two alphabetical dictionaries, English-Latin and Latin-English. Though the size of the topical part is grossly out of proportion relative to the other two, it shows what a comprehensive dictionary would look like in the future (Stein 1985: 333–52).
3. Multilingual so-called nomenclators appeared on the Continent in great numbers and sometimes of a quite monumental size. Among them was Hadrianus Junius's *Nomenclator, omnium rerum propria nomina variis linguis explicata indicans* of 1567, which was adapted to English by John Higgins in 1585. Its original worked with nine languages. It is an erudite and monumental work, devoted to academic encyclopedism rather than language teaching.

By the beginning of the seventeenth century, the lexicographical patterns for onomasiological dictionaries were firmly set. They appeared in combination with other works and independently. The most elaborate combination of an alphabetical and an onomasiological dictionary is certainly James Howell's (?1594–1666) *Lexicon Tetraglotton*

(Howell 1660; Hüllen 1999: 203–42). The book has some 1,000 (unnumbered) folio pages. The topical part is divided into 52 sections. Their order is less philosophical and more geared to the lifestyle of the genteel, who were obviously envisaged as the potential users.

Howell worked on an earlier French-Italian-Spanish model by Guilleaume Alexandre de Noviliers (1629), which he complemented with English translations. But the botanist John Ray (1627–1705) compiled his own topical dictionary in English, Latin, and Greek, the *Dictionariolum trilingue* (Ray 1675). It was meant for English boys who were learning Latin and/or Greek (Hüllen 1999: 293–9). It has some 2,660 entries printed on 91 pages. His 32 topical clusters cover all the conventional domains that are important for a language learner, but the way in which he explains names, in particular those of plants, shows the eager botanist and naturalist.

Although these dictionaries developed in England out of their own resources, the tradition received a strong boost from the work of William Bathe (1564–1614), an Irish Jesuit living in Salamanca, who published his *Janua linguarum* in 1612. The book consists of 1,200 sentences in Latin and Spanish and a wordlist of 5,300 lexemes. These sentences are broken down into "centuries" of one hundred, devoted to various topics. They are rather loosely connected. Each word occurs in one sentence only. The idea was that merely by memorizing them a scholar would learn the Latin language. The book became famous on the whole Continent and was adapted in many European languages (Hüllen 1999: 377–82), including English. In 1631 and 1633, Johann Amos Comenius (1592–1670) published his own version as the *Janua linguarum reserata*, at first in Czech and Latin. Its order was strictly modeled on the image of his own religious ideas of the world and therefore nearer to the onomasiological principle. It surpassed even Bathe's success. It was received in England and all over Europe and translated accordingly.

Dictionaries of synonyms and Roget's Thesaurus

It could easily be shown that the distinguishing and weighing of synonyms against each other in the service of logical precision, refinement of style, and drama of speech has been a (largely unreflected) technique well known since the Platonic dialogues. There were also theoretical deliberations on this phenomenon, starting with Prodikos of Keos (b. 470 BCE). Important names in this tradition are Cicero (106–43 BCE) and Quintilian (ca. 35–ca. 99 CE), Isidore of Seville (ca. 560–636), John of Garland (ca. 1195–1258 [?1272]), Erasmus of Rotterdam (?1469–1536), Simon Pelogromius (1507–?), and others.

The more recent treatment of synonyms is linked to the French Abbé Gabriel Girard (?1677–1748). In 1735 and 1736 he published books on French synonyms which were repeatedly issued (e.g., Girard 1718) and which caused many similar books to appear in France and in many other European countries and languages. His aim was to refine the art of conversation according to the rules of *proprieté* and *clareté*,

the French ideals of style following classical rhetoric. His own style was modeled accordingly. In England, John Trusler (1735–1820), Hester Lynch Piozzi (1741–1821), and William Taylor (1765–1836) were Girard's followers. Like his, their books were neither serious linguistic treatises nor dictionaries in the formal sense. But they ushered in a whole series of such. All of the dictionaries of synonyms that appeared subsequently were arranged according to the alphabet of the headword of each row of synonyms. Most – but not all – of them had comments on the use of synonymous words. They grew in the numbers of lexemes treated and in the refinement of their definitions. Among them were comprehensive and influential works like William Perry's (fl. 1805) *The Synonymous, Etymological, and Pronouncing English Dictionary* (1805) and George Crabb's (1778–1851) *English Synonyms, Explained; In Alphabetical Order* (1816). They stimulated the growing interest in semantics and laid many psychological intricacies open which lie hidden in the meanings of words, above all of verbs (Hüllen 2005).

Peter Mark Roget (1779–1869) – the medical doctor who wrote the *Thesaurus* as a retiree – set a new tone, because he collected in his book synonyms without any comparing comments and arranged them according to the principles of onomasiology. He wanted to be understood as a prompter for native speakers who cannot find the right word for their ideas *in situ*. He trusted them to understand meanings correctly and precisely when they saw the words printed on the page. He arranged the whole English vocabulary into six classes (1. *Abstract relations*, 2. *Space*, 3. *Matter*, 4. *Intellect*, 5. *Volition*, 6. *Affections*), broken down into 24 sections, each with a varying number of subsections, and altogether exactly 1,000 entry articles, most of which were juxtaposed as positive and negative meanings (antonyms). Each entry article had paragraphs according to word classes (nouns, verbs, adjectives, adverbs, phrases) and each row of synonyms consisted of groups which were separated by a semicolon and which indicated that the degree of synonymy was denser within than between them.

The book was an unbelievable success, at first with re-editions every year, later with editions at somewhat longer intervals but also in the US and in other parts of the English-speaking world. Just as unbelievable is the fact that Roget's original macrostructure as well as the microstructure of the entry articles proved to be feasible for all subsequent editions. The anniversary edition of 2002 (Davidson 2002) is structured thus: 1. *Abstract relations*, 2. *Space*, 3. *Matter*, 4. *Intellect: the exercise of the mind*, 5. *Volition: the exercise of the will*, 6. *Emotion, religion, and morality*. Even the sections and subsections as well as the sequence of headwords allowed the subsequent editors to group the ever new and ever more numerous vocabulary in their traditional slots. Moreover, the paragraphing of the entry articles is still the same. But the number of words is by now ten times as many as it was in 1852. Although the term *thesaurus* – "storehouse, treasure" – already came into use for dictionaries in the second half of the sixteenth century (e.g., Thomas Cooper: *Thesaurus linguae romanae et brittanicae*, 1565), it is nowadays almost exclusively used to denote the type of book which Roget founded.

Onomasiological Dictionaries, Thesauri, and Recent Semantics

Onomasiological dictionaries and thesauri have much in common, above all the semantic ordering of their entries. The former are more interested in the meaning definition of individual lexemes, whereas the latter have the relationships between synonyms as their focus. But there are books where the comments on lemmata are such that it would be difficult to clearly draw a line between the one and the other.

Both onomasiological dictionaries and thesauri present the lexis of English (or of any other language) as a complex web in which meaning is constituted by differences between words. This makes them, as it were, the practical forerunners of certain theoretical concepts of the twentieth century that had the ambition of including semantics in a theory of language. To them belong the concepts of the semantic field, of the configuration of semantic features, and of semantic models like frames (scenes) or scripts. Though different in their basic assumptions and terminology, they have the aim in common of showing that the vocabulary of a whole language is not merely an amorphous mass of words, but an ordered arrangement – whether determined by the facts of culture (as the protagonists of semantic fields maintained), by autonomous linguistic structures (as the protagonists of semantic features did), or by the cognitive conditions of the human mind (as is explained by the representatives of frame semantics). However, this is exactly what the authors of onomasiological dictionaries and thesauri also assumed and showed. In doing so, they followed certain basic assumptions of their time. In the beginning and for many centuries, they maintained that the order of lexis mirrored the order of the world, as it was described in philosophical treatises. After the Cartesian turning point and in particular under the influence of John Locke's work, the order of lexis was seen as following human ideas on reality rather than reality itself. The traditional philosophical background of onomasiology came to the fore when John Wilkins (1614–72), who devised a universal language for mankind (1668), organized its semantic part in the form of an all-embracing wordlist in which every slot was precisely defined by categories. The philosophical structuring was here taken to an extreme so that the whole vocabulary of all natural languages appeared as one perfect terminology with precisely defined relations of its members. Roget mentioned him as one of his predecessors. After Wilkins, the onomasiological paradigm had obviously exhausted itself and works on synonyms predominated.

Apart from the permanent re-editions of *Roget's Thesaurus*, the production of onomasiological dictionaries and thesauri did not play a major role in the twentieth century compared to that of semasiological ones. Best known are *The Longman Lexicon of Contemporary English* (ed. by Tom McArthur, 1981) and the *Random House Word Menu* (ed. by Stephen Glazier, 1992). There are, of course, many new alphabetical dictionaries of synonyms. But Roget has outgrown them all.

As a rule, dictionaries are consulted for local information. Perhaps the necessity of having to find one's way through the whole verbal world, in order to gain knowledge

of one or several words, is found to be too demanding. The search, therefore, pursues an arrangement that preserves the advantages but decreases the demands. The solution is a "dictionary thesaurus," which combines the alphabetical wordlist, at least, with the method of clustering synonyms. This is done by inserting "boxes" at the spot where the headword of a row of synonyms appears in the course of the alphabet and then cross-referencing each lexeme inside the "box" with its appearance in the alphabet. With the help of this arrangement it is possible for readers to spot every word alphabetically. After that they are automatically led to the cluster of synonyms of which it is a member. The arrangements of an alphabetical dictionary and a dictionary of synonyms are, thus, dovetailed. The onomasiological (i.e., essentially philosophical) character of the dictionary, however, is lost – to the book and also to the readers who draw their linguistic knowledge from it. The first to have done this was obviously Francis Andrew March with *A Thesaurus Dictionary of the English Language, designed to suggest immediately any desired word needed to express exactly any given idea* (1911). Similar mixtures of the lexicographical design are to be found in the *Longman Language Activator* (1993) and the *Compact Oxford Dictionary Thesaurus* (2001), where each page is divided into an upper and a lower half, with the upper devoted to words in alphabetical arrangement and the lower devoted to their synonymous complementation. Working with these means gaining time but losing linguistic insight.

REFERENCES AND FURTHER READING

Davidson, G. (2002). *Roget's Thesaurus of English Words and Phrases*. 150th Anniversary edn. London: Penguin.

Fischer, D. J. V. (1989). *The Anglo-Saxon Age c. 400–1042*. New York: Longman.

Girard, G. (1718). *La Justesse de la langue françois*. Paris: Houris.

Gneuss, H. (2002). Aelfrics Grammatik und Glossar: Sprachwissenschaft um die Jahrtausendwende in England. In W. Hüllen & F. Klippel (eds.), *Holy and Profane Languages: The Beginnings of Foreign Language Teaching in Western Europe* (pp. 77–92). Wiesbaden: Harrassowitz.

Green, J. (1997). *Chasing the Sun: Dictionary Makers and the Dictionaries They Made*. London: Pimlico.

Howell, J. (1660). *Lexicon Tetraglotton, An English-French-Italian-Spanish Dictionary. . . .* London: J. G. for Cornelius Bee.

Hüllen, W. (1999). *English Dictionaries 800–1700: The Topical Tradition*. Oxford: Clarendon Press.

Hüllen, W. (2005). *A History of Roget's Thesaurus: Origin, Development, and Design*. Oxford: Oxford University Press.

Hunt, T. (ed.) (1991). *Teaching and Learning Latin in Thirteenth-Century England*. 3 vols. Rochester: D. S. Brewer.

Ray, J. (1675). *Dictionariolum trilingue: secundum locos communes, nominibus usitatoribus Anglicis, Latinis, Graecis ordiné parallelos dispositis*. London: Andrea Clark for Thomas Burrel.

Roget, P. M. (1852). *Thesaurus of English Words and Phrases Classified and Arranged so as to Facilitate the Expression of Ideas and Assist in Literary Composition*. London: Longman, Green, Longman, Roberts, & Green.

Rossebastiano, A. (2000). La Tradition des manuels polyglottes dans l'enseignement des langues. In S. Auroux, E. F. K. Koerner, H. Niederehe, & K. Versteegh (eds.), *History of the Language Sciences: An International Handbook of the Evolution of the Study of Language from the Beginnings to the Present*. Vol. 1 (pp. 688–98). Berlin: de Gruyter.

Starnes, De W. T. & Noyes, G. E. (1991 [1946]). *Renaissance Dictionaries English-Latin and Latin-English*. New edition with an introduction and

a select bibliography by G. Stein. Amsterdam: Benjamins.

Stein, G. (1985). *The English Dictionary before Cawdry*. Tübingen. Niemeyer.

Stein, G. (1997). *John Palsgrave as Renaissance Linguist: A Pioneer in Vernacular Language Description*. Oxford: Clarendon Press.

Swanton, M. (ed. and trans.) (2000). *The Anglo-Saxon Chronicle*. New edn. London: Phoenix Press.

Withals, J. (1553). *A shorte Dictionarie for yonge begynners gathered of good authours, specially of Columel, Grapald, and Plini.* . . . London: Lewis Evans.

Wright, T. & Wülcker, R. P. (eds.) (1884). *Anglo-Saxon and Old English Vocabularies*. 2 vols. London: Trübner. Reprint: Darmstadt: Wissenschaftliche Buchgesellschaft 1968.

Zupitza, J. & Gneuss, H. (eds.) (1966). *Aelfrics Grammatik und Glossar*. 2nd edn. Berlin: Weidmannsche Buchhandlung.

11

Johnson, Webster, and the *Oxford English Dictionary*

Charlotte Brewer

What part does a dictionary play in the development of the language? This is a hard question to answer. Samuel Johnson's *Dictionary of the English Language* (1755), Noah Webster's *Dictionary of American English* (1828), and the *Oxford English Dictionary* (*OED*; first edition completed 1928) have all exercised a strong influence on the historical narratives of the language that speakers and commentators have chosen to construct: but the extent to which the language would be different had these dictionaries not been written is arguable (and impossible to prove one way or another). Remarkably, all three dictionaries became patriotic symbols from the moment they were published: all caught the national imagination and came to represent what was finest about the English – or American – tongue, and therefore about the country itself. Johnson's former pupil, the actor David Garrick, composed a complimentary epigram to accompany his dictionary's publication, which lauded English prowess over French whether in the sword or the pen: "Johnson, well-arm'd like a hero of yore Has beat forty French and will beat Forty more!" (the point being that the French national dictionary, first published in 1694, had taken over forty Frenchmen forty years to compile, while the superior Johnson's *Dictionary* emerged after only nine years' gestation from a single hand). Webster and his dictionary symbolized America's break with corrupt old Europe and the recently formed nation's minting of new customs, new laws, and new language. The *OED*, most comprehensive, scholarly, and the biggest of the three works, exemplified the triumph of nineteenth-century methods of empirical scientific investigation, and reassured the nation that England was at long last catching up with its old rival Germany in philological vigor and achievement. All three dictionaries turned to literary texts as exemplars of language usage, and one of the most important roles of the *OED* in particular has been as storehouse of the nation's cultural (literary, historical, philosophical, theological) treasures, in the form of quotations illustrating how a word had been used from its earliest days up to its last ones. This link with what the nineteenth-century critic Mathew Arnold called "the best that has been known and thought" established all three dictionaries as

cultural icons, and whether or not they have had an identifiable effect on day-to-day
language, all three have certainly, in their different ways, influenced individual writers
and the literary canon.

Johnson

In his discussion of one of Johnson's most famous works, his *Lives of the Poets*, Arnold
identified Johnson's critical biographies as a central point of reference for the study
of English literature: Johnson provided, he said, "a fixed and thoroughly known centre
of departure and return" (1878: xii). That the same can also be claimed for Johnson's
Dictionary was a lucky outcome for the group of London publishers who in 1746
signed up this comparatively unknown writer to compile a dictionary. Existing monolingual English dictionaries were very different from the work that Johnson eventually
produced. These had begun appearing from 1604 onwards, and as their title pages
made clear were originally designed to satisfy the needs of "unskilful persons" (children, youths, or women) trying to deal with the influx of unfamiliar and difficult
words into the vocabulary from classical and contemporary European languages. By
the early eighteenth century these dictionaries had grown in volume and also scope,
to include ordinary as well as abstruse words, but they did not resolve the intense
anxieties regularly voiced by intellectuals about the imperfections, "abuses and absurdities" that had crept into the language as its vocabulary had expanded over previous
centuries. Complaints like that of Jonathan Swift in his "Proposal for Correcting,
Improving and Ascertaining the English Tongue" (1712) about the unregulated circulation of these words and about the instability of the English tongue – whether
its vocabulary or its grammar – were frequent by the 1740s, and Johnson's *Dictionary* was seen by contemporaries as an answer to the problem. As his patron Lord
Chesterfield put it,

> The time for discrimination seems to be now come. Toleration, adoption and naturaliza-
> tion have run their lengths. Good order and authority are now necessary . . . We must
> have recourse to the old Roman expedient in times of confusion, and chuse a dictator.
> (Crystal 2004: 380, 365–418)

It is certainly true that Johnson pronounced on matters of usage, and that he was in
turn taken as an authority on them. In his beautifully written Preface, he said his
"chief intent" was "to preserve the purity, and ascertain [i.e., fix] the meaning of our
English idiom." Johnson also said other things indicating that he recognized that this
prescriptive aim was impossible for his dictionary to achieve (for example, that "words
are hourly shifting their relations, and can no more be ascertained in a dictionary,
than a grove, in the agitation of a storm, can be accurately delineated from its picture
in the water"); nevertheless the reception of his work – which sold extraordinarily
well both during and after his lifetime – established it as a symbol of rectitude and

fixity in language. Two much-quoted exempla illustrate this: *Vanity Fair* heroine Becky Sharp tossing it out of the window of her carriage as she sped away from Mrs. Pinkerton's academy for young ladies, and the historian Lord Macaulay preserving a copy on his desk, over a hundred years after it was first published, "to keep his diction up to the classic standard, and to prevent himself from slipping into spurious modernisms."

But when Johnson said that certain words – *abominable*, or *adorer*, or *bang*, or *coax* – were examples of "low" language, was he describing the response to such vocabulary of the educated and socially sophisticated stratum of society his dictionary's readers might wish to emulate, or was he instead delivering a snobbish judgment out of touch with contemporary usage? Was he, in other words, being *descriptive* or *prescriptive*? Dictionaries tend to be regarded as prescriptive even when they explicitly set out to describe how language is, not determine what it should be; and Johnson's dictionary was probably no exception (see Lynch & McDermott 2005).

Although Johnson is often, quite erroneously, described as the father of English lexicography, he was enormously dependent on previous dictionaries, and initially worked from an interleaved copy of his most successful precursor (and subsequent dictionary rival), Nathan Bailey's *Dictionarium Britannicum*, published in 1730. (What we now would think of as plagiarism – ruthless plundering of previous works for words, definitions, and etymologies – was a long established lexicographical tradition: Johnson was plundered in his turn by numerous successors, including Webster and the *OED*.) It was in utilizing the products of his own reading, in the form of excerpted quotations, that Johnson broke new ground, for it led him to construct his definitions from examples of real usage rather than from the uncontextualized wordlists in previous dictionaries. Scrutiny of words embedded in their contexts enabled him to identify and discriminate a wide range of different senses, on a far greater scale than his lexicographical predecessors (as comparison with any of them, page by page, will demonstrate), and doubtless also facilitated the precise and pithy definitions in which Johnson so excelled, and which were often adopted wholesale by subsequent lexicographers.

Even in the inclusion of quotations, though, Johnson was not original. As someone who had helped catalogue the vast collection of learned books in the Harley library, he was familiar with European encyclopedias and bi-lingual dictionaries, many of which had also illustrated their entries with nuggets of wisdom and gems of literature taken from great works of the past. Consequently he recognized the part that quotations from major authors could play in substantiating his definitions, and knew how word-books of this sort could function as cultural vade-mecums.

In choosing quotations, Johnson preferred "writers of the first reputation to those of an inferiour rank," and when possible, he printed excerpts which gave "pleasure or instruction, by conveying some elegance of language, or some precept of prudence or piety." So it was not apt exemplification of language usage alone that guided his selection, but also aesthetic and moral considerations. Johnson explains that he sought his examples in the main "from the writers before the restoration, whose works I

regard as the wells of English undefiled": in the event, just seven sources furnished nearly half the quotations in his *Dictionary*: Shakespeare (15.5 percent), Dryden (10 percent), Milton (5.7 percent), and Bacon, the Bible, Addison, and Pope – the last two both post-Restoration – (under 4.5 percent each; Schreyer 2000).

Confining the provenance of his quotation sources was undeniably significant for the type of dictionary Johnson produced. As commentators have noted, "By selecting the domain of research, Johnson limited both the kind of English and the kind of knowledge his book could contain" (DeMaria 1986: 90). Nevertheless it was probably this characteristic as much as anything else – the wealth of citation from great writers that substantiated his definitions and celebrated intellectual and literary culture – that ensured Johnson's continued dominance in the field seventy years and more after the first publication of his *Dictionary*.

Noah Webster

One of the things that Johnson did not do was carp at his predecessors as a way of puffing his own work. The same cannot be said of Noah Webster, who launched a savage attack on Johnson in the initial announcements of his work and in the dictionary itself, despite his adoption of Johnson's material on virtually every page.

Disputes about the origin of his work and the extent of his borrowings dogged Webster from the start of his career (entertainingly anatomized in Micklethwait 2000). The best known and most influential of his earlier publications was the "blue-back" spelling book, first published in 1783, the year America's War of Independence against England ended. Over the next few decades this seminal textbook, reputed to have sold up to 100 million copies, taught most of educated America their letters. As the eventual president of the Confederation, Southerner Jefferson Davis, wrote in 1859, "We have a unity of language no other people possess, and we owe this unity, above all, to Noah Webster's Yankee Spelling-Book" (Webster 2002: 26). The swift establishment of the spelling-book across the country meant that by the time his first dictionary, the *Compendious*, appeared in 1806, Webster was a household name. In 1828, when the *American Dictionary* was published, it assumed a cultural prominence and lexicographical centrality against which his various dictionary rivals could make little impact. Webster's posthumous life has been longer even than Johnson's, owing partly to the Webster family and publishers' ability to capitalize on their initial market position (through deft exploitation of copyright privileges Webster himself had been concerned to create and strengthen in American law), partly to the quality and market dominance of the numerous subsequent dictionaries produced by the publishing house Merriam-Webster.

It is easy to see where the attraction of a home-grown dictionary might lie in America's struggle for cultural as well as political independence from England. As Webster wrote in 1778, "Europe is grown old in folly, corruption and tyranny," and it was consequently "the business of Americans" to emancipate themselves from

Europe, not least by "diffus[ing] an uniformity and purity of language" (Webster 2002: 11).

As Micklethwait shows, Webster built up a wordlist from a number of different sources, but the resulting dictionary has a strong stamp on it both of Webster himself and of American culture. The differences between the law and customs of England and America naturally gave rise to differences in language: as Webster explained in his Introduction – hawking, hunting, heraldry, and "the feudal system of England" originated terms which in the US "can only be known to us as obsolete or as foreign words." By contrast, "the institutions in this country which are new and peculiar, give rise to new terms or to new applications of old terms, unknown to the people of England," such as *land-office*, *land-warrant*, *consociation* [of churches], *senate*, *congress*, etc.

Such examples clearly illustrate the political and cultural program of the dictionary. And one can see the results as one turns over the pages (Webster's copy of Johnson, reproduced in Micklethwait 2000: 319, shows the word *tomahawk* noted in Webster's hand for insertion in his own dictionary). One of the ways in which Webster extended the function of his dictionary was to supply far more encyclopedic information than had Johnson, and this gave him the opportunity to locate the dictionary both geographically and culturally, as well as giving examples of how a word is used in a real-life context. Thus the entry for *source* refers to the St. Lawrence River and the Great Lakes of America; that for *denationalize* explains "A ship built and registered in the United States, is *denationalized* by being employed in the service of another nation."

Other comments on words taken from Johnson (whether or not mediated by other sources) indicate the status of vocabulary in relation to its American context:

HABITUDE, *n.* 2. Frequent intercourse; familiarity. [*Not usual.*] To write well, one must have frequent *habitudes* with the best company. *Dryden.*
SOWINS, *n.* Flummery made of oatmeal somewhat soured. [*Not used, I believe, in America*]
SOWL, *v.t.* To pull by the ears. *Shak.* [*Not used in America*]

These examples are also typical in their treatment of the individual features of Johnson's entries. Webster's definitions are virtually identical, word for word, with Johnson's, but the entry as a whole is much shortened, so while Webster reproduced Johnson's four separately distinguished senses of *habitude*, he printed only one quotation in full, compared with Johnson's ten. In general, Webster was much more sparing in his use of quotations than Johnson, and was often content (as under *sowins* and *sole*) to cite the author by surname alone and leave the quotation out. "One of the most objectionable parts of Johnson's Dictionary," he felt, was "the great number of passages cited from authors, to exemplify his definitions. Most English words are so familiarly and perfectly understood, and the sense of them so little liable to be called in question, that they may safely be left to rest on the authority of the lexicographer without examples."

Since he had already reaped much of the advantage, in the form of discriminated senses, that Johnson had got from his profusion of quotations, one can see his point. Nevertheless, Webster was clearly not insensible to the value of citations, and skillfully adapted this aspect of Johnson's *Dictionary* for the cultural purposes of his new nation. As he declared in his Introduction, quoting Johnson, "The chief glory of a nation . . . arises from its authors"; consequently it was "with pride and satisfaction" that he named Franklin, Washington, and other distinguished American writers as his authorities on the same page as writers like Hooker, Milton, and Dryden.

An enormous number of the quotations Webster did print come not from contemporary or older writers but from the Bible, reflecting his unshakable commitment to Congregationalism from 1808 onwards. This pervasive biblical content led to the publication in 1967 of a handsome facsimile edition of his *Dictionary* by the Foundation for American Christian Education. Many times reprinted, this edition also forms the basis for the dictionary's current online availability (stripped of quotations from non-biblical sources) via a number of internet Bible sites. As the Preface to the facsimile says, "One cannot read [Webster's] quotations nor study his discussion of the grammatical construction of our language without encountering at every point a Scriptural Christian philosophy of life." Webster's own strongly moralistic streak was no doubt responsible for the rigid stance the dictionary took on "vulgar and obscene words," of whatever sort: Webster simply excluded them, in line with his previous declaration that omitting such words was part of his intention in writing a dictionary in the first place (Micklethwait 2000: 191). Thus his dictionary was, like Johnson's, more prescriptive than descriptive, though there is nothing in Webster's long Introduction that suggests he grappled as thoughtfully with this issue, and with the nature of language itself, as did Johnson in his Preface.

OED

Both Johnson and Webster hoped to record the best examples of usage and create a standard by which future developments in language could be judged and to which future writers might aspire. By contrast, the editors of the *OED* set out to do something at once more humble and more ambitious: to record all the words in the English language without discrimination or interference of any sort. In the words of one of their founders, R. C. Trench, they planned to cast a swoopnet across the language, catching every word that had ever been used, recording its usage from its first use to its last and thus enabling it "to tell its own story." The new dictionary was to be an objective and impartially assembled "inventory": "It is no task of the maker of it to select the *good* words of the language . . . If he fancies that it is so, and begins to pick and choose, to leave this and to take that, he will at once go astray . . . He is a historian of [the language], not a critic" (Murray 1977: 136, 195).

This magnificent and extraordinarily optimistic scheme was first set in motion in 1857, but stopped, started, and dawdled for some years owing to a variety of setbacks

(including the death of the first editor and the difficulties of establishing satisfactory methods for collecting and processing material). It began to make steady progress when J. A. H. Murray became editor in 1879. The first instalment appeared in 1884, and the last in 1928. The intervening period took a terrible toll both on the editors, eventually four in all (Henry Bradley, C. T. Onions, and W. A. Craigie subsequently joined the enterprise), and on the publishers Oxford University Press, for whom the project had looked at times to become an expensive white elephant which might never realize its original aims.

As already indicated, Murray drew on material in both Johnson – the direct source of nearly 3,000 quotations and at least 723 definitions for the first edition of *OED* (Silva 2005) – and Webster (whose contribution is as yet unquantified). The latter dictionary, in its 1864 "Unabridged" edition, played an additionally significant, indeed baleful, role in the creation of the *OED*, acting as a benchmark by which the publishers measured the progress of Murray and his team as they toiled away, treading the path of the alphabet with what seemed sometimes unduly sluggish resolution. Murray had originally agreed to keep to a scale of six times the equivalent text in Webster's, allowing him sufficient space to rewrite the American dictionary's etymologies, include quotations, identify more senses, and of course increase the word-stock. This procrustean limit occasioned antagonism and anguish on both sides as the Oxford lexicographers surpassed Webster in scholarship and industry and produced copy ten times, or on one occasion twenty times, as long as Webster's, which the publishers insisted they must cut back. But the result was a dictionary that still towers above others in the English language, not least on account of its size – 10 volumes, 15,490 pages, 252,200 entries, 1,861,200 quotations in the first edition of 1928; 20 volumes, 21,730 pages, 291,500 entries, and 2,436,600 quotations in the second edition of 1989.

The total inclusiveness originally aimed at by the *OED* was an unattainable ideal. It would have been impossible to read all available written sources in the English language, and it was therefore impossible to be sure of including all words. Moreover, many of the words which were known to the lexicographers turned out to be unsuitable for inclusion: some because they were too specialized or too eccentric, some because they were obscene, some because they were insufficiently attested, some because there was no room. The gradual erosion of the ideal of inclusiveness – and the consequent shift away from descriptiveness to, in effect, prescriptiveness, since every decision to exclude a word is a departure from the purist ideal of descriptive lexicography so confidently stated by Trench and the others – is a fascinating feature of the early stages of the *OED*.

The lexicographers flung their nets over a wide range of texts (relating not just to literature, history, philosophy, and theology, but also commerce, crafts, trades, and pastimes). This produced a bank of five million quotations, of which around two million were printed in the dictionary, forming what the lexicographers later described (in the Preface to the 1933 edition) as "the only possible foundation for the historical treatment of every word and idiom which is the *raison d'être* of the work." The "consistent pursuit of this [quotation] evidence," they continued, "has worked a revolution

in the art of lexicography." This is undeniably the case. But the quotations gathered in were dependent on the sources available. Unsurprisingly, the editors amassed less evidence for the medieval period than for the post-medieval, reflecting the increases in English vocabulary from 1500 onwards. But did their far greater numbers of words and quotations from the sixteenth and nineteenth centuries indicate more word-production over these years? Or instead that the readers and lexicographers had searched texts from this period more intensively than they had those written in the intervening years, and consequently recorded more items from them? (see further Brewer, *Examining the OED*).

The enormous range of cited sources is apparent to any casual browser turning the pages of the *OED*, but here too the lexicographers favored some more than others. Electronic searches now available online reveal their preferences for canonical literary texts as quotation sources: Shakespeare is the single most cited authority, followed by the Bible, Walter Scott, *Cursor Mundi* (a Middle English poem of nearly 30,000 lines containing a summary of universal history), Milton, Chaucer, Dryden, Dickens, and Tennyson. Were these the giants that have most contributed to the English language? Or were they the ones most favored, for a variety of different reasons, by the lexicographers? To what extent does this preference (as with Johnson) determine the quality and nature of the language the dictionary records?

Even aside from the selection of sources, prescriptiveness of varying types crept into the dictionary elsewhere too. Racist and sexist definitions, unexceptionable at the time they were written, can easily be found (see entries for *hubbub, savage, housekeeper, learned* (sense 2b)), and so can occasions on which common usage is castigated (as in entries for *ambient* (sense 6), *allude* (sense 5), *stole* (n1 sense 1d)) rather than deferred to as evidence to be recorded rather than proscribed.

Reservations of this sort appear insignificant, however, when seen in the context of the *OED*'s achievement and its advance on its predecessors. The crispness and precision of the definitions, the erudition displayed in the etymologies and other comments on words and word formations, and the formidable analyses of semantic development and change found in the enumeration of senses (enabled by all these quotations), are evident on every page.

A twentieth-century supplement was merged with the parent dictionary to create a second edition in 1989, after which the *OED* began a slow but fundamental transformation, still in progress. Revision of the entire dictionary, most of it untouched since 1928, is now taking place under a team of lexicographers who are rewriting every entry, drawing on the vast quantity of linguistic scholarship that has appeared since the dictionary was first compiled, and putting to use thousands of freshly amassed quotations. This task – quite as daunting and ambitious as that originally undertaken by Murray and his fellow-pioneers – is both complicated and enabled by the conversion of the *OED* into electronic form (www.oed.com/). The consequent revolution in dictionary-making, and dictionary-using, has returned Oxford to the pinnacle of world lexicography which it occupied on the first edition's completion in 1928. The nature and implications of this revolution have yet to be fully measured.

References and Further Reading

Arnold, M. (1878). *Six Chief Lives from Johnson's 'Lives of the Poets'*. London: Macmillan.

Brewer, C. (2007). *Treasure-House of the Language: the Living OED*. New Haven, CT: Yale University Press.

Brewer, C. (2005). *Examining the OED*. www.oed.hertford.ox.ac.uk/main/.

Crystal, D. (2004). *The Stories of English*. London: Allen Lane.

DeMaria, R. (1986). *Johnson's Dictionary and the Language of Learning*. Oxford: Clarendon Press.

Lynch, J. & McDermott, A. (eds.) (2005). *Anniversary Essays on Johnson's Dictionary*. Cambridge: Cambridge University Press.

Micklethwait, D. (2000). *Noah Webster and the American Dictionary*. London: McFarland.

Mugglestone, L. (2000). *Lexicography and the OED*. Oxford: Oxford University Press.

Murray, K. M. E. (1977). *Caught in the Web of Words*. New Haven, CT: Yale University Press.

Schreyer, R. (2000). Illustrations of authority: quotations in Samuel Johnson's *Dictionary*. *Lexicographica*, 16, 58–103.

Silva, P. (2005). Johnson and the *OED*. *International Journal of Lexicography*, 18, 231–42.

Starnes, D. T. & Noyes, G. E. (1991). *The English Dictionary from Cawdrey to Johnson, 1604–1755*. Amsterdam: John Benjamins.

Webster, N. (2002). *Noah Webster's First Edition of an American Dictionary of the English Language*. San Francisco: Foundation for American Christian Education.

Part IV
Pre-history of English

Introduction

The following chapters consider the pre-history of English by placing the language in the Indo-European and Germanic groups and compare it with genetically connected languages in each of these groups (by Philip Baldi and R. D. Fulk, respectively).

English is an Indo-European language having approximately 140 sister languages. Some of these languages, like Old Church Slavic, Pāli, and Hittite, are now extinct, whereas others, like Spanish, Russian, and Hindi-Urdu, are spoken in areas with large populations. Indo-European is not the biggest family in terms of the number of affiliated languages. The Austronesian family of the Pacific, for instance, includes about 800 genetically connected languages, and the Bantu family of Africa about 400. Yet the Indo-European language family is arguably the most significant in terms of distribution and geopolitical influence in today's world.

Because English is one of the least conservative Indo-European languages, it is sometimes difficult to recognize its family resemblances with sister languages. There are nonetheless several criteria that demonstrate the genetic tie between English and the rest of the Indo-European family. By far the most discernible is the existence of cognates in core vocabulary such as numerals, body parts, and personal pronouns. The English word *three*, for instance, is *tráyaḥ* in Sanskrit and *teri-* in Hittite. The English *foot* corresponds with the Gothic *fōtus* and the Greek *podós*. The first-person singular *I* is *ich* in German, *ego* in Latin, and *ahám* in Sanskrit. Another criterion concerns morphological structure: Old English, like Greek and Sanskrit, declines adjectives according to case, number, and grammatical gender.

Theoretically speaking, all Indo-European languages derive from one linguistic source. Such an ancestral language has not been attested, however, and various efforts have been made to reconstruct this common speech known as Proto-Indo-European. The Indo-European language family may be pictured as a tree seen from above, with differently shaped branches, like Indo-Iranian, Greek, and Celtic, radiating out from the center. Some of the branches (also called "subgroups") of Indo-European come with written records documenting the derivation of daughter languages. The Italic subgroup, for instance, has Latin as a parent language and Romance varieties like Italian and French as daughter languages. Other subgroups of Indo-European have no records for earlier generations. The Germanic subgroup, for instance, has many attested sister languages, including Gothic, Old Icelandic, and Old Low Franconian, but there are no records for their parent language, Proto-Germanic.

The feature that most clearly distinguishes Germanic from other Indo-European languages is its phonological system. For instance, words for "heart" in Germanic all begin with the *h* sound (a voiceless fricative), like *haírtō* in Gothic and *herza* in Old High German, whereas their cognates in other Indo-European languages usually begin with the *k* sound (a voiceless stop), like *kardíā* in Greek and *kard-* in Hittite. Such a systematic correspondence of consonants between Germanic and the rest of Indo-European was first formulated as a set of rules by Jacob Grimm. Germanic also differs

from other Indo-European languages in terms of innovative morphological features such as the definite article (English *the*) and the dental suffix as a past tense marker (English *-ed*).

Haruko Momma

12
English as an Indo-European Language

Philip Baldi

Like most of the more than 5,000 languages in the world, English belongs to a language family, that is, a group of languages that are related to each other genetically and share a common ancestry. The "genes" they share are inherited linguistic features which have been transmitted through time over the history of the languages in question. The notion of a language family is founded on the observation that two or more languages may contain features of lexicon (vocabulary), phonology (sound), morphology (word structure), and syntax (grammar) which are too numerous, too fundamental, and too systematic to be due to chance, to general features of language design (typology), or to borrowing through contact. The language family to which English belongs is known as the Indo-European (IE) language family, and the common ancestor from which the Indo-European languages derive is called Proto-Indo-European (PIE). The subgroup within Indo-European to which English belongs is Germanic, specifically West Germanic.

As we begin our exploration of English as an IE language, we will first spend some time discussing the methods by which languages are classified genetically, how these methods help us to separate linguistic structures that are inherited from those which are not, and how they are used to access the past, including the preliterary past, of languages such as English.

How do we know that languages share "genetic material," and are therefore to be grouped within the same language family? We begin with a few simple illustrations with languages which will be familiar to most readers.

Everyone knows that the "Romance" languages (such as French, Italian, and Spanish) are all in some way descended from Latin. What this means is that the Romance languages are all "sister" languages, and that they stem from a common ancestor, thereby forming a genetic group (more specifically a subgroup). We know this on independent factual grounds, based on the documented history of the Roman Empire and its spread throughout early Europe. But even in the absence of historical records tracing the spread of the Romans and their language in its various forms, we

Table 12.1   *One* through *ten* in some Romance languages

	Italian	French	Spanish	Portuguese	Rumanian	Latin
one	uno	un	uno	um	unu	unus
two	due	deux	dos	dois	doi	duo
three	tre	trois	tres	tres	trei	tres
four	quattro	quatre	cuatro	quatro	patru	quattuor
five	cinque	cinq	cinco	cinco	tint	quinque
six	sei	six	seis	seis	sase	sex
seven	sette	sept	siete	sete	sapte	septem
eight	otto	huit	ocho	oito	optu	octo
nine	nove	neuf	nueve	nove	nao	novem
ten	dieci	dix	diez	dez	dzate	decem

Table 12.2   *One* through *ten* in some Germanic languages

English	Dutch	German	Swedish	Yiddish
one	een	eins	en	eyns
two	twee	zwei	två	tsvey
three	drie	drei	tre	dray
four	vier	vier	fyra	fir
five	vijf	fünf	fem	finf
six	zes	sechs	sex	zeks
seven	zeven	sieben	sju	zibn
eight	acht	acht	åtta	akht
nine	negen	neun	nio	nayn
ten	tien	zehn	tio	tsen

would arrive at the same conclusion of linguistic relatedness through the comparison of the modern languages. Consider, for example, the lower numerals in selected "major" Romance languages (table 12.1), written in standard orthography (which may obscure features of pronunciation).

Of course the existence of similarities among these five Romance languages is easy to explain. They share a common ancestor language (Latin), and have inherited the lower numerals directly from this source; i.e., the words are "cognates" and the languages are "sisters." But there are equally compelling data from languages whose ancestor can only be inferred because, unlike Latin, it was never written down. Consider the modern members of the Germanic subgroup (table 12.2).

Despite the obvious relatedness and common ancestry in the Romance and Germanic examples just cited, such connections are not always obvious. And even when it is convincingly established that the languages in question are in some sort of historical relationship, it is by no means an easy step to determine what the ancestor

might have looked like, when and where it was spoken, or what other languages might be related, perhaps more distantly (i.e., as "cousins" rather than "sisters"). The Latin-Romance connection is deceptively simple because of what we know about the lines and stages of transmission between the historical end points (Latin and Italian, for example). The Germanic case is somewhat more difficult because of the absence of an attested ancestral language (there are older Germanic languages, such as Gothic or Old Icelandic, but these are not proto-systems). Nonetheless, the evidence for relatedness among these languages is just as powerful as with the Romance languages. We just don't have a written ancestor.

Are such resemblances enough to prove a genetic relationship among languages? Are we forced to conclude from these displays of vocabulary in a limited field (here, lower numerals) that the languages in each group are derivable from some common ancestor? Surely there are other explanations available to account for the likenesses – borrowing through language contact, for example. Languages exchange vocabulary without regard for family membership; need and prestige are the two primary factors which govern the borrowing process. The languages which make up the respective Romance and Germanic subgroups have been in close cultural and geographical contact for millennia, so might it not be conceivable that they all just borrowed the numbers 1–10 from one or the other of them, or perhaps some other language?

For the lexicon to be used even as a preliminary guide to possible genetic relationships, we need more examples of potential cognates than a few (admittedly impressive) sets of numerals. In particular we need vocabulary items which, like the numerals, are part of the "core" vocabulary, i.e., words which are unlikely to have been borrowed, and which exist in sufficient quantity to exclude the possibility of chance (see table 12.3).

Like the numerals, these words come from deep in the core of the lexicon. They are not technical terms, like *computer* or *fax*, nor do they represent culturally transportable items such as *pizza* or *sushi*. And there are countless numbers of sets like them, eliminating the factor of chance. The only reasonable way to account for these similarities is to treat the words as cognates, and to assume that they are derived from a common source. We call that source language "Proto-Germanic."

Table 12.3 Some "core" Germanic vocabulary

English	Dutch	German	Swedish	Yiddish
love	liefde	Liebe	ljuv "sweet"	libe
to live	leven	leben	leva	lebn
to fly	vliegen	fliegen	flyga	flien
hand	hand	Hand	hand	hant
house	huis	Haus	hus	hoyz
my, mine	mijn	mein	min	mayn
mother	moeder	Mutter	mo(de)r	muter
name	naam	Name	namn	nomen

Classifying languages based on vocabulary similarities represents only the first step in the historical process. To complete the task, we have to take a closer look at the properties of the words we have assembled to determine the degree of systematicity which holds across the languages. If the languages are indeed related (as we know these to be), the correspondences in vocabulary should be matched by systematic correspondences in phonology and morphology as well (syntax is somewhat more problematic). The principle of regularity is the cornerstone of the comparative method, by which linguists reconstruct the parent language and its intermediate stages based on the comparative analysis of the descendant languages. So, if say English and Swedish are related, and if there is a correspondence such that Eng. /m/ corresponds to Swed. /m/ in a given phonetic environment, then it should be the case for every /m/ (see the examples for "my," "mother," "name"); likewise for /l/ (see "love," "live," "fly") or for /v/ and /b/ (see "love" and "live" in English and German). As we work out the details of such correspondence sets we make inferences about the ancestral sound, which in the first two cases would be postulated as *m and *l (with the * designating a hypothetical reconstructed segment). For every set of words in which Swed. /m/ corresponds to Eng. /m/ in a given phonetic environment, we claim that both derive from a common proto-sound *m in Proto-Germanic. The same principle holds as we work to progressively more distantly related languages, such as Latin and (Old) English, or Greek and Sanskrit, using the oldest available data as we work backwards in time, all the way to PIE. Needless to say the correspondences become less and less obvious with deeper time spans and the need for auxiliary explanatory mechanisms such as analogy and secondary sound change increases, but the method is sophisticated enough that it can reveal correspondences over millennia of distance in first attestation, say between Old English (ca. 600 CE) and Ancient Greek (ca. 800 BCE) or Hittite (ca. 1750 BCE).

The Indo-European Language Family

The term "Indo-European" refers to a family of languages which by about 1000 BCE were spoken over a large part of Europe and parts of southwestern and southern Asia (see figure 12.1).

The dating and location of a unified PIE is controversial in many respects, but the most widely held opinion among specialists puts the protolanguage in the area of the Pontic-Caspian steppes north of the Black and Caspian Seas at about 3500 BCE, after which it began to diversify into the descendant subgroups through phases and stages which are matters of debate (more than a few locales and time horizons have been proposed). Though the concept of "Indo-European" is linguistic, the term is originally geographic, referring to the location of the easternmost (India) and westernmost (Europe) languages at the time the family was securely identified in the eighteenth and nineteenth centuries. In comparison with some of the other 250–300 language families of the world, the IE family is relatively small. It contains about 140 languages

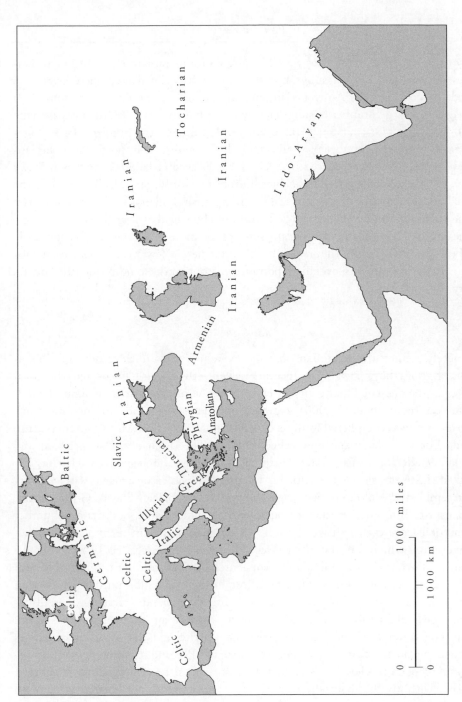

Figure 12.1 Distribution of Indo-European Languages, circa 500–1000 BCE (from P. Baldi (2002) *The Foundations of Latin*. New York: Walter de Gruyter; map 1, p. 37). Reprinted with permission

(many extinct), more than 90 of which belong to Indo-Iranian; these 140 or so languages are classified into 11 subgroups, one of which is Germanic, where English is located. By contrast, the Austronesian language family of the Pacific has some 800 languages in a large number of subgroups, and the Bantu family (Africa) has as many as 400 languages. Of course it is important to distinguish the number of languages in a family from the number of speakers, or the geopolitical importance of the languages in question (as evidenced by their status as second languages, or as a *lingua franca*). By these latter criteria the Indo-European family, specifically through the colonial and global languages such as French, Spanish, and especially English, has a unique standing among the language families of the world.

The family tree represents graphically some of the more important and recognizable members of the IE family (figure 12.2). We offer here a few words about each subgroup, its dating, and its overall importance for our understanding of PIE and its history.

Anatolian

Completely extinct, the Anatolian languages were unknown until archeological excavations in Boğazköy, Turkey in the early twentieth century uncovered the royal archives of the ancient Hittite city of Hattušaš. The original trove of about 10,000 clay tablets (now about 25,000), dating from the seventeenth to the thirteenth centuries BCE, was deciphered from its cuneiform script and shown to be representing an Indo-European language now called Hittite. The discovery, classification, and eventual detailed analysis of the Anatolian languages, but especially Hittite, has impacted IE studies significantly. Before Hittite, PIE was reconstructed with a "look" that resembled the older IE languages, in particular Baltic, Slavic, Greek, Latin, and Sanskrit. But Hittite, though demonstrably older, does not share a number of structural features with the "classical" IE languages, and in many cases displays characteristics which can be shown to significantly predate those in other IE languages. Two of the more famous of these archaisms were the existence of several sounds (called "laryngeals") that had been lost in the other subgroups, often leaving a trace; and the absence of the "classical" three-way gender system (masculine-feminine-neuter) in substantives in favor of a two-way animate-inanimate system. Accounts of differences such as these between Hittite and the other IE languages have challenged the traditional look of reconstructed PIE and its chronology, prompting some scholars to view the Anatolian languages as sisters, rather than daughters, of PIE, with both descending from a more remote protolanguage called "Indo-Hittite."

Indo-Iranian

This subgroup contains two closely related subdivisions, namely Indic (Indo-Aryan) and Iranian.

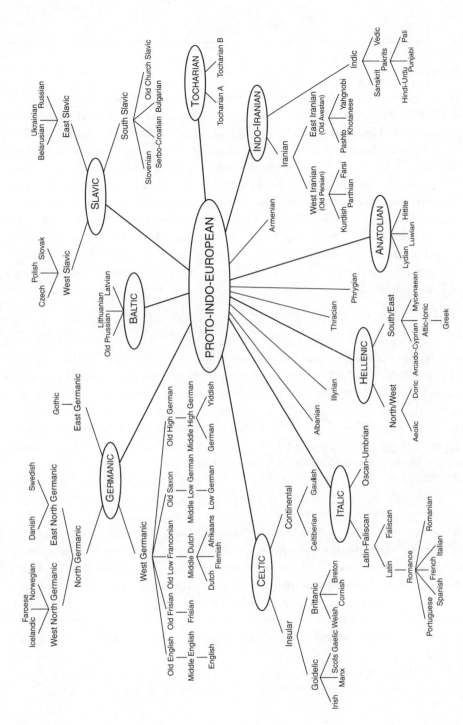

Figure 12.2 Major Indo-European branches and languages

Indic (Indo-Aryan)

The languages of the Indic group are classified into three historical periods, namely Old Indic (1500–600 BCE), Middle Indic (600 BCE–1000 CE), and Modern Indic (since 1000 CE). The most ancient language is Vedic, an archaic form of Sanskrit whose oldest documents are dated by some to about 1200–1000 BCE, though others consider them to be older. A closely related form of Vedic is Classical Sanskrit, which was codified in the work of the grammarian Pāṇini ca. 500 BCE, and in which several important literary texts are written. The oldest Middle Indic texts are in Pāli (sixth to fifth century BCE), followed by the Aśoka inscriptions (ca. 250 BCE) and some Jainist religious writings from about the same period. Modern Indic is one of the largest and most heterogeneous of the IE subgroups, with perhaps as many as ninety different languages. Among the best known of them are Hindi-Urdu, Marathi, Punjabi, and Gujurati.

Iranian

Ancient Iranian has two important representatives. The chief one of these is Old Avestan (also known as Gathic Avestan), dating from about 600 BCE, possibly earlier. The second important member of Ancient Iranian is Old Persian, a Western Iranian language, which may date to as early as 500 BCE. Western Middle Iranian is represented by Middle Persian (Pahlavi) and Parthian, while the Eastern Middle Iranian languages are Sogdian, Khotanese, Khorasmian, and Bactrian. Modern descendants of Iranian are Modern Persian (Farsi), Pashto, and Kurdish.

Greek

Also known as Hellenic, the Greek branch contains some of the oldest testaments of Indo-European. Attested inscriptionally from as early as the eighth century BCE, Greek has textual monuments in the Homeric epics the *Iliad* and the *Odyssey*, which may be as old as 800 BCE. Even older than these are the Linear B tablets from Crete, Pylos, and other ancient locales which represent a form of Greek called Mycenaean and may be from as far back as the fourteenth century BCE. The two principal subdivisions are between South/East Greek (comprising Attic-Ionic, Arcado-Cyprian, and Mycenaean), and North/West Greek (comprising Aeolic and Doric). The main dialect of Greek is Attic, the literary language of Athens in which standard Classical Greek literature was composed. Standard Modern Greek developed from Attic-Ionic.

Italic

The Italic subgroup of Indo-European consists of many genetically connected languages from ancient Italy which share certain distinctive characteristics. There are two main Italic subdivisions. The more important of the two, Latin-Faliscan, is

represented chiefly by Latin, one of the most important IE languages and arguably the most important language in the development of Western Civilization. Latin is identifiable in some short inscriptions from the seventh century BCE, though the first continuous literature stems from the third century BCE. Faliscan is known only from inscriptions, the oldest of which dates to the early seventh century BCE. Latin survives in the modern Romance languages, which developed from spoken varieties of the language in various parts and at different times and social circumstances in the history of the Roman Empire and beyond. The best known of the Romance languages are Italian, French, Spanish, Portuguese, Catalan, and Rumanian; less well known are Dalmatian, Rhaeto-Romansch, Ladino, Sicilian, Sardinian, Occitan, and many other local and social varieties. The second Italic subdivision is called Osco-Umbrian (also Sabellic or Sabellian). There are no modern descendants of this branch, which comprises Oscan (attested as early as the fifth century BCE), Umbrian (perhaps as early as 300 BCE), South Picene (fifth to sixth century BCE), and a number of fragmentary languages. Some classification schemes put Italic in a special subunity with Celtic known as "Italo-Celtic."

Germanic

The Germanic subgroup, which includes English among its members, is widespread geographically and is internally heterogeneous. The oldest attestations of Germanic are the Scandinavian Runic inscriptions, the oldest of which dates from the first century CE. The Germanic languages are conventionally separated into three geographic subdivisions. The first, East Germanic, contains only a single well-attested language, Gothic. Gothic is the language with the oldest continuous documents in Germanic, the biblical translation by Bishop Wulfila from around the second half of the fourth century CE. The second subdivision of Germanic is North Germanic, whose principal representative is Old Icelandic (also called Old Norse). Apart from the Runic inscriptions, the oldest material in North Germanic comprises Norwegian and Icelandic sagas and legal texts from the ninth century. Modern North Germanic languages are Icelandic, Faroese, and Norwegian in one group, and Danish and Swedish in another. The final group, West Germanic, is the most expansive and internally diverse of the Germanic languages; its descendants include German, Yiddish, Dutch, Flemish, Afrikaans, and English, with its many varieties worldwide. (See further ENGLISH AS A GERMANIC LANGUAGE.)

Celtic

The languages of the Celtic subgroup are traditionally divided into two main geographical sections, the Continental and the Insular. The Continental group, made up of Celtiberian (Hispano-Celtic), Lepontic, and Gaulish, is extinct. The oldest material from the Continental group is from the sixth century BCE. The Insular Celtic languages show up materially somewhat later. Split into two groups, Goidelic and

Brittanic (Brythonic), the Insular languages are first attested in some Ogham Irish sepulchral inscriptions from around 300 CE. The Goidelic group is made up of Irish, Scots Gaelic, and the extinct Manx. Brittanic comprises Welsh, the most robust of the modern Celtic languages, Breton, spoken in Brittany (France), and the extinct Cornish. Some classification schemes put Celtic in a special subunity with Italic known as "Italo-Celtic."

Tocharian

Discovered in archeological excavations around the turn of the twentieth century in Chinese Turkestan, the two varieties of Tocharian (usually called simply "A" and "B") have added modestly to the Indo-European base. The documents of the languages, mostly religious and some commercial, are relatively late, stemming from the period of about 500–700 CE.

Baltic

Sometimes grouped with the Slavic languages to form a composite intermediate branch called "Balto-Slavic," the Baltic subgroup survives in two modern languages, Lithuanian and Latvian (Lettish), which together make up the East Baltic subdivision. Many other Baltic languages have become extinct, including a language called Old Prussian, which was spoken until the early eighteenth century and represents the West Baltic subdivision. The oldest Baltic material, the Old Prussian Basel Epigram, dates to as early as 1369 CE, while the oldest Lithuanian texts stem from the early sixteenth century, and the oldest Latvian material is probably datable to 1585.

Slavic

Often grouped with Baltic as "Balto-Slavic," the Slavic languages fall into three geographical subdivisions. The first, South Slavic, comprises Bulgarian, Macedonian, Serbian, Croatian, Slovenian, and the extinct Old Church Slavic, in which the bulk of the oldest (tenth century) Slavic materials are written. The second Slavic subdivision is West Slavic, which comprises Czech, Slovak, Polish, Kashubian, and some others. And finally there is East Slavic, made up of Russian, Ukrainian, and Belarussian.

Armenian

Armenian is first attested in religious documents and translations from the fifth century CE. It shows a great deal of influence from neighboring languages, including Greek, Arabic, Syriac, and Persian, so much so in fact that it was first misclassified as a dialect of Iranian.

Albanian

Unknown linguistically until the fifteenth century CE, Albanian shows a great deal of influence from neighboring languages such as Greek, Slavic, and Turkish, as well as from Latin. This made its secure identification as a branch of Indo-European somewhat problematic when the IE languages were being classified in the eighteenth and nineteenth centuries. The first document in Albanian is a baptismal formula from the fifteenth century. There are two principal dialects, Gheg and Tosk.

Fragmentary languages

In addition to the 11 major subgroups, there are also many apparently unaffiliated languages which survive only in fragments such as glosses and sporadic inscriptions. These languages provide enough information to be classified as IE, but not much beyond that. Included among the fragmentary IE languages are Ligurian (northern Italy, possibly related to Celtic), Messapic (southern Italy, possibly connected with Illyrian), Sicel and Sicanian (Sicily), Venetic (northeastern Italy), Thracian (in the area of modern Bulgaria and southern Romania), Phrygian (in the area of modern central Turkey), Illyrian, from the Dalmatian coast area of the Adriatic), and several others.

Aspects of the structure of PIE

The extensive comparison of the daughter languages and their analysis according to the comparative method and other established methodologies has led to a protolanguage that has been reconstructed in considerable detail. In this section we will identify some of the more prominent features of reconstructed "classical" PIE, especially those relevant for the history of English, largely omitting revisions, including laryngeals, based on Anatolian evidence.

Phonology

Table 12.4 shows the correspondences between selected consonant and vowel segments in several ancient IE languages and the oldest Germanic languages. Reconstructed PIE initiates the correspondences.

Table 12.5 provides a few illustrative lexical reconstructions. (See further PHONOLOGY: SEGMENTAL HISTORIES.)

Morphology

Nominal and pronominal morphology

"Classical PIE," that is, the PIE reconstructed before the integration of Anatolian evidence into the protolanguage, is considered to be an inflectional (fusional) language

Table 12.4   Phonological correspondence among some PIE languages

PIE	Hitt.	Skt.	Lat.	Gk.	Goth.	OIc.	OHG	OE
p	p	p	p	p	f	f	f	f
t	t	t	t	t	þ	þ	d	þ
k	k	ś	k	k	h(j)	h	h	h
k^w	ku	k/c	qu	p/t/k	hw/w	hv	hw/w	hw
b	p	b	b	b	p	p	p/pf	p
d	t	d	d	d	t	t	z	t
g	k	j	g	g	k	k	k	k
g^w	ku	g/j	gu/u	b/d/g	qu	kv	q	cw/k
b^h	p	bh	f(b)	ph	b	b	b	b
d^h	t	dh	f(d)	th	d	d	t/d	d
g^h	k	h	h	kh	g	g	g	g
g^{wh}	ku	gh/h	f	ph/th/kh	w	w	w	w
s	s	s	s	s	s	s	s	s
m	m	m	m	m	m	m	m	m
n	n	n	n	n	n	n	n	n
l	l	l/r	l	l	l	l	l	l
r	r	r/l	r	r	r	r	r	r
w/u	w	v	v	Ø	w	v	w	w
y/i	y	y	j	h/z	j	Ø	j	g(y)
a	a	a	a	a	a	a	a	æ
e	e, a	a	e	e	i	e	e	e
i	i	i	i	i	i	i	i	i
o	a/ā	a	o	o	a	a	a	æ
u	u	u	u	u	u	u	u	u
ā	ā	ā	ā	ā/ē	ō	ō	ō	ō
ē	ē	ā	ē	ē	ē	ā	ā	ǣ
ō	ā	ā	ō	ō	ō	ō	ō	ō

(Hitt. = Hittite; Skt. = Sanskrit; Lat. = Latin; Gk. = Greek; Goth. = Gothic; OIc. = Old Icelandic; OHG = Old High German; OE = Old English)

in which case markers on nominals (nouns, adjectives, pronouns) indicate their grammatical relationship to other words in a sentence, and mark gender and number agreement among words in phrases. The protolanguage is traditionally reconstructed with eight (occasionally nine) cases which indicate grammatical and semantic distinctions such as subjecthood, objecthood, direction towards, dislocation from, temporality, exchange, possession, agency, and instrumentation. The cases are known as the

Table 12.5 Some PIE reconstructions, based on "core" vocabulary from IE languages

	Hitt.	Skt.	Lat.	Gk.	Goth.	OIc.	OHG	OE	PIE
three	teri-	tráyaḥ	trēs	treîs	þreis	þrīr	drī	þrī	*trei-
seven	šipta-	saptá	septem	heptá	sibun	siau	sibun	seofon	*septm̥
cow	wa-wa-(i)-ˣ	gáuḥ	bōs	boûs	⊕	kýr	chuo	cū	*gʷou-
I	ūk	ahám	ego	egṓ(n)	ik	ek	ih	ic	*eg-
foot	pata-ˣ	pā́t	pedisº	podósº	fōtus	fōtr	fuoz	fōt	*ped-
heart	kard-	⊕	cordisº	kardíā	haírtō	hjarta	herza	heorte	*kerd-
sheep	ḫawi-ˣ	áviḥ	ovis	o(w)is	⊕	ǣr	ouwi	ēowu	*owi-

ˣ The form is Hieroglyphic Luwian.
º The genitive case reveals the stem.
⊕ The cognate form is not found in this language.

Table 12.6 A sample noun declension (Lat. *servus* "servant")

Case	Singular	Plural
Nominative	*servus*	*servī*
Genitive	*servī*	*servōrum*
Dative	*servō*	*servīs*
Accusative	*servum*	*servōs*
Ablative	*servō*	*servīs*
Vocative	*serve*	*servī*

nominative, genitive, dative, accusative, ablative, locative, instrumental, and vocative. Number refers to the quantification of entities in a phrase; the protolanguage had three numbers (singular, dual, and plural), as well as three genders (gender is an unfortunate term which simply means a kind of noun class), namely masculine, feminine, and neuter. Adjectives followed the same pattern of inflection as nouns, and agreed in gender and number with their head noun. Pronouns are marked by their own more-or-less unique endings. Latin provides a useful analog to the PIE system, though without the locative and instrumental (table 12.6).

In the Latin sentence *Marcus servum vocat* "Marcus calls the servant," Marcus' role as subject is marked by the ending *-us* and the servant's role as object is indicated by *-um*. The order of the words is grammatically irrelevant (Latin, like PIE, usually puts the verb at the end). When words occur as members of a constituent (word group), their membership is indicated by shared endings marking case, number, and gender, as in *velōcī equō* "to the swift horse" [dative-singular masculine], *malōrum animālium*

"of the bad animals" [genitive-plural-neuter], or *ab aliīs fēminīs* "from the other women" [ablative-plural-feminine]. (See further HISTORY OF ENGLISH MORPHOLOGY.)

Verbal morphology

PIE verbs are synthetically complex amalgamations of meaningful elements which indicate grammatically and semantically significant categories. The PIE verb encoded two voices, active and mediopassive (voice reflects the role of the subject); a number of tenses (tense locates the verbal action temporally: at least the present, imperfect, aorist, perfect, and possibly a future are usually postulated); and mood, which indicates the factual content of the utterance from the speaker's point of view: at least the indicative, imperative, and optative moods are reconstructed, and occasionally the subjunctive. Voice, tense, and mood markers are attached to stems indicating aspectual categories (e.g., whether the action is continuous or punctual), and the entire complex is indexed to the subject by means of person/number markers. Verbs can be transitive (i.e., they can govern an object as in "Mary sees Bill") or intransitive ("Sarah walks to school"), though there is no specific formal marking on the verb to distinguish the transitive and intransitive types.

Once again Latin can be instructive, though it is not a perfect replica of PIE: a verb form like *am-ā ba-t* in *rēx amābat* "the king used to love" contains a stem form (*am-*), which indicates the lexical meaning "love"; a mood marker (*-ā-*), marking indicative (factual) mood; a tense/aspect marker (*-ba-*) which marks continuous past action; and finally a person/number/voice marker (*-t*), which indicates third person singular in the active voice. If we change the example to the passive *rēx amābātur* (*am-ā -bā -t-ur*) "the king used to be loved," the marker of passivity is the final *-ur*; in the plural *rēgēs amābantur* (*am-ā -ba-nt-ur*) "the kings used to be loved" note that the person/number marker is now *-nt-*.

Syntax

Fusional languages like PIE and many of its descendants (including Old English, though not to the same extent as Latin, Greek, or Sanskrit) have fundamentally different syntactic patterns from languages like Modern English or French. The reason has much to do with word order, and the fact that a good deal of the syntax of fusional languages is conveyed in morphological expressions, such as case endings. In Modern English, for example, the order of elements in a sentence is grammatically fixed: except in stylistically marked utterances such as "Bagels, I like," the subject precedes the verb, and the object follows the verb in simple sentences. It is not grammatical to say "Him John sees" or "Sees him John" to mean "John sees him." But in fusional languages like PIE, word order is a stylistic, not a grammatical device. Latin is illustrative again: *Marcus mē vocat* "Marcus calls me" represents the preferred (unmarked) order of elements, but *mē vocat Marcus* or *Marcus vocat mē* have the same semantic value as

Marcus mē vocat. That is because the grammatical indication of subject (*Marcus*) and object (*mē*) is being carried by the endings, not the position of the words relative to each other; furthermore, the verb *vocat* is indexed by the final *-t* to the third person nominal subject *Marcus*, and couldn't possibly go with *mē*. PIE (like Old English) was dominantly verb-final (*John him sees*). Verb-final languages have certain properties such as: they use postpositions (*the world over*); adjectives typically precede the noun they modify (*the proud winners*), also true for genitives (*Susie's exam*); comparative constructions have the order standard-marker-adjective (*Louis than taller* [= *taller than Louis*]); and relative clauses precede the noun they qualify (*who teach English professors* [= *professors who teach English*]). (See further HISTORY OF ENGLISH SYNTAX.)

The ways in which many of these features of PIE descended into Germanic and on to English are discussed in ENGLISH AS A GERMANIC LANGUAGE, in this volume.

ACKNOWLEDGMENT

Thanks to Richard Page and Aaron Rubin, who commented on an earlier version of this chapter.

REFERENCES AND FURTHER READING

Fortson, B. W., IV (2004). *Indo-European Language and Culture: An Introduction*. Oxford: Blackwell.

Mallory, J. P. & Adams, D. Q. (1997). *Encyclopedia of Indo-European Culture*. London: Fitzroy Dearborn.

Onions, C. T. (1969). *The Oxford Dictionary of English Etymology*. Oxford: Clarendon Press.

Pokorny, J. (1951–9). *Indogermanisches etymologisches Wörterbuch*. Bern: Francke.

Ramat, A. G. & Ramat, P. (eds.) (1998). *The Indo-European Languages*. London: Routledge.

Szemerényi, O. (1996). *Introduction to Indo-European Linguistics*. 4th edn. Oxford: Oxford University Press.

Watkins, C. (2000). *The American Heritage Dictionary of Indo-European Roots*. 2nd edn. Boston: Houghton Mifflin.

13
English as a Germanic Language

R. D. Fulk

Although English has borrowed much vocabulary from non-Germanic languages, particularly French and Latin, it remains a Germanic language not just in its core vocabulary of everyday words, but in its sounds and in its structure. The Germanic roots of the language are nowhere plainer than in its phonology. In 1822, Jacob Grimm (1785–1863) demonstrated a regular phonological difference between the Germanic family of languages and the other Indo-European languages. In general, voiceless stop consonants such as /p, t, k/ in the other Indo-European languages appear as the corresponding voiceless fricatives in the Germanic languages: for example, Latin *pater*, *trēs* = Present-Day English (PDE) *father*, *three*. Likewise, voiced stops such as /b, d, g/ in the other languages correspond to Germanic voiceless stops /p, t, k/, as with Latin *duo*, *gens* = PDE *two*, *kin*. And the Indo-European consonants reconstructed as the voiced aspirated stops /bh, dh, gh, gh^w/ appear in Germanic as voiced fricatives: to Sanskrit *mádhu-*, *nábhas-*, compare Icelandic *mjǫðr* 'mead', Old English *nifol* 'dark' (where *f* represents a voiced sound [v]), though at the beginning of a word or after a nasal consonant we find instead voiced Germanic stops, as in *bear* and *bind* (compare Sanskrit *bhárati* and *bándhati*, respectively). The correspondences are the result of a phonological change, now referred to as "Grimm's law," that affected Proto-Germanic, the prehistoric Indo-European language from which the Germanic languages descend. The law is charted in table 13.1, where /þ/ and /ð/ represent the sound of PDE *th* in *think* and *this*, respectively; /χ/ is a voiceless velar fricative (developing to *h* where preserved in PDE) like that in Scottish *loch* and German *Nacht*; /ɤ/ is the voiced equivalent of this (as in Danish *kage*); and /ß/ is similar to /v/ (to which it develops in PDE), but it is formed with both lips rather than with teeth and lips together (as in Spanish *cabo*).

So regular is the correspondence of sounds that it made a profound impression, inspiring the formulation of similar "sound-laws" and the reconstruction of protolanguages – in essence spawning Western linguistics as a science, since diachronic change and consistency of explanation were the preoccupations of nineteenth-century linguistics.

Table 13.1 Grimm's law (somewhat simplified)

	Proto-Indo-European				→ Germanic				
	labial	dental	velar	labialized		labial	dental	velar	labialized
Voiceless stop	p	t	k	k^w	→ Voiceless fricative	f	þ	χ	$χ^w$
Voiced stop	b	d	g	g^w	→ Voiceless stop	p	t	k	k^w
Aspirated stop	bh	dh	gh	gh^w	→ Voiced fricative/ stop	ß/b	ð/d	ɣ/g	$ɣ^w/g^w$

English shares with the other Germanic languages a number of further phonological innovations that differentiate it from the rest of the Indo-European family. The resonants /l, r, m, n/ could be syllabic in Proto-Indo-European (PIE) (as they are word-finally, for instance, in PDE *bottle*, *mitten*, etc.), with various results in non-Germanic languages; only in Germanic do the syllabic varieties regularly become /ul, ur, um, un/, as in *spurn* (compare Sanskrit *spṛṇóti* 'wards off') and Old English *wulf* 'wolf' = Sanskrit *vṛkaḥ* < PIE *wḷk^wos*. Among other vowel changes, PIE *o* became Germanic *a*, as expressed in the PDE spellings *yard* (= Old Icelandic *garðr*, compare Latin *hortus*, Greek χόρτοσ) and *what* (= Old Icelandic *hvat*, German *was*, compare Latin *quod*). Likewise, PIE *ā* became Germanic *ō*, spelt *o* in PDE *mother* (= Old Icelandic *móðir*, compare Latin *māter*) and (*el*)*bow* (= Old Icelandic *bógr*, compare Doric Greek πᾶχυσ).

A certain prosodic (accentual) change had a more profound effect: in Proto-Germanic, the accent shifted to the initial syllable in most word classes, but to the root syllable in verbs. The regularity is less clearly observable in PDE than in some other Germanic languages, due to the later influx of foreign (chiefly Romance) vocabulary; but to the verbs *undergó*, *outwéigh*, *uplíft*, with unstressed prefixes, compare the nouns *úndertow*, *óutbuilding*, *úpdraft*, with initial stress. A result of the shift of accent is that final and other unstressed syllables tended to weaken and disappear over time, making most native English words relatively short by comparison to their cognates (their near genetic relations in other Indo-European languages). For example, the monosyllabic verb *melts* is equivalent to trisyllabic Sanskrit *márdati*, and *young* is cognate with trisyllabic Latin *juvencus*. The accent shift also is implicated in a change known as "Verner's law" (named after the Danish linguist Karl Verner, 1846–96), whereby the fricative consonants /f, þ, s, χ/ were voiced after originally unstressed vowels. This explains many seeming exceptions to Grimm's law, for example Old English *soden* 'boiled, sodden' (instead of expected **sožen*) < PIE **sutonós*. Alternations caused by Verner's law were still found in Old English, but in PDE (where Germanic /z/, voiced from /s/ by Verner's law, has become /r/) the only remaining alternations are between <s> and <r> in the spellings *was*:*were* and *lose*:*forlorn*.

The morphology of English and its Germanic relatives also differs from that of other IE languages in systematic ways. The verb system in PIE was particularly rich and complex, expressing two voices, four moods, and perhaps as many as six tenses. Aside from a few relic formations, the Germanic languages have reduced this system to one voice (active, though Gothic, the most conservative of the Germanic languages, also preserves the medio-passive voice), three moods (indicative, subjunctive, imperative), and two formal tenses (present and preterite [i.e., past], though English has subsequently developed further distinctions by the use of auxiliaries). More important, methods of forming verb stems in Proto-Indo-European were remarkably varied. For example, a present stem might be characterized by reduplication of the initial consonant and insertion of a vowel, creating an extra, initial syllable (e.g., Greek δί-δω-μι 'I give', root δω-) or by infixation of *n* in the root (e.g., Latin *frangō* 'I break'; compare perfect *frēgī*, without the *n*; PDE has the similar relic *stand*: *stood*) or by the addition of a suffix such as *-sk-* or *-yo-* before the personal ending (e.g., Latin [*g*]*nō-sc-ō* 'I get to know' : perf. [*g*]*nō-vī*; Sanskrit *náh-ya-ti* 'binds') or by use of the bare root (e.g., Sanskrit *é-ti* 'goes') or root plus connecting vowel (e.g., Sanskrit *bhár-a-ti* 'bears'). In addition, in different moods and tenses the root might show "ablaut" – the term refers to the alternation of vowels in PIE itself – resulting in PDE series like *ride, rode, ridden* and *grow, grew, grown*. This complex PIE system was simplified considerably in Germanic, where stem types came to be characterized less by infixes and stem-forming suffixes than by a limited number of ablaut types (in essence, seven). Thus, for example, all verbs that resembled Proto-Germanic **rīðanan* (PDE *ride*, like *drive, rise, write*, etc.) formed their tenses the same way. These seven classes of verbs correspond roughly to the PDE "irregular verbs," though the distinctions among the seven classes are much harder to discern in PDE than in OE, and now the principal parts of these verbs must for the most part be learned individually rather than deduced from comparison to similar verbs.

Yet even in Proto-Germanic these seven classes of "strong" verbs came to be closed classes, in the sense that although they contained verbs that formed their principal parts the same way (the way PDE *sing, sang, sung* is analogous to *ring, rang, rung*), they were unproductive: new verbs could not be added to these classes. Rather, new verbs entering the language were added to the classes of "weak" verbs, a morphological innovation that distinguishes the Germanic languages from the rest of the Indo-European group. These are the verbs that in PDE add *-ed* in the past tense and the passive participle, along with any others that add an alveolar (dental) stop consonant in the past tense, such as *bring, brought*; *have, had*; and *make, made* (even though these are now treated as "irregular verbs"). Thus, like PDE *nail, nailed* are German *nageln, nagelte*, Danish *nagle, naglede*. The origin of the dental suffix used in the past tense is disputed, but one explanation often advocated is that it is a form of the verb *do*. If this is correct, then a past tense form like *nailed* could be said to derive from the Proto-Germanic equivalent of *nail-did*.

Another morphological characteristic of the Germanic group is the development of preterite-present verbs. Already in Proto-Indo-European some perfect forms had

present meaning, e.g. **woida* 'I know', literally 'I have seen', a perfect form of the root **wid-* (cf. Latin present *videō* 'I see'). In Germanic, because these verbs were perceived as expressing present-tense meanings, new preterites of the weak variety were developed for them, though the presents were still largely inflected like preterites – that is, they followed the ablaut alternations of preterite verbs and had preterite endings attached. For example, the Old English verb *sceal* 'shall', inflected in the present tense like the preterite of a strong verb, has the preterite *sceolde*, inflected like a weak verb. In PDE, several of these verbs survive as modal auxiliaries, chiefly *can*, *may* (past *might*), *must*, and *shall*. These modal auxiliaries are set apart from other verbs in that they take no ending *-s* in the third person singular of the present (e.g., *she can* vs. *she writes;* this is a relic of preterite inflection in the present tense), they do not require the support of the verb *do* to form a question or a negative statement (e.g., *Must they?* vs. *Do they know?* and *they must not* vs. *they do not know*), and accompanying infinitives are not preceded by *to* (e.g., *can go* vs. *wants to go*). In addition to *can*, *may*, *must*, and *shall*, some other, moribund relics of the Old English preterite-present verbs are found, including some of the older uses of *dare* and *need* (as in *Dare I say it?* and *Need this be a bad sign?*).

In regard to the declension of nouns and adjectives – that is, the addition of endings to indicate grammatical relations within the sentence – PIE had a system of at least eight cases, as in Sanskrit. In Germanic the number was reduced, so that in Old English we find, really, four cases (nominative, accusative, genitive, and dative, which are the cases of the subject, direct object, possessor, and indirect object, respectively), though there are scant remains of a fifth (instrumental, indicating means). With the loss of inflectional endings over the course of the medieval period, English relinquished all case endings in adjectives and all but the possessive ending *-s* (now spelt *-'s* and *-s'*) in nouns, though a wider variety of case-forms survives in pronouns (*I*, *me*, *my*, *mine*, etc.). Germanic developed another "strong" and "weak" distinction, quite different from the one in verbs, in regard to the inflection of adjectives. Thus, for example, the adjective *gōd* 'good' is inflected as follows in the singular with strong masculine endings: nominative *gōd*, accusative *gōdne*, genitive *gōdes*, dative *gōdum*. With weak endings, however, the forms are nominative *gōda*, accusative, genitive, and dative *gōdan*. Nearly all early Germanic adjectives may bear either strong or weak inflections, depending on whether or not nouns they modify are definite. A noun is definite when it refers to a particular individual or item or subset of the totality of extant items. Thus, for example, in PDE, nouns preceded by *the*, *this*, *that* or a possessive pronoun like *my* or *their* are definite, while nouns preceded by *a(n)* or no article are usually indefinite (exceptions: *Shakespeare, Chicago, outer space*). In some Germanic languages, weak adjectives are still used with definite nouns and strong with indefinite ones, for example German *der junge Mann* 'the young man' vs. *ein junger Mann* 'a young man'. This was the situation in Old English (compare *se gōda mann* 'the good person': *gōd mann* 'a good person'), though the endings of all English adjectives were gradually lost in the course of the Middle Ages, resulting in elimination of the distinction. Even the definite article itself is an innovation in Germanic, since Proto-Indo-European had

no articles. PDE *the* developed from a PIE demonstrative pronoun whose reflex (result-ing form) in OE might still be rendered 'that' or 'this', or not at all (as in *þā hwīle þe wē þæt līf habbað* '[for] the while that we have life', i.e., 'for as long as we live'). The rise of definite articles is clearly a late development in Germanic, as shown by the fact that the articles differ considerably from one Germanic language to another: in Ice-landic, for example, the definite article derives from a source distinct from the source of PDE *the*, and it is commonly attached as a suffix, as in *bók-in = the book*.

As for the order of elements in clauses and sentences, the most notable feature is the general tendency in the Germanic languages for finite verbs (i.e., verb forms other than infinitives and participles) to appear as the second constituent in independent clauses (so-called V2 order). The first constituent may be a word or a phrase, for example a prepositional phrase, as in *þȳ ilcan gēare forðfērde Carl Francena cyng* '[In] that same year died Charlemagne, king of the Franks'. In Old English, V2 order was a strong tendency rather than a firm rule (as it is in Icelandic and German). Element order in English has subsequently become fixed in the pattern subject-verb-object (SVO), but in PDE there survive relics of the older, less rigid system, with an element other than the subject before the verb, for example *In the tree lived two owls* and *Up jumped the prosecutor* and *"Hello," said the parrot.* The Germanic languages are also inno-vative in respect to methods of forming relative clauses.

The differences between the Germanic languages and the rest of the Indo-European group – and only a few such differences have been described above – are thus fairly striking. There are similarly regular differences among the Germanic languages them-selves, and although these differences are usually a bit subtler, they point to certain subgroupings within the Germanic family. The family can be sectioned into three subdivisions, East, North, and West Germanic. The East Germanic division is repre-sented by Gothic only (hence it is extinct), the North Germanic by the Scandinavian languages (excluding Finnish and Lappish, which are not Indo-European), and the West Germanic by German (High and Low), Yiddish, Dutch, Flemish, Afrikaans, Frisian, English, and older varieties of these, such as Middle English and Old Low Franconian (a type of older Dutch). The relations among the three Germanic groups are debated, since there are certain features that East Germanic shares only with West Germanic (e.g., the form of the verb 'have': Gothic *haban*, German *haben*, etc., vs. Icelandic *eiga*, Swedish *äga*, etc.), and certain ones that it shares only with North Germanic (e.g., the ending *-t* in the second person singular preterite of strong verbs: Gothic and Old Icelandic *namt* 'you took' vs. OE *nōme*, OHG *nāmi*, etc.). But the most striking resemblances are those between North and West Germanic, leading most linguists to assume that the two groups descend from a common protolanguage, Northwest Germanic, from which East Germanic was separated at a fairly early date. This analysis is represented by the *Stammbaum* or genealogical tree in figure 13.1.

A few of the most obvious commonalities are these. Gothic retains the Proto-Indo-European method of reduplication (addition of an initial syllable that begins with the same consonant as the verb root, as explained above in regard to Greek δί-δω-μι) to mark the preterite of certain verbs (those of the seventh ablaut class): for example,

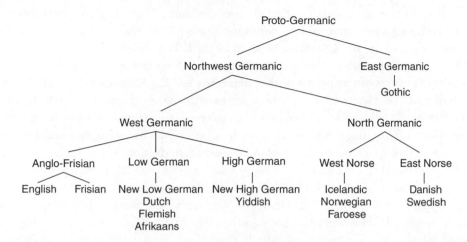

Figure 13.1 One version of a genealogical model (*Stammbaum*) of the descent of the Germanic languages

Gothic *haitan* 'command' has the pret. sg. *haihait.* In Northwest Germanic, although there are a few relic reduplicated forms, the system of forming the preterite of these verbs has been changed fundamentally, so that we find, for example, OE *hēt* 'commanded' beside the rare older, reduplicated *heht.* A few of the other developments common to Northwest Germanic are loss of the medio-passive voice (mentioned above as preserved in Gothic); development of /z/ to /r/ ("rhotacism"), as in PDE *more,* Old Icelandic *meira* = Gothic *maiza;* retention of Verner's law alternations (lost in Gothic); backing of Proto-Germanic *ē* to *ā* (to Gothic *rēdan* 'advise', compare Old Icelandic *rāða,* German *raten*); and the development of umlaut vowels, i.e., front varieties of back vowels when *i* or *j* followed in the next syllable (e.g., to German *Brüder,* Old Icelandic *brœðir,* PDE *brethren,* with front vowels in the first syllable, compare Gothic *brōþrjus,* with a back vowel). But chronological differences may be involved in the rise of some of these features, and linguistic changes may extend over wide swaths of territory, affecting more than one language group at once, so that the genetic or "Stammbaum" model of a language's direct descent from a protolanguage, without horizontal contact among languages in a family tree, is an oversimplification of the way that languages actually develop. It may be, after all, that there never was a Northwest Germanic protolanguage.

As for developments specific to West Germanic, distinguishing it from both Gothic and the Scandinavian languages, a simple difference is the development of *ð* to *d*: to Icelandic *ríða, glaður* compare PDE *ride, glad.* But the most significant phonological development characterizing West Germanic is consonant gemination (doubling) between a short vowel and a resonant consonant, particularly /j/: to Gothic *satjan,* Old Icelandic *setja* 'set', compare Old English *settan,* Old Saxon *settian;* and to Old Icelandic *epli* 'apple', compare Old English *æppel,* Old Frisian *appel.* Before /j/, only /r/ is not so geminated; hence Gothic *nasjan, harjōs* = Old English *nerian* 'save' (with rhotacism), *herias* 'armies'.

The West Germanic group comprises three divisions, Anglo-Frisian, Low German, and High German, often said to correspond roughly to the tripartite division of *Ingaevones*, *Istaevones*, and *Herminones* asserted by the Roman historian Cornelius Tacitus in his *Germania* (ca. 98 CE). (The term "Ingvaeonic," assuming Tacitus' *Ingaevones* is a spelling error, is often applied in the literature to all the West Germanic languages excluding High German, though now it tends to be employed less usefully as a synonym for "Anglo-Frisian." The Low German varieties in question show Ingvaeonic features to varying degrees.) The Anglo-Frisian group includes English and Frisian, a language now restricted to about 300,000 speakers in the northwestern Netherlands, including coastal islands, though formerly the Frisians occupied the entire coast from the Zuider Zee to southern Jutland. English and Frisian share several features that set them apart from the other West Germanic languages. For example, both show fronting of long and short West Germanic *a* (to German *Saat*, *Sack*, the latter with the sound [a], roughly as in *father*, compare PDE *seed*, *sack*, Frisian *sied*, *sek*); monophthongization of Germanic *ai* (to German *breit*, compare PDE *broad*, Frisian *breed*); and palatalization and affrication of velar consonants adjacent to certain front vowels and glides (to German *gelten*, *Kirche*, with initial stop consonants, compare PDE *yield*, *church*, Frisian *jilde*, *tsjerke*). Frisian is thus the language most closely related to English. The similarities between the two have sometimes been overstated in the popular literature, but a Frisian rhyme puts the matter succinctly: *Buuter, breea, in griene tjiiz / is goe Ingels in goe Fries* 'Butter, bread, and green cheese / is good English and good Frisian'.

Among the West Germanic languages, English and Frisian are the most clearly differentiated from High German; languages like New Low German and Dutch show High German features in varying degrees. One High German feature is preservation of the postvocalic consonant clusters *mf*, *ns*, *nþ*. In Anglo-Frisian and in some Low German varieties, the nasal consonant in these groups is lost, with compensatory lengthening of the preceding vowel: to PDE *soft*, *five*, *us*, *mouth*, with loss of the nasal consonant, compare Old High German *samfto*, *fimf*, *uns*, *mund*. But the feature that most markedly sets off the High German dialects from the rest of the West Germanic group is the High German Consonant Shift, a systematic change of consonants comparable to Grimm's law. Word-initially, the stop consonants /p, t, k/ become affricates: to PDE *pipe*, *tide* compare German *Pfeife*, *Zeit*. Elsewhere in the word they become fricatives: to PDE *ship*, *water*, *make* compare German *Schiff*, *Wasser*, *machen*. And voiceless geminate stops become affricates: to OE *æppel*, *settan* compare German *Apfel*, *setzen* 'apple, set'. Of some further developments in this consonant shift, those still attested in the modern standard language are the change of initial /d/ to /t/ (to PDE *drink*, compare German *trinken*) and of /þ/ to /d/ (to PDE *thank*, compare NHG *danken*).

Thus, already in the Old English period, English occupied a relatively peripheral position in the West Germanic division. This is because the features that most clearly define the Anglo-Frisian group are consistently linguistic innovations, evidencing evolution away from the remainder of the West Germanic group, such as fronting of /a/ to /æ/ (as in *hat*, *thatch*) and affrication of original /k, g/ (as in *church*, *singe*). The

peripheral status of English becomes even clearer when changes specific to Old English and to the later language are taken into account (on which see PHONOLOGY: SEGMENTAL HISTORIES).

REFERENCES AND FURTHER READING

Bammesberger, A. (1992). The place of English in Germanic and Indo-European. In R. M. Hogg (ed.), *The Cambridge History of the English Language, Vol. 1: The Beginnings to 1066* (pp. 26–66). Cambridge: Cambridge University Press.

Beekes, R. S. P. (1995 [1990]). *Comparative Indo-European Linguistics*. Trans. UvA Vertalers & P. Gabriner. Amsterdam: Benjamins.

Braune, W. (1987). *Althochdeutsche Grammatik*. 14th edn. revd. by H. Eggers. Tübingen: Niemeyer.

Brunner, K. (1965). *Altenglische Grammatik nach der angelsächsischen Grammatik von Eduard Sievers*. 3rd edn. Tübingen: Niemeyer.

Campbell, A. (1959). *Old English Grammar*. Oxford: Clarendon Press.

Collinge, N. E. (1985). *The Laws of Indo-European*. Amsterdam: Benjamins.

Fulk, R. D. (1998). The chronology of Anglo-Frisian sound changes. *Amsterdamer Beiträge zur älteren Germanistik*, 49, 139–54.

Gallée, J. H. (1993). *Altsächsische Grammatik*. 3rd edn. revd. by H. Tiefenbach. Tübingen: Niemeyer.

Hogg, R. M. (1992). *A Grammar of Old English, Vol. 1: Phonology*. Oxford: Blackwell.

Hopper, P. J. (1975). *The Syntax of the Simple Sentence in Proto-Germanic*. The Hague: Mouton.

Krahe, H. & Meid, W. (1969). *Germanische Sprachwissenschaft*. 7th edn. 3 vols. Berlin: de Gruyter.

Luick, K. (1914–40). *Historische Grammatik der englischen Sprache*. 2 vols. Stuttgart: Tauchnitz.

Noreen, A. (1923). *Altisländische und altnorwegische Grammatik*. 4th edn. Halle: Niemeyer.

Prokosch, E. (1938). *A Comparative Germanic Grammar*. Baltimore: Linguistic Society of America.

Robinson, O. W. (1992). *Old English and Its Closest Relatives*. Stanford: Stanford University Press.

Russ, C. V. J. (1978). *Historical German Phonology and Morphology*. Oxford: Clarendon Press.

Steller, W. (1928). *Abriss der altfriesischen Grammatik*. Halle: Niemeyer.

Streitberg, W. (1900). *Urgermanische Grammatik*. Heidelberg: Winter.

Szemerényi, O. J. L. (1996 [1990]). *Introduction to Indo-European Linguistics*. Trans. D. M. Jones & I. Jones. Oxford: Clarendon Press.

Wright, J. (1954). *Grammar of the Gothic Language*. 2nd edn. revd. by O. L. Sayce. Oxford: Clarendon Press.

Part V
English in History: England and America

Section 1
Old English in History
(ca. 450–1066)

Introduction

The idea of English as "the language of England" goes back to the fifth and sixth centuries when a large number of people migrated from the North Sea region to Britain. Since these migrants belonged to different Germanic tribes like the Angles and the Saxons, they probably spoke several varieties of North Sea Germanic. By the time Bede completed the *Ecclesiastical History of the English People* in 731, however, the descendants of these settlers could be identified as *gens anglorum* ("English people"), a group unified through their common language. Bede nevertheless wrote the *Ecclesiastical History* in Latin so that his work would be read throughout Western Christendom. Even when Bede referred to a short poem composed by Cædmon, the first named English poet, he did not quote Cædmon's Old English original but instead paraphrased it in Latin prose. For Bede, a Northumbrian monk writing only a century after the conversion of the Anglo-Saxons, parchment and ink were reserved for Latin composition, whereas English poetry, even when it dealt with Christian themes, was designated for memory and oral performance (see also THE ANGLO-SAXON POETIC TRADITION). In the time of Bede, such an attitude towards the vernacular was probably not an anomaly. Despite the political supremacy of Northumbria and Mercia in the early Anglo-Saxon period, only a few specimens of dialects remain from these northern kingdoms. The paucity of texts written in the Northumbrian and the Mercian dialects (collectively known as the Anglian dialect) may be due in part to the Viking invaders who ravaged churches and monasteries in northern regions. It is likely nonetheless that the vernacular did not have status as a written language in the earlier parts of the Old English period (see TOPICS IN OLD ENGLISH DIALECTS).

A turning point in the cultural history of English took place when King Alfred of Wessex (r. 871–99) launched a series of vernacular projects after his successful defense of his kingdom against the Vikings. Alfred himself translated at least four Latin texts into English and invited others to join him in promoting vernacular literacy among all Englishmen of the free class. Alfred's ambitious plan enhanced new ideas about the vernacular: English was good enough for prose composition and worthy enough for parchment. Most of the English texts from Alfred's generation were written in Early West Saxon, the dialect of his realm (see EARLY OLD ENGLISH). West Saxon continued to be a privilege dialect in the tenth century when Alfred's successors consolidated West Saxon supremacy and supported intellectual movements led by the Church. Until this point, Old English dialects had corresponded mostly to geographical variety, like Northumbrian, Mercian, and Early West Saxon. With the monastic reform in the royal seat of Winchester in the late tenth century, however, the Late West Saxon dialect became the standard written vernacular to be used for manuscripts produced even outside Wessex. Late West Saxon, which accounts for the majority of the extant Old English corpus, is characterized by highly regulated orthography (see LATE OLD ENGLISH). The following West Saxon version of Cædmon's *Hymn* is probably more familiar to students of Old English today than the early Northumbrian version printed on page 159:

Nu sculon herigean   heofonrices weard,
meotodes meahte   and his modgeþanc,
weorc wuldorfæder,   swa he wundra gehwæs,
ece drihten,   or onstealde.
He ærest sceop   eorðan bearnum
heofon to hrofe,   halig scyp pend;
þa middangeard   moncynnes weard,
ece drihten,   æfter teode
firum foldan,   frea ælmihtig.

Old English manuscripts continued to be read after the Norman Conquest of 1066. In some cases, new copies were made well into the twelfth century.

Haruko Momma

14
Early Old English (up to 899)

Daniel Donoghue

The first chapter of Bede's *Ecclesiastical History of the English People* begins with a geographical survey of the island of Britain followed by a listing of the five languages spoken there: "These are the English, British, Irish, Pictish, as well as the Latin languages; through the study of scriptures, Latin is in general use among them all" (McClure & Collins 1999: 10). By "British" Bede means what is now called Welsh; Pictish, now extinct and evidenced only in scattered bits such as place-names, was spoken in northern Scotland; Irish was spoken in Ireland, of course, but also in many areas of Northumbria and Scotland; English needs little comment here, except that like Welsh and Irish it has undergone extensive changes since the eighth century. Latin was different. It was no one's native tongue, but a common language among the educated elite of western Europe, almost all of whom were churchmen like the monk and priest Bede (d. 735), who was one of the greatest scholars of early medieval Europe.

For Bede, there was no question that he should write in Latin. His choice had little to do with the linguistic features of his native vernacular, a northern dialect of what we now call Old English, but the most "literary" use to which it was put at the time was oral poetry, which sustained a tradition stretching back centuries. Bede was "familiar with English poetry" according to one of his disciples, and indeed he probably drew from oral legends to fill in some details in his *History* (McClure & Collins 1999: 300). But Bede and his contemporaries gave little thought to writing down Old English poems, and a tradition of prose had yet to develop.

Although Latin never relinquished its pre-eminence as a literary and scholarly language, the uses of written English began to expand in the second half of the ninth century. Dominating this period is the figure of Alfred, king of Wessex and a scholar in his own right. His reign began in a state of crisis because an invading army threatened to obliterate his kingdom. Alfred gradually won back and expanded the territory of Wessex. Beyond his political and military accomplishments, Alfred has an equally important role in the history of English literature, as the second half of this essay shows.

Early England

The cultural diversity of early England arose after the withdrawal of the last Roman legions as the late empire was contracting. Bede narrates how mercenary forces led by Hengest and Horsa (both names mean "horse") arrived in 449 at the behest of a British king named Vortigern. After a number of successes on the battlefield they turned against their British employers and invited more of their tribesmen to join them in taking the land for themselves. While recent studies show that the migration and linguistic patterns were more complex, Bede's account became the defining narrative of the arrival of the Angles, the Saxons, and the Jutes. He locates the settlement of the Jutes in and around Kent; the Saxons in Wessex, Sussex, Essex; and the Angles in East Anglia, Mercia, and Northumbria. But by the eighth century he could speak of them as a single *gens* who spoke the same language.

While most details about the Germanic invaders remain obscure, it is clear they were not Christian, while the British they supplanted were. We know relatively little about their theology (although the names of their gods Tiw, Woden, Thor, and Frig are still enshrined in our days of the week), so "pagan" often means little more than "not Christian" for both medieval and modern historians. Christianity remained active, however, in those parts of Britain that the Anglo-Saxons did not conquer, including what is now Wales and Cornwall, and of course in Ireland. Ireland is a notable case because Latin learning remained vigorous there even while most of western Europe entered what has been called the "Dark Ages."

Two significant events mark the beginning of the Christianization of Anglo-Saxon England. In the 560s an Irish monk named Columba established a monastic settlement on Iona, an island off the west coast of Scotland. It became the launching point for missionary and monastic activity around Northumbria and accounts for the pervasive influence of Celtic traditions there. And in 597 a Roman monk named Augustine, sent by Pope Gregory, led a mission to Kent where they were welcomed by King Æthelberht, whose wife Bertha came from a Christian Frankish family. Augustine's mission was, according to Bede, a resounding success, so that he not only baptized King Æthelberht but also 10,000 Anglo-Saxons by the end of 597. Across England, however, conversion was often a faltering process, especially in the first century after Augustine's mission.

While Bede could speak of a single *gens Anglorum* the political reality was that from the earliest years "England" consisted of a patchwork of separate kingdoms, which came to be known as the Heptarchy: Kent, Essex, Sussex, Wessex, East Anglia, Mercia, and Northumbria. At any given time one kingdom might assert over-lordship over others, which Bede called *imperium*, later called *bretwalda* in Old English. The seven kingdoms are more than political designations, because they provide a template for distinguishing the four regional dialects of Old English: Northumbrian, Mercian, Kentish, and West Saxon (see TOPICS IN OLD ENGLISH DIALECTS).

From Cædmon to Alfred

A famous passage in the *Ecclesiastical History* tells the story of how in a dream Cædmon, a lay peasant who worked for a double monastery (with separate quarters for monks and nuns) led by Abbess Hild, miraculously received an ability to create new poems. Cædmon, Bede tells us, had lived

> until he was well advanced in years and had never learned any songs. Hence sometimes at a feast, when for the sake of providing entertainment, it had been decided that they should all sing in turn, when he saw the harp approaching him, he would rise up in the middle of the feasting, go out, and return home.
>
> On one such occasion when he did so, he left the place of feasting and went to the cattle byre, as it was his turn to take charge of them that night. In due time he stretched himself out and went to sleep, whereupon he dreamt that someone stood by him, saluted him, and called him by name. "Cædmon," he said, "sing me something." Cædmon answered, "I cannot sing; that is why I left the feast and came here because I could not sing." Once again the speaker said, "Nevertheless you must sing to me." "What must I sing?" said Cædmon. "Sing," he said, "about the beginning of created things." Thereupon Cædmon began to sing verses which he had never heard before in praise of God the Creator, of which this is the general sense: "Now we must praise the Maker of the heavenly kingdom, the power of the Creator and his counsel, the deeds of the Father of glory and how He, since he is the eternal God, was the Author of all marvels and first created the heavens as a roof for the children of men and then, the almighty Guardian of the human race, created the earth." This is the sense but not the order of the words which he sang as he slept. For it is not possible to translate verse, however well composed, literally from one language to another without some loss of beauty and dignity. When he awoke, he remembered all that he had sung while asleep and soon added more verses in the same manner, praising God in fitting style. (McClure & Collins 1999: 214–15)

The miracle that attracts Bede's attention is that Cædmon received not just the gift of poetry, but rather the gift of creating Christian poems in the vernacular. Before Cædmon, Old English verse was practiced as an oral tradition using formulaic phrasing and traditional (non-Christian) subjects. Poems might be memorized in their entirety or new ones invented by skilled poets (scops), but the ability to recite poems in the traditional meter was apparently widespread. One minor detail in Bede's story gives a rare glimpse into the folk habits of the time that is otherwise missing in the written record. While everyone else at the farmworkers' feast takes turns handling the harp and reciting poems in the traditional way, as if it were the most common thing in the world, only Cædmon, remarkably, cannot participate. Even if we grant some exaggeration for the sake of a good miracle story, it seems clear that the ability to recite poems was a widespread skill (see THE ANGLO-SAXON POETIC TRADITION).

When Abbess Hild heard of Cædmon's dream and his poem, she arranged for a group of scholars to test whether the new gift was divine. So they told Cædmon a

story from the Bible and asked him to turn it into poetry. He went away overnight, and like a cow chewing cud, ruminated on the story. Returning to Hild and her scholars the next day, he gave it back to them "in excellent verse." With Hild's encouragement he took vows and entered the monastery, where he learned stories from all of sacred history and turned them into Old English poetry.

While Bede never claims that Cædmon's interlocutors transcribed anything he said, a number of the Latin *Ecclesiastical History* manuscripts contain a copy of what is now called "Cædmon's Hymn." (For reproductions of 21 versions, see Robinson & Stanley 1991 and O'Donnell 2005.) The relatively large number of copies attests to the widespread belief that these nine lines fairly represent what Cædmon uttered in front of Hild and her Whitby scholars. Some of the manuscripts can be dated to within a few years of Bede's death, such as the Moore Manuscript (Cambridge University Library MS. Kk. 5. 16), which has preserved on its final folio the following, glossed here with an overliteral translation:

nu scylun hergan	hefaenricaes uard
now let us praise	*the heavenly-kingdom's protector*
metudæs maecti	end his modgidanc
the creator's might	*and his purpose*
uerc uuldurfadur	sue he uundra gihuaes
the work of the glorious-father	*as he every wonder*
eci dryctin	or astelidæ
the eternal lord	*the beginning established*
He aerist scop	aelda barnum
He first created	*for the children of men*
heben til hrofe	haleg scepen
heaven as a roof	*the holy creator*
tha middungeard	moncynnæs uard
then middle-earth	*the protector of mankind*
eci dryctin	æfter tiadæ
eternal lord	*later created*
firum foldu	frea allmectig
for men the world	*the lord almighty*

What Bede's Latin says indirectly is that only after the traditional verse form was adapted to Christian themes did it stand a chance of passing from a purely oral medium to one that was written down. Cædmon's innovation was to take the traditional oral formulaic language and tweak it so that, for example, epithets for earthly kings became applied to the Christian deity. Thus his phrase *eci dryctin* ("eternal lord," used twice in the nine lines) was based on an older formula like *eorla dryctin*, "lord of men." It was a simple change with far-reaching consequences.

The version printed here retains several scribal features from the manuscript, such as the absence of punctuation and a solitary capitalized letter (i.e., slightly larger than

its neighbors), but in two respects it is quite different. The scribe wrote out the poem in three long lines stretching from margin to margin, and most of the words are run together, so it does not conform to our expectations for the visual presentation of a poem, with word breaks, line breaks, and punctuation. It is as though the scribe expected readers to be so familiar with the language and conventions of poetry that they could navigate the continuous text without anything resembling today's array of visual cues. The lack is particularly disorienting for modern readers because of the convoluted syntax, which was perfectly conventional for poetry.

At this early date the spelling conventions were still developing, as some of the scribe's choices reveal. While the Anglo-Saxons had made use of the runic alphabet (called futhorc) for inscriptions of various kinds, Christianity brought with it the Latin alphabet as well as the important technology of writing. Because the first efforts to transcribe Old English faced the problem of using a system of writing developed for one language (Latin) to transcribe another (Old English), the scribes had to improvise graphemes for some sounds. Latin, for example, had no separate letter for the consonant /w/, but it had developed a convention to allow the letter <u> to do double duty as vowel and consonant, which the scribe of the Moore manuscript adopts (e.g., *uurc uuldurfadur*, where the first <u> of each word represents the consonant /w/). The scribe used the digraph <th> to represent the voiceless interdental fricative /θ/ (which by coincidence is in line with today's spelling convention). The sound /æ/ is sometimes represented by the digraph <ae> and sometimes the ligature <æ> (also called *ash*); and the digraph <sc> is used for the sound /ʃ/. Scribes in later decades would turn to the *futhorc* runes to supplement the Latin alphabet with the letters *wynn* <ᚹ> for /w/ and *thorn* <þ> for the interdental fricatives /θ, ð/; as an equivalent to <þ> they also created a new letter <ð> (today called *eth*,) modified from an insular form of the letter <d>. The letters <ᚹ, þ, ð, æ> and the digraphs <sc> and <cg> (for the sound /dʒ/, not found in "Cædmon's Hymn") became standard around the year 800.

Some time around the year 900, Bede's *Ecclesiastical History* was translated from Latin into Old English as part of an ambitious program sponsored by King Alfred (d. 899). The treatment of the Cædmon episode is fairly literal, but one telling change is worth comment here. When Hild's scholars recognize the miraculous nature of his poetic gift, Bede's Latin says that "his teachers became in turn his audience"; but the Old English goes further and claims that "his very teachers learned and wrote from his spoken words [lit. from his mouth]." The West Saxon translator recognized the practical and symbolic importance of committing Cædmon's words to writing, whether or not Hild's scholars transcribed his oral performances. (Bede is silent on the point.) As we will see, the written word was a central part of Alfred's program of translation.

Mercia and the Vikings

Between the death of Bede (735) and the birth of King Alfred (849), political dominance shifted to a sequence of powerful Mercian kings, but because so few of their

written records survive we know relatively little about them (Toon 1983: 17–43). Yet some centers of learning must have flourished because Alfred recruited Mercian scholars to his court. Viking attacks and occupation spelled the end of Mercian political dominance and lay behind the loss of whatever written records the Mercian scholars produced.

The vikings appeared with a terrifying suddenness, or as the Anglo-Saxons may have said, they came *unþinged*. In 789 a West Saxon reeve approached three ships that landed near Portland. He assumed they were traders and intended to take them to the king's residence. It was the last mistake he ever made. They were vikings from Norway, who killed him and his men on the spot. A few years later another viking raid plundered the island monastery of Lindisfarne (Whitelock 1979: 181). The Anglo-Saxon Chronicle entry for 793 portrays the event against a backdrop of apocalyptic signs:

> In this year dire portents appeared over Northumbria and sorely frightened the people. They consisted of immense whirlwinds and flashes of lightning, and fiery dragons were seen flying in the air. A great famine immediately followed those signs, and a little after that in the same year, on 8 June, the ravages of heathen men miserably destroyed God's church on Lindisfarne, with plunder and slaughter. (Campbell 1962)

At first the vikings were content with "smash and grab" raids, but by the middle of the ninth century they formed larger forces that wintered over in England. In 866 one such force was large enough that the Chronicle-writer called it a *micel hæðen here* "a great heathen army."

By the time Alfred came to the throne in 871 the vikings had effective control over all of England except for part of Wessex. But after crucial victories on the battlefield and some skillful diplomacy, Alfred eventually won back control of Wessex and expanded it. An important turning point came in 878, when Alfred defeated the invading viking army, and as part of the terms of surrender its leader Guthrum agreed to be baptized with Alfred as his sponsor. About ten years later Alfred and Guthrum signed another treaty that recognized a boundary running northwest roughly from London to Chester, along the old Roman road called Watling Street. North of that line was the Danelaw, and the extent of Scandinavian settlement there is clear from the number of placenames like Woodthorpe and Grimsby which contain Norse or Danish elements (see figure 14.1). After the ninth century, as the vikings and their descendents settled, their native speech began to influence the local dialects with far-reaching results in the later history of the English language.

Alfred and Literacy

We know many details about Alfred because he was careful to use the written word in matters of state. "The variety of written sources for Alfred the Great," observes Simon Keynes, "is at once the product, the expression, and the symbol of what was

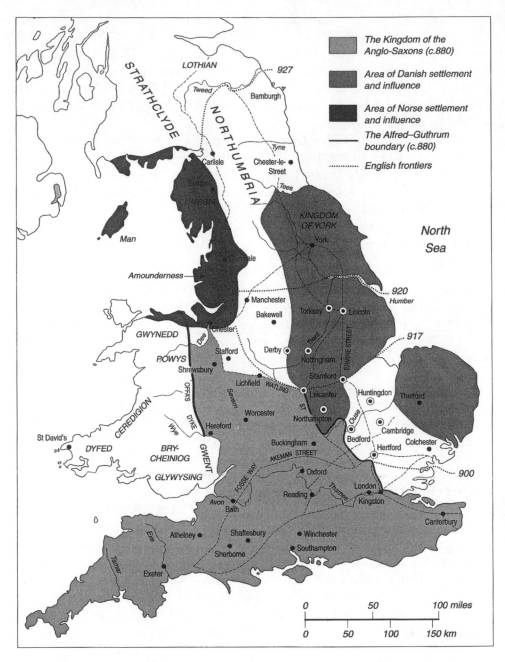

Figure 14.1 Anglo-Saxon England, late ninth century (from M. Lapidge (ed.) (1999) *The Blackwell Encyclo-paedia of Anglo-Saxon England.* Oxford: Blackwell; map 11, "The Kingdom of the Anglo-Saxons (c. 900)")

so distinctive about Alfred's kingship and royal government" (Keynes 2003: 175). But he had to build his scribal centers from the ground up, because when he took the throne Alfred claims he found the state of learning in a deplorable condition. Reaching outside of Wessex he attracted to his court an impressive collection of scholars from Mercia and Gaul. He also recruited Asser, a Welsh monk who wrote a Latin *Life of King Alfred*, which provides a wealth of information about the king's life and his reign.

One of Alfred's greatest innovations, however, was his promotion of English as a *written* language. From our perspective today the advantages of using the vernacular may seem obvious, but to Alfred's contemporaries literacy was primarily restricted to Latin, so his decision to elevate Old English must have seemed unconventional. The "Alfredian Canon" includes the Anglo-Saxon Chronicle, a group of annals that derive from a common source in the early 890s; it also includes translations from three Latin texts: Bede's *Ecclesiastical History*, the Orosius's *Seven Books of Histories against the Pagans*, and Gregory the Great's *Dialogues*. Of these we know the translator of only the *Dialogues*, a Mercian scholar named Werferth. Alfred himself, however, translated Augustine's *Soliloquies*, Boethius's *Consolation of Philosophy*, Gregory's *Pastoral Care* (*Regula Pastoralis*), and the first fifty Psalms; he also compiled a law code in Old English, for which he wrote a preface (Bately 2003; but now see Godden 2007). In a letter sent with his translation of *Pastoral Care*, Alfred sketches a brief history of the decline of learning in his kingdom and his steps to redress it, including the translation of those texts "most necessary for all people to know." The same passage outlines a program to teach lay people how to read, thus opening up the advantages of literacy beyond the ranks of the clergy.

Such royal attention gave impetus to developing the conventions of Old English prose, which were neither those of the spoken language nor those of Latin. With no prose models to guide them, Alfred and his fellow translators had to forge new practices, at times with happier results than others. Many of the early Chronicle entries, for example, lack syntactic complexity; and the anonymous translator of Bede's *History* often hews awkwardly close to the Latin syntax (Donoghue 2004: 101–3). But many passages in these and the other Alfredian texts display an increasing confidence in the new medium, without which the triumphs of Ælfric's and Wulfstan's prose in the following centuries could not have taken place.

While the conventions of verse were established well before those of prose, we know comparatively little about the state of poetry before 900 because few early texts survive. Most of the surviving 30,000 lines of Old English verse are preserved in six manuscripts dating from the mid-tenth century or later, and most of those poems concern religious topics (see LATE OLD ENGLISH). While untold numbers of poems were preserved in memory, how many were ever transcribed? When Alfred was a boy, according to Asser's biography, his mother awarded him a book of Old English poems because he had memorized its contents. Was this book an anomaly? We will never know, but many poems extant today must have been transcribed from earlier exemplars. What seems clear is that the genre of poetry favored anonymous authorship, oral techniques of composition, and transmission by memory.

References and Further Reading

Bately, J. (2003). The Alfredian canon revisited: one hundred years on. In T. Reuter (ed.), *Alfred the Great* (pp. 107–20). Aldershot: Ashgate.

Donoghue, D. (2004). *Old English Literature, A Short Introduction.* Oxford: Blackwell.

Godden, M. (2007). Did King Alfred write anything? *Medium Ævum* 76: 1–23.

Hogg, R. M. (1992). Phonology and morphology. In R. M. Hogg (ed.), *The Cambridge History of the English Language, Vol. 1: The Beginnings to 1066* (pp. 67–167). Cambridge: Cambridge University Press.

Keynes, S. (2003). The power of the written word: Alfredian England 871–999. In T. Reuter (ed.), *Alfred the Great* (pp. 175–97). Aldershot: Ashgate.

Keynes, S. & Lapidge, M. (eds. and trans.) (1983). *Alfred the Great.* London: Penguin.

McClure, J. & Collins, R. (eds. & trans.) (1999). *Ecclesiastical History of the English People.* New edn. Oxford: Oxford University Press.

Mitchell, B. & Robinson, F. C. (2001). *A Guide to Old English.* 6th edn. Oxford: Blackwell.

O'Donnell, D. P. (2005). *Cædmon's Hymn.* Woodbndge: D. S. Brewer.

Reuter, T. (ed.) (2003). *Alfred the Great: Papers from the Eleventh-Centenary Conferences.* Aldershot: Ashgate.

Robinson, F. C. & Stanley, E. G. (eds.) (1991). *Old English Verse Texts from Many Sources: A Comprehensive Collection.* Copenhagen: Rosenkilde and Bagger.

Toon, T. E. (1983). *The Politics of Early Old English Sound Change.* New York: Academic Press.

Whitelock, D., et al. (eds. & trans.) (1961). *Anglo-Saxon Chronical: A Revised Translation.* New Brunswick: Rutgers University Press.

15
Late Old English (899–1066)

Mechthild Gretsch

The outer limits of the period we are concerned with in this chapter are determined by two historical events: the death of King Alfred the Great and the Norman Conquest. It is not unusual to define periods in the history of a language by historical events, but it is less often the case that linguistic history, historical events, and the intellectual climate in which they unfolded are considered in their interactions. It is an approach which will be adopted here. The history of a language cannot be adequately written by describing exclusively its sound shifts, the development of its morphological and syntactical subsystems, and the changes which occurred in its lexicon – important as these aspects no doubt are when reviewing the history of English or of any other language. But we will have to bear in mind that language in its spoken and written form at a given time plays a crucial part in the culture of its speakers at that time, that feelings of group identity or national identity were often forged in a decisive way by the bond of a common language, and that, especially in the early periods, linguistic phenomena may relate to political situations, or to a scholarly and/or political interest taken in the state of a language, to a degree that these phenomena cannot be sufficiently understood in terms of purely linguistic criteria. We also have to bear in mind that English was not the only language in which texts were written in Anglo-Saxon England. As everywhere in the medieval West, Latin was the prime language of religion, scholarship, and literature, enjoying unrivalled prestige. In Anglo-Saxon England in the tenth and the early eleventh centuries, however, there is a characteristic tendency (unique in a European context) to supplement Latin texts with texts written in the vernacular in practically all domains where Latin had been prevalent. The implication of this situation is that the shaping influence of Latin (and contemporary Anglo-Latin in particular) on the various linguistic and stylistic levels of Old English merits our close attention. With these preliminaries in mind, let us now turn to the beginning of our period.

No pronounced caesura was marked by the death of King Alfred on October 26, 899, neither in the affairs of the state, nor, for all we know, in the prevailing

intellectual climate, and certainly not in matters of language. The political entity, the Kingdom of the Anglo-Saxons, created by Alfred in the wake of his decisive victory over Guthrum's Danish army at Edington, in 878, continued to exist (within ever-expanding boundaries) under his son and successor Edward the Elder (899–924) and during the first years of the reign of his grandson Æthelstan (924–39), until, during this reign, it was succeeded by a larger and more ambitious polity: the first "Kingdom of all England." During the latter part of Alfred's reign, the Kingdom of the Anglo-Saxons comprised Wessex, Sussex, Kent, and that part of the former Mercian kingdom which had not succumbed to the Danish attacks; towards the end of King Edward's reign its territory appears to have embraced most of England south of the Humber. This emerging late-ninth- and early-tenth-century Southumbrian polity very possibly had important philological implications.

The assumption that no marked change occurred in the intellectual preoccupations after King Alfred's death and throughout Edward the Elder's reign rests decisively on manuscript evidence. We have no knowledge how soon after the king's death Alfred's circle of scholars dispersed and whether any of the "Alfredian" texts was composed after 899, but it is important to note that two of the four manuscripts which traditionally have been assumed to represent Alfredian (that is Early West Saxon) English were wholly or partly written during Edward's reign, presumably at some point in the 920s. These manuscripts comprise the two oldest texts of Alfred's translation of Pope Gregory's *Regula pastoralis*, datable to the last decade of the ninth century; the A-version of the Anglo-Saxon Chronicle in its earlier parts (up to and including the annal for 920); and the earliest manuscript of the translation of Orosius's *Historiae aduersus paganos*. The Orosius and the annals 892–920 of the Chronicle are datable to the 920s (the earlier annals are datable to s. ix/x), and both texts were written in the same scriptorium (probably located at Winchester) and presumably by the same scribe. Also during the 920s this scribe very possibly wrote most of the text in Oxford, Bodleian Library, Junius 27, a Latin psalter with a continuous gloss in Old English. We may add, therefore, the Junius Psalter with its Old English gloss to the four received manuscript witnesses to Early West Saxon English.

It has long been noted that a characteristic feature of the four received witnesses to Early West Saxon is a substantial admixture of Anglian dialect forms, and these are duly recorded in our standard grammars of Old English. Various explanations have been adduced for this pronounced Anglian admixture, such as the linguistic influence of King Alfred's literary helpers of Mercian extraction, Mercian spelling conventions, or reflexes from West Saxon subdialects, where those Anglian forms were supposed to have been indigenous. None of these explanations is wholly satisfactory. Could the four Mercian helpers really have exerted such a pervasive influence on the language as is testified (incompletely, we must assume) by the chance survival of the Early West Saxon manuscripts, especially when we reflect that a substantial part of these manuscripts was written during the later years of King Edward's reign, when (with one possible exception) none of these Mercian scholars will still have been alive? How

likely is the adoption of "Mercian spelling conventions" (for which there is no hard evidence) in West Saxon texts, when a close reproduction of spoken sounds seems to have been axiomatic for most Old English scribes? And are we to assume that most of the scribes and authors of the Early West Saxon texts came from the West Saxon–Mercian borderlands, where West Saxon subdialects, in which Anglian forms could have been indigenous, would have to be located?

A different, and perhaps more convincing, explanation may be offered by a closer look at the fifth of the Early West Saxon manuscripts: the Junius Psalter. It is an explanation which takes us back to the political order of the 920s, when the Junius Psalter was written: the Kingdom of the Anglo-Saxons. The Junius gloss is a copy of the first surviving Old English psalter gloss, preserved in London, BL, Cotton Vespasian A. i and dated s. ix^{med}. Interestingly, the Junius gloss is a comprehensive "West-Saxonization" of the Vespasian gloss, which is one of our few representatives of the Mercian dialect. The Junius glossator's transcription of his Mercian exemplar into his own dialect is pervasive and pertains to the phonological and the lexicological level; but it is not entirely systematic. Often, Anglian dialect features remain untouched, such as Anglian forms of *i*-mutation (e.g., *fœran* instead of West Saxon *feran* 'to go') or Anglian dialect words, such as *leoran* 'to go' or *æswic* 'deceit'.

In short, the Junius gloss throws into much sharper relief than the other Early West Saxon manuscripts the linguistic situation prevailing in early tenth-century Winchester, the political center of the Kingdom of the Anglo-Saxons. If, as seems clear, the purpose of the gloss was to transcribe a Mercian exemplar into the West Saxon dialect, why is such tolerance shown towards Anglian forms and words, which no doubt the glossator had recognized as Anglianisms, since he eliminated them in many of their occurrences? The answer may be that this reflects a situation in which the West Saxon political élite saw reason to respect Mercian attitudes. Mercia was the junior partner in the Kingdom of the Anglo-Saxons, but Mercians were prominent in Edward's court circles, as they had been in Alfred's. The Anglo-Saxon Chronicle, in spite of the chroniclers' attempts to glorify the West Saxon dynasty and in spite of a rather moderate interest in Mercian internal affairs, reveals no anti-Mercian bias. Moreover, there are clear indications that in leading West Saxon circles a certain prestige seems to have been conceded to Mercian scholarship, the most prominent of these indications being King Alfred's famous remark that, in the early years of his reign, Mercia was the only place where he had encountered some Latin learning and some expertise in rendering Latin texts into the vernacular. The mélange of West Saxon and Anglian dialect forms which is shown (albeit in varying degrees) in the five Early West Saxon manuscripts would sit squarely with the political and intellectual ambience I have briefly touched upon. What is not clear, in the present stage of our knowledge, is whether this dialect mix was consciously produced, perhaps at royal instigation and for political reasons, or whether it simply mirrors the political, social, and linguistic reality obtaining during Edward's reign, at least in the royal entourage, where numerous Mercians, alongside native West Saxons, attended to their various

military, administrative, ecclesiastical, and scholarly duties. Whatever the answer may be, in these Early West Saxon manuscripts we meet for the first time in the history of English a supradialectal language, which, though not a standard, reflects in one way or another the contemporary political order. An admixture of Mercian dialect forms remains noticeable in basically West Saxon manuscripts up to the last quarter of the tenth century. We will have to bear this in mind when we come to consider the rise of Standard Old English.

Standard Old English – its origin, nature, and dissemination – is one of the two phenomena which loom large in any discussion of Late Old English; the second of these phenomena is known by the term "Winchester vocabulary." Both phenomena have in common a concern for forging and refining the vernacular, but they originated in quite different political and intellectual circumstances. Let us first consider the Winchester vocabulary. Beginning with two works which probably originated in the 940s and which are attributed to one of the principal proponents of the Benedictine reform, Æthelwold, bishop of Winchester (963–84), a group of texts shows a pronounced tendency in a number of semantic fields to prefer certain words, the "Winchester words," to their synonyms. The two early texts are the interlinear gloss to the psalter in London, BL, Royal 2. B. V and the translation of the *Regula Sancti Benedicti*; to the later group belong the works of Ælfric and about ten late-tenth- or early-eleventh-century prose texts or continuous interlinear glosses. All these texts can be shown, on grounds other than philological ones, to have some connection with Winchester. Just one example must suffice to give a glimpse of how Winchester usage functions: for Latin *ecclesia* in the abstract sense 'the Catholic Church' the Winchester word would be *gelaþung* and the non-Winchester synonyms would be *cirice* or *gesamnung*. Like *gelaþung*, the majority of the Winchester synonyms pertain to the language of the Christian religion; further examples are: *cyðere* 'martyr', *miht* 'virtue; strength, power', *ege* 'the fear of the Lord', *behreowsung* 'repentance', *wuldorbeag* 'crown' (in a metaphorical sense: 'crown of eternal life' etc.), and the word-family *modig* for the concept of *superbia*, 'sinful pride'. The implication of this is of course that Winchester usage was introduced and established to reproduce Latin Christian terminology and that it is, therefore, a stylistic rather than a linguistic phenomenon, and cannot be adequately assessed in terms of dialect vocabulary. Interestingly, in the case of *gelaþung* 'the Catholic Church', authors employing Winchester words are in a position to distinguish lexically between the two meanings which are covered by one word, *ecclesia*, in Latin: in their usage, *cirice* 'church' would be the word denoting the church building. This and other such examples betray an intense scholarly preoccupation with a precise rendering of important Christian concepts, and occasionally greater lexical precision was achieved than was possible in Latin. Close analysis of the Winchester words further reveals that they often respond to prevailing political and intellectual conditions. Thus, there are intricate relationships (which space forbids tracing here) between the Winchester term *wuldorbeag* 'crown (of eternal life etc.)' and contemporary political reality (where, from the reign of Æthelstan onwards, crowns were beginning to play an ever-increasing role in the coronation and the portraiture

of kings), psalm exegesis, Benedictine liturgy, and the tenth-century iconography of crowns.

To put it briefly: in their sum, Winchester words reveal the active interest of the circle of scholars responsible for them in the lexical structure of the vernacular, in the resourcefulness of Old English word-formation and in the interface between words and ideas. Who were these scholars? The established terminology points to Winchester in the late tenth century; for all we know, the supreme intellectual center in late Anglo-Saxon England, and the only center for which – in Bishop Æthelwold's famous cathedral school at the Old Minster – an intense interest in working with and refining the vernacular is amply attested. But we have seen that Winchester words make their first appearance long before Æthelwold became bishop there (in 963), namely in texts dating from the 940s and associated with him. This takes us back to the circle of the new Benedictines, gathering around Dunstan (the later archbishop of Canterbury) and Æthelwold during their years at Glastonbury, eagerly pursuing their scholarly interests there. These interests did not only embrace the study of patristic authors, but also of Latin grammar and metrics, and of Aldhelm (d. 709 or 710), the most famous Anglo-Latin proponent of the hermeneutic style (see below), who was to emerge from these studies as the favorite curriculum author in Late Anglo-Saxon schools.

If we want to understand why the earliest practitioners of Winchester usage revealed such an ingrained interest in words, attempting to differentiate in a sophisticated fashion some of the key terminology of the Christian belief, in a language that was still in its intellectual infancy, we have to go back still beyond Glastonbury to the court of King Æthelstan (924–39). This court culture was permeated with imperial aspirations, here apparent for the first time in English history and encouraged by the unification of England under West Saxon supremacy in 927 and by the triumphant assertion of this supremacy in 934 and 937 against a powerful northern alliance. Furthermore, King Æthelstan's court was a meeting point for numerous foreign scholars, who contributed decisively to its intellectual life. In this ambience young Dunstan and Æthelwold spent their formative years, and it left an indelible impression on the future leaders of the Benedictine reform. With regard to Winchester vocabulary it is probably significant that the Late Anglo-Saxon flair for the hermeneutic style first becomes tangible at King Æthelstan's court. This Latin style, which was practiced in England from the 930s onwards to the exclusion almost of any other style, is character-ized by an ostentatious display of unusual, even arcane, vocabulary. The hermeneutic style thus reveals a fascination with words: the vocabulary rather than the syntax is the hallmark of this style. There is no direct link between the hermeneutic style and Winchester vocabulary: Winchester words do not create a hermeneutic style in English. But the Glastonbury circle (and later, the Winchester school) by their active interest in Latin vocabulary, by their training in searching glossaries and the works of specific authors for recherché and unusual words, and by their training in coining learned and flamboyant Latin terms, may well have been prompted to enrich the vernacular through their lexical experiments with Winchester vocabulary.

We may now turn, in conclusion, to the phenomenon of Standard Old English. The term refers to phonological and morphological forms of Late West Saxon, occurring in a regularized orthography in manuscripts dating from the late tenth to the early twelfth century, and originating in all parts of England, not only the West Saxon dialect area. As a corollary of these standardizing tendencies, the merger of unaccented vowels (a, e, o, u) in inflexional endings in indistinct /ə/, occurring in the course of the tenth century, is largely masked in Old English texts attempting to conform to the standard. The standard thus presents an inflexional system which no longer existed in spoken English, not even in spoken West Saxon. It seems clear, therefore, that Standard Old English was confined to writing, and that no standardization and concomitant exportation of West Saxon forms took place on the level of spoken English. It needs stressing that the systematic Anglo-Saxon endeavors to produce a written standard have no parallel in any of the European vernaculars for many centuries to come. As a plausible model for such endeavors we should, once again, turn to Latin. In Medieval Latin, too, a written standard existed, alongside numerous regional varieties of the spoken language. Furthermore, the practitioners of Standard Old English seem to have attached more importance to the representation of a correct and consistent inflexional morphology than to a rigorous consistency in the orthography of stressed vowels. This again points to Medieval Latin, where some amount of variation is found in the writing of vowels and consonants, but inflexional morphology is left largely untouched by such spelling vagaries.

Once again: who were the scholars who developed the program for standardizing English? If King Æthelstan's court was an inspirational force for the Winchester vocabulary, could not the same be assumed for the notion of Standard Old English? The evidence points away from such an assumption. Manuscripts exhibiting the phonological and morphological forms of Standard Old English do not appear before the last quarter of the tenth century. Furthermore, a strong Mercian element makes itself felt in Æthelstan's entourage. He therefore probably saw no reason to disapprove of the supradialectal literary language which had developed during King Edward's reign, and to encourage an exclusively West Saxon literary language. We have to go to the early 970s, the concluding years of King Edgar's reign (957/9–75) to find the political and intellectual climate in which the notion of Standard Old English would sit well. It was only during these years that a kingdom of all England, unified under West Saxon rule, gained general recognition as a stable political entity and became established in the awareness of its political and intellectual élite. This new awareness was accompanied by strong normative tendencies in various domains. Space permits mention of only the two most important manifestations of these tendencies: first, the promulgation of the *Regularis concordia*, in about 973, with the aim to regulate life and liturgy in the monasteries all over the country. Its declared principle for such regulation was: "one Rule, one country." Also in about 973, was launched what is known as "King Edgar's reform of coinage," and what was a drastic change in the monetary system of England, whereby a uniform currency was introduced in the entire kingdom, which admitted no local variation in the design of coins.

Even from these cursory remarks it is obvious that a standardized form of English would be wholly consonant with the normative tendencies of the early 970s. It is also obvious that, as with the *Regularis concordia* or the reform of coinage, the implementation of a linguistic uniformity all over England would have been dependent on a strong central authority, in other words, the king. But King Edgar himself and his political, administrative, or military advisers would have been unlikely to conceive the idea of a standardized vernacular and to select the linguistic forms for its implementation. A scholarly cast of mind and an interest in working with the English language was needed for such a project. This is where Bishop Æthelwold and his, meanwhile, Winchester circle and school enter the tenth-century linguistic scene for a second time: Æthelwold had been Edgar's teacher, and he was one of his intimate advisers. We may, therefore, be permitted to assume that in the promotion of Standard Old English Æthelwold and Edgar collaborated closely, and that Æthelwold's school at the Old Minster was the home of England's first standardized language.

Standard Old English and Winchester vocabulary aim to forge and refine a language with only a nascent literary culture after the model of the most prestigious and sophisticated language in the European West. They thus reveal the confidence which scholars in late Anglo-Saxon England placed in the potential of their vernacular to be developed into a medium of scholarly discourse, which, eventually, would be on a par with Latin. We may assume that such confidence was made possible by the Alfredian literary and linguistic legacy, which decisively shaped the early decades of the tenth century. We may also assume that this confidence was boosted by the periods of political grandeur which England enjoyed in the tenth century, by the process of its unification, and by the scholarly patronage of two tenth-century kings of all England, Æthelstan and Edgar.

REFERENCES AND FURTHER READING

Gneuss, H. (1972). The origin of Standard Old English and Æthelwold's school at Winchester. *Anglo-Saxon England*, 1, 63–83; rptd. with add. Gneuss, H. (1996). *Language and History in Early England*. Aldershot: Ashgate, no. I.

Gretsch, M. (1999). *The Intellectual Foundations of the English Benedictine Reform*. Cambridge Studies in Anglo-Saxon England 25. Cambridge: Cambridge University Press.

Gretsch, M. (2000). The Junius Psalter gloss: its historical and intellectual context. *Anglo-Saxon England*, 29, 85–121.

Gretsch, M. (2001). Winchester Vocabulary and Standard Old English: the vernacular in Late Anglo-Saxon England. The T. N. Toller Memorial Lecture 2000, *Bulletin of the John Rylands University Library of Manchester*, 83, 41–87.

Hofstetter, W. (1988). Winchester and the standardization of Old English vocabulary. *Anglo-Saxon England*, 17, 139–61.

Keynes, S. (1995). England, 700–900. In R. McKitterick (ed.), *The New Cambridge Medieval History, Vol. 2: c. 700–c. 900* (pp. 18–42). Cambridge: Cambridge University Press.

Keynes, S. (1999). England, 900–1016. In T. Reuter (ed.), *The New Cambridge Medieval History, Vol. 3: c. 900–c. 1024* (pp. 456–84). Cambridge: Cambridge University Press.

Yorke, B. (ed.) (1988). *Bishop Æthelwold: His Career and Influence*. Woodbridge: Boydell.

16
Topics in Old English Dialects

Lucia Kornexl

Old English dialectology can boast of a long and fruitful tradition. As early as 1705, George Hickes in his *Thesaurus Grammatico-Criticus et Archaeologicus* (I, 87f.) identified a distinctly Northern English variety in the areas influenced by the viking invasions. Systematic research into the linguistic diversification of pre-Conquest England started in the second half of the nineteenth century. Since then, Old English dialect studies have made considerable progress. At the same time, there has been a growing awareness of the complexity of the field and of the limitations imposed upon modern researchers by the great distance in time and the fragmentary nature of the extant material.

The Old English Dialect Names and Their Significance

Grammars and handbooks of Old English usually distinguish four major dialects, roughly located in the following regions:

- Northumbrian, north of the Humber.
- Mercian, in the Midlands, stretching from the Humber to the Thames.
- Kentish, in the Southeast, covering Kent and Surrey.
- West Saxon, in the South and Southwest of England.

Due to a number of common dialect features, Northumbrian and Mercian have traditionally been classed together as Anglian.

The four major varieties listed above are named after four early Anglo-Saxon kingdoms, while the terms "Anglian" and "Saxon" refer to the largest tribal groups among the fifth-century Germanic invaders from the Continent. Being both suggestive and notoriously hard to contextualize, these dialect names are scarcely apt to capture the complex linguistic reality in Britain during the more than six centuries from the

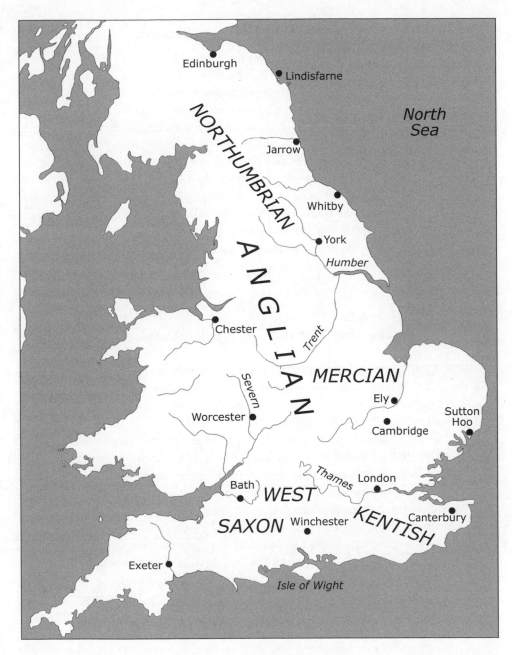

Figure 16.1 Dialect map of Anglo-Saxon England (from B. Mitchell & F. Robinson (2007) *A Guide to Old English*, 7th edn. Oxford: Blackwell; "Map of Anglo-Saxon England," p. viii)

Germanic invasion to the Norman Conquest (cf. Hogg 1998). After all, political and linguistic boundaries in Anglo-Saxon England were by no means coextensive and moved over time, quite independently of each other. Neither can the relationship between tribal and speech communities be determined in any exact way. Among the established varieties, Kentish and Mercian have proved especially difficult to define. Modern scholars in search of a more refined and more coherent nomenclature are, however, subject to much the same material restrictions as the pioneers of Old English dialectology, who did invaluable work in charting the linguistic map of Anglo-Saxon England. It therefore does not come by surprise that, despite many reservations, the traditional classification is still almost universally adhered to. The ongoing critical discussion about the aptness of the conventional designations and their territorial significance has nevertheless helped to sharpen the theoretical outlook of the discipline and enhanced its critical potential.

The Origin of the Old English Dialects

The dialectal diversity of Old English becomes apparent in the written material available from the early eighth century onwards. When and where these distinctions originated is, however, a longstanding and much disputed question. Did the Germanic invaders bring over their different varieties from the Continent, or are these varieties basically a post-migration development? Bede's famous account of the tribal settlement of England in his *Historia ecclesiastica* (I, 15), which has frequently been cited in this context, does not really yield relevant information with respect to linguistic conditions, because the three powerful groups of Germanic settlers Bede mentions by name – the Angles, the Saxons, and the Jutes – are assigned to geographically rather than to linguistically defined areas (see EARLY OLD ENGLISH).

More recent research into the matter has shed new light on the relationship between the Continental Germanic languages and the Old English dialects, though the subject remains a controversial one. Thus on the basis of a newly discovered manuscript – the so-called "Straubing *Heliand* fragment" – special lexical affiliations between the Old Saxon language of this text and the Anglian dialect of Old English have been postulated (Korhammer 1980), while from a morphological and phonological point of view such a connection has explicitly been denied (Nielsen 1991). Another hypothesis holds that early dialectal differences in Anglo-Saxon England result from the chronological differences between an earlier, "Saxon," and a later, "Anglian" migration wave from the same Continental homeland in Northern Germany (Kortlandt 1986). However great or small the amount of variation that was imported from the Continent, it is safe to assume that extralinguistic conditions in Britain such as geographical barriers, tribal affiliations, and political circumstances exerted a shaping influence on the development of the linguistic landscape there.

The Character and Distribution of the Surviving Materials

In comparison to other Germanic languages, Old English is remarkably well attested. The extant documents are, however, very unevenly distributed over place and time. Thus one of the most conspicuous blind spots on the dialect map of Anglo-Saxon England is East Anglia – the area which at the end of the Middle English period was to assume a crucial role in the formation of modern Standard English. Besides, the surviving materials do not always readily yield comparable data so that only an incomplete picture of the dialect situation in Old English emerges.

For early Northumbrian, we have merely a few brief texts, mainly of the eighth century, such as the runic inscriptions on the Ruthwell Cross and on the Franks Casket, and the evidence contained in the early Latin manuscripts of Bede's *Historia ecclesiastica* – the famous hymn by the lay poet Cædmon and a number of place and personal names. Later Northumbrian is preserved in three interlinear glosses added to the Latin texts of the *Lindisfarne Gospels*, to parts of the *Rushworth Gospels* (Ru¹), and to the *Durham Ritual* during the second half of the tenth century. Largely unaffected by the prevailing trend towards standardization, these documents also provide valuable insights into the leveling of inflexional endings which was operative in all varieties of Late Old English but seems to have been most pronounced in the linguistically more progressive areas of viking settlement in the northern parts of the country.

Mercian is again chiefly evidenced by gloss materials such as the late seventh-century *Épinal Glossary* and the early ninth-century *Corpus Glossary*, and by the interlinear glosses to the *Vespasian Psalter* (ninth century) and the non-Northumbrian sections of the *Rushworth Gospels* (Ru²; later tenth century). The fact that during the late ninth and well into the tenth century Mercian exported its features into West Saxon texts has been taken as an indication of its temporary status as a prestige dialect, boosted by linguistic and extralinguistic factors that still await clarification (see LATE OLD ENGLISH).

Kentish is only sparsely attested by some eighth- and ninth-century charters and three witnesses from the tenth century, transmitted together in one manuscript (BL Cotton Vespasian D.vi): the *Kentish Hymn*, the *Kentish Psalm*, and the interlinear glosses to the *Kentish Proverbs*. These glosses exhibit a considerable admixture of West Saxon forms, while the charters show a distinctly Mercian influence. Conversely, sporadic Kenticisms have been traced in quite a number of Old English texts and manuscripts of different dialectal shape.

West Saxon is by far the best documented of all Old English varieties, though we have scarcely any evidence from before ca. 900. There is a conventional distinction between Early West Saxon, represented by a group of late ninth and early tenth-century manuscripts that are associated with the literary activities of King Alfred and his court, and Late West Saxon, which begins to take shape in the latter half of the tenth century and is considered to be represented most purely in the works of Ælfric,

the eminent Late Old English prose writer (ca. 1000). The kind of straightforward evolutionary development suggested by the terminological contrast between "early" and "late" West Saxon is, however, not borne out by the surviving material. Matters are further complicated by the fact that during the latter half of the tenth century written West Saxon became increasingly subject to conscious regulation and turned into a supradialectal literary norm – a *Schriftsprache* – adhered to by scribes all over the country (see LATE OLD ENGLISH).

Defining Old English Dialects on the Basis of the Available Evidence

With reference to Old English, the term "dialect" is normally used in the core sense of a regionally distinctive variety, because we lack the necessary amount and range of data for a systematic study of other types of variation such as socially determined "class dialects" or language use according to variables like age, gender, education, and occupation. The extant documents were produced by a small élite of scribes working mainly in ecclesiastical centers and monastic scriptoria. But even for manuscripts that can be localized with reasonable certainty, dialectal attribution remains difficult: manuscripts as well as scribes could travel between different dialect areas and a scribe's dialect may have considerably differed from that of the text he copied. The degree to which local peculiarities, scriptorial decisions, or individual habits shaped a particular text – often in a process of multiple copying – is usually beyond reconstruction. The lack of internal consistency found in quite a number of Old English texts from different areas also reminds us that dialect mixing must have been just as normal a part of the linguistic reality of Anglo-Saxon England as it is of modern speech communities in contact with each other. New approaches developed in modern dialectology, with both synchronic and diachronic orientation, offer an opportunity to gain new insights from the available data. Valuable impulses have, for example, come from the theoretical and methodological innovations of the *Linguistic Atlas of Late Mediaeval English* and from current work on its companion piece, the *Linguistic Atlas of Early Middle English*, which will eventually bridge the gap between Old and Middle English dialectology.

Attempts to build up a more precise picture of dialectal variation in Old English include the study of place-names and the search for distinctive variables in the boundary clauses of Anglo-Saxon land charters that can be compared to corresponding forms in literary texts (see Kitson 1995; for a current project to collect these descriptions of the boundaries of land units in a web-driven database, see www.langscape.org.uk). As potentially datable and localizable sources, charters are also expected to yield information on the nature of the spoken dialects of the respective regions. The linguistic value of the Anglo-Saxon charter evidence must, however, be viewed with due caution, as most of these documents are only preserved in much later copies and need not necessarily be representative of the language of the area to which they relate in geographical terms.

Old English dialect distinctions have primarily been established on the basis of spelling variants that are assigned specific phonetic values. The underlying assumption is that in the absence of a written norm the average Old English scribe would aim at a faithful reproduction of spoken sounds, though on the basis of exclusively written sources the relationship between speech and writing can of course only approximately be defined. Still, phonological features have traditionally been regarded as particularly significant dialect markers in historical dialectology, not least because they are much more frequent and more easily traceable than instances of morphological, lexical, or syntactic variation. The provision of the complete corpus of Old English texts in a searchable electronic form by the *Dictionary of Old English* Project (see www.doe.utoronto.ca) has substantially aided scholarly research on an extended range of supposed dialect variables on all linguistic levels.

Old English Word Geography

Research in the dialect vocabulary of Old English has mainly focused on lexical differences between Anglian and West Saxon. Pertinent studies have shown that identifying dialect words is a laborious task that requires careful diagnostic work: lexical and semantic considerations have to be supported by other linguistic criteria and by contextual information about the origin, contents, and transmission of the relevant texts in order to avoid circular reasoning. Distributional patterns for particular Old English vocabulary items have in fact quite frequently been found to cut across traditional dialect boundaries. This accords with the findings of modern dialectology that no two linguistic features are fully identical in their geographical extension. To arrive at a more precise classification of the Old English lexicon, it is also important to develop reliable criteria that help to distinguish genuine regionalisms from words that are marked in a different way, for instance as reflections of older usage (archaisms) or of stylistic preferences (see A HISTORY OF THE ENGLISH LEXICON).

The complex patterning of semantically related lexical choices has, for example, been demonstrated in a comprehensive analysis of the Old English vocabulary for "pride" (Schabram 1965). For the concept of "sinful pride," expressed by Latin *superbia* – the first and worst of the seven deadly sins – a basic distinction between Anglian *oferhygd* and West Saxon *ofermod* emerged, while the language of Ælfric and other Late West Saxon texts related to Winchester exhibit a striking preference for *modignes* and other members of the *mod* word-family. This so-called "Winchester vocabulary" has been shown to be the result of a deliberate attempt at standardization mainly guided by stylistic considerations (see LATE OLD ENGLISH). The question to what extent this educated written usage of terms that mainly relate to the sphere of religious culture is indebted to the local dialect of Winchester and other Southern English subdialects has been the subject of an intensive scholarly discussion (e.g., Seebold 1992; Kitson 2004).

The "Dialect" of Old English Poetry

Most of what survives of Old English poetry is preserved in the four great poetic manuscripts produced in the late tenth and early eleventh centuries. These verse texts show predominantly Late West Saxon traits, but they also contain quite a number of Anglian features. This led earlier scholars to the assumption that the bulk of Old English verse originated in Anglian territory, presumably prior to the viking invasions, and received its West Saxon coloring through transliteration by scribes who were trained in the Late West Saxon prestige variety. Factual support for this hypothesis was, for example, found in the transmission history of the earliest known English poem, Cædmon's hymn, which survives in multiple copies both in the poet's native Northumbrian dialect and in later West-Saxonized versions (see EARLY OLD ENGLISH: O'Donnell 2005).

In a seminal article, Kenneth Sisam (1953) rejected the view that virtually all early English poetry was Anglian and proposed the idea of a "general Old English poetic dialect" which he described as "artificial" and "archaic," with a common vocabulary of probably mixed origin and a conservative inflexional system. The notion of a "dialect" that was used by all Anglo-Saxon poets regardless of place and date stands in marked contrast to the usual understanding of the term sketched out above. Recent scholarship has criticized the liberal application of Sisam's hypothesis by some authors and especially by editors when confronted with the problem of determining the dialect status of heterogeneous Old English verse texts (e.g., Godden 1992; Megginson 1995). Though the existence of a distinctively poetic idiom and style is undisputed, the concept of a general poetic dialect remains open to question. The complex distribution of dialectal features in individual pieces of Old English verse and prose and between them offers a continued challenge for historical linguists in their search for a more adequate and more precise description of linguistic variation in Old English.

REFERENCES AND FURTHER READING

Campbell, A. (1959). Introduction. In *Old English Grammar* (pp. 1–11). Oxford: Clarendon Press.

Crowley, J. (1986). The study of Old English dialects. *English Studies*, 67, 97–112.

Godden, M. R. (1992). Literary language. In R. M. Hogg (ed.), *The Cambridge History of the English Language, Vol. 1: The Beginnings to 1066* (pp. 490–535). Cambridge: Cambridge University Press.

Hogg, R. M. (1992). Introduction. In *A Grammar of Old English, Vol. 1: Phonology* (pp. 1–9). Oxford: Blackwell.

Hogg. R. M. (1998). On the ideological boundaries of Old English dialects. In J. Fisiak & M. Krygier (eds.), *Advances in English Historical Linguistics (1996)* (pp. 107–18). New York: Mouton de Gruyter.

Kalbhen, U. (2003). Kentische Glossen und kentischer Dialekt im Altenglischen. Mit einer kommentierten Edition der altenglischen Glossen in der Handschrift London, British Libary, Cotton Vespasian D.vi. Frankfurt am Main: Lang.

Kitson, P. R. (1995). The nature of Old English dialect distributions, mainly as exhibited in

charter boundaries. In J. Fisiak (ed.), *Medieval Dialectology* (pp. 43–135). New York: Mouton de Gruyter.

Kitson, P. R. (2004). On margins of error in placing Old English literary dialects. In M. Dossena & R. Lass (eds.), *Methods and Data in English Historical Dialectology* (pp. 219–39). New York: Lang.

Korhammer, M. (1980). Altenglische Dialekte und der *Heliand. Anglia*, 98, 85–94.

Kortlandt, F. (1986). The origin of the Old English dialects. In D. Kastovsky & A. Szwedek (eds.), *Linguistics across Historical and Geographical Boundaries. In Honour of Jacek Fisiak on the Occasion of his Fiftieth Birthday. Vol. 1: Linguistic Theory and Historical Linguistics* (pp. 437–42). New York: Mouton de Gruyter.

McIntosh, A., Samuels, M. L., & Benskin, M. (eds.) (1986). General introduction. In *A Linguistic Atlas of Late Mediaeval English*. 4 vols. (Vol. 1, pp. 1–36). Aberdeen: Aberdeen University Press.

Megginson, D. (1995). The case against a 'general Old English poetic dialect'. In M. J. Toswell (ed.), *Prosody and Poetics in the Early Middle Ages: Essays in Honour of C. B. Hieatt* (pp. 117–32). Toronto: University of Toronto Press.

Nielsen, H. F. (1991). The Straubing Heliand-Fragment and the Old English dialects. In P. Sture Ureland & G. Broderick (eds.), *Language Contact in the British Isles: Proceedings of the Eighth International Symposium on Language Contact in Europe, Douglas, Isle of Man, 1988* (pp. 243–73). Tübingen: Niemeyer.

O'Donnell, D. P. (2005). *Cædmon's Hymn: A Multimedia Study, Edition and Archive*. Woodbridge: D. S. Brewer.

Sauer, H. (1992). Old English word geography: some problems and results. In W. G. Busse (ed.), *Anglistentag 1991 Düsseldorf: Proceedings* (pp. 307–26). Tübingen: Niemeyer.

Schabram, H. (1965). *Superbia: Studien zum altenglischen Wortschatz. Teil I: Die dialektale und zeitliche Verbreitung des Wortguts*. Munich: Fink.

Seebold, E. (1992). Kentish – and Old English texts from Kent. In M. Korhammer (ed.), *Words, Texts and Manuscripts: Studies in Anglo-Saxon Culture Presented to Helmut Gneuss on the Occasion of His Sixty-Fifth Birthday* (pp. 409–34). Woodbridge: D. S. Brewer.

Sisam, K. (1953). Dialect origins of the earlier Old English verse. In K. Sisam (ed.), *Studies in the History of Old English Literature* (pp. 119–39). Oxford: Clarendon Press.

Stanley, E. G. (1994). The dialect origins of Late Old English verse. *Poetica*, 42, 1–21.

Section 2
Middle English in History (1066–1485)

Introduction

The next three chapters concern the history of Middle English, a period that lasted approximately four hundred years from the late eleventh to the late fifteenth centuries. In this volume, 1066 is treated as a symbolic beginning of the period because of the significance of several events that took place in that year. In the fall of 1066, the last Anglo-Saxon king, Harold Godwineson, fought two battles. In the first, he defeated a Norwegian army at Stamford Bridge. In the second battle, fought at Hastings a few weeks later, Harold and his army were defeated by the Normans led by Duke William. These two battles virtually put an end to the Scandinavian ambition to reclaim the English throne. By this time, however, a large population of Scandinavians had long settled in northern England (see also EARLY OLD ENGLISH and LATE OLD ENGLISH). Their language, known collectively as Old Norse, subsequently seeped into the English vernacular and most likely gave momentum to the series of grammatical innovations that generally moved from north to south in the Middle English period (see also HISTORY OF ENGLISH MORPHOLOGY; HISTORY OF ENGLISH SYNTAX; A HISTORY OF THE ENGLISH LEXICON). With the arrival of the Normans, the ruling class of England became predominantly French speaking. English, though still spoken by the majority of the population, occupied the lower tier of the language pyramid. Confined to local function with limited usage, written English now reflected regional speech and relied on individual talent unbridled by regularization from higher authority.

When England became politically isolated from the Continent in the thirteenth century, however, more and more members of the ruling class turned to the insular vernacular. Consequently English was placed under French influences, absorbing Romance vocabulary and experimenting with continental poetic forms. The Gallicism known as the polite *ye* – in which second-person plural forms (*ye*, *you*, etc.) were used for the second-person singular (instead of *þou*, *þe*, etc.) to register deference – spread with remarkable rapidity and consistency (see EARLY MIDDLE ENGLISH). The cultural history of Middle English is a history of elaboration through which the language responded to the demand for a greater social application. Chaucer's reputation as a distinguished English author among his contemporaries and near contemporaries may largely come from his rhetorical elaboration upon the vernacular (see VARIETIES OF MIDDLE ENGLISH; also CHAUCER'S LITERARY ENGLISH).

In the late Middle English period a written standard began to develop in the metropole, where the original regional dialect was constantly modified by the dialects of new migrants. Writing in London during the late fourteenth century, Chaucer showed sensitivity to the way his work was copied by his scribe. During the earlier decades of the fifteenth century, a new London dialect was cultivated at Chancery for the production of governmental documents. This language of administration became a literary standard when William Caxton used it to print works of Chaucer, Malory, and other English authors (see LATE MIDDLE ENGLISH; also EARLY MODERN ENGLISH

PRINT CULTURE). While written English was being standardized, spoken English continued to accommodate diatopic diversity. Given the widening gap between written and spoken English in the fifteenth century, we may need to reconsider the tidy and simple diagram traditionally used to explain a series of phonetic changes known as the Great Vowel Shift (see PHONOLOGY: SEGMENTAL HISTORIES). The end of the Middle English period is set, again symbolically, in 1485 when the Wars of the Roses concluded with the ascension of the first Tudor king, Henry VII. Henry was also the first Welshman to assume the English throne (see also ENGLISH IN WALES).

Haruko Momma

17

Early Middle English (1066–ca. 1350)

Thorlac Turville-Petre

Speech and Writing

Following the Norman Conquest, England was a country with three main languages, and English was the least prestigious of the three. Before 1066 English coexisted with Latin, the language of the Church; after that it competed with an alternative vernacular, Norman French, which in England developed its own features as Anglo-Norman. The Normans represented a relatively small proportion of the population, but their language came to have a disproportionate impact upon society, since they were in positions of power. French terms began to infiltrate English as Norman lords married English ladies and employed English bailiffs with whom they needed to communicate if their estates were to be run effectively. Those who had estates across the Channel would have considered themselves as people of a Norman realm rather than specifically English until Normandy was lost to France in 1204, at which point they had to choose to commit themselves to one nation or the other. The aristocrats attached to the court, and those who, like a succession of English kings, took wives from the Continent, continued to speak French at some level well into the fourteenth century (Rothwell 1976).

As a written language English had to establish a role side by side with Latin and French. Before the Conquest royal documents were written in English, but the Normans had no tradition of writing documents in the vernacular and continued to use Latin. Not until the mid-thirteenth century does French become common for official documents, and not until the early fifteenth century does English make regular appearance as a language of official record (Clanchy 1993). Neither French nor English ever displaced Latin entirely in documentary use. Latin, always the language of monastic learning, particularly for writings aimed at a wider European readership, now also increased its hold as the learned language (Rigg 1992). In the twelfth century the Angevin empire ruled by the "English" king included all of western France from Normandy to Gascony and the court was truly international and constantly

peripatetic. Learned Latin authors wrote histories, epics, beast-fables, advice for both courtiers and recluses, lives of saints, satires, and works on law and politics, philosophy and theology.

The range of writings in Anglo-Norman matched and overlapped those in Latin to a considerable degree (Dean 1999). The differences are principally to be accounted for by the nature of the readership. Latin was learned and studied in the schools and universities in England and on the Continent. Most of those who had become proficient in Latin were those with a clerical education, and were consequently men, though women Latinists were not unknown. Those who read Latin had privileged access to a world of ancient writers as well as to the intellectual debates of the age. French was read by a wider range, including the laity from the upper social strata, both male and female. There is ample evidence for women as patrons of Anglo-Norman in the twelfth century.

Early Anglo-Norman writers focused on narratives of the pre-Conquest past: on histories of the ancient Britons and the Anglo-Saxons, on stories of English heroes and lives of Anglo-Saxon saints, initially regarded with contempt by the settlers but soon identified as part of their new cultural heritage (Crane 1986; Short 1991). Through such narratives the Normans, having redefined themselves as "English," appropriated an identity that linked them with the land and the traditions they had inherited from a past generation of heroes and saints.

Those with the ability and leisure to read and who could afford to own manuscripts were likely to opt for the languages that had status, Latin and French. Yet by the later thirteenth century, some preferred English and were finding French something of a struggle. At the same time as the first English translations of Anglo-Norman romances were appearing, Walter of Bibbesworth compiled a treatise designed to improve the French of those whose first language was English (Rothwell 1990). The practical value as well as the social cachet of French encouraged gentry families to brush up their language skills, even though English was their mother tongue. From this period also come manuscripts preserving texts in the three languages. It was a period when English texts were becoming much more numerous, but French and Latin were still understood and enjoyed widely enough to be preferred for many topics. Two case studies will demonstrate the importance of appreciating the trilingual context of early Middle English writings (Salter 1988).

Laȝamon's Brut

For the history of Britain from the earliest settlement until the domination of the Anglo-Saxons, the Middle Ages relied on Geoffrey of Monmouth's Latin *History of the Kings of Britain*, completed in 1136. With its account of the reign of King Arthur it became so popular that over two hundred copies still survive, so that its influence penetrated deeply into historical and non-historical works of the Middle Ages. It gave the British a noble Trojan ancestry and a glorious past, and although Geoffrey's

purpose was to serve the interests of his Norman patrons, his history could also be interpreted as an encouragement to the political aspirations of the Welsh and, by a blatant misappropriation of the legend, the English as well.

An early translator of Geoffrey's *History* was the Norman cleric Wace, completing his version in French couplets in 1155, expanding the work considerably, and romanticizing it by emphasizing contemporary chivalric interests, for example introducing the story of Arthur's creation of the Round Table. Wace's *Roman de Brut* is the direct source of Laȝamon's *Brut*, probably written around 1200, surviving in two late thirteenth-century manuscripts (Brook & Leslie 1963, 1978).

Laȝamon's is an extraordinary work, a highly ambitious recasting of its source. Nothing similar survives from the period, and although we may have lost other works that would set it in some context, it is doubtful that there was ever anything truly to compare with it. Its verse-form is an eclectic melding of the ancient alliterative line with French rhymed verse. The meter is so flexible that its features are difficult to analyze in a formal way, but the fundamental unit is the half-line, usually of two stresses, with alliteration and/or rhyme. Over long passages the meter is strangely hypnotic.

The vocabulary of the poem is also remarkable. By Laȝamon's time words of Norman origin were embedded in the English language, but they are scarcely present in Laȝamon's vocabulary, despite the fact that he was translating a French source. This must mean that words of Norman origin could still be identified and that Laȝamon deliberately excluded them in favor of Anglo-Saxon words. The most striking of these were drawn from the heroic vocabulary of Old English, such as (for "knight, man") *beorne, gume, kempe, leode, haleþe, rink, segge, scalc*; (for "people," "court") *hired, duȝeþe; blonke* for "horse," and *apele* for "noble." Laȝamon makes effective use of another notable feature of the Old English verse tradition, the poetic compound-noun, as *here-feng*, "battle-capture," i.e., "booty," *here-scrud*, "battle-garment," i.e., "armour," *leod-cwide*, "nation-language," i.e., "English," *leod-scome*, "national shame," *leod-swike*, "traitor to his country." This vocabulary is preserved in one manuscript, BL Cotton Caligula A.IX, but must have been recognized as a peculiar and archaic feature of Laȝamon's style, since it is revised wholesale in BL Cotton Otho C.XIII, where much of the distinctive vocabulary is removed and replaced by more commonplace words, sometimes of French derivation. Thus *rink, segge*, and *scalc* are replaced by *man* or *cniht*, *grith* by *pais* "peace," *leod-swike* by *wikede*, and so on (Cannon 1993; Stanley 1969).

In his choice of verse-form and vocabulary Laȝamon is writing English epic, an aspect of his work that is reinforced by other stylistic features. Just as *Beowulf* (and, for that matter, Homeric epic) does, he makes great use of the formula, a half-line consisting of a repeated expression or syntactic structure:

> Ærst sweor Arður, aðelest kingen (11,410)
> Al for Arður æiȝe, aðelest kingen (11,418)
> Hail seo þu, Arður, aðelest kinge (11,425)
> [*Ærst sweor* First swore; *aðelest kingen* noblest of kings; *æiȝe* respect for;
> *Hail seo þu* Greetings to you]

These expressions are formal signatures of epic style, where what matters about a hero is his heroic nature shared with other heroes throughout the ages, and where every villain is most hateful of all men, "laþest alre monne."

Another striking feature of Laȝamon's style is his use of poetic similes, some particularly elaborate and running over as many as 16 lines. These similes are prominent in the section of the poem dealing with Arthur's battles against the Saxons. Often they liken the combatants to animals, birds, or fish. So in one passage the Saxons wander like the crane in the moor-fen, pursued by hawks, attacked in the reeds by dogs, safe neither on land nor in water. In the end:

> Havekes hine smiteð, hundes hine biteð;
> þenne bið þe kinewurðe foȝel fæie on his siðe. (10,066–7)
> [Hawks strike him, hounds bite him; then the kingly bird is on the road to death.]

The inspiration must have been Latin heroic poetry, the classical epic of Virgil and Statius, as well as twelfth-century epics such as Walter of Châtillon's *Alexandreis* and other Latin poems praising rulers and their victories (Salter 1988: 48–70).

Drawing on models in English, Latin, and French, Laȝamon constructed a national epic with Arthur at its center, a war-leader from a heroic past. He was the first but not the last to fashion Arthur into a national hero, for kings from Edward I onwards used the example of Arthur to ratify their own ambitions. At the culmination of the story, as Arthur is ferried to Avalon, Merlin prophesies that he will return "Anglen to fulste" (14,297) – to help the English. This is not a solecism, confusing Arthur with his Saxon enemies, but an artful re-visioning of the hero, dissolving the historical division between British and English. Laȝamon defines the nation by its territory, and *leode* means both "land" and "people, nation." In this first English account of Arthur, Laȝamon paves the way for the celebration of Arthur as a national icon.

The Owl and the Nightingale

The Owl and the Nightingale must be situated just as firmly within a multilingual context (Cartlidge 2001). It belongs, first of all, to a European tradition of debate poems, between summer and winter, the body and soul, water and wine – some learned, some frivolous, often witty, many in Latin and others in French. The poem is usually dated soon after 1189, though the two manuscripts in which it survives (BL Cotton Caligula A.IX and Jesus College, Oxford, 29) are from the second half of the thirteenth century. Both manuscripts are miscellanies of English and Anglo-Norman and both include *Le Petit Plet*, "the Little Debate" (Merrilees 1970). Like *The Owl and the Nightingale*, the Anglo-Norman poem is written in octosyllabic couplets, a measure that English learnt from Anglo-Norman. Both poems proclaim their Englishness, but in significantly different ways. *Le Petit Plet*, overtly nationalistic, asserts the superiority of English women over French and the greater beauty of the flowers

and meadows of England. The setting reflects this idealized view: an orchard with a clear spring purling over the gravel, tall trees to offer shade, birds singing sweetly. *The Owl and the Nightingale* describes an everyday English scene: a secluded spot in a summer valley, where the Nightingale hides in an impenetrable hedge, and the Owl, true to its nature, sits on an old stump "mid ivi al bigrowe" (27). Still more down to earth is the Nightingale's singing station (according to the Owl):

> I mai þe vinde ate rumhuse
> Among þe wode, among þe netle;
> þu sittest and singst bihinde þe setle. (592–4)
> [I can find you at the privy among the weeds, among the nettles;
> you sit and sing behind the seat.]

In both poems the arguments are supported by the authority of proverbs. These formulas of traditional wisdom can have a literary and biblical heritage, or contrastingly can be an evocation of popular wisdom passed down from generation to generation. In *Le Petit Plet* many of them are drawn from Seneca and from a Latin school-text, the *Distichs of Cato*, quoted by name (154–6). In *The Owl and the Nightingale*, on the other hand, the proverbs are frequently ascribed to King Alfred, thus presenting them as the wise sayings inherited from a great figure from the Anglo-Saxon past:

> Vor soþ hit is þat seide Alvred:
> "Ne mai no strengþe aȝen red." (761–2)
> [For it is true as Alfred said: "Might can do nothing against cleverness."]

Why was such a cosmopolitan poem composed in English? By this time Anglo-Norman was for most of its potential audience a language that had to be learnt. Even though serious and weighty issues are debated, *The Owl and the Nightingale* is, above all, funny: its comic effect lies in our awareness of the poem's incongruities: the bad-temper and shrill invective of the debaters within the formal and legalistic structure of the debate genre. Even more incongruously, the debaters are birds. A leading element of the comedy of the human birds is that their verbal exchanges are in language that imitates speech. The poet calls our attention to the nature of everyday exchanges when he refers to shepherds' *schitworde* (286), and occasionally the language of the birds is no better than that: "A tort ne ȝive ich for ow alle" (1686) – "I don't give a turd for any of you," says the Owl. Often the exchanges are strikingly colloquial:

> Lat me nu habbe mine þroȝe!
> Bo nu stille and lat me speke! (260–1)
> [Let me have my turn now! Be quiet now and let me speak!]

Anglo-Norman literature is quite capable of low repartee, as evidenced in some obscene fabliaux, but by the thirteenth century a provincial audience would be peering

at it through the veil of a second language rather that associating its vocabulary with the English sounds around them.

Social Register

Not available to earlier writers in English were certain indicators of polite speech and social difference borrowed from French. These included not only a range of vocabulary, but also, most telling of all, the use of 'ye' to address a single individual. In Old English 'ye' and 'you' were plural; an individual was addressed as 'þou' and 'þe'. During the thirteenth century the practice of using the plural pronoun as a mark of deference began to be copied from French custom. It became a wonderfully useful way for a writer to indicate both the social awareness of the speaker and the relationship between the speaker and the person addressed. Peasants would not know the distinction; nobles would understand its social complexities and would display deference where it was due. Among the social factors that come into play are context, rank, age, gender, and familiarity (Burnley 1989: 19–21).

The earliest sustained example of the practice is not from fashionable London but surprisingly from the romance *Havelok* composed around 1300 (Smithers 1987). The hero, an exiled Danish prince, arrives penniless on the Lincolnshire coast. In order to survive, he goes barefoot to Lincoln to find a job at the castle, and there the earl's cook spots him:

> And seyde "Wiltu ben wit me?
> Gladlike wile ich feden þe.
> Wel is set þe mete þu etes,
> And þe hire þat þu getes." (906–9)
> [And said "Wilt thou be with me? I will gladly feed thee.
> The food thou shalt eat and the wages thou shalt get shall be well spent."]

Havelok replies:

> "Goddot!" quoth he, "leve sire,
> Bidde ich you non oþer hire,
> But yeveþ me inow to ete.
> Fir and water y wile you fete. (910–13)
> ["By God!" he said, "dear sir, I don't ask you for any other wages;
> just give me enough to eat. I'll fetch fire and water for you."]

In this context it pays to be deferential, even if you are a prince in disguise speaking to a cook. The surprise at this date is that the provincial writer pays attention throughout his text to the convention and expects his audience to observe the irony of the situation. Certainly, consistent usage is not standard until considerably later, when Chaucer, Gower, and the *Gawain*-poet take full advantage of it. In *Sir Orfeo* (ca. 1340),

where the courtly setting as well as the London audience might have encouraged its consistent use, the polite *ye* is found just once, at the significant moment when the court acknowledges Orfeo as the king they had believed dead: "ʒe beþ our lord, sir, and our king!" (582).

REFERENCES AND FURTHER READING

Brook, G. L. & Leslie R. F. (eds.) (1963, 1978). *Laʒamon: Brut*. EETS 250, 277. London: Oxford University Press.

Burnley, D. (1989). *The Language of Chaucer*. Basingstoke: Macmillan.

Cannon, C. (1993). The style and authorship of the Otho revision of Laʒamon's *Brut*. *Medium Ævum*, 62, 187–209.

Cartlidge, N. (ed.) (2001). *The Owl and the Nightingale*. Exeter: Exeter University Press.

Clanchy, M. T. (1993). *From Memory to Written Record*. 2nd edn. Oxford: Blackwell.

Crane, S. (1986). *Insular Romance: Politics, Faith, and Culture in Anglo-Norman and Middle English Literature*. Berkeley: University of California Press.

Dean, R. J. (1999). *Anglo-Norman Literature: A Guide to Texts and Manuscripts*. ANTS Occasional Publications Series 3. London: ANTS.

Merrilees, B. S. (ed.) (1970). *Le Petit Plet*. ANTS 20. Oxford: Oxford University Press.

Morris, R. (ed.) (1874–93). *Cursor Mundi*. EETS 57, 59, 62, 66, 68, 99, 101. London: Oxford University Press.

Rigg, A. G. (1992). *A History of Anglo-Latin Literature 1066–1422*. Cambridge: Cambridge University Press.

Rothwell, W. (1976). The role of French in thirteenth-century England. *Bulletin of the John Rylands Library*, 58, 445–66.

Rothwell, W. (ed.) (1990). *Walter de Bibbesworth, Le Tretiz*. ANTS Plain Texts Series 6. London: ANTS.

Salter, E. (1988). *English and International: Studies in the Literature, Art and Patronage of Medieval England*. Ed. D. Pearsall and N. Zeeman. Cambridge: Cambridge University Press.

Short, I. (1991). Patrons and polyglots: French literature in twelfth-century England. *Anglo-Norman Studies*, 14, 229–49.

Smithers, G. V. (ed.) (1987). *Havelok*. Oxford: Oxford University Press.

Stanley, E. G. (1969). Laʒamon's antiquarian sentiments. *Medium Ævum*, 38, 23–37.

Turville-Petre, T. (1996). *England the Nation: Language, Literature, and National Identity, 1290–1340*. Oxford: Oxford University Press.

Turville-Petre, T. (2007). *Reading Middle English Literature*. Oxford: Blackwell.

18
Late Middle English (ca. 1350–1485)

Seth Lerer

By "late Middle English," I mean the vernacular as spoken and written from roughly the death of Geoffrey Chaucer in 1400 to the rise of printing at the close of the fifteenth century. This chapter will therefore focus mainly on English in the fifteenth century. (For English in the second half of the fourteenth century, see CHAUCER'S LITERARY ENGLISH.) English men and women were acutely conscious of their language changing at this time. French was progressively disappearing as both the language of official record and of social prestige (Strang 1970; Baugh & Cable 2002; Williams 2004). The stirrings of the Great Vowel Shift (see PHONOLOGY: SEGMENTAL HISTORIES) were being recorded in the orthography of both private correspondence and public documents (Lass 1999; Davis 1955). The rise of Chancery as the organ of royal and parliamentary writing was affecting the conventions of spelling as well, defining standards that would be absorbed into the publications of William Caxton and his successors (Fisher 1977, 1984, 1996). English literature, to a large degree, remained under the sway of Chaucerian imitation and obeisance, as writers such as John Lydgate, Stephen Hawes, and John Skelton preserved many of that poet's idioms even as the language of the everyday was changing (Lerer 1993, 1997; Trigg 2002, 2006). By 1490, Caxton himself, writing in the preface to his *Eneydos*, could note that "our langage now vsed varyeth ferre from that whiche was vsed and spoken what I was borne."

Late Middle English, then, remains a period of both remarkable linguistic change and equally remarkable social awareness of that change. My purpose in this chapter is to detail some of these key changes but, more broadly, to illustrate ways in which particular fifteenth-century men and women gave voice to or recorded in their writing a vernacular consciousness. In the course of this chapter, too, I hope to raise some larger questions about methods for the study of this period and suggestions for future research.

Ever since Otto Jespersen coined the term "Great Vowel Shift" in 1909, this change in English pronunciation has been seen as the defining moment in the history of the

language. "The greatest revolution that has taken place in the phonetic system of English is the vowel-shift," he wrote in his *Modern English Grammar* (Jespersen 1909: 231). Recent scholarship, however, has queried the impact of this change (Lass 1999; Giancarlo 2001). Was the raising and fronting of the vowels truly a systemic change, or was it something that, only in retrospect, seems to have sorted itself out in response to contact among regional and class dialects? Matthew Giancarlo, in a recent critique of the philological debates around the Great Vowel Shift, summarizes what may be a new scholarly consensus:

> The 'standardization' described by the GVS may simply have been the social fixation upon one variant among several dialectical options available in each case, a variant selected for reasons of community preference or by the external force of printing standardization and not as a result of a wholesale phonetic shift. (Giancarlo 2001: 35)

As French began to disappear as the prestige language for England, some form of English itself had to emerge as the social standard. As dialects came into contact in the cities, different pronunciations vied for social prominence. The sounds of English thus may have changed in the course of the fifteenth and sixteenth centuries as part of a larger, social process of replacing a lost prestige *language* with a new prestige *dialect*: a dialect not keyed to region but to social class, to education, or to wealth.

Along with changes in pronunciation, there were changes in the look of written English. The development of what has come to be known as "Chancery Standard" had the most vivid and long-lasting effect. Originating in the household of the medieval English kings, Chancery emerged out of the mix of domestic administration to come to control the production of official documents by the middle of the fourteenth century (Fisher 1977; Fisher et al. 1984). It was a kind of Secretariat of State that not only produced texts but trained scribes to write them. From the 1380s until the 1450s, Chancery taught a house style of spelling, grammatical forms, lexical usage, and idiom that characterized the papers coming out of many of the royal offices (those of the Signet, the Privy Seal, and Parliament). Among the features of that writing were the preservation of historical forms, even in the face of changes in pronunciation (for example, spellings such as *high*, *ought*, *slaughter*, *right*, *though*, and *nought*). Other features include what would have been, for Middle English speakers, Northernisms. At least some of Chancery's scribes came from the North, and such young men would have been part of the great fifteenth-century migration of the children of the gentry, commercial, or rural families to the metropolis. Their regional preferences appear in such forms as the preference for the Northern form *–ly*, rather than the Midlands form *–lich*, for the adverbial ending; for the ending *–s*, instead of *–eth*, for the ending of the third person singular of verbs; and for certain forms of the verb "to be."

Chancery English had an impact on the rise of printed documents in Britain. When Caxton set up his print shop in Westminster, he located his business not in the commercial part of London (the old City) but the site of court. Caxton adopted Chancery-style spellings and word forms when he came to print not just official or intellectual texts but literary ones as well. His early volumes of the English authors Chaucer,

Gower, Lydgate, Malory, and others, calibrated themselves not to the older spelling habits of the scribe but to the newer conventions of Chancery. Caxton's achievement was to take a standard of official writing for a literary standard. In so doing, he contributed to what we see, in retrospect, as the "modernization" of English (Fisher 1984).

But, in addition, by maintaining certain Chancery conventions, Caxton contributed to the growing divorce between the sound of spoken English and the ways in which it was written. As John Hurt Fisher puts it, "the most important development of the [fifteenth] century was the emergence of writing as a system coordinate with, but independent from, speech." While during the Middle English period writing was largely regional or individual, "during the fifteenth century an official standard began to emerge. . . . Speech is not writing" (Fisher et al. 1984: 26). This split between the voice and hand (or type) had become so great that by 1569 the scholar John Hart could lament in his *Orthographie*:

> In the modern and present manner of writing there is such confusion and disorder, as it may be accounted rather a kind of ciphering, or such a darke kinde of writing, as the best and readiest wit that euer hath bene could, or that is or shal be, can or may, by the only gift of reason, attaine to the ready and perfite reading thereof, without a long and tedious labour. (Hart 1569: 2)

What we might say, then, is that Middle English marks its end not so much with a signal shift in sound or with some signifying political date, but with an attitude towards speech and writing: a recognition that the English of the page is no longer the English of the voice.

Throughout the fifteenth century we can see these tensions between page and voice as writers struggle with both changing sounds and changing conventions of writing. The vast collection of the letters and papers of such families as the Pastons, the Celys, and the Stonors has long been used as a mine of evidence for charting such changes (Davis 1955). Members of these families represent, to varying degrees, levels of vernacular literacy for the late Middle English period, and they share in an emerging, late-medieval and early modern epistolary culture. In reading through these letters, we see tensions both linguistic and social. For the letter was the place of personal expression. Epistolary manuals taught parents and children, lovers, diplomats, and business people how to shape themselves in writing (Jardine 1993; Lerer 1997). And that shaping went on in a world acutely aware of shifting language, as well as of shifting class and cultural forms.

The Pastons in particular provide brilliant examples at all these levels. Their letters illustrate how members of the family used the conventions of Middle English spelling to represent changes in pronunciation that we now see, in retrospect, as features of the Great Vowel Shift. Thus, throughout their mid-fifteenth century correspondence, we may find in spellings such as *myte* for the word "meet," or *hyre* for the word "hear," the use of the *y* grapheme to indicate the high front vowel /i:/. Such spellings offer evidence that the old, Middle English open and close *e* (the phonemes /ɛ:/ and /e:/) would have

been raised and fronted. Spellings such as *abeyd* for the word "abide" indicate that the Middle English /i:/ sound has become a diphthong (probably pronounced, at this time, as /ei/). The word "our" is often spelled *aur*, "out" appears as *owt*, and "house" appears as *hows*, all indicating that the Middle English high back vowel /u:/ has diphthongized. Spellings such as *mayd* for the word "made" have been taken to indicate that the Middle English long back vowel /a/ has been raised and fronted (at this point, probably pronounced as a kind of diphthong, something like /ai/ or /ɛi/).

Behind these ad hoc spellings we can see people coping with their language changing in their own lifetimes. But behind other kinds of spellings, we can see writers aspiring to official standards. Chancery forms appear throughout the Paston correspondence, especially in the letters of John Paston II and John Paston III (after they took up court positions in London in the 1460s). As Davis and Fisher point out, they began to use the Chancery-sanctioned (and ultimately, Northern dialectical) forms *them* and *their*, instead of the Midlands and Southern Middle English *hem* and *hir*. They maintained the old spellings such as *right* and *thought*, even though some other members of their family were spelling these kinds of words according to new pronunciations (often with a *–th* or a *–ʒt*, implying that the old velar fricative had disappeared from pronunciation, and that the vowel had lengthened in response: thus, instead of Middle English /rixt/ we have /ri:t/, the sound that would eventually diphthongize into /rait/).

More than just illustrating details of linguistic use, these letters reveal writers measuring their writing against new standards of speech or spelling. They represent encounters with vernacular authority. But to appreciate their understanding of vernacular authority more broadly, we need to look closely at their letters in full. Take, for example, Agnes Paston, the brilliant and affluent matriarch of the family, who wrote to her son John in a letter dated October 29, 1465. It has the rich simplicity of a biblical homily, tempered by allusions to the poetry of Chaucer and popular proverb. It hews closely, as many of the Paston letters do, to the conventions of medieval epistolarity: the greetings, the signatures, the forms of address are all formulaic (and, indeed, were found in many of the manuals of letter-writing circulating at the time). Still, it remains a deeply personal appropriation of the conventions of written English.

> Sonne, I grete ʒow wele and lete ʒow wete þat, for as myche as ʒoure broþir Clement leteth me wete þat ʒe desire feythfully my blyssyng, þat blyssyng þat I prayed ʒoure fadir to gyffe ʒow þe laste day þat euer he spakke, and þe blyssyng of all seyntes vndir heven, and myn, mote come to ʒow all dayes and tymes. And thynke verily non o þer but þat ʒe haue it, and shal haue it with þat þat I fynde ʒow kynde and wyllyng to þe welfare of ʒoure breþeren.
>
> Be my counseyle, dyspose ʒoure-selfe as myche as ʒe may to haue lesse to do in þe worlde. ʒoure fadyr sayde, 'In lityl bysynes yeth myche reste. þis worlde is but a þorughfare of woo, and whan we departe þer-fro, riʒth nouʒght bere with vs but oure good dedys and ylle. And þer knoweth no man how soon God woll clepe hym, and þer-for it

is good for euery creature to be redy. Quom God vysyteth, him he louyth.

And as for ʒoure breþeren, þei wylle I knowe certeynly laboren all þat in hem lyeth for ʒow.

Oure Lorde haue ʒow in his blyssed keying, body and soule.

Writen at Norwyche þe xxix day of Octobyr.

By ʒoure modir A. P.

(Davis 1971: 43–4)

At the linguistic level, Agnes's letter is a mix of seemingly advanced and conservative forms. First off, it appears that the language is moving to accept the *you*-forms as the standard second person pronoun. Throughout the Paston correspondence, in fact, everyone addresses each other using this old, formal form. The few exceptions are reserved for moments of true anger or contempt, and reading through the correspondence we can sense not that this is a particularly formal family, but that *you*-forms of the second person were becoming, by the close of the fifteenth century, the normative, or unmarked manner of address. Some of her spellings, too, indicate changes in pronunciation or particulars of local dialect (for example, spelling "blessing" as *blyssyng*, and "much" as *myche* suggests that the short –e- and the short –u- sounds of Middle English were similar in her speech). She is also spelling the word "right" as *riʒth* to indicate the new pronunciation without the velar fricative. But this letter also shows some old fashioned forms. The third person pronoun is *hem*, rather than *them*; plurals of verbs end in *–en* (*laboren*); and there is a markedly un-French vocabulary in this letter (*counseyle* stands out as one of the very few words of obvious French origin).

What we might say is that this letter is an essay in vernacularity itself: an engagement with the everyday Englishness of English as it comes through proverb and quotation. "In lityl bysnes lyeth mych reste." Agnes introduces this maxim as a saying of the boy's father; but these are the words not just of the father of the family but the father of English poetry. In Geoffrery Chaucer's little poem, "Truth," by all accounts the most widely circulated of his lyrics in the fifteenth century, he advises: "Gret rest stant in little besiness" (note that one manuscript of "Truth," Corpus Christi College, Oxford, 203, replaces the word "Gret" with "Meche"; this must have been the version alluded to in Agnes's letter). And in the *Knight's Tale* from his *Canterbury Tales*, Chaucer has Egeus, the old father of King Theseus, give the son this advice for living:

> This world nys but a thurghfare ful of wo,
> And we been pilgrymes, passynge to and fro. (ll. 2847–8)

These lines find their echo in Agnes's advice, too. At her most parental, then, she turns to some of the most famously parental and advisory of Chaucer's lines, not simply to give counsel to her son but to appropriate the voice of vernacular counsel itself: the voice of Chaucer.

Now, compare Agnes's straightforward and affirmative vernacularity with the complex syntax and polysyllables of Agnes's son John, who writes on June 27, 1465 to his own wife, Margaret, about their son. Here is an excerpt from his letter.

> Item, as for yowre sone: I lete yow wete I wold he dede wel, but I vnderstand in hym
> no dispocicion of polecy ne of gouernans as a man of the werld owt to do, but only
> leuith, and euer hath, as man disolut, with-owt any prouicion, ne that he besijth hym
> nothinge to vnderstand swhech materis as a man of lyuelode must nedis vnderstond. Ne
> I vnderstond nothing of what dispocicion he porposith to be, but only I kan think he
> wold dwell ageyn in yowr hows and myn, and ther ete and drink and slepe . . . As for
> yowr sone, ye knowe well he neuer stode yow ne me in profite, ese, or helpe to valew
> of on grote, . . . (Davis 1971: 132)

There is more of interest here than sound shift. When John writes about the behavior
of a "man of the werld," he uses the resonant vocabulary of French legalism: "I vnder-
stand in hym no dispocicion of policy ne of gouernans." His son may live, but he does
so "disolut with-owt any prouicion." He claims not to understand "what dispocicion
he porposith to be," but he can only imagine that he would simply like to live in
their house and only "ete and drink and slepe." These sentences arc from elaborate
French to basic English. They set up high expectations, only to dash them. From the
rich polysyllables of politeness, we end with the blunt monosyllables of failure: eat
and drink and sleep. From the claims of parental expectation ("euery gentilman that
hath discrecion"), we wind up with a child who isn't worth a groat.

But there are difficulties, too, for in this letter, written in John Paston's own hand,
we can see him struggling for the right expression. In Norman Davis's edition of the
Paston Letters and Papers, the word *disolut* ("dissolute") appears in half brackets, indicating that it is an interlinear addition to the letter. Davis's notes make clear that
John first wrote "as a man fownd of." Apparently, John was going to write that his
son was a man fond of something (or maybe even fond of nothing). But he crossed
that out, and over it wrote "disolut." Then he wrote "hauing nothing" next to it, but
crossed that out, too. John's self-correcting replaces familiar, vernacular expressions
with newer terms of French or Latin origin. Instead of being fond of something, John's
son is "dissolute," a word that first appears in the early fifteenth century originally
from the Latin, *dissolutus* (untied, set apart). The use of the word meaning "unre-
strained in behavior," or "wanton," is not attested until 1460, while the sense of being
morally loose or debauched (what the *OED* calls "the current sense") is not attested
until 1513. Clearly, John Paston's use is very new, a word emerging into vernacular
consciousness. So, too, the everyday phrase "hauing nothing" becomes "with-owt any
prouicion." *Provision* came from the Latin, by way of the French, and originally connoted the ability to see ahead, to plan for the future. From this sense, the word's
meaning extends to embrace those things that we provide for the future (i.e., provisions). The word emerges, according to the *OED*, in the first third of the fifteenth
century, but does not take on its modern, extended meaning until the end of the
century. Again, for Paston writing in 1465, it is a new word.

John Paston has, in these lines, effectively translated commonplace, vernacular
expression into an exotic, new vocabulary. What he is saying is that his son lives from
day to day, without making any plans for the future – and he says it in a language

whose imported newness, whose polysyllabic technicality, not only damns the son but elevates the father. His letter, in short, is a study in character: his own, as well as his son's. John comes off as a figure of both social and linguistic authority, a man of the word as well as of the world.

And this, it seems to me, lies at the heart of the late Middle English experience. More than just looking at details of sound or spelling, texts such as the Paston letters show us writers grappling with vernacular expression. To see Agnes Paston invoking Chaucer's lines says a great deal about the impress of Chaucerian literary authority on an everyday, literate populace. To see John Paston recasting his Gallicized English says a great deal about the changing registers of social usage. We see these writers locating themselves in a changing vernacular and, in the process, giving worldly voice to the forms of late Middle English words.

References and Further Reading

Baugh, A. C. & Cable, T. C. (2002). *A History of the English Language*. 5th edn. Englewood Cliffs, NJ: Prentice-Hall.

Davis, N. (1955). The language of the Pastons. *Proceedings of the British Academy*, 40, 119–44; rpt. in J. A. Burrow (ed.) (1989), *Middle English Literature: British Academy Gollancz Lectures* (pp. 45–70). Oxford: Oxford University Press.

Davis, N. (1971, 1976) *The Paston Letters and Papers of the Fifteenth Century*. 2 vols. Oxford: Clarendon Press.

Fisher, J. H. (1977). Chancery and the emergence of Standard Written English. *Speculum*, 52, 870–89; rpt. in J. H. Fisher (1996), *The Emergence of Standard English* (pp. 36–64). Lexington: University Press of Kentucky.

Fisher, J. H. (1984). Caxton and Chancery English. In R. F. Yeager (ed.), *Fifteenth-Century Studies* (pp. 161–85). New Haven: Archon; rpt. in J. H. Fisher (1996), *The Emergence of Standard English* (pp. 121–44). Lexington: University Press of Kentucky.

Fisher, J. H. (1996). *The Emergence of Standard English*. Lexington: University Press of Kentucky.

Fisher, J. H., Richardson, M., & Fisher, J. F. (1984). *An Anthology of Chancery English*. Knoxville: University of Tennessee Press.

Giancarlo, M. (2001). The rise and fall of the Great Vowel Shift? The changing ideological intersections of philology, historical linguistics, and literary history. *Representations*, 76, 27–60.

Hart, J. (1569). *An Orthographie*. Facsimile reprint in R. C. Alston (ed.) (1969), *English Linguistics 1500–1800*. No. 209. Menston: Scolar Press.

Jardine, L. (1993). *Erasmus, Man of Letters*. Princeton, NJ: Princeton University Press.

Jespersen, O. (1909). *A Modern English Grammar on Historical Principles, Vol. 1: Sounds and Spellings*. Copenhagen: Munskaard.

Lass, R. (1999). Phonology and morphology. In R. Lass (ed.), *The Cambridge History of the English Language, Vol. 3: 1476–1776* (pp. 56–186). Cambridge: Cambridge University Press.

Lerer, S. (1993). *Chaucer and His Readers: Imagining the Author in Late-Medieval England*. Princeton, NJ: Princeton University Press.

Lerer, S. (1997). *Courtly Letters in the Age of Henry VIII*. Cambridge: Cambridge University Press.

Strang, B. M. H. (1970). *A History of English*. London: Methuen.

Trigg, S. (2002). *Congenial Souls: Reading Chaucer from Medieval to Postmodern*. Minneapolis: University of Minnesota Press.

Trigg, S. (2006). Chaucer's influence and reception. In S. Lerer (ed.), *The Yale Companion to Chaucer* (pp. 297–323). New Haven, CT: Yale University Press.

Williams, D. (2004). *The French Fetish from Chaucer to Shakespeare*. Cambridge: Cambridge University Press.

19

Varieties of Middle English

Jeremy J. Smith

Introduction

Middle English is often characterized as the "dialectal phase of English" (Strang 1970: 224), but this description needs careful unpacking. Scholars no longer look on the history of English as synonymous with the history of standard English, in which only the standard has a structure and legitimate history. What is meant by "dialectal phase" is that, during the Middle English period, variation in all levels of language (speech, lexicon, grammar) is reflected in writing.

The reason for this situation relates to the function of Middle English during much of the medieval period: as in so many fields, the forms of a language relate to its communicative functions. Broadly, the functions of Middle English were generally local; folk used English when communicating with their neighbors. It was therefore economical, when developing written forms of the language, to map the writing-system closely onto local speech.

Communication on a national level was generally carried out using other languages altogether. As indicated in Thorlac Turville-Petre's chapter (EARLY MIDDLE ENGLISH), the language of record and of international culture, since the Norman Conquest, was Latin; varieties of French, notably Anglo-Norman, also developed special functions, notably in literature. The aristocracy seems to have persisted in speaking French for some time after the Conquest, though there is debate about how far and for how long French remained their native tongue; it seems that French in England for much of the Middle Ages was a social accomplishment, rather like in pre-revolutionary Russia (cf. Tolstoy's *War and Peace*).

English culture was multilingual, therefore, to an extent which now might seem strange, but which is explicable in contemporary terms. English is now a global language, but during the Middle Ages it was spoken by comparatively few people in part of a small island on the edge of the corner of the world known to Europeans. A parallel might be drawn with some of the "smaller" languages spoken in modern

Europe; Finnish and Dutch speakers are remarkably multilingual – astonishingly so to monoglot modern Britons or Americans – but this relates to the fact that outsiders comparatively rarely learn Finnish or Dutch.

Of course, the description just given is over-simple because static. The situation was in reality fluid, varying both diachronically (i.e., through time) and diatopically (i.e., from place to place). A key factor here is the degree of elaboration of the language at a given time and place, using the term "elaboration" to refer to a language's or variety's functional range. As discussed in earlier chapters, Old English was in some ways more elaborated than Middle English, and thus a variety of Old English with certain national functions had emerged by the end of the Anglo-Saxon period: Classical Late West Saxon (see LATE OLD ENGLISH). At the beginning of the period, during the eleventh and twelfth centuries, material written in this variety continued to be copied, with comparatively little variation, in conservative scriptoria in the west of England. Many texts in Early Middle English, as described by Thorlac Turville-Petre (see EARLY MIDDLE ENGLISH), attempted to recuperate this Anglo-Saxon past, albeit in locally restricted vernaculars (e.g., Laȝamon's *Brut*).

Towards the end of the Middle English period, English began to take on more functions and thus became more elaborated. English began to be used for some government records; it took on more literary and other cultural uses, as described by Seth Lerer (LATE MIDDLE ENGLISH). In short, it was beginning to develop a capacity for "eloquence" in the same way as French and Italian had done, even though Latin learning remained a crucial cultural accomplishment. This elaboration of English had implications for its written form: it began to undergo a process of standardization. More belatedly, prestigious varieties of speech began to emerge, though much of the evidence for this latter process derives from the Early Modern period and is thus not strictly relevant for this chapter. (See VARIETIES OF EARLY MODERN ENGLISH.)

In what follows, the issues raised above will be developed. First, the meaning of the term "dialect" will be examined. Some characteristic features of Middle English varieties will then be discussed. The chapter concludes with further discussion of the standardization processes which English underwent towards the end of the period.

What Were the Dialects of Middle English?

Middle English textbooks often provide a list of dialects as follows: Northern, West Midland, East Midland, South-Western, South-Eastern. Such a typology is helpful operationally, but modern dialectological study indicates that it is an over-simplification. Present-day language-varieties shade into each other, forming a continuum; the same situation obtained for Middle English.

The Middle English dialect-continuum has been mapped in the major work on Middle English dialects, the *Linguistic Atlas of Late Mediaeval English* (LALME). LALME, superseding previous dialectological work on Middle English, provides a conspectus of local usages which makes it possible to localize a text – with a degree

of variation depending on the culture of the locality – to approximately a 10-mile radius on a map. (It should be noted that localizing a text means placing that text within the Middle English linguistic typology, a point not always clearly understood; scribes did move about, and took their language with them, so to state that the language of a given text can be localized *to* X does not mean that it was necessarily physically written *at* X.)

LALME shows that clear-cut boundaries between dialects are not to be had. Nevertheless, it is possible to offer a brief sketch of usages prototypical of particular regions within the Middle English dialect continuum.

Spellings and Sounds

It is sometimes stated that, during the Middle English period, folk "wrote as they spoke." Such a statement is an over-simplification; given that writing-systems are attempts to give permanent form to something evanescent, viz. speech, we must expect a degree of conventionalization. Nevertheless, the statement does capture an important fact about written Middle English: the writing-systems of the period were phonographic.

In phonographic languages, sounds (syllables, speech-segments) map onto letters. This notion was known in antiquity, as demonstrated by the Greek and Roman doctrine of *littera*. According to this doctrine, a letter (*littera*) consists of a sound (*potestas* "power"), a written symbol (*figura* "figure"), and a name (*nomen*). This doctrine underpins the traditional approach to the teaching of reading known as "phonics": "C says /k/, A says /a/, T says /t/, /k/ – /a/ – /t/ says CAT."

In phonographic languages which distinguish speech-segments, the relationship between sound and written symbol is one where phoneme maps onto grapheme: a maximally economical mapping. (An attempt to develop a system where allophonic distinctions are fully represented by allographic distinctions would be impossibly unwieldy for general communicative purposes, though specialized writing-systems have been developed to represent allophones, e.g., the phonetic alphabet developed by the International Phonetic Association.)

In the transition from Old to Middle English, the inherited writing-systems of the Anglo-Saxon period were modified to become more phonographic. Given the local functions of Middle English, this strategy made sense; teaching reading by the ancient "phonic" method was easier if there was a direct mapping between phoneme and grapheme, and this was possible if the graphemic system could be mapped onto the phonological system of a particular locality. As a result, it is possible (in principle, with all sorts of caveats) to use the writing-systems of Middle English as evidence for parallel sound-systems.

The details of these systems are given in standard textbooks (e.g., Mossé 1959; Burrow & Turville-Petre 1997; Horobin & Smith 2002; Wright & Wright 1928), but some exemplification is possible here:

1. The dialectal distribution of fricatives.
2. Reflexes of Old English initial *hw-*.
3. Reflexes of Old English (West Saxon) *y*.

(1) The phonemicization of the distinction between voiced and voiceless fricatives is a feature of the transition from Old to Middle English. In Old English, the pairs [v, f], [z, s], and [ð, θ] were allophones, in what is called complementary position. Voiceless forms (cf. /f, s, θ/ in Present-Day English *fail*, *sail*, *thing*) appeared word-initially and word-finally, while voiced forms (cf. /v, z, ð/ in Present-Day English *veil*, *zap*, *that*) appeared intervocalically. We might compare [v] for <f> in Old English *hlāford* "lord" with [f] for <f> in Old English *hlāf* "loaf (of bread)." The phonemicization of these pairs seems to derive at least in part through contact with French, which, as loanwords, introduced into English "minimal pairs" such as *seal/zeal*, *fine/vine*, where the voiceless/voiced distinction meant a change in meaning.

However, there were native sources of voiced fricatives in word-initial position. There are Middle English records of forms such as *vox* "fox," *zenne* "sin," etc. from dialects over a wide area in the south of England, from Kent in the east to Devon in the west. A few of these forms have entered the standard language, e.g., *vixen* "female fox," but most have not. Voicing of initial fricatives is in Present-Day English a recessive feature found in southwestern dialects; it is a feature of "Mummerset," the stage-dialect adopted by actors to reflect rural, unsophisticated usage.

(2) By contrast, another feature with apparently restricted currency in Middle English has spread much more widely. The distinction between /w/ and /ʍ/ in pairs such as *wile* "trick"/*while* seems to have been comparatively restricted in Middle English dialects; spellings such as *wan* "when," and back-spellings such as *where* "were," are a characteristic of southern varieties but not found consistently in Midland or Northern usage. In Present-Day English, however, the distinction seems to be disappearing fast, though occasionally sustained by conservative, spelling-induced habits derived from the <w->/<wh-> distinction. Even in Scotland, where the /w/-/ʍ/ distinction has been considered an important feature of local usage, the distinction is dying out among younger speakers for whom pairs such as *witch/which* sound the same.

(3) It is important to recognize that such developments typically happen word-by-word and not globally, and this process of development – often described as "lexical diffusion" – may be illustrated by a third example: the history of the reflexes of Old English (West Saxon) *y*, which in Old English was a close front rounded vowel [y], much like the "u" in Present-Day French *tu*. It is usual to state that, in Middle English dialects, Old English *y* developed in three directions: as *i* in northern and east midland dialects, as *u* in western and west midland dialects, and as *e* in the southeast. But the evidence of Present-Day standard written English demonstrates that this simple pattern was in reality more complex. We might take the forms *busy* (from Old English *bysig*), *bury* (from Old English *byrian*), and *merry* (from Old English *myrig*) as examples. With *busy*, a southwestern spelling maps onto a northern and east midland

pronunciation; with *bury*, a southwestern spelling maps onto a southeastern pronunciation; and a southeastern spelling and pronunciation has become standard in *merry*. It is clear that the boundary-lines between the reflexes of Old English *y* are porous, and we must expect residues of variant usages to appear outside their alleged place of origin (see PHONOLOGY: SEGMENTAL HISTORIES).

Of course, these comparisons with later dialectal usage do not draw on the evidence of the standard language, and there is a functional reason for this: Present-Day standard written English does not allow any more than trivial variation (cf. the US/British distinction between *–or* and *–our* in *honor*, *honour*). The global function of English means that symbol-sound mapping is no longer possible; one writing-system has to cater for a range of distinct phonological systems. We will return to this point below.

Lexicon and Grammar

Similar patterns may be observed in the lexicons and grammars of Middle English. A general picture can be swiftly described: northern innovation, relating to contact with Norse, and southern conservatism.

In the lexicon, the Middle English evidence clearly shows dialectal distinction in vocabulary. Perhaps the most famous discussion of such differences is to be found towards the end of the period, in a famous anecdote told by William Caxton in the preface to his translation of *Eneydos* (1490), a text cited briefly by Seth Lerer in his chapter below:

> And that comyn englysshe that is spoken in one shyre varyeth from a nother. In so moche that in my dayes happened that certayn marchauntes were in a shippe in tamyse [i.e., the River Thames] for to haue sayled ouer the see into Zelande [i.e., Zealand, in the Low Countries]/ and for lacke of wynde thei taryed atte forlond [i.e., the North Foreland, the westernmost point on the coast of modern Kent]. and wente to lande for to refreshe them And one of theym named sheffelde a mercer cam in to an hows and axed [i.e., asked] for mete [i.e., food]. and specyally he axyd after eggys And the good wyf answerde. That she coude speke no frenshe. And the marchaunt was angry. for he also coude speke no frenshe. but wold haue hadde egges/ and she vnderstode hym not/ And thenne at laste a nother sayd that he wolde haue eyren/ then the good wyf sayd that she vnderstod hym wel/ Loo what sholde a man in thyse dayes now wryte. egges or eyren/ certaynly it is harde to playse euery man/ by cause of dyuersite & chaunge of langage. (Cited from Crotch 1928: 108–9)

This famous passage is interesting for several reasons, but, most obviously, it illustrates diatopic variation in the lexicon, and thus may be taken as an early comment on Middle English word geography. The Middle English records show that different forms vary in diatopic distribution in Middle English. Thus *kirk* 'church' and *stern* 'star', both Norse-derived words, appear in Northern Middle English but not in the south; and

bigouth 'began' appears in Older Scots but not in Middle English, where *gan* and *can* were preferred. Interestingly, *kirk* is recessive in the history of English; now used only in Scotland and in parts of northern England near the border, the Middle English evidence demonstrates that it was once much more widespread in the Midlands as well. It is still found there in place-names (e.g., Ormskirk, Kirk Ella, etc.).

Dialectal variation in Middle English grammar can be illustrated from one text: Chaucer's *Reeve's Tale*. The reason for this is that Chaucer was attempting in this tale to reflect Northern usage; comparison with surviving northern texts suggests that he was an accomplished linguistic observer.

The story of the *Reeve's Tale* is swiftly told: two young Northern students avenge themselves on a scheming Cambridge miller by one having sex with his wife and the other with his daughter. The interest for our purposes lies in Chaucer's technique of characterization through dialect, which may be illustrated from the following passage:

> Aleyn the clerk, that herde this melodye,
> He poked John, and seyde, "Slepestow?
> Herdestow evere slyk a sang er now?
> Lo, swilk a complyn is ymel hem alle,
> A wilde fyr upon thair bodyes falle!
> Wha herkned evere slyk a ferly thyng?
> Ye, they sal have the flour of il endyng.
> This lange nyght ther tydes me na reste;
> But yet, nafors, al sal be for the beste."
> (A.4168–4176, after Benson et al. 1988)

Several grammatical features may be noted here: the use of *tydes*, with the northern *-es* inflexion in place of contemporary southern *tydeth*, or the use of Norse-derived *thair* where the best Chaucerian manuscripts, such as the Ellesmere and Hengwrt Manuscripts of the *Tales* now known to have been copied by Chaucer's "own scribe" Adam Pinkhurst (Mooney 2006), would use Old English-derived *here*. The pronoun *they*, also Norse-derived, seems to have reached southern England earlier than the other parts of the third-person plural paradigm, possibly because subject-form pronouns have a more important grammatical ("thematic") role and more distinctive forms tend therefore to be selected.

More subtly, the editor has intervened, arguably unnecessarily, in the phrase *This lange nyght*. The authority for this usage is the Ellesmere Manuscript, but, in this instance the reading is problematic. The Hengwrt Manuscript of the *Tales*, also written by Pinkhurst and arguably more authoritative, reads *This lang nyght*, which represents northern grammar more precisely. Final *-e* in many adjectives was, in southern Middle English of Chaucer's day, used to distinguish "strong" adjectives (i.e., those not preceded by *the*, *this*, *that*, etc.) from "weak" and plural adjectives; cf. the Present-Day German distinction between *der alte Mann* and *der Mann ist alt*. This distinction fell out of use in southern varieties after Chaucer's death. In Northern

varieties it had disappeared some time before. It is intriguing that Adam Pinkhurst in the Hengwrt Manuscript uses -*e* to distinguish weak and strong singular adjectives everywhere except in his representation of northern speech in the *Reeve's Tale*, and it is possible that an attempt is being made to reflect rhythmic patterns characteristic of northern speech, foregrounded for southern listeners. If so, it seems Pinkhurst took to heart Chaucer's invocation: *after my makyng thou wryte more trewe* ("you should write more faithfully according to my composition," from Chaucer's short poem *Wordes unto Adam, his owne scriveyn*, line 4). (For further discussion, see Horobin 2003: 58.)

Standardization

The processes of standardization of the written mode in the fourteenth and fifteenth centuries have been much studied over the last thirty years, especially by contributors to LALME. The classic study remains that by Samuels (1963), who distinguished "types" of so-called "incipient standard" from the fourteenth and fifteenth centuries. It is significant that the origins of a number of these types correlate with the parts of the country where population had undergone a considerable increase since the Conquest; these areas were the source of the immigrants to London who brought the advancing forms with them to the capital.

These types are as follows:

1. Type I, in use from the middle of the fourteenth century onwards, is found in the majority of manuscripts attributed to Wycliffe and his followers, although it is not restricted to them. Otherwise known as "Central Midlands Standard," its importance is testified by its use in a large number of texts, not only religious, which have survived in it. Characteristic Type I forms, common in the Central Midland counties in Middle English times, include *sich* "such," *mych* "much," *ony* "any," *silf* "self," *stide* "stead," *ʒouun* "given," *siʒ* "saw."

2. Type II forms are found in a set of mid-fourteenth-century texts from what might be described as the "Greater London area," including the well-known Auchinleck Manuscript. Characteristic Type II forms derive from Norfolk and Suffolk, e.g., -*ande* present participle, the word *þerk* "dark," etc.; these forms seem to correlate with a pattern of mid-fourteenth-century immigration into the capital which shows a marked influx from East Anglia. Other characteristic forms include *werld* "world," *þat ilch(e)*, *ilch(e)* "that very," *noiþer, noþer* "neither," *þei(ʒ)* "though," *þai, hij* "they."

3. Type III forms appear most characteristically in manuscripts copied by Adam Pinkhurst. Its characteristic features reflect a shift in immigration patterns at the end of the century, whereby newcomers to the capital originated in the Midlands and brought their forms with them. Frequently attested forms include *world*, *thilke*, *that ilk(e)* "that very," *neither*, *though*, *they*, *yaf* "gave," *nat* "not," *swich(e)* "such," *bot* "but," *hir(e)* "their," *thise* "these."

4. Type IV is the language used in the mass of government documents after ca. 1430, for which reason it has been labeled "Chancery Standard" (the term is in many ways unfortunate; see further Benskin 2004 and references there cited). It shows the impact of yet further waves of immigrants from the Midlands, who included in their linguistic repertoires some originally North Midland forms. Characteristic forms include *gaf* "gave," *not* "not," *but*, *such(e)*, *theyre*, etc. "their," *thes(e)* "these," *thorough/ þorowe* "through," *shulde* "should."

It is important not to overstate the status of these types. Even Adam Pinkhurst will use non-Type III forms as minor variables (e.g., *noght* "not" alongside *nat* in the Ellesmere Manuscript). As a number of scholars have pointed out, these types are not uniform in the same way that Present-Day written Standard English is uniform; rather, "seen against the perspective of Middle English dialects overall, each type comprises closely similar samples from the cline that is the total range of dialectal variation" (Sandved 1981: 39). In other words, the types represent focusing in the written mode in the same way that, for example, Received Pronunciation represents focusing in the spoken mode in Present-Day English: a norm to which particular users tend rather than a set of shibboleths from which any deviation is stigmatized.

Indeed, the process of written standardization seems, as suggested at the beginning of this chapter, to have been essentially driven by communicative needs (see further Samuels 1981; Benskin 1991). As English became elaborated and took on a number of national roles, the written variation which had characterized it hitherto became inconvenient, and "grosser provincialisms" were expunged in favor of those with more common currency. Later on, in the Early Modern period, the early printers established norms which were subsequently reified as the norm for educated persons; such a development also correlated with the rise of standardized forms of speech. These issues will be covered in later chapters. (See VARIETIES OF EARLY MODERN ENGLISH; EARLY MODERN ENGLISH PRINT CULTURE.)

REFERENCES AND FURTHER READING

Benskin, M. (1991). Some new perspectives on the origins of standard written English. In J. A. van Leuvensteijn & J. B. Berns (eds.), *Dialect and Standard Language/Dialekt und Standardsprache, in the English, Dutch, German and Norwegian Language Areas* (pp. 71–105). Amsterdam: Koninklijke Nederlandse Akademie van Wetenschappen Verhandelingen, Afd. Letterkunde, Nieuwe Reeks, deel 150.

Benskin, M. (2004). Chancery Standard. In C. Kay, C. Hough, & I. Wotherspoon (eds.), *New Perspectives on English Historical Linguistics II: Lexis and Transmission* (pp. 1–40). Philadelphia: Benjamins.

Benson, L. et al. (eds.) (1988). *The Riverside Chaucer.* Oxford: Oxford University Press.

Burrow, J. & Turville-Petre, T. (1997). *A Book of Middle English.* Revd. edn. Oxford: Blackwell.

Crotch, W. (ed.) (1928). *The Prologues and Epilogues of William Caxton.* London: Early English Text Society.

Horobin, S. (2003). *The Language of the Chaucer Tradition.* Cambridge: Brewer.

Horobin, S. & Smith, J. (2002). *An Introduction to Middle English.* Edinburgh: Edinburgh University Press.

LALME = McIntosh, A., Samuels, M. L., & Benskin, M., with Laing, M. & Williamson, K.

(1986). *A Linguistic Atlas of Late Mediaeval English*. Aberdeen: Aberdeen University Press.

Mooney, L. (2006). Chaucer's scribe. *Speculum*, 81, 97–138.

Mossé, F. (1959). *A Handbook of Middle English*. Trans. J. Walker. Baltimore: Johns Hopkins University Press.

Samuels, M. L. (1963). Some applications of Middle English dialectology. *English Studies*, 44, 81–94.

Samuels, M. L. (1981). Spelling and dialect in the late and post-Middle English periods. In M. Benskin & M. L. Samuels (eds.), *So Meny People Longages and Tonges: Philological Essays in Medi-*

aeval English and Scots Presented to Angus McIntosh (pp. 43–54). Edinburgh: Benskin & Samuels.

Sandved, A. (1981). Prolegomena to a renewed study of the rise of Standard English. In M. Benskin & M. L. Samuels (eds.), *So Meny People Longages and Tonges: Philological Essays in Mediaeval English and Scots Presented to Angus McIntosh* (pp. 31–42). Edinburgh: Benskin & Samuels.

Strang, B. (1970). *A History of English*. London: Methuen.

Wright, J. & Wright, E. M. (1928). *An Elementary Middle English Grammar*. 2nd edn. Oxford: Oxford University Press.

Section 3
Early Modern English in History (1485–1660)

Introduction

Though relatively short, the early modern period saw English widen its scope in more than one way. To begin with, the number of English-speakers increased dramatically between the late fifteenth century and the year 1660: the population of England jumped from two to five million; the size of London octupled to 400,000; the same number of people emigrated to Ireland and North America. During the same period, English vocabulary grew at an unprecedented speed with the expansion rate reaching its peak in around 1600. The first monolingual dictionary, *A Table Alphabeticall*, was published in 1604 to explain difficult words in plain English. Writers like Shakespeare were responsible for adding hundreds of words to the English lexicon. An even greater number of neologisms were created in science and other areas of learning. Since many of the new words were borrowed or coined from classical languages, Latin and Greek comprised a superstructure within the already stratified English lexicon. Those who tried to block the foreign influences criticized the bookish nature of these new words by calling them "inkhorn" terms. (See EARLY MODERN ENGLISH; also A HISTORY OF THE ENGLISH LEXICON.)

At the beginning of the Tudor dynasty, in 1485, English was already a language of Parliament, governmental documents, and print. In the next two centuries, English further elevated its social status by playing a role in the unfolding of events of great significance such as the Reformation, the intellectual movements known as humanism and the Renaissance, the colonial expansion, and the Civil War. To take the role of English in print technology for an example, the Great Bible was authorized by the Protestant King Henry VIII in opposition to the Latin Vulgate. After Henry, different versions of the Bible, both vernacular and Latin, were endorsed by different monarchs until the compilation of the King James Bible in 1611 (see also EARLY MODERN ENGLISH PRINT CULTURE). In the seventeenth century, political debates were often conducted through the bandying of pamphlets. New formats such as news-sheets, newspapers, and periodicals were also on the rise. Thanks to the growing print industry, English orthography was more or less established by the 1590s. Standard pronunciation of English was yet to be established, however, and people tolerated regional dialects within the national border. Syntax and lexis served as a social marker instead, since these discourse-related features were considered to reveal one's rank and education. As for a privilege dialect, aspiring poets were encouraged to emulate the speech of London and especially of the court (see VARIETIES OF EARLY MODERN ENGLISH). With a few notable exceptions, women received less formal education than men. Only 2 percent of printed material produced in seventeenth-century England is known to be by women authors (see also ISSUES OF GENDER IN MODERN ENGLISH).

Haruko Momma

20
Early Modern English (1485–1660)

Terttu Nevalainen

Setting the Scene: People and Cities

The period from 1485 to 1660 spans the Renaissance and the Restoration in Britain. In 1485 the first Tudor monarch, Henry VII, ascended the throne, and 1660 marks the restoration of the Stuart monarchy as Charles II returned to the throne following ten years of Oliver Cromwell's rule after the English Civil War (1640–9). The world of the early Tudors differed in many ways from that of the late Stuarts, as did their language. This chapter discusses the social and cultural issues that shaped the directions in which the English language evolved during this period.

Population growth and urbanization

In the late fifteenth century the vast majority of the English people, only some two million in all, lived in the countryside. The largest city was London with a population of about 50,000 inhabitants. Other large towns were Bristol, Canterbury, Coventry, Exeter, Norwich, Salisbury, and York, whose populations varied between 5,000 and 9,000. By 1660, the population of England and Wales exceeded five million. The growth of London in particular had been spectacular: with a population of 400,000 it had become one of the largest cities in Europe, second only to Paris and Constantinople. The prophetic words of James I at the beginning of the century had come true, and London had become "all England" (Beier & Finlay 1986; Dyer 1991).

As the center of England's political and economic life, culture, and fashion, London attracted both migrants and short-term visitors from all over the country. It has been estimated that one adult in six had some experience of life in London in the latter half of the seventeenth century (Wrigley 1967). For visitors, London's attractions included the latest fashions as well as an unequalled marriage market, as suggested by the letters of Henry Oxinden, a Kentish gentleman, cited in (1) and (2).

(1)   I sent thee the newest and best fashion stuffe in London on Tuesday last for a gound and petticoate, because I thought nothing too good or too deare for thee. (CEEC, Henry Oxinden 1647; OXINDEN, 114)

(2)   Pray if my sister Elizabeth may marry well in London, not to neglect itt: for good husbands are hard to bee gott here. (CEEC, Henry Oxinden 1639; OXINDEN, 144)

However, because of epidemic and endemic diseases, living in the capital also meant health hazards: on average, more people died in London than were born there. The bubonic plague, which was feared most, could claim the lives of hundreds of people almost overnight. In (3), Philip Henslowe, the theatre financier and owner of the Rose and Fortune playhouses, records the toll of one such epidemic in 1593.

(3)   I eand praysinge god that it doth pleass hime of his mersey to slacke his hand frome visietinge vs & the sittie of london for ther hath abated this last two weacke of the sycknes iiij hundreth thurtie and five & hath died in all betwexte a leven and twealle hundred this laste weack wch I hoop In the lord yt will contenew in seasynge euery weacke . . . (CEEC, Philip Henslowe 1593; HENSLOWE, 281)

London was where news was made and circulated. The first printed news-sheets started to appear in the 1620s, and the first official English newspaper in 1665. But even in the seventeenth century, domestic news passed by word of mouth or private letter more quickly than it could be printed. In (4) Otwell Johnson, a London wool merchant, gives his brother an eyewitness account of the public execution of Katherine Howard, the fifth wife of King Henry VIII, in the Tower of London in 1542.

(4)   And for newes from hens, knowe ye that even according to my writing on Sonday last, I se the Quene and the Lady Betcheford [*sic*] suffer within the Tower the day following, whos sowles (I doubt not) be with God, for thay made the moost godly and Christyan's end that ever was hard tell of (I thinke) sins the worlde's creation, uttering thayer lyvely faeth in the blode of Christe onely, with wonderfull pacience and constancye to the death; (CEEC, Otwell Johnson 1542; JOHNSON 4)

The power and prestige attached to the Royal Court, however, attracted new media from early on: to be close to the Court, William Caxton set up the first printing press in England at Westminster in 1476. Politics was inseparable from religion throughout the period, but particularly in Henry VIII's reign (1509–47), when the Catholic country was transformed into a Protestant one. The Reformation affected many aspects of society, from land ownership to the language of devotion (Brigden 1989; see p. 212).

Overseas expansion

In the late fifteenth century English was spoken only in England and to some extent in Ireland and Wales, while Scots had their own distinct idiom, Scots-English (see ENGLISH IN IRELAND; ENGLISH IN WALES; ENGLISH IN SCOTLAND). By the 1660s, an

estimated 400,000 English speakers had emigrated to Ireland and North America, founding their first permanent settlements in Virginia (1607) and New England (1620). There were not many towns on the map of North America in the first half of the seventeenth century, among the first being Jamestown (Virginia), Boston and Plymouth (New England). New York – or New Amsterdam, as it was known to contemporaries – only came into English possession in 1664. Charles II writes to his sister Minette about this new acquisition:

> (5)   You will have heard of our takeing of New Amsterdame, which lies just by New England. 'Tis a place of great importance to trade, and a very good towne. It did belong to England heeretofore, but the Duch by degrees drove our people out of it, and built a very good towne, but we have gott the better of it, and 'tis now called New Yorke. He that took it, and is now there, is Nicols, my brother's servant, who you know very well. (CEEC, Charles II, 1664; CHARLES 2 95)

Because of the short time English had been spoken in North America, few differences had arisen between the English and American varieties by 1660. We also have to bear in mind that those who emigrated to the New World came from different regions of the mother country: most of the people who settled in Massachusetts in the first half of the seventeenth century were from East Anglia, but those destined for Virginia mostly came from the south of England (Fischer 1989).

In fact more happened to Scots English in the sixteenth and seventeenth centuries. Apart from regional changes within Scots, the distinct process of anglicization which had begun in the sixteenth century was accelerated on the accession of King James VI of Scotland to the throne of England in 1603 as James I of England and Scotland (Devitt 1989). One important factor in the process was the publication in 1611 of the Authorized Version of the Bible (King James Bible), which became the version of the scriptures preached throughout the realm.

Vernacularization

In the late Middle Ages, England had been trilingual, with French and Latin serving many of the official functions that English came to occupy in the Renaissance. This expansion of use paved the way for English becoming a full-fledged standard language. In the administration, vernacularization began in the royal writing offices in the early fifteenth century, and spread to other domains as diverse as religion, philosophy, science, and literature. They were all enriched by translations from the classical and continental languages. A number of literary landmarks appeared in the sixteenth and seventeenth centuries: Virgil's *Aeneid* was translated by Henry Howard, Earl of Surrey in the 1540s; Castiglione's *The Courtier* by Sir Thomas Hoby (1561); Ovid's *Metamorphoses* by Arthur Golding (1567); Plutarch's *Lives* by Sir Thomas North (1579); Montaigne's *Essays* by John Florio (1603); and Homer's *Iliad* and *Odyssey* by George Chapman (1611 and 1614–16, respectively).

Illustration: language of religion

Religion was one of the domains where the use of English expanded in the sixteenth century. In the Middle Ages, England was a Catholic country, and followed the rest of western Europe in the use of the dominant language of the Church, Latin. There was an English translation of the Bible based on the Latin Vulgate instituted by John Wycliff in the 1380s, but it did not have the authorization of the Church.

The first complete English translation of the Bible from the original Hebrew and Greek appeared in 1534. Much of it was based on the work of William Tyndale, who had translated the New Testament and parts of the Old Testament in the 1520s. However, in this age of religious turmoil, Church authorities branded many of the terms introduced by Tyndale as heretical. Despite contemporary disapproval, his work became the cornerstone for later Bible translations, the King James Bible in particular. A large number of Tyndale's terms such as *Jehovah*, *Passover*, *scapegoat*, and *atonement* have lived on, as have his phrases, including *my brother's keeper* (Genesis 4), *the salt of the earth* (Matthew 5), and *a law unto themselves* (Romans 2) (McGrath 2001: 75, 79).

The Church exerted a strong influence on everyday life in Renaissance England, and a large proportion of all printed texts were in the domain of religion. The King James Bible and the Book of Common Prayer – first translated into English in 1549, reissued with modifications in 1552 and revised in 1662 – had larger print runs than any other contemporary books. Some aspects of their grammar were already obsolete or deviated from general use at the time. These forms include the second-person singular pronoun *thou*, the old subject pronoun *ye* (as opposed to *you*), and the third-person singular verb ending -(*e*)*th* (as opposed to -*s*). They became part of the language of religion, recognizable as such even today. The excerpt in (6) comes from the King James Bible.

> (6)   7 Marueile not that I saide vnto
> thee, Ye must be borne againe.
> 8 The winde bloweth where it listeth,
> and thou hearest the sound thereof,
> but canst not tel whence it commeth,
> and whither it goeth: So is euery one
> that is borne of the Spirit.
> (*The New Testament*; John 3:7–8)

Enrichment of the Written Language

Gaining ground in many new functions as a literary language, English was significantly enriched by lexical creativity and intake. Tyndale had wanted his translations to be accessible to ordinary people, including the legendary "boy that driveth the plough," but this was not a possible or even desirable aim for all translators. Specialist

terms were needed in all fields that began to use the vernacular, and different strategies were available to achieve this end, including borrowing (Nevalainen 1999).

Illustration: medical vocabulary

One of the fields where significant word-formation activity took place was the language of science. To get an idea of the variety of processes available to specialists at
the time, we may look at terms for sicknesses and body parts in medical treatises
between the last quarter of the fifteenth and the first half of the sixteenth century
(Norri 2004).

A very common process was adopting a new word from another language, often
from French but especially from Latin, or one that appeared in both. As a result of
such borrowing, new names of sicknesses came into English in this period including,
for instance, *fracture*, *indigestion*, *inflammation*, and *tension*, while body-part names were
enriched by terms such as *extremities*, *hymen*, *mandible*, *membrane*, *tendon*, and *testicle*.
Another common way of introducing a new term was using native processes of word-
formation such as compounding or affixation. Compound words consist of two independent words, such as *oliphant sickness* 'elephantiasis'. Affixation is a process by which
a prefix or a suffix is added to an already existing word, as in *misdeed* (*mis-* + *deed*,
'impotence') and *grinders* (*grind* + *-er*, 'molars'). Besides *-er*, the *-ing* ending was
common in these formations, as in *fainting*, *putrefying*, *vomiting*.

The meaning of an existing word could also be extended to create a new term. In
The Breuiary of Helthe (1547: 140v.), Andrew Boorde introduced the word *blast*
meaning a sudden eye-condition caused by "an euyl wynde or else of some contagiouse
heat." Similarly *pox* (plural of *pock*, 'pustule on the skin') was a popular metonymic
term for *syphilis*. However, many of these new words did not become a lasting part
of English medical terminology. A large number of them were later replaced, e.g.,
pedicoun ('epilepsy'), *mappa ventris* ('diaphragm'), *outcoming* ('dislocation'), as well as
oliphant sickness and *misdeed*, mentioned above.

The Inkhorn Controversy

The same processes of borrowing, word-formation, and extension of meaning were
employed in other fields of specialization, including literary language. In the course
of the sixteenth century, borrowing words from the classical languages, Latin in particular, reached such proportions that it gave rise to a heated debate known as the
Inkhorn Controversy (*inkhorn* 'inkwell', with reference to bookishness). Those who
opposed excessive borrowing argued that one should rely on native sources of vocabulary instead, in order to be intelligible to the uneducated. Some conservatives even
advocated the use of obsolete and dialectal words (Barber 1997).

The concern for intelligibility was particularly acute in a period when only a small
proportion of the population had access to a classical education, and an even smaller
percentage continued their studies in the two universities, Oxford and Cambridge, or

obtained legal training in the Inns of Court at London. The vast majority of the ordinary English people were not literate in the sixteenth century, although there were more people who could read at least the printed word than those who could both read and write. Londoners were on average more literate than people elsewhere. Although there were notable exceptions – Queen Elizabeth I (1533–1603) translating, for instance, Boethius' *De consolatione philosophiae* – women's average level of literacy was much below that of men's (Cressy 1980). (See ISSUES OF GENDER IN MODERN ENGLISH.)

Towards a Standard Language

The purists lost the battle against loan words, and there was an upsurge of new words adapted from Latin, French, and other European languages in specialist fields ranging from theology and science to literary language. For teaching purposes, wordlists were appended to popular textbooks such as Edmund Coote's *English Schoole-maister* (1596). The monolingual English dictionaries were all "hard-word" dictionaries recording borrowed lexis. The first one, *A Table Alphabeticall*, compiled by Robert Cawdrey, came out in 1604. Its title page addresses its intended readership (7):

> (7)   A Table Alphabeticall, conteyning and teaching the true writing, and vnderstand-
> ing of hard vsuall English wordes, borrowed from the Hebrew, Greeke, Latine, or
> French, &c. With the interpretation thereof by plaine English words, gathered for the
> benefit & helpe of Ladies, Gentlewomen, or any other vnskilfull persons, Whereby they
> may the more easilie and better vnderstand many hard English wordes, which they shall
> heare or read in Scriptures, Sermons, or elswhere, and also be made able to vse the same
> aptly themselues.

Spelling became the target of another major language debate in the sixteenth century. As shown by Cawdrey's title in (7), even printers and professional writers did not have a fully standardized spelling system. Shakespeare, for one, could sign his name in several different ways. Despite this relative diffuseness of the contemporary norm, a debate arose between reform and convention. (See CLASS, ETHNICITY, AND THE FOR-MATION OF "STANDARD ENGLISH.")

Orthoepists felt that spelling and pronunciation had drifted too far apart, and efforts were made to bridge the gap. In *The Opening of the Unreasonable Writing of Our Inglish Toung* (1551), John Hart criticized spelling practices that had no match in pronunciation: superfluous letters appeared in words such as *authorite* (<h>), *eight* (<g>), and *people* (<o>). The silent word-final <e> was used inconsistently: it indicated a long preceding vowel in words like *spake*, *take*, and *before*, but created an extra syllable in words spelled with a double consonant (*sunne*, *sonne*). To remedy such short-comings, Hart proposed a more phonemic system, also containing new letters, for instance, for the initial sounds in words like *chain* and *thimble*.

Although spelling reformers found some support, they more often met with staunch opposition. In his popular teaching manual, *The Elementarie* (1582), Richard Mulcaster argued that there was too much variation in speech, both regionally and socially, to make it a suitable basis for spelling. He therefore joined those who preferred established usage as the norm, suggesting that "[t]he vse & *custom* of our cuntrie, hath allredie chosen a kinde of penning, wherein she hath set down hir relligion, hir lawes, hir priuat and publik dealings" (1582: 98).

By 1650, the printed word had already reached a high degree of orthographic uniformity. Fixed spelling had become an area of technical specialization in the printing trade, and these printers' norms were imposed on manuscripts to be published (Scragg 1974). There are only a few conventions that make late seventeenth-century texts look different from ours. They include contracted verb forms ('*d* for -*ed*); spelling -*ick* for -*ic* and -*or* for British English -*our*; and the use of capital letters to mark foregrounded words.

The period from the Renaissance to the Restoration did not, however, try to fix English grammar or pronunciation. Linguistic prescriptivism became part of the standardization process only in the long eighteenth century (see BRITISH ENGLISH IN THE LONG EIGHTEENTH CENTURY).

REFERENCES AND FURTHER READING

Barber, C. (1997). *Early Modern English*. Edinburgh: Edinburgh University Press.

Beier, A. L. & Finlay, R. (1986). Introduction. In A. L. Beier and R. Finlay (eds.), *London 1500–1700: The Making of the Metropolis* (pp. 1–33). New York: Longman.

Brigden, S. (1989). *London and the Reformation*. Oxford: Clarendon Press.

CEEC = The Corpus of Early English Correspondence; see Nevalainen & Raumolin-Brunberg, 2003.

Cressy, D. (1980). *Literacy and Social Order: Reading and Writing in Tudor and Stuart England*. Cambridge: Cambridge University Press.

Devitt, A. (1989). *Standardizing Written Language: Diffusion in the Case of Scotland 1520–1659*. Cambridge: Cambridge University Press.

Dyer, A. (1991). *Decline and Growth of English Towns, 1400–1600*. London: Macmillan.

Fischer, D. H. (1989). *Albion's Seed: Four British Folkways in America*. Oxford: Oxford University Press.

McGrath, A. (2001). *In the Beginning: The Story of the King James Bible*. London: Hodder & Stoughton.

Nevalainen, T. (1999). Early Modern English lexis and semantics. In R. Lass (ed.), *The Cambridge History of the English Language, Vol. 3: 1476–1776* (pp. 332–458). Cambridge: Cambridge University Press.

Nevalainen, T. (2006). *An Introduction to Early Middle English*. Edinburgh: Edinburgh University Press.

Nevalainen, T. & Raumolin-Brunberg, H. (2003). *Historical Sociolinguistics: Language Change in Tudor and Stuart England*. London: Longman/Pearson Education.

Norri, J. (2004). Entrances and exits in English medical vocabulary, 1400–1550. In I. Taavitsainen & P. Pahta (eds.), *Medical and Scientific Writing in Late Medieval English* (pp. 100–43). Cambridge: Cambridge University Press.

Scragg, D. G. (1974). *A History of English Spelling*. Manchester: Manchester University Press.

Wrigley, E. A. (1967). A simple model of London's importance in changing English society and economy 1650–1750. *Past and Present*, 37, 44–70.

21
Varieties of Early Modern English

Jonathan Hope

The Early Modern period saw the re-establishment of English as a multi-functional language, used in spoken and written contexts throughout England, and in parts of Wales, Scotland, and Ireland. The language was also used in different contexts at all points on the social scale. This situation contrasts directly with the Middle English period (see MIDDLE ENGLISH IN HISTORY), where the use of English in written contexts was relatively restricted (Latin and Anglo-Norman being more common), and the use of spoken English was not automatically associated with the highest social classes. The contrast with the Old English period is less clear-cut, since English at that time was employed in many written contexts (albeit in competition with Latin), and was the normal spoken language throughout Anglo-Saxon society.

As a language extends its functionality, its geographical spread, and its medium (that is, as it develops written forms), we expect an increase in the number of its varieties, defining "variety" as a form of the language associated with a particular function, social or geographical context, or medium. A variety consists of a set of forms – which may be phonetic, lexical, morpho-syntactic, and discourse-related – which predictably co-occur. Varieties may be characterized by only one factor: for example, accounts and court records show relatively little geographical variation in the period, so we can say that they constitute almost wholly functional varieties (the linguistic features which occur are determined by the function of the text). More commonly, varieties are characterized by the variable interaction of more than one factor: for example, letters share certain structural features (openings, closure, signatures) which can be ascribed to function, but they also vary in terms of orthography, lexis, morpho-syntax, and discourse features, according to geographical and social factors associated with the producer (and sometimes the recipient). In the following sections, I give an overview of some of the varieties of Early Modern English divided into functional varieties, geographical varieties, and discourse/social varieties, but it should be remembered that these are not exclusive categories, since the factors of function, geography, social class, and medium potentially interact.

Inevitably, I will concentrate on written varieties here, since the only direct evidence we have for the varieties of Early Modern English is in this form, but it is possible to use evidence from written texts to make some comment on spoken varieties: court records sometimes attempt to reproduce actual conversations; plays and jest books give fictional representations of speech; Early Modern orthoepists made very detailed studies of the sounds of some Early Modern English varieties (see Dobson 1968).

Functional Varieties

Although the evidence from the Middle English period is less full, it is a reasonable assumption that the range of functional varieties supported by English grew in the Early Modern period as English was adopted for use in contexts which had previously used mainly Latin or Anglo-Norman. In many cases, English was used alongside other languages: legal texts (1) often shift between Latin questions and framing material, and English reports of witness statements; business records (2) commonly show mixing of words and even morphemes from a wide range of languages, though English, Latin, and Anglo-Norman are the most common (Wright 1996).

> (1)　Add iiij[tum] Interrogatorio dicit that he was in the stokkis but he seith that he neuer harde ne knewe the wordis conteyned in the first parte of the article/ et quo ad georgium villeris dicit q[d] master hughe Asseton and the seid george came to this deponent sittyng in the stokkis [. . .] and askid hym as he dede
> (Cusack 1998: 109; from the Bishop of Lincoln's 1525 Visitation of Newarke College and Hospital, Leicester)

> (2)　Item to will knoll and denbolde for worke　　　　　　　　　vj s ix d
> Item to Schaptor for carriage　　　　　　　　　　　　　　　　　ij s
> Item domino willielmo austyn in nominee rewardi de computi　xij d
> Item to Iohn Gye　　　　　　　　　　　　　　　　　　　　　　　xxxiij s iiij d
> (Cusack 1998: 47; from the accounts of the churchwardens of Ashburton, Devon for 1500–1)

Functional varieties like this are often highly formulaic in structure, showing little temporal or geographical variation. Formulae here include the Latin references back to an original list of questions ('Add iiij[tum] Interrogatorio dicit' = 'to the fourth question he says . . .'), the Latin phrases which introduce each new answer ('et quo ad georgium villeris . . .'), and, in the accounts, the structuring of entries using the Latin term 'Item' and ending with the amount paid ('vj s ix d' = six shillings, nine pence). Although such texts are relatively invariant in their structure, they have considerable interest for historians of Early Modern English because, in the case of depositions, they often record something close to actual speech, and, in the case of accounts, they often give us access to everyday vocabulary items which are unrecorded elsewhere (Wright 1996).

Court records in particular have been studied by historians, literary scholars, and linguists (see, for example, Wrightson 1982; Hope 1993; Jardine 1996; Syme forthcoming (a), (b)).

Geographical Varieties

Whereas depositions and accounts have a highly predictable form and register, diaries and letters are far more varied both in terms of their physical form and linguistic features – so although they can be considered primarily as functional entities, letters and diaries often give us access to evidence for geographical varieties of Early Modern English. Diaries range from externalized and relatively impersonal lists of notable events (for example, those of Henry Machyn, 1550–63 – edited by Nichols 1848, and Thomas Rugge, 1659–61 – edited by Sachse 1961) to more personalized accounts of the concerns of the diarist (Roger Lowe 1663–78 – edited in Winstanley 1994), and extracts from each of these diaries will be found in Cusack (1998: 158–79); on diaries generally, see Findlay (2002); Jajdelska (2007, ch. 5).

Letters, even those from individuals of very high social class, can provide evidence for geographical variety (3):

(3)   Madame and dearest sister, The suddaine pairting of this honorable gentleman, youre ambassadoure, upon thaise unfortunatt and displeasant neuis of his onkle, hes mouit me with the more haist to trace theis feu lynes unto you; first, to thanke you, as uell for the sending so rare a gentleman unto me, to quhose brother I was so farre beholden; as also, for the tayce sending me such summes of money, quhiche, according to the league, I shall thankfullie repaye with forces of men, quensoeuer youre estait sall so require . . .
(Görlach 1991: 353; James VI of Scotland to Elizabeth I of England, September 1588)

Here, James VI of Scotland (who was to become James I of England) writes to Elizabeth I using a range of Scottish English features: '-it' for past participle endings: 'mouit' = moved; 'qu-' for 'wh-': 'quhose' = whose, 'quhiche' = which, 'quensoeuer' = whensoever. The appearance of these Scottish English features not only illustrates one geographical variety of Early Modern English, but demonstrates that there was no single written standard at this time. Nevalainen and Raumolin-Brunberg (1996, 2003) constitute a major investigation of varieties and variation in Early Modern letters.

Geographical varieties are represented in Early Modern plays, though interestingly, most of the representations are of national, rather than regional, varieties. In Shakespeare's *Henry V* (1599), for example, we have representations of Scottish, Irish, and Welsh English in the speech of three captains:

(4)   *Welsh.*   Captaine *Iamy* is a maruellous falorous Gentleman . . .
(5)   *Irish.*   By Chrish Law tish ill done: the work ish giue ouer . . .
(6)   *Scot.*   It sall be vary gud, gud feith, gud Captens bath . . .
(Shakespeare, *Henry V*, folio TLN1195, 1206–7, 1220 – act 3, scene 2 in modern editions)

And the same author's *Merry Wives of Windsor* (1597/8) again has Welsh English, alongside non-native speaker English (French). In fact, as Paula Blank notes, there are surprisingly few representations of regional English varieties in Early Modern English drama, and no consistent representation of any phonetic features that might be associated with lower-class London accents, despite the frequent appearance of such characters in the drama (Blank 1996: 40). It is possible, of course, that Shakespeare and other playwrights verbally directed their fellow-actors when a regional or lower-class accent was intended, so did not consider it necessary to imitate the accent in writing, but this hypothesis is made unlikely by the fact that Shakespeare does transliterate accent when he depicts national varieties of English. Blank's hypothesis that constant migration into London at this time meant that there was no consistent lower-class accent, might accord with what we know of population movements (see EARLY MODERN ENGLISH), but runs counter to the findings of modern sociolinguistic studies of rapidly growing towns. Although it is an unfamiliar notion to most present-day speakers of English (especially British varieties), the literary evidence seems to suggest that Early Modern culture was very tolerant of linguistic variation, and certainly did not automatically associate regional English with lack of education or low social class (Barber 1997: 103). On this hypothesis, regional and class varieties are largely absent from literary representations not because they did not exist, but because they were not stigmatized. In support of this hypothesis is the one clear-cut use of regional English in Shakespeare, which occurs in *King Lear* (1605/6). In act 4, scene 6, the noble character Edgar, already in disguise as a beggar, puts on a rustic dialect when confronted by Oswald, a steward:

(7)   *Edg.*   Good Gentleman goe your gate and let poore volke passe: and
'chud ha'bin zwaggerd out of my life, 'twould not ha'bin zo long as 'tis, by a vortnight.
Nay, come not neere th'old man: keepe out che vor'ye
(Shakespeare, *King Lear*, folio TLN 2690–3; act 4, scene 6 in modern editions)

Although the features of this dialect can be found in Kent and Somerset English (the 'ich' first person forms, and fricative voicing), this is in fact an almost wholly literary variety, traceable at least from the medieval *Second Shepherds' Play* of the Wakefield cycle, through Golding's translation of Ovid in 1565, and beyond *King Lear* into song books and jest books in the seventeenth century.

It seems therefore that geographical varieties of English are used in literature only as rather crude badges of identity, establishing national identity (Scottish, Irish, Welsh) or very broad social identity (rural versus urban). There is no sense of a

fine-grained social order associated with regional dialects, nor of an upper/lower-class split (despite the claims of Fox 2000: 55, 60; see also THE RISE OF RECEIVED PRONUNCIATION). I will return to this important, and perhaps surprising, claim in the section on standardization below.

Discourse/Rhetorical Varieties

If I am right in the claim that geographical variation was not identified with social variation to the extent that it is in the later history of English, what evidence is there for social varieties in Early Modern English? Stigmatization of regional variety is almost wholly absent from Early Modern drama, and is only ambiguously present in contemporary comment on language. There is, however, substantial evidence that higher-level, discourse features are used as an indicator of level of education, and therefore social class (or rank).

In Shakespeare's *King Lear*, Gloucester responds to a change in his disguised son's speech with the comment

(8)   Me thinkes thy voice is alter'd, and thou speakst
In better phrase, and matter then thou didst.
(Shakespeare, *King Lear*, folio TLN 2440–1 – act 4, scene 6 in modern editions)

Edgar has also just switched from prose to verse, often a key indicator of social class in drama. In Shakespeare's *Romeo and Juliet* (1595), Mercutio responds to Romeo's joining in with a game of complex quibbling on a series of words with the telling phrase

(9)   now art thou sociable, now art thou Romeo: now art thou what thou art by Art
as well as by Nature
(Shakespeare, *Romeo and Juliet*, folio TLN 1190–1 – act 2, scene 4 in modern editions)

Romeo confirms his rank by demonstrating the ability to manipulate language consciously (by art) as well as naturally (by nature). This is a difficult value-system for us to grasp, since we tend to favor linguistic behavior that is, or represents itself as being, spontaneous. Education in the Early Modern period however consisted of rigorous training, in Latin, in the manipulation of language according to a set of predetermined rhetorical structures, often learned by rote (Baldwin 1944). Educated individuals could recognize each other by identifying modes of discourse rather than particular accents. We tend to assume that Ben Jonson's comment in *Timber* that "language most shows a man: speak that I may see thee" refers to phonology – in truth, it is more likely to refer to much higher-level features of discourse: lexis, syntax, and the deployment of formal rhetorical figures of speech.

Standardization: Contemporary Comment on Variation and Varieties

The Early Modern period sees, in printed texts at least, what could be called the triumph of standardization. By 1660, books and pamphlets produced by the London printing houses show a very low degree of orthographic variation, while the major morpho-syntactic changes in English appear, from the evidence of print, mainly to be complete by around 1600: after this date, outgoing features such as 'thou', third person singular '–th', and unregulated use of auxiliary 'do' (for this terminology, see Barber 1997: 193–6) are largely confined to formulaic, archaic, and poetic contexts.

We should be wary, however, of projecting this print standardization onto the language as a whole. Printers standardized the orthography of their manuscript copy as a matter of course (Davis & Carter 1958), and the wide range of different types of manuscript material that survives from the Early Modern period shows that there remained a high degree of variation both within and between the idiolects of individuals. The rapid standardization of orthography in print from the 1590s onwards is impressive, but it masks continued variation outside the printing house, and even printed texts show a high degree of register variation (mainly in the areas of lexis and syntax) based on their perceived audiences.

It is also crucial when considering standardization to differentiate between standardization and the ideology of standardization: that is, the identification and stigmatization of certain features or varieties (see the essays in Wright 2000, esp. Milroy 2000). As we have seen, standardization itself is largely complete in printed Early Modern texts by the early 1600s. However, the type of comment on language which introduces the ideology of standardization is not unambiguously present until around 1660. Earlier comment on the varieties of English has been used to support the notion that a spoken standard was emerging (Fox 2000: 53, 55, 60), but such contemporary comment has to be read carefully: much of it is by schoolmasters, who had a financial interest in spreading linguistic insecurity; it is not always clear when written, rather than spoken English is being referred to; selective quotation can ignore other pronouncements which are very relaxed about variety. For example, George Puttenham's much repeated recommendation to poets about which variety they should use, "the usual speech of the court and that of London and the shires lying about London within lx miles," is actually very open indeed, and makes no explicit attempt to exclude basilectal varieties in London or the shires.

Resources

The extensive printed and manuscript materials which come down to us from the Early Modern period mean that we have direct access to a wide range of written varieties, and second-hand access to some spoken varieties via court records, informal

letters, plays, and jest books. The best place to start work on written varieties is the manual to the Helsinki corpus (Kytö 1996); the follow-up corpora of letters (Nevalainen & Raumolin-Brunberg 2003) and Scottish-English (Meurman-Solin 1993) introduce some manuscript and regional material. Cusack (1998) contains careful transcriptions of selected court records, letters, diaries, accounts, and presentments, which introduce the reader to the main types of manuscript material to be found in county and city record offices throughout the United Kingdom, even including some texts from Early Modern America. The Helsinki corpora are available via ICAME, while Cusack (1998) also acts as a guide to some of the printed editions of manuscript material, and an introduction to some of the city and county record offices that hold manuscripts from the period.

References and Further Reading

Baldwin, T. W. (1944). *William Shakespeare's Small Latine and Lesse Greek*. 2 vols. Urbana: University of Illinois Press.

Barber, C. (1997). *Early Modern English*. 2nd edn. Edinburgh: Edinburgh University Press.

Blank, P. (1996). *Broken English: Dialects and the Politics of Language in Renaissance Writings*. London: Routledge.

Cusack, B. (1998). *Everyday English 1500–1700: A Reader*. Edinburgh: Edinburgh University Press.

Davis, H. & Carter, H. (eds.) (1958). *Joseph Moxon 1683–4 Mechanick Exercises on the Whole Art of Printing*. Oxford: Oxford University Press.

Dobson, E. J. (1968). *English Pronunciation 1500–1700*. 2nd edn. 2 vols. Oxford: Clarendon Press.

Fox, A. (2000). *Oral and Literate Culture in England 1500–1700*. Oxford: Oxford University Press.

Findlay, E. (2002). Ralph Thoresby the diarist: the late seventeenth-century pious diary and its demise. *Seventeenth Century*, 17 (1), 108–30.

Görlach, M. (1991). *Introduction to Early Modern English*. Cambridge: Cambridge University Press.

Hope, J. (1993). Second person singular pronouns in records of Early Modern "spoken" English. *Neuphilologische Mitteilungen*, 94 (1), 83–100.

Jajdelska, E. (2007). *Silent Reading and the Birth of the Narrator*. Toronto: University of Toronto Press.

Jardine, L. (1996). *Reading Shakespeare Historically*. London: Routledge.

Kytö, M. (1996). *Manual to the Diachronic Part of the Helsinki Corpus of English Texts*. 3rd edn. Helsinki: Department of English, University of Helsinki.

Meurman-Solin, A. (1993). *Variation and Change in Early Scottish Prose: Studies Based on the Helsinki Corpus of Older Scots*. Helsinki: Academia Scientiarum Fennica.

Milroy, J. (2000). Historical description and the ideology of the standard language. In L. Wright (ed.), *The Development of Standard English 1300–1800* (pp. 1–28). Cambridge: Cambridge University Press.

Nevalainen, T. & Raumolin-Brunberg, H. (eds.) (1996). *Sociolinguistics and Language History: Studies Based on the Corpus of Early English Correspondence*. Amsterdam: Rodopi.

Nevalainen, T. & Raumolin-Brunberg, H. (2003). *Historical Sociolinguistics: Language Change in Tudor and Stuart England*. London: Longman.

Nichols, J. G. (ed.) (1848). *The Diary of Henry Machyn, Citizen and Merchant-Taylor of London, from AD 1550 to AD 1563*. Camden Society Original Series, vol. 42. London: J. B. Nichols and Son.

Sachse, W. L. (ed.) (1961). *The Diurnal of Thomas Rugg 1659–1661*. Camden Society, 3rd series, vol. 91. London: Offices of the Royal Historical Society.

Syme, H. S. (forthcoming, a). Becoming speech: voicing the text in Early Modern English courtrooms and theatres. *Compar(a)ison* (special issue on law and literature).

Syme, H. S. (forthcoming, b). Royal depositions: Richard II and Early Modern textuality. *Shakespeare Quarterly*.

Winstanley, I. (ed.) (1994). *The Diary of Roger Lowe of Ashton in Makerfield, Lancashire 1663–1678*. Ashton in Makerfield: Picks Publishing.

Wright, L. (1996). *Sources of London English: Medieval Thames Vocabulary*. Oxford: Oxford University Press.

Wright, L. (ed.) (2000). *The Development of Standard English 1300–1800*. Cambridge: Cambridge University Press.

Wrightson, K. (1982). *English Society 1580–1680*. London: Hutchinson.

Section 4
Modern British English in History (1660–present)

Introduction

The following three chapters consider English in the modern era. Carey McIntosh's essay spans 1660 to 1830, a period known as the "long" eighteenth century. Like other cases of periodization, the identification of the long eighteenth century as a historical period is somewhat arbitrary. It begins with the Restoration of the Stuart monarchy after a protracted Civil War. It ends with a combination of events ranging roughly from the death of the Romantic poet Byron in 1824 to the ascension of Queen Victoria in 1837. The blurriness of its boundaries notwithstanding, the long eighteenth century comprises a bridge between "the world of Shakespeare" and "our world." Richard W. Bailey's essay on modern British English begins in 1834, when Michael Faraday collaborated with the polymath William Whewell to coin Greek-based terms like *electrolysis*, *cathode*, and *ion*. By this time, English had become a language of culture equipped with monolingual dictionaries and normative grammar, full-blown print culture, gender debates, and fictional characters like Elizabeth Bennet who used impeccable diction in their upper-middle-class household (see also JOHNSON, WEBSTER, AND THE *OED*; EARLY MODERN ENGLISH PRINT CULTURE; ISSUES OF GENDER IN MODERN ENGLISH; JANE AUSTEN'S LITERARY ENGLISH).

Modern Britain was also an age of meritocracy. Faraday and Whewell, the men who jointly invented vocabulary for electrochemistry, were sons of a blacksmith and a carpenter, respectively. The Earl of Chesterfield was willing to give up his privileges in English to Samuel Johnson, the son of a poor bookseller. As British society became more and more democratic in its outlook, the demand for standardizing English became greater and more complex. In the early modern period, the standardization of English was mostly limited to print orthography, and very little stigma was attached to regional varieties of spoken English (see also VARIETIES OF EARLY MODERN ENGLISH). Even Johnson, the bastion of correct diction, was disinclined to give up his provincial articulation. In contrast, his young biographer James Boswell, as Lynda Mugglestone notes, sought instructions from a renowned elocutionist to remove the "defects" of his Scots accent. Boswell was among a large number of people, often of Scottish or Irish origin, who emulated the pronunciation of metropolitan English. In theory, the promotion of standard speech had egalitarian purposes. In reality, this cultural project privileged one variety of London English while turning all other varieties into social markers (see also CLASS, ETHNICITY, AND THE FORMATION OF "STANDARD ENGLISH"). In the late nineteenth century, the geographically non-localized variety of English spoken by the educated men and women across Britain was dubbed Received Pronunciation (RP). Virtually a class dialect, RP rapidly gained recognition and assumed the voice of authority when it was adopted by the BBC. The development of standard English corresponded with the expansion of the political influence of England first to other parts of Britain and to Ireland and then to its

overseas colonies where new varieties of English arose (see AMERICAN ENGLISH IN HISTORY; PART VI: ENGLISH OUTSIDE ENGLAND AND THE UNITED STATES; PART VIII: ISSUES IN PRESENT-DAY ENGLISH).

Haruko Momma

22

British English in the Long Eighteenth Century (1660–1830)

Carey McIntosh

Much of what happened to the English language during the long eighteenth century can be related to an extraordinary growth of language consciousness in those 160 years. In the 1660s, only a handful of people worried about English. There were no real English grammars and nothing we would recognize as an English dictionary, no daily newspapers, no "media" at all. No one studied English in school, except to learn to read. But by the early nineteenth century "correctness" in speech and writing was almost a national obsession. Hundreds of grammars and dozens of dictionaries had been published and purchased, with no sign that the British public's appetite for them had been sated. Browse through R. C. Alston's ten volumes of bibliographies to get a sense of how many different kinds of books on the English language were written before 1800 (for example, dialect collections, dictionaries of thieves' cant), and how rapidly their numbers increased after 1700.

The growth of language consciousness was certainly accelerated by the enormous steps Britain took in this period towards becoming a fully literate print culture (see Eisenstein 1983; McIntosh 1998). In the 1660s, most people did not read or write. Language was primarily an oral phenomenon, transmitted from mouth to ear. The most powerful national communications systems were the sermons and speeches and readings that people heard every week in church or chapel. But by 1830 all the (pre-electronic) institutions of literacy were going full steam: dictionaries, magazines, anthologies, advertisements, newspapers, cartoons, lending libraries, book reviews, women writers, and feminist tracts. The "canon" of English literature (starring Shakespeare) was being studied, and elocutionists like Thomas Sheridan got rich by telling Scots and Irish how to talk like educated Londoners.

It is tempting to think of the years from 1660 to 1830 as a kind of hinge between the world of Shakespeare and our world. During this time many modernities came into being: the natural sciences; global capitalism; money as credit, not just gold and silver; the modern sexual identities of men and women (Hitchcock & Cohen 1999); the social sciences (economics, anthropology, sociology); feminism; noble savages and

Byronic heroes; musical comedy; tourism; statistics; fashion plates (McKendrick et al. 1982); sports as a business; trade unions; Romanticism; steam engines; public art exhibits; the British Empire.

Wars of Truth

Just because the Civil War had ended doesn't mean that Restoration England was stable or confident or secure. Almost everyone welcomed Charles II as king over a newly peaceful nation, but these were turbulent times: bubonic plague in 1665, the Great Fire of London in 1666, war with Holland in 1667, a Popish Plot to kill Charles in 1678, a successful revolution in 1688 (booting out an anointed king), war against the Irish in 1690, war against France in 1697 and then again from 1701 to 1713.

English continued to feel the effects of the Civil War, in conflicts and contrasts between the language (and values) of the court, and the languages of other people, including Dissenters. Royalists exercised a good deal of control over publication in general because they administered the Licensing Act, and yet Quaker women were preaching in public and writing tracts as no women ever had before (Foxton 1994). "High" culture was cultivated in the shadow of Catholic France. John Dryden adapted precepts of the Académie Française by which to "correct" his own prose; the superheroes of his plays resemble those of Corneille and his literary criticism echoes Le Bossu and Rapin. Meanwhile, chapbooks and other popular, cheap publications continued to be written and read by the thousands (Spufford 1981).

The English language was also affected by reactions against the Civil War. The repudiation of "enthusiasm" in religion was paralleled by a repudiation of enthusiastic language – Dryden tried to abandon the metaphysical "conceit," and John Locke attacked not only metaphor but also rhetoric in general. Members of the Royal Society (founded 1663) denounced all "amplifications, digressions, and swellings of style: to return back to the primitive purity, and shortness, when men deliver'd so many things, almost in an equal number of words" (Sprat 1667, cited in Adolph 1968: 114). Some bold thinkers who valued simplicity and clarity in language went so far as to design artificial languages modeled on mathematics (e.g., John Wilkins; see Land 1986).

The New Literacy

In 1695 the Licensing Act expired, which meant that anyone could publish anything without government permission. The first daily newspaper dates from 1702; periodical publication exploded with *The Tatler* (1709) and *The Gentleman's Magazine* (1731). Only four towns could boast of printing presses in 1700 (London, Oxford, Cambridge, and York). By the early nineteenth century books, broadsides, ads, posters, handbills,

labels, tickets, indentures, and such were being printed in every sizable town in Britain, and London alone had 52 newspapers. The first modern copyright law was passed in 1709. Literacy rates among women rose from about 10 percent in 1660 to about 50 percent in 1750; among men, from 30 percent to 67 percent (see EARLY MODERN ENGLISH PRINT CULTURE).

Politicians embraced the new print culture. Swift's brilliant tracts and slashing satires have been credited with creating the Peace of Utrecht (1713). A long series of publications by the new-born "loyal opposition" (*Cato's Letters*, *The Craftsman*, Junius, Burke's speeches) were read throughout the century and formed in America a basis for revolutionary thought. Step by step, the political life of the nation became a matter of public record – that is, it appeared in print.

Language consciousness increasingly took the form of public embarrassment at the unregulated condition of English. Swift complained in 1712 that "our Language is extremely imperfect," subject to "daily Corruptions," and full of "Absurdities"; his "Proposal for Correcting, Improving and Ascertaining the English Tongue" lamented the absence of just the institutions France had created in the mid-seventeenth century, a national academy and a comprehensive dictionary. Joseph Addison devoted a *Spectator* essay to relative pronouns, "who," "which," and "that" (No. 78, 1710). Alexander Pope corrected his own correspondence for publication by deleting slang and substituting more correct and elegant expressions. Henry Fielding ridiculed bad grammar in Colley Cibber's prose (*The Champion*, April 29, 1740).

The idea that certain forms of a natural language are better than others (called "prescriptivism"), though sanctioned by classical rhetoric and inchoate in Ben Jonson and John Dryden, did not gain a real foothold in British culture till the eighteenth century. Practical English grammars began to appear around 1710 (Alston 1974; Michael 1970), and the English dictionaries published in 1706 and 1721 identified "Country" words – rural and provincial terms. In 1747 Samuel Johnson published a plan for the first historical dictionary of English and promised a campaign against "barbarisms" and "cant" (see JOHNSON, WEBSTER, AND THE *OED*). The most influential grammar of the century (by Robert Lowth) did not appear till 1762, but it opened the floodgates of prescriptivism – and it gave a first, in some cases a definitive form to many of the same rules as are still taught all over the world to people learning to write English. Prescriptive or "normative" grammar can be used as an instrument of class oppression (see CLASS, ETHNICITY, AND THE FORMATION OF "STANDARD ENGLISH"), but these grammars can also liberate, enabling people to rise out of poverty or oppression – William Cobbett's autobiography (1796) credits Lowth's grammar with enabling him to become something more than a mere foot-soldier.

"A Polite and Commercial People"

Despite wars and revolutions, famines, riots, and strikes, Britain grew and prospered under the first three Hanoverian kings. During George II's reign (1727–60) the value

of British exports to America quadrupled and the value of exports to India septupled (Langford 1989: 168). Sarcastic references to the extravagance and wealth of "Nabobs" just back from India begin in the 1720s (Sambrook 1986: 76). Agricultural reform increased the yield of basic crops, but it also pushed people off the land into towns, some of which were becoming genuine cities, with street lights, police, sidewalks, and slums. The industrial revolution changed the workplace, and it changed private homes, where factory-made utensils and furniture gradually displaced hand-made. New roads and canals enabled the transportation of heavy materials, such as coal and slate; there were 2,223 miles of canals in Britain by 1790 (Langford 1989: 410–17).

Gradually, class replaced rank as a social discriminator. Money began to count almost as much as land ownership. Horsemanship, swordsmanship, and wit gave way to politeness and sensibility, as upper-class virtues (Barker-Benfield 1992). By summarizing many of these changes as a "feminization" of culture, we recognize the increasingly important role that women played during this period. The "first feminists" emerged in the eighteenth century (Astell, Montague, Wollstonecraft: see Ferguson 1985), and more women wrote and published than ever before – in women-oriented genres, in romantic and sentimental novels, familiar letters, children's books, courtesy books. I have argued that the language of ordinary prose was affected by these changes, becoming more polite, correct, periphrastic, nominal, abstract (McIntosh 1998).

Such changes contributed to the "standardization" of English (Milroy & Milroy 1985). School texts and book reviews castigated every word and usage they considered non-standard. The government tried to eradicate regional variation and local languages in Scotland and Wales (Sorensen 2000; see also ENGLISH IN SCOTLAND; ENGLISH IN WALES). David Hume and James Boswell and other equally famous Scots fretted over Scotticisms in their writing and speech. The developing self-consciousness about language shows up in the novel and in plays where non-standard speakers are almost uniformly comic characters, someone to laugh at, e.g., Squire Western in *Tom Jones* (1749) or Win Jenkins in *Humphry Clinker* (1771) (see Blake 1981: 1988). But of course there was much more variation than the novelists knew (for a useful and comprehensive summary, see Görlach 1999).

A powerful change during our period was urbanization. In 1670, only one place in Britain had more than 20,000 people, London with 475,000; the next four largest were rather small towns of 12–20,000. In 1841, London was twice as big as Paris, with 2,239,000 inhabitants, and six other towns had more than 100,000 inhabitants (Sweet 1999: 3–4). Although this unprecedented growth brought luxury and high culture to the provinces (Borsay 1989), it also deepened the division between rich and poor. In the early nineteenth century, two thirds of town-dwellers owned little more than the clothes they stood up in and lived in tiny, dark, unventilated slums. Sewerage scarcely existed before 1850. The word "slum," adopted from cant or slang, is first used in print in its modern sense in 1825, which is roughly the time that Cockney-speakers first appear in literature.

Enlightened Views and Romantic Vistas

The English Civil War that immediately preceded our period was only one of the "wars of truth" in seventeenth-century Europe. France, Germany, Spain, Denmark, Sweden, and Austria all fought in the Thirty Years War (1618–48) between Catholic and Protestant powers, a bloody, drawn-out affair that left Germany "in ruins," the Empire "a hollow shell," and France "the chief power in Europe" (Bridgwater 1953). What later came to be known as the Enlightenment can be seen as yet another reaction against those religious wars. Such various and varying thinkers as Bayle, Leibniz, Newton, Voltaire, Locke, and Shaftesbury all agreed that the architect of the universe was a reasonable being, who presided over cosmic harmony, not sectarian strife. Deistic thought celebrated the astonishing orderliness of the Newtonian universe and welcomed new discoveries produced by new sciences, e.g., oxygen, electricity, and Halley's comet (Porter 1990).

The Enlightenment made its mark on language largely through new words, new technical terms (see BRITISH ENGLISH SINCE 1830), but its love of orderliness can also be detected in the way it organized linguistic phenomena. Dictionaries of the late eighteenth century are more precise and systematic than earlier dictionaries, most of which defined words in an informal, even colloquial style and still included (for example) the magical powers of gems. Encyclopedias before about 1730, such as Chambers', explain certain things in scholastic (Aristotelian) terms, whereas the first edition of the *Encyclopedia Britannica* (1768–71) draws substantially on recent discoveries in mathematics, physiology, and biology (McIntosh 1998: 184–94). Modern linguists still rely on the scheme of organization for languages and language families ("Indo-European") that was invented or discovered by Sir William Jones in the 1780s.

Romanticism had its seeds in the eighteenth century (Berlin 1999), but it did not emerge in Britain as a dominating set of attitudes till around 1800. "I am certain of nothing but of the holiness of the Heart's affections and the truth of the Imagination," wrote John Keats in 1817. According to Sir Isaiah Berlin, romanticism places the highest value on "integrity, sincerity, readiness to sacrifice one's life to some inner light" (p. 8). This is a radical change in that it abandons the idea that human action should always aim at forms of good and right which are known and public (p. 13). Romanticism sanctions a belief in minorities, in failures, in unrecognized genius.

A romantic (or pre-romantic) mindset will therefore be attracted to the study of minority languages, dialects, and exotic tongues. John Ray published the first collection of British dialect words in 1674. Allan Ramsay began a series of anthologies of poetry in the Scots language in 1721. Thieves' cant featured in such comedies and satires as John Gay's *The Beggar's Opera* and Fielding's *Jonathan Wild*. Macpherson's *Ossian* (1760) and Percy's *Reliques* (1765) were wildly popular, igniting new researches into ballads and other folk literature all over Europe. The Scots English of Robert Burns' poems (1786) and of Walter Scott's Waverley novels (1814ff.) attracted hun-

dreds of thousands of readers. An interest in unfamiliar foreign languages generated English publications on Chinese (1761), Icelandic (1763), Welsh (1764), and Danish (1770), all of which anticipated Herder's widely influential thoughts on the "original language" (*Ursprache*) of a nation or people as the outward expression of its inner essence. Wordsworth's 1800 Preface to the Lyrical Ballads, which many historians designate as the beginnings of full-fledged British Romanticism, announces a preference for the language of real men [and women], peasants, simple people – which is as much an attempt to find words to express essential humanity, as it is a revolt against eighteenth-century poetic diction.

I think that by the early nineteenth century, language consciousness in Britain had perceptibly liberated and opened up. The only major new dictionary of this era came from America (Webster's magnum opus of 1828), but scholars were assimilating the truly historical perspectives on language change developed by the Neogrammarians in Germany; spadework for the *OED* would soon be under way. Compare Byron's language world with Johnson's or Swift's: "My current tongue is Levant Italian, which I gabble perforce, my late dragoman spoke bad Latin, but having dismissed him, I am left to my resources which consists in tolerably fluent Lingua Franca, middling Romaic [modern Greek] and some variety of Ottoman oaths" (Byron 1982: 46). Though all three men delighted in word-play, Johnson and Swift disapproved of colloquialisms and slang; they took for granted the classical and neo-classical principles of seventeenth-century scholars like Vossius and Rapin. The word "slang" itself, which meant "jargon, cant" as a new word in the 1750s, developed a less pejorative sense by 1818, "the highly colloquial non-standard speech of young people." In Byron's lifetime slang could be fashionable when used by swells or bang-ups or jehus (so called because they drove their chariots hard and fast). Prescriptivism was by no means dead or dying, however; there was no escaping Lowth's and Murray's grammars in school. Elizabeth Bennet, the wonderful heroine of Jane Austen's *Pride and Prejudice* (1813), speaks with exemplary correctness, and we recognize her sister Lydia as an air-head by her slangy and ungrammatical speech: "I was in such a fuss!" and "my uncle and aunt were horrid unpleasant."

REFERENCES AND FURTHER READING

Adolph, R. (1968). *The Rise of Modern Prose Style*. Cambridge, MA: MIT Press.

Alston, R. C. (1974). *A Bibliography of the English Language from the Invention of Printing to 1800*. Ilkley: Janus Press.

Barker-Benfield, G. J. (1992). *The Culture of Sensibility: Sex and Society in Eighteenth-Century Britain*. Chicago: University of Chicago Press.

Berlin, I. (1999). *The Roots of Romanticism*. Princeton, NJ: Princeton University Press.

Blake, N. F. (1981). *Non-Standard Language in English Literature*. London: Andre Deutsch.

Borsay, P. (1989). *The English Urban Renaissance: Culture and Society in the Provincial Town, 1660–1770*. Oxford: Clarendon Press.

Bridgwater, W. (ed.) (1953). *The Columbia-Viking Desk Encyclopedia*. New York: Viking Press.

Byron, G. G. (1982). *Selected Letters and Journals*. Ed. L. Marchand. Cambridge, MA: Harvard University Press.

Eisenstein, E. L. (1983). *The Printing Revolution in Early Modern Europe*. Cambridge: Cambridge University Press.

Ferguson, M. (ed.) (1985). *First Feminists: British Women Writers, 1578–1799*. Bloomington: Indiana University Press.

Foxton, R. (1994). *"Hear the Word of the Lord": Quaker Women's Writing 1650–1700*. Melbourne: Bibliographical Society of Australia and New Zealand.

Görlach, M. (1999). Regional and social variation. In R. Lass (ed.), *The Cambridge History of the English Language, Vol. 3* (pp. 459–538). Cambridge: Cambridge University Press.

Hitchcock, T. & Cohen, M. (1999). Introduction. In T. Hitchcock and M. Cohen (eds.), *English Masculinities 1660–1800* (pp. 1–22). London: Addison Wesley Longman.

Land, S. K. (1986). *The Philosophy of Language in Britain: Major Theories from Hobbs to Thomas Reid*. New York: AMS Press.

Langford, P. (1989). *A Polite and Commercial People: England 1727–1783*. Oxford: Clarendon Press.

McIntosh, C. (1998). *The Evolution of English Prose 1700–1800: Style, Politeness, and Print Culture*. Cambridge: Cambridge University Press.

McKendrick, N., Brewer, J., & Plumb, J. H. (1982). *The Birth of a Consumer Society: The Commercialization of Eighteenth-Century England*. Bloomington: Indiana University Press.

Michael, I. (1970). *English Grammatical Categories and the Tradition to 1800*. Cambridge: Cambridge University Press.

Milroy, J. & Milroy, L. (1985). *Authority in Language: Investigating Language Prescription and Standardisation*. London: Routledge & Kegan Paul.

Page, N. (1988). *Speech in the English Novel*. London: Macmillan.

Porter, R. (1990). *The Enlightenment*. London: Macmillan.

Sambrook, J. (1986). *The Eighteenth Century: The Intellectual and Cultural Context of English Literature, 1700–1789*. London: Longman.

Sorenson, J. (2000). *The Grammar of Empire in Eighteenth-Century British Writing*. Cambridge: Cambridge University Press.

Spufford, M. (1981). *Small Books and Pleasant Histories: Popular Fiction and Its Readership in Seventeenth-Century England*. Athens: University of Georgia Press.

Sweet, R. (1999). *The English Town, 1680–1840*. London: Longman.

23
British English Since 1830

Richard W. Bailey

In 1834, William Whewell introduced the word *scientist* to the English language, having formed it by analogy with *artist*, to describe "students of knowledge of the material world."

In the spring of that year, Whewell (1794–1866) was sought out by Michael Faraday (1791–1867) for advice on naming, and Faraday began his letter by writing: "I wanted some new names to express my facts in Electrical science without involving more theory than I could help." Farady had just coined the noun *eletrolyte* and then the verb *electrolyze* "instead of saying that water is *electro chemically decomposed*." But he was puzzled by what to call the *electrodes* (itself a Faraday coinage): "the two surfaces . . . by which the current enters into & passes out."

New Names for New Facts

Whewell had been present at the Royal Society when Faraday had presented his ideas and had heard the new words. Whewell was glad to be consulted: "I was rejoiced to hear [the new terms], for I saw or thought I saw that these novelties had been forced upon you by the novelty of extent and the new relations of your views."

In an exchange of letters, the two scientists discussed various Greek-derived words before coming to the solution. "If you take *anode* and *cathode*," Whewell wrote, "I would propose for the two elements resulting from *electrolysis* the terms *anion* and *cation* . . . and for the two together you might use the term *ions*." In the course of these letters, Faraday thought of words that would be even less likely to imply theory than *anode* and *cathode*: *Voltode* and *Galvanode*. These would have the further merit of memorializing Allesandro Volta (1745–1827) and Luigi Galvani (1737–98), and they mirror some coinages for electrical phenomena recently come into English use: *voltaism* (1811) and *galvanism* (1797). Whewell found *Voltode* and *Galvanode* objectionable: on the one hand, they are "not only entirely but ostentatiously arbitrary"; on the other,

"it will be very difficult for anybody to recollect which is which." Someone led Faraday to fear that *anode* might be construed as "no way," but Whewell assured him that *anados* and *cathodos* were genuine Greek words and that the idea that *anode* means "no way" would be rejected by anyone with "any tinge of Greek" (James 1993: 2, 177–86; see also Hamilton 2002: 259).

So the matter was settled. In the fortnight beginning on April 24, 1834, Faraday and Whewell settled on terms that would become and remain part of *electro-chemical analysis* (a term that had been introduced by Faraday's mentor, Humphrey Davy, in 1807): *anode*, *cathode*, *anion*, *cation*, and *ion*.

New Words: Who's in Charge?

What is remarkable in this episode in English word-formation is that the way of selecting these terms was in some respects new to the nineteenth century.

In 1712, Jonathan Swift had proposed that the Earl of Oxford undertake to chair a committee for "improving" the English language, a task much needed, Swift wrote, because "its daily Improvements are by no means in proportion to its daily Corruptions" (Bolton 1966: 108). Swift alleged that cutting away corruption would lead to perfection, "*fixing* our Language for ever, after such Alterations are made in it as shall be thought requisite" (Bolton 1966: 117). A generation later, another earl – the Earl of Chesterfield – echoed the same theme: "Toleration, adoption and naturalization have run their lengths. Good order and authority are now necessary" (Bolton 1966: 126). Chesterfield was willing, he wrote, to surrender "all my rights and privileges in the English language" to the son of a provincial bookseller, Samuel Johnson. In proposing to compile a dictionary, Johnson had hoped that the work might achieve Swift's goal, serve to "fix" English, and dispose of the need for change. But in a spasm of pre-publication gloom, Johnson despaired of that idea, and alleged that no dictionary could secure a language "from corruption and decay" (Bolton 1966: 151; see also JOHNSON, WEBSTER, AND THE *OED*).

The Reformation of Authority Over Words

By the 1830s, a new optimism appeared. Progress was seen everywhere. No more the old notion that the language had declined from an earlier stage of *purity*. No more the idea that English would be better with fewer words.

Scientists needed new words for new ideas, and Faraday (among others) was free-ranging in considering candidates. Aristocrats were no longer in charge of English; merit – which could be found almost anywhere – was in the ascendant.

Faraday was self-taught and the son of a London blacksmith; Whewell was the son of a Lancashire carpenter who was ridiculed for his rusticity when he took up his studies at Cambridge. Faraday was undoubtedly the scientific genius of his age;

Whewell was a polymath who in 1841 was named to the most prestigious academic post in England, Master of Trinity College, Cambridge. That was just a year after he had coined the word *physicist* for scientists who studied "force, matter, and the properties of matter."

The fact that intellectuals from humble backgrounds had taken charge of English was just one expression of the radical changes taking place in the Anglo-American world in the 1830s: the Reform Bills extending democracy; Chartism to empower the working class; Jacksonianism, in the United States, shifting power from the eastern élites to unruly westerners.

Whewell exulted in the opportunity to create a new world of words to match the creativity of his times:

> Such a coinage [of words] has always taken place at the great epochs of discovery; like the medals that are struck at the beginning of a new reign: – or rather like the change of currency produced by the accession of a new sovereign; for their value and influence consists of their coming into common circulation. (Quoted by Hamilton 2002: 261)

Faraday and Whewell took charge of making English words, and the methods they employed were in many ways new. Greek-derived borrowings into English had long been important in theology and rhetoric, but *ion* and the like presaged the international scientific vocabulary whose creation emerged as a global enterprise drawing on Greek and Latin for a "systematic" and "scientific" vocabulary.

Faraday was fond of compounds like *magneto-electric* (1831), but he also used ordinary words in special senses, like his coinage of *magnetic field* (1845) that made a scientific metaphor of *field*. As was proposed with *Voltode* and *Galvanode*, personal names could yield scientific terms. In his own lifetime, Faraday became such a word: *Farad* (1861), a measure of capacitance. With the addition of suffixes, this memorial word exfoliated into many scientific nouns, verbs, and adjectives: *faradaic* (1875), *faradic* (1878), *faradism* (1876), *faradization* (1867), *faradize* (1864).

In the twentieth century, words connected with Michael Faraday flourished, particularly as capacitance became a central idea in the circuitry of the electronic age. Whewell had emphasized the significance of new words "coming into common circulation," but a huge community of specialists may use words freely even though those words never surface in general-purpose dictionaries. Thus, many prefixes have been attached to *farad*: *abfarad, attofarad, centifarad, decifarad, dekafarad, exafarad, kilofarad, megafarad, microfarad, millifarad, nanofarad, pelofarad, picofarad, stratfarad, terafarad*. However mysterious to the literary, these are English words with English meanings, and their absence from dictionaries is only evidence of the inadequacy of dictionaries in representing the full capacity of English.

Compound nouns were increasingly important in the English wordstock. Here are some that appear in the *OED* (with dates of first known use): *Faraday cage* (1916), *Faraday's constant* (1931), *Faraday('s) dark space* (1893), *Faraday('s) disk* (1886), *Faraday effect* (1889), *Faraday('s) ice-pail experiment* (1888), *Faraday's law* (1850),

Faraday's line (1857), *Faraday tube* (1893). As a search of scientific writing readily displays, there are far more compounds using *Faraday* than these, and there are all sorts of abbreviations as well: *mfd* "microfarad"; pF "picofarad." The impulse of scientists to collapse and abbreviate words, just as Faraday had coined *electrolize* to replace the cumbersome *electro chemically decompose*, was a new and productive way of creating the "new names" required by science. In the twenty-first century, this word-making by abbreviation and acronym had became an unremarkable part of technical English: FIFCE "Filtered Faraday Cup Experiment"; SFWE(M) "Static Feed Water Electrolysis (Module)." (As the phrases behind these initialisms show, there was an enormous increase during the twentieth century in the practice of piling up nominal modifiers.)

Faraday, a member of a Protestant denomination proclaiming biblical inerrancy, must have seen himself on the model of Adam in the Garden: "whatsoever Adam called every [thing], that was the name thereof" (Genesis 4:19).

The Counter-Reformation

The unnoticed story of British English since 1830 is the explosive growth in words from science, medicine, and technology. Only a fraction of these are found in even the largest general-purpose dictionaries, and the reason is not far to seek: they have been purposively excluded. In an essay published in 1860, the scholar most responsible for the design of the great dictionaries of the past century and a half provided a rationale for omitting them:

> Nothing is easier than to turn to modern treatises on chemistry or electricity, or on some other of the sciences which hardly or not at all existed half a century ago, or which, if they existed, have yet been in later times wholly new-named – as botany, for example – and to transplant new terms from these by the hundred and the thousand, with which to crowd and deform the pages of a Dictionary; and then to boast of the vast increase of words which it has gained over its predecessors. (Trench 1860: 57–8)

However right the practical implications of the decision, this view is hard to reconcile with the principle that dictionaries are obliged to consider every word: "It is no task of the maker of it to select the *good* words of a language," Trench had written: "The business which he has undertaken is to collect and arrange all the words, whether good or bad, whether they do or do not commend themselves to his judgment" (Trench 1860: 4–5). Excepting, of course, words from the study of chemistry and electricity.

If Whewell and Faraday saw this policy as a deliberate rejection of their efforts to provide new words for new ideas, they would have been right. Throughout his career as a public scientist, Faraday had wasted time refuting the allegations of persons who believed in table-turning, spirit-rapping, and other projections of the supernatural into the natural. That lexicographers might give more weight to unsub-

stantiated imaginings than to the empirical findings of science would not have surprised him.

Language historians have too often seen English through the narrow portals of dictionaries, as if these works represented the language without fear or favor. By doing so, they have overlooked the most abundantly creative efforts to enlarge the wordstock by any means imaginable: creation, borrowing, affixation, blending, abbreviation, sense-shifting, and compounding among them.

Of course, the idea that English was in decline, that corruption and instability were a threat to it, had by no means disappeared in the nineteenth century. If anything

Figure 23.1 Grim-visaged grammar glares from atop the chair full of symbols in this image used as the frontispiece of George Jackson's *Popular Errors in English Grammar* (1830). While it makes sport of instruction in Latin, the ideas behind the satire applied with equal force to English. The crest on the back of the seat shows Richard Busby (1606–95), headmaster of Westminster School, who was said to have used a scourge of birch twigs (shown below the portrait) on all but one of the pupils sent to him for education. The faces on the arms and legs of the chair represent the four parts of grammatical study: orthography, etymology, syntax, and prosody. The three figures at the lower back represent verbs: active, passive, and neuter. Above Busby's portrait are two figures: on the left, the *noun substantive* which can stand alone; on the right, the *noun adjective* which inclines toward the *substantive* which is necessary to its existence. The etching had been published in 1802 in imitation of an earlier work by Peter Lely. The sour impressions on all the faces reminded Jackson's readers that the study of language is far from sweetness and light. This image used here by permission of the National Portrait Gallery, London

there was a counter-reformation in which the views of Swift and Chesterfield were revived with ever-increasing ferocity. At the very time Whewell and Faraday were debating just which new words to use for Faraday's new ideas, W. H. Savage published a work titled: *The Vulgarisms and Improprieties of the English Language*. Books of this sort have poured from British printing presses ever since. One of them had the arresting title, *Don't* (Bunce 1883).

Savage recognized that emergent democracy threatened the linguistic influence of the learned and the courtly: "This want of fixity [in English] creates an everlasting contention, and leaves to the arbitrary caprice of individuals a power, in which the ignorant assume a right of claim equally forcible with that of the learned; and in which barbarism and vulgarity so far prevail, as to render the contention of ambiguous determination" (Savage 1833: v). As many others down to the present would repeat, Savage saw the threat to English in fluidity (rather than fixity), innovation (rather than stability), impropriety (rather than decorum).

Views like Savage's flourished, and it was taken as commonplace that sensitivity to linguistic nuance (and a willingness to speak out on behalf of the good) was a responsibility of cultivated English people. Avoiding errors in one's own speech, and attacking it in the speech of others, remains a British cultural value into the twenty-first century. English newspapers regularly carry reports of anger over usages and despair over the likelihood of improvement. These linguistic prejudices are expressed without the reservations now typical of criticism in such other domains of life as nationality, race, and religion.

The Ascendant Standard

From the late eighteenth century to the present, the idea of a *standard* English has been mostly subtractive. The standard does not include multiple strings of negatives within a clause: "I cannot go no further" (Shakespeare, *As You Like It*). It does not include *ain't* as a negative contraction of *are not* (or *am not*). It does not include usages formerly standard like "I felt sure that you was angry with me" (Jane Austen, *Sense and Sensibility*). Books like Savage's do not instruct readers in what they should do but in what they ought not to do.

As democracy spread in nineteenth-century Britain, it became ever more necessary to identify positive models of usage, and even more so in the twentieth when the founding of the BBC in 1922 projected a "national" voice to Great Britain. John Reith (1889–1971), first manager and then director general of the BBC, was particularly sensitive to the obligation of the radio to promote good English, and he commissioned guides to usage that would be rule books for broadcasters. Works of this sort have continued to be influential, both directly and indirectly, in defining a standard, particularly in pronunciation but also in other aspects of English usage. (See Bridges 1929; Lloyd James 1935; Burchfield 1982; see also THE RISE OF RECEIVED PRONUNCIATION.)

Another idea that emerged in the post-World War I period was that bad English was connected with bad morals. The 1921 Newbolt Report on the Teaching of English expressed this idea in vivid language:

> The great difficulty of teachers in Elementary Schools in many districts is that they have to fight against the powerful influence of evil habits of speech contracted in the home and street. The teachers' struggle is thus not with ignorance but with a perverted power. (Quoted by Mugglestone 2003: 256)

Non-standard speech, once seen as an arena for pedantic squabbling, suddenly became central to the restoration of values massacred in the horrors of the Western Front.

With unprecedented power to pick and choose among usages, the authorities were obliged to be frank about their choices. The Merton Professor at Oxford from 1920 to 1945, H. C. Wyld (1870–1945), was particularly attuned to nuance and frank to explain his views even "[a]t the risk of offending certain susceptibilities" (1936b, 2). For Wyld, "received standard English" was rarely encountered since the English of nearly everyone was tainted by region or class. RSE was the natural way of speaking among those whose families had emerged to prominence in the seventeenth century. Were he asked to locate this sort of English, Wyld declared that he would seek it "among Officers of the British Regular Army": "The utterance of these men is at once clear-cut and precise, yet free from affectation, at once downright and manly, but in the highest degree refined and urbane" (Wyld 1934: 614; see also Wyld 1936a: xvi).

While many things changed in Britain in the second half of the twentieth century, attitudes toward English changed little. Though the BBC may tolerate greater variety among newsreaders today, it is still an accepted belief that "only about 3 percent of the English population speak RP" (Hughes & Trudgill 1979: 3) and their preferences and whims must be acknowledged by the national broadcasting services. Even a book promoting a sympathetic understanding of language variety is marketed under the title: *Bad Language* (Andersson & Trudgill 1990).

Language Variety in Literature

With the marriage market no longer regulated by one's title, property, or (obvious) wealth, the small hints of "background" that might emerge in speech became crucial indicators. (Sociolinguists call such indicators *markers* rather than *stereotypes*.) Charles Dickens was among the first of the prominent novelists to draw on ways of speaking for this purpose with a Uriah Heep immediately recognizable as a villain by his English. British fiction writers have been unusually concerned with the power of linguistic detail, and the futuristic fiction of Anthony Burgess's *A Clockwork Orange* (1962) and Russell Hoban's *Riddley Walker* (1980) makes much of the connection between brutish behavior and non-standard English.

In the past quarter century, Britain has become both multicultural and polylingual. Some poets and a few novelists are beginning to explore the rich map of language variety in literature; more are sure to follow.

REFERENCES AND FURTHER READING

Andersson, L. & Trudgill, P. (1990). *Bad Language*. Oxford: Blackwell.

Bolton, W. F. (ed.) (1966). *The English Language: Essays by English and American Men of Letters, 1490–1839*. Cambridge: Cambridge University Press.

Bridges, R. (1929). *The B. B. C.'s Recommendations for Pronouncing Doubtful Words*. Society for Pure English, tract 32. Oxford: Clarendon Press.

Bunce, O. B. (1883). *Don't: A Manual of Mistakes & Improprieties More or Less Prevalent in Conduct & Speech*. London: Ward.

Burchfield, R. W. (1982). *The Spoken Word: A BBC Guide*. New York: Oxford University Press.

Hamilton, J. (2002). *A Life of Discovery: Michael Faraday, Giant of the Scientific Revolution*. New York: Random House.

Hughes, A. & Trudgill, P. (1979). *English Accents and Dialects*. London: Edward Arnold.

Jackson, G. (1830). *Popular Errors in English Grammar*. 3rd edn. London: Effingham, Wilson.

James, F. A. J. L. (ed.) (1993). *The Correspondence of Michael Faraday: Letters 525–1333*. London: Institute of Electrical Engineers.

Lloyd James, A. (1935). *The Broadcast Word*. London: K. Paul, Trench, Trubner.

Mugglestone, L. (2003). *"Talking Proper": The Rise of Accent as Social Symbol*. Oxford: Oxford University Press.

Savage, W. H. (1833). *The Vulgarisms and Improprieties of the English Language*. London: T. S. Porter.

Trench, R. C. (1860). *On Some Deficiencies in our English Dictionaries*. London: John W. Parker.

Wyld, H. C. (1934). *The Best English: A Claim for the Superiority of Received Standard English*. Society for Pure English, tract 39. Oxford: Clarendon Press.

Wyld, H. C. (1936a). *The Universal Dictionary of the English Language*. New edn. London: Herbert Joseph for Selfridge & Co.

Wyld, H. C. (1936b). *A History of Modern Colloquial English*. 3rd edn. Oxford: Blackwell.

24
The Rise of Received Pronunciation

Lynda Mugglestone

In his *Plan of a Dictionary of the English Language*, Samuel Johnson confidently declared his intention to "ascertain" or fix pronunciation, "the stability of which is of great importance to the duration of a language" (1747: 11). By the time his *Dictionary* was published eight years later, such attempts at control had nevertheless been abandoned. Entry words were equipped only with an indication of stress-position, hence CO'MELY or INDETERMINA'TION. Furthermore, Johnson now affirmed the impossibility of trying to "enchain syllables" which he compared to attempts to "lash the wind" – both, he added, were "the undertakings of pride, unwilling to measure its desires by its strength." (See JOHNSON, WEBSTER, AND THE *OED*.)

Yet "lashing the wind" in this context was, in fact, to emerge as a major topos of the late eighteenth and nineteenth centuries as writers such as John Walker, Thomas Sheridan, Robert Nares, and Benjamin Smart (among many others) strove to establish national norms of "good" usage for speech. The title-page of Sheridan's *Dictionary*, published in 1780, affirmed that "One Main Object . . . is, to Establish a Plain and Permanent Standard of Pronunciation." Walker's *Critical Pronouncing Dictionary* (1st edn. 1791) provided a detailed transcription of each entry-word, using a combination of phonetic respelling and numerical diacritics; it was, as his obituary in *The Athenaeum Magazine* later affirmed, to become "the statute book of English orthoepy" (Obituary 1808: 81). Orthoepy – literally "speaking correctly" – was central both within this new genre of lexicography and in the escalating popularity of elocution. It played a salient role too in the manuals of linguistic correctness which also proliferated at this time.

"Consciousness can be awaken'd only by information," Sheridan had written in his own favorably received *Course of Lectures in Elocution* (1762: 38). While information was thereby provided in abundance (Walker's dictionary, for example, went through four editions in his lifetime and remained in print throughout the nineteenth century, often being recommended for school as well as individual use), it was consciousness – a shift in language attitudes towards pronunciation – which was perhaps of greatest

significance. Johnson's reluctance to change his native Staffordshire articulations had revealed, for instance, a clear lack of "consciousness" in this respect. The decision of his young Scottish biographer, James Boswell, to take elocution lessons from Sheridan himself instead confirmed the contrary. Sheridan was explicit on the "defects" of Scots articulation; Walker's dictionary likewise contained a specific section proffering remedy for those afflicted by a Scots accent. The Scottish barrister Sylvester Douglas further endorsed this shift in normative language attitudes; Scots, he declared, was merely to be seen as "a provincial and vicious dialect of English"; failure to accommodate to London norms brought "lasting ridicule" and conspicuous "disadvantages" (1991: 99). Other regional varieties were placed in similarly negative paradigms; lengthy sections on the "vices" of the Irish and on the phonetic failings of lower-status speakers in London were included in Walker's *Dictionary*. In the interests of standardization, all were depicted as in need of reform.

Relevant images of "standard" pronunciation rested on a complex interplay of ideas. On one hand, notions of demerit were firmly attached to localized forms of speech. In dominant prescriptive ideologies, regional marking of this kind (which revealed the geographical origins of the speaker) were – in another version of that subtractive methodology already discussed by Bailey (see BRITISH ENGLISH SINCE 1830) – therefore to be displaced by the assimilation of metropolitan standards. While "good" London English had long been singled out as superior in tone and style, contemporary agendas of standardization meant that emphasis was now placed on its specification as a reference model for the entire nation. Pronouncing dictionaries (as well as the associated disciplines of elocution and speech-training) were hence made integral to the diffusion and dissemination of its norms in ways which might, as Sheridan himself stressed, ultimately bring to an end the divisions which differences of accent often seemed to enact. As he admitted, the "right" accent could operate as a social testimony ("a sort of proof that a person has kept good company"); the standard that he (and others) prescribed was located only among "people of education" at the Court and those "who have constant opportunities of conversing with them." Yet, he argued, this "good" speech of London was "ardently desired by an infinite number of individuals." Socio-cultural assumptions about prestige (seen, however, only from a top-down perspective) stressed emulatory paradigms in which it was taken for granted that those without such an accent would willingly adopt its forms. In the grandeur of Sheridan's prescriptive visions, by eliminating enunciations which served to betray local allegiances speakers would "no longer have a variety of dialects, but as subjects of one king, like sons of one father, have one common tongue. All natives of these realms would be restored to their birthright in commonage of language, which has been too long fenced in, and made the property of a few" (1762: 261–2). In spite of the negatively loaded metalanguage which was often deployed, the ultimate aim was portrayed as profoundly egalitarian.

Standardization was thereby made to reside in the intentional provision of a single (and ultimately fixed) national accent for all speakers, just as – in the public domains of print – each word was assuming an increasingly invariant norm. Variation, in

keeping with mainstream prescriptive ideologies, was regarded as aberrant. "Needless irregularity is the worst of all deformities," as Nares categorically declared (1784: iv), adding that "it is disgusting to hear continually the same words differently pronounced in the mouths of different speakers" (p. vii). The rhetoric of standardization seized on the proscription of certain elements and the prescription of others in what became a popular set of dyads. Most prominent was, perhaps, the "proper" use of /h/; a sound regarded with comparative indifference earlier in the century (see Mugglestone 2007: 95ff.). Other dyads focused on "good"/"bad" articulations of *ing* (as /ɪŋ/ not /ɪn/) or *wh* (as /ʍ/ not /w/), and on the "proper" distribution of sounds such as /ʌ/ and /ʊ/ (as in southern enunciations of *cut* and *full*, respectively).

In a further strand of consciousness-raising in this context, such dyads were also often equipped with explicit appeals to notions of cognitive ability (features such as /h/-dropping or the regionally marked /ʊ/ in words such as *cut* were, for instance, explicitly specified as indicators of "Defective Intelligence" by the educationalist John Gill). Appeals to the social sensibilities of readers also featured highly. Benjamin Smart's *Practical Grammar of English Pronunciation* (1810) is typical in this respect:

> There are two pronunciations even in London, that of the well-bred, and that of the vulgar; and the difference does not consist merely in the various manner of pronouncing particular words, but often with the latter in a corruption of fundamental sounds. In short, it is owing to the one being cultivated, and the other neglected. The cultivated speaker employs a definite number of sounds which he utters with precision, distinctness, and in their proper places; the vulgar speaker misapplies the sounds, mars or alters them.

As Smart's pronouncing dictionary later specified, "a man displaying [a rustic accent] must have a huge portion of natural talent or acquired science, who surmounts the prejudice it creates" (1836: xl). The aim instead was the acquisition of a form of speech "in which all marks of particular place of birth and residence are lost."

As in the practical observance of Sheridan's dictates by Boswell, it is the evidence of individual response which can be most telling. Smart's lectures in London were, for example, attended by the young Michael Faraday in 1818. Born in 1791, his native characteristics were clearly those of Smart's "vulgar speaker." The son of a blacksmith, he bore "the accent of the streets" (Hamilton 2002: 1), as well as a clear tendency, in Smart's terms, to "misapply" /w/, referring, for instance, to his elder brother as "Wobert" rather than "Robert." Ambitious, intelligent, and determined upon self-improvement, he made copious notes – over 150 pages – of the information he gleaned on good delivery from Smart's lectures; in the many lectures which Faraday himself gave in the course of his later scientific career, it was the effectiveness of his delivery which was often singled out for praise. Smart was to attend some of these lectures, being invited by Faraday and explicitly urged to monitor the speech-style deployed, noting any aspects which required additional adjustment.

"Received Pronunciation"

Michael Faraday exemplifies in a variety of ways the shift of "consciousness" which had taken place by the early nineteenth century. The spoken language had come to be seen as a site of active intervention; Johnson's tolerance of regional variation was, at least in prescriptive rhetoric, placed firmly in the past. Lectures such as those delivered by Smart and Sheridan, elocution lessons, countless manuals of instruction which ranged from the expensively bound volume to the cheap penny pamphlet, all formed part of this intended dissemination of ideas, urging convergence towards national standards of speech. Images of linguistic propriety (and its converse) frequently infused the representation of speech in nineteenth-century novels, as well as in popular journals. Stereotypes of "talking proper," for instance, recurrently appear in the socio-historical record which *Punch*, launched in 1845, provides: "'Ow, 'Arry ! I s'y ! *H'yn't* 'e a Ugly Cowve," comments the Cockney 'Arriet to an equally /h/-less 'Arry in a cartoon in July 1887. Both are drawn standing before a Crystal Palace tableau (depicting some particularly noble-looking native Indians). While the tableau is tellingly headed "Development of Species under Civilisation," it is, however, the mangled aspirates, occluded diphthongs, and prominently displayed non-standardness of spelling which here serve to confirm the image, and the limits, of Cockney "civilisation" – and the distance of such localized speakers (in social as well as geographical terms) from "standard" norms. The linguistic infelicity – and cultural ignorance – of the nouveaux riches (another popular nineteenth-century stereotype (see Mugglestone 2007: 64ff.) is given prominence in *Punch* in the following month (see figure 24.1). As in Sheridan's earlier appeals for convergent behavior in speech, the "right accent" clearly remained "a proof that one has kept good company"; here, by implication, it is the converse which is true, infelicities of accent being made to reveal a social origin which no wealth can disguise.

While these popular images of norm and deviation hence emphasized contemporary interest in phonetic nuance (and attendant social meanings) in a variety of ways, the reality of language practices was, as ever, far more complex. The phonetician Alexander Ellis, writing in the late nineteenth century, for example, confirmed the existence of a geographically non-localized mode of speech – here labeled, for the first time, "received pronunciation" (RP): "In the present day we may . . . recognise a received pronunciation all over the country; not widely differing in any particular locality, and admitting a certain degree of variety" (1869: 23). Nevertheless, while he acknowledged that, in historical terms, "there has never been so near an approach to a uniform pronunciation as that which now prevails," Ellis also stressed that, rather than constituting an inviolable and national standard, it was evident that "a large number of words are pronounced with differences very perceptible to those who care to observe, even among educated London speakers" (1869: 629). Moreover, as one moved outside the capital, and especially lower down the social scale, the range of variations increased.

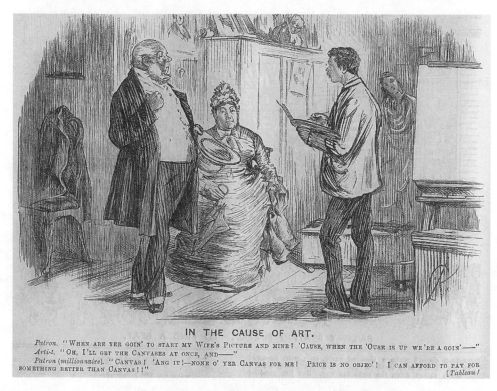

IN THE CAUSE OF ART.

Patron. "WHEN ARE YER GOIN' TO START MY WIFE'S PICTURE AND MINE? 'CAUSE, WHEN THE 'OUSE IS UP WE'RE A GOIN'—"
Artist. "OH, I'LL GET THE CANVASES AT ONCE, AND—"
Patron (millionnaire). "CANVAS! 'ANG IT!—NONE O' YER CANVAS FOR ME! PRICE IS NO OBJEC'! I CAN AFFORD TO PAY FOR SOMETHING BETTER THAN CANVAS!!"
[*Tableau!*

Figure 24.1 Affiliations of accent and status are prominent in the nineteenth-century caricaturing of the nouveaux riche. In spite of newly acquired wealth, it is the lower-status associations of /h/-dropping, missing 'g's, and elided /t/s which therefore predominate (here alongside other images of cultural deficit which focus on a comic ignorance about the role of canvas in the art of portraiture). It is perhaps by no means coincidental that the word *snobbishness*, according to the *OED*, is first recorded in *Punch*. (Illustration: *Punch, or the London Charivari*, August 27, 1887, p. 94)

Rather than the egalitarian norm which Sheridan had intended all speakers to use, irrespective of their social or regional circumstances, the emergent RP of the late nineteenth century instead seemed to be, as the phonetician Henry Sweet affirmed, "a class-dialect more than a local dialect . . . the language of the educated all over Great Britain" (1881: 7). If non-localized, it was therefore socially restricted, an image further consolidated by Daniel Jones in the first edition of his influential *English Pronouncing Dictionary* (*EPD*) where he described its characteristic use by "the families of Southern English persons whose men-folk have been educated at the great public boarding-schools" (as well as by "a considerable proportion of those who do not come from the South of England but who have been educated at these schools" (1917: viii)). Jones's preferred label for this form of speech was "Public School Pronunciation" (PSP) – a term which, by its specification of a set of fee-paying boarding schools with a non-localized intake of pupils from all over the country, also effectively served to

convey certain crucial aspects about the socio-cultural identity of this non-regional and undoubtedly élite accent. Rather than Sheridan's model of "one accent fits all," Jones's descriptions (especially in early editions of the *EPD*) instead suggest the continued – and perhaps even heightened – divisiveness of accent difference by the early twentieth century.

Broadcast Voices

Attitudes of this kind were perhaps only to be reified further by the introduction of broadcasting and the adoption of RP as the accent of authority on the airwaves. While Sheridan had seen print – especially in the form of the pronouncing dictionary – as the only means of securing non-localized dissemination for his preferred model of speech ("this would be making a noble use of the art of printing," as he had declared in 1762), the potential of broadcasting was radically different, not least since it transmitted the spoken voice itself. RP swiftly gained a monopoly in news broadcasting, and the anonymity of the early announcers was aided by speech-training in RP which ensured a striking consonance in the pronunciations they employed. In the early days of the BBC, mispronunciation could indeed be grounds for dismissal; as Allighan notes, rendering *indicted* as "indick-ted" led to the termination of the broadcasting career of one unfortunate news announcer (1938: 238). From 1926 the BBC Advisory Committee on Spoken English sought to clarify accepted – and expected – norms (among which "indick-ted" was not included). Varieties of English on the airwaves continued to foster popular language attitudes in many respects; the institutional image of standard English spoken with an RP accent (hence securing a formal propriety of phrasing and phoneme alike) was used for "serious" broadcasting; regional varieties, especially on the National Programme, connoted instead comedy and "light" entertainment, in what was to be a well-established cultural hierarchy.

Though John Reith, the first director general of the BBC, disclaimed prescriptive intent in the speech styles selected for broadcasting, a range of comments nevertheless suggest his commitment to these popular ideologies of correctness. As he wrote in *Broadcast over Britain*, "No one would deny the great advantage of a standard pronunciation of the language, not only in theory but in practice. Our responsibilities in this context are obvious" (1924: 161). "So long as the announcer is talking good English, and without affectation, I find it much to be desired that the announcer should be copied," he continued, discussing evidence that broadcasting was already being observed to act as a linguistic model for children. Reith's "Good English," however, presumably once again excluded the regional for which emulation was not, at least within this particular paradigm, to be desired at all (see further Mugglestone 2007: 265–81; 2008).

It was nevertheless to become clear that even broadcasting would not, in reality, secure the dominance of RP in actual language practice. Johnson had early criticized Sheridan for the limits of linguistic exposure which his work would achieve ("What

influence can Mr. Sheridan have upon the language of this great country, by his narrow exertions," he had caustically asked Boswell; "it is burning a farthing candle at Dover, to shew light at Calais"). Though the same could not be said of broadcasting, which eventually made its way into virtually every home in Britain, even exposure to RP on this scale would not secure the national homogeneity of accent which many had desired. Indeed, over time, it is clear that RP has come to be a minority accent in this context too; the introduction of commercial broadcasting in the 1950s led to a far greater democratization of purpose, coverage, and ultimately of accent too (even in the traditional and authoritative domains of news broadcasting).

Instead, accent has continued to function as a complex signifier of identity – social, geographical, and cultural. Standard English – as a non-localized variety in terms of lexis, grammar, and syntax (see Trudgill 2002: 159–70) – can, in fact, be spoken in any accent. RP, as a non-localized mode of pronunciation, has become a common reference model in dictionaries and in the teaching of English as a foreign language and, as Cruttenden notes, it can still be described as an "implicitly accepted social standard of pronunciation" (in Gimson 1994: 78), usually associated with those at the apex of the social pyramid. (See EARNING AS WELL AS LEARNING A LANGUAGE.) Yet, as Ellis and indeed Jones had stressed (especially in his later work), RP is far from monolithic and, rather than being a fixed standard, remains – here precisely like all other varieties of English – open to change and variation. Cruttenden (1994: 80) confirms the existence of "General RP," "Refined RP," and even Regional RP ("the type of speech which is basically RP except for the presence of a few regional characteristics"). Moreover, in the twenty-first century a diminishing pressure for non-RP speakers to acquire RP because of its perceived social advantages is also increasingly evident. Coming full circle from Sheridan's earlier prescriptive persuasions, regional modes of speech can attest a growing (and committed) loyalty from their users, while traditionally disfavored articulations – such as the glottal stop – are concurrently making their way into RP of younger generations.

REFERENCES AND FURTHER READING

Allighan, G. (1938). *Sir John Reith*. London: Stanley Paul.

Douglas, S. (1991 [1799]). *A Treatise on the Provincial Dialect of Scotland*. Ed. C. Jones. Edinburgh: Edinburgh University Press.

Ellis, A. J. (1869–89). *On Early English Pronunciation*. 5 vols. London: Trübner.

Gill, J. (1857). *Introductory Text-Book to School Management*. London: Longman.

Gimson, A. C. (1994). *Gimson's Pronunciation of English*. 5th edn. Revd. A. Cruttenden. London: Edwin Arnold.

Hamilton, J. (2002). *Faraday: The Life*. London: Harper Collins.

Johnson, S. (1747). *The Plan of a Dictionary of the English Language*. London: J. & P. Knapton.

Johnson, S. (1755). *A Dictionary of the English Language*. 2 vols. London: W. Strahan.

Jones, D. (1917). *English Pronouncing Dictionary*. London: Dent.

Mugglestone, L. C. (2007). *"Talking Proper:" The Rise of Accent as Social Symbol*. 2nd extended edn. Oxford: Oxford University Press.

Mugglestone, L. C. (2008). Spoken English and

the BBC. In the beginning. In J. R. Rainer, D. Maillat, and C. Mair (eds.), *Broadcast English.* Aubeiten aus Anglistick und Amerikanistik 33, G. Narr, Tübingen.

Nares, R. (1784). *Elements of Orthoepy.* London: T. Payne.

Obituary of Distinguished Persons: Mr. John Walker. (1808). *The Athenaeum Magazine* 3, 77–84.

Reith, J. C. W. (1924). *Broadcast over Britain.* London: Hodder & Stoughton.

Sheridan T. (1762). *A Course of Lectures on Elocution together with two Dissertations on Language.* London: W. Strahan.

Sheridan T. (1780). *A General Dictionary of the English Language.* London: Printed for J. Dodsley, C. Dilly, and J. Wilkie.

Smart, B. H. (1810). *A Practical Grammar of English Pronunciation.* London: John Richardson.

Smart, B. H. (1836). *Walker Remodelled. A New Critical Pronouncing Dictionary of the English Language.* London: T. Cadell.

Sweet, H. (1881). *The Elementary Sounds of English.* London: printed for the author.

Trudgill, P. (2002). *Sociolinguistic Variation and Change.* Edinburgh: Edinburgh University Press.

Section 5
American English in History

Introduction

The British first attempted to establish mercantile colonies in North America in the late sixteenth century. The colonies did not survive, but the later successes of James-town in 1607 and the Pilgrims' landing at Plymouth Rock in 1620 gained the English language its first real footholds in the New World. American English was thus sub-sequently defined largely in economic and religious terms: those who wished to dis-tinguish their language from British English did so as part of a larger program of separation from the home country, while those who strove to maintain an English identity resisted changes in the language.

The authors in this section explore the developing political and socio-cultural role of language in America. Beginning with Thomas Jefferson's linguistic choices while drafting the Declaration of Independence, David Simpson considers what was at stake in American writers' ongoing linguistic dialogue with British lexicographers and language mavens. This dialogue echoes, but does not simply replicate, the Scottish struggle to define a language of their own following the Acts of Union of 1707 (see ENGLISH IN SCOTLAND). Scottish linguists would go on to play a central role in American schoolmasters' attempts to define a curriculum in rhetoric appropriate to American students (see ENGLISH, LATIN, AND THE TEACHING OF RHETORIC). The desire for an American English would reach its apotheosis in Noah Webster's *American Dictionary of the English Language*.

As exemplified in Webster's dictionary project, the ideal of an American language has been a strong force in American history, serving in turn as a tool for practitioners of both class oppression and uplift, both expansion and unification, both international-ism and xenophobia. American English can serve such divided masters because its speakers have developed a sensitivity to dialect that rivals that of British speakers. As Walt Wolfram explains, dialect sensitivity can be traced to the effects of both the Civil War and Westward Expansion in the nineteenth century, as well as to various population shifts and immigration patterns throughout the history of the United States. Gavin Jones explores the "politics of power and identity" that inhere in any discussion of dialect, tracing the role the perception of dialect as fragmentation has played in the long history of cultural expansion and assimilation in the United States. Jones points out that the Eastern fear of incomprehensible rural countrymen in the Western territories and the fear of a growing babel of urban immigrants shared an outlet in caustic satires of ethnolinguistic difference.

The term "American English," much like "English" itself, asserts a unity belied by the multiplicity it actually represents. Ironically, the growing perception of a dominant global "American English" coincides with increasing apprehension within the United States that the language is fragmenting into socio-culturally defined ethnolinguistic sub-dialects (see LATINO VARIETIES OF ENGLISH; MIGRATION AND MOTIVATION IN THE DEVELOPMENT OF AFRICAN AMERICAN VERNACULAR ENGLISH). The English-Only movement is only one sign of this growing concern. At the same

time, much as the printing press made standardization of English spelling both necessary and inevitable, increasingly easy travel and real-time communication with otherwise remote parts of the country is resulting in less, not more, variation, even as it increases awareness, and even acceptance, of variation itself.

Michael Matto

25

American English to 1865

David Simpson

> When in the course of human events it becomes necessary for one people to dissolve the
> political bands which have connected them with another, and to assume among the
> powers of the earth the separate & equal station to which the laws of nature and of
> nature's god entitle them, a decent respect to the opinions of mankind requires that
> they should declare the causes which impel them to the separation.[1]

Thus Thomas Jefferson introduces his famous list of truths that are self-evident, and
begins the draft of the *Declaration of Independence*. The most and therefore least obvious
aspect of this document is that it is in English. It is immediately intelligible to those
against whom it is directed and from whom it declares itself disaffiliated. No act of
translation is required. The *Declaration* speaks the language of the tyrant power, opposing from a common linguistic contract the "long train of abuses & usurpations" which
that power had so often used the language to implement. At the same time, Jefferson's
draft perhaps signals its common ground with the republican tradition that was
thought to have brought about the most precious liberties of the British themselves.
He was not the first English-speaker to react against the threats of an "absolute
despotism."

But if Jefferson writes in English, it is a particular *kind* of English, one that appears
to the modern reader as marked by inconsistent and even whimsical spellings. He
uses the forms *-ising* and *-izing* without any apparent sense of contradiction (*organising,
agonizing, naturalization*), and also alternates *-our* with *-or* (*honour, tenor, endeavored*),
setting up options that still inform the distinctions between modern American and
British English. Additionally, he proffers spellings we might regard as merely out of
date (*compleat*), or as idiosyncratic (*paiment, wholsome, souldiers*), or as just plain slips of
the pen (*unacknoleged*). He consistently prefers *independant* over *independent*.

In the published text of the *Declaration*, which does not include all of Jefferson's
original sentences and adds some others, we are at once aware of changes in orthography.[2] All nouns are capitalized, in the standard eighteenth-century (but not

nineteenth-century) way. Jefferson's *organising* becomes *organizing*, to conform with *Naturalization*. *Payment, wholesome*, and *unacknowledged* appear in their familiar forms, and *independent* is preferred throughout. But *compleat* stands as before, and some asymmetry remains in the relation of *-our* and *-or*. The printed text reads *endeavoured* (twice) and *neighbouring* but oddly changes Jefferson's *honour* to *Honor*.

Going back a year in time, and perhaps (in the eyes of the nation about to be) several centuries in political philosophy, we find one of Samuel Johnson's contributions to the American crisis: "Taxation No Tyranny; an Answer to the Resolutions and Address of the American Congress" went through four editions in 1775, and was, of course, conceived to preempt Jefferson's putting pen to paper some months later.[3] Johnson is eloquent in the defence of the status quo, speaking against "these lords of themselves, these kings of *Me*, these demigods of independence" (p. 429). By such independence "the whole fabrick of subordination is immediately destroyed, and the constitution sunk at once into a chaos" (p. 425). He yet hopes that the rebellious spirits of the colonies "may be subdued by terrour rather than by violence" (p. 452).

Johnson's spellings again are striking, and this time they are quite self-conscious, as Jefferson's presumably were not. The author of the great (though not the first) *Dictionary* was adamant in his preference for *-our* and *-ick* forms, and this preference is related to larger political and social convictions. Johnson aimed to tidy up the language, and to do so according to conscious procedures. But even Johnson's text is inconsistent. The spelling *governors* (p. 420) coexists with *governours* (p. 440), and *terrour* is answered by *error* (p. 441), against the *Dictionary*'s attempt to legislate for *-our* endings in each case. The slips are probably not Johnson's own, but those of a typesetter. Nevertheless, the suggestion is that the language is too undisciplined to be efficiently restrained, too devious and ambiguous for the ambitions of rational reform. Johnson himself says as much in his voice as author of "The Plan of a Dictionary of the English Language" in admitting that "language is the work of man, of a being from whom permanence and stability cannot be derived" (Johnson, 1957, p. 130).

It might seem ironic that the published text of the *Declaration* in fact does so much to conform Jefferson's spelling with Johnson's models, given that the two belong on opposite sides of the political fence. There are hints here of a pattern that will recur often in the period under study (and indeed beyond it): the most independent and patriotic sentiments in America may be published in a language that continues to be governed by the conventions and strictures of metropolitan London, even as the British Parliament has lost political control, and may indeed even be in political opposition. But at the same time we must note the final world of the text: *Honor*, not *honour*. Johnson loses this one. If we cannot suppose this to be a conscious victory for the American printer, it is nevertheless a prophecy of the American English to come.

The year 1776 was a momentous one in literary and philosophical terms, as well as in national politics. It saw the first publication of the great books of Adam Smith and Edward Gibbon, as well as of important works by Paine, Price, Campbell, and

Bentham. Looking at some of these texts, we find that the same pattern of moderate chaos is repeated, one that seldom threatens understanding yet does startle the modern eye.

Paine's *Common Sense* both fav*ors* and fav*ours* independ*ance* (not independ*ence*). A comparison of the orthography of the first and the first revised edition reveals a range of inconsistencies. I have not checked every case, but from a brief examination it seems that the first edition uses consistent *-our* forms, whereas the second alternates quite frequently.[4] It also switches between *connexions* and *connections* (e.g., pp. 15, 17). Once again, as in the draft and printed version of the *Declaration*, the language of liberty is a somewhat scrambled one. Paine's book, printed in Philadelphia, does not reveal any striking differences from the spelling habits of Richard Price's *Observations on the Nature of Civil Liberty*, which was reprinted in the same city, though presumably from the London edition. In neither case does there seem to be any connection between spelling and political sentiment.

In the case of Adam Smith, whose *Wealth of Nations* (another book not unconnected with the political crisis) also appeared for the first time in 1776, the question of language is further complicated by the fact that he was a Scotsman. Most of the quarrels over the Scots language in the eighteenth century had to do with pronunciation and dialect; the claims of Gaelic or Lallans to separate status were not much attended to in metropolitan culture, as they are not to this day. Nevertheless, Hume had felt himself obliged to delete the Scotticisms from his *History of England*, for the question of the Scots language and diction was a definite point of contention in the general task of subjugating and incorporating Scotland after the Act of Union in 1707.[5] As so often occurs, and as in the case of the United States in 1776 (though less dramatically here), this was a union only in name. The two Jacobite rebellions were the most spectacular instances of continuing discontent, but the Scottish problem was an enduring part of English political consciousness. Samuel Johnson, on his tour of the Highlands, noted:

> Of what they had before the late conquest of their country, there remain only their language and their poverty. Their language is attacked on every side. Schools are erected, in which *English* only is taught, and there were lately some who thought it reasonable to refuse them a version of the holy scriptures, that they might have no monument of their mother-tongue (1957, p. 701).

John Witherspoon, a Scotsman who emigrated to America, claimed to have coined the prophetic word *Americanism* from the analogy with *Scotticism* (1802, 4:460). Had Scotland remained independent, he remarks, no shame would have been attached to the term:

> But by the removal of the court to London, and especially by the union of the two kingdoms, the Scottish manner of speaking came to be considered as provincial barbarism; which, therefore, all scholars are now at the utmost pains to avoid (p. 461).

America will have a quite different fate, he predicts: "we shall find some centre or standard of our own, and not be subject to the inhabitants of that island, either in receiving new ways of speaking, or rejecting the old."

Adam Smith seems to have managed to put forth a largely acceptable "English" style, or so it would seem from a brief inspection. His orthographic habits are not dissimilar from those already encountered. The recent definitive edition of *The Wealth of Nations* (1976) lists (2:952f.) among its variants many of the words already familiar: *independent/-ant, compleat/-ete, public/-ick*, and so forth. A good sense of Smith's own habits, rather than those of printers or other hands, can be derived from a glance at the edition of the *Correspondence* (1977). The letters written during 1776 are especially fascinating, although the American crisis merits only the briefest mention. Smith is preoccupied with the affecting sight of his friend Hume dying, and with the resulting uncertainties over the publication of the notorious *Dialogues Concerning Natural Religion*. In those letters printed by the editors from holograph sources, Smith alternates *expell* and *expel* (p. 201), uses *Collonel* for *Colonel* (p. 203) and *dyed* for *died* (p. 203; but *die* on p. 206), and the forms *alledge* (p. 204), *antient* (p. 201), and *chearfulness* (pp. 206, 203). He seems to use *-our* consistently over *-or*.

The point has surely been made, though further examples could be adduced. Except for Samuel Johnson, no one in 1776, on either side of the ocean, seems to show much concern for a standard spelling practice, whether in personal drafts or printed texts. This view of the situation is not only supported but almost prescribed by a glance at the dictionaries. Nathan Bailey's *Dictionarium Britannicum*, published in London in 1730, Johnson's more famous successor, and John Entick's *New Spelling Dictionary* (first published in 1764, then edited by William Crakelt and reprinted in 1784 and 1791) cover between them most of the variable spellings seen so far, with the exception of obvious idiosyncrasies. Entick and Bailey give both *compleat* and *complete*, while Johnson decides for the second; Johnson has *allege* for Entick's and Bailey's *alledge*, and opts (with Bailey) for *honour* and *publick* (against Entick). Bailey does declare that *honorable* is "the truest Spelling" of the word he lists as *honourable*, and bravely tries to discriminate between *inferior* (as adjective) and *inferiour* (as noun). The diligent language user of 1776 would, in other words, search in vain for complete agreement among the authors of the dictionaries themselves. Noah Webster, who produces what is arguably the first significant American dictionary in 1806 (though he will not use the title until 1828), does not depart from the above options in his transcriptions of these words.

Noah Webster is, however, a radical in the realm of language, and is the first major challenger of the linguistic hegemony of the British in general and of Johnson in particular (see JOHNSON, WEBSTER, AND THE *OED*). Although, many of Webster's claims were made on conservative grounds, so that putative Americanisms were consistently explained as true English words defunct in the mother country, it is yet impossible, after Webster, to be unaware of the argument about language as a *national* argument. After Webster, inconsistencies cannot be assumed to imply the same apparent insouciance that marks the language of 1776. They continue to occur,

of course, and we encounter all the familiar ones and some new ones in the letters of James Fenimore Cooper. But the context for these vagaries is different after Webster, so that we must question whether Cooper might be consciously or unconsciously ignoring the potential for a consistently American language in a way that no writer of 1776 would have been. There are various ways of accounting for this, from the reductive explanation (which contains some truth) suggesting that Cooper was so dependent on the British market that he could not afford any belligerently American linguistic identity, to the more substantial and complex one that involves an assessment of Cooper's own politics and sociolinguistic insights (see Simpson 1985: 149–201).

As 1776 did not usher in a new language, so neither did it invent a new literature or a new philosophy. It did, however, impose the demand that these prospects be examined and worked for, and it determined that the traditional Enlightenment preoccupations persisting or arising in the early years of independence should take on a consciously national resonance, whether for or against innovation and novelty. Thus, although ambitions for changing, fixing, or analyzing to its roots the quixotic spirit of language had been commonplace in the eighteenth century, they become focused as part of the *American* ideal after 1776. Not for the first time Webster announces:

> *Now* is the time, and *this* the country, in which we may expect success, in attempting changes favorable to language, science and government (1790a, p. 80).

And he does so in various kinds of English. The preface to his *Collection of Essays and Fugitiv Writings*, also published in 1790, advertises

> Essays and Fugitiv Peeces, ritten at various times, and on different occasions, az will appeer by their dates and subjects (1790b, p. ix).

That Webster's plan for a coherently innovating American English ultimately had only a heavily modified success should not allow us to underestimate the ramifications and implications of its claims. And, three years later, William Thornton makes the nationalist claim even more vociferously:

> You have corrected the dangerous doctrines of European powers, correct now the languages you have imported, for the oppressed of various nations knock at your gates, and desire to be received as your brethren. As you admit them facilitate your intercourse, and you will mutually enjoy the benefits. – The AMERICAN LANGUAGE will thus be as distinct as the government, free from all the follies of unphilosophical fashion, and resting upon truth as its only regulator (1793, pp. v–vii)

"I perceive no difficulties," says Thornton, continuing to address his countrymen: "if you find any, I trust they are not without remedy." Side by side with this preface, he gives the text entire in his reformed mode of spelling, beginning thus:

Iu hav ᴋoʀᴇᴋtid ᴆᴐ deendjrᴐs doᴋtrinz ov Iuropiiᴐn
pᴐuᴐrz . . .

There lie the difficulties! But if none of the schemes of which this is an example came
to anything, and if they seem intrinsically madcap to us now, they yet had their place
in a varied and widespread argument about the prospects for an American English.

For by the middle of the nineteenth century such a linguistic practice, if not quite
a "language," had come into being. Its conventions were, as they still are, much less
completely differentiated from the British norms than many good patriots would have
liked. But they were at the same time somewhat too distinctive for the Anglophiles,
and for the British themselves. The arguments about the relative features and qualities
of British and American English have not ceased, except that the boot is now often
on the other foot; since the end of World War II, it is Great Britain that has felt the
need to defend itself against the incursions of an American English. But however
familiar these issues are to us now, they have certainly become much less obsessive
than they were in the period from independence to the middle of the next century.
During these years, the formative years of the new nation, it seems to have been
impossible for any traveler to cross the Atlantic in either direction without weighing
in on one side or the other of the language debate.

Returning to the *Declaration* of 1776, it is worth noting that not one word in the
printed text or in Jefferson's draft could be thought of as an Americanism. The silence
of the document in this respect is a good indication of the gravity of its message, as
well as of the state of the language at the time it was written. Of course, few of the
words that were to become the object of obsessive self-consciousness in the succeeding
years—*bison, sleigh, creek, bluff,* and so forth—would have fitted into it anyway. A word
like *caucus* would have been too innovative in a document of such historical weight;
and, however much prior caucusing there might have been, the assembly did after
all meet in *congress*. In this respect the *Declaration* is not prophetic, for very few
written works of the following century or so were to escape scrutiny, supportive or
otherwise, for the presence of Americanisms, and a great number of them produced
such words.

Finally, there is the matter of the American speech. What would Jefferson have
sounded like, reading over the draft aloud to himself? Evidence on this subject is thin
and contentious. It was and continued to be a nationalistic commonplace that there
were no dialects in America, and that the Americans spoke a clearer and more uniform
English than the British themselves. This was surely true, to a degree, and American
English is still more uniform than the language spoken in Britain. Nevertheless, hints
of qualification exist, and they are there from the early years of the new nation. Once
again, Webster is informative. From his *Dissertations* (1789a, pp. 103–13) we can infer
that Jefferson, as a Virginian, might have said *holpe* for *help* and *tote* for *carry* (though
perhaps not in a public assembly!) and that he might have "almost" omitted "the
sound of r as in *ware, there.*" If the Adams contingent, arriving in Philadelphia in
1776, had noticed and perhaps sneered at these or other speech habits, then Jefferson

might have reciprocally registered the oddity of the men of Massachusetts saying *keow* for *cow*, and *marcy* for *mercy*. They might have shared with the local Philadelphians the habit of saying *wessel* for *vessel*, if not the tendency to pronounce *drop* as *drap* or *crop* as *crap*.

One might guess that all these features that Webster notices among "that class of people who do not travel" would have been either absent or considerably softened in the speech of the learned delegates. But Webster makes clear that dialects do exist; he even goes on, like a true son of the Enlightenment, to connect them with particular social configurations. Thus the "drawling nasal manner of speaking in New England" is deduced from the features of local government and the prevailing distribution of property. New England has no slaves and few "family distinctions," so that the speech patterns are consequently hesitant and diffident. No one must trespass on the rights of another, or imply that he might be anything less than an equal. So, for the New Englander, "Is it not best?" replaces "you must."

It must further be stressed that dialect in general is an important and highly contested ingredient of the American literary language well before Twain and his immediate precursors. When we see the same phenomena in British literature, we do not usually have to look very far to note its implications in class struggles and self-definitions. The issue is less emphatic in American literature, but it is still important, whatever level of comic celebration might enliven it. As America becomes a nation, or declares itself one, it is perhaps already *not* one nation, at least under the gods of speech. The working out of this question in, for example, Cooper's *The Pioneers*, produces a complex intensity with clear social and historical functions. At one extreme it is a matter of translation – from Delaware to English, from poetry to prose. At the other, less tragical pole it is a struggle for linguistic hegemony between a range of ethnic and special interest groups. Cooper's melting pot is one that is still a very long way from the liquefying temperature, and in the heating process the cracks already appear. The struggle he projects is one in which even silences are eloquent.

But Cooper writes his first novels almost fifty years after the *Declaration of Independence*, and he emerges from a tradition that is still insufficiently familiar to literary critics and historians. The coming into being of an American language and an American literature during this period was a considerably less self-confident process than that most commonly described as occurring in the 1850s.

NOTES

1 Citations of the draft and of subsequent orthographic details are from Jefferson (1950–: I.315–19). A convenient reprint can be found in Wills (1978: 374–9).

2 The original sheet is reproduced in facsimile in Boyd (1945: plate X).

3 The standard text of this work is in Johnson (1977: 401–55).

4 The first edition was published in Philadelphia by R. Bell on January 10, 1776; the "New Edition" was published by W. and T. Bradford on February 14, 1776.

5 See Boswell (1970: 404). Boswell himself planned but never published a dictionary of words "peculiar to Scotland": see Read (1937: 193). Howell (1971: 156–9) notes how many of the superintendents of the English language were themselves Scotsmen – Campbell, Blair, and Kames among them. On the decline of the Scots language during the eighteenth century, see Tulloch (1980: 171–81).

REFERENCES AND FURTHER READING

Bailey, N. (1730). *Dictionarium Britannicum: Or, a Compleat Etymological English Dictionary, being also an Interpreter of Hard and Technical Words.* London: Cox.

Baron, D. E. (1982). *Grammar and Good Taste: Reforming the American Language.* New Haven, CT: Yale University Press.

Boswell, J. (1970). *Life of Johnson.* Ed. R. W. Chapman. Corrected edn. J. D. Fleeman. Oxford: Oxford University Press.

Boyd, J. P. (ed.) (1945). *The Declaration of Independence: The Evolution of the Text as Shown in Facsimiles of Various Drafts by Its Author, Thomas Jefferson.* Princeton, NJ: Princeton University Press.

Dillard, J. L. (1992). *A History of American English.* New York: Longman.

Dillard, J. L. & Blanton, L. (1985). *Toward a Social History of American English.* Berlin: Mouton.

Entick, J. (1791). *Entick's New Spelling Dictionary.* Ed. W. Crakelt. London: J. Mawman.

Gustafson, T. (1992). *Representative Words: Politics, Literature and the American Language.* Cambridge: Cambridge University Press.

Howell, W. S. (1971). *Eighteenth-Century British Logic and Rhetoric.* Princeton, NJ: Princeton University Press.

Hume, D. (1932). *The Letters of David Hume.* 2 vols. Ed. J. Y. T. Greig. Oxford: Clarendon Press.

Jefferson, T. (1950–). *The Papers of Thomas Jefferson.* Ed. J. P. Boyd et al. 29+ vols. in progress. Princeton, NJ: Princeton University Press.

Johnson, S. (1957). *Johnson: Poetry and Prose.* 2nd edn. Ed. M. Wilson. London: R. Hart-Davis.

Johnson, S. (1977). *Political Writings.* Ed. D. J. Greene. The Yale Edition of the Works of Samuel Johnson, vol. 10. New Haven, CT: Yale University Press.

Paine, T. (1776). *Common Sense: Addressed to the Inhabitants of America.* Philadelphia: R. Bell.

Price, R. (1776). *Observations on the Nature of Civil Liberty, the Principles of Government, and the Justice and Policy of the War with America.* London: T. Cadell; Philadelphia: R. Bell.

Read, A. W. (1937). Projected English dictionaries, 1755–1828. *Journal of English and Germanic Philology,* 36, 188–205; 347–66.

Shell, M. (1993). Babel in America. *Critical Inquiry,* 20, 103–27.

Simpson, D. (1985). *The Politics of American English, 1776–1850.* Oxford: Oxford University Press.

Smith, A. (1976). *An Inquiry into the Nature and Causes of the Wealth of Nations.* 2 vols. Ed. R. H. Campbell, A. S. Skinner, W. B. Todd. The Glasgow Edition of the Works and Correspondence of Adam Smith. Oxford: Clarendon Press.

Smith, A. (1977). *The Correspondence of Adam Smith.* Ed. E. C. Mossner and I. S. Ross. The Glasgow Edition of the Works and Correspondence of Adam Smith. Oxford: Clarendon Press.

Thornton, W. (1793). *Cadmus; or a Treatise on the Elements of Written Language.* Philadelphia: R. Aitken & Son.

Tulloch, G. (1980). *The Language of Walter Scott: A Study of his Scottish and Period Language.* London: Deutsch.

Webster, N. (1789). *Dissertations on the English Language, with an Essay on a Reformed Mode of Spelling.* Boston: I. Thomas.

Webster, N. (1790a). *Rudiments of English Grammar; being an Introduction to the second Part of the Grammatical Institute of the English Language.* Hartford, CT: Elisha Babcock.

Webster, N. (1790b). *A Collection of Essays and Fugitiv Writings on Moral, Political, Historical and Literary Subjects.* Boston: I. Thomas & E. T. Andrews.

Webster, N. (1806). *Compendious Dictionary of the English Language, in which Five Thousand Words*

are added to the number found in the best English Compends. Hartford, CT: Hudson & Goodwin; New Haven, CT: Increase Cooke.

Webster, N. (1828). *An American Dictionary of the English Language*. 2 vols. New York: S. Converse.

Wills, G. (1978). *Inventing America: Jefferson's Declaration of Independence*. New York: Vintage Books.

Witherspoon, J. (1802). *The Works of the Rev. John Witherspoon, D.D., L.L.D.* 2nd edn. 4 vols. Philadelphia: William W. Woodward.

26
American English Since 1865

Walt Wolfram

The State of American English in 1865

By the time the Civil War ended in the mid-1860s, the United States had established language norms independent of the British Isles and significant patterns of internal diversification within North American English had evolved. As one observer of language variation at the time put it, "Let a man 'go to Congress,' as we say, and he will soon find that he is amid a variety of dialects" (Burt 1878: 411). On a grassroots level, the Civil War brought soldiers together from different regions of the North and South, raising greatly the level of awareness about regional language differences in the process.

The best portrait of the diverse dialect landscape of North America at the conclusion of the Civil War is provided by the earliest dialect surveys conducted under the aegis of the Linguistic Atlas of the United States, which began in the early 1930s (Kurath 1939). In these surveys, the selection of older, lifetime residents representing different regions, who would have learned their variety of English during the mid- and later 1800s, provided a convenient picture into American English during the second half of the nineteenth century. The first surveys focused on New England and the Atlantic States, reflecting their primary role in the early European settlement history of North America. Hans Kurath (1949), one of the early pioneers in this survey effort, provided a landmark map of the Atlantic States that showed three major dialect regions at the time, the North, Midland, and South, as well as a number of significant subregions within this overarching tripartite delimitation. Kurath's map is reproduced in figure 26.1.

The connection to the original settlement history of the US in figure 26.1, the so-called "Founder Effect" (Mufwene 1996, 2001), is transparent in Kurath's map. It indicates, for example, the early influence of cultural hearths in Boston (Northern), Philadelphia (Midland), and Charleston (South), as well as the outward spread of distinctive varieties from these focal points. It also depicts a Southern region that showed

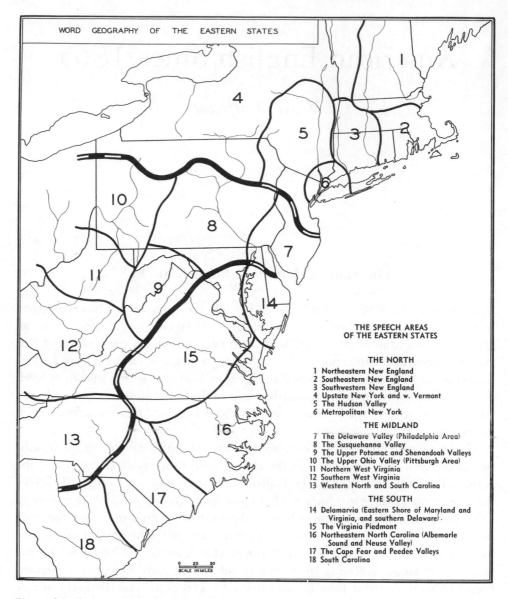

Figure 26.1 Dialect areas in the United States: mid- and late-nineteenth century (from H. Kurath (1949) *Word Geography of the Eastern United States*. Ann Arbor: University of Michigan Press; figure 3, "Speech Areas of the Eastern States"). Reprinted with permission

significant diversity. In fact, the linguistic unity of the South symbolically represented today in shared traits such as the stereoptypical second person plural *y'all*, the ungliding of the /ai/ vowel of *time* as *tahm*, the use of double modals (e.g., *He might could do it*), and lexical differences such *tote* for "carry" or *fixing to* for "intend or plan to" (*She's fixing to go now*) is largely a post-Civil War phenomenon (Bailey 2001), no doubt

inspired by the durable cultural divide between the North and South that resulted from the Civil War.

The Westward Extension

For the most part, European settlers and their descendents moved directly westward, taking their varieties of English and other languages with them. The expansion of dialect areas resulting from this movement is shown in figure 26.2 (Carver 1987), which used data from a major nationwide lexical dialect survey of American English carried out between 1965 and 1970, the *Dictionary of American Regional English*, or *DARE* (Cassidy 1985; Cassidy & Hall 1991, 1996; Hall 2002). Carver's summary map gives a good picture of the diversity of American English in the early and mid-twentieth century, building on and complementing the earlier surveys of the Linguistic Atlas of the United States and Canada.

Europeans and their descendants in New England and New York began pushing westward beyond New York into Ohio, driven by overcrowding, high land prices, steep taxes, and the religious and social conservatism of the Northeast. In general, the northern US is largely a region of New England expansion. The westward expansion of the American Midland was accomplished chiefly by three groups of speakers: those from the upper South, from the Mid-Atlantic States, and from the New England/New York dialect area. For the most part, the three streams remained separate, at least up to the Mississippi River, giving rise to a three-tiered settlement and primary dialectal patterns, most notable in Ohio, Indiana, and Illinois. Settlers from the upper South had pushed into the heart of Tennessee and Kentucky by the latter part of the eighteenth century and from there continued into Southern Missouri and Northern Arkansas.

At the same time that the Northern and Midland dialect boundaries were being extended westward, the South was expanding as well. Several dialect lines were laid in Georgia, since settlement was halted at several rivers for a number of years. Alabama is sometimes considered a separate sub-dialectal area, since it was settled rather late in comparison with the majority of the South and since its settlers tended to be from both lower and upper Southern dialect regions. However, Mississippi is lowland Southern in character. Southern Oklahoma and Texas are Southern as well, though central Texas has developed its own brand of Southern speech, probably due in some measure to Texans' strong sense of cultural distinctiveness.

The most recent portrait of language variation in the US comes from a telephone-based survey (TELSUR) of vowel differences conducted in the 1990s by William Labov and his associates (Labov et al. 2006). Although a number of factors have certainly led to modifications in the dialects of American English in the twentieth century, the three major dialect divisions indicated by early dialect geographers (e.g., Kurath 1949) are still apparent. A summary map of the most recent survey representing American English language variation at the turn of the twenty-first century is given in figure 26.3.

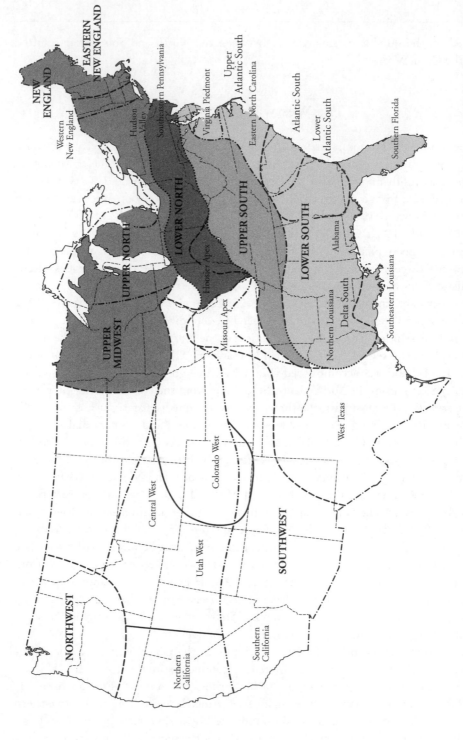

Figure 26.2 Dialect areas in the United States: mid-twentieth century (from C. M. Carver (1987) *American Regional Dialects: A Word Geography*. Ann Arbor: University of Michigan Press, p. 248). Reprinted with permission

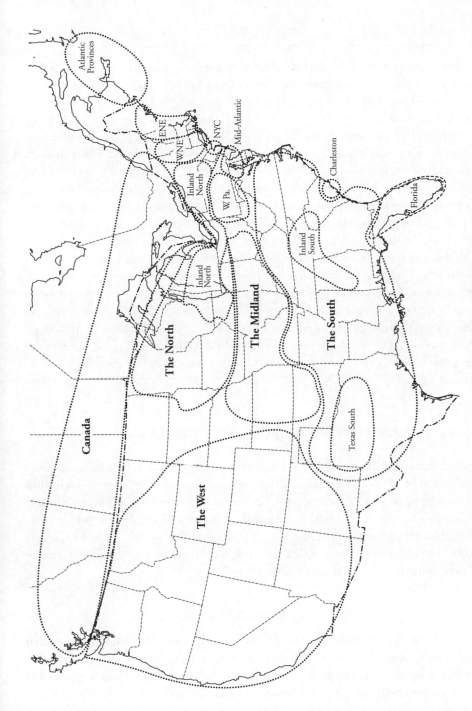

Figure 26.3 Regional map of American English at the end of the twentieth century (from W. Labov et al. (2006) *Atlas of North American English*. New York: Mouton de Gruyter; map 11.15, "An Overall View of North American Dialects," p. 148). Reprinted with permission

The basic separations in the East and Midwest are still between a Southern dialect area, a Midland region (characterized by the merger of the [ɑ] and [ɔ] vowels in word pairs such as *Dawn* and *Don*), and a Northern area, which Labov (1994) calls the Northern Cities area since the pronunciations that characterize this region are most prominent in the large cities. In addition, we see the emergence of some new dialect areas in recent decades, particularly in the West. Some West Coast dialects are even leading the spread of certain features across the US at this point. For example, West Coast speech, led by Southern California, is increasingly characterized by the fronting of back vowels, so that the vowel of *boot* sounds like *biwt* and *good* sounds like *gid*. Similarly, the use of so-called UPTALK – that is, rising or "question" intonation on declarative statements – is now becoming a prominent trait of West Coast dialects ranging from Los Angeles to Portland. Though once associated with the "Valley Girl" talk of teenage girls in the San Fernando Valley area of California, uptalk has spread far beyond its apparent West Coast origins and is now prevalent in the speech of young people of both sexes in many parts of the US. In more recent decades, innovations such as uptalk and the use of *be like* and *go* to introduce quotes (e.g., *He's like, "What are you doin'," and I go, "What do you think I'm doin'?"*) in American English spread from west to east rather than the converse, earlier patterns of diffusion.

Parameters of Change in American English

Changes in American English over the past century and a half reflect demographic, socio-historical, and socio-cultural transformations in American society, including shifting patterns of population movement; changing patterns of immigration and language contact; shifting cultural centers and socio-cultural ideologies; and increasing interregional accessibility and mobility. Variation also reflects independent, internally motivated linguistic changes that have taken on regional and social significance in the diversification of American English.

Shifting population patterns

In the twentieth century there were major population movements along north-south lines to complement the earlier east-west migratory flow. Beginning in the post-World War I years, for example, large numbers of rural southern African Americans began migrating northward into such major cities as Chicago, Detroit, and New York. The descendants of the African Americans who migrated northward, particularly those of the working class, remained relatively isolated from surrounding white speakers so that there has been limited cross-assimilation between African American and European American speech varieties in America's large northern cities. Accordingly, the Southern roots of African American English are still quite evident in these transplant communities.

Changing immigration and language contact patterns

During the twentieth century, immigrants continued to pour into America. Many were members of the same cultural groups who came in large numbers in the nineteenth century (e.g., Germans, Italians, Irish), while others were new to the US or arrived in significant numbers for the first time. The languages brought by these new immigrant groups affected general American English, in some cases leaving a substrate effect on English. For example, the use of syntactic constructions such as *Are you going with?* in southeastern parts of Pennsylvania is a permanent imprint of the historical German influence, and the ungliding of the *o* in the pronunciation *Minnesota* is a linguistic remembrance of the Scandinavian influence. Other languages have also served as the foundation for the creation of new socio-cultural varieties of English in the latter part of the twentieth century.

Changing cultural centers and socio-cultural ideologies

As Americans during the twentieth century began leaving the rural countryside in large numbers for the economic opportunities offered by the nation's large cities, older and newer metropolitan areas took on increased social, political, and cultural significance. Today, these metropolitan areas are the focal points for many current linguistic innovations. In the process, dialect features that were formerly markers of regional speech have been transformed into markers of social class, ethnicity, or urban-rural distinctions. For example, the Northern Cities Vowel Shift discussed below is clearly centered in large metropolitan areas, where younger, European American suburban lower-middle-class women tend to take the lead in its shift, showing the intersection of regionality, ethnicity, class, and gender.

We also find changing cultural relations among members of different ethnic groups manifested in linguistic variation. It might be expected that the result of institutionalized desegregation of the US in the last half century would lead to the erosion of ethnic dialect boundaries, but this is not always the case. In fact, some ethnolinguistic boundaries are intensifying rather than dissipating. If, for example, ethnic dialects become an important component of cultural and individual identity, then language divergence may follow. Thus, distinct socio-cultural varieties such as African American English (see MIGRATION AND MOTIVATION IN THE DEVELOPMENT OF AFRICAN AMERICAN VERNACULAR ENGLISH), Hispanic English (see LATINO VARIETIES OF ENGLISH), Cajun English (Dubois & Horvath 1998; Melançon 2006), and even some varieties of Native American English (Wolfram & Dannenberg 1999) are maintaining and intensifying their distinctiveness as symbols of ethnic identity. In fact, one of the feature stories of American English in the latter half of the twentieth century is the significance of ethnolinguistic varieties of English as emblems of socio-cultural identity.

Accessibility and mobility

The ever-widening network of transportation and intercommunication now provides access to even the remotest of speech communities in the US. The development of major interstate highways in the mid-twentieth century, as well as the paving of roads and building of bridges, broke down formidable geographic barriers so that once-remote regions have been transformed into havens for tourists and other outside visitors. Cable and satellite television, mobile telephones, and internet communications are also bringing Americans from across the country into closer communicative contact than ever before. Just a few years ago it was hard to imagine that a linguist might contact a speaker in a remote mountain or island community by email or instant messaging to ask questions about language, but such is the nature of present-day communication networks and linguistic fieldwork.

One of the most important linguistic consequences of this increasing contact has been the significance of dialect endangerment. As some of the more remote areas are opened to intercommunication and persistent contact with the outside world, their distinctive language varieties, fostered in isolation and spoken by relatively small numbers of people, may be overwhelmed by encroaching varieties of English. Such a fate is currently befalling a number of island communities on the Eastern Seaboard that have become increasingly accessible to tourists and new residents during the latter half of the twentieth century. Studies of island communities on the Outer Banks of North Carolina (Wolfram & Schilling-Estes 1997; Wolfram et al. 1999) and in the Chesapeake Bay (Schilling-Estes 1997; Schilling-Estes & Wolfram 1999) indicate that some of these dialects are in a moribund state. But there may also be dramatically different responses to dialect endangerment, ranging from the rapid decline of traditional American English varieties within a couple of generations of speakers to the intensification of dialectal distinctiveness as a traditional variety dies. Thus, while some dialect areas of the Outer Banks in North Carolina are rapidly losing most of their time-honored dialect features, residents of Smith Island, Maryland, in the Chesapeake Bay, are actually escalating their use of distinguishing dialect traits. For example, younger generations of speakers in Smith Island show much more frequent use of distinct dialect patterns such as the leveled use of past tense *be* as *weren't* (e.g., *I/you/ (s)he/we/you/they weren't*) and dramatic increases in the pronunciation of the /au/ vowel in *sound* more like *saind* (phonetically [æɪ]). Even though the dialect is intensifying rather than weakening, it is in danger of dying out through sheer population loss, since the maritime industry of the island is rapidly vanishing. Most likely, this intensification is due to an increasing sense of solidarity as fewer and fewer islanders remain to follow the traditional Smith Island way of life.

Linguistically Based Diversification

One of the most significant changes in American English over the past half century involves a large portion of the vowel system. Investigations of vowel systems

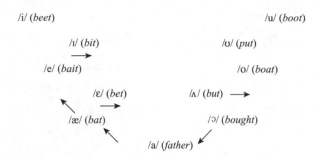

Figure 26.4 Northern Vowel Shift (from W. Wolfram & N. Schilling-Estes (2006) *American English: Dialects and Variation*, 2nd edn. Oxford: Blackwell, p. 366)

conducted in the past couple of decades (Labov 1994; Labov et al. 2005) have un-covered two major changes currently underway in the US; each is associated with regional and social factors. The basis for this change appears to reside in the inherent, rotational scheme of vowel trajectories, although it has now taken on primary regional and social meaning. The resulting shift in the vowel systems is so significant that it has been likened to the Great Vowel Shift that affected English from approximately 1300 through 1600 (see PHONOLOGY: SEGMENTAL HISTORIES).

One pattern of change is called the Northern Cities Vowel Shift. In this vowel rotation, the low long vowels are moving primarily forward, and then upward, and the short vowels are moving downward and backward. For example, a vowel like the /ɔ/ in *coffee* is moving towards the /a/ vowel of words like *father*. The /a/ vowel, in turn, moves towards the /æ/ of *bat*, which then moves upward towards the vowel /ɛ/ of *bet*. At the same time, the /ɛ/ vowel of words like *bet* moves backward towards the /ʌ/ vowel of *but*, which is then pushed backward towards the vowel of *bought* /ɔ/. Diagrammatically, the shift may be represented in figure 26.4. For convenience, "key words" in terms of idealized standard American English phonemes are given. The arrows indicate the direction in which the vowels are moving in this shift pattern.

Regionally, the vowel rotation pattern in figure 26.4 starts in Western New England and proceeds westward into the northern tier of Pennsylvania; the extreme northern portions of Ohio, Indiana, and Illinois; Michigan; and Wisconsin. It is more concentrated in the larger metropolitan areas, typically in the suburbs. More advanced stages of this change can be found in younger women in the largest metropolitan areas such as Buffalo, Cleveland, Detroit, and Chicago. Its diffusion from these focal points tends to follow a hierarchical or cascading pattern. From large, heavily populated cities that are cultural centers, the changes spread first to moderately sized cities that fall under the influence of the large, focal city, leaving nearby sparsely populated areas unaffected. Gradually, innovations filter down from more populous, denser areas to less densely populated areas, affecting rural areas last, even if such areas are quite close geographically to the original focal area of the change.

In the Southern Vowel Shift, the short front vowels (the vowels of words like *bed* and *bid*) are moving upward and taking on the gliding character of long vowels. In

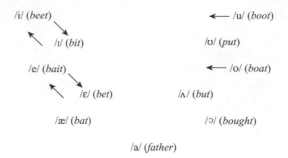

Figure 26.5 Southern Vowel Shift (from W. Wolfram & N. Schilling-Estes (2006) *American English: Dialects and Variation*, 2nd edn. Oxford: Blackwell, p. 367)

standard American English, a vowel like the long *e* of *bait* actually consists of a vowel nucleus [e] and an upward glide into an [ɪ], so that it sounds more like *bay-eat*. A vowel like the short *e* [ɛ] of *bet* does not have this gliding character, at least not in the idealized standard variety. In the Southern Vowel Shift, the vowel of *bed* moves up toward [e] and takes on a glide, becoming more like *beyd* [beɪd]. Meanwhile, the front long vowels (the vowels of *beet* and *late*) are moving somewhat backward and downward, and the back vowels are moving forward. The rotational patterns that characterize the Southern Vowel Shift are indicated in figure 26.5

Because the Southern Vowel Shift and Northern Cities Vowel Shift move the vowels in very different rotational directions, the varieties characterized by these vowel shifts are becoming increasingly different from one another. In fact, this differential rotation is the major reason why some dialectologists now claim that Southern and Northern speech are, in fact, diverging rather than converging. The Southern Vowel Shift, unlike the Northern Cities Vowel Shift, is more advanced in rural areas of the South than in metropolitan areas and appears to be receding. The focal area of change for the Southern vowel system is therefore the converse of that observed for the Northern system, where changes radiate outward from and are most advanced in metropolitan areas.

The Future of American English

As some traditional dialects of American English are receding, new ones are emerging, reflecting the changing dynamics of American demography, social structure, and language ideology. At the same time, the present contours of variation in American English are deeply embedded in its historical origins, and the development and future developments will no doubt take their cues from the present dialect profile. Variation in American English continues to mark the regional, social, and cultural cartography of the US as poignantly as any other cultural artifact, and there is no reason to expect that it will surrender its emblematic role in the future.

REFERENCES AND FURTHER READING

Bailey, G. (2001). The relationship between African American Vernacular English and White vernaculars in the American South: a sociocultural history and some phonological evidence. In S. L. Lanehart (ed.), *Sociocultural and Historical Contexts of African American English* (pp. 53–92). Philadelphia: Benjamins.

Burt, N. C. (1878). *Appleton's Journal*, New Series 5 (July–Dec), 411–17.

Carver, C. M. (1987). *American Regional Dialects: A Word Geography*. Ann Arbor: University of Michigan Press.

Cassidy, F. G. (editor-in-chief) (1985). *Dictionary of American Regional English, Vol. 1, A–C*. Cambridge, MA: Harvard University Press, Belknap.

Cassidy, F. G. & Hall, J. H. (eds.) (1991). *Dictionary of American Regional English, Vol. 2, D–H*. Cambridge, MA: Harvard University Press, Belknap.

Cassidy, F. G. & Hall, J. H. (eds.) (1996). *Dictionary of American Regional English, Vol. 3, I–O*. Cambridge, MA: Harvard University Press, Belknap.

Dubois, S. & Horvath, B. (1998). From accent to marker in Cajun English: A study of dialect formation in progress. *English World-Wide*, 19, 161–88.

Hall, J. C. (editor-in-chief) (2002). *Dictionary of American Regional English, Vol. 4, P–Sk*. Cambridge, MA: Harvard University Press, Belknap.

Kurath, H. (1939). *Handbook of the Linguistic Geography of New England*. Providence: Brown University Press.

Kurath, H. (1949). *Word Geography of the Eastern United States*. Ann Arbor: University of Michigan Press.

Labov, W. (1994). *Principles of Linguistic Change, Vol. 1: Internal Factors*. Oxford: Blackwell.

Labov, W., Ash, S., & Boberg, C. (2006). *Atlas of North American English*. New York: Mouton de Gruyter.

Melançon, M. E. (2006). Stirring the linguistic gumbo. In W. Wolfram & B. Ward (eds.), *American Voices: How Dialects Differ from Coast to Coast* (pp. 238–43). Oxford: Blackwell.

Mufwene, S. S. (1996). The development of American Englishes: some questions from a creole genesis hypothesis. In E. W. Schneider (ed.), *Focus on the USA* (pp. 231–64). Philadelphia: John Benjamins.

Mufwene, S. S. (2001). *The Ecology of Language Evolution*. Cambridge: Cambridge University Press.

Schilling-Estes, N. (1997). Accommodation versus concentration: dialect death in two post-insular island communities. *American Speech*, 72 (1), 12–32.

Schilling-Estes, N. & Wolfram, W. (1999). Alternative models for dialect death: dissipation vs. concentration. *Language*, 75 (3), 486–521.

Wolfram, W. (2006). Dialects in danger (Outer Banks, NC). In W. Wolfram & B. Ward (eds.), *American Voices: How Dialects Differ from Coast to Coast* (pp. 189–95). Oxford: Blackwell.

Wolfram, W. & Dannenberg, C. (1999). Dialect identity in a tri-ethnic context: the case of Lumbee American Indian English. *English World-Wide*, 20, 79–116.

Wolfram, W. & Schilling-Estes, N. (1997). *Hoi Toide on the Outer Banks: The Story of the Ocracoke Brogue*. Chapel Hill: University of North Carolina Press.

Wolfram, W. & Schilling-Estes, N. (2006). *American English: Dialects and Variation*. 2nd. edn. Oxford: Blackwell.

Wolfram, W., Hazen, K., & Schilling-Estes, N. (1999). *Dialect Maintenance and Change on the Outer Banks*. Publications of the American Dialect Society 81. Tuscaloosa: University of Alabama Press.

27

American English Dialects

Gavin Jones

To focus on dialect as a category always engages a politics of power and identity that pitches a theoretically standard language against the non-standard varieties which surround it. Acknowledgment that the United States has its own regional, social, and ethnic kinds of English has often worked to sanction class and cultural hierarchies while naturalizing English in a multilingual nation by distracting attention from the non-English languages that might threaten it. Yet awareness of dialect has equally tended to provoke fears over the quality and coherence of English in America. Questions concerning the origin of American English dialects – were colonial settlement patterns or the influence of non-English speakers most responsible for vernacular variety? – could make dialect seem at once a sign of cultural stability and degeneration. We can think of dialect as a linguistic frontier, one that marks the power of a certain type of English to maintain cultural dominance by assimilating difference, but more significantly a frontier that marks a cultural intermixture whereby that dominant language bears traces of the non-English speakers, the marginal ethnic and racial groups, and the lower social classes with which it comes into contact.

Regional differences in American English were clearly noted by the mid-eighteenth century, though the early national period saw the first sustained debate over the socio-political implications of dialectal diversity. Fearing the status hierarchy that dialects encouraged, the great lexicographer Noah Webster advocated a common language based on the idealized speech of a New England "yeoman" class of independent land-holders, a dialect that he believed to embody inherently rational and Saxon powers that would naturally overcome other dialects and thus ensure social and political harmony in the nation. For Webster, provincial *pronunciation* was the big issue, as it was for many of his peers. They tended to stress relatively minor issues of accent over deeper differences in grammar or vocabulary, yet they nevertheless feared (to a degree of paranoia) the power of these phonetic differences to splinter American English into mutually incomprehensible varieties. Because Webster believed that language behaved like a democracy, his linguistic analysis echoed anxieties over the direction of the

national experiment at large: suspicion of dialect intertwined with anxieties that the federalist nation may fragment into antagonistic regions (as of course it did with the Civil War, another era in which political conflicts were traced to a confusion of different dialects in political discourse), and with anxieties that democracy was degenerating into rampant individualism or into a vulgarized mainstream. Hence Alexis de Tocqueville in *Democracy in America* (1835) and James Fenimore Cooper in *The American Democrat* (1838) would downplay the importance of regional speech differences and would emphasize instead the corruptive effect of unregulated and unstable signification that stemmed from a situation where every person seemed to have a dialect of their own. The flipside of sociolinguistic leveling was a belief that spoken quality was in decline. According to C. A. Bristed, in an important 1855 overview of English in America:

> The English provincialisms *keep their place*; they are confined to their own localities, and do not encroach on the metropolitan model. The American provincialisms are more equally distributed through all classes and localities, and though some of them may not rise above a certain level of society, others are heard everywhere. (Bristed 1855: 61–2)

In terms of social class, the linguistic center could not remain impervious to marginal influence, which meant that even the prestige varieties of English seemed distinctly regional in tone.

The literary growth of regional dialect humor in the 1820s and 1830s points to a broad public awareness by this time of regional differences in speech, especially between the Northeast and the South. Literary evidence also suggests recognition of the effects of language contact in producing various ethnic Englishes (Welsh, Dutch, Irish, Scots) as well as Native American pidgin English and African American Vernacular English. The pressures of language contact helped unsettle any understanding of American dialect as regional, in the European sense of relatively static and persistent local speech distinctions. Indeed, recognized speech types such as the Yankee, at least when they appeared in literature, were as much markers of a marginal political identity as they were reflections of a regional culture. A case in point here is the western dialect that became prominent in the Jacksonian era, as politicians began to speak with a folksy democratic vigor designed to subvert effete gentility. Vernacular language was central to the construction of political personalities that marked a shift in the moral character of the constructive citizen, away from the elite and toward acceptance of the popular. These speech types were strongly associated with the frontier, though less as a place, with its own vocabulary and accent, and more as a *process of language creation* itself – a "tall talk" resonating with linguistic exuberance. According to the philologist Maximilian Schele de Vere in 1872, the dialect of the West is marked by vigor, freedom, hyperbole, and hearty sounds that emerge from the gigantic proportions of the environment and the purity of the air, from the fast pace of life, and from a lack of conservative cultural institutions. For less romantic and more conservative critics, the western speaker was a windy lunatic, yet the point remained that the western

dialect, for good or ill, was defined by an attitude toward language more than by vocabulary or accent. This dialect was really a style of discourse that nevertheless seemed partly incomprehensible to many eastern auditors – a style purportedly rooted in the individual's independent character and in the violence and vastness of western experience. A further influence on this western dialect was the pronounced contact on the frontier between English and other languages. According to the mid-nineteenth-century grammarian, William Chauncey Fowler:

> As our countrymen are spreading westward across this continent, and are brought into contact with other races, and adopt new modes of thought, there is some danger that, in the use of their liberty, they may break loose from the laws of the English language, and become marked not only by one, but by a thousand Shibboleths. (Fowler 1868: xiii)

An 1869 article by Socrates Hyacinth accordingly observed words from Italian, Spanish, and German as active parts of the Texan dialect.

Literary and spoken dialects should be understood as separate strains, and care must be taken in assessing the reliability of literary evidence for actual speech varieties. The apparent dialect voices that carried debate between North and South during the antebellum and Civil War periods, for example, were less reflections of regional speechways than rhetorical counterlanguages whose abuse of the written conventions of linguistic propriety powered harsh political satires of sectional interests. A more serious attention to regional dialects developed in the postbellum period, as a desire for concrete evidence replaced the often idealistic celebration of lowly speech within mid-century romantic philology. After the war, James Russell Lowell added a long introduction to his *Biglow Papers* (a series of dialect poems and other pieces, written to satirize the Mexican War of 1848 and later the Civil War) that sought to establish the authenticity of the Yankee dialect but that tended to underscore the much looser sense of dialect already operating in an American context. For Lowell, Yankee speech – which barely constituted a dialect at all – comprised occasional archaisms, newer coinages, moments of raciness, and strong cultural connections both with older British English and with the "refined" language. Lowell was at the vanguard of renewed scholarly interest in the varieties of American English during the last quarter of the nineteenth century, ironically at a time when the forces of linguistic standardization were taking hold in the public school system and in other cultural institutions. The so-called local color fiction that sought to represent New England, Appalachian, Hoosier, "Pike County," and a host of other dialects from virtually every state of the union, can be understood as linguistic nostalgia in the face of de-regionalization, or as a means to imply an ideal standard language by demonstrating clearly what it was not. Attempts to represent dialects accurately in print were sanctioned by scholarly linguists such as William Dwight Whitney, who argued that all languages were really dialects whose relative status was a function of political power rather than inherent linguistic quality. Analysis of the printed voices within regional literature suggests

that a literary meal was being made of relatively minor regional differences in vocabulary and grammar (pronunciation, at least, did seem to vary more widely between the Northeast, the South, and the West). The cultural work performed by this dialect writing tended to outweigh its status as evidence of linguistic variety.

This cultural work targeted distinctions between social classes more than between regions because dialect speakers were usually understood as lower class, irrespective of their local affiliations. In this regard, the apparent relativism of scholars such as Whitney and Thomas Lounsbury was strictly limited by their belief that the dialect of the cultivated class should remain dominant because of an inherent superiority that rested on the cultivation and education of its speakers. The Gilded Age obsession with language questions thus involved three vague speech varieties, or meta-dialects, associated with the lower classes (the speakers of the less standard speech varieties that attracted the attention of regional writers), with the educated classes (whom Lounsbury called the "intellectually good"), and with a broad middle class whose loose kind of speech occupied so-called verbal critics such as Richard Grant White (1870), one of a legion of self-appointed linguistic detective police anxious about the nation's alleged decline in linguistic standards. This middling way of speaking can be thought of as another kind of frontier dialect, a contact zone between the high and the low, or rather a zone in which the high always seemed threatened by the forces of vulgarity, poor tone, pretentiousness, and by virtually meaningless words that White described as "living a precarious life on the outskirts of society, uncertain of their position, and a cause of great discomfort to all right thinking, straightforward people" (p. 201).

The other major impact on this mainstream dialect, at least in the urban context that occupied verbal critics and other observers, came from the massive influx of immigrants from southern and eastern Europe, who spoke Italian and Yiddish among a multitude of other tongues. The potential impact that non-English languages were understood to have on American English helps to explain something of a contradiction in the study of dialect: the combined beliefs that the United States has a uniformity of idiom unknown in world history *and* that it lies on the brink of a sudden increase in dialectal diversity that could rapidly overthrow the written language. For E. S. Sheldon (1896), first president of the American Dialect Society (established 1889), the causes of diversity lay in the contact between English speakers and the speakers of "foreign" languages. Sheldon points to a futurist sensibility common within American awareness of its dialects, a belief – which sanctioned cultural pessimism for many – that substantive dialect divergence was always just about to happen. (See LATINO VARIETIES OF ENGLISH.)

According to Schele de Vere's *Americanisms* (1872), the assimilation of non-English speaking groups into an English-speaking culture had left specific traces in certain regional vocabularies of American English, as heard in the Dutch influence on New York, the French influence on Louisiana, and the Spanish influence on California. Literary evidence suggests a clear awareness of hybrid forms of "German-English" dialect in Pennsylvania and Chinese pidgin English on the west coast. By the turn of

the century, the new frontier of American English was the east-coast city, particularly the melting-pot of lower Manhattan, where the efforts of non-English speaking immigrants to master English were creating a number of informal ethnic dialects of English. Rather than remaining separate subvarieties, however, these new speech types seemed to be combining into a "New Yorkese" dialect that was both a slangy language of class difference and an international synthesis, both a native English and – in the words of William Dean Howells (1896) – "a thing composite and strange to our present knowledge." The vaudeville stage became an important site in which the linguistic processes of the immigrant city were informally translated and analyzed. A part-anxious, part-frustrated, part-reckless humor was discovered in the mutual unintelligibility of different ethnic dialects of what claimed to be a common tongue. Established Irish brogues collided with burlesque versions of Italianized, Yiddishized, and Germanized English, as well as Chinese pidgin English. Frequently, the vaudeville comedian or actor would fuse multiple ethnic dialects into a single speech act, thus representing individually the bewildering array of language-contact situations that were shaping American English. Any understanding of this multicultural situation again necessitates a broad definition of American dialect as ethnic process rather than regional product – a process whereby the acquisition of English creates ways of speaking that are culturally significant precisely because they are unstable and transitional hybrids.

A staple of both literary and stage humor throughout the nineteenth century and well into the twentieth was African American Vernacular English (AAVE) – unique among American English dialects in its depth of grammatical and phonetic difference, its historical persistence, and its cultural prominence. The recognition that slaves (as well as free blacks in the North) spoke in a distinct vernacular often descended into the ridiculous parodies of black speech on the blackface minstrel stage, parodies that may have worked to bond diverse working-class audiences into a sense of white superiority, or else to make black speech seem separate and unequal in spite of prominent observations in the 1840s that southern whites (particularly women) actively imitated the speech patterns of their black slaves. The explosion of national interest in AAVE immediately after the Civil War brought renewed efforts both to demean and to understand a dialect whose power was undeniable. James A. Harrison's essay "Negro English" (1884) offers a remarkably complex analysis of the difference of AAVE, found in its patterns of intonation and word order, its densely figurative expressions, its "hybridization" and lengthening of conventional English words, its protective ambiguity, and its creative capacity to generate pungent "Negroisms." In terms of origins, most accounts described AAVE as a partly archaic, partly incorrect imitation of white English that encoded a black intellectual deficit and thus sanctioned social segregation. Yet the case of Gullah, the creole language spoken on the Sea Islands of Georgia and the Carolinas which gained national attention in *Slave Songs of the United States* (1867) and elsewhere, presented observers with such a degree of consistent grammatical and lexical difference that the explanation of African influence broke through even the most racist descriptions of the language, such as Ambrose Gonzales's preface to

his dialect sketches *The Black Border* (1922). Recognition of African influence on Gullah may even have been suppressed intentionally at the turn of the century, perhaps because of the implications such a recognition held amid debates over the possible influence of black speech on white English in the South. Not until the anthropological work of Melville Herskovits in the 1930s and 1940s, and Lorenzo Turner's *Africanisms in the Gullah Dialect* in 1949, was Gullah tied to an African substratum of syntactical, morphological, lexical, and phonological features. If Gullah has been recognized as a complex combination of British, American, Caribbean, and African language varieties, then AAVE in general has provoked debate over its geographical origins. According to some linguists, AAVE probably descends from a creole language – something like Gullah – originally spoken throughout the US, which originated in a west African pidgin language that emerged as a *lingua franca* among speakers of different African (and European) languages. It remains difficult to assess the degree of African influence on AAVE because historical evidence is unclear concerning which of many African languages may have predominated in the Americas, and because influence may have taken place in less quantifiable areas such as tone, loan-translations, and communication styles.

The mid-1990s debate over whether Ebonics should be taught as a foreign language in Oakland (California) schools, can be understood as the sharp end of broad historical attitudes toward differences within American English. Arguments for the institutional recognition of Ebonics as a systematic and rule-governed language variety presuppose that different languages represent different worldviews, an assumption that can equally entertain fears that such dialects encourage cultural conflict, or else perpetuate class hierarchies by trapping individuals in a socially stigmatized speech community. If Ebonics has a grammatical base in African language varieties then it encapsulates a major trend in the creation of American English dialects: the process whereby new vernaculars emerge from the clash of different languages. The twenty-first-century competition between English and Spanish in the US continues to yield multiple and less formalized varieties of English spoken as a second language. Situated on a frontier between social mobility and social stratification, between the powers of assimilation and of ethnic difference, the dialects of American English continue to fire heated political debates in which unequal social access to the prestige varieties of English confronts the cultural rights of individuals and groups to resist mainstream norms of speech. (See MIGRATION AND MOTIVATION IN THE DEVELOPMENT OF AFRICAN AMERICAN VERNACULAR ENGLISH.)

REFERENCES AND FURTHER READING

Bristed, C. A. (1855). The English language in America. In *Cambridge Essays, Contributed by Members of the University* (pp. 57–78). London: J. W. Parker.

Fowler, W. C. (1868). *English Grammar: The English Language in its Elements and Forms*. New York: Harper.

Harrison, J. A. (1975 [1884]). Negro English. In

J. L. Dillard (ed.), *Perspectives on Black English* (pp. 143–95). The Hague: Mouton.

Howells, W. D. (1896). New York low life in fiction. *New York World*, July 26, 18.

Hyacinth, S. (1869). South-western slang. *Overland Monthly*, 3, 125–31.

Jones, G. (1999). *Strange Talk: The Politics of Dialect Literature in Gilded Age America*. Berkeley: University of California Press.

Lippi-Green, R. (1997). *English with an Accent: Language, Ideology, and Discrimination in the United States*. London: Routledge.

Lowell, J. R. (1890). *The Biglow Papers: The Writings of James Russell Lowell in Ten Volumes. Poems II*. Vol. 8. Boston: Houghton, Mifflin.

Mufwene, S. S. (ed.) (1993). *Africanisms in Afro-American Language Varieties*. Athens: University of Georgia Press.

Schele de Vere, M. (1872). *Americanisms: The English of the New World*. New York: Charles Scribner.

Simpson, D. (1986). *The Politics of American English, 1776–1850*. Oxford: Oxford University Press.

Sheldon, E. S. (1896). What is a dialect? *Dialect Notes*, 1, 286–97.

White, R. G. (1870). *Words and Their Uses*. New York: Sheldon.

Section 6
Topics in History

Introduction

The previous sections devoted to English in History moved chronologically from Old English through the beginning of the twentieth century. But within that chronology are embedded a number of additional stories, each offering its own special insight into the interaction of language and history. This section tells six of those stories.

Over the centuries English has been expressed through many physical media, including voice, manuscript page, printed page, loudspeaker, and LCD screen. Any new medium relies on the conventions of its predecessor even as it slowly replaces them, subtly but fundamentally altering the public's relationship to its language. In "Early Modern English Print Culture," John King describes the technological innovations of the late-fifteenth through seventeenth centuries that made possible the mass-production of printed material, replicating the manuscript's customary appearance on the page while nevertheless ushering in a new culture of print. Alan Bell and Philippa Smith take up a similar story in the early twentieth century with "English in Mass Communication: News Discourse and the Language of Journalism." Here we see how the mechanics of print are supplemented by other advances in communication – telegraph, telephone, radio, and satellite – in ways that not only speed up the dissemination of information, but actually shape how news stories are understood and told.

Public perception of language is also a common thread that runs through the other four essays in this section. In "Issues of Gender in Modern English" Deborah Cameron asks whether historical evidence is available to determine objectively the differences between men's and women's English at a given time, or whether only public *perceptions* of difference can be known. Using the methods of historiography and corpus linguistics (see CORPUS-BASED LINGUISTIC APPROACHES TO THE HISTORY OF ENGLISH), Cameron compares conduct-book proscriptions to the evidence of the written record to uncover women's roles in language innovation and codification. Tony Crowley's "Class, Ethnicity, and the Formation of 'Standard English'" also considers standard and non-standard usage, outlining the cultural forces that elevate certain pronunciations, syntactic constructions, and vocabulary, while denigrating others. The editors of the *OED* had set out to limit the dictionary's scope to the "standard language," meaning the usage of representative authors writing in popular, not technical or specialized, registers. But "standard language" has become conflated with "standard English," a concept rooted in class and ethnic elitism defined as the "best" English spoken by highly educated urbanites (see also A HISTORY OF THE ENGLISH LEXICON; JOHNSON, WEBSTER, AND THE *OED*). Similar to Cameron, Crowley untangles the strands of actual usage that have been densely interwoven with the claims of codifiers and language mavens.

Language standards are passed on through education and reinforced through both official and public pressure to conform. English has not always been a language deemed worthy of intense study or important enough to codify in rules (see EARLY

MODERN ENGLISH; VARIETIES OF EARLY MODERN ENGLISH), but as Michael Matto's "English, Latin and the Teaching of Rhetoric" tells us, once English replaced Latin as the dominant language of study in the schools and in international commerce, public concern with the teaching of a specifically English rhetoric rises to the fore, greatly affecting American secondary and post-secondary education. Internationalism itself is the focus of Andrew Gonzalez's "The Transplantation of American English in Philippine Soil." During America's late-nineteenth-century imperial expansion into the Philippines, English teachers were sent via military transports to take over Filipino school instruction. Language can thus be seen as a primary tool for colonial control. As happens in other colonized areas (see Part VI: "English Outside England and the United States"), the subsequent history is one of balancing national identity and pride in local languages with the cultural capital of speaking "standard English."

Michael Matto

28

Early Modern English Print Culture

John N. King

The craft of printing had a belated arrival in the British Isles when William Caxton (d. 1492) established the first printing enterprise in England circa 1476. Even though claims that the advent of printing had a revolutionary impact on the production and sale of books and on practices related to reading have not withstood scrutiny (see Grafton, Eisenstein, & Johns 2002), it did encourage the growth of literacy, dissemination of books on a scale more massive than previously possible, and important developments in English political, religious, social, and cultural life. A full generation earlier, Johannes Gutenberg had established the printing house in Mainz where he produced his 42-line Bible (ca. 1455), the earliest European book printed with movable type. During ensuing years, printing spread rapidly to major cities including Cologne, Basel, Rome, and Venice. Older than fifty years of age when he initiated the printing trade in England, Caxton had spent more than two decades abroad as a Merchant Adventurer. Although he had resided primarily at the Flemish port of Bruges, he probably learned the trade of printing from Johannes Veldener in Cologne in 1471–2. On returning to Bruges, he established the press on which he joined Colard Mansion in printing the earliest extant book printed in the English language, his own translation of Raoul Le Fèvre's *History of Troy* (1475?).

Returning to England soon after this inaugural publication, Caxton set up a printing operation that differed in no material respect, except for its smaller scale, from those operated by Gutenberg and great continental publishing magnates such as Anton Koberger of Nuremberg. Indeed, the technology of hand-press book production remained essentially unchanged until industrial printing superseded it early in the nineteenth century. A goldsmith like many other early printers, Gutenberg applied his expertise at metallurgy in his invention of the casting of movable type that enabled the rapid production of multiple copies of documents. Although this move constituted an innovation in European book production, printing with movable type had been in use in China for many centuries. Gutenberg devised an ingenious type mold into which a matrix bearing a reversed and indented character was inserted.

The type caster then poured a molten alloy composed of lead, tin, and antimony into the mold at the same time that he jerked it in order to force the metal into contact with the matrix. Finished type was stored in upper and lower cases that respectively contained capital and non-capital letters cast in founts of different typefaces and sizes. Provision of type was a challenging responsibility because of its considerable expense.

Like Gutenberg before him, Caxton discharged what the seventeenth-century printer and publisher Joseph Moxon defines as "the office of a master-printer [in] . . . providing materials to work withal, and successive variety of directions how and in what manner and order to perform that work." If he followed the ideal procedure set forth by Moxon, Caxton established a well-lighted establishment with a "solid and firm foundation and an even horizontal floor" that provided stable support for printing presses (Moxon 1962: 15–17). As a master who combined the functions of printer, publisher, and retailer, Caxton coordinated all aspects of his business, including securing capital investment, negotiating with authors and editors, establishing house style, acquiring paper, fitting different books into a more-or-less efficient pattern of concurrent printing, paying wages, warehousing, and selling books both to stationers and to retail customers. He engaged in gathering collected works, wrote prefaces for some books, and probably assisted with proofreading.

Like their continental colleagues, Caxton and his English successors printed books in the form of codices that consisted of sheets of paper folded into pages that binders cut along edges, assembled into gatherings or quires, and sewed at the spine. Even during the time of electronic publication, codices still represent what readers think of as "books." The first stage in the printing of a book involved the master's determination of book format, which was contingent to a considerable degree upon the length and generic nature of the exemplar. Formats range from broadsheets that consisted of a single unfolded sheet of paper, to folios made with a single fold that produced four pages, quartos made with a double fold that produced eight pages, octavos with sixteen pages, duodecimos with twenty-four pages, and so forth from sixteenmos to 124^{mos}. Broadsheets were appropriate to proclamations and popular ballads, folios to substantial works of scholarship or collections of poetry, quartos to non-ephemeral writings geared to a polite readership, and octavos to relatively inexpensive editions of sermons, handbooks, devotional manuals, and popular literature. Duodecimo format lent itself to genteel books of about the size of a deck of cards, such as collections of prayers and meditations, which readers might slip into pockets, folds in a garment, or valises. Smaller formats tended to be curiosities. Like broadsheets, at the other end of the scale, tiny books were highly ephemeral. Few books were published ready-bound, because it was customary for purchasers to commission bindings from specialized tradesmen who employed limp forel, parchment, or calfskin.

The cost of books varied in direct relationship to the number of sheets of paper required for their production. Because book production required a significant investment of capital, publishers typically secured loans to supplement their own resources. The major means by which the master could limit the consumption of paper, and

therefore the relative price of books, was selection of the type fount to be used for the body of the text. For any given text, use of a larger fount consumed more paper for the same number of copies. The master then had to determine the amount of paper needed. This involved casting off the exemplar by estimating the quantity of text and computing the number of perfected sheets required for its printing. Effective casting off also required determination of the amount of white space and placement of illustrations, tables, and other paratext. Although paper production existed on a small scale in England, the meagerness of domestic production forced publishers such as Caxton to rely on paper mills located in continental Europe, which were able to produce large quantities of affordable 100 percent rag content white paper.

Following the casting off of text and acquisition of paper stock, compositors began by selecting type from the upper and lower cases for placement in composing sticks before laying lines out on an imposing stone. In accordance with the format of the book, compositors set type in pages that they assembled in inner and outer formes for printing on the respective sides of each sheet of unfolded paper. The absence of sufficient quantities of type to keep pages standing necessitated the standard practice whereby compositors broke up and redistributed type to the cases after the printing of sheets and before composing new pages. The high cost of type stock meant that only a very few pages could be set in type at any one time. Constant redistribution of type necessitated rapid proofreading during the course of printing. Scrutinizing pages as they came off the press, proofreaders introduced stop-press corrections as printing was in progress. Discovery of errors after the distribution of type resulted in the insertion of pen and ink corrections, cancel slips (i.e., printed words that were pasted over errors, cancellation of whole pages or sheets, and/or lists of errata).

Employing a modification of the ancient screw press, pressmen placed formes of type on a press stone within a wooden frame known as a coffin. Laid upon a movable carriage, this assembly slid paper and type in and out of the printing press. Prior to its insertion, workers smeared it with printer's ink, an amalgamation of varnish and lampblack or another coloring agent, with pairs of leather balls. In order to keep sheets of paper in proper alignment, workers affixed them to pins that projected from a movable frame called a tympan. Attached to it was a frisket that held a piece of heavy paper or parchment that swung down in order to protect the margins of paper sheets from being smudged with ink as they moved in and out of the press. A plate-like wooden or metal device known as a platen pressed inked type onto the paper when a pressman pulled with substantial force on the handle of the screw to which it was affixed. Because paper made out of cloth had to be dampened in order to accept the impression of ink, it was later hung out to dry.

The older idea that print culture supplanted manuscript culture has not held up under scrutiny (Love 1993; Marotti 1995). Indeed, scriptoria continued to flourish long after the advent of printing. Fifteenth-century printed books or incunabula, a term derived from the Latin word for swaddling-clothes, resemble manuscript codices through the inclusion of foliation, incipits and explicits, guide letters to enable scribes to add initial capitals, and broad margins and woodcuts that invite illumination by

hand. It is not so much that early printers emulated the conventional form and appearance of manuscripts as that they lacked other models for the construction of codices. Regardless of whether they are in manuscripts or print, books share common formats and styles of binding and decoration. Indeed, libraries continued to shelve books and manuscripts side by side. Distinction between books and manuscripts in library catalogs represented a late development (McKitterick 2003: 12–17). It is no accident, then, that designers modeled black-letter type on manuscript hands in common use. Purchasers of books commissioned decoration that included hand rubrication that differed in no material respect from the inscription of colored inks in order to supply emphasis in manuscripts. Although parchment was the standard medium for late medieval manuscripts, it was unsuitable for use in printing. Nevertheless, printers would sometimes employ it to produce unique or very rare copies of books designated for presentation to actual or would-be patrons. It requires a discerning eye to distinguish between manuscript and print in such cases. It is true that texts moved from manuscript into print, but many individuals continued to inscribe long extracts from printed books in manuscript form until well into the seventeenth century. Some hybrid books contained both manuscript and print. The tendency of aristocrats to regard print as an unseemly medium for publication encouraged the circulation of elite verse and prose within coterie circles.

When Caxton began to print, publish, and sell books at the sign of the Red Pale within the precincts of Westminster Abbey, he recognized that he could not compete with the continental trade in books in Latin. He therefore supplied a need by publishing material that was otherwise unavailable, namely books in the English vernacular and some Latin books specific to England (e.g., books of hours of the use of Sarum). In adopting this insular trading strategy, he "set the pattern for the printed book in Britain for several centuries" (Hellinga 1999: 67–8). Furthermore, he established a typographical standard that endured for more than a century by importing matrices for a French style of black-letter type fashionable in Flanders during his residence at Bruges. Although it did not endure on the Continent, black letter remained the norm for English vernacular typography until the widespread shift to roman type at the end of the sixteenth century for most, but not all, categories of books.

Westminster constituted an ideal location for Caxton to market books to aristocrats and courtiers who circulated within the environs of the Yorkist court. His continued reliance on aristocratic patronage is notable in his close association with Anthony Earl Rivers, whose translation of *Dicts or Sayings of the Philosophers* he printed in 1477. Not only did Caxton remain in favor during the reigns of Edward IV and Richard III, he also thrived after Henry VII established the Tudor regime following his victory at the battle of Bosworth Field in 1485. Integrating the activities of printing, publishing, and retailing of books in the manner of other early master printers, he took on some printing jobs for others. Although the earliest extant example of printing in England is an indulgence, religious material represented a minor component of his production. For the most part, however, he catered to élite taste for translations of French romances and historical texts that were fashionable at the Burgundian court

from which Caxton initially received patronage. Aristocratic fashion also determined his selection of works of English poetry, history, romance, and other kinds of writing.

Linguistic considerations supplemented aristocratic taste in Caxton's decision to publish one of England's best-known texts, Geoffrey Chaucer's *Canterbury Tales*, in addition to texts such as the *Morte Darthur* by Sir Thomas Malory and poetry by John Gower and John Lydgate. They represent the fruit of the replacement of French and Latin by the English vernacular as the normative language for verse and prose. In concentrating on vernacular books for a middle-class and aristocratic readership, Caxton intensified the dominance that the London dialect of Middle English enjoyed due to the city's population density, commercial activity, and proximity to the royal court. A century later, George Puttenham's *Art of English Poesy* (1589) advised would-be poets that northern English "is not so courtly nor so current as our southern English is, no more is the far western man's speech: ye shall therefore take the usual speech of the court, and that of London and the shires lying about London within sixty miles, and not much above" (p. 145). Sociolinguistic considerations of this kind help to explain Caxton's failure to publish writings such as William Langland's *Piers Plowman*, a difficult and highly allusive alliterative allegory written in a Midlands dialect of Middle English.

Caxton acknowledges his explicit desire to avoid increasingly archaic language in his preface to *Eneydos* (ca. 1490), which states:

> I doubted that I should not please some gentlemen which late blamed me saying that in my translations I had over-curious terms which could not be understand of common people and desired me to use old and homely terms in my translations. And fain would I satisfy every man, and so to do took an old book and read therein; and certainly the English was so rude and broad that I could not well understand it.

Even more telling is his anecdote about the difficulty experienced by a traveler in communicating with a speaker of a non-London dialect when he

> came into a house and asked for meat and specially he asked after eggs. And the good wife answered that she could speak no French. And the merchant was angry for he also could speak no French, but would have had eggs; and she understood him not. And then at last another said that he would have eyren; then the good wife said that she understood him well. Lo! What should a man in these days now write, 'eggs' or 'eyren'? Certainly it is hard to please every man because of diversity and change of language.

Acknowledging that he caters not for a "rude [and] uplandishman" reader, but rather to "a clerk [learned man] and noble gentleman that feeleth and understandeth in feats of arms, in love and in noble chivalry," Caxton self-consciously strives to achieve a "a mean between both" regional and London dialects by translating "this said book into our English not over-rude nor curious, but in such terms as shall be understanden by God's grace according to my copy" (Blake 1973: 79–80).

Caxton's death in 1492 did not disrupt the production of books that flowed unabated from the premises that he had founded. His successor, Wynkyn de Worde, continued his master's policy of bringing archaic or regional wording into conformity with London English. In publishing the second edition of the *Book of Hawking, Hunting, Fishing and Blasing of Arms* (1496), for example, he or his employees consistently changed non-standard forms contained in the original printed at St. Albans six years earlier. They accordingly replaced "needis" with "need," "bot" with "but," "flowris" with "floures," "waar" with "were," and so forth (Hellinga 2007: 101). (See EARLY MODERN ENGLISH; VARIETIES OF EARLY MODERN ENGLISH.) De Worde made a momentous decision in 1500/1 when he moved from Westminster to Fleet Street. Some years later he also opened a retail shop at St. Paul's Churchyard. Contemporary printers such as Richard Pynson, Peter Treveris, and Julian Notary followed suit by establishing printing houses at close-by locations. These sites have demarcated the epicenter of the British book trade until the present day. In abandoning Caxton's aristocratic book list, de Worde emphasized books suitable to the sizable population of the City of London. In addition to grammar books, de Worde also published collections of popular poetry. Far more than Caxton, de Worde engaged in the publication of religious books. Patronage that he received from Lady Margaret Beaufort, the mother of Henry VII, may have encouraged him to adopt this lucrative shift in strategy. Pynson's shop at Temple Bar positioned him at an ideal location to sell the legal books in which he specialized to students and barristers at the nearby Inns of the Court.

As de Worde realized, clerical and lay readers constituted a lucrative market for religious publications. Indeed, they comprised a majority of books published in sixteenth- and seventeenth-century England. Early generations of English printers turned out edition after edition of indulgences, books of hours, sermons, primers, missals, breviaries, collections of hymns, litanies, saints' lives, and other Latin rite liturgies. Nevertheless, it was not until 1535 that Thomas Berthelet, the King's Printer, published the first and only edition of the Vulgate Bible printed in early modern England. Printers held back until then because of the technical superiority and lower cost of continental editions of books in Latin. After all, the majority of books in Latin and Greek were printed abroad. Furthermore, it was illegal to print or read the Bible in the vernacular because of the conservatism of church and state under Henry VIII. For this reason, William Tyndale went into exile in order to publish his epochal translation of the New Testament (1525). It is a remarkable coincidence that the first complete translation of the English Bible, compiled by Miles Coverdale, was published in the same year as Berthelet's Vulgate version. Although the Coverdale Bible was patronized by Thomas Cromwell, vicegerent for religious affairs during the aftermath of Henry VIII's revolutionary schism from the Church of Rome, it lacked official authorization. In company with Thomas Cranmer, Archbishop of Canterbury, Cromwell attempted to move England in the direction of Protestant reform. Not only did Cromwell preside over the Dissolution of the Monasteries, which led to widespread destruction and dispersal of "papist" books, but he joined Cranmer in furthering

publication of the first authorized translation, which was known as the Great Bible (1539) because of its large size. During the thorough-going Protestant regime under Henry VIII's son, Edward VI, a torrent of Protestant books swamped recently banned Roman Catholic books that were subject to widespread iconoclastic attack. Cranmer oversaw production of vernacular service books, the Book of Homilies and Book of Common Prayer, which joined the Great Bible in supplanting the traditional Latin rite. When Edward VI's sister, Mary I, attempted to reverse changes in religion introduced by Henry VIII and Edward VI, authorities banned the English Bible and Protestant books and returned to the Vulgate Bible and Latin rite. Not only did the regime of Elizabeth I undo these changes, but it attempted to counter the popularity of the unauthorized Geneva Bible (1560) favored by Puritans with a new authorized version known as the Bishops' Bible (1568). It was replaced in turn by the King James' Bible (1611), which was regarded by many readers as the only acceptable version of the English Bible until the middle of the twentieth century.

Black-letter typography characterized the great majority of sixteenth-century English Bibles except for the Geneva Bible. This striking exception resulted from a chasm that had opened between the increasingly old-fashioned practices of English printers, who continued to follow Caxton's practice of printing vernacular books in black-letter type, and printers in the Low Countries, Switzerland, France, Italy, and Spain. The latter had long since shifted to roman and italic type for printing books written in both Latin and vernacular languages. In doing so, they shifted from the original use of roman and italic type and for printing classical Latin and humanistic texts. Translated by Protestants who migrated to Switzerland to escape persecution under Mary I, the Geneva Bible contains typography that had become standard in the city in which it was printed. Many succeeding editions of this version and other English Bibles continued to be printed in black letter after ca. 1590, when the English printers shifted en masse to roman type. Despite the survival of many black-letter Bibles after this date, a steady trend moved in the direction of roman typography. Black letter retained an increasingly vestigial presence in certain classes of popular books and in the vernacular component of John Foxe's *Book of Martyrs* (1563), which was one of the most widely read and influential English books of the Early Modern era. By the 1680s, however, virtually all English books, including the Bible and the *Book of Martyrs*, were printed in roman type. By the time of the Glorious Revolution, therefore, English books had taken on an appearance that differs little from that of books printed in the twenty-first century.

From the time of Caxton onward, English printers employed woodcuts in order to enhance the appearance, comprehensibility, and salability of books even though the presence of illustration tends to increase book prices. Printers tended to share woodblocks that moved freely among London printing houses because it was less expensive to share generic woodcuts than to commission woodcuts whose use was confined to specific texts or portions of text. The year 1535 represents a turning point, because a ban on religious pictures made most older blocks useless. It is inappropriate, however, to conclude that Protestant iconoclasts were opposed to the use of visual

imagery in general. A new generation of woodcuts came into use in the 1540s and 1550s as sanctioned illustrations for Protestant books. For example, the reputation of Foxe's *Book of Martyrs* is inseparable from its highly affective pictures of martyrs being burnt at the stake. Its publisher, John Day, was unusual in maintaining proprietary control over woodcuts that he employed in publishing the best illustrated books of his time. Despite the view that the use of illustration in Bibles and other religious books declined after 1580, at a time when Puritans attacked vestiges of Catholicism in the Church of England, we do not encounter a sharp break from the Protestant practice of replacing unsanctioned pictures with "pure" alternatives. During the seventeenth century, woodcuts gave way to copperplate engravings as the dominant mode of book illustrations. Although intaglio plates were superior in quality to woodcuts, they were little used during the sixteenth century because of the added expense of using a copperplate press to add engravings to pages already printed on a hand-press.

Despite some changes in the production, financing, and marketing of books, the technology of the English book trade remained remarkably stable from the time when William Caxton began to produce books on hand-presses at Westminster until the shift to the machine-press at the beginning of the nineteenth century. As noted above, major developments during this period included concentration of English printing and publication in the vicinity of Fleet Street and St. Paul's Cathedral, expansion of literacy, growth of a middle-class readership, publication of Bibles, abandonment of black letter in vernacular printing, and the shift from woodcuts to engravings in the illustration of most books. The late sixteenth and seventeenth centuries witnessed a shift from domination of the London book trade by earlier master-printers (e.g., Caxton, de Worde, Pynson, and Day), who had successfully integrated printing, publication, and marketing, to the growth of syndicates of booksellers who shared capitalization, profits, and losses on books whose printing they commissioned from job printers. Publishers managed risk for major book projects through the sale of subscriptions and publication in fascicles. Pamphlets had always been a staple of the London book trade, but the period of circa 1620–95 witnessed sustained growth in periodicals. Indeed, thriving sales of periodical essays sustained writers such as Joseph Addison, Richard Steele, and Samuel Johnson during the eighteenth century. The final phase of hand-press publication also witnessed the growth of prescriptive orthography, grammar, and usage in a marked shift from the decided lack of standardization prior to 1700. Publication of Dr. Johnson's *Dictionary* (1755) played an important role in this development. (See BRITISH ENGLISH IN THE LONG EIGHTEENTH CENTURY.)

NOTE

This essay makes silent reference to *English Short Title Catalogue* and the *Oxford Dictionary of National Biography*. Quotations are modernized.

REFERENCES AND FURTHER READING

Barnard, J. & McKenzie, D. F. (eds.) (2002). *The Cambridge History of the Book in Britain, Vol. 4: 1557–1695*. Cambridge: Cambridge University Press.

Blake, N. F. (ed.) (1973). *Caxton's Own Prose*. London: Andre Deutsch.

English Short Title Catalogue (Online) (1992). London: British Library.

Gaskell, P. (1985). *A New Introduction to Bibliography*. Rpt. with corrections. Oxford: Clarendon Press.

Grafton, A., Eisenstein, E. L., & Johns, A. (2002). AHR Forum: How revolutionary was the print revolution? *American Historical Review*, 107, 84–128.

Hellinga, L. (1982). *Caxton in Focus: The Beginning of Printing in England*. London: British Library.

Hellinga, L. (1999). Printing. In L. Hellinga & J. B. Trapp (eds.), *The Cambridge History of the Book in Britain, Vol. 3: 1400–1557* (pp. 65–108). Cambridge: Cambridge University Press.

Hellinga, L. (compiler) (2007). *Catalogue of Books Printed in the XVth Century Now in the British (Museum) Library (BMC)*, Part 11 (English incunabula). 't Goy-Houten, Netherlands: Hes & De Graaf Publishers.

Hellinga, L. & Trapp, J. B. (eds.) (1999). *The Cambridge History of the Book in Britain, Vol. 3: 1400–*

1557. Cambridge: Cambridge University Press.

Kilgour, F. G. (1998). *The Evolution of the Book*. New York: Oxford University Press.

King, J. N. (2006). *Foxe's* Book of Martyrs *and Early Modern Print Culture*. Cambridge: Cambridge University Press.

Love, H. (1993). *Scribal Publication in Seventeenth-Century England*. Oxford: Oxford University Press.

Luborsky, R. S. & Ingram, E. (1998). *A Guide to English Illustrated Books, 1536–1603*. 2 vols. Tempe, AZ: Medieval & Renaissance Texts & Studies.

McKitterick, D. (2003). *Print, Manuscript and the Search for Order, 1450–1830*. Cambridge: Cambridge University Press.

Marotti, A. (1995). *Manuscript, Print, and the English Renaissance Lyric*. Ithaca, NY: Cornell University Press.

Moxon, J. (1962). *Mechanick Exercises on the Whole Art of Printing (1683–4) by Joseph Moxon*. 2nd edn. Ed. H. Davis and H. Carter. Oxford: Oxford University Press.

Oxford Dictionary of National Biography (Online). (2004–). Oxford: Oxford University Press.

Puttenham, G. (1936 [1589]). *The Arte of English Poesie*. Ed. G. D.Willcock and A. Walker. Cambridge: Cambridge University Press.

29
Issues of Gender in Modern English

Deborah Cameron

Introduction: Attitudes and Evidence

In the introduction to his influential text *Growth and Structure of the English Language*, Otto Jespersen remarked: "There is one expression that continually comes to mind when I think of the English language and compare it to others: it seems positively and expressly *masculine*, it is the language of a grown-up man and has very little child-ish or feminine about it" (Jespersen 1912: 2). Whatever this means in linguistic terms, it is clearly meant to be a compliment. Masculinity is a desirable attribute; femininity is not.

English has always, of course, been the language of women as well as men. But today, when students of the history of English ask how those women might have influenced the development of the language in the past, or what differences there might have been between their use of it and men's, one obstacle standing in the way of a sensible answer is the prevalence among scholars until very recently of attitudes like Jespersen's. Before anything else can be said about gender and the history of English, it is necessary to draw attention to the problematic nature of the evidence available to us – one problem, though not the only one, being the way pro-masculine biases have historically shaped the construction of knowledge.

Since it was not possible to preserve direct evidence of the spoken language until the advent of audio-recording, for most of its history our knowledge about English is based on evidence from written sources – more exactly, from those written sources that survived for long enough to be consulted. One result is a body of evidence in which male-authored texts far outnumber female-authored ones. The further back in time one goes, the more difficult it is to locate enough female-authored source materi-als to support general claims about women's use of English. In the pre-modern era fewer women than men were in a position to produce any kind of writing: studies of "signature literacy" (the ability to sign one's name rather than making one's mark on documents) suggest that by 1,500 about 10 percent of English men were minimally

literate, but for women the corresponding figure was only 1 percent. Literacy rates rose during the early modern period, but still the genres of writing in which literate women would have been best represented – such as personal letters – have survived less well than printed texts. Women produced just 2 percent of the texts printed in England during the seventeenth century.

To the extent that it reflects realities, such as the gap that once existed between male and female literacy rates, the predominance of evidence about men's English is itself a piece of evidence illuminating the historical relationship between language and gender. Yet questions may be asked about whether this predominance is entirely a faithful reflection of the historical facts. It has been argued that some of the most important tools historians of language have to work with were shaped by the kind of unselfconscious masculism Jespersen's comment on English, quoted above, exhibits. Consequently we cannot always tell how far the absence, under-representation, marginalization, or devaluation of women relative to men is a product of the conditions of those women's own time, and how far it is an artifact of the prejudices of later scholars.

Consider, for instance, the *Oxford English Dictionary* (*OED*), a monumental work of historical scholarship that sets out to document the origins and uses of every word in the English language from its first traceable appearance to the lexicographers' own time (see JOHNSON, WEBSTER, AND THE *OED*). One of the distinctive features of the *OED* is its copious use of quotations to illustrate the changing senses of words. There is at present no accurate and exhaustive listing of all the sources quoted in the dictionary, so it is not possible to give a definitive figure for the proportion of quotations taken from texts written by women. However, by hand-counting quotations in an indicative sample, Charlotte Brewer (private correspondence; see also Baigent et al., 2005) has estimated that this proportion is approximately 5 percent. Even making due allowance for the effect of women's limited access to textual production in the medieval and early modern periods (when for reasons already noted, an even lower percentage might reasonably be expected), this figure is arguably so low as to suggest an editorial bias in favor of men.

Support for this suspicion comes from John Willinsky's (1994) analysis of which authors are quoted and with what frequency in the twentieth-century Supplement to the *OED*. In this period there was no shortage of suitable female-authored source material. Nevertheless, the twelve most-quoted authors in the Supplement are all men: the most-quoted woman (and thirteenth most-quoted author overall) is Charlotte Yonge with 676 citations, and the next most-quoted women with around 400 citations each are the three popular mystery writers Agatha Christie, Ngaio Marsh, and Dorothy Sayers.

In addition to under-representing women, this selection of female authors – none of them considered major literary figures in their own time or subsequently – seems at odds with the dictionary's policy of favoring high-quality literary sources. Again, that can hardly be because there were no women publishing work of acknowledged literary merit in the twentieth century. Virginia Woolf, for instance, is quoted, but

only half as often as Agatha Christie. One could argue that "middlebrow" formula fiction such as Christie's is more typical of twentieth-century English usage than the writing of a high modernist like Woolf; but the *OED* had always placed literary value above representativeness as a criterion for selecting sources. In this respect it is evident, however, that the Supplement treats women differently from men. And before the twentieth century, even the most uncontroversially "great" female literary figures are in most cases quoted sparingly (Jane Austen, for example, gets fewer citations than Charlotte Yonge). The result is that the *OED* tells us less than it might about the contribution of women writers to the development of English as a literary language, even in those periods when their contribution was clearly substantial.

Making women "invisible" is not the only way in which the historical record distorts their role as language-producers. That record may be impoverished in terms of the direct evidence it provides of women's ways of using English in successive eras, but it contains a wealth of commentary on women's alleged linguistic shortcomings – a kind of indirect evidence about their use of English, largely produced by men and often incorporating an obvious anti-feminist bias.

In the eighteenth century, for instance, the period in which most effort went into the "ascertainment" of English (that is, codifying and fixing norms for its correct use), we find many commentators bemoaning the vacuous chatter of women with their wanton disregard for grammar and logic and their susceptibility to fashionable neologisms. Below I reproduce a well-known example from the writing of Lord Chesterfield:

> Language is indisputably the more immediate province of the fair sex: there they shine, there they excel. The torrents of their eloquence, especially in the vituperative way, stun all opposition, and bear away, in one promiscuous heap, nouns, verbs, moods and tenses. If words are wanting, which indeed happens but seldom, indignation instantly makes new ones; and I have often known four or five syllables that never met one another before, hastily and fortuitously jumbled into some word of mighty import. (Chesterfield 1777, quoted in Bailey 1992: 253)

Scholars contemplating this kind of commentary have to ask what status to accord it as evidence. Should we consider the possibility that what Chesterfield describes here was a "real" tendency, perhaps arising from the inferior quantity and/or quality of education received by the class of women he is talking about? Or should we treat this sort of comment as purely ideological, evidence only of stereotypes that were prevalent at the time, and for which there may have been little or no basis in reality?

The linguistic shortcomings ascribed to women by commentators do not remain consistent throughout history. What does remain largely constant until very recently, however, is the devaluation of whatever is represented as "feminine." Eighteenth-century commentators like Chesterfield lamented women's tendency to innovate (his being an age in which linguistic change was widely considered inherently undesirable), but later commentators, who had come to regard language change as a natural

and necessary process of adaptation, often represented men as the innovators who actively "renew" language while women remain conservative or passive (this view appears for instance in Otto Jespersen's 1922 survey of gender differences, 'The woman') (Jespersen 1998). It is not difficult for present-day readers to notice the persistent anti-feminist bias, but it is more difficult to know what the relationship might have been between such attitudes and the actual linguistic practice of women or men.

There are, then, particular difficulties facing scholars who want to investigate the historical influence of gender on the development and use of English. Clearly there is a need for awareness, and for caution, in the interpretation of evidence and the evaluation of claims. But that does not mean we can say nothing about women as users (and creators) of the English language in periods before our own. In the following section I will examine one instance where scholars have tried to address the issues just discussed.

Using the Present to Illuminate the Past (and vice versa)

One way to approach the question of gender-linked variation in past forms of the English language is to begin with observations for which there is plentiful evidence in the present, and investigate — by adapting the relevant synchronic methods to diachronic study — whether and to what extent the same tendencies can also be observed in data taken from earlier sources. If it is found that certain well-attested present-day tendencies do *not* appear in earlier historical periods, that may prompt researchers to look for explanations in changing social conditions for men and women; this has the potential to shed light on the underlying reasons for gender-linked linguistic variation.

In non-historical research on the relationship between language and gender undertaken since the early 1970s there have been many attempts to generalize about male-female differences in the use of English, but few of the generalizations proposed have been supported by a convincing body of empirical evidence. One finding that is widely regarded as robust, however, concerns the patterning of gender in relation to linguistic variation and change, which has been studied for 40 years by variationist sociolinguists. It has been a recurrent, albeit not exceptionless, finding that women tend to be more advanced than men in the use of prestige standard variants, and to lead in "change from above" where there is a shift in the direction of prestige variants and away from stigmatized non-standard variants. More recently (see Labov 1990), it has also come to be the orthodox variationist view that women typically lead in "change from below," where an innovative non-standard variant is displacing another, more traditional one, as well as in change from above.

The synchronic evidence, then, does not support the claim made by Jespersen and others that women are uniformly conservative language-users, while linguistic innovation is the province of men. William Labov has characterized women's behavior in

present-day speech communities as paradoxical, observing that they "conform more closely than men to sociolinguistic norms that are overtly prescribed, but conform less than men when they are not" (Labov 2001: 293). But is it possible to find the pattern he identifies in earlier periods of history? Has it always existed, or does it depend on relatively recent developments affecting the position of men and women?

This question has been systematically explored for the late medieval/early modern period (ca. 1410–1681) by the historical sociolinguists Terttu Nevalainen and Helena Raumolin-Brunberg (2003), working with data from the Corpus of Early English Correspondence (CEEC), a collection of personal letters which these two researchers, with their colleagues at Helsinki University, were instrumental in compiling. Though inevitably, given the conditions of the period it covers, female-authored material makes up a smaller proportion of the corpus than male-authored material (168 women contribute around 1,000 letters amounting to 0.45 million running words, while 610 men contribute around 5,000 letters amounting to 2.26 million running words), the CEEC compilers made deliberate efforts to amass women's correspondence in sufficient volume for a quantitative analysis of gender-linked tendencies to be meaningful.

The linguistic phenomena Nevalainen and Raumolin-Brunberg examine are a series of morphosyntactic changes affecting early modern English. Obviously, written data cannot so readily be used to study the sound changes which have always dominated the synchronic study of variation and change. However, letters were selected for particular attention because of their closer relationship to the spoken language, where most innovations originate. The grammatical changes analyzed include the shift in third person singular present tense verb inflections from –*eth* to –*s*, the decline of multiple negation, the replacement of subject-pronoun *ye* by *you* and of the possessives *mine/thine* by *my/thy*, the introduction of possessive *its* (where *his* had previously been used with inanimates) and the use of periphrastic *do* both in negative sentences (where it still occurs in present-day English, e.g., 'I do not like his prices') and in affirmatives (e.g., 'I did send it to my brother', where *do* would now be used only to mark emphasis, as in 'you say I didn't, but I *did* send it to my brother').

Nevalainen and Raumolin-Brunberg find that gender had an impact on the progress of these changes. Like their counterparts today, early modern women appear to have led in many changes from below, including for instance the shift from –*eth* to –*s* (which was a case of a northern dialect form becoming more widely diffused and ultimately displacing the southern variant). On the other hand, in this period it was men rather than women who led in changes from above, an example being the decline of multiple negation, which seems to have been a conscious move away from a progressively more stigmatized construction. Nevalainen and Raumolin-Brunberg suggest that women as a group in Tudor and Stuart times did not promote the spread of variants that "emanated from the world of learning and professional use" (2003: 130), because they did not have sufficient contact with that world: although there were occasional exceptions (such as Queen Elizabeth I), most women did not receive an extensive education, and they were excluded by their sex from learned professional circles.

This historical finding is of interest not only to students of grammatical change in the early modern period, but also to sociolinguists seeking to explain what underlies gender differences in the present. One longstanding explanation for the role of women in changes from above is that women are more "status-conscious" linguistically than men, and that this reflects their more limited access to the domains of activity, such as education and work, from which men derive social status directly (women's social status, by contrast, is said to be derived largely from that of their husbands or fathers). In other words, women's punctilious use of "correct" language is a symbolic way of compensating for their lack of independent status in the real social world. This observation might seem at least as relevant for the women of earlier centuries, who had even less opportunity to gain status in non-symbolic ways; but as the CEEC evidence shows, early modern women, at least, did not make use of the same strategy. The implication, arguably, is that women only have the "symbolic compensation" option when they are not, in fact, completely excluded from certain spheres of activity. And that might lead us to wonder whether the gender-linked sociolinguistic patterns most commonly reported in (Western) societies today are actually of rather recent origin, reflecting conditions which would not have obtained in most other times and places.

Using Ideological Evidence

The work of Nevalainen and Raumolin-Brunberg exemplifies a "direct" approach to the question of how gender affected language-use in earlier historical periods, in that their evidence comes from a sizeable sample of the actual writing produced by men and women in Tudor and Stuart England. Other evidence bearing on gender is more "indirect," however, drawn from texts in which the speech of men and women is represented and commented on by contemporary observers. The historical record is rich in observations on women's speech like Lord Chesterfield's, quoted above; it is also rich in texts advising women on the proper use of language. Women are of course not the only targets of prescriptive advice on language-use, but historically they have been favored targets for advice literature of all kinds, and particularly for the kind of advice that focuses on properly *gendered* behavior. These points can be understood as reflecting two important social realities: the particularly strong impetus that exists in male-dominated societies to control and discipline the behavior of women, and the principle that femininity is "marked" relative to masculinity. That markedness is encapsulated in the eighteenth-century convention of referring to women as "the sex": men are imagined as the default category of human beings, not defined for most purposes by their gender, whereas for women their gender does largely define them. They are thus felt, unlike men, to be in need of specific guidance on all aspects of their role as women. What, though, can we learn from this kind of discourse on language and gender?

I have already suggested that this is a complicated issue. Language and gender scholars today often make a distinction between "ideology" (beliefs about and

representations of masculine and feminine linguistic behavior) and "practice" (the actual language-use of real men and women), and warn against taking ideological representations as straightforwardly descriptive of practice. For historians of language, this may be a real temptation. Consider, for instance, something like Chesterfield's comment that women's combined volubility and ignorance caused them to "jumble" syllables into outlandish neologisms. Quite a number of his contemporaries made similar remarks, and it is tempting to apply the principle "no smoke without fire": in other words, to reason that if many different sources remark on a certain phenomenon at a certain time, we are justified in supposing that it existed. Yet if we think for a moment about the statements that are commonly made about language and gender in our own time, it is evident that not all of them correspond to real facts. In many cases they are not even intended as factual statements: their force is normative, not descriptive. When someone says, for instance, that "women don't swear," what they usually mean is that they think women shouldn't swear, or wish they didn't. In research on present-day English it is possible to investigate systematically how far ideological statements correspond to the evidence of practice (on gender and swearing, see for instance McEnery and Xiao's 2004 study using the British National Corpus, which found that both genders use *fuck* and its variants, though men in the BNC sample use these items with significantly higher frequency than women). But the ideological beliefs of earlier periods may be more difficult to assess. For instance, to test the claims made by Chesterfield and others about eighteenth-century women we would need data from the conversational speech situations in which the relevant tendencies were presumably observed, supposing they existed; but of course, we do not have that kind of data.

Where there is no direct evidence of practice to corroborate an ideological statement about how men or women spoke, it is obviously necessary to be cautious about citing it as evidence in a descriptive analysis. Perhaps less obviously, though, it is also necessary to be cautious about interpreting its significance as ideology. To understand ideological documents fully, we need to know – or at least try to discover – the answers to such questions as: "In the context of the time, what motivations might there have been for people to make assertions X, Y and Z? Who were the people making the assertions, and whom were they addressing? How common were their beliefs, and what competing ideas would their readers have been familiar with?"

Let us consider an illustrative example. Feminist critics since the 1970s have repeatedly drawn attention to the "silencing" of women – to restrictions on and disapproval of their speech and writing, especially their public speech and published writing – as an important aspect of women's subordination. Feminist linguistic historians have pointed to the ideological contribution made to the silencing of women by prescriptive texts and critical comments which equate "normal" femininity with loquacity (as does Chesterfield in his sarcastic reference to women's "torrents of eloquence") while at the same time equating female virtue with the opposite, reticence or silence. In some feminist writing, this kind of ideological silencing has been portrayed as a timeless, monolithic tradition, extending unbroken from Aristotle ("silence is a woman's glory") through St. Paul ("the woman should be silent in church") to

1950s etiquette guides and marriage manuals ("women should develop the ability to be good listeners"). It has also been suggested that this tradition had, and perhaps still has, a negative impact on women's own attitudes and behavior, making them tentative and insecure as public speakers and writers.

Yet this may be something of an over-simplification. In the first place, we cannot infer from the existence of numerous texts prescribing silence to women that women were, in reality, silenced. We might even want to draw the opposite inference – that the prescription was repeated so frequently because its targets were not complying! (Similarly, historians of pronunciation treat the existence of innumerable prescriptive texts instructing readers to pronounce their initial h-sounds as indirect evidence suggesting that in practice h-dropping was common.) But in addition, if we ask who was writing for whom and why, we may discover that the prescription of silence to women is not as timeless and monolithic as some discussions have made it seem.

In their introduction to a collection of essays about conduct literature – a genre of writing produced from the Middle Ages onward to instruct people on various aspects of proper behavior – Nancy Armstrong and Leonard Tennenhouse (1987: 8) quote a striking example of women being instructed to keep silence. It comes from a text entitled *A Godly Forme of Householde Gouernment*, which was published in 1614, and which uses the formal device of laying out the duties of wives and husbands in two columns, like this:

Husband	*Wife*
Deal with many men	Talk with few
Be "entertaining"	Be solitary and withdrawn
Be skillful in talk	Boast of silence

It would be possible to read this as just restating the ancient patriarchal prejudice against women talking. But Armstrong and Tennenhouse argue that to understand it properly, we also need to read it in the context of ideological struggles that were taking place in England in the early seventeenth century. Addressed to a bourgeois and puritan readership, *A Godly Forme of Householde Gouernment* is part of an ongoing struggle for cultural ascendancy between the class its authors and readers represented, and the dominant aristocratic class. Ideas about the proper place of women, including ideas about when and how women should speak, were being used in the text not only to instruct bourgeois women, but also to attack, by implication, the immoral and decadent culture of the aristocracy, whose women were not subject to the same restrictions. At the European royal courts, for instance, courtiers of both sexes were expected to engage in public displays of verbal skill, often in mixed company and not infrequently on subjects that were sexually and politically charged. The representation of women in bourgeois conduct texts was calculated to underline their supposed moral superiority to aristocratic women, as well as their difference from bourgeois men. Hence the contrasting linguistic norms summarized by Ann Rosalind Jones in the formula "the court lady was required to speak; the bourgeois wife was enjoined to silence" (Jones 1987: 40).

This reading of a particular prescription addressed to women illustrates two points of more general significance. One is that gender interacts with other social differences, such as class, race, ethnicity, nationality, and religious and political affiliation. There are no generic "women" (or "men"), and it is therefore important to consider what particular subset of women or men is being talked about, or talked to, in a text that talks about gender. In the modern period, our knowledge about both ideology and practice is heavily skewed towards the upper and middle classes. Not only is the record dominated by their linguistic production, it is also dominated by texts written for and about them. For reasons already discussed (our dependence on written sources and thus literate informants) we cannot correct that bias; but we should certainly be conscious of it.

Another point illustrated by the discussion of seventeenth-century English conduct texts is that there were, during the period in question, conflicting views rather than just one view on what constituted proper linguistic behavior for women. This can be related to the point just made about the interaction of gender with other social divisions – in this case, class and religious ones. But even within one section of society, beliefs and attitudes will vary. In the past as in the present, we should not assume there was a single set of views to which "everyone" uncritically subscribed. What survives will tend to be evidence of the attitudes held by those people who had most power, influence, and access to print: but it does not follow that those people's views were the only views in existence, or that they reflected the beliefs of a majority of their contemporaries, any more than it would be true to say that mass-market texts like John Gray's *Men are from Mars, Women are from Venus* (1992) represent some general consensus among English-speakers today.

In some cases, evidence of dissent has survived. The view that women corrupted English through their ignorance and carelessness (as advanced by Lord Chesterfield, among others) was vigorously contested, for instance, in an anonymous *Essay in Defence of the Female Sex* published in 1697. The author (thought by many scholars to be Judith Drake), argued that far from being impaired by their ignorance of Latin and Greek, women's proficiency in English was enhanced by vernacular education:

> For Girles after they can read and write . . . are furnished among other toys with Books, [which] . . . give 'em very early a considerable Command both of Words and Sense; which are further improved by their making Visits with their Mothers, which gives them betimes the opportunity of imitating, conversing with, and knowing the manner and address of elder Persons . . . These advantages the Education of Boys deprives them of, who drudge away the Vigour of their Memories at Words, useless ever after to most of them, and at Seventeen or Eighteen are to begin their Alphabet of Sense, and are but where the Girles were at Nine or Ten. (Anon. 1697: 57–8)

This author makes no bones about the ideological function of her argument as propaganda: she writes quite explicitly "in defence of the female sex" (though once again, we should notice that she is not talking about all women, but only women of the

educated classes). Ideological statements intended to disparage women or keep them in their place should be seen in a similar light: their authors are not just describing reality or summarizing prevailing wisdom, but making calculated interventions in particular arguments. Those arguments were seldom only about language, even if they were conducted on linguistic terrain. For centuries, language and gender has been contested territory: to understand discourse relating to it, past or present, we must place it in its broader historical (social, political, and intellectual) context – and read it with a critical eye for the interests that were at stake.

References and Further Reading

Anon. [?Judith Drake] (1697). *An Essay in Defence of the Female Sex*. London: Roper & Wilkinson.

Armstrong, N. & Tennenhouse, L. (eds.) (1987). *The Ideology of Conduct: Essays on Literature and the History of Sexuality*. New York: Methuen.

Baigent, E., Brewer, C., & Larminie, V. (2005). Women and the archive: the representation of gender in the *Dictionary of National Biography* and the *Oxford English Dictionary*. *Archives: Journal of the British Records Association*, 30, 13–35.

Bailey, R. (1992). *Images of English: A Cultural History of the Language*. Cambridge: Cambridge University Press.

Gray, J. (1992). *Men are from Mars, Women are from Venus*. New York: Harper Collins.

Jespersen, O. (1912). *Growth and Structure of the English Language*. 2nd edn. Leipzig: Teubner.

Jespersen, O. (1998 [1922]). The woman. Reprinted in D. Cameron (ed.), *The Feminist Critique of Language: A Reader* (pp. 225–41). London: Routledge.

Jones, A. R. (1987). Nets and bridles: early modern conduct books and 16th-century women's lyrics. In N. Armstrong & L. Tennenhouse (eds.), *The Ideology of Conduct: Essays on Literature and the History of Sexuality* (pp. 39–72). New York: Methuen.

Labov, W. (1990). The intersection of sex and social class in the course of linguistic change. *Language Variation and Change*, 2, 205–54.

Labov, W. (2001). *Principles of Linguistic Change, Vol. 2: Social Factors*. Oxford: Blackwell.

McEnery, A. & Xiao, Z. (2004). Swearing in modern British English: the case of *fuck* in the BNC. *Language and Literature*, 13, 235–68.

Nevalainen, T. & Raumolin-Brunberg, H. (2003). *Historical Sociolinguistics*. London: Longman.

Willinsky, J. (1994). *Empire of Words: The Reign of the OED*. Princeton, NJ: Princeton University Press.

30

Class, Ethnicity, and the Formation of "Standard English"

Tony Crowley

Introduction: Renaissance Origins

The emergence of the English vernacular as a culturally valorized and legitimate form took place in the Renaissance period. It is possible to trace in the comments of three major writers of the time the origins of a persistent set of problems which later became attached to the term "standard English." Following the introduction of Thomas Wilson's phrase "the king's English" in 1553, the principal statement of the idea of a centralized form of the language in the Renaissance was George Puttenham's determination in 1589 of the "natural, pure and most usual" type of English to be used by poets: "that usual speech of the court, and that of London and the shires lying about London, within lx miles and not much above" (Puttenham 1936: 144–5). In the following decade the poet and colonial servant Edmund Spenser composed *A View of the State of Ireland* (1596) during the height of the decisive Nine Years War between the English colonists in Ireland and the natives. In the course of his wide-ranging analysis of the difficulties facing English rule, Spenser offers a diagnosis of one of the most serious causes of English "degeneration" (a term often used in Tudor debates on Ireland to refer to the Gaelicization of the colonists): "first, I have to finde fault with the abuse of language, that is, for the speaking of *Irish* among the *English*, which, as it is unnaturall that any people should love anothers language more than their owne, so it is very inconvenient, and the cause of many other evils" (Spenser 1633: 47). Given Spenser's belief that language and identity were linked ("the speech being *Irish*, the heart must needes bee *Irish*"), his answer was the Anglicization of Ireland. He therefore recommended the adoption of Roman imperial practice, since "it hath ever been the use of the Conquerour, to despise the language of the conquered, and to force him by all means to use his" (Spenser 1633: 47).

There are several notable features to be drawn from these Renaissance observations on English, a language which, it should be recalled, was being studied seriously and codified in its own right for the first time in this period. The first point is the social

and geographic basis of Wilson and Puttenham's accounts. Wilson's phrase "the king's English" was formed by analogy with "the king's peace" and "the king's highway," both of which had an original sense of being restricted to the legal and geographic areas which were guaranteed by the crown; only with the successful centralization of power in the figure of the monarch did such phrases come to have general rather than specific reference. Puttenham's version of the "best English" is likewise demarcated in terms of space and class: his account reduces it to the speech of the court and the area in and around London up to a boundary of 60 miles. A second point to note is that Puttenham's definition conflates speech and writing: its model of the written language, to be used by poets, is the speech of courtiers. And the final detail is the implicit link between the English language and English ethnicity which is evoked by Spenser's comments on the degeneration of the colonists in Ireland. These characteristics of Renaissance thinking on English (its delimitation with regard to class and region, the failure to distinguish between speech and writing, and the connection between language and ethnicity) were characteristics which would be closely associated with the language throughout its modern history.

The Problem of the Dictionary

The first lexicographical attempts to codify English also date from the Renaissance. Richard Mulcaster's *Elementarie* (1582) appealed for an effort to "gather all the words which we use in our *English* tung, whether naturall or incorporate, out of all professions, as well learned as not, into one dictionarie" in order to ascertain their "right writing" and determine their "naturall force and their proper use" (Mulcaster 1925: 274). The aim of the first monolingual English dictionary proper, Robert Cawdry's *A Table Alphabeticall* (1604), was to help "Ladies, Gentlewomen, or any other unskilfull persons" in their reading of scriptures, sermons, or other texts by facilitating the "understanding of hard usuall English wordes, borrowed from the Hebrew, Greeke, Latine, or French. &c." by way of explanations in "plaine English wordes" (Cawdry 1604: title page). The appearance of these works signaled an increasing confidence in the English vernacular; linked to the rise of Protestantism by the technological and economic forces of print capitalism, the language became a central factor in the development of the recently centralized and increasingly assured English nation (Anderson 1991: 37–46). But it is important not to be misled by the nature of these works: despite Mulcaster's call for a "dictionarie" of English, texts such as the *Table Alphabeticall*, and others like it, were no more than developed glossaries. Given the task of explaining meaning and settling orthography, they were in effect aids to reading for newly literate groups by means of their translations of "hard words" (glossae) into "plaine" English. There is a tension, however, between Mulcaster's call and Cawdry's response: Mulcaster asked for a work ("a perfit English dictionarie") which would collect *all* of the words of the English language; what Cawdry produced was a list of specialized words which were judged to cause difficulty in reading.

This conflict between comprehensiveness and selectivity was one which bedeviled English lexicographers. Despite the use of adjectives such as "complete," "general," "universal," and the promise that a particular text contained "all" of the words of English, seventeenth- and eighteenth-century dictionaries did not in fact attempt to record and define the lexicon of the English language. Even Johnson's great dictionary, the most comprehensive to date, was quite clear that there were parts of the language which simply did not merit inclusion. The "Plan of a Dictionary of the English Language" (1747) expressed the desire to "preserve the purity" of the language, considered "so far as it is our own" and with regard to "the words and phrases used in the general intercourse of life" or in the compositions of "polite writers," and Johnson organized his work accordingly (Johnson 1793a: 161). The terms used by workers in their everyday activities, for example, were specifically excluded; he offered no apology for the omission in the Preface to the finished work:

> Of the laborious and mercantile part of the people, the diction is in a great measure casual and mutable; many of their terms are formed for some temporary or local convenience, and though current at certain times and places, are in others utterly unknown. This fugitive cant, which is always in a state of increase or decay, cannot be regarded as any of the durable materials of a language, and therefore must be suffered to perish with other things unworthy of preservation. (Johnson 1793b: 195)

Despite this blithe assertion, both the Plan and the Preface evince Johnson's anxiety about what precisely ought to be found in a dictionary. For although his work stood as the model for almost a century and a half, it exemplified the central problem which had faced dictionary-makers from the start: how to decide what to include and what to leave out. Johnson's most difficult task, as he admitted in the Preface, was "to *collect* the *Words* of our language" (Johnson 1793b: 184). Though it seemed more complex, the working-out of etymologies, a notoriously unreliable field of knowledge at the time, was the more simple labor.

What was it exactly that worried not just Johnson but the serious lexicographers who followed him? Why was the collection and recording of the items of the English lexicon so complicated? Johnson's discovery was that in order to "ascertain" the language he had to make a whole series of judgments on particular words: were they obsolete, archaic, foreign, slang, fleeting, dialectal . . . ? Or were they current, established, assimilated, general, attested, literary . . . ? Which is to say that the problem was not simply that of finding words which looked and sounded English, but of deciding which of them "properly" belonged to the English language. His answer was to resort to what was effectively a set of stylistic preferences and prejudices. For example, as well as the exclusion of the supposedly ephemeral language of the working and mercantile class, Johnson left out words derived from proper names and those he found only in previous dictionaries and not in his own reading. More significantly, he used as his model of literary decorum a defined set of writers from a specific period which were selected according to his political and aesthetic taste. Thus in order to

avoid the supposed Gallicizing tendencies of his age, Johnson "endeavoured to collect examples and authorities from the writers before the restoration, whose works I regard as the *wells of English undefiled*, as the pure sources of genuine diction" (Johnson 1793b: 191). Writing from the period which stretched from the late sixteenth century to the Restoration (with particular attention to the texts of Hooker, Spenser, Raleigh, the King James Bible, Bacon, and of course Shakespeare) was taken to exemplify the highest standards of language and thus to be authoritative.

Despite his prescriptive and proscriptive delimitations, Johnson spent much of the latter part of the preface to the dictionary justifying its faults and errors. His chief comfort was that "if our language is not here fully displayed, I have only failed in an attempt which no human powers have hitherto completed" (Johnson 1793b: 200). He was right in various respects: he had failed, but only in a way that others had failed, and the reason for the lack of success was that it was simply impossible to achieve what was being attempted: to display the language fully. Or at least that was how the field of lexicography stood before the *New/Oxford English Dictionary*-makers started their work in the mid-to-late nineteenth century.

The Invention of "Standard Language" and "Standard English"

The origins of the *N/OED* lie in a recognition of the inadequacies of the English lexicographical tradition. In 1857 the Philological Society passed a resolution at the behest of Richard Chenevix Trench, Dean of Westminster and future Archbishop of Dublin, to form an "Unregistered Words Committee" in order to publish a supplement to the works of both Johnson and his principal successor, Charles Richardson. It soon became apparent that the scope of the task had been underestimated and thus in the *Proposal for the Publication of a New English Dictionary* (1859) it was argued that "instead of the Supplement to the standard English Dictionaries . . . a New Dictionary of the English Language should be prepared under the authority of the Philological Society" (*Proposal* 1859: 7–8). This was the beginning of the monumental project whose object, in the words of the preface to the first volume, was to gather materials "for a Dictionary which, by the completeness of its vocabulary and by the application of the historical method to the life and use of words, might be worthy of the English language and English scholarship" (*Preface* 1888: v). Two significant changes had occurred since Johnson had started his work more than a century before. The first was the development of the historical method of comparative philology, and the second, a consequence of the first, was the lexicographer's aim of inclusiveness. The plan set out in the *Proposal* consisted of five main points: that the dictionary should (1) "contain every word in the literature of the language it professes to illustrate" and should not be "an arbiter of style"; (2) "admit as authorities all English books"; (3) set the historical limits of "English" and thus the limits of possible quotation; (4) trace the history of each word in the language and the development of its senses; (5) settle the

etymological origins of the word and its cognate history. The methodological care with which the dictionary-makers set out their task has been explored in detail elsewhere (Crowley 2003: ch. 3). Underpinning the endeavor is a principle which the lexicographers did not spell out, but which is implicit in the five points of the plan. This was that the dictionary was to be a study, within the limits set for it, of the vocabulary of English literature (in the broadest sense of the term). When the editors referred to the dictionary as an account of the English language they were using deceptive shorthand; what they meant was that the text was to be a record of the forms used in English writing. In order to help to clarify this methodological principle they invented a concept which could guide them in their complex and laborious endeavors: the "standard language." Thus the *Proposal* noted that "as soon as a standard language has been formed, which in England was the case after the Reformation, the lexicographer is bound to deal with that alone" (*Proposal* 1859: 3). It was the *N/OED* which necessitated the need for the "standard language" and not, as is usually thought, the "standard language" which created the need for the *N/OED*.

In this sense then the "standard language" was clear: it was a concept which evolved from the work of lexicographers and linguistic historians and referred to the uniform and commonly accepted written form of the English language. There was, however, a closely related term which developed at around the same time and which was to cause a tremendous amount of difficulty and to have very unfortunate social and educational consequences. This was the phrase "standard English," which is recorded in the second edition (1989) of the *N/OED* as first appearing in a philological sketch on the history of the language in the *Quarterly Review* in 1836: "it is, however, certain that there were in [the fourteenth century], and probably long before, five distinctly marked forms, which may be classed as follows: 1. Southern or standard English, which in the fourteenth century was perhaps best spoken in Kent and Surrey. . . ." There are a number of significant points in this illustration of the term: it refers to the spoken language; the definition is regional; and it includes an evaluation whose basis is unclear. It is in fact very close to the definition of the "best" English produced by Puttenham some three hundred years previously.

It is important to note that the term "standard" in "standard language" (as used by the lexicographers) and "standard English" (used by the *Quarterly Review* contributor) has different meanings. In the first case the sense is that of something which is widely practiced and accepted, or common and uniform (as in standard procedures or standard fittings). So the "standard language" refers to a relatively stable form of the written language which had evolved and which had been commonly used over a period of time. In the second example, however, the sense is that of something which exemplifies a particular level of achievement and which is therefore valorized (as in not meeting the required standard, or falling standards). So "standard English" refers to a form of the language which has been evaluated and judged to be superior to others. And it is this second sense which appears in the first entry on "standard" in regard to language in the supplement to the first edition *N/OED* (1933):

Applied to a variety of the speech of a country which, by reason of its cultural status and currency, is held to represent the best form of that speech. *Standard English* that form of the English language which is spoken (with modifications, individual or local), by the generality of the cultured people in Great Britain.

One of the quotations used to illustrate the sense was from Henry Sweet's *The Sounds of English* (1908): "Standard English, like Standard French, is now a class dialect more than a local dialect; it is the language of the educated all over Great Britain." There is no reference at all to "standard language" in the entry (though the first quotation is that of the coinage of the term in the dictionary proposal) and what the definition and its illustration demonstrate is a definite shift from a term and concept which was clear and delimited to one which was unclear and controversial. It is important to consider why "standard language," meaning a form of the written language able to be described and recorded in terms of a set of identifiable features, was displaced by "standard English," meaning a form of the spoken language identified not in terms of specific intrinsic features but in terms of the social characteristics of its poorly defined speakers (the "cultured" or the "educated").

"Standard English" and the Politics of Language

Like the Renaissance commentators on the language with which this essay began, linguists and literary critics in the late nineteenth and early twentieth centuries were contributors to the politics of language of their society. And as with their Renaissance counterparts, two of the concerns which characterized their thinking on language were class and ethnicity. The way in which professional linguists contributed to the development of a socially inflected definition of "Standard English" has been demonstrated in a previous work (Crowley 2003: ch. 5). But what became particularly marked in the early twentieth century was the deployment of "Standard English" in a series of debates which emerged from moments of historical crisis and which centered on the articulation, propagation, and reception of specific forms of identity. Henry Wyld's influential account of "Received Standard English" (RS) for example presents a model of patrician and patriarchal culture:

> It is characteristic of RS that it is easy, unstudied, and natural. The 'best' speakers do not need to take thought for their utterance; they have no theories about how their native tongue should be pronounced, nor do they reflect upon the sounds they utter. They have perfect confidence in themselves, in their speech, in their manners. For both bearing and utterance spring from a firm and gracious tradition. 'Their fathers told them' – that suffices. Nowhere does the best in English culture find a fairer expression than in RS speech. (Wyld 1934: 614)

The archetype of such speech is to be found among the British officer class since their utterances are "at once clear-cut and precise, yet free from affectation; at once

downright and manly, yet in the highest degree refined and urbane" (Wyld 1934: 614). "Standard English" was defined repeatedly in the works of linguists in this period as the language of a particular social group: the educated, cultured, and civilized. It also happened to be the language of the dominant class of one of the ethnic groups which constituted British society. In a clear rearticulation of Puttenham's definition of "good English," the phonetician Daniel Jones specified that it was "the form which appears to be most generally used by Southern English persons who have been educated at the great English public boarding-schools" (Jones 1922: 4). A definition by Wyld on the other hand appeared to exclude regionality, proposing that "standard English"

> Is a kind of English which is tinged neither with Northern, not Midland, nor Southern peculiarities of speech, which gives no indication, in fact, of where the speaker comes from – the form of English which is generally known as *good English*. It is the ambition of all educated persons in this country to acquire this manner of speaking, and this is the form of our language which foreigners wish to learn. If we can truthfully say of a man that he has a Scotch accent, or a Liverpool accent, or a Welsh accent, or a London accent, or a Gloucestershire accent, then he does not speak 'good English' with perfect purity. (Wyld 1907: 48)

But Wyld's account revealed nothing more than that the role of embodying the language and culture, which had earlier been ascribed to the privileged inhabitants of a particular region, was now occupied by members of the national ruling class in Post-Renaissance Britain. It just so happened that the national ruling class was composed by men who had been educated at English private schools.

"Standard English" and the Education Debates

The use of the term and concept "Standard English" has been most controversial within British education debates. In one of the most important inquiries into the role of English in the school curriculum, the Newbolt Report (*The Teaching of English in England*, 1921) set an agenda which exercised a profound influence on language teaching in Britain. In a useful assertion of the centrality of language instruction to education, the report commented that "the first and chief duty of the Elementary School is to give its pupils speech – to make them articulate and civilized beings, able to communicate themselves in speech and writing, and able to receive the communication of others" (Newbolt 1921: 60). The stress on communication skills is important, but it is undermined by the social prejudices which center around the term "civilized":

> It must be remembered that children, until they can readily receive such communication, are entirely cut off from the life and thought of the race embodied in human words. Indeed, until they have been given civilized speech it is useless to talk of continuing their education, for in a real sense, their education has not begun. (Newbolt 1921: 60)

It is hard to imagine that the writers of the report considered children at the age of four or five to be literally *in fans* (without speech) and thus cut off from human life and thought, and when analyzed closely it is clear that what is meant is that children (it would have been more accurate for the report to have said *most* children) had not been exposed to "civilized speech." Thus noting that "it is emphatically the business of the Elementary school to teach all its pupils who either speak a definite dialect or whose speech is disfigured by vulgarisms, to speak standard English," the report prescribed language lessons for children under the age of eleven which included recognizing "errors of pronunciation," observation of how the speech organs function, and practice in producing the sounds of "standard English" properly (Newbolt 1921: 65). The "civilized speech" referred to by the report meant the "Standard English" speech of the English ruling class, as a definition offered by one of the compilers of the Newbolt Report revealed:

> There is no need to define standard English speech. We know what it is, and there's an end on't . . . If any one wants a definite example of standard English we can tell him that it is the kind of English spoken by a simple, unaffected young Englishman like the Prince of Wales. (Sampson 1925: 41)

It is important to note the different modes of failure engendered by the use of "standard English" in the discourses surrounding British education in the twentieth century. The first is the impossibility of the state's attempt to achieve cultural hegemony through the inculcation of a common linguistic culture. The fact that the spoken language to be taught in all schools was, by definition, the preserve of a privileged ethnic élite meant that the idea of a national language project was exposed as a sham. This is part of the explanation for that otherwise puzzling obsession that the British have with speech differences as social markers of class and regionality. The second failure is the damage done to generations of children whose education in language was based on the idea that their speech was defective and that they needed to be taught to ape the accents of their social betters. And the third educational malfunction was in the effect that the confusion between a "standard language" and "standard English" had on literacy. Though it is impossible to know how much time was spent on pointless lessons in trying to teach all children how to sound like English public school boys, members of the officer class, or the Prince of Wales, it is clear that the time would have been much better spent in learning to read and write with confidence and fluency.

It would be comforting to imagine that the mistakes of the past have been recognized and rectified. But the definition of "standard" when used of language in the latest (1989) edition of the *OED* suggests otherwise: "Applied to that variety of a spoken or written language of a country or other linguistic area which is generally considered the most correct and acceptable form, as *Standard English, American,* etc.; Received Standard; also, standard pronunciation = *received pronunciation.*" Though the definition attempts to be clearer than the 1933 entry, it is in fact obscure in various

ways. If "Standard English" (there is no mention of "standard language") is a written form of the language, then what does it mean to refer to it as "the most correct and acceptable form"? As opposed to what? What are the less correct and less acceptable written forms of the language which need to be contrasted with "Standard English" ("standard," it might be noted, now appears to merit capitalization)? If this means dialect writing then it refers either to forms which are no longer used or to forms which are used in contemporary literature such as Irvine Welsh's *Trainspotting* in order to represent the speech of a region or class (in this example the speech of working-class Scots). In either case it is difficult to see why these would be described as incorrect or unacceptable. Perhaps the phrase means any instance of writing which does not conform to the rules of "Standard English," in which case, unless the rules admit of a great number of exceptions, a good deal of literature in the English language must be deemed not quite correct and not quite acceptable. If on the other hand "Standard English" refers not to writing but to speech then other questions are raised: what precisely does it mean to call one variety of speech "the most correct and acceptable form"? Most correct (as opposed to correct?) in whose hearing? And most acceptable to whom?

The confusions of the past are being repeated as a result of the difficulties which surround the term and concept "standard English." The use of the phrase by reactionary ideologists in the 1980s, and the way in which it is still deployed in an uncritical fashion by contemporary linguists of note, has been demonstrated elsewhere (Crowley 2003: chs. 7–8). What is unfortunate is that the term continues to function in Britain, with all its imprecision and its history of social prejudice, in the vitally important sphere of education. The latest version of the National Curriculum prescribes that "written standard English" and "spoken standard English" be taught to all schoolchildren. And referees for candidates for teacher-training are now asked to certify that they are able to use "spoken and written standard English" (no such requirement is specified to applicants in advance). The fact that such a confusing term (does it refer to speech or writing? to a uniform common language or a form of excellence? is it the language of a specific class or ethnic group?) continues to be used is testimony to the fact that the exclusive social interests which first articulated a partial account of English in the Renaissance period still manage to influence the way in which the language is defined today. Questions of class and ethnicity remain attached to "standard English"; that is surely cause for concern to linguists, educators, and anyone concerned with social justice. (See further JOHNSON, WEBSTER, AND THE *OED*; THE RISE OF RECEIVED PRONUNCIATION.)

REFERENCES AND FURTHER READING

Anderson, B. (1991). *Imagined Communities: Reflections on the Origin and Spread of Nationalism.* London: Verso.

Barker, E. (1927). *National Character and the Factors in its Formation.* London: Methuen.

Barrell, J. (1983). The language properly so-called:

the authority of common usage. In J. Barrell, *English Literature in History 1730–80: An Equal, Wide Survey* (pp. 110–75). London: Hutchinson.

Beal, J. C. (1999). *English Pronunciation in the Eighteenth Century: Thomas Spence's Grand Repository of the English Language.* Oxford: Clarendon Press.

Cawdry, R. (1604). *A Table Alphabeticall, contayning and teaching the true writing and vnderstanding of hard vsuall English wordes.* London.

Crowley, T. (1996). *Language in History: Theories and Texts.* London: Routledge.

Crowley, T. (2003). *Standard English and the Politics of Language.* 2nd edn. Basingstoke: Palgrave Macmillan.

Gibson, A. (2002). *Joyce's Revenge: History, Politics and Aesthetics in Ulysses.* Oxford: Oxford University Press.

Gill, A. (1972 [1619]). *Logonomia Anglica.* Pt. 2. Stockholm: Almqvist & Wiksell.

Graddol, D., Leith, D., & Swann, J. (1996). *English: History, Diversity and Change.* London: Routledge.

Johnson, S. (1793a [1747]). *The Plan of a Dictionary of the English Language.* In *The Works of Samuel Johnson.* Vol. 1. Dublin.

Johnson, S. (1793b [1755]). "Preface to the English Dictionary." In *The Works of Samuel Johnson.* Vol. 1. Dublin.

Jones, D. (1922). *An Outline of English Phonetics.* Cambridge: Cambridge University Press.

Leith, D. (1983). *A Social History of English.* London: Routledge & Kegan Paul.

Mugglestone, L. (1995). *"Talking Proper:" The Rise of Accent as Social Symbol.* Oxford: Clarendon Press.

Mulcaster, R. (1925 [1582]). *Elementarie.* Ed. E. T. Campagnac. Oxford: Clarendon Press.

Newbolt, H. (1921.) *The Teaching of English in England.* London: HMSO.

'Preface' (1888). In *A New English Dictionary on Historical Principles.* Vol. 1. Oxford: Clarendon Press.

Proposal for the Publication of a New English Dictionary (1859). Appendix to the *Transactions of the Philological Society,* London: Philological Society.

Puttenham, G. (1936 [1589]). *The Arte of English Poesie.* Ed. G. D. Willcock & A. Walker. Cambridge: Cambridge University Press.

Sampson, G. (1925). *English for the English.* Cambridge: Cambridge University Press.

Skeat, W. W. (1895). "The Proverbs of Alfred." *Transactions of the Philological Society* (1895–8). London: Philological Society.

Spenser, E. (1633 [1596]). *A View of the State of Ireland.* In J. Ware (ed.), *The Historie of Ireland Collected by Three Learned Authors.* Dublin.

Watts, R. J. & Bex, A. (eds.) (1999). *Standard English: The Continuing Debate.* London: Routledge.

Watts, R. J. & Trudgill, P. (2002). *Alternative Histories of the Language.* London: Routledge.

Wright, L. (2000). *The Development of Standard English 1300–1800: Theories, Descriptions, Conflicts.* Cambridge: Cambridge University Press.

Wyld, H. C. (1907). *The Growth of English.* London: Murray.

Wyld, H. C. (1934). The best English: a claim for the superiority of Received Standard English. Society for Pure English, Tract 39, 603–21.

31

The Transplantation of American English in Philippine Soil

Br. Andrew Gonzalez, FSC*

Several varieties of American English were transplanted in Philippine soil with the colonization of the Philippines by the United States of America in 1898, made legal by the Treaty of Paris on December 10, 1898. Except for a few members of the Filipino élite who had traveled abroad and spent some time in the British Empire or who had visited the United States (as had the Philippines' national hero, Jose Rizal), acquaintance with the English language was practically nil. However, those who had studied abroad in Europe were aware of the prominence of the British Empire under Queen Victoria and realized the importance of the English language, although they may not have been personally competent in it.

Rizal urged his sister Saturnina to learn English and wrote letters to her in his textbook variety of English. In the educational plan of the Malolos Republic in 1898, largely under the authorship of President Emilio Aguinaldo's intellectual adviser, Apolinario Mabini, the importance of the English language was recognized in the prominent use to be accorded to it in the proposed Academy under the new Republic, thereby largely displacing Spanish.

The first teachers of English were a group of soldiers under General Elwell Otis, recruited for the purpose by the chaplain, a Catholic priest named William D. McKinnon, assuming unofficially the functions of an officer-in-charge of education during the pacification of the islands until a military government could be established (Churchill 2001).

When the Organic Act of the Philippines was passed in 1901 by the second Philippine Commission under William Howard Taft, the Department of Public Instruction was set up. Although President William McKinley (through his Secretary of War Elihu Root, who was in charge of the colonies) urged the study of the local languages along with English, in effect the English language became the sole medium of instruction in the schools, and thus the educational system became the main agency for the teaching of the language. The first teachers in the system were recruited from all over the United States and arrived on board the USS *Thomas* on August 21, 1901; hence

the word "Thomasites" became synonymous in Philippine education usage with teachers recruited from the United States largely to teach the English language. Almost from the beginning, however, local teachers who knew enough English to be able to aid the Thomasites were pressed into service. These were teachers of Spanish who had trained in the former Spanish normal schools (one in Manila: the Escuela Normal Superior of the Ateneo for male teachers; and the other one in Bicol in southern Luzon: the Escuela Normal Superior of Santa Isabel in Naga for female teachers) as well as bright students who soon acquired competence in the language and were recruited to teach in the primary grades after completing elementary school. These talented students continued their secondary education in the public schools and subsequently at the Philippine Normal School, which offered a post-secondary school Spanish-type baccalaureate and an elementary teaching certificate. To qualify to teach in high school, they needed a bachelor's degree in education, which was offered at the College of Education of the University of the Philippines beginning in 1913.

The methods of teaching, by today's applied linguistics standards, were inadequate, based mostly on the grammar analysis method of the American schools themselves, using readers written for Americans with cultural content that was American. Only in 1918 were the first adaptations (using Filipinizing elements, substituting Filipino names like Pepe and Pilar for American names, and replacing fruits like apples and pears with bananas and pineapples) printed and distributed, but with the same frame of reference for phonics and little oral practice. Beginning in 1919, a school teacher and pensionado (scholar sent to the United States for studies), Camilo Osias, wrote the first series of *Philippine Readers* with Philippine cultural content, and not just Philippine realia.

From the beginning, the transplantation resulted in adaptation to the local environment. The 1925 Monroe Survey described the children as speaking like birds to depict their accented English, showing the influence of the local Austronesian languages (mostly Tagalog), but noted that they were reading relatively well, two grades below their native-speaker counterparts in America.

Acquisition of competence in English was rapid, to judge from self-reported competence. Based on the 1903 survey, 305,417 people (or 4 percent of the population) aged 10 years and above were able to speak English (see Salinger et al. 1905). Compare this finding with that of the last census of the Philippines under the United States, during the Commonwealth Period, in 1939, where the number of Filipinos 10 years and above reported to have competence in English was 26.6 percent of a population of 16,000,303. The steady and fast growth of English speakers in the country can be seen in table 31.1.

Continuing with Moag's (1982) metaphor of transplantation, the language was planted on native soil, has grown, become institutionalized, and taken on local features in phonology, grammatical structure, and especially lexicon. (For a description of the phonology of Philippine English, see Llamzon 1969, 1997; Tayao 2004; for a description of its structural features, see Gonzalez 1997; Bautista 2000, 2005; for a description of its lexicon, see Cruz & Bautista 1995; Bautista 1997.) More importantly, as

Table 31.1 English language speakers in the Philippines

Year	Population	Percentage of English speakers
1903	7,635,426	4.00
1918	10,314,310	8.70
1939	16,000,303	26.60
1948	19,234,582	36.96
1960	27,087,685	38.96
1970	36,648,486	44.80
1980	48,098,960	64.50
1990	60,487,185	56.00
2000	76,800,000	no data

early as 1910, creative and scholarly writing in English by Filipinos at the university level appeared, especially at the University of the Philippines with the publication of the first *College Folio*, containing poems and short stories by Filipino writers. During the Commonwealth Period, at a literary contest sponsored by the government, young writers presented prize-winning essays (Salvador P. Lopez), long poems (Rafael Zulueta da Costa), and short stories (Jose Garcia Villa); these and others constituted the first generation of literary writers in English. The tradition of creative writing in English has continued uninterrupted – this was true even during the Japanese Period (1941–5) – so that at present, one can speak of a flourishing or flowering of Philippine literature in English. This is especially evident in the best entries to the annual Palanca Awards (awards named in honor of a philanthropist, Carlos Palanca) in poetry, short stories, novels, dramas, and screenplays, both in English and in Tagalog (or Filipino), with more entries for English than for Filipino.

Moreover, the institutionalization of a Philippine variety of English has been recognized now for the past twenty years; descriptions of this variety have been made, with lists of local usages called Filipinisms and local idioms included in the *Anvil-Macquarie Dictionary of Philippine English for High School* (2000) and in collections such as those of Cruz and Bautista (1995). But in the publishing industry and in universities, the standard non-local variety forms are still taught and insisted upon. What has become acceptable is the oral variety of Philippine English with its local pronunciation, but with the written form still maintaining at least notionally the traditional rules of American English grammar without the peculiar Philippine English features which are present in the writing of even the most educated. Very often, editors and copyeditors are not aware that these forms are non-standard American English and let them go, which will make their institutionalization even in the more conservative print medium simply a matter of time.

One foresees that the differentiation of Philippine English as one variety of English derived from American English will continue, although the natural check on excessive differentiation will be provided by the mass media and formal communications. For

English to continue to be the world language, there has to be a measure of mutual intelligibility, which will then act as a brake to over-differentiation. And Filipinos, like speakers of other varieties of non-native English, will have to learn to be multi-dialectal in English, reserving a standard form for mutual intelligibility with other non-native and native English language speakers, and using a local variety, probably derivable from the code-switching variety so prominent at present, for informal and consultative styles (Joos 1967) of communication among themselves. In élite schools, the world standard that is in the process of formation will continue to be approximated, but in the less endowed universities, the code-switching and the local variety will be used more and more, even in classes. The picture is quite complex and does not admit of simplistic descriptions.

Post-Colonial Philippine English

One of the concerns of the American colonial government on the eve of independence before the Commonwealth Period was the maintenance of English in the educational system. Hence, it was made a condition in one of the earlier versions of the independence law that the English language would continue to be used in the school system after independence, since the colonial government believed that the acquisition of English as a world language would be an asset for the Philippines, and since at that time no national language had been selected. The mandate to select and develop a national language came from the 1935 Constitution.

It must be emphasized, however, that this policy was not a unilateral decision of the United States, but had the consent and approval of the Filipino administrators as well as the presenters themselves. The reasons for "hanging on to English" were not the cultural maintenance of American influence or a special affection for things American. The Filipinos were pragmatists then, just as they are now. As in the past, their main motivation for continuing to study and use the English language is instrumental, not integrative – and for educational purposes now made more imperative with the development of technology (for surveys, see Gonzalez & Bautista 1986; for later data, see Gonzalez & Sibayan 1998).

After it was selected to be the basis of a national language in 1937 (following the national language law of the Commonwealth in 1935), Tagalog was renamed Wikang Pambansa, then Pilipino, now Filipino. The national language Filipino has been widely propagated so that the latest census of 2000 (National Statistics Office 2000) shows 85 percent of the population are speakers of Filipino. It is taught as a separate subject and, under the bilingual education scheme of the Department of Education, it is used as a medium of instruction for some subjects (those falling under Social Studies) together with English (English Language, Mathematics, Science). Hence, there is near-unanimous acceptance of Filipino as the national language. There is at present a flourishing literary output in Filipino, but this is not the case in the scientific register, where English is still used, and in the printed mass medium, where most

newspapers are still in English. This reality makes it quite clear that presently the adherence to English is instrumental and pragmatic, especially for university and graduate work, for international business, for conducting transactions at the highest social levels, and for world communication, especially in science and mathematics and now information technology.

However, transplanted English has been cultivated, has grown and developed, has become institutionalized. At one time, in view of the manifest nationalism among intellectuals in the 1970s, it looked like there was a domination of Filipino over English in all registers. This was not to be, however, breaking Moag's paradigm. After a seeming period of neglect, from the time of President Corazon Aquino on, the concern of all has been the "deterioration" in the standards of English because of the poor quality of English instruction, especially in rural areas. Hence, since 1986, there have been concerted efforts to renew the teaching of English and to continue its use especially at the university level, with emphasis now placed on reading and writing skills more than listening and speaking skills.

Since the 1970s, there has been an acceptance of a Philippine variety of spoken English with its distinctive pronunciation patterns influenced mainly by the native vernacular. This pronunciation is slowly being adopted as a standard and is propagated not so much by mass media but by the schools. It is considered élitist, such that the upper-class *dialect* of the Philippine variety of English derives from this standard, with the *cline* changing according to the *edulect* of students and the schools where they came from (see Honey 1991, who called attention to this; the evidence was gathered from various publications of Gonzalez and Bautista). The accepted standard for Philippine pronunciation is syllable-timed intonation, absence of the vowel reduction rule and a tendency toward spelling pronunciation, and collapsing of some phonemic distinctions, e.g., [a] and [ə], [o] and [ow], [i] and [iy], [e] and [ey], [s] and [š], [z] and [ž].

In grammar a restructuring of some grammatical subsystems of English is emerging, notably: articles for different types of general and specific statements expressed, unusual use of tense and aspect, and unusual combinations of two-word or three-word verbs. Editors usually stay with the traditional rules and try to correct texts when they copyedit items for publication, but the peculiar usages persist even among the best writers of English (Bautista 2000, 2005).

Writing style has been studied by Gonzalez (1985) and shows a mixing of languages according to degree of intimacy. In general, however, Filipino students are taught rhetoric and composition in the traditional way and have developed what Gonzalez (1991) calls a classroom writing style, like neo-Victorian essays with an elegant but limited register that is quite formal. There is much creativity, however, in poetry and in fiction in English (Gonzalez 1987).

Literary writing in English continues and has produced writers who have made their names internationally; the methods and techniques tend to be imitative of American innovative writers, however, and the models can almost be pinpointed, although with some more creative writers a special style of writing fiction is now emerging.

Thus, to continue Moag's organic metaphor, the American English language in the Philippines faces not decline and extinction, but rather new growth based on the climate specific to the society. And therefore the term should be *evolution*, in line with world communication situations, which must be studied to predict which direction the evolution may go. The tree is fully grown but looks different from its original roots because of over 100 years of use in a multilingual society (vernacular and English).

With this evolution, Filipinos have developed different -*lects* which are best seen as products of the education of the speakers, since in the Philippines speakers learn English in school and are very much influenced by the models they are acquainted with there. One informal variety uses American-type slang and colloquial slang words, but the more informal style is a code-switching style between Filipino and English; the formal or foreign style is usually reserved for writing and speeches; the intimate style is hardly used because the home language serves better for this (although there is now an increasing number of English-speaking households where the parents speak with their children in English but the household helpers use the local vernacular).

Uses of English in Philippine Daily Life

The Social Weather Stations survey (1994), commissioned by the Linguistic Society of the Philippines and involving a nationwide sample of 1,200 respondents, indicated that approximately 56 percent of the population claim to speak some version of English; many can read, understand, and write better than they can speak, as the results in table 31.2 show.

For a time, during the heady days of nationalism in the 1970s, the domains of English appeared to have become restricted and the domains of Filipino more expansive. Among the upper classes, entertainment used to be only in English; during recent times even the upper classes watch movies and videos in Filipino. However, the proliferation of CDs and VCDs and DVDs at cheap prices has renewed interest in English and widened its domain once more in entertainment.

In the mass media, most of the radio programs are in English, while 80 percent of TV is English in the VHF channels (Dayag 2004) – the rest are in Filipino. In the print medium, national daily newspapers and two national tabloids are in English, the other national tabloids are in Filipino, with some weekly magazines in Filipino and in three other vernaculars, Cebuano, Ilocano, and Hiligaynon. Scholarly publications are approximately 90 percent English, with some scholarly books and dissertations now written in Filipino.

Table 31.2 Competence in English in the Philippines

Speak	56%
Read	73%
Write	59%
Understand	74%

In the world of business and international communication as well as scholarship, English has a monopoly. Daily business transactions at the market and the grocery store are in Filipino; in upper-class department stores, especially in Makati City, the use of English is more common. At the office, most communication is in Filipino, including some friendly letters, but formal letters are always in English and transactions with one's superiors are usually in English. Meetings are often bilingual with some code-switching, although the main language is English; at formal board meetings, everything is usually in English. Of course, for international contacts and international negotiations, as well as for conferences abroad, English is used. In spite of efforts made by some universities (Gonzalez & Bautista 1981, 1985) to use Filipino as a medium of instruction, and in spite of requirements at Philippine Normal University and at the University of the Philippines for some departments to submit masters' theses and doctoral dissertations in Filipino, the language of academic discourse continues to be English, although in lectures there can be code-switching between Filipino and English. Scholarly publications in the Philippines are 95 percent in English, and of course international journals are for the most part published in English. In any case the more formal the occasion, the more English is used.

Conclusion

Thus, the first foray of American English has given birth to specific varieties of "English as spoken in the Philippines." The language has been institutionalized, so it is now legitimate to speak of a Philippine variety of American English, which is called Filipino English or Philippine English.

There were many varieties of American English brought to the Philippines by the American military and civil servants (especially the Thomasites), and resulting from this transplantation are equally varying local varieties of English. The varieties vary depending on the first language of the speakers and their native vernacular, which has effects on the phonology of American English as spoken in the Philippines. There is more uniformity in the written form and in the formal varieties of the oral language based on a written script (as in lectures and speeches) because grammar is learned in the schools. This variety is now in a process of standardization, even in its pronunciation, so that among the well educated who speak a standardized form of Philippine English, it is difficult to tell where the vernacular is coming from, whether Cebuano, Tagalog, Ilocano, or any of the other Philippine languages. Some lexical items and idioms as well as loan translations have been legitimized by extensive local use, but changes in the article system and tense-aspect system have not yet been fully accepted, hence written Philippine English in scientific and scholarly publications is much akin to the standard written variety of American English (or, for that matter, other native varieties of English – Canadian, British, Australian, and New Zealand). One surmises that a world standard will emerge and that Filipinos who want to be part of the modernizing moment of internationalism will have to add this variety of World English to their individual repertoires.

The social situation in the Philippines is one of stable bilingualism for the educated, with restricted domains for English as already described. Part of the burden of post-colonial societies including the Philippines is to live down the cultural domination of the colonial presence, a task that the Philippines has found hard to accomplish. At one time the English language from the United States was considered part of this cultural baggage that had to be unloaded. It seems that the early soothsayers who predicted the demise of English in the Philippines were incorrect, for now the English language as Filipinos have acquired it has returned with a vengeance, and there is a scramble to improve English language teaching in both formal schooling and non-formal arrangements such as special schools.

The main reason for this, at the present time, is the economic advantage it offers – good English skills are needed for enterprises such as local call centers and for overseas work. The number of jobs for Filipinos in the call-center industry in the Philippines is predicted to rise to between 250,000 and 310,000 by 2009 (Hernandez 2004, as cited by Keitel 2005). It is no wonder that the Secretary of the Philippines' Department of Labor and Employment has characterized the call-center industry as "a sunshine industry that represents a window of growth for the country" (Department of Labor and Employment, as cited by Keitel 2005). On the other hand, overseas Filipino workers – Filipinos working abroad either as temporary workers or as official or unofficial immigrants – are estimated to number over eight million, and they live and work in 194 countries and territories all over the world (Department of Labor and Employment, as cited by Lorente 2005). A recent Asian Development Bank report places the remittances from migrant Filipino workers at US$14 billion to US$21 billion, a sum that amounts to 32 percent of the country's Gross National Product (Wehrfritz & Vitug, 2004, as cited by Lorente 2005). The Philippine comparative economic advantage seems now to be in human services more than in industrial or agricultural products; obviously, essential to the marketability of such human services is competence in English.

Still, the cultural burden of American English is slowly being discarded and Asian, specifically Philippine, cultural concerns are being introduced. Philippine English is being used to express these new cultural realities, which are, like the language they are expressed in, a mixture of the traditional and the modern. (See also WORLD ENGLISHES IN WORLD CONTEXTS.)

NOTE

* The author, Andrew Gonzalez, FSC, passed away on January 29, 2006, while in the final stages of completing this essay; it is our honor to publish it posthumously. We would like to thank his anonymous colleague in the Philippines for preparing the final manuscript. The editors of this volume have since made changes to that manuscript to produce the present version; any errors should be so attributed.

REFERENCES AND FURTHER READING

Anvil-Macquarie Dictionary of Philippine English for High School (2000). Pasig City: Anvil Publishing.

Bautista, M. L. S. (1996). An outline: the national language and the language of instruction. In M. L. S. Bautista (ed.), *Readings in Philippine Sociolinguistics*. 2nd edn. (pp. 223–7). Manila: De La Salle University Press.

Bautista, M. L. S. (1997). The lexicon of Philippine English. In M. L. S. Bautista (ed.), *English is an Asian Language: The Philippine Context* (pp. 49–72). Sydney: Macquarie Library.

Bautista, M. L. S. (2000). *Defining Standard Philippine English: Its Status and Grammatical Features*. Manila: DLSU Press.

Bautista, M. L. S. (2005). Validating the putative features of Philippine English, with cross-reference to other Englishes. Paper presented at the 11th Annual Convention of the International Association of World Englishes, Purdue University, West Lafayette, Indiana, July 23.

Churchill, B. (2001). Education in the Philippines at the turn of the 20th century: background for American policy. Unpublished manuscript.

Cruz, I. & Bautista, M. L. S. (compilers) (1995). *A Dictionary of Philippine English*. Pasig City: Anvil Publishing.

Dayag, D. T. (2004). The English-language media in the Philippines. In M. L. S. Bautista and K. Bolton (eds.), *World Englishes Special Issue on Philippine English: Tensions and Transitions* (pp. 47–58). Oxford: Blackwell.

Department of Labor and Education (DOLE) (2002). Call center industry continues to boost employment. Retrieved October 22, 2005 from www.dole.gov.ph/news.

Department of Labor and Education (DOLE) (2005). OFW deployment breaches .5 million mark in 1st semester, July 2. Retrieved August 27, 2005 from www.dole.gov.ph/news.

Gonzalez, A., FSC. (1985). Studies on Philippine English. Occasional Papers no. 39. Singapore: SEAMEO Regional Language Center.

Gonzalez, A., FSC. (1987). Poetic imperialism or indigenous creativity: Philippine literature in English. In L. Smith (ed.), *Discourse Culture*

Strategies in World English (pp. 141–56). New York: Prentice-Hall.

Gonzalez, A., FSC. (1991). Stylistic shifts in the English of the Philippine print media. In J. Cheshire (ed.), *English Around the World: Sociolinguistic Perspectives* (pp. 333–63). Cambridge: Cambridge University Press.

Gonzalez, A., FSC. (1997). Philippine English: A variety in search of legitimation. In E. Schneider (ed.), *English Around the World, Vol. 2: Caribbean, Africa, Asia, Australia*. Studies in honor of Manfred Görlach (pp. 205–12). Philadelphia: John Benjamins.

Gonzalez, A., FSC & Bautista, M. L. S. (1981). Towards intellectualization: The use of Pilipino as a medium of instruction in Philippine tertiary institutions. In A. H. Omar & N. M. Noor (eds.), *National Language as Medium of Instruction: Papers Presented at the Fourth Conference of the Asian Association on National Languages, May 1977* (pp. 111–60). Kuala Lumpur: Dewan Bahasa dan Pustaka.

Gonzalez, A., FSC & Bautista, M. L. S. (1985). *Aspects of Language Planning and Development in the Philippines*. Manila: Linguistic Society of the Philippines.

Gonzalez, A., FSC & Bautista, M. L. S. (1986). *Language Surveys in the Philippines (1966–1984)*. Manila: De La Salle University Press.

Gonzalez, A., FSC & Sibayan, B. P. (1998). Philippine educational surveys revisited. *Perspective* (Centennial Issue), 18.1, 40–55.

Hernandez, B. (2004). Philippine outsourced call center industry growth forecast: opportunities and challenges. Speech delivered at the American Chamber of Commerce.

Honey, J. (1991). The concept of 'Standard English' in first and second language contexts. In M. L. Tickoo (ed.), *Languages and Standards: Issues, Attitudes, Case Studies*. RELC Anthology Series no. 26 (pp. 23–32). Singapore: SEAMEO Regional Language Center.

Joos, M. (1967). *The Five Clocks*. New York: Harcourt, Brace & World.

Keitel, R. (2005). Call centers: implications for Philippine education. Paper given at monthly meeting of the Foundation for Upgrading the

Standards of Education, Century Park Hotel, Manila, January 25.

Llamzon, T. A. (1969). *Standard Filipino English.* Quezon City: Ateneo de Manila University Press.

Llamzon, T. A. (1997). The phonology of Philippine English. In M. L. S. Bautista (ed.), *English is an Asian Language: The Philippine Context* (pp. 41–8). Sydney: Macquarie Library.

Lorente, B. (2005). In the grip of English: labor migration from the Philippines and the making of English-speaking servants of globalization. Unpublished manuscript.

Moag, R. T. (1982). The life cycle of non-native Englishes: a case study. In B. Kachru (ed.), *The Other Tongues: English Across Culture* (pp. 270–88). Urbana: University of Illinois Press.

Monroe, P. (1925). *A Survey of the Education System of the Philippine Islands.* Manila: Bureau of Printing.

National Statistics Office (2000). *Census of Population and Housing. Report No. 2. Socio-economic and Demographic Characteristics Philippines.* Manila: National Statistics Office.

Salinger, J. P. et al. (1905). *Censo de las Islas Filipinas 1903, Vols. 1–4.* Washington, DC: Oficina del Censo de los Estados Unidos de America.

Social Weather Stations (1994). Survey findings on the use of English language. *Philippine Journal of Linguistics*, 25.1&2, 85–93.

Tayao, M. L. G. (2004). The evolving study of Philippine English phonology. In M. L. S. Bautista & K. Bolton (eds.), *World Englishes Special Issue on Philippine English: Tensions and Transitions* (pp. 77–90). Oxford: Blackwell.

Wehrfritz, G. & Vitug, M. (2004). Philippines: workers for the world. *Newsweek* (international edition). October 4. www.msnbc.msn.com/id/6100244/site/newsweek.

32

English, Latin, and the Teaching of Rhetoric

Michael Matto

From public legal oratory to private poetic displays of wit, from pastors' sermons to business letters, from elegies for princes to schoolboy declamations of lessons, the art of rhetoric has been called to serve many discursive genres. Rhetoric is most simply defined as "the art of persuasion," but a single definition for such a protean concept is reductive. Instead of seeking a simple definition, we might trace the historical contexts in which the term has been invoked (or, as often, disparaged) within the English-speaking world. Debates over the purpose of rhetoric tend to arise during times that attitudes towards language are in flux, and so mark key moments in the history of English.

The twin histories of rhetoric and of the English language together illustrate the social and cultural roles language plays. Among its many roles, rhetoric has been most significantly and consistently a component of Western education. Today, rhetoric is paired with the teaching of standard English grammar and called "composition." Virtually every college and university in the United States requires some form of English composition course for first-year students. However, this was not always the case. The first-year course in English in its current form began in earnest only in the last quarter of the nineteenth century, at Harvard College. Before Harvard's new program, writing in English was secondary to learning Greek and Latin, and rhetoric was properly studied alongside the ancient languages. By the turn of the century, however, virtually all American colleges and universities had dropped Latin as a requirement for admission and begun teaching English composition in the first year of college. This shift in emphasis from Latin to English as the primary language of education and as a language worthy of linguistic and rhetorical study has altered fundamentally our ideas about English. To understand this change and its place within the history of the English language, we will touch upon a number of topics: classical rhetoric, the growth of English as a prestige language, the professionalization of American education, and the attempts to define good English style.

Roots of Rhetoric

Rhetoric was originally an ancient Greek art which dealt in the main with oral performance, not written text. Today, oral presentation has largely disappeared as a required
course in American colleges, replaced almost entirely by a focus on the written, representing a fundamental shift in rhetoric's focus. (However, the pendulum may be swing-
ing back towards the oral as more colleges begin to specify "improved communication
skills" rather than "writing skills" as the goal of first-year English courses.)

Rhetoric as outlined by the Greeks and codified by the Romans was traditionally
broken into five parts, now generally known by their Latin names: *inventio* ("invention," or selecting argumentative strategies); *dispositio* ("arrangement," or structuring
the argument); *elocutio* ("style," or putting the argument into specific language);
memoria ("memory," or learning the argument by heart); and *pronuntiatio* ("delivery";
or performing the argument). The art of rhetoric was fundamental to ancient Greek
culture because of the high value the Greeks placed on political and litigious public
interaction – so much so that the earliest teachers of rhetoric, the Sophists, could
claim that learning to speak well even made one more virtuous.

At the same time, however, rhetoric's power was also considered suspicious. If
rhetoric is the art of persuasion, what is to be done about those who can persuade
others of falsehoods? Plato in his *Gorgias* has Socrates dismiss rhetoricians as practitioners of a sophisticated but ultimately empty art, able to convince listeners of their
positions through appeals to emotion and faulty logic, aiming not for truth but merely
for results (even as today we will call a politician's speech or lawyer's argument "mere
rhetoric," full of impressive language but empty of meaning). For example, Plato
charged that a talented rhetor with no medical training could nevertheless convince
a patient that the advice of his doctor was wrong.

Aristotle, in contrast, defined rhetoric as an adjunct to logic, claiming that the best
practitioners would find that the most convincing arguments were also those grounded
in the truth, which itself could only be discovered through logical reasoning. He
therefore emphasized *inventio* (the original Greek term is *heuresis*) as the most significant part of rhetoric. Strategies for invention were related to his study of *topoi*, or
"topics" (literally, "places"), the elements through which logical arguments were
constructed, and the forerunner to our current idea of a "commonplace" or shared bit
of conventional wisdom. For instance, one might prove that *Aristotle was a mammal*
by drawing on the premise that *all human beings are mammals*, an example of the topic
genus and *species*. Other *topoi* include cause and effect, degrees of comparison, part to
whole, citing authority, and many others (for a convenient compendium, see Burton
1996/2004). For Aristotle, rhetoric was necessary and useful because it represented
the application of higher-order philosophical dialectic (logic) to the more pragmatic
needs of legal and political culture. Aristotle therefore did not dispute that rhetoric
might be used for unethical ends, but such a use would be simply faulty rhetoric by
his reckoning, not a reason to condemn the entire enterprise.

At issue was rhetoric's relation to ethics on the one hand and logic on the other. Is rhetoric a form of logic, or merely language manipulated to engage the emotions? Plato and Aristotle's disagreement on this point laid the groundwork for much of the discussion of rhetoric that was to follow in Western history, particularly in relation to language teaching in schools. Today we expect education and the production of knowledge to arise from empirical experimentation and the scientific method, but in the Middle Ages, when such methods were yet to be invented, the right means of discerning and expressing truths was through disputation and dialectical thinking, called scholasticism. The foundation for education within this epistemological framework was a system made up of two parts: the *trivium* ("the three ways") and the *quadrivium* ("the four ways"). Rhetoric was one part of the more basic *trivium*, which also consisted of grammar and logic. The *quadrivium* followed, which covered arithmetic, geometry, music, and astronomy. Within this system we find an interesting conflation of Aristotelian and Platonic ideas about rhetoric. While rhetoric remained the art of persuasion, the study of rhetoric in the Middle Ages was largely based on the extensive list of tropes and figures of speech found in Roman treatises (particularly Quintilian's *Institutio Oratoria* and the *Rhetorica ad Herennium*). This focus on figures of *speech* (metaphor, onomatopoeia, vivid description, understatement, etc.) echoed but varied significantly from Aristotle's *topoi*, or figures of *thought*, which he considered part of logic. *Elocutio* (speech) thus came to dominate *inventio* (thought) (see Murphy 1974; Kennedy 1980). Because of this, though rhetoric was based mainly on Aristotelian ideas, it became equated with mere ornamentation, the flowery metaphors and clever turns of phrase that were to clothe one's ideas. As such, the study of rhetoric was once again subject to the Platonic critique of being frivolous.

Latin Rhetoric and English Style

During the medieval period it was simply assumed that any educated person throughout Europe was educated in Latin, not his (or less commonly, her) mother tongue. More than the language of the Church, within most European kingdoms Latin was also the language of law, business, education, and often government. Latin thus served as more than a *lingua franca* between peoples; it was the language of power in medieval European society. In England after the Anglo-Saxon period (during which Old English had been the language of state within the various kingdoms), much of the history of English is as the second or third player within the spheres of influence, behind Latin and, for a good while, French as well. English does not become widely used for government purposes again until the fifteenth century (see EARLY MIDDLE ENGLISH), and even then it shares duties with Latin. After the fifteenth century, English gradually climbs to the top of the prestige ladder, with the largest obstacle to its ascent being the entrenchment of Latin in the schools.

The sixteenth and seventeenth centuries, however, still see English writers striving to legitimize their native language through twin exercises in translation and original

composition. Translators go to work turning the Latin and Greek classics into poetic, literary English, while writers like Spenser and Milton set out to compose their own epics in their mother tongue to rival the very classics being translated (see Adamson 1999). This period also sees the production of authorized English Bibles, including the great King James Bible in 1611 (see EARLY MODERN ENGLISH). At the same time, treatises on rhetoric, once written almost exclusively in Latin, began to appear in English as well (e.g., Thomas Wilson's *The Arte of Rhetorique*, 1553), as were guidebooks on writing poetry (e.g., George Puttenham's *The Arte of English Poesie*, 1589). But even in tackling ever more difficult material, English writers were still trying to prove themselves by measuring their successes against the established prestige of Latin.

Still, the new poetic guidebooks in particular helped English to carve out its own niche by redefining rhetoric as *style*, not meaning an over-emphasis on *elocutio*, but rather a move away from persuasion and towards composition and clarity of exposition. The dawn of the seventeenth century in England saw the coming of a movement (now known as the Scientific Revolution) which sought to break from medieval pedagogy and its underlying philosophy of scholasticism, and to replace it with a philosophy of empiricism. A language vacuum was thus created in the learned world, since Latin represented the language of the old medieval scholasticism. By the 1660s the newly formed Royal Society of London for the Improvement of Natural Knowledge argued for an English style appropriate to its own empirical philosophy, which was itself drawn from Francis Bacon (d. 1626), empiricism's chief advocate in England. The Royal Society's motto *nullius in verba* ("On the words of no [master]") indicated their devotion to experimentation rather than adherence to the authority of those who came before or the commonplace wisdom they had passed down. The Royal Society was therefore skeptical of *topoi* and of figures of speech used as ornament, and argued for an English style as clear and straightforward as mathematical representation. The desire for a literal language with one-to-one correspondence between its words and things in the natural world was very compelling. In 1668 Royal Society member Bishop John Wilkins was inspired to undertake his monumental *Essay Toward a Real Character and a Philosophical Language* which attempted to create a system of reference that would assign a single non-polysemous, non-arbitrary sign for every thing in the world. Needless to say, his system did not catch on, but the spirit of Wilkins' efforts can be found in the Society's promotion of a plain, direct style for English prose, and in such later onomasiological works as Roget's *Thesaurus* (see ENGLISH ONOMASIOLOGICAL DICTIONARIES AND THESAURI).

English was now coming into its own as a language of prestige and modern learning. Once English was established as a proper vehicle for both rhetorically sound prose and well-formed poetry, English began to matter enough to warrant the attention of language mavens. Eighteenth-century grammarians and lexicographers set out to apply to English the same level of grammatical and syntactic study as had been previously afforded Latin (see BRITISH ENGLISH IN THE LONG EIGHTEENTH CENTURY). But in one sense, Latin still retained pride of place. Many grammarians assumed that

English should conform to the linguistic structure of Latin. They made this assumption for one of two reasons: they either believed in the notion of a "universal grammar" to which all languages must conform, and saw Latin, as codified in the classical period, as a perfect representative of that grammar; or they did not subscribe to the theory of universal grammar, but still saw Latin as a model by which to adjudicate disagreements about English usage. Latin grammar was often difficult to apply in practice to a Germanic language such as English, leading to debates about when to use "who" versus "whom," the propriety of ending sentences with prepositions, the proper construction of verbal phrases, and other ongoing grammatical controversies. Representative here as a somewhat moderate voice is Robert Lowth and his *Short Introduction to English Grammar* (1762), an early attempt to systematize and perfect English by codifying its rules in accordance with both logic and Latin precedent. Lowth downplayed his reliance on Latin grammar for his judgments, but the twin criteria of "logic" and "Latin" are often a redundancy for Lowth, who would have looked to Latin as a model precisely because of its perceived perfect and logical structure. The somewhat awkward fundamental grammatical terminology for English (e.g., the complex verb tense system of present, perfect, pluperfect, future perfect, etc.) derives ultimately from the application of Latin and Greek grammar to English. But most telling in Lowth's book, and representative of the age, is his procedure of quoting from canonical English writers not to provide examples of good usage, but rather to point out their pernicious errors. English was not defined by actual usage, but in terms of an abstract structure for all languages based on the classical grammars (see Leonard 1929).

While the prescriptivists were writing their rule books and dictionaries, the question of the correct place of rhetoric in education was raised once again. Eighteenth-century Scottish rhetoricians were particularly influential; especially noteworthy are George Campbell's *The Philosophy of Rhetoric* (1776) and Richard Whately's *Elements of Rhetoric* (1828). But more influential than these in American schools was Hugh Blair's text *Lectures on Rhetoric and Belles Lettres*, first published in 1783. Blair dismissed *inventio* from the purview of rhetoric, but not because he thought it belonged to the domain of logic (as Aristotle had); Blair was skeptical of the whole notion of teaching the *topoi* as a method of invention. He argued that good ideas are the product of an innate genius, not the application of a systematic theory. Taking this position meant that the still widely valued discipline of logic was not available to help Blair save rhetoric from either the Platonic critique of false persuasion or the empirical critique of excessive ornamentation. Blair was, however, able to turn to the innate value of good taste and the aesthetics of belletristic writing as an alternate defense. Acknowledging that the art of rhetoric was perceived to be "ostentatious and deceitful," and its subject "minute and trifling," he writes his lectures to counter the "corruption . . . of good taste and true eloquence," insisting that

> it is equally possible to apply the principles of reason and good sense to this art [rhetoric], as to any other that is cultivated by men. If the following Lectures have any merit, it will consist in an endeavor to substitute the application of these principles in the

place of artificial and scholastic rhetoric; in an endeavor to explode false ornament, to direct attention more towards substance than show, to recommend good sense as the foundation of all good composition, and simplicity as essential to all true ornament. (Blair 2005: 4)

Blair thus rescues rhetoric from the charge of excess ornamentation not by stressing *inventio* as Aristotle did, but rather by emphasizing his idea of "good taste." Because Americans valued social mobility, made possible by the industrial revolution in the eighteenth and nineteenth centuries, good taste became a practical concern, as it was one route to a rising social status (Bledstein 1976). Blair's justification for studying rhetoric relies on this desire to represent oneself as cultured and accomplished. Subjecting the excesses of nature to the constraints of a well-developed "art" was for Blair the very definition of civilization, and rhetoric was the application of artful restraint to natural language. Importantly, Blair's ideal of taste and common sense derived not from an appreciation of Latin (at least, not in any conscious way), but from his understanding of other fine arts. Blair's criterion of taste, as well as his explicit emphasis on belletristic *writing* as opposed to speaking, marked a break from the Latin-rooted rhetorics of the past, and made his a favorite textbook in American schools for much of the nineteenth century.

The Nineteenth-Century American High School

The structure of modern education, made up of compulsory primary and secondary schooling followed by optional college and graduate study, must seem inevitable to the average American. But the modern high school is an invention of the nineteenth century, designed to serve the changing needs of an industrial economy. The medieval universities, designed to prepare lawyers, clergy, and physicians, had taken on instruction in Latin grammar and the other subjects of the *trivium* and *quadrivium* as well, as their students needed such instruction to succeed. Their education was rooted in a tradition that reached back to the Greeks, with logical disputation at its center and the authority of tradition, as codified in Latin writings, the final arbiter. With the scientific and industrial revolutions, however, came a drastic shift in the very idea of a university, one that enacted the motto of the Royal Society: *nullius in verba*. "Where once libraries had been the center and only essential component of cathedral schools, monasteries, colleges, and universities, now botanical gardens; arboretums, physical, chemical, and geological cabinets and museums; and engineering laboratories and agricultural experiment stations appeared and altered the academic landscape" (Herbst 1996: 5). Laboratory work and experiments, not logic and dialectic, defined the modern university bent on producing experts for the new industrialized economy. As universities became more specialized, the "basics" (i.e., the things learned from schoolbooks) became relegated to the lower schools. Thus "grammar schools" were so-called

precisely because they focused on teaching Latin grammar, the first art of the old *trivium*. In colonial America, grammar schools were generally seven year programs for boys ages seven to fourteen, at which point they entered college. By the end of the eighteenth century, grammar school had been reduced to four years, and some Boston students entered Harvard as early as ten years old (Herbst 1996: 13). This seeming too young, nineteenth-century educators and local governments conceived the idea of a post-grammar school other than college.

While there was general agreement that such a post-grammar school was a good idea, by the 1820s a debate ensued over whether such a "secondary" school would function as preparatory for university education, or as an alternative to college for those not destined to study in the higher professions. Today, modern secondary schools serve many functions simultaneously: students are placed on "tracks" leading them to college, vocational school, or neither. In the early nineteenth century, however, proponents of secondary schools imagined they might serve only one of two possible functions: schools could prepare students for the colleges, or for the new businesses developing within the industrial market economy. The former demanded continued emphasis on the equivalent of the *trivium* and *quadrivium*, freeing university faculty to dedicate themselves to the production of the specialized knowledge that was useful in the new economy as one source of technical innovation, but also continuing the university's traditional function of producing doctors, lawyers, and clergy. The latter needed practical courses in math, science, and English (as opposed to Latin) grammar, as well as classes in such skills as bookkeeping, in order to produce potential employees: urban clerks and merchants, surveyors, mechanics, and other middle-class workers in an industrial market economy. Determining the proper function of the high school was thus an epistemological debate: What kind of knowledge is desirable in a culture that defines itself as a meritocracy, where anyone can rise as high as ability and desire allow? And what role could Latin play in such a culture? Benjamin Rush, a medical doctor known as "the father of American psychiatry," voiced the suspicions of many utilitarian Americans when he mused in 1789, "Do not men use Latin and Greek, as the scuttlefish emit their ink, on purpose to conceal themselves from an intercourse with the common people?" (Reese 1995: 92).

Such sentiment against Latin and the élitist classical education it represented only grew in the nineteenth century. The ancient Greek pedagogical ideal of *paideia*, which emphasized developing students into fully realized human beings and citizens, had been invoked centuries before by the Sophists who claimed that learning the rhetorical arts helped students become more virtuous. The same claim had been made in Renaissance Europe on behalf of humanist education, itself rooted in the study of grammar and rhetoric. While defenders of classical education since the nineteenth century have made a similar humanistic argument, they have been forced to add that learning Latin is also *practical* as it exercises the mind and cultivates mental discipline. A typical example of this dual argument is the following from a Connecticut school inspector's report in 1872:

It is true that men do not make bargains in Latin or Greek, or talk French in the market, or plough with the syllogism, or compute the value of stocks by the propositions of Euclid, or rake hay with the principles of morals. . ... Yet the man whose mind has been sharpened, and drilled, and enlarged by such exercises, is not only a wiser and more skillful man of business, but a nobler and better man in his various relations of life. (Reese 1995: 99–100)

To be accepted, the high school curriculum had to satisfy both the practical needs of business and the expectations of the majority of Americans who wanted the schools to instill in their children the values of the capitalist market economy. Schoolwork had not only to be demonstrably utilitarian, but also to instill bourgeois values. Math teachers presented scenarios that had students calculate how much money to deduct from a lazy worker's paycheck, or (conversely) how much a benevolent gentleman gave to a beggar. After simple algebra, students applied higher mathematics to analyze the performance of stocks and bonds and to compute compound interest and foreign exchange rates (Reese 1995: 114–15). Textbooks in the humanities were written to serve capitalist interests as well. Grammar books offered example sentences that strove to instill good taste (echoing Blair), a disdain for idleness, and a desire to aspire. The following sentences, for instance, were to be corrected for syntax and punctuation: "Idleness and ignorance is the parent of many vices"; "By the unhappy Excesses of Irregular Pleasure in Youth how many amiable Dispositions are corrupted or destroyed How many rising Capacities and Powers are suppressed How many flattering Hopes of Parents and Friends are totally extinguished" (Murray, quoted in Reese 1995: 115). The inclusion of moralizing in the grammar school textbook was nothing new; Latin grammars since the classical period had drawn their examples from lists of proverbs and conventional wisdom. What is telling is the emphasis on the ethical nature of good *economic* behavior.

Translation English

Much as English filled a vacuum identified by the Royal Society in the late seventeenth century by offering a medium for the plain style appropriate to their empirical bent, so would "correct English" now supplant "correct Latin" as a sign of prestige in the new economy. We can see this supplantation most clearly in the methods for teaching both languages. Since the seventeenth century in America, college education had increasingly admitted English into the schoolroom alongside or in place of Latin, both as a language of instruction and a subject of study. While this shift was slow and motivated by many things, the change itself is telling. In 1662 John Brinsley in Virginia established a plan for a school and college for the colony. In a list of the purposes for language study, the classical languages were to be learned largely for their own sakes, while English was mentioned only in the context of learning good Latin or Greek style. It was assumed that a student's English would improve by

studying Latin, but this was hardly the purpose of such study (Halloran 1990: 151–3). By 1923, the relative value of Latin and English had been fully reversed, with the teachers of Latin forced to validate their subject matter by demonstrating that Latin instruction improves students' production and comprehension of English. In its report on the state of teaching Latin in the 1920s, the American Classical League defined fully six of its eight "Aims and objectives in the teaching of secondary Latin" in terms of improving students' English, not their Latin – for example: "3. Increased ability to understand the exact meaning of English words derived directly or indirectly from Latin, and increased accuracy in their use"; "5. Increased ability to speak and write correct and effective English through training in adequate translation"; "7. Increased knowledge of the principles of English grammar, and a consequently increased ability to speak and write English grammatically correct" (American Classical League 1924–5: 45). While a contemporary study showed no actual effect of learning Latin on students' English (Miller & Briggs, 1923), improvement in the vernacular remains a favorite justification for continued teaching of Latin and other foreign languages.

An opposed argument decrying Latin's deleterious effects on English could also be heard in the late nineteenth century: the complaint against so-called "translation English." In 1874 Harvard began requiring of all applicants an examination in English. By this time the colleges and universities had accepted that English, not Latin, was the language every college graduate would be expected to master, but were finding that the incoming students needed more instruction in English grammar and rhetoric than the colleges were willing to give over time to teach. While the application exam was designed to sort the incoming class, the poor results also shamed the lower schools for their graduates' poor writing style and lack of familiarity with the classics of English literature. In 1888, fourteen years into Harvard's experiment with the English examination, Le Baron Russell Briggs wrote an analysis of the program that was less than glowing; the students' writing simply does not meet his standards. Some of his complaints from over a century ago are still heard today: "The apostrophe is nearly as often a sign of the plural as of the possessive; the semicolon, if used at all, is a spasmodic ornament rather than a help to understanding; and – worst of all – the comma does duty for the period, so that even interesting writers run sentence into sentence without the formality of full stop or of capital" (Briggs 1995: 64–5). Less familiar is his complaint that the students' style has been adversely affected by the translation exercises commonly assigned in language classes: "many [school masters] suffer their pupils to turn Greek and Latin into that lazy, mongrel dialect, 'Translation English'" (p. 62). He offers as an example the sentence "One of the strangers having been informed of the youth's mission, set out to find the sought for uncle of the youth." The tortured syntax, produced not as a translation but as a native English sentence in a student composition, is the result of years of rendering Latin into English without fully understanding the content of the Latin, leading to overly literal rendering of Latin syntactic constructions, particularly the ablative absolute. This construction is made up of a noun and a verb in its participle form, both in the ablative case: *Caesar, acceptis litteris, nuntium mittit* ("Caesar, the letter having been received, sends

a messenger"; Allen & Greenough 1983: §419). A more idiomatic English sentence might read, "After receiving the letter, Caesar sends a messenger." Likewise, Briggs would have preferred the student write something like "After learning of the youth's mission, one of the strangers set out to find the uncle whom the youth had been seeking." Latinate style was not always disparaged, however; Milton had imitated the ablative absolute and other Latinism in his writing, as in the clause "us dispossessed" in the following lines from *Paradise Lost* (see Hale 1997):

> This inaccessible high strength, the seat
> Of deity supreme, us dispossessed,
> He trusted to have seized.
> (VII 141–3)

Briggs' invection against "Translation English" reveals that by the end of the nineteenth century, good style in English was no longer contingent on the rules of Latin.

Conclusion

The story of English replacing Latin as the language of instruction in American schools and colleges is the story of a language being in the right place at the right time. If Latin rhetoric represented the medieval scholastic mindset, English style represents the new world order: relentlessly practical, plainspoken, rule-governed but flexible, and most importantly, accessible to all: solid, like a piece of mission-style furniture. The plain style is best represented in the United States by William Strunk and E. B. White's slim English guide *The Elements of Style*. Strunk's original of this classic work was a mimeographed style sheet he gave to his mystified students at Cornell in 1918. Expanded and published as *The Elements of Style* in 1959 by his former student E. B. White, the writing guide has never been out of print. Its promise is to deliver good writing to the masses: follow a few simple rules, apply some common sense, dedicate a bit of time to thinking about your writing, and you will write well. Strunk and White represent the *telos* of both the Royal Society's call for plain language and Hugh Blair's belletristic project, putting a particularly pragmatic American spin on the notion of good taste in writing.

REFERENCES AND FURTHER READING

Adamson, S. (1999). Literary language. In R. Lass (ed.), *The Cambridge History of the English Language, Vol. 3: 1476–1776* (pp. 539–653). Cambridge: Cambridge University Press.

Allen, J. H. & Greenough, J. B. (1983). *Allen and Greenough's New Latin Grammar for Schools and Colleges: Founded on Comparative Grammar*. New Rochelle, NY: Caratzas Brothers.

American Classical League (1924–5). *The Classical Investigation: Conducted by the Advisory Committee of the American Classical League.* Part one (of three). Princeton, NJ: Princeton University Press.

Berlin, J. (1984). *Writing Instruction in Nineteenth-Century American Colleges.* Carbondale: Southern Illinois University Press.

Blair, H. (2005 [1783]). *Lectures on Rhetoric and Belles Lettres.* Landmarks in Rhetoric and Public Address. Ed. L. Ferreira-Buckley & S. M. Halloran. Carbondale: Southern Illinois University Press.

Bledstein, B. J. (1976). *The Culture of Professionalism: The Middle Class and the Development of Higher Education in America.* New York: W. W. Norton.

Briggs, L. B. R. (1995 [1888]). The Harvard admission examination in English. In J. C. Brereton (ed.), *The Origins of Composition Studies in the American College, 1875–1925: A Documentary History* (pp. 57–73). Pittsburgh: University of Pittsburgh Press.

Burton, G. O. (1996/2004). *Silva Rhetoricae: The Forest of Rhetoric.* Brigham Young University. www.rhetoric.byu.edu.

Hale, J. (1997). *Milton's Languages.* Cambridge: Cambridge University Press.

Halloran, S. M. (1990). From rhetoric to composition: the teaching of writing in America to 1900. In J. J. Murphy (ed.), *A Short History of Writing Instruction: From Ancient Greece to Twentieth-Century America* (pp. 151–82). Davis, CA: Hermagoras Press.

Herbst, J. (1996). *The Once and Future School: Three Hundred and Fifty Years of American Secondary Education.* New York: Routledge.

Kennedy, G. (1980). *Classical Rhetoric and its Christian and Secular Tradition from Ancient to Modern Times.* Chapel Hill: University of North Carolina Press.

Leonard, S. A. (1929). *The Doctrine of Correctness in English Usage: 1700–1800.* Madison: University of Wisconsin Press; rpt. 1962, New York: Russell & Russell.

Michael, I. (1987). *The Teaching of English: From the Sixteenth Century to 1870.* Cambridge: Cambridge University Press.

Miller, S. R. & Briggs, T. H. (1923). The effect of Latin translation on English. *School Review*, 31, 756–62.

Murphy, J. J. (1974). *Rhetoric in the Middle Ages: A History of Rhetorical Theory from St Augustine to the Renaissance.* Berkeley: University of California Press.

Murphy, J. J. (ed.) (2001). *A Short History of Writing Instruction: From Ancient Greece to Twentieth-Century America.* 2nd edn. Davis, CA: Hermagoras Press.

Reese, W. J. (1995). *The Origins of the American High School.* New Haven, CT: Yale University Press.

33
English in Mass Communications: News Discourse and the Language of Journalism

Philippa K. Smith and Allan Bell

Before the invention of the printing press and before literacy existed on a grand scale, attempts to communicate to a mass audience were limited. Town criers, bards, or simply "word of mouth" relied on speech as the only means of communication with face-to-face interactions defining and organizing the "scope of social life" (Lorimer & Scannell 1994: 1). However, technological advances over time enabled a capability to print words, transmit information by telegraph and telephone, broadcast sound through radio and both sound and images through television, movies, satellite and the Internet. All have had a major influence on the way we are informed today.

A human thirst for knowledge about "other" people and about events happening beyond our front door, within communities and societies, and across nations has provided an impetus for mass communication, as have the concepts that "information is powerful" (Hiebert et al. 1991: 217) and that language is power (Fairclough 1989; Fowler 1991; McQuail 1987). From these have grown the phenomena of the "news" industry – the vehicle by which information is gathered, reported on, disseminated, and consumed, with the pursuit of timeliness at the heart of its production (for a historical overview of news media in Britain and the USA, see Allan 1999).

While there are numerous areas about the news to be studied, in this essay we have chosen to examine the influence technology and journalistic practice have on news discourse. That is, we look at how language is used to convey the news.

Technology, Media, and Language

The invention of the telegraph was the first crucial step in the development of modern news practices and forms because of its ability to speed up both the delivery of news and its productivity. Its use became widespread in the mid-nineteenth century and this coupled with other influences, such as the creation of international news agencies,

helped establish modern patterns of news. Along with the development of an industry that realized the profitability of communicating to mass audiences, a particular discourse of news, fed by the language of journalism, evolved. The quest to get the story first, before one's competitors, and the use of a non-chronological format for writing stories were central to the production of news.

Echoing McLuhan's often quoted phrase "the medium is the message" (1964: 7), Hartley says that the news is shaped mostly by the characteristics of the medium, whether radio, newspapers, or television:

> . . . collectively, we make up "reality" as we go along, perceiving it as meaningful to the extent that it can be made to resemble the expectations we bring to it from the ordered language-system of the news. However, it must be said at once that the news, whether heard on radio, read in newspapers or seen on television, gains much of its "shape" from the characteristics of the medium in which it appears. (Hartley 1982: 5)

Equally, however, it is important to note that the English language has also impacted on the media globally as the forms of modern journalism were largely developed in the English language. The rise of daily newspapers in English-speaking countries laid the groundwork for journalistic practice in the way news was gathered, written, edited, produced, and interpreted. The international news agencies, mainly in English, were instrumental in disseminating such practices on a global scale and supplied a large proportion of content for media organizations (Bell 1996).

Analyzing News Discourse

McLuhan attributes the idiosyncrasies of "headlines, journalese and telegraphese" to the telegraph – all phenomena he claims "dismay the literary community with its mannerisms of supercilious equitone that mime typographic uniformity" (1964: 223). However, it is the codes and conventions of news discourse that we have learned to recognize which enable us to become "news-literate" and interpret the "world at large" (Hartley 1982: 5). Acknowledging that "news is a very specific example of 'language-in-use,' of socially structured meaning" (Hartley 1982: 7), it is important to realize that it is shaped by technology, deadlines and times restraints, restrictions on space or air time, journalistic practices, gatekeeping by editors and sub-editors, media ownership, and a myriad of other influences to which the majority of the audience is oblivious. Establishing how realistic the world is as portrayed through journalistic representation has led academics to pay greater attention to its construction. An examination of the language of news can be both revealing and enlightening. As Lule comments:

> The language of news is what matters. Readers – even journalists themselves – often don't have the time to really concentrate on the words of news, to fully understand *what is being said*, to probe all the possible meanings and implications of the language. Yet the news, as Hamlet told Polonius, is "words, words, words." (Lule 2001: 5)

Linguists (particularly applied and sociolinguists) and discourse analysts have been intrigued by the language of news media. They have been aided by the accessibility of language data from the media, but also by a recognition that the media as language-producing institutions are significant, that media use language in linguistically interesting ways, and that media institutions and their discourses play an important role in shaping culture, politics, and social life.

In the burgeoning research field of discourse analysis a number of frameworks have developed to assist investigation into media use of language. Bell (1998), recognizing that the "story" is central to the news, developed a guide that examines event structure, relating this to actors, times, and places contained within an article. Such analysis "shows up inconsistencies, incoherence, gaps and ambiguities within the story, conflicting forces during the story's production by journalist and copy-editor, and implications for readers' comprehension" (Garrett and Bell 1998: 9). Bell's text *The Language of News Media* (1991) draws on the author's experience as a journalist and editor, including analysis of news stories written or edited by himself or journalistic colleagues. Three themes are central in this approach: the processes that produce media language, the notion of the news story, and the role of the media audience. Van Dijk (1985, 1988a, 1988b, 1991) proposes an analytical framework for the structures of news discourse by bringing together production and interpretation of discourse as well as its textual analysis, including examining the conventions and rules that organize content and the complexity of news themes. Van Dijk's (1988a) analysis of newspaper stories in many languages found few significant differences in news discourse structure. Fairclough has emphasized several trends towards change in the discourses of contemporary society, particularly in the media and including a shift to increased informality of language. Fairclough (1995) developed a three-tier model within a methodology known as critical discourse analysis. At the core is an examination of the text in areas such as structure and vocabulary, which then overlaps into discourse practice (text production and consumption), followed by socio-cultural practice involving an examination of the outside influences or powers affecting the text.

News Discourse Across the Twentieth Century: A Case Study

Three polar expeditions that occurred at different times across the twentieth century provide an ideal case study to compare the way their news reached the world and how it was reported by the New Zealand media. (The relevance of confining the study to the media of one country is that New Zealand is the home country to two of the expedition leaders, and has always been the main departure point for expeditions because of its proximity to Antarctica.) This case study is based on research previously conducted by Bell (2002, 2003) that compares the parallel stories of exploration and hardship under Captain Scott (1910–13), Sir Edmund Hillary (1956–8), and Peter Hillary (1998–9) in the way their news reached the world.

These three polar expeditions were all tales of adventure and challenge in the harsh conditions of the southern continent. The British expedition led by Captain Robert Falcon Scott hauled its own sledges 1,000 miles across the world's severest environment in an effort to be the first humans to get there. On reaching their destination on January 18, 1912 there was bitter disappointment among the party to find that the Norwegian Roald Amundsen had reached the Pole just a month before them. The return journey was harrowing in extreme conditions and Scott and his party died well short of their base many months before they were discovered.

In 1957 Sir Edmund Hillary – the first person, with Norgay Tensing, to climb Mount Everest four years previously – led a team of New Zealanders in the Antarctic purely to support a British expedition intent on making the first crossing of Antarctica by land. However, with the British expedition making slower than expected progress from the opposite side of the continent, Hillary decided that instead of turning back as planned, he and his team, driving modified New Zealand farm tractors, would keep going to reach the Pole, which they accomplished on January 3, 1958.

Forty-one years later, Peter Hillary, Sir Edmund's son, led the three-person Iridium Ice Trek to the South Pole, taking 84 days and arriving on January 26, 1999. The expedition pulled sleds nearly 1,500 kilometers from Scott Base with the explicit aim to recreate Scott's man-hauled journey to the Pole, and to complete the trek back. Although they were successful in reaching the Pole, the return trip was abandoned because of hardship and the lateness of the season; the team members flew back instead.

So what influenced *how* and *when* the news of the outcome of each expedition was reported? How had changing technologies over the century, in combination with the basic journalistic desire to be first to deliver the news to a mass audience, altered the discourse of news? A brief analysis of the initial news coverage of each expedition enables these questions to be answered.

Captain Scott: 1912/1913

It took a whole year for news of Scott's expedition reaching the Pole and its eventual fate to be made public. Members of the expedition's relief ship *Terra Nova* telegraphed the news in secret to London when they arrived in a small New Zealand coastal town in February 1913. Local reporters, in true journalistic form, wanted to be "first" to break the news but were rebuffed. Instead the story was circulated from London and published in the world's newspapers, including the *New Zealand Herald*, the country's largest daily, on February 12, 1913.

Like most newspapers in 1913 the *New Zealand Herald* news items were embedded within, rather than appearing on, the front page. News of Scott's demise appears on page seven, while the first six pages carry columns of advertisements ranging from births, deaths, and marriages to jobs wanted or vacant, and shipping news. The actual coverage of the expedition, however, fills some two pages, nearly half of the area allocated for news. It consisted of a number of short pieces with headlines such as HOW

THE NEW ZEALAND HERALD, WEDNESDAY, FEBRUARY 12, 1913.

JAPANESE RIOTS

; LOST IN TOKIO.

[ERS CHARGE MOB.

POLITICAL CRISIS.

)SITION MEMBERS CHEERED.

ɔh.—Press Association.—Copyright
ived February 11, 11.30 p.m.)

TOKIO, February 10.
:ical crisis which arose in
t week developed into seri-
ıg in the vicinity of the
ıtary Buildings to-day.
s were made to wreck and
ɜ bureaucratic newspaper

mes attacked the rioters
es. Six of them were killed
rs severely wounded.
kado, in a rescript, ordered
Minister (Marquis Saionji)
d alleviate the situation in
:ion of securing the aban-
of the motion of censure on
·nment. Two members of
Cabinet are in favour of
e with the rescript. The
ɜ unwilling to compromise.
d subsequently surrounded
Parliament) Buildings, and
he arrival of members of
sition, who were wearing
:s. They hooted the Minis-

ice repeated their charges,
rsons were injured.
·ipt has been issued sus-
he sitting of the Diet for
·s.
crowds assembled in the
nd the police were unable
with the disorder. The
were then summoned.
ırowing occurred, and a re-
the melee followed. The
ain attacked the newspaper
d the staff replied with
shots. One rioter was

DEATH IN ANTARCTIC

FATE OF CAPT. SCOTT AND PARTY

THRILLING OFFICIAL NARRATIVE.

MISFORTUNE FOLLOWS MISFORTUNE.

EVANS DIES FROM ACCIDENT.

OATES SEVERELY FROSTBITTEN.

DIES THAT OTHERS MIGHT PROCEED.

IN A BLIZZARD FOR NINE DAYS.

SHORTAGE OF FUEL AND FOOD.

A DEPOT ONLY ELEVEN MILES AWAY.

THE news from the South Pole, so carefully guarded on the arrival of the Terra Nova at Oamaru yesterday, is the most tragic in the history of Antarctic exploration. Captain Scott reached the Pole, but the

BODIES AND RE(

CAPTAIN OA1

OTHERS REFU

WALKED INTO 1

By Telegr

The chief search par
ber 30 last. It was org
of two divisions. Dr. A
and Dimitri, and Mr. W
Messrs. Nelson (biologis
Officers Crean, Williams
They had seven Indian
months, expecting an ex
One Ton Camp was four
Proceeding along the
Wright's party sighted,
it were found the bodie
tenant Bowers.
From their records t

DEATH OF EVANS

The first death was t
Royal Navy (official num
foot of the Beardmore
concussion of the brain, s
time before.

GALLANT DEATH

Captain L. E. G. Oa
His feet and hands were l
on heroically, his comrad
approaching. He had b
plaint, and he did not
Captain Scott writes,
the night, hoping not to
blowing a blizzard. Oa
be some time.' He went
him since."
Captain Scott adds,
death, but though we tri
of a brave man and an E
On March 16, Oates
could not leave him.

THREE PERISH W

Figure 33.1 Ten-deck headline from the *New Zealand Herald*, 1913; reprinted with permission

FIVE BRAVE EXPLORERS DIED and CAPTAIN SCOTT'S LAST MESSAGE TO THE PUBLIC. The news discourse of the time tended to report such sub-events as a myriad of short stories, unlike newspapers of today which mainly incorporate the information into fewer, longer stories.

The lead story itself has ten decks of headlines (see figure 33.1). Although this is an extreme example because of the scale of the story, five decks were not uncommon in the *New Zealand Herald* at this period. The headlines told the story and in some cases referred to other sidebar stories separate from the story above which they were placed. In terms of the time structure of news stories these ten headlines themselves

form an inverted pyramid of time so that the latest and most newsworthy aspects of the story appear in the first two decks. The headlines proceed by going back to the most distant chronological event in the fifth deck, then working chronologically through the subsequent sequence of events towards the present in the remaining decks.

It is interesting that the paper chose to focus on the tragedy of the expedition rather than the success of reaching the South Pole. In fact the headlines neglect to mention Scott's success of reaching the Pole, which is left to the second sentence in the lead paragraph. The drama is further enhanced in the headlines with the use of words such as *death*, *thrilling*, *misfortune*, *severely*, *blizzard*, and *shortage* contributing to a classic late-imperial story of heroism for Britain and the Empire.

Sir Edmund Hillary: 1958

Sir Edmund Hillary reached the Pole at 8pm, and reported the arrival by radio to Scott Base. He was interviewed by radio at the Pole by a reporter back in McMurdo Sound and the news relayed to Wellington, New Zealand's capital city. It is possible that this very local news story was – like Scott's – first broadcast back to New Zealand from the mother country. The main New Zealand radio stations lacked their own independent news service and still relayed the BBC World Service news from London. Archival recordings of the radio broadcasts do not exist, so we can only assume that the first news of Hillary's arrival at the South Pole was disseminated by radio. Hard copy of newspaper coverage, however, has been retained and indicates that the New Zealand Press Association wired the news around New Zealand newspapers and the world at 10.19pm on Friday, January 3. The *New Zealand Herald* ran it as its lead story the next morning, January 4, 1958, the same day the explorers flew back to Scott Base.

The newspaper's style, to embed the story with other news items inside the paper, is still the same as in 1913, though this time the story appears on page 8. However, only about a third of a page is devoted to the story, suggesting that Antarctica was now deemed less of an unknown and unconquerable continent with the establishment of airfields and a South Pole base. In addition the time lag between the news event and its reporting has shrunk vastly compared with 1913 which, coupled with the fact that this story was devoid of tragedy, makes it less of a dramatic tale.

A three-deck headline runs along with the copy across 3–5 columns (see figure 33.2). The top headline appears staid and formal while the second deck has crisp, tight, modern phrasing. The third headline, while attempting to inject some drama into the story, strikes one as dated and rather wordy with two prepositions. Note the contrast and the alliteration in the use of the word *First* in headline two and *Final* in headline three, which serve to heighten the sense of achievement surrounding the expedition, particularly since the British expedition was still delayed.

The lead paragraph relates the arrival of Sir Edmund Hillary and his party at the South Pole and makes much of the fact that they were the first party to reach the Pole

Sir Edmund and Party Reach Pole

FIRST TEAM OVERLAND SINCE SCOTT

Final March of 70 Miles In One Day

Sir Edmund Hillary and his party of four men and three tractors arrived last night at the South Pole—the first party to reach the Pole by land since Captain Scott made his tragic sledge journey 46 years ago.

A New Zealand Press Association flash, received in Auckland at 10.19 p.m., read: "Hillary Arrived at Pole." It was the end of a cold, hazardous 1200-mile haul along the Ross ice-shelf, up Skelton Glacier and over the treacherous, crevasse-torn polar plateau.

With Sir Edmund are Mr Murray Ellis, of Dunedin, Mr Peter Mulgrew, of Lower Hutt, Mr Jim Bates, of Morrinsville, and Mr Derek Wright, of Wellington. This brings the number of people at the Pole to 22—the New Zealand party plus the 17 Americans stationed there.

Sir Edmund, who is the third Antarctic expedition leader in history to reach the Pole by land, has arrived in plenty of time to celebrate the anniversary of Scott's arrival on January 18, 1912. Amundsen, the first man to reach the Pole, got there on December 14, 1911.

Among the stores on one of the sledges are two New Zealand flags. These will be planted at the Pole to mark the New Zealand effort in Antarctic exploration. Already at the Pole is a cardboard New Zealand flag dropped there when the former Minister of Railways, Mr McAlpine, flew over last October.

Depots Set Up

Sir Edmund left Scott Base with three tractors and a "weasel" on October 15. The vehicles towed seven sledges loaded with supplies and fuel, most of which was used in establishing a string of depots in preparation for the New Zealand party's return with Dr Vivian Fuchs and his British Transantarctic Expedition.

As well as sledges the New Zealand expedition took a special caravan designed by Sir Edmund to provide "comfortable living" in the bitter cold and tearing blizzards of the Polar Plateau. The tractors, 26-horse-power Fergusons, were fitted with little cabins and with crawler-type web tracks over the wheels.

A few days after the tractor party left Scott Base Mr R. Miller and Dr Marsh were flown to the foot of Skelton Glacier with their dog team to dig out a supply base established there last February. They accompanied Sir Edmund up the glacier to Depot 180, where they were joined by another dog team flown in with Mr R. Ayres and Mr R. Carlyon.

Most of the trek was made in never-ending daylight. The party travelled at "night" when temperatures dropped a little and snow surface became harder, and slept during the "day" when the air was warmer. Each march started about 5 p.m. and finished the following morning.

Rivalry Developed

In the first stages of the trek the dog teams lagged behind the vehicles. Friendly rivalry developed between the men with the dogs and those with the tractors. Then, gaining the lead in the first days of December, the dog teams scouted ahead and radioed details of the ice-country. The dog teams reached Depot 700 just 48 hours ahead of the tractor party.

Sir Edmund's original plans were to meet Dr Fuchs 350 miles from the South Pole, at Depot 700. But the British party, which met appalling weather and difficult terrain between Shackleton Base and South Ice, was at the time still 600 miles from the Pole. After days of uncertainty Sir Edmund made his now world-famous statement: "We are heading hell-bent for the South Pole, God willing and crevasses permitting."

The New Zealand tractor party pushed on alone across the bleak, 9000-feet high plateau. The "Weasel" and dog teams were left at Depot 700.

NO REPORT FROM DR FUCHS

Although Dr Fuchs spoke to Sir Edmund by radio yesterday morning, his party's position is not known. The position was not relayed to Scott Base.

An N.Z.P.A.—Reuters message from London says it is believed the British party has overcome the worst part of the journey and there is now a reasonable prospect of speedy progress to the Pole.

ONE DRUM OF FUEL LEFT

Leader Tells Of Journey

Press Assn.   Scott Base

The New Zealand Antarctic party reached the South Pole at 8 o'clock last night after a 24-hour forced march of 70 miles.

In a radio message, Sir Edmund Hillary told Scott Base conditions had been misty and unpleasant during the long run at three miles an hour from the previous camp.

"Steering by the sun from earlier fixes, we came bang on the base," said Sir Edmund. "We are all very tired but well, and very pleased to have arrived.

"The success we have had could not have been possible without the help we have had from everyone from the time the expedition was first planned. My thanks go in particular to every member of the expedition whose support in Antarctica has put us where we are now."

The tractor train arrived at the Pole with one unused drum of fuel.

"This was sufficient for 20 miles, so we were cutting it rather fine due to the very soft snow experienced," said Sir Edmund. "The Ferguson tractors are showing signs of wear and tear, but they have gone magnificently in quite unsuitable conditions."

The tractor train arrived at the Pole with all three tractors, the caboose and two sledges.

The tired but very happy party will to bed at the Pole about two miles from the American base and this morning the tractor train will trundle forward to meet the Americans.

J. G. Bates   M. Ellis   P. D. Mulgrew   D. Wright

Traveller on Raft Within 30 Miles of Goal

Own Corres.   Wanganui

Mr Fred Cookson, of Auckland, who is travelling down the Wanganui by raft, yesterday passed Koroniti, 30 miles from Wanganui. He expects to reach Wanganui on Monday or Tuesday.

Mr Cookson, a gardener, means to settle in the city.

The 98 Boy Scouts travelling down the river are making good progress. They are living on tinned food, eels, goats caught on the banks and pigs given by Maoris.

THREE FAMILIES SOUGHT

Typhoid Fever Check

Radio calls were made yesterday for three Taumarunui families, believed to be in the Auckland district, to report immediately to the Health Department.

Officers of the department explained that this was a routine check following the admission of a case of typhoid fever to hospital.

A doctor said last night that a cream supply was regarded as a possible source of the fever. The people sought by radio were thought

WOMAN KILLED ON CROSSING

The previous group to reach the South Pole by land—Captain Scott and his party at the Pole 46 years ago. Left to right are Dr E. A. Wilson, Captain R. F. Scott, Petty-Officer E. Evans, Captain L. E. G. Oates and Lieutenant H. R. Bowers. This picture was taken on January 18, 1912.

Price Control Over To Business Men

Parliamentary Reporter   Wellington

Price control will be imposed on goods "only where necessary," said the Minister of Industries and Commerce, Mr Holloway, yesterday. The Minister had been asked for his policy on price control for goods manufactured in New Zealand and receiving protection as a result of the Government's new import selection policy.

"Whether there is any extension of price control by the Government depends entirely on the policy of the New Zealand manufacturers and traders," said Mr Holloway. "So long as prices are not unreasonable, and are related to genuine costs, there will be no need for direct action."

A Press Association message from Wellington said that questions on price control and the purchase of cars with funds held privately overseas were discussed by the Prime Minister, Mr Nash, at his press conference yester-

ernment's part to approve such transactions.

The question had not yet been considered by the Government, which might, however, not be happy about incurring future liabilities. Also, it would have to be considered if people should be able to obtain things which other people had to do without.

£30 MILLION CUT NEEDED FOR

ROYAL PLANE MAY BE TOO LARGE

Late Whenuapai Discovery

Staff Reporter   Wellington

It is possible that the British Overseas Airways Corporation DC-7C airliner which is to bring the Queen Mother to New Zealand on February 1 may not be able to land fully loaded at Whenuapai. An urgent exchange of messages is going on between the Civil Aviation Administration and BOAC in London.

A decision from BOAC is expected in Wellington on Monday.

There are two courses open. The aircraft could arrive at Whenuapai without a full load, or it could be diverted to Ohakea or Harewood. The

Figure 33.2   Three-deck headline and associated stories from the *New Zealand Herald*, 1958; reprinted with permission

by land since Captain Scott made his tragic sledge journey 46 years before. However, much of the remaining story is in fact background about Hillary's expedition accompanied by archival photographs of the expedition members, and one historic shot of Scott's team who had perished earlier that century. Detail is given of Hillary's decision to head for the South Pole ahead of the British who were delayed by the Antarctic conditions, which suggests a certain post-imperial independent-mindedness in deciding to head for the Pole himself. A second shorter story on the same page (under the heading ONE DRUM OF FUEL LEFT) is likely to have been the latest incoming news that was quickly added before the printing deadline. But the main difference from 1913 is the reduction in the time between the event and the news. This time the news is in print the next day rather than the next year.

Peter Hillary: 1999

In stark contrast to the other expeditions, Peter Hillary used a satellite phone to give to the media daily progress reports of his 1999 Iridium Ice Trek expedition (named for its sponsor, the ill-fated communications company Iridium). The team also recorded a video diary of the journey as they went. The world heard within minutes of their arrival at the Pole at 5.17pm on January 26, 1999. An hour after arriving at the South Pole at 6.20pm, Peter Hillary was being interviewed live by telephone by the male and female news anchors on Television New Zealand's early evening network news on Channel One:

John Hawkesby (news anchor)
Returning now to the Iridium ice trekkers and news they have finally reached the South Pole.
    It's been one of the toughest treks in history through one of the world's most hostile environments. But after 84 days and nearly fifteen hundred kilometers the Iridium ice trekkers have finally achieved their goal.
Judy Bailey (news anchor)
Along the way Peter Hillary, Eric Phillips, and Jon Muir have conquered bad weather, illness, and frostbite. But within the last hour they've put all that behind them, reaching the world's southernmost point.
    And joining us now live by phone from the South Pole is Peter Hillary: Peter, congratulations to you all. Has it been worth it?
Peter Hillary
Oh look it's – I must say having got here – ah – to the South Pole – everything seems worth it, Judy.
    I'm sitting on my sled at exactly 90 degrees south, it's nearly 30 degrees below zero, but I wouldn't – I wouldn't want to be anywhere else.
    It's just fantastic . . .

The impact of television on news discourse is immediately obvious when compared with the media of the former expeditions. Both anchors use a friendly, informal,

conversational tone as they break the news, taking turns to create drama in the story with words such as *finally*, *toughest treks in history*, and *hostile*, and highlighting the *bad weather*, *illness*, and *frostbite* which the expedition has had to *conquer*. The interview is presented in the manner of a scoop – the two main channels in New Zealand are intensely competitive and the *New Zealand Herald*, because of the timing of the expedition's arrival, was faced with running the story the following day. It delegated 12 short paragraphs on the front page. (Newspapers now featured the news on the front page while classifieds ran at the back.)

However, the discourse on television, rather than focusing on news, has taken on a different tack. It runs along the lines of a live congratulatory welcome with a sense of familiarity emphasized by the use of first names between Hillary and the anchors as if they were old friends. The body language of the female anchor Judy Bailey oozes with enthusiasm as she lets her hands fall to the desk in delighted emphasis, and smiles incessantly. Even her phrase "and joining us now . . ." instills a sense of collective pride on behalf of the New Zealand audience who, watching television in the comfort of their homes, are well aware that Peter Hillary is following in the footsteps of his father as a national hero.

One of the most remote places on earth has an almost domesticated feel as the technology enables people who are there to appear, live and co-present on screen. A sense of distance and inaccessibility is lost, which contrasts remarkably with Scott, who had no way out except to walk. The program goes on later to provide a live link between Hillary and his wife Yvonne at home in New Zealand, their conversation broadcast to thousands of viewers in a voyeuristic manner. Although considered a news item, such coverage of this polar expedition is largely lacking in informational content but high on profuse emotion.

A Question of Time

Examining the news coverage of these three expeditions is revealing about change and continuity in time and place, and their relationship across the twentieth century. In spite of the differences between the era of the press and the era of television, the news coverage of all the expeditions is driven very much by the journalistic desire to "scoop" the news and to produce the copy within the media deadline. The time lapse between the news event and its reporting also shrinks considerably from months to hours to minutes. The source of the news too changes from an official handout to the live interview.

Alongside these changes can be seen shifts in news presentation, discourse, and language. The positioning of news items changed from being buried in the midst of the newspaper to the front page, and the number of headlines reduced, thereby rearranging the structure of the story. A move towards linguistic compression is seen, noticeably in the headlines, where function words are dropped and replaced with

shorter, sharper lexical items. Such compression across the century characterizes the development of news discourse. It continues to be a major force in changing news language and is affected by greater competition for space in the media from other stories and a desire to produce items that attract the eye of the reader and sell the product.

Nationalist and imperial overtones raise their heads in all three expeditions, but a shift in how they are demonstrated is also apparent. The self-assured imperialism of the British Empire dominates at the start of the twentieth century, to be taken over by a hardy New Zealander confident in his ability to reach the Pole regardless of whether the British wanted to get there first, and finally to the celebration of a local hero amidst a media frenzy of national pride.

Conclusion

What is significant when comparing these expeditions is the response of language to the methods of mass communication available at the time. News discourse responds to advancing technology, the speed with which information is received and sent, the sources it can be derived from, and the locations to which it can be disseminated. But it is also the social, political, and historical conditions surrounding the production and consumption of the discourse that Hartley comments "will shape what it says, the way it develops, the status it enjoys, the people who use it, the use to which it is put and so on" (1982: 6).

While we have concentrated on media in the twentieth century, it is worthwhile noting the speed with which news discourse has continued to change. Examples of the impact of new media are already evident with hundreds of television channels now transmitting across national boundaries and the Internet embracing globalization through online news organizations, podcasts, blogs, and countless websites, each with its own particular discourse and agenda. The public too has taken on a new role of not just being the audience, but also becoming reporters of the news. Coverage of events such as the devastating tsunami in Indonesia in 2004, the 9/11 New York terrorist attacks in 2001, the Madrid train bombings in 2004 and the London Underground in 2005, involved contributions (often live) from "on-the-spot" civilians. Using mobile telephones and video cameras, they were able to give eyewitness accounts, take photographs, or send video footage via the Internet direct to news organizations even before local journalists could get there.

Keeping track of the effects that such changes may have on news discourse globally can be overwhelming. In 1998 Bell and Garrett identified that gaps of research into news language existed, and that same sentiment can be expressed today. In order to see how language shapes the news, to understand the real meanings behind the words, and to recognize how this affects our view of the world, ongoing attention needs to be paid to the language of mass communication.

NOTE

The authors wish to recognize the passing of Sir Edmund Hillary on January 11, 2008, at the time when this book was going to press.

REFERENCES AND FURTHER READING

Allan, S. (1999). *News Culture*. Buckingham: Open University Press.

Bell, A. (1991). *The Language of News Media*. Oxford: Blackwell.

Bell, A. (1996). Text, time and technology in news English. In S. Goodman & D. Graddol (eds.), *Redesigning English: New Texts, New Identities (The English Language, Past, Present and Future, Book 4)* (pp. 3–26). Milton Keynes and London: Open University and Routledge.

Bell, A. (1998). The discourse structure of news stories. In A. Bell & P. Garrett (eds.), *Approaches to Media Discourse* (pp. 64–104). Oxford: Blackwell.

Bell, A. (2002). Dateline, deadline: journalism, language and the reshaping of time and place in the millennial world. In J. E. Alatis, H. E. Hamilton & A. H. Tan (eds.), *Georgetown University Round Table on Languages and Linguistics 2000 – Linguistics, Language and the Professions: Education, Journalism, Law, Medicine, and Technology*. Washington, DC: Georgetown University Press.

Bell, A. (2003). Poles apart: globalization and the development of news discourse across the twentieth century. In J. Aitchison & D. M. Lewis (eds.), *New Media Language* (pp. 7–17). London: Routledge.

Bell, A. & Garrett, P. (eds.) (1998). *Approaches to Media Discourse*. Oxford: Blackwell.

Fairclough, N. (1989). *Language and Power*. London: Longman.

Fairclough, N. (1995). *Media Discourse*. London: Edward Arnold.

Fowler, R. (1991). *Language in the News: Discourse and Ideology in the Press*. London: Routledge.

Garrett, P. & Bell, A. (eds.) (1998). Media and discourse: a critical overview. In P. Garrett & A. Bell, *Approaches to Media Discourse* (pp. 1–20). Oxford: Blackwell.

Hartley, J. (1982). *Understanding News*. London: Routledge.

Hiebert, R., Ungurait, D., & Bohn, T. (1991). *Mass Media VI: An Introduction to Modern Communication*. New York: Longman.

Lorimer, R. & Scannell, P. (1994). *Mass Communications: A Comparative Introduction*. Manchester: Manchester University Press.

Lule, J. (2001). *Daily News, Eternal Stories: The Mythological Role of Journalism*. New York: Guilford Press.

McLuhan, M. (1964). *Understanding Media*. London: Routledge & Kegan Paul.

McQuail, D. (1987). *Mass Communication Theory: An Introduction*. London: Sage.

Van Dijk, T. A. (1985). Structures of news in the press. In T. A. van Dijk (ed.), *Discourse and Communication* (pp. 69–93). Berlin: De Gruyter.

Van Dijk, T. A. (1988a). News analysis: case studies of international and national news in the press. Hillsdale, NJ: Lawrence Erlbaum Associates.

Van Dijk, T. A. (1988b). *News as Discourse*. Hillsdale, NJ: Lawrence Erlbaum Associates.

Van Dijk, T. A. (1991). *Racism and the Press*. London: Routledge.

Part VI

English in History: English Outside England and the United States

Section 1
British Isles and Ireland

Introduction

This section considers the early colonial role of the English language within the British Isles and Ireland. The three essays in this section tell the political, cultural, and linguistic stories of English in Wales (Marion Löffler), Scotland (J. Derrick McClure), and Ireland (T. P. Dolan), respectively, following its legacy from the Middle Ages until the present as a both creative and destructive force among the Celtic languages. Compared with the global exportation of English to the Americas, Africa, South Asia, and the South Pacific (discussed in the following sections), the early movement of English within the British Isles and Ireland might seem minimal. But the compressed geography created a pressure cooker, intensifying the effects of language contact within and among these islands.

Though these essays are divided along geographic and national lines, the Celtic and English variants spoken throughout the region remain cross-connected. For instance, the Scots spoken in Scotland is closely related to the Ulster-Scots of Northern Ireland, just as many of the shared idioms and phonological features between Scottish English and Hiberno-English can be traced to the influence of the Gaelic languages they largely (but by no means completely) supplanted. These essays therefore provide histories that are similar in their overall shape but unique in their specific details.

We find, for example, in Wales and Ireland the shared irony that invasions sponsored by Norman French-speaking rulers (the Norman invasion of England in 1066 for Wales, and the Cambro-Norman invasion of Ireland in 1171) should result in English, not French, becoming the dominant language. In both cases, the language of the invading ruling élite was French, but English was the effective language of communication between the English speakers who settled the land and the Celtic speakers who were displaced. Similarly, we find throughout the islands recurring attempts to exact control by outlawing Celtic languages and through compulsory education in English.

Despite such efforts to Anglicize the people, the Gaelic languages affected significantly the English spoken in the respective areas, albeit to differing degrees. Dolan demonstrates that the phonology, vocabulary, and syntax of Irish so conditioned the English in Ireland that Hiberno-English is best understood as a "fusion" of Old Irish and Old English. In contrast, Löffler finds no real benefit to defining a "Welsh English," even though many (but certainly not all) distinguishing features of the English spoken in Wales can be traced to Welsh influence. McClure marks a middle road, referring to a "Scottish variety of international English."

Spoken English and written English do not always share the same distinguishing features. Dolan points out that while all Irish speakers of English speak Hiberno-English both privately and professionally, they will generally *write* the standard British English learned in school. In the same way, the distinctive pronunciation of Scottish English is not reproduced in writing. The exceptions historically have been

class-based satires that ridicule non-standard dialects. More recently, however, local English pronunciation and speech patterns have been celebrated in print, part of a post-colonial nationalism that is accepting not of colonial English, but local English. This is a pattern of adaptation and adoption that we will see repeated throughout the following sections on English outside England and the United States.

Michael Matto

34
English in Wales

Marion Löffler

The territory of Wales was first determined from the outside, in 778, when King Offa ordered a dyke to be erected to protect his kingdom, Mercia, against intrusion from the Brythonic Celts who inhabited the lands bounded by the Irish Sea in the west and the estuaries of the rivers Dee in the north and east and Wye and Severn in the south and east. They were already calling themselves *Cymry* (compatriots) and their country *Cymru*, although the Germanic population east of Offa's Dyke called them *Wealas*, a term denoting Romanized strangers. From this developed the modern English appellations "Welsh" for the people and their language, and "Wales" for the country. Despite Wales's early incorporation into the emerging English state with the Acts of Union (1536/1543), it was not until the twentieth century, and through a process fraught with conflict and resentment, that English became the majority language in Wales. An Anglo-Welsh literature developed only from the 1920s and the existence of a present-day "Welsh English" remains questionable. Although Wales is a bilingual country in which, according to the 2001 Census, English was claimed to be spoken by nearly all of its 2.8 million inhabitants but Welsh by only about 20.5 percent, the Welsh language remains a stronger marker of national identity than its "Welsh Englishes." The present status quo is grounded in the history of Wales.

English in Wales before 1891

The English language came to Wales, alongside Norman French, in the wake of the Conquest of 1066. Only a year later Anglo-Norman barons began to expand beyond Offa's Dyke to build mighty strongholds around which English craftsmen and traders were settled, notably in the east and the south of Wales. The burghers in these "English boroughs" were granted generous privileges while the indigenous population was often forcibly moved to different locations. Moreover, Welshmen were forbidden to acquire land in the English boroughs, to carry weapons there, and to marry into

borough families. Baronies were often divided into an "Englishry" and a "Welshry" in which different laws and customs prevailed (Jenkins et al. 1997: 54). When, in 1282, north Wales was conquered by the English crown following the death of Llywelyn the Great, the last indigenous Prince of Wales, Edward I and his successors emulated the baronial policy of castle-building, settlement, and separation of the populations. Following the quashing of the last national rebellion, led by Owain Glyn Dŵr from 1400 to ca. 1415, additional penal laws against the Welsh were passed.

English thus became the language of town life and commerce (while French remained the language of law and court), but the populations rarely mixed and therefore English did not make significant territorial gains. The Welsh gentry continued to patronize native poets and storytellers who upheld the medieval Welsh standard language. Following the Wars of the Roses in the fifteenth century, many nobles followed Henry Tudor, the Welshman who was to become England's King Henry VII, to the court in London, where they soon became Anglicized, thus establishing English as the language of the Welsh upper classes. Through the so-called "language clause" of the first Act of Union in 1536, English was made the language of the legal domain (Jenkins et al. 1997: 62–5). On the other hand, the presence of Welshmen at court meant that a strong lobby existed when Elizabeth I made Protestantism the state religion, which entailed promoting vernacular versions of the scriptures. The translation of the Bible into Welsh in 1588 fixed its standard and prevented it from disintegrating into a collection of dialects, as was the fate of medieval Irish and Scottish Gaelic. The smaller editions of the Welsh Bible available from the 1630s facilitated the official and private use of the language in the religious domain and thus lent it some prestige.

It has been estimated that, by the end of the eighteenth century, over 70 percent of the inhabitants of Wales were still Welsh-speaking and had no knowledge of the English language (Jenkins et al. 1997: 48). The Welsh language was dominant in the religious sphere. English, spoken by the upper classes, dominated the official domain, commerce, and the small sector of private secular education (Jenkins et al. 1997: 73–6). Geographically, English had been established in south Pembrokeshire since a colony of Englishmen and Flemings had been settled there by Henry I, and it had slowly been advancing from Offa's Dyke into the eastern counties of Breconshire, Radnorshire, and Denbighshire (Jenkins et al. 1997: 56–8). At this crucial point, the onset of the industrialization of northeast and south Wales encouraged the surplus rural population to migrate to these new urban areas, thus avoiding the need for overseas emigration which so strongly affected Ireland and Scotland. This internal population movement resulted in the emergence of numerically strong and literate urban communities of Welsh-speakers who worshipped in their own language in Methodist, Presbyterian, Baptist, Quaker, and Unitarian chapels. These communities were thus separated by language and by religion from the English-speaking upper classes, who tended to belong to the Anglican Church (Thomas 2000). But the onset of compulsory schooling following the Primary Education Act of 1870, the dominance of the English language in the legal, educational, and commercial domains, and the

high rate of immigration from England during the last two decades of the nineteenth century, were already preparing the way for the major language shift of the twentieth century.

English in Wales 1891–2001

In 1891, when the Census on the Population of Great Britain first included a question regarding language use in Wales, less than half of the Welsh population claimed to be able to speak English. A hundred years later, less than 20 percent of the population claimed to use Welsh in their daily lives, while the overwhelming majority was English-speaking (Aitchison & Carter 2000). By the last decades of the nineteenth century, the indigenous population had no longer been able to satisfy the increasing demand for labor in the Welsh coal mines and steel works. Between 1890 and 1910, south Wales in particular experienced very high rates of in-migration from neighboring English areas. Within two generations this influx, coupled with the high prestige of English as the language of education, law, and state, facilitated the linguistic anglicization of a large part of the population in the industrial areas.

The rural west and north of Wales, although subject to continued depopulation, was slower to yield to language change. By the 1920s an "inner Wales" or *Y Fro Gymraeg* (Welsh-speaking heartland) and an anglicized "outer Wales" had emerged. Following World War II, the English language, aided by radio, television, and the onset of mass tourism, had also begun to encroach on *Y Fro Gymraeg*. By 2001, it had been reduced to a number of language islands in the north and west of Wales (Aitchison & Carter 2000: 48, 49, 94, 96). Throughout the twentieth century the advance of the English language was resisted by Welsh language movements (Löffler 2000) which brought about the establishment of Welsh-medium education (1939), the creation of Welsh-language radio stations (1974) and television channels (1982, 1998), and the Welsh Language Act of 1993, which made Welsh an official language in Wales alongside English. Since the last decades of the twentieth century, Welsh language organizations have focused on the preservation of *Y Fro Gymraeg*, including attempts to bilingualize English speakers and to strengthen the rural economy.

By the beginning of the twenty-first century, therefore, English was the majority language in Wales but its image as a colonial language had not been fully overcome. Studies conducted in the 1970s and 1980s suggested that some monolingual English speakers in south Wales as well as bilinguals further west perceived an ability to speak Welsh to be indicative of strong positive personality traits and of Welshness, and some were learning Welsh in an attempt to assert their Welsh identity (Bourhis et al. 1973: 456; Giles et al. 1977: 174; Giles 1990: 263–6). However, these and more recent studies of the English spoken in south Wales also demonstrate that "on many traits such as trustworthiness, friendliness and sociability, the mere possession of a Welsh accent appeared sufficient to secure for its speakers ratings as favourable as

those accorded the Welsh-language speakers" (Giles 1990: 264; Coupland & Ball 1989: 24). In addition to these long-inherited complexities of Welsh-English relations in Wales, the characteristics and use of English by more recent immigrant groups, such as the West Indian population of Cardiff, await further investigation (Giles 1990: 267–8).

The "Welsh Englishes"

Awberry has described the varieties of English spoken in Wales as, firstly, those common in "Welsh Wales," secondly, those used in "Longstanding English Areas," notably southern Pembrokeshire, the Gower, and the border country, and, thirdly, those spoken in the "Conurbations," notably the Barry-Cardiff-Newport area (Awberry 1997: 86–8). The first variety is mainly used by bilingual speakers and may show direct interlingual interference from the Welsh language. Its most obvious feature is its "sing-song" speech pattern, which differs markedly from the "stepping pattern" found in standard English (Connolly 1990: 126). Other features include the dropping of "w" in word-initial position, so that, for example, "wood" becomes "ood," and the retaining of some full vowels in unstressed syllables where standard English reduces those vowels to "schwa." A common grammatical feature is the generalized use of the tag "isn't it" independent of the tempus and person of the preceding clause. An example might be, "They are singing beautifully, isn't it." Its lexicon includes Welsh words of endearment, such as "cariad" (love) and "bach" (little), and cultural institutions such as the national *eisteddfod*, an annual cultural festival.

Awberry's second and third categories comprise varieties which are independent of the Welsh language. Although the "Survey of Anglo-Welsh Dialects" conducted by Swansea University has, since 1977, provided geographical and historical overviews (Parry 1977, 1979a; Penhallurick 1991), most descriptions of the English spoken in Wales have concentrated on Awberry's "Longstanding English areas" (Parry 1990; Penhallurick 1994) and the "Conurbations" (Coupland 1988; Parry 1978, 1979b). These studies have shown that the English spoken in southern Pembrokeshire, the Gower, and along the English border shows few signs of Welsh-language influence but maintains close linguistic links with neighboring areas of England and their dialects (Awberry 1997: 94–5; Jenkins et al. 1997: 55), with which they share the rhoticity of their accents and certain lexical items. The variety of English spoken in Cardiff shares this lack of distinctively Welsh features, since the Vale of Glamorgan has been anglicized for hundreds of years (Collins & Mees 1990; Coupland 1988).

The varieties used in the adjacent valleys of post-industrial south Wales, however, have retained more distinctively Welsh features. In many cases, their speakers' grandparents or even parents were still Welsh-speaking, and a growing number of Welsh speakers have moved to live in these areas while working in the capital city, Cardiff. Such varieties, like the English spoken in Port Talbot, east of Swansea, thus share

features with some of the varieties used in areas where the Welsh language is still an everyday presence. For instance, clear "l" is employed in all positions, words such as "near" and "cure" are disyllabic, since the diphthongs have been dissolved into two successive monophthongs, and the pronunciation of "blue" differs from "blew," the latter featuring the diphthong "iu" (Connolly 1990: 122–5). Grammatical features include the use of auxiliary verbs in unmarked declarative sentences, such as "We did see the film," and the fronting of verb forms, as in "coming home he was." Welsh lexical items such as "cam" (step) and "crachach" (posh people) are used, and other items such as "venter" (bet), also have their roots in Welsh, in this case in the verb "mentro" (to venture) (Connolly 1990: 127–8).

The postulation of a Standard Welsh English on the basis of these distinctively Welsh varieties of English is questionable, however, since each expresses quite local values and exhibits different linguistic features. Coupland (1990: 243–52) has suggested that these different varieties of Welsh English have been used to signify ideologically different political stances. Thus, although the "Welsh Englishes" are an acknowledged feature of the sociolinguistic situation in Wales, their social role is neither clear-cut nor simple.

"Welsh English" in English and Anglo-Welsh Literature

Outside Wales, some features of the English employed by Welsh speakers, which are still found in some of the varieties described above, have been used since the sixteenth century to characterize the Welsh in English literature. The inability of Welsh speakers to conform to English rules of grammar and pronunciation was expressed in a Welsh "stage English" whose main features were taken to be the omission of word-initial "w," the substitution of "s" for "sh" in words like "wish," the pronunciation of words like "cheese" as "sheese," and the replacement of voiced by voiceless consonants. The famous Fluellen in Shakespeare's *Henry V*, for instance, praised "Alexander the Pig"(Hughes 1924: 33–4) and the lampoon character "Unnafred Shones, wife to Shon-ap-Morgan" referred to God as "Cod" (Lord 1995: 51). Although it has been argued that these were convenient stereotypes, there is no denying that Shakespeare's Stratford-upon-Avon, like many other English towns and cities, was home to a sizeable Welsh population which provided ample material for observers, authors, and satirists (Hughes 1924: 27; Harries 1991: 154; Jenkins et al. 1997: 95).

The practice of characterizing and satirizing lower-class Welshmen through their distinct use of English remained common until the nineteenth century. In 1915 the pioneer Anglo-Welsh writer Caradog Evans, whose first short story collection *My People* caused a scandal (Evans 1987: 37–42), attempted to coin for his characters a biblical English whose lexicon and word order were heavily influenced by Welsh:

> Don't say then! Pity that is. Am I not taking the old Schoolin's pig to Castellbryn on Friday too? Went you to all the old nests, woman fach? (Evans 1987: 66).

But it was only during the second half of the twentieth century that Welsh authors writing in English were accepted into the national fold. As late as 1939 the famous Welsh playwright Saunders Lewis had publicly doubted whether an Anglo-Welsh literature existed (Harris 2000: 451–2), and the first studies of such writers were not published until the 1970s. Dylan Thomas, perhaps internationally the most famous Anglo-Welsh author, employed subtle echoes of the Welsh language and its poetic conventions in his work. *Under Milkwood* features alliterative patterns in its descriptive passages about "streets rocked to sleep by the sea" (Thomas 1995: 17) and English language structures heard to this day in Welsh-speaking seaside towns and villages, such as New Quay in Ceredigion, in which Thomas spent some time:

> Remember last night? In you reeled, my boy, as drunk as a deacon with a big wet bucket and a fishfrail full of stout and you looked at me and you said, "God has come home!," you said, and then over the bucket you went, sprawling and bawling, and the floor was all flagons and eels. (Thomas 1995: 26).

More recently, Anglo-Welsh playwrights from the urban south, notably Ed Thomas and Ian Rowlands, have employed stylized forms of the varieties of English spoken in south Wales in order to reinforce their plays' (south) Welsh identity. The acclaimed film *House of America* (1997), which was based on the play by Ed Thomas and set in Banwen in the Neath valley, made use of the English spoken there in characterizing south Wales and its working-class culture. But Anglo-Welsh playwrights have not flinched from tracing the fault lines of a complex bilingual situation in which, for example, a son learning the language of his deceased father may be misunderstood by the Anglo-Welsh community in which he lives and despised by other family members:

> "I've said it all along, and I'll say it again, that Welsh school is just an Academy of Fascists." He relished the word "fascist" as only a bigot can. "I'd rather hack my leg off than learn Welsh mun. No bugger speaks Welsh in the Valleys, face it." I wanted to say "Don't be so stupid," but I didn't have a leg to stand on. I shed my language each night like a linguistic snake, most of my friends did. (Rowlands 2001: 92)

The heavy industries of the valleys of south Wales, which facilitated the emergence of tightly knit communities and the rise of distinct dialects of Welsh in the nineteenth century and of English in the twentieth century, have long gone. Increased population mobility within both Britain and the European Union, as well as the influence of the modern mass media, are accelerating the rate at which languages and linguistic geographies change. In Wales the continued out-migration of young people in search of work, coupled with the influx of significant numbers of English speakers from England and from new EU members states, is set both to further the advance of English into hitherto Welsh-language areas, and to shape the varieties of English spoken there in the near future.

References and Further Reading

Aitchison, J. & Carter, H. (2000). The Welsh Language 1921–1991: A Geolinguistic Perspective. In G. H. Jenkins & M. A. Williams (eds.), *"Let's Do Our Best for the Ancient Tongue": The Welsh Language in the Twentieth Century* (pp. 29–107). Cardiff: University of Wales Press.

Awberry, G. (1997). The English language in Wales. In H. C. Tristram (ed.), *The Celtic Englishes* (pp. 86–100). Heidelberg: Universitätsverlag C. Winter.

Bourhis, R. Y. & Giles, H. (1976). The language of cooperation in Wales: a field study. *Language Sciences*, 42, 13–16.

Bourhis, R. Y., Giles, H., & Tajfel, H. (1973). Language as a determinant of Welsh identity. *European Journal of Social Psychology*, 3, 447–60.

Collins, B. & Mees, I. (1990). The phonetics of Cardiff English. In N. Coupland (ed.), *English in Wales: Diversity, Conflict and Change* (pp. 87–103). Clevedon: Multilingual Matters.

Connolly, J. H. (1990). Port Talbot English. In N. Coupland (ed.), *English in Wales: Diversity, Conflict and Change* (pp. 121–9). Clevedon: Multilingual Matters.

Coupland, N. (1988). *Dialect in Use: Sociolinguistic Variation in Cardiff English*. Cardiff: University of Wales Press.

Coupland, N. (1990). "Standard Welsh English": a variable semiotic. In N. Coupland (ed.), *English in Wales: Diversity, Conflict and Change* (pp. 232–57). Clevedon: Multilingual Matters.

Coupland, N. & Ball, M. J. (1989). Welsh and English in contemporary Wales: sociolinguistic issues. In G. Day & G. Rees (eds.), *Contemporary Wales: An Annual Review of Economic and Social Research, Volume Three* (pp. 7–40). Cardiff: University of Wales Press.

Evans, C. (1987). *My People: Edited by John Harris*. Bridgend: Seren.

Giles, H. (1990). Social meanings of Welsh English. In N. Coupland (ed.), *English in Wales: Diversity, Conflict and Change* (pp. 258–82). Clevedon: Multilingual Matters.

Giles, H., Taylor, D. M., & Bourhis, R. Y. (1977). Dimensions of Welsh identity. *European Journal of Social Psychology*, 7(2), 165–74.

Harries, F. J. (1991). *Shakespeare and the Welsh*. Felinfach: Llanerch.

Harris, J. (2000). The war of the tongues: early Anglo-Welsh responses to Welsh literary culture. In G. H. Jenkins & M. A. Williams (eds.), *"Let's Do Our Best for the Ancient Tongue": The Welsh Language in the Twentieth Century* (pp. 439–61). Cardiff: University of Wales Press.

Hughes, W. J. (1924). *Wales and the Welsh in English Literature*. Wrexham: Hughes and Son.

Jenkins, G. H., Suggett, R., & White, E. M. (1997). The Welsh language in early modern Wales. In G. H. Jenkins (ed.), *The Welsh Language Before the Industrial Revolution* (pp. 45–122). Cardiff: University of Wales Press.

Löffler, M. (2000). The Welsh language movement in the first half of the twentieth century: an exercise in quiet revolutions. In G. H. Jenkins & M. A. Williams (eds.), *"Let's Do Our Best for the Ancient Tongue": The Welsh Language in the Twentieth Century* (pp. 181–216). Cardiff: University of Wales Press.

Lord, P. (1995). *Words with Pictures: Welsh Images and Images of Wales in the Popular Press, 1680–1860*. Aberystwyth: Planet.

Parry, D. (1977). *The Survey of Anglo-Welsh Dialects, Vol. 1: The South-East*. Swansea: University of Wales Swansea.

Parry, D. (1978). *Notes on the Dialect of Gwent*. Swansea: University of Wales Swansea.

Parry, D. (1979a). *The Survey of Anglo-Welsh Dialects, Vol. 2: The South-West*. Swansea: University of Wales Swansea.

Parry, D. (1979b). *Notes on the Glamorgan Dialects*. Swansea: University of Wales Swansea.

Parry, D. (1990). The conservative English dialects of south Pembrokeshire. In N. Coupland (ed.), *English in Wales: Diversity, Conflict and Change* (pp. 151–61). Clevedon: Multilingual Matters; Cardiff: University of Wales Press.

Penhallurick, R. J. (1991). *The Anglo-Welsh Dialects of North Wales*. Frankfurt am Main: Peter Lang.

Penhallurick, R. J. (1994). *Gowerland and Its Language: A History of the English Speech of the Gower Peninsula, South Wales*. Frankfurt am Main: Peter Lang.

Rowlands, I. (2001). Marriage of convenience. In M. Jenkins, E. Thomas, I. Rowlands, F. Vickery, & R. Williams, *One Man, One Voice: Plays* (pp. 83–116). Cardiff: Parthian Books.

Thomas, B. (2000). A cauldron of rebirth: population and the Welsh language. In G. H. Jenkins (ed.), *The Welsh Langauge and Its Social Domains, 1801–1911* (pp. 81–100). Cardiff: University of Wales Press.

Thomas, D. (1995). *Under Milkwood: The Definitive Edition*. London: Everyman.

35
English in Scotland

J. Derrick McClure

Any examination of *English* in Scotland must take account, from the outset, of the fact that the term *English* has two distinct applications. The Insular West Germanic dialect referred to as Old English, or Anglo-Saxon, had extended its range north of the Tweed by the seventh century: that is, it had become established in what is now Scotland. Long before the Kingdom of Scots had taken its present form, and long before a Kingdom of England had come into existence at all, the ancestor of the language universally known as English was spoken within the bounds of present-day Scotland. In the tenth and eleventh centuries the domain of the Kings of Scots expanded to include this Germanic-speaking territory; and continuously since then, the presence of this speech-form has been an integral part of the social, cultural, political, and linguistic history of Scotland – or to shift the emphasis, the history of the language in Scotland is an integral part of the general history of English. That is non-controversial; yet at the time of this writing, a speech-form called *Scots*, which stands as clearly as does international standard English in a direct line of descent from Anglo-Saxon, is officially recognized as a language by the European Bureau of Lesser-used Languages; and both the government of the United Kingdom and the Scottish government are under legal obligation to give it the recognition and support due to an indigenous language (and have provoked strong criticism for their failure to do so with any degree of adequacy; though in February 2008 the Scottish goverment announced plans for a national audit of provisions for Scots in education and the media, with a view to raising the profile and status of the language). This *Scots* is clearly distinct from the international English language as spoken in Scotland: which in itself is individual enough to be universally recognized.

Until the question was answered by an official ruling (and even now, regrettably, for some people) the status of Scots as an independent language or a set of dialects of English was a topic for endless, impassioned, and sometimes woefully ill-informed argument. The facts of language history are perfectly straightforward: as Old English changed and fissiparated, the dialects spoken from the northern to the southern

extremity of its domain became increasingly divergent; and as two kingdoms took shape in the island of Britain the dialects spoken in London and in Edinburgh acquired the status of national languages. The northern form, which enjoyed a distinctive and largely independent development during the period of the Scottish monarchy, survived Scotland's loss of political independence; and to this day has a vigorous existence as both a literary medium and a vehicle for everyday spoken communication. To a detached observer, there might seem to be nothing in any way exceptionable in recognizing the existence of "Scots" as a well-defined and long-established set of dialects within the great range of forms referred to collectively as "English."

Yet two factors exist which inevitably complicate the issue. The first is the presence, already referred to, of a distinctively Scottish form of international English. This has its origin in the social developments of the seventeenth and eighteenth centuries: in summary, as peaceful intercourse between the two kingdoms increased, first the aristocracy and then the ordinary citizens of Scotland found it desirable to become fluent in metropolitan English; and what had at first been the attempts of native Scots-speakers to master a language which, if not entirely "foreign" (since Scots and English had never been mutually unintelligible), was certainly a very different one from their own, rapidly became institutionalized as a distinct form of the language (precisely comparable to the emergence of Indian or Nigerian English as autonomous forms in more recent times). "Scottish English" is the recognized, and indeed the only rational, term for this speech-form; but since Scottish English is not Scots (and indeed came into existence precisely because its speakers wished *not* to use Scots), the term carries the implication that "Scots" is not English at all.

The second factor exists in the more subjective, but equally real, domain of cultural and political attitudes. A dynamic literary efflorescence in twentieth-century Scotland was marked by a vigorous insistence, on the part of its most active and most brilliant contributors, on the status of Scots as a national language, and the need to recover for Scots the place which it had once held among the great literary languages of Europe. The key figure in the movement, soon dubbed the "Scottish Renaissance," was Hugh MacDiarmid (pseud. Christopher Grieve), whose revolutionary influence on the entire Scottish cultural scene has lasted to the present day. The ardent political, as well as cultural, nationalism which inspired the Renaissance made of Scots a strongly promoted symbol of national identity. (It also gave rise to some of the finest poetry written in Scots since the eighteenth century, and to a deliberately planned and notably successful attempt to extend the language in the largely undeveloped field of drama.) The present-day controversy regarding the amount of official recognition and support that should be given to Scots has an unmistakable political dimension: patently, the disgraceful foot-dragging of the government in the first two terms of the Scottish parliament was motivated by fear that support for the Scots language would be seen as encouraging the movement for Scottish political independence.

There is an element of irony in this patriotic association of Scots with "Scottishness," in that during the period of the independent Scots-speaking monarchy, which is also the period of some of the greatest literary achievements in the language, there

was *no* strong and widespread sense that Scottish national identity was in any way bound up with the use of the distinctive Scots tongue. The first major writer to make a patriotic point of the fact that his work was *writtin in the langage of the Scottis natioun*, which he called *Scottis*, was Gavin Douglas, writing in 1513: previously, Scottish poets – even the two who celebrated in epic verse the heroic defenders of Scotland's freedom against English military aggression, John Barbour in *Brus* and Blind Harry in *Wallas* – had been completely untroubled by the practice of referring to the language as *Inglis*. However, factitious though it is, the perception of "Scots" as the language in which Scotland's identity is enshrined, and concomitantly a tendency to repudiate with vigor any suggestion that it should be discussed under the heading of "English," is now well-established in Scotland: at least among writers and scholars.

Among ordinary users of the language, the picture is somewhat different. In some areas, the local form of Scots not only is vigorously alive as the community language but is underpinned by a conscious pride in its status as a marker of regional identity, and often also by local cultural traditions. One example is the Borders: in fact, an excellent example of the common truth that regional distinctiveness is most deliberately maintained in areas close to a linguistic or cultural frontier. Local customs such as the Riding of the Marches, a well-preserved folk memory of the region's stirring and bloodstained history (until the seventeenth century warfare was unending in the Borders: even when the monarchies were officially at peace mutual raiding was the normal way of life, and when not fighting the English the Scottish Border families indulged in feuds with each other), eagerly supported sporting events, and a flourishing culture of local literature and folk song combine to keep the dialects in rude health. Another is the Northeast, where a highly distinctive farming culture, which survived until within living memory, came to be commemorated in a local dialect literature of exceptional scope and quality, and where the dialect, known as "the Doric," is the mainspring of "Doric nichts" in pubs and an annual Doric Festival in which performances of dialect poetry both traditional and freshly composed, local folk songs and ballads and monologues by experienced and often outstandingly gifted dialect raconteurs are received with enthusiastic appreciation. In such instances, however, it is notable that Scots is seen as part of a *regional* rather than a *national* identity: its speakers, if questioned, would be seen to regard the fact that they *are* Scottish as a complete matter of course, needing no discussion; but the identity which they proudly proclaim by their use of their native speech is that of *their own part* of Scotland rather than that of the country as a whole: indeed, the affectation of being unable to understand the dialect of speakers in the next town or village is notably common. In the Northern Isles, which did not become part of the Scottish kingdom till 1472, this attitude assumes a paradoxically contrasting form: there, the most strongly differentiated of all Scots dialects are cherished as part of a cultural identity which the islanders insist is not Scottish at all: they are, exclusively, Orcadians and Shetlanders; and though their dialects are linguistically Scots, albeit permeated with Scandinavian influence on not only their lexis but their phonology, they forcefully repudiate any suggestion that this, or anything else, makes them Scottish.

The situation is different, too, in urban areas: the social and cultural status of the local speech-forms there, in fact, is one of the most vexed issues concerning the Scots tongue. The traditional dialects of rural Scotland arose as part of regional cultures which developed over centuries, and were intimately associated with the local ways of life (the vocabulary relating to the seasonal round of labor on the big Aberdeenshire arable farms is truly remarkable in its scale and precision): indeed, the decline or demise of the traditional rural culture is in many regions recognized as a threat to the dialect, not only because of the resultant decline in population and exodus of the young but because there is simply no occasion any longer to use the words associated with the old ways of life. In the cities, by contrast, the distinctive urban sociolects are of relatively recent development (that of Glasgow and the Clyde conurbation is by far the longest-established and the most clearly recognized as an autonomous speech-form) and lack the traditional prestige of the rural dialects; but far from being under threat they develop apace, acquiring new words and idiomatic expressions; and in a different and more subversive respect, being associated with a class rather than a region, they are also a strongly maintained mark of group identity. One of the most conspicuous cultural developments in recent years has been the literary exploitation of the urban dialects. Glasgow led the way, writers such as Tom Leonard in poetry and Alan Spence in prose fiction capitalizing not only on the distinctiveness of the urban basilect itself but on the well-established image of Glasgow as a tough working-class city; that Edinburgh, perceived (certainly by its own citizens) as several cuts above Glasgow in respectability, also possesses a dialect-speaking underclass has by now also been dramatically illustrated in local fiction and poetry, notably Irvine Welsh's brutally realistic evocations of the gutter-talk of drug addicts and petty criminals; Aberdeen has traditionally been seen as the heart of the traditional North-east Doric but, with the rapid growth of the city and loss of the ancient symbiotic relationship with its rural hinterland, is unmistakably acquiring an urban patois of its own which awaits its literary celebration. On the other hand, these relatively new speech-forms are often contrasted unfavorably with the traditional rural dialects, which are held to represent "real" Scots in contrast with the "just slovenly speech" of the conurbations. This attitude is still an orthodoxy in educational circles; hardly excused by the certain fact that it is far easier for teachers to act on the old simplistic assumption that urban speech is fit for nothing but eradication than to incorporate into educational practice the recognition by linguistic researchers that the rise of an urban sociolect is a commonplace development with parallels throughout the world.

Using the word *English* in its all-inclusive sense, the picture of "English in Scotland" is remarkably complex and diverse. Several recognizable layers exist. First, the Scottish form of international English occupies the unchallenged place of the prestige language: diglossia with Scottish Standard English as the "high" and one or another of the Scots dialects as the "low" form is so common as to be virtually a norm in non-Gaelic Scotland. Accents associated with England, such as traditional RP or the so-called "Estuary" accent, now very commonly heard in the media, carry no particular prestige in Scotland and are certainly not regarded as models: some linguists have

recently claimed to detect "Estuary" influence in Scottish urban speech, for example in the replacement of [θ] by [f] instead of the traditional [h] (i.e., *think* pronounced "fink" instead of "hink," *nothing* pronounced "nuff'n" instead of "nuh-h'n") or the use of *innit* as an all-purpose question tag; but if the suggestion of influence is correct its effects are very limited and assuredly do not portend a linguistic takeover. Despite its unchallenged status as the prestige *spoken* form in Scotland, however, Scottish Standard English as such has no conspicuous *literary* presence. This is not because of any dearth of literary works by Scots writing in English, for there *is* no such dearth: it is simply because the English used, imagined, and represented by Scottish writers has relatively few features which could be conveyed in written form. Scottish Standard English is instantly recognizable by characteristics of pronunciation (e.g., rhoticity, retention of vowel distinctions before [r], monophthongal [i e o u]) and a large number of distinctive vocabulary items (e.g., *asbet* (large dish), *bonnie* (handsome), *blether* (talk nonsense), *bramble* (blackberry), *cleg* (horsefly), *rone* (roof gutter), *swither* (hesitate)), but the unobtrusive though pervasive features of grammar and phrasing which are equally part of its unique identity (*are you not* rather than *aren't you*, *what age is he* rather than *how old is he*, *everybody hasn't got one* rather than *not everybody has one*, etc.) are in the nature of things unlikely to appear in numbers in written texts. Robert Louis Stevenson's *To S. R. Crockett* opens with the following verse:

> Blows the wind today, and the sun and the rain are flying,
> Blows the wind on the moors today and now,
> Where about the graves of the martyrs the whaups are crying:
> My heart remembers how!

— where the word *whaups* (curlews) is the only *linguistic* clue to the fact that the writer was a Scot. As a modern example, a professional Glasgow crime boss in William McIlvanney's *The Papers of Tony Veitch* says:

> I'm going to find this Tony Veitch. Just for starters. If it's him, he's dead. And anybody that gets in my road'll get hurt sore. I wouldn't like to think Hook was being less than helpful.

— the expression *in my road*, the passive in *get* and the adverbial *sore* being unobtrusive signs that the speaker, though certainly using English, is a Scot. Other examples abound, from the eighteenth century to the present day, of novels and poems with a Scottish setting as an integral feature, but with little or nothing specifically Scottish about the actual language on the page. (The case of drama is of course different: in a valid production, Scottish characters in a play would speak with Scottish accents; and it is noteworthy that in the fields of film and television, in recent years, not only has the presence of audibly Scottish actors become much more widespread but the voices of Scottish characters in dramas can now be expected to be authentic: the

lamentable travesties of "Scotty" and the like now appear, mercifully, to be a thing of the past.)

At the other extreme from Scottish Standard English are the long-established rural dialects, still an integral part of community life in many areas. Their future survival is often seen as precarious and certainly cannot be complacently taken for granted: the fact that they are at last, though belatedly and even now with infuriating slowness, acquiring an increasing degree of recognition and even encouragement in the primary and secondary school system is, so far at least, a dubiously adequate defense against the threats posed by the Anglo-American-centered media, the decline of the rural communities, and the obstinate indifference of the Scottish government – at least until the replacement of the Labour-Liberal Democrat coalition by the Scottish National Party as the governing party in 2007. However, they are assuredly far from lost. The following example, from Shetland, is from an anthology of new dialect writing published in 2003:

A laar o soodaest wind wis makkin a agg aroond da shore. Da sea swilled in among da waarie bleds an filled da treenkies inby Wylkie Geo. Da owld man wis hard pit tae ta keep his feet among da slob o waar at lay brookit up aa da wye alang da beach.

"Can you no scrime yon muckle bit o wid, Daw?" Saandy took a tighter grip apo his staff an glindered doon owre, bit aa he could see wis da wattir mirlin afore his een. Wi a gaff da twa boys nippit doon da beach. Dey clickit da batten oot o da skoom an beguid ta haal him up abön da shoormal.

Features which mark this dialect are phonological, such as *d* for voiced *th* (*da* for *the*, etc.) and the front rounded vowel in *abön* (above); grammatical, such as *him* for "it" (referring to the *batten*, log), and above all lexical: *laar* "gentle breeze," *agg* "slight swell," *treenkies* "channels between rocks," *waar* "seaweed," *brookit* "piled up," *scrime* "see with difficulty," *glindered* "peered," *mirlin* "shimmering," *gaff* "shout of laughter," *shoormaal* "foreshore." The dialects of the archipelago have a wealth of words relating to the sea and shore, and to conditions of wind and tide. From a different dialect and a different register is the following extract from a weekly newspaper column by Robbie Shepherd in the *Aberdeen Press and Journal* (August 20, 2005):

It wis an enterin mornin, the wifie remarkit, as we dreeve oot the country last wikk an seen we were back amon scythes, binders an stooks wi aa the back-brakkin darg attach't till't.

Is a fairmer's dochter, es wis aye the upcome o her faither fin the wither sattle't an they cwid get on wi the hairst. A picter took wir een, tee, in a local hotel wi the men fowk reddin roads wi the scythe, githerin the corn intae bunnles an wippin roon aboot tae form the shaives.

Here too local phonological features are conspicuous: *dreeve* "drove," *seen* "soon," *is* "as," *es* "this," *fin* "when," *wither* "weather." (*Brak* "break," *faither* "father," *fowk* "folk,"

roon "round," etc., are not Northeastern but common Scots: the same is true of *stooks* "stands of bound sheaves," *darg* "labour," and *reddin* "clearing.") *An enterin mornin* is a local expression meaning a good morning for starting a task. The regular publication of passages such as these demonstrates clearly the enduring strength of the local dialects in their communities.

The vocabulary of urban Scots, in contrast to the rural dialects, is characterized by words from a modern slang register rather than traditional Scots lexemes; and its pronunciation by strongly marked accents rather than anciently established phonological changes. The boundary between Scots and Scottish English is much less clearly marked in the case of the urban dialects; a fact which gives at least the hint of an objective basis to the persistent question whether they are entitled to be classified as Scots. This example is from *The Rubai'iyat of Omar Khayyam in Scots* by Rab Wilson, published in 2004:

> Imagine this big amazin Universe that we leeve in;
> Imagine it lik a great big cinema:
> The Sun – the projector; the world – the screen;
> An oor brief lives flittin briefly across it aa.
>
> Every wan o us leaves here empty-haundit;
> Oor only reward, loss an ruin –
> Naethin; that's aa it's goat tae oaffir,
> Aathing in the world – it aa adds up tae naethin.

The only linguistic features which differentiate this, on the page, from English are of pronunciation, whether phonetic (*wan*, *goat*) or phonological (*oor*, *naethin*, *aa*). On the other hand, this evocation of a plebeian voice is as much an integral part of the blunt, hard-hitting tone of the lines as is the deliberate mock-naivety of *this big amazin Universe* or the irony of *aa it's goat tae offir*: a reader who could not imaginatively *hear* the hectoring tones of a Glasgow pub philosopher would lose much of the intended effect.

The enormous variety of Anglo-Saxon-derived speech forms currently alive in Scotland, varying in their social connotations as widely as in their regional shibboleths, has provided fuel for an extraordinarily rich and fascinating range of literary experiments. The hopes of MacDiarmid and his immediate successors (Sydney Goodsir Smith, Tom Scott, Alexander Scott, Alasdair Mackie, and Robert Garioch, to mention only a few of the greatest) that a more or less standardized "Synthetic Scots," maximally differentiated from English and containing the full range of vocabulary from all the literature of the past, would establish itself as a national language for all purposes have not come to fruition (a fact which in no way diminishes the magnitude of their poetic achievements); and at the time of writing some of the most interesting developments are in the use of naturalistic renderings of urban patois for literary purposes: Edwin Morgan's translation of Racine's *Phèdre* into Glasgow demotic must represent a kind of apotheosis for this literary movement. What may be predicted with total confidence is that Scotland will continue to be the site of lively and highly

individual developments, in both literary and conversational usages, of its national form of standard English as well as of Scots.

REFERENCES AND FURTHER READING

Aitken, A. J. (1979). Scottish speech: a historical view. In A. J. Aitken & T. McArthur (eds.), *Languages of Scotland* (pp. 85–119). Edinburgh: Chambers.

Aitken, A. J. (1981). The good old Scots tongue: does Scots have an identity? In E. Haugen, J. D. McClure, & D. S. Thomson (eds.), *Minority Languages Today* (pp. 72–90). Edinburgh: Edinburgh University Press.

Corbett, J. (1997). *Language and Scottish Literature*. Edinburgh: Edinburgh University Press.

Corbett, J., McClure, J. D., & Stuart-Smith, J. (eds.) (2003). *The Edinburgh Companion to Scots*. Edinburgh: Edinburgh University Press.

Devitt, A. J. (1989). *Standardizing Written English: Diffusion in the Case of Scotland 1520–1659*. Cambridge: Cambridge University Press.

Görlach, M. (ed.) (1985). *Focus on Scotland*. Varieties of English Around the World General Series G5. Amsterdam: Benjamins.

Görlach, M. (2002). *A Textual History of Scots*. Heidelberg: C. Winter.

Graham, J. J. (1979). *The Shetland Dictionary*. Stornoway: Thule Press.

Jones, C. (ed.) (1997). *The Edinburgh History of the Scots Language*. Edinburgh: Edinburgh University Press.

Macafee, C. (1983). *Glasgow*. Varieties of English Around the World Text Series T3. Amsterdam: Benjamins.

Macafee, C. (1994). *Traditional Dialect in the Modern World: A Glasgow Case-Study*. Frankfurt-am-Main: Peter Lang.

McClure, J. D. (1994). English in Scotland. In R. Burchfield (ed.), *The Cambridge History of the English Language, Vol. 5: English in Britain and Overseas* (pp. 23–93). Cambridge: Cambridge University Press.

McClure, J. D. (2000). *Doric: The Dialect of North-East Scotland*. Varieties of English Around the World Text Series T8. Amsterdam: Benjamins.

McClure, J. D. (2000). *Language, Poetry and Nationhood: Scots as a Poetic Language from 1878 to the Present*. East Linton: Tuckwell.

Williamson, I. K. (1982, 1983). Lowland Scots in education: a historical survey. *Scottish Language*, 1, 54–77, & 2, 52–87.

36
English in Ireland

Terence Patrick Dolan

Introduction

The English language has been spoken in Ireland since the twelfth century, at first by the English-speaking retinues of the Norman invaders. Up to the nineteenth century the principal language of most of the population was Gaelic (Denvir 2006: 547–50; Crowley 2005: 96–163). The relationship between the two languages is symbolized in the term used to describe the form of English used in Ireland, Hiberno-English, that is, a fusion of two independent, totally different languages, each with a powerful identity and a political symbolism in its own right, from Old Irish and Old English. The term Irish English, based on the analogy of American or Australian English, is not appropriate to the Irish situation because the English language in those countries did not experience a long process of symbiosis between the native tongue and that of the immigrant settlers as has happened in Ireland.

The Irish learnt English, as best they could, through a process of translation from the Irish language, which involved substituting Irish vowels and consonants for the nearest English ones. James Joyce selected the words *home*, *Christ*, *ale*, and *master* (*Portrait of the Artist*) to exemplify phonetic differences between a Dubliner and an English priest, for instance, with the "o" vowel in home, the "st" sound in Christ, the clear "l" in ale, and the rhotic observance of the "r" in master. The substratal influence from Irish still affects the lexicon and grammar of the English language in Ireland. The number of people who use Irish for their everyday communication is relatively small, according to the 2002 Census, and this in spite of generous financial support from the government (*Census of Ireland 2002*: 12, 27, 72). Nowadays there are possibly as many speakers of Polish in Ireland as of Irish, which in recent years has been in decline, even in those areas known as the Gaeltacht (a term originating in Scotland, meaning a district where Gaelic is spoken, used in Ireland since the late 1900s). Article 4 of the Constitution of the Irish Free State specifies the status of the two languages: "The national language of the Irish Free State (Saorstat Eireann) is the Irish

language, but the English language shall be equally recognized as an official language" (Crowley 2005: 166). Public acknowledgment is paid to the native language with the use of bilingual signposts, notices, and titles in Irish (e.g., *Taoiseach*, leader of government), as well as the establishing of Irish-only schools and of a Gaelic television station. All Irish people speak Hiberno-English, not just in the home but professionally and socially, but they write "Standard" English, which they learn at school, unless when representing their vernacular in creative writing.

History

English won the battle for dominance over Irish, but only to a certain extent and from a certain point of view. In 1171 Henry II invaded and incorporated Ireland with the earlier written connivance of the only English pope, Adrian IV (1154–9), formerly Nicholas Breakspear. The invaders brought in two new languages, Norman-French and English, to accompany the native Irish and the universal ecclesiastical Latin. The Norman overlords and their immediate retainers spoke French and the lower orders spoke English. Norman-French was used in England for diplomatic correspondence up to the reign of Henry IV (1399–1413). In Ireland, its use declined earlier, roughly coinciding with King John's loss of Normandy in 1204, but not before it had contributed a number of words to the lexicon of Irish, for example, *dinnéar* from French *diner* [dinner]. It seems not to have contributed to place-names in Ireland, though it has been claimed that Buttevant, a town in County Cork, is from the French "*Boutez en avant*" (Push Forward), the war-cry of the local de Barry family. The early fourteenth-century Irish manuscript, British Library MS Harley 913, contains several items written in French as well as in Latin and English (Lucas 1995; Dolan 1999).

The Irish language was the sole vernacular in most parts of the country, apart from the English Pale (the area in the eastern counties of Kildare, Meath, Louth, and Dublin, centered on the city of Dublin and ruled over by Dublin Castle) and a few large towns; as well as the linguistically distinctive area in southeast Wexford comprising the baronies of Forth and Bargy (Dolan and Ó Muirithe), whose English has been described as Chaucerian because of its medieval English component; and another north of Dublin, in Fingal (Archer), whose characteristic use of English, with its high Irish complement, survived until recent times. So concerned were the authorities in England at the increasing Gaelicization of the English colony that Prince Lionel, Duke of Clarence, son of King Edward III, and incidentally Geoffrey Chaucer's first employer, was sent over to preside over a Parliament in the city of Kilkenny which issued a Statute in 1366, written in French in 36 chapters. This attempted by legislation to deter the ruling élite from adopting and encouraging Irish cultural practices, such as riding horses in the Irish fashion, entertaining minstrels, inter-marrying, and speaking Irish. An infringement would result in the guilty persons having their lands and tenements seized and not released till the offending party had learnt how to use

English again. This legislation was unsuccessful, but not repealed until the Parliament of 1613–15.

From the mid-sixteenth century onwards, the prestige of the Irish language began to decline. This was in no small way due to the plantation-scheme introduced by the Tudors, which destroyed the self-esteem of the Gaelic patrons of native poetry, and by so doing the bardic tradition itself, and also extended English rule outside the Pale. For the first time Irish country people had no longer to consider the rulers as a remote class residing in Dublin and the English Pale, but as people setting up plantation-homes in their own localities. The natives had to learn some basic words of English as quickly as possible, with difficulty, in order to receive instructions from their employers. There was constant contamination from Irish, giving rise to the Stage Irish character, whose eccentric speech, often exaggerated, attracted derision. From this period, the literary use of Hiberno-English, though fictional, establishes it as a distinct spoken variety of English.

The status of English was all the time rising, for practical reasons. The old image of Irish as the language of nationhood, nationalism, and Catholicism was discarded. English was the key to survival and success. Politicians needed English to pursue their careers in Westminster after the passing of the Act for the Legislative Union of Ireland with Great Britain in 1800. Daniel O'Connell, though fluent in Irish, used English in his great rallies. In 1831 a system of primary school education was introduced, with English as the medium of instruction (aided by the threat of beatings for speaking Irish, recorded on personal tally sticks). Priests educated in St. Patrick's College, Maynooth, a seminary founded in 1795, addressed their congregations in English, while, counterproductively, members of other faiths, Anglican, Methodist, Presbyterian, tried to proselytize through Irish. One of the effects of the Great Famine was the death of multitudes of monoglot Irish speakers, a further blow to the native language. More and more people from the island of Ireland were emigrating to far-flung parts and, to an appreciable extent, were influencing the language of their new countries. For example, emigrants from Northern Ireland enriched the lexicon of the Appalachians in the United States (Montgomery 2006), others that of Newfoundland English (Story et al. 1990; also Hickey 2004). The Chicago journalist F. P. Dunne (1867–1936) was the first American author to fully exploit the grammar, lexicon, and pronunciation of Hiberno-English, as authentically represented in his Mr. Dooley.

Northern Hiberno-English reflects the history of the original Province of Ulster. The fact that six of the original nine counties of the Province now form what is known as Northern Ireland, with the remaining three parts of the Republic, confirms its peculiar status on the island of Ireland. Settlers from southwest Scotland and from the northwest Midlands and southwest of England came to live in Ulster on land confiscated from the native Irish-speaking population during the seventeenth century as part of the Plantation of Ulster (Adams 1986; Harris 1984, 1985). There were far more Scottish than English settlers, a ratio of about six to one, and the predominating influence of the larger community of planters has had a defining effect on Northern Hiberno-English (Traynor 1953; Corrigan 1990; McCafferty 2000; Kirk 1997; Mallory 1999).

In recent times the Good Friday Agreement granted and guaranteed "parity of esteem" to the Irish language and also to a distinct variety of Northern Hiberno-English called Ulster Scots, or Ullans (Görlach 2000; Fenton 2000; Robinson 1997). To some this looks like *realpolitik*, since it attempts to address the competing cultural claims of nationalists and loyalists. Ulster-Scots has a symbolical value well beyond the relatively few people who use it as their daily language, and the Irish language has similar prestige among the nationalists, whether or not they speak it. The Irish language has retained its presence in the West of the Province, in coastal Donegal, but, in recent times, it has enjoyed a recurrence of usage in other Ulster counties. Knowledge of Irish is associated with nationalism. Although Ullans is a variety of Scots, its recently acquired political status has contentiously encouraged claims for it to be termed a language in its own right. It has had a literary tradition since the eighteenth century, but much of its distinctive vocabulary and syntax are the same as those of Northern Hiberno-English (Dolan 2002).

Grammar

The main source of the distinctive features of Hiberno-English grammar is the grammar of the Irish language (Filppula 1999), although some scholars argue for an English dialectal substrate (Lass 1990). In Irish the verb heads all sentences. Thus, a British English speaker would say, "The wedding takes place today," whereas a Hiberno-English speaker could say, "Well, it's the day that's in it for the wedding," based on the Irish. There is no verb "have" in Irish, giving rise to the pattern of "I'm just after eating my dinner" (McCafferty 2006). Sentences such as "I have read the book" are rendered "I have the book read" in Hiberno-English, reflecting the separation of verb and past participle in Irish (Kallen 1990). Irish has a habitual form of the verb "be" that enables a speaker to make a distinction between "I am here today" and "I do be here every Monday."

The Irish language also affects Hiberno-English obliquely, as in the absence of "shall" to form the future. Irish has a distinct future-form and so Irish speakers took the "will" form and used it on all occasions ("Will I wet [make] the tea?"). The future with "shall" is rarely heard. In Irish, indirect questions, which are normally introduced in Standard English by "if" or "whether," retain the inversion of the original Direct Question and this carries over into Hiberno-English ("She asked him was he motting [dating]?").

The conjunction "and" (*agus* in Irish) has a greater range of use in Hiberno-English, giving non-standard formations which are acceptable in Irish, such as "She interrupted me and me reading the paper," where the "and" could be equivalent to adverbial conjunctions such as "when," "while," "although," and so forth. To outsiders this sounds like bad grammar.

Other features include the frequent use of preposition-plus-pronoun ("Put your coat on you," based on the Irish idiom); distinctive adverbs ("Is it yourself that's in it"); ubiquitous use of the adverb "there" as a clincher ("I saw him here, there,

yesterday"); singular verb with plural subject ("Those stairs is steep, so they are," owing to the verb *ta* in Irish meaning both "is" and "are," and not changing for the plural); translations from Irish as in "He fell out of his standing" for "He fell over"; absence of "yes" and "no" (hence, "Did you read the book?" is answered by "I did not read it," following Irish usage); clefting as in "It's Brigid saw James"; fronting as in "Three operations I had in the hospital"; omission of the relative pronoun as in "It was John wrote that play"; use of "till" to express purpose as in "Come here till I comb your hair."

In Ulster-Scots the main divergence in grammar is the use of Scottish and Northern English forms such as the determiner "thon" for "yonder," and the distinctive negatives, "nae" added as a suffix ("A didnae think" for "I didn't think") and "no" meaning "not" (Robinson 1997; Fenton 2002). Otherwise, many allegedly Northern features are to be found south of the Border (Dolan 2002). Take, for example, the use of "but" at the end of clauses as in Tom Paulin's poem *Seize the Fire,* "I'm trapped, but" (31). It is also to be found in the Dublin English of Roddy Doyle's characters ("Make it a Guinness, but," "What about the sweet but?" in *The Van*). It is also included in Robinson's (1997) *Ulster-Scots Grammar* ("A'm for toon thenicht, scho's no cumin but," p. 178).

Many authors have used Hiberno-English in their writings, for local color, or to produce humor, or just to belittle the speakers. Rendering Hiberno-English into other languages has caused problems as regards accuracy and authenticity, mainly owing to the fact that translators tend to regard Hiberno-English as slang, rather than as a sophisticated member of the family of Englishes, with its own grammar and lexicon (Dolan 2003).

Vocabulary

The vocabulary of Hiberno-English has two distinctive features. It retains dialectal, often obsolete, English words and incorporates lexical items from the Irish language. The closer an area is to locations in which Irish was spoken up till recently, the more Irish words are used in the English sentence as, for example, in East Kerry or North Mayo. Words still in use, especially among older speakers, include "hames" (make a hames, a mess, something), "cog" (joke), "oxter" (armpit), "fornenst" (facing, in front of), and "disremember." Some words have the Irish diminutive suffix "-een" attached, registering either affection ("girleen"), or contempt ("jackeen," a little John Bull, a Dubliner). The Irish words add an extra dimension to the language, covering meanings not indicated by English words, such as "gombeen," "bohereen," "kithogue" (left-handed, awkward), "meas" (respect, as in "I put no meas on him"), and "sleeveen" (smooth-tongued trickster). Some English words are used as if they were their Irish equivalents. "Bold," for example, always means "mischievous" ("Don't be bold"), because the equivalent Irish word *dana* includes the dual meanings of courageous and ill-behaved. Irish people, unconsciously translating from their native language, "fire"

a stone, meaning "throw" it, and speak of someone being "in it," meaning "alive," or their bedroom being "all through-other," translating from the Irish word for "untidy." "The party was black" in Hiberno-English means that it was a very crowded party, with the word "black" translating the Irish phrase "dubh le daoine" (black with people). The meanings of even very common words slightly differ. For instance, "evening" starts in the middle of the afternoon, and "couple" means a few, never two. Idiomatic features include the use of phrases like "Your man," referring to "that person in your company."

Ulster-Scots includes many words used by Hiberno-English speakers north and south of the Border, such as "thole," "crack," "scallion," "farl," "lug," and so forth. "Oxter" (armpit) is to be found throughout the island of Ireland, and so, too, are "lock," meaning a quantity of something ("a lock of books"), and "messages" (groceries).

Irish has had very little influence on the lexicon of British English. The remarkably short list includes "galore," "shenanigan," "cantankerous," "Tory," "slew" and its cognate "slogan," "gombeen," "esker," and "whiskey," to name the most common. "Crack" is English in origin, so, too, are "smithereens" and "smashing," though claims have been made for purely Irish origins for them, as also for "kibosh," "phoney," and "so long," all mistakenly.

Hiberno-English has a distinctive form of slang, which in the nature of such a variety is constantly being expanded. Many older words are still in use, for example, "strides" (trousers), "hoor" (English "whore," in this form used affectionately of males), "mot" (a girl-friend, which is also found in the verbal form "motting," dating). The old word "yoke," meaning contrivance ("Give me that yoke"), has taken on a new life, in plural form meaning Ecstasy tablets. The obsolete English word "crack," which is nowadays also applied to a drug, still retains its old meaning of noisy entertainment, either spelt "crack" or in its fake Irish form "craic" (given spurious affirmation by an entry under "craic" in the *Foclóir Gaeilge-Béarla* [Irish-English Dictionary], 1978). New usages include "a ride and a rasher" (an intimate night followed by breakfast), as well as many examples of rhyming slang, the form imported from England, but given an Irish touch, such as "in the Margaret," meaning "in the bed," based on rhyming slang for "scratcher," bed, rhyming with Thatcher. The four-letter "f-word" is common in Hiberno-English, together with the euphemistic forms "feck" and "frig," often used as intensives, without deliberately intending to offend. For the first time, *The New Partridge Dictionary of Slang and Unconventional English* (2005) includes Hiberno-English.

Sometimes incorrectly referred to as slang, the language of the Traveling Community known variously as Gammon, Shelta, or Cant (the preferred term of the Travelers themselves; Kirk & Ó Baoill 2002b) is an important sub-variety of English in Ireland. Formed during the seventeenth century by traveling bilingual groups, it uses the word-order and grammar of English, with a lexicon that includes many words from Irish, fewer from English, as well as words deliberately disguised (for instance, "abuse" is re-formed as "rabuse"). The wider community is now absorbing cant words, such as "wide" (aware, in the know).

Pronunciation

English speakers came to Ireland from various parts of the English-speaking world, bringing with them their various dialects, which affected how the Irish learned to speak English from them (Hogan 1927: 62–77; Bliss 1979: 186–252; Hickey 2005: 28–92). The sound systems of the two languages differ, and Irish people pronounced English words according to the sound system of their own dialect of Irish, approximating to the sounds they heard from native speakers of English, hence the distinctive pronunciation of *home*, *Christ*, *ale*, and *master* noted by Joyce in *Portrait*, referred to above. There are four basic divisions of Hiberno-English, roughly following the boundaries of the four provinces, Leinster, Munster, Connaught, and Ulster, as Joyce identifies in *Finnegans Wake*: "derry's own drawl" (Ulster), "corksown blather" (Munster), "doubling [Dublin] stutter" (Leinster), "gullaway [Galway] swank" (Connaught) (Joyce 1988: 197.2–6).

The *Dictionary of Hiberno-English* provides a guide for the pronunciation of each entry, following the system of the International Phonetic Association (IPA). Most of the sounds are based on Irish, such as the Northern word "spalter," to walk in an awkward way, pronounced "shpalter," or "them," pronounced almost like "dem." Irish influence also causes the ubiquitous epenthetic vowel ("elum" for "elm," "filum" for "film"), and the rendering of "idiot" as "eejit" which is much less critical in meaning. Other words retain older English pronunciations, such as "easy" pronounced "aisy" or "queer" as "quare." "Wh" is differentiated from "w," hence "Wales" and "whales" are distinguished. "Produce" and similar forms with "du" are pronounced "projuce." In western parts of Ireland, "column," "minute," and the like are pronounced "minyute" and "colyum." The stress patterns are markedly different from other forms of English. Words tend to be stressed later, giving rise to *committ-ee*, *archi-tecture*, *in-fluence*, and so forth, which carry earlier stress in other forms of English (Bliss 1979: 194–8).

The pronunciation of Northern Hiberno-English is the most complex because of its origins in Irish, Northern English, and Scottish Gaelic (Harris 1984, 1985; Robinson 1997), a mixture which led to a tripartite division of the language of Ulster into Ulster Scots, South Ulster English, and Mid Ulster English, which takes in Belfast.

Sociolinguistic Changes

Interesting changes are taking place in the Irish use of English at present. Dublin English has been influenced by continual immigration from Britain, and from rural parts of Ireland, which has given it a strong character of its own (Hickey 2005). Recently the self-confidence conferred by the Celtic Tiger economy has encouraged some of its citizens, especially young females, to create a new form of Hiberno-English, mainly in its pronunciation, by which they hope to distance themselves from

the traditional "brogue" which characterized Hiberno-English up to recent times: "Oh my God! I, like, totalled my caw on the rindabite." It is a mixture of vogue expressions heard on American soap-operas pronounced with what they mistakenly think is a Home-Counties accent from London. In some respects it reminds one of the absurdly pretentious "London" accent affected by Lady Clonbrony in Maria Edgeworth's *The Absentee* (1812). It is called a Dublin 4 or D4 accent, the most prestigious postal district in the capital, where the national broadcasting station RTE, and the largest university, University College Dublin, some of whose students have invented their own accent, grander still, are situated. I think that it may just be a linguistic rite of passage and that the more outlandish pronunciations will be dropped as speakers mature. Certainly, a slight erosion of localisms is noticeable, owing to the spread of new Dublin Hiberno-English beyond the capital, and also because of the universal influence of American English. Other changes signal cultural change in Ireland. The use of religious expressions is declining, in company with the decline of the power of the Church, and references to rural phenomena. Declining, too, is the frequency of proverbs quoted in Irish in conversation. More substantial changes may be expected from the significant numbers of immigrants coming to Ireland with the expansion of the European Union. My research so far into this phenomenon shows that the immigrants retain their own language but when they speak English their sounds and stress-patterns approximate to those of Hiberno-English. So far, words from their countries of origin have not been identified in the English of Ireland.

Conclusion

The English language in Ireland is distinguished by its retention of archaic and dialectal forms from British English, the substratum of Irish, and a different way of using language, more indirectly, emotionally, and rhetorically. It comprises many strands, supported by communities wishing to preserve individual cultures, but much of the lexicon is common to the island as a whole. As it evolves, totemic linguistic divisions will be subsumed.

REFERENCES AND FURTHER READING

Adams, G. B. (1986). *The English Dialects of Ulster*. Holywood, Co. Down: Ulster Folk and Transport Museum.

Archer, P. (1975). *Fair Fingall*. Dublin: An Taisce Fingall.

Bliss, A. (1979). *Spoken English in Ireland 1600–1740*. Dublin: Cadenus Press.

Census of Ireland [for 2002] (2004). Vol. 11 – Irish Language. Dublin: Stationery Office.

Corrigan, K. P. (1990). Northern Hiberno-English: the state of the art. In T. P. Dolan (ed.), *The English of the Irish: Special Issue, Irish University Review*, vol. 20 (pp. 91–119).

Cronin, M. (1996). *Translating Ireland: Translation, Language and Identity*. Cork: Cork University Press.

Cronin, M. & Ó Cuilleanain, C. (eds.) (2002). *The Languages of Ireland*. Dublin: Four Courts Press.

Crowley, T. (2000). *The Politics of Language in Ireland 1366–1922*. London: Routledge.

Crowley, T. (2005). *Wars on Words: The Politics of Language in Ireland 1537–2004*. Oxford: Oxford University Press.

Dalzell, T. & Victor, T. (2005). *The New Partridge Dictionary of Slang and Unconventional English*. 2 vols. London: Routledge.

Denvir, G. (2006). Literature in Irish, 1800–1890; from the Act of Union to the Gaelic League. In M. Kelleher & P. O'Leary (eds.), *The Cambridge History of Irish Literature*, vol. 1 (pp. 544–98). Cambridge: Cambridge University Press.

Dolan, T. P. (ed.) (1990). *The English of the Irish: Special Issue, Irish University Review*, vol. 20 (pp. 91–119).

Dolan, T. P. (1999). Writing in Ireland. In D. Wallace (ed.), *The Cambridge History of Medieval English Literature*. Cambridge: Cambridge University Press.

Dolan, T. P. (2002). Language policy in the Republic of Ireland. In J. M. Kirk & D. P. Ó. Baoill (eds.), *Language Planning and Education* (pp. 144–56). Belfast: Cló Ollscoil na Banríona.

Dolan, T. P. (2003). Translating Irelands: the English language in the Irish context. In M. Cronin & C. Ó Cuilleanáin (eds.), *The Languages of Ireland* (pp. 78–92). Dublin: Four Courts Press.

Dolan, T. P. (2005). The compilation of a *Dictionary of Hiberno-English*. In H. Gottlieb, J. Mogensen, & A. Zettersten (eds.), *Symposium on Lexicography XI, Proceedings of the Eleventh International Symposium on Lexicography May 2–4, 2002*, University of Copenhagen (pp. 207–15). Tubingen: M. Niemeyer.

Dolan, T. P. (2006). *A Dictionary of Hiberno-English: The Irish Use of English*. Revd., expanded edn. Dublin: Gill & Macmillan.

Dolan, T. P. & Ó Muirithe, D. (eds.) (2006). *The Dialect of Forth and Bargy, County Wexford*. Dublin: Four Courts Press.

Fenton, J. (2002). *The Hamely Tongue, A Personal Record of Ulster-Scots in County Antrim*. Revd., expanded edn. Belfast: Ullans Press.

Filppula, M. (1999). *The Grammar of Irish English, Language in Hibernian Style*. London: Routledge.

Görlach, M. (2000). Ulster-Scots: a language? In J. Kirk & D. Ó Baoill (eds.), *Language and Politics* (pp. 13–31). Belfast: Cló Ollscoil na Banríona.

Harris, J. (1984). English in the north of Ireland. In P. Trudgill (ed.), *Language in the British Isles* (pp. 115–34). Cambridge: Cambridge University Press.

Harris, J. (1985). *Phonological Variation and Change: Studies in Hiberno-English*. Cambridge: Cambridge University Press.

Hickey, R. (1983). Syntactic ambiguity in Hiberno-English. *Studia Anglica Posnaniensia*, 15, 39–45.

Hickey, R. (2002). *A Source Book for Irish English*. Amsterdam: J. Benjamins.

Hickey, R. (ed.) (2004). *Legacies of Colonial English: Studies in Transported Dialects*. Cambridge: Cambridge University Press.

Hickey, R. (2005). *Dublin English, Evolution and Change*. Amsterdam: J. Benjamins.

Hogan, J. J. (1927). *The English Language in Ireland*. Dublin: Educational Company of Ireland.

Joyce, J. (1988). *Finnegans Wake*. London: Faber and Faber.

Joyce, P. W. (1988). *English as We Speak it in Ireland*. Intro. T. P. Dolan. Dublin: Wolfhound.

Kallen, J. (1990). The Hiberno-English perfect: grammaticalisation revisited. In T. P. Dolan (ed.), *The English of the Irish: Special Issue, Irish University Review*, vol. 20 (pp. 120–36).

Kelleher, M. & O'Leary, P. (eds.) (2006). *The Cambridge History of Irish Literature*. 2 vols. Cambridge: Cambridge University Press.

Kiberd, D. (1993). *Synge and the Irish Language*. 2nd edn. London: Macmillan.

Kirk, J. M. (1997). Ulster English: the state of the art. In H. Tristram (ed.), *The Celtic Englishes I* (pp. 135–79). Heidelberg: Universitätsverlag C. Winter.

Kirk, J. M. & Ó Baoill, D. P. (eds.) (2002a). *Language Planning and Education: Linguistic Issues in Northern Ireland, the Republic of Ireland, and Scotland*. Belfast: Cló Ollscoil na Banríona.

Kirk, J. M. & Ó Baoill, D. P. (eds.) (2002b). *Travellers and their Language*. Belfast: Cló Ollscoil na Banríona.

Lass, R. (1990). Early Mainland Residues in Southern Hiberno-English. In T. P. Dolan (ed.), *The English of the Irish: Special Issue, Irish University Review*, vol. 20 (pp. 137–48).

Lucas, A. (ed.) (1995). *Anglo-Irish Poems of the Middle Ages*. Dublin: Columba Press.

Macafee, C. I. (1966). *A Concise Ulster Dictionary*. Oxford: Oxford University Press.

McCafferty, K. (2000). *Ethnicity and Language Change: English in (London)Derry, Northern Ireland*. Amsterdam: J. Benjamins.

McCafferty, K. (2006). *Be after V-ing* on the past grammaticalisation path: how far is it after coming. In H. Tristram, *The Celtic Englishes IV* (pp. 130–51). Potsdam: Universitätsverlag Potsdam.

Mallory, J. P. (ed.) (1999). Language in Ulster. *Ulster Folklife*, 45.

Montgomery, M. (2006). *From Ulster to America, the Scotch-Irish Heritage of American English*. Belfast: Ulster Historical Foundation.

Moreno, C. P. A. (2006). *An Analysis of the Early Novels of Patrick MacGill: Bilingualism and Language Shift from Irish to English in County Donegal*. Lewiston, NY: Edwin Mellen Press.

Ó Donaill, N. (ed.) (1978). *Foclóir Gaeilge-Béarla*. Dublin: Oifig an tSoláthair.

Ó Siadhail, M. (1989). *Modern Irish: Grammatical Structure and Dialect Variation*. Cambridge: Cambridge University Press.

O'Rahilly, T. F. (1932). *Irish Dialects, Past and Present*. Dublin: Browne and Nolan.

Paulin, T. (1990). *Seize the Fire: A Version of Aeschylus's 'Prometheus Bound'*. London: Faber and Faber.

Robinson, P. (1997). *Ulster-Scots: A Grammar of the Traditional Written and Spoken Language*. Belfast: Ullans Press.

Story, G. M., Kirwin, W. J., & Widdowson, J. D. A. (1990). *Dictionary of Newfoundland English*. 2nd edn. with supplement. Toronto: University of Toronto Press.

Traynor, M. (1953). *The English Dialect of Donegal: A Glossary Incorporating the Collections of H. C. Hart MRIA*. Dublin: Royal Irish Academy.

Tristram, H. (ed.) (2006). *The Celtic Englishes IV*. Potsdam: Universitätsverlag Potsdam.

Section 2
English in Canada, Australia, and New Zealand

Introduction

This section focuses on English in Canada (John Edwards) and in Australia and New Zealand (Pam Peters). Currently known as "Commonwealth realms," these countries recognize the English monarch as their own but are politically autonomous (unlike the rest of the United Kingdom – see the previous section, "British Isles and Ireland"). Also historically called "settlement colonies" of England, these countries have complex political, cultural, and linguistic relationships with their erstwhile homeland.

Like other colonial Europeans, the British established their "settlement colonies" overseas in lands that settlers imagined to be "open"; their intent was to claim property and establish new homesteads. Over the generations settlers and their descendants developed national and cultural identities distinct from their British ancestors and pressed for political independence, either by force, as did the United States, or through slow political processes. Canada, Australia, and New Zealand did not gain full political autonomy until the mid-twentieth century. (Such settlement colonies can be distinguished from the so-called "exploitation colonies" of South Asia, Africa, and the Caribbean, in which the British intended not to establish homesteads but rather to profit from indigenous natural and, sadly, human resources; see the next section: "Colonial and Post-Colonial English").

Though sharing a history as settlement colonies, Canada, Australia, and New Zealand each has its own unique relationship to England and to the English language. Canada, as Edwards recounts, was originally a dominantly French colonial destination, but was overtaken by English settlers in the late eighteenth and nineteenth centuries. Canada officially remains a bilingual nation of English and French speakers, though only a small minority of the citizenry is actually bilingual. Further, these are not the only two languages spoken; Canada has long been a "receiving country," attracting a large number of immigrants, originally from Europe, but increasingly from all over the world. The history of the English language in Canada thus offers a case study in governmental policies designed to both accommodate and constrain a bilingual and multicultural society.

British settlement of Australia began in the late eighteenth century, and of New Zealand some fifty years later. Australia does not have the same bilingual history as Canada, nor did the many aboriginal languages (as many as 300 at the time of settlement) have any systematic impact on the English of Australians. The history of Australian English is therefore best understood in terms of its early divergence from Standard British English in vocabulary and pronunciation and the later influence of the American English of film, television, and other media. Peters refers to the "cultural cringe" felt through the mid-twentieth century by many middle-class Australians when confronted with the differences between their English and that of England. New Zealand English, while following a history similar to Australia's, additionally has felt the influence of Maori, the language of the earlier Polynesian settlers of the islands.

Maori loanwords, spellings, and pronunciations have entered English through both everyday contact and, more recently, an affirmative "maorification" campaign.

The future of Canadian, Australian, and New Zealand English will be determined by governmental policies, economic globalization, and populous nationalism. Australians, for instance, must decide whether they want to foster an "Australian-flavored" English as a kind of national branding, or if they will promote a less identifiable, globally homogeneous English for their exports. Canada's language issues are more internal, and will hinge on immigration and education policies as well as the pragmatic choices made by citizens hoping to capitalize on the global economy.

Michael Matto

37
English in Canada
John Edwards

Introduction

Although English came to Newfoundland (a British colony until it joined Canada in 1949) in the late fifteenth century, French was the first European language on the mainland, arriving with fishermen and explorers in the early sixteenth century. By the end of the eighteenth century, however, the English conquest of New France, the deportations of French speakers from Acadia (now the Maritime provinces of Canada) and the influx of American "loyalists" during and following the revolution of 1776 laid the foundations for the ascendancy of English in Canada – and the eclipse of French dominance. Mackey (1998) provides some telling numbers:

> At the time of the American revolution – when the English population of Canada was less than 9,000 (as against 65,000 French) – the number of American anti-revolutionaries . . . numbered upward of 100,000 . . . By the 1870s, when the population of Canada was just over three and a half million, two million were speakers of English . . . During the following century, almost ten million people immigrated to Canada, most of them English-speaking. (pp. 22–3)

Besides the predominance of English-speaking immigrants, the assimilation of French speakers in many parts of the country has proved significant; most of the French-origin population outside Quebec and New Brunswick (the only officially bilingual province), for example, no longer speak French. And the vast waves of continental-European immigrants – the "allophones," whose mother tongue was neither French nor English – have typically moved towards the latter. While it has been suggested that a Canadian "mosaic" exists, rather than the "melting pot" to the south, the reality is that – on both sides of the border – anglo-conformity has been the historical norm.

The story of English in Canada is in some sense a familiar and predictable one. As in other "receiving" countries of the new world – notably the United States, Australia,

and New Zealand – the power of the language has followed the twin flags of conquest and commerce, and the global power of English, a phenomenon that has become particularly evident in the last half-century or so, has only amplified pre-existing local tendencies. As the wider world has become increasingly made safe for Anglophones, so too has Canada.

Canadian Anglophones don't all sound the same, of course: there are regional differences in language and speech. Chambers (1998) points to the Scots roots of rural speech in Nova Scotia, for instance, and to the Irish influences on Newfoundland dialects. Nonetheless, English in Canada is much less regionally diversified than it is south of the border, especially at "standard" level. The historical patterns of internal immigration and mobility have given rise to a linguistic conservatism greater than that found in other new-world Anglophone societies – all of which tend, in any event, to be less regionally diverse in their speech patterns than the mother country from which they emerged. Standard Canadian English – overwhelmingly an urban, middle-class dialect – is virtually the same across the entire breadth of the country. Australia – another "receiving" society in which the distances are vast, another country with "more geography than history" (as the early-twentieth-century Canadian Prime Minister, Mackenzie King, once put it) – has a "Broad Australian" accent (think of Paul Hogan), a lower-class but non-regional variant that coexists across the continent with "General Australian" (Russell Crowe) (see AUSTRALIAN AND NEW ZEALAND ENGLISH); but there is no counterpart in Canada. It is apparent that the most interesting part of the story of Canadian English is not its internal variety.

English: Dominance and Accommodation

The real story of English in Canada – the one that differs from those in other parts of the Anglophone world – involves its relationship with French: neither can be understood without the other. Canada's social mainstream has always run in twin language channels, and, even as English strengthened its position, French continued to be an important player on the national stage. Francophone political power, for example, has remained strong, reflected in the careers of many of the country's most prominent leaders – from Wilfrid Laurier (prime minister from 1896 to 1911), to Pierre Trudeau (1968–84), to Jean Chrétien (1993–2003). The contemporary sovereigntist aspirations of nationalist *Québécois* are sometimes seen – in the rest of the country, and beyond its borders – as a "problem" to be "solved." These are not new phenomena, however; on the contrary, such aspirations have been a feature of the political landscape from the beginning (although, naturally enough, their prominence has waxed and waned with social and political circumstance). More important is the widespread failure to see that the very fabric of the country involves such "dualism" (the "two solitudes," as novelist Hugh MacLennan (1945) dubbed them, drawing the term from a poem by Rilke). Politically and linguistically, Canada is an ongoing experiment in the accommodation of two nations under one state roof. (This common

description prescinds, of course, from consideration of the indigenous nations whose presence in Canada long predates that of the two European "charter" groups. In contemporary assessments, it is also necessary to pay attention to the ethnonationalist sentiments of those many immigrants who are neither Francophone nor Anglophone.)

The fact that one of these nations (Quebec) is more classically delineated, that the other is so heterogeneous (if based essentially on an English "stream") that the very idea of *nation* is hardly appropriate, and that neither adequately understands the nature of the social solidarity felt by the other – these are some of the reasons recent Canadian discourse is often less a dialogue than competing monologues.

The social discourse involves other important players in the drama, too. The allophones, for example, are a very sizeable presence: recent census figures show that, collectively, they now constitute 42 percent of the overall Canadian population. Those of British ethnic origin make up 32 percent, and those of French background 24 percent. As with many census details, these figures are not entirely clear-cut. The 42 percent allophone presence, for example, includes 16 percent whose backgrounds also involve French, British, or Canadian (an "ethnic" category now available on census forms, but one which research suggests is almost completely chosen by people who would otherwise have reported French or British origins – i.e., *not* allophones). The figures just noted for those of French and British backgrounds also include this "Canadian" category. Fuller details and explanatory notes can be found in Pendakur and Hennebry (1998) and Pendakur and Mata (1998). The final 2 percent of the general population is of aboriginal ethnic origin. This group, however – the fourth important player in the ongoing Canadian drama – has an importance, largely due to its historical presence, which numbers alone would not suggest. To further complicate the picture, it must be remembered that none of the major groups – Francophones, Anglophones, allophones, and aboriginals – is itself a monolithic or seamless entity. The social and linguistic stage in Canada is thus a contentious area, indeed – and what makes it even *more* fractious is that all the action takes place against the huge backdrop of the United States.

The point here is a central one – for socio-political life in general, and for the power and scope of English in particular: in Canada, as elsewhere, sociolinguistic contact and struggle are essentially about power and, more specifically, *identity*. The tensions here remind us that language is much more than an instrumental medium; it has a symbolic significance that is closely tied to the heritage and the circumstances of its speakers. It would be difficult enough for Canada – huge, sparsely populated, historically young, and so on – to deal with such powerful internal tensions, even if it did not share a very long border with the world's most potent and expansive regime. As it is, the interior wrangling occurs within a country traditionally uncertain of itself, unsure of its social and cultural allegiances, without a strong "national" identity. And this, of course, is largely attributable to the relationship between Canadian geography and demography, and those south of the border. The most popular question for more than a century has been "Who are we?" and the most common response has been one

born out of comparison with America. It is arguably the case that no new-world "receiving" country is yet a nation, in the classic sense of the term, but there are degrees of unity. Some identifiable quantity called "American culture" has greater substance, for example, than a Canadian counterpart. A fairer comparison for the latter, however, might be Australia. Similar to Canada in many aspects of social and political development, it is nonetheless different in two pivotal ways: its population does not lie along a hundred-mile-wide border with the modern leviathan; and its dominant (non-indigenous) linguistic heritage is a singular one.

On the contemporary Canadian stage, the main antagonists are nationalist *Québécois* Francophones and Anglophone federalists. Most readers will be aware of the continuing tensions here, tensions most recently focused in Quebec's 1995 referendum on independence. Fewer, perhaps, will know that the other players, as mentioned above, also have strong stakes in the piece. Indeed, within the general picture I have sketched here, the most recent and most sensational debates have led to broad examination of virtually *all* aspects of the Canadian political, social, cultural, and linguistic fabric. Going beyond the desire of nationalists in Quebec to achieve sovereignty – and the reaction to this in other constituencies – other matters now under the collective microscope include the cultural and political rights of indigenous "first nations" and the policies and practices involving bilingual and multicultural accommodations. All such matters are politically highly charged, but it should be remembered that all reflect deep concerns about the maintenance and continuity of group identity.

The Canadian setting represents, in many ways, a "purer" example of linguistic and national struggle than is often found. That is, while disputes over language and culture are always of intrinsic interest, they are sometimes mainly symbolic – they signal other fundamental intergroup problems (of economic or political nature, for instance). In contemporary Canada, however, while powerful symbolic marking is of course at work, the forces of ethnonationalism are, in fact, central to the debate. It is not economic deprivation or lack of adequate political representation that most accurately characterizes the current drive for Quebec sovereignty, for example – or, more generally, the visceral determination to protect the French language and culture. It is, rather, a more "classic" sense of nationalism, in which the coincidence of nation with state is the paramount concern. This profound yearning – entirely understandable, and with many historical parallels – is now allied with a sense that a sovereign Quebec could, in fact, prosper. This accounts for the potency of current manifestations – and it also suggests something of the continuing story of the inter-linguistic tensions that flesh out the story of English in Canada.

Social Engineering

Some of these inter-linguistic tensions can be traced through federal policies of "social engineering." Following the findings of a royal commission in the 1960s, an Official Languages Act was passed in 1969 (since revised and updated). Its main thrust is

institutional bilingualism, provision of government services in both languages, and so on. No individuals – apart from civil servants – are required to become bilingual, although the expansion of personal repertoires is naturally seen to be desirable. Mother-tongue education (in French or English, that is) is mandated "wherever numbers warrant" (an elastic term that has often proved contentious).

The commissioners had closely examined both the "personality" and the "territorial" principle – in the first, linguistic rights attach to individuals wherever they live within the state; in the second, rights vary regionally, and the outcome is commonly some sort of "twinned unilingualism." Largely on political grounds, the commissioners and the government opted for the "personality" approach. Nonetheless, social and demographic forces have brought about a *de facto* territorialism. As noted above, Francophones outside Quebec (and Anglophones within the province) have undergone either language or physical shift. Apart from a "bilingual belt" in those parts of Ontario and New Brunswick which border Quebec, the tendency is for greater linguistic polarization. The idea – perhaps the dream – of a truly bilingual country has faded.

As second languages, both French and English are required in public education, of course, and census figures reveal almost five million self-reported bilingual individuals – about 17 percent of the total population. Bilingualism rates are highest in Quebec (at 38 percent) and New Brunswick (33 percent), and thus in other regions rates are considerably below the overall 17 percent rate (see Marmen & Corbeil, 1999). But census figures rest upon reported ability to conduct conversations in both languages – a loose measure, indeed. A more fine-grained investigation by Statistics Canada, for instance, has shown that, when people are asked if they "can carry on a fairly long conversation on different topics," there is a noticeable decline in reported bilingual ability (see Edwards 1995).

Official bilingualism has essentially been a peripheral entity for most Canadians, particularly for Anglophones outside Quebec. Consequently, the federal policy has received largely passive acceptance – with more active resentment against its manifestations in some quarters, particularly in regions furthest from Quebec. In any event, however, the policy has always been contentious. Was it truly intended to give official substance to the actual state of affairs, in which French and English mainstreams were to continue and, where possible, intertwine via bilingual adaptations? Or, was it a bone thrown by an increasingly powerful Anglophone community? These are extremes, and accuracy is probably found somewhere between them. It is, of course, an irony that, since the country became officially bilingual, Quebec itself has steadily supported French dominance.

The same royal commission which led to the Official Languages Act also gave rise to the Canadian multiculturalism policy – outlined by Pierre Trudeau in 1971 and formalized in legislation in 1988. Its general aim is to aid cultural groups (essentially, the allophones), both in their own development and in their contribution to wider society. A specific feature is assistance in learning one (or both) of the two official languages. Thus, a multicultural program is embedded in a *bilingual* framework – that

is, there is no particular support for allophone languages. With only the two "charter" languages emphasized, many wondered from the outset if some enduring difference between the status of the allophonic "others," and that of the English and the French, was to be enshrined. Given what has been discussed above, it could also be the case that a multicultural policy that speaks in only French or English is, in some "net-outcome" sense, a *de facto* supporter of English. (And there is, of course, a more general objection still: policies supportive of culture are curious beasts, to say the least, if they have no explicit linguistic component.)

As with official bilingualism, the multiculturalism initiative has been seen as politically opportunistic, in a country in which the "others" are collectively so numerous. Indeed, the most recent figures (see Department of Canadian Heritage, 2000) emphasize how strong these "others" are, particularly in the urban landscape. In 1996, for instance, 48 percent of the population in all Canadian metropolitan areas reported "at least one ethnic origin other than British, French, Canadian [see above] or Aboriginal" (p. 5). In Toronto, the figure is 68 percent, in Vancouver 64 percent, and even in the Montreal/Ottawa region it reaches almost one-third. Given such powerful concentrations, it is easy to understand government attention to diversity. It is also easy to see why criticism of multicultural policy has been particularly marked in Quebec. There, the fear has been of gradual relegation to the status of "other," of "Francophone" becoming one of the many subspecies of "allophone." The recent sovereigntist activity among nationalist *Québécois* gave a sharper edge to this – on referendum night (in 1995), then premier Jacques Parizeau spoke of the narrow loss: "It's true," he said, "we have been defeated, but basically by what? By money and the ethnic vote" (see Edwards 1997).

English vis-à-vis French Today

Of the two official languages, then, English is very much the stronger; and each of the two is increasingly geographically delimited. While the proportion of the population of generally British provenance has declined with the immigration of allophones, this latter group is of course very fragmented in terms of both origins and languages. Consequently, English remains the single most dominant variety, the linguistic destination for most allophones, and the most potent – or threatening – variety for Francophone and aboriginal groups. A language of ever-increasing global significance, English is a medium which tends to attract speakers, not lose them. Even among Quebec Anglophones, whose French competence has enlarged in recent years, the place of English, in a bilingual accommodation, is generally not at risk. For speakers of other languages in Canada, however, bilingualism is often a way-station on the road to a new monolingualism.

Recent census figures (as reported by Castonguay 1998, for example) show that, while mother-tongue proportions for English, French, and "Other" are about 60 percent, 24 percent, and 15 percent, the actual home-language *use* figures are 68

percent, 23 percent, and 8 percent. The trend is clear. Statistics also reveal the linguistic polarization already referred to: the "official" minorities (i.e., the English in Quebec and the French outside that province) are both in decline. Outside Quebec, for example, 78 percent report English as the mother tongue, while home-language use is about 88 percent. Inside Quebec, on the other hand, the French mother-tongue and home-language use figures are essentially identical (at roughly 82 percent). There is no reason to think that these tendencies are about to alter. French in Quebec has "gained" – not least because of Anglophone out-migration – while Francophones in the rest of the country continue to undergo anglicization. Due to government policies, allophone immigrants to Quebec now tend to end up more on the Francophone side of the linguistic ledger, but allophones in other regions are subject to anglicization.

The "bilingual belt" (noted above) accounts for about 75 percent of the roughly one million Francophones found outside Quebec. Of this percentage, about half a million live in Ontario (where they represent about 5 percent of the provincial population) and the other quarter million live in New Brunswick, where they constitute about 35 percent of the population. It is sometimes forgotten that the bilingual belt crosses provincial borders. Thus, 85 percent of Quebec's Anglophones live close to Ontario (most of them, more specifically, in the western part of Montreal island) or north of the American border.

No discussion of English in Canada, however brief, would be complete without a mention of French immersion programs (see Edwards 1994; Genesee 1998). This is because – even though they involve the teaching of *French* – these programs reveal the attitudes and aspirations of an influential section of the dominant group, secure in its own linguistic context and without any fear that learning a new language might mean the loss of the original one. Unlike traditional language instruction at school, Anglophone youngsters in immersion classrooms receive all their schooling – at least in the earliest years – through the medium of French. Their mother tongue is hardly put at risk, given its commanding national and global role. The origins of immersion education – at least in this modern incarnation – are found in Montreal in the 1960s, where Anglophone parents were dissatisfied with the French learned by traditional methods. Immersion programs are designed to capitalize on young children's abilities, relative unselfconsciousness and attitudinal openness. Communicative purposes are emphasized throughout, thus capturing (so far as possible) something of the atmosphere of first-language acquisition. Immersion education is typically associated with well-motivated and enthusiastic parents and teachers.

There is a large and often technical literature on immersion methods and outcomes. Overall, however, the programs can be counted a success, inasmuch as children gain a more native-like command of French than do their more traditionally taught schoolmates – and without losing ground across subject areas or, indeed, in English-language development. Surveys suggest that, even in the current political climate, support for this type of education remains strong. It is a curiosity (noted by de Bot 1994, among others) that a country which is increasingly linguistically polarized, and in which the separation of Quebec would likely lead to the abandonment of official

bilingualism in fairly short order, is also a country in which voluntary enrolment in immersion programs remains broadly attractive.

Beyond its purely pedagogical goals, immersion education was also meant to provide something of a bridge between the "two solitudes," and here success has been rather less marked. Studies have suggested that those students with immersion experience often seem not to make fullest use of their competence, and their rationale for learning French remains more "instrumental" than "integrative" – that is, their motivations are generally pragmatic and do not derive from powerful desires for cultural shift or accommodation. Although better and more comfortable with conversational French than are their more traditionally instructed counterparts, immersion graduates are not markedly more likely to seek out or initiate "cross-group" encounters – even in contexts, like Montreal, where opportunities abound (see Edwards 1994).

A Concluding Note

Canada is a society in flux. A country long regarded as a bastion of democracy and tolerance came to the verge of fracture a decade ago – and rumblings are now being heard again in the nationalist corridors of Quebec. The apparently perennial nature of tensions between sovereigntists and federalists rests upon the enduring linguistic duality of the country. In other Anglophone contexts – the United Kingdom, the United States, Australia, and so on – the social and political fortunes of English may fluctuate with those of the global Anglophone community. This is also true in Canada – but there, the story of English *also* unfolds against the backdrop of another powerful internal variety. This arrangement makes Canada unique among new-world societies.

REFERENCES AND FURTHER READING

Castonguay, C. (1998). The fading Canadian duality. In J. Edwards (ed.), *Language in Canada*. Cambridge: Cambridge University Press.

Chambers, J. (1998). English: Canadian varieties. In J. Edwards (ed.), *Language in Canada*. Cambridge: Cambridge University Press.

de Bot, K. (1994). Comment. *International Journal of the Sociology of Language*, 110, 193–201.

Department of Canadian Heritage (2000). *Annual Report on the Operation of the Canadian Multiculturalism Act*. Ottawa: Canadian Heritage

Edwards, J. (1994). *Multilingualism*. London: Penguin.

Edwards, J. (1995). Monolingualism, bilingualism, multiculturalism and identity: Lessons and insights from recent Canadian experience. *Current Issues in Language and Society*, 2, 5–37.

Edwards, J. (1997). French and English in Canada: before and after the Quebec referendum of 1995. In W. Wölck & A. de Houwer (eds.), *Recent Studies in Contact Linguistics*. Bonn: Dümmler.

Genesee, F. (1998). French immersion in Canada. In J. Edwards (ed.), *Language in Canada*. Cambridge: Cambridge University Press.

Mackey, W. (1998). The foundations. In J. Edwards (ed.), *Language in Canada*. Cambridge: Cambridge University Press.

MacLennan, H. (1945). *Two Solitudes*. Toronto: Collins.

Marmen, L. & Corbeil, J.-P. (1999). *Languages in Canada: 1996 Census.* Ottawa: Canadian Heritage.

Pendakur, R. & Hennebry, J. (1998). *Multicultural Canada: A Demographic Overview.* Ottawa: Multiculturalism & Citizenship Canada.

Pendakur, R. & Mata, F. (1998). *Patterns of Ethnic Identity and the "Canadian" Response.* Ottawa: Multiculturalism & Citizenship Canada.

38

Australian and New Zealand English

Pam Peters

Introduction: The Early Immigration Phase

The Englishes of the South Pacific have much in common, past and present. Both owe their origins to the immigration of a large core of British settlers, though the settlement years for Australia were from the 1780s, whereas New Zealand began to be settled from about 1840. In both places, the mixing of immigrants from many different dialect areas of Britain is thought to have resulted in a kind of koineization of speech. The first generation of Australians was heard to speak remarkably "harmonious" English, meaning that their speech was not colored by any particular dialect (Dixon 1822, in Blair 1975: 18). It nevertheless owes most to southeastern British speech, in being nonrhotic (i.e., pronouncing 'r' only before a vowel sound), and having the wide diphthongs /aɪ/ and /aʊ/ (Mitchell & Delbridge 1965). Some admixtures from southwestern dialects, northern (including Scottish) and Irish can be found in the lexicon, but they do not seem to have impacted on the Australian accent. Australian speech is remarkably homogenous throughout the country, with only slight variations in the distribution of the same phonemic alternates, e.g., /a/ and /æ/ in words like *chance, demand, graph* from Hobart to Brisbane (Bradley 2003:148).

New Zealand English probably owes something to early Australian English, with Australian immigrants moving east across the Tasman Sea. But with numerous British settlers there too, the mix of dialects seems to have produced similar phonological traits, which was positively evaluated as "purer than can be found in any given district at home" (McBurney 1887; in Leitner 2004: I.97). It presents a similar phonemic system except in the realization of short vowels (see below), and in residual rhoticism in the speech of those at the southernmost point of the South Island (= Southland), where Scottish settlement was most intense (Gordon & Maclagan 2004: 604–5). Otherwise, through the center and north of the South Island, and all through the North Island, New Zealand accents are also remarkably homogenous. Despite the lack

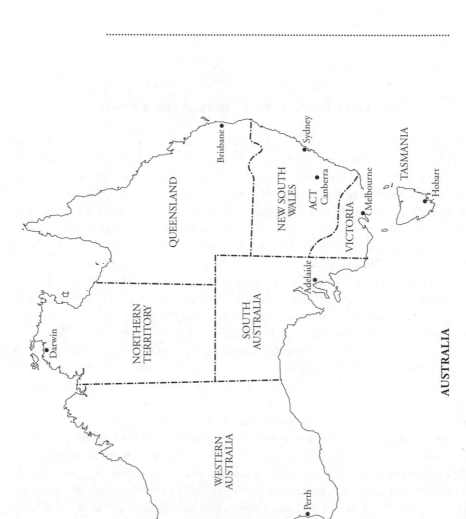

NEW ZEALAND

AUSTRALIA

Figure 38.1 Australia and New Zealand

of fully fledged regional accents, there are regionalized elements in the lexicons of Australian and New Zealand English (discussed below).

Australian and New Zealand Accents

Some of the first comments on the speech of Australians and New Zealanders in the nineteenth century are remarkably positive, as we have seen. But with the implementation of universal education during the nineteenth century, Australian and New Zealand accents began to come under scrutiny by teachers and school inspectors, whose adverse criticisms on the pronunciation of particular vowels and consonants were reported annually as an Appendix to the *Journal of the House of Representatives* (Maclagan & Gordon 2004: 45). In 1912 the Principal of Wellington College noted that the New Zealand accent had become "much worse in the last ten years" (p. 46). A 1926 pamphlet of the Australian English Association (i.e., the association for Australian teachers of English) passes judgment on national speech as "ugly" (Bernard 1969). These comments dating from the later nineteenth and earlier twentieth century must be set against the backdrop of the rise of RP in Britain, based on southern British English. Both Australian and New Zealand accents, as reflexes of southern British, were judged unfavorably against it. The fear that antipodean accents would be unfavorably received overseas was one aspect of the so-called "cultural cringe," whereby middle-class Australians (and New Zealanders) up to the mid-twentieth century took for granted the superiority of external linguistic and cultural reference points, and would return "home" to England to refresh their connections with the Mother Country. The Australian Broadcasting Commission (later Corporation) founded in 1932 employed only southern British radio announcers until well into the 1960s. "Educated" Australian English was by then better supported as the ABC's prestige model, through the pioneering work of Mitchell (Leitner 1984: 68–72). Yet research on popular attitudes to the Australian accent (Bradley & Bradley 2000) puts the decline of the cultural cringe somewhat later, tailing off through the 1980s and 1990s. In New Zealand it could still be found in the 1990s (Bayard 2000: 321).

A nationwide study of the speech of Australian adolescents (Mitchell & Delbridge 1965) helped to document variation within the Australian accent, and to show that it ranged from "broad" to "cultivated," with most individuals between those extremes as "general" speakers. Broad speakers tended to widen the diphthongs /eɪ/ and /oʊ/ to /ʌɪ/ and /ʌʊ/; to front /əɪ/ and /aʊ/ to /æɪ/ and /æʊ/; and to diphthongize /i/ and /u/ into /əɪ/ and /əʊ/ respectively. Some variation between metropolitan and rural speech emerged, with relatively more "broad" speakers in rural areas; and between males and females: more males than females were "broad" speakers. More complex patterns of sociolectal variation have been found in subsequent small-scale research with adult metropolitan speakers (Bradley 1991: 228–31), and larger-scale work in Sydney (Horvath 1985) with adults and children, using vowel and consonant variables.

However, these accent variations have yet to be satisfactorily correlated with lexico-grammatical variation, *pace* Leitner (2004: I.239), as distinct sociolects.

The most characteristic feature of the New Zealand accent is its raising of short front vowels, so that /æ/ is pronounced as /ɛ/, /ɛ/ as /ɪ/, and /ɪ/ becomes centralized as /ə/, sounding like a close form of schwa. This linked set of rising vowels resembles the rising of long front (and back) vowels in the Great Vowel Shift (see PHONOLOGY: SEGMENTAL HISTORIES). In addition, the front centering diphthongs of this nonrhotic accent, /ɪə/ and /ɛə/, are often merged. The effect is turned into numerous puns by New Zealanders themselves, as in the hairdresser's business name "Hair today, gone tomorrow." In that case, the two centering diphthongs seem to neutralize on the lower form, but this varies somewhat regionally and sociolinguistically (Batterham 2000). Ongoing changes in New Zealand speech have been found to have sociolinguistic correlates (Gordon & McLagan (2004: 607–12).

The consonant repertoire in Australian and New Zealand English is very similar, in their nonrhoticity, except for the residual postvocalic /r/ in New Zealand's Southland, and their use of dark /l/ in postvocalic positions. Some Australian speakers tend to vocalize this dark /l/, as in /miuk/ for *milk* (Borowsky 2000: 72–7). Most Australian speakers have dispensed with /ʍ/ in *where*, *which*, etc., merging it with /w/, as shown in their pronunciations in the *Macquarie Dictionary* (1981 and later); and its use is receding in New Zealand (Bauer & Warren 2004: 596). In Australia /h/ dropping is a minority feature (Horvath 1985: 101–2), while in New Zealand it is rare.

A distinctive intonational pattern found in both Australian and New Zealand English is the use of a high rising terminal (HRT) in declarative statements. It occurs as the speaker/narrator solicits the continued attention of the listener, and signals with HRT that there is more to tell (Horvath 1985: 121–2, 131–2). Its users are most likely to be young females from lower-working-class backgrounds. In New Zealand it also correlates with Maori ethnicity.

Australian and New Zealand Grammar and Usage

The standard grammar of writing in Australia and New Zealand is much like that of the major varieties of English in the northern hemisphere. There are however differences of degree which can be traced through comparative studies based on parallel corpora (= text databases of varieties of English). Corpus-based research shows numerous points of syntax on which contemporary Australian and New Zealand English norms do not coincide exactly with those of British English (Collins & Peters 2004).

The use of the present (mandative) subjunctive (e.g., *They insisted that the child be accompanied by a parent*) is one syntactic variable whose use is notably stronger in both Australian and New Zealand English than in contemporary British English. The mandative seems indeed to have fallen into disuse in Britain through the mid-twentieth century, reflecting perhaps the advice of Henry Fowler to avoid it (Peters

2004: 520–1). At any rate, it had become stylistically marked as rather formal British English by the 1980s, although its use remained steady in the US throughout the century. Meanwhile its use in Australia and New Zealand towards the end of the twentieth century was closer to the American norm than the British (Peters 1998; Hundt et al. 2004: 569–70). This raises the question as to whether this reflects fresh American influence, or "colonial lag." Australia and New Zealand were further removed from any Fowlerian influence that might have reduced the ordinary use of the mandative.

Another notable syntactic variable of Australian and New Zealand English is the combination of the present perfect with specific past time reference points, as *he's done it yesterday*. Though noted elsewhere as a vagary of speech (Trudgill 1984: 42), it can be heard in scripted New Zealand and Australian radio news (Bauer 1989: 70–1; Engel & Ritz 2000). Its use in broadcasting could of course be explained in terms of the need to lend immediacy to news events, though it may also owe something to underlying spoken usage, which radio journalists are encouraged to reflect. If so, it helps to exemplify the way in which features of speech are more readily absorbed into written usage than elsewhere in the world. The fact that contractions such as *it's* and *don't* appear in a wider range of Australian prose than American or British (Peters 2000: 168–75) is a further demonstration.

Verb morphology in Australia and New Zealand still tends to endorse the less regular forms. One example is that the *–ed* marker of past tense and past participle gives way to the irregular *–t* forms, in *dreamt, spelt*, etc., although British English is now more inclined to the regular *dreamed, spelled*, etc., as is American English (Hundt et al. 2004: 562). There is some endorsement of the *–en* participle in New Zealand newspapers, in both active and passive use of *proven*. In Australia, substantial support for *gotten* was found in a survey carried out by the magazine *Australian Style* in 2002 (Collins & Peters 2004: 596). In intransitive use (*she had never gotten so angry*), it gained 45 percent of the vote across the age range (10–65+), and 69 percent from younger Australians (under 25). In these examples of tending towards *–en*, Australian and New Zealand English are closer to American English, as in the trend among younger speakers to use *shrunk, sprung, sunk* for the past tense, instead of *shrank, sprang, sank*.

Research shows reduced morphological distinctions among the personal pronouns by Australians and New Zealanders, and a tendency to prefer the so-called "common case," i.e., the accusative where it is an option. In written usage, the accusative is often selected over the genitive before a gerund, as in *the idea of you coming with me . . .* (Peters 2006: 772–4). And in informal spoken usage, the accusative *me* commonly appears instead of the nominative *I* in coordinated phrases, as either second or first coordinate (Peters, forthcoming).

In both Australian and New Zealand non-standard usage, *yous* serves as an informal second person pronoun, especially for the plural. In the forms *yiz* and *yez*, its existence is documented in Australian light fiction of the 1960s, and it is widely used among younger and rural speakers. In New Zealand it was first documented in the 1970s among school children; and more recently among Maoris (Johnston & Robertson

1993). They maintain a three-way distinction between *you* (one person), *youse* (two people), *youse fullas* (more than two) which is also found in Aboriginal English (Harkins 1994: 50–2), and reminiscent of the Old English pronoun system.

Lexical Resources and Lexicography

Both Australian and New Zealand English inherited the common vocabulary of British English, and have used and adapted it in their own distinctive environments. Many British terms for flora and fauna were applied to antipodean species, usually unrelated. So the Australian *bluebell* and *heath* and the New Zealand *beech* and *birch*; the antipodean *heron, kingfisher, magpie, robin*; and the South Pacific *bream, flounder, salmon, whiting* are different species than their northern referents – though they bear some superficial likenesses to them.

Topographic terms diverge somewhat from the sets used in Britain. The British English word *creek* refers to an estuary, but in Australia and New Zealand it becomes the general term for a stream, reflecting no doubt the earliest patterns of exploration from the coast inland. Regional British terms such as *brook, beck, burn* are not used at all. *Gully* (*OED* "small ravine") is used generally for an eroded water course, or a narrow valley, especially where alluvial gold was found (*Australian National Dictionary* (*AND*) 1988; *Dictionary of New Zealand English* (*DNZE*) 1997). The term *bush* is used in both Australia and New Zealand for land covered with natural vegetation, and thus typically connotes mixed eucalyptus in the first, and native rain forest in the second. This generic usage of *bush* seems to reflect the use of the Dutch *bosch* in South Africa, though it was also thus on the American frontier. *Bush* is very frequent in Australian and New Zealand compounds, with 12–15 large dictionary pages devoted to them in *AND* and *DNZE*, capturing aspects of frontier life, from the *bush whacker* to the *bush telegraph*.

Compounding was the early strategy for naming many indigenous Australian animals. The word *native* was put to use in *native bear* (koala), *native cat* (quoll), *native dog* (dingo), *native hedgehog* (echidna), *native hyena* (Tasmanian devil). Aboriginal loan-words were eventually used in some cases (*dingo, koala, quoll*), yet relatively few overall have been taken up in Australian English. Those that have are particularly terms for fauna and flora, and relatively few referring to aspects of Aboriginal culture and society are current in modern Australian English (Dixon et al. 1990). With the expansion of agricultural frontiers across Australia, there was little peaceable contact with Aborigines; and Aboriginal cultures and communities were deconstructed by relocation of the remaining populations, especially in southern Australia. The many different Aboriginal languages (estimated to have been 300 at the time of the first British settlement) also went against the settlers acquiring much understanding of Aboriginal words, and contributed instead to the formation of Aboriginal pidgin Englishes. In New Zealand the Maori language was much the same throughout the country, and settlers had much more continuous contact with Maori people. Hence the larger

proportion of loanwords reflecting Maori culture and lifestyle: *hangi* "earth oven," *hongi* "touching of noses as a salutation," *marae* "enclosed space and meeting house," *poi* "small ball on string, swung or twirled to the rhythm of a song or dance." Apart from its stronger historical base, the use of Maori loanwords in New Zealand English has been reinforced by recent efforts to affirm the Maori names for species which had acquired English ones. So the red pine is *rimu*, the black pine *matai*, the white pine *kahikatea*. This is part of an affirmative campaign which has also seen "maorification" of the spelling and pronunciation of older loanwords and placenames. (See CREOLES AND PIDGINS.)

Informal usage in Australia and New Zealand is alike in making considerable use of abbreviation, much more so than in the US or the UK. In Auckland street signs, *peds* "pedestrians" are warned to watch for traffic; and *bach* is the general word for a small holiday house (a place where you batch) – except in Southland, where it is a *crib*. In Australia *rels* is the common abbreviation for "relatives," and *demo* for "demonstration." Abbreviated forms are used and invented in everyday discourse, especially words formed with the suffix *–ie* (*-y*), attached to abbreviated compounds and longer words so that *budgerigar* becomes *budgie*, *football* becomes *footie*, and the *cockatoo farmer* (i.e., "small farmer") a *cocky*. For Australian and New Zealand adults they are solidarity markers and not confined to talking with children (Simpson 2004: 643). The suffix *-o* is also used this way (though not as frequently) to produce *arvo* ("afternoon"), *journo* ("journalist"), etc. The same hypocoristic suffixes are used in informal names for people (*Robbie*, *Robbo*) and places (*Brizzie* for Queensland capital *Brisbane*, *Paddo* for *Paddington*) (Simpson 2000). Many hypocoristics are local and context-bound, for example the use of *vollies* for "volunteers" in a Northern Territory newspaper headline. By the same token, a hypocoristic may carry different meanings in different places. Around Canberra, Australia's capital city, *ambo* is used to refer to an ambassador; elsewhere it means an "ambulance officer."

Publishing and the Media in Australia and New Zealand

Both Australian and New Zealand English have relatively short histories, evolving below the level of consciousness through most of the last 150–200 years. There have been occasional peaks of recognition, as with the conspicuous articulation of Australian identity through the *Bulletin* magazine's use of Australian English in the 1880s and 1890s (Moore 2001: 49); and Henry Lawson's writing features distinctive terms from Australia and New Zealand. Participation in two world wars has also been the key to self-recognition, when the Australia and New Zealand Army Corps forces, extracted from the home environment, were suddenly made aware of their contrasting cultural and linguistic identity. The growth of indigenous literary writing has undoubtedly helped to articulate it since World War II, with Australian authors such as Patrick White and David Malouf, and New Zealanders such as Katherine Mansfield and Janet Frame, establishing international reputations.

A further factor was the establishment of local (Australia and New Zealand) publishing by international publishers in recent decades, where previously only very limited publishing of Australian fiction had been done by the Melbourne-based firm of Angus and Robertson (Alison 2001). But during the 1970s Penguin Books established a profitable paperback publishing business in Melbourne, Australia, which for a time subsidized the British parent company (Dutton 1996: 52). Allen and Unwin produced fiction and non-fiction very successfully in Sydney in the 1980s, and in 1990 the Australian office bought itself out of its London parent company to become an independent publisher. Queensland University Press meanwhile started from a local base in the early 1950s, publishing a wide range of Australian works, and increasing the exposure of Australian authors. Publishing ventures like these, and other niche players in that volatile industry, have undoubtedly helped to affirm national identity and language – against the challenge of global publishing empires.

Indigenous media have also helped to support national and cultural identity in Australia, through a requirement that 60 percent of what the national broadcaster puts to air must be locally produced. Meanwhile the three commercial channels only occasionally make or buy local programs, and much American-made material is aired, from the excellent children's program *Sesame Street* to the trashy *Jerry Springer Show* for dysfunctional adults. New Zealanders overall are exposed to much more American programming, with no restrictions on the amount of overseas material (Bayard 2000: 298), and a greatly reduced role for the New Zealand national broadcaster through funding cuts in the 1990s.

Given the amount of American-produced television watched by Australians and New Zealanders, it is hardly surprising if Americanisms are picked up and assimilated. While younger citizens seem to absorb such words and expressions without qualms, surveys conducted through *Australian Style* in 2001–2 suggest that older Australians are more disquieted by them. Complaints about the "Americanization" of Australian English have long been a commonplace of letters written to the ABC's Standing Committee on Spoken English (Leitner 1984: 73–8), and to New Zealand's newspapers (Gordon & Deverson 1989). Yet many so-called "Americanisms" from *okay* to *guy* were established in British English before reaching Australia (Peters 2001: 307). Their appearance in the antipodes could therefore result from combined northern hemisphere influence, or "international English," rather than "American" influence per se.

Conclusion: National Identity and Globalization

Through the twentieth century, both Australians and New Zealanders have developed distinctive accents and vocabulary to forge their own independent varieties of English. There are dictionaries to describe them (Australia also has its own government style manual, and several usage guides). They are therefore endonormative varieties (Schneider 2003). At the same time they are connected into the global economy, and

need global markets for their publishing and media products. It is then a conundrum as to whether such products may sell by virtue of their local flavor/local language, or are more likely to do so if "translated" into a more international form of English – or at least one which is fully accessible to readers to northern hemisphere markets. Australian editors generally regard it as part of the business, though some resist, on the grounds that it amounts to stifling national identity. It is arguable that translating Australian and New Zealand books into more global forms of English for readers overseas will have no impact on the local forces that contribute to the individuality of Australian/New Zealand English. The need to describe local southern hemisphere phenomena – social, cultural, environmental – is not going to change, but will remain a stimulus to diversification of the language. The deeply rooted preference for more informal modes of expression is not likely to disappear; and as long as the written medium is permeable to spoken idiom, colloquialisms will establish themselves within the standard. They are no longer voluntarily suppressed as part of a cultural cringe, but strongly affirmed. The Englishes of the South Pacific can thus coexist with the major varieties of English in the northern hemisphere.

Appendix: Select entries from Karl Lentzner's *Dictionary of the Slang-English of Australia and of Some Mixed Languages*, published in 1892

Cockatoo (up-county). Also *cockatoo* farmer or settler, a small settler. Sometimes termed *cocky*. So called to compare them with the common sulpher-crested white *cockatoos*, which come down on the newly sown cornfields in myriads.

> The *cockatoo* settlers or free selectors fight desparately for the privilege of picking out any piece of land they may fancy.
> *A. C. Grant: Bush Life in Queensland*
>
> A *cockatoo* fence is one on a cockatoo's farm.
> The trees themselves, . . . woven with their branches into the stout cockatoo fence.
> *Blackwood's Magazine: C. T., Impressions of Australia*

Colonial (Australian and American), unsettled, because in the early days of the colonies men dressed and behaved unconventionally, and life and property were by no means so secure as they are now. Also rude, rough, ungainly, awkward, used in this sense more in England than in Australia. An Englishman will say very or thoroughly *colonial* in a contemptuous way.

Jackaroo (up-country), the name by which young men who go to the Australian colonies to pick up colonial experience are designated (A. C. Grant's "Bush Life"). Like *bossaroo*, a slang word coined on the model of kangaroo.

Mia-mia (up-country), a bed, pronounced *my-my*, rest. *Mia-mia* or *gunyah* is the hut the Australian blackfellow constructs for himself by making a sloping screen of leafy branches. It has passed into white men's slang. Australians say, "I'm going to my *mia-mia*," meaning "I'm going to bed" or "going to rest."

Within our leafy *mia-mia* then we crept,
And ere a man could fifty count we slept.
Keighley Goodchild: On the Tramp

Shake, to (popular), to steal. Originally imported by convicts into New South Wales, this word has passed into universal use among schoolboys, bushmen, shepherds, &c. When "taking" is stealing, it is called *shaking*. When "taking" is only a breach of etiquette, it is called "jumping"; you would *shake* a person's watch, but you would only "jump" the seat which he had engaged in a railway carriage.

REFERENCES AND FURTHER READING

Alison, J. (2001). Publishers and editors: Angus and Robertson, 1888–1945. In M. Lyons & J. Arnold (eds.), *A History of the Book in Australia 1891–1945* (pp. 27–36). Brisbane: University of Queensland Press.

Australian Style (1992 on). A national bulletin on issues in Australian style and English in Australia. Sydney: Dictionary Research Centre.

Batterham, M. (2000). The apparent merger of the front centring diphthongs – EAR and AIR – in New Zealand English. In A. Bell & K. Kuiper (eds.), *New Zealand English* (pp. 111–45). Amsterdam: John Benjamins.

Bauer, L. (1989). The verb *have* in New Zealand English. *English World-Wide*, 10 (1), 69–83.

Bauer, L. & Warren, P. (2004). New Zealand English: phonology. In B. Kortmann et al. (eds.), *A Handbook of Varieties of English*. 2 vols. (pp. 580–602). Berlin: Mouton de Gruyter.

Bayard, D. (2000). The cultural cringe revisited: changes through time in Kiwi attitudes toward accents. In A. Bell & K. Kuiper (eds.), *New Zealand English* (pp. 297–324). Amsterdam: John Benjamins.

Bell, A. & Kuiper, K. (eds.) (2000). *New Zealand English*. Amsterdam: John Benjamins.

Bernard, J. (1969). On the uniformity of spoken Australian English. *Orbis*, 18, 62–73.

Blair, D. (1975). On the origins of Australian pronunciation. *Working Papers of the Language Research Centre* (Macquarie University), 1 (2), 17–27.

Blair, D. & Collins, P. (eds.) (2000). *English in Australia*. Amsterdam: John Benjamins.

Borowsky, T. (2000). The vocalisation of dark /l/ in Australian English. In D. Blair & P. Collins (eds.), *English in Australia* (pp. 69–88). Amsterdam: John Benjamins.

Bradley, D. (1991). /AE/ and /a:/ in Australian English. In J. Cheshire (ed.), *English Around the World* (pp. 227–34). Cambridge: Cambridge University Press.

Bradley, D. (2003). Mixed sources of Australian English. *Australian Journal of Linguistics*, 23 (2), 143–50.

Bradley, D. (2004). Regional characteristics of Australian English: phonology. In B. Kortmann et al. (eds.), *A Handbook of Varieties of English*. 2 vols. (pp. 645–55). Berlin: Mouton de Gruyter.

Bradley, D. & Bradley, M. (2000). Changing attitudes to Australian English. In D. Blair & P. Collins (eds.), *English in Australia* (pp. 271–86). Amsterdam: John Benjamins.

Britain, D. (1992). Linguistic change and innovation: the use of high rising terminals in New Zealand English. *Language Variation and Change*, 4, 77–104.

Collins, P. & Peters, P. (2004). Australian English morphology and syntax. In B. Kortmann et al. (eds.), *A Handbook of Varieties of English*. 2 vols. (pp. 593–610). Berlin: Mouton de Gruyter.

Dixon, R., Ramson, W., & Thomas, M. (1990). *Australian Aboriginal Words in English*. Melbourne: Oxford University Press.

Dutton, G. (1996) *A Rare Bird*. Melbourne: Penguin Books Australia.

Engel, D. M. & Ritz, M.-E. A. (2000). The use of the present perfect in Australian English. *Australian Journal of Linguistics*, 20 (2), 119–140.

Gordon, E. & Deverson, T. (1989). *Finding a New Zealand Voice*. Auckland: New House Publishers.

Harkins, J. (1994). *Bridging Two Worlds*. Brisbane: Queensland University Press.

Hundt, M., Hay, J., & Gordon, E. (2004). New Zealand English morphosyntax. In B. Kortmann et al. (eds.), *A Handbook of Varieties of English*. 2 vols. (pp. 560–92). Berlin: Mouton de Gruyter.

Gordon, E. & Maclagan, M. (2004). Regional and social differences in New Zealand English: phonology. In B. Kortmann et al. (eds.), *A Handbook of Varieties of English*. 2 vols. (pp. 603–13). Berlin: Mouton de Gruyter.

Horvath, B. (1985). *Variation in Australian English: The Sociolects of Sydney*. Cambridge: Cambridge University Press.

Johnston, L. & Robertson, S. (1993). Hey, You! The Maori–NZE interface in sociolinguistic rules of address. *Te Reo*, 36, 115–27.

Kortmann, B. & Schneider, E., together with Burridge, K., Mesthrie, R., & Upton, C. (2004). *A Handbook of Varieties of English*. 2 vols. Berlin: Mouton de Gruyter.

Leitner, G. (1984). Australian English or English in Australia – linguistic identity or dependence in broadcast language. *English World-Wide*, 5 (1), 55–85.

Leitner, G. (2004). *Australia's Many Voices*. 2 vols. Berlin: Mouton de Gruyter.

Lentzner, K. (1892). Wörterbuch der Englischen Volkssprache in Australien und einiger Englischen Mischsprachen (*Dictionary of the Slang-English of Australia and of some Mixed Languages*). Halle-Leipzig: Ehrhardt Karras.

Lyons, M. & Arnold, J. (eds.) (2001). *A History of the Book in Australia 1891–1945*. Brisbane: University of Queensland Press.

Maclagan, M. & Gordon, E. (2004). The story of New Zealand English: what the ONZE project tells us. *Australian Journal of Linguistics*, 24 (1), 41–56.

Mitchell, A. & Delbridge, A. (1965). *The Speech of Australian Adolescents*. Sydney: Angus & Robertson.

Moore, B. (ed.) (2001). *Who's Centric Now? The Present State of Post-Colonial Englishes*. Melbourne: Oxford University Press.

Orsman, H. (ed.) (1997). *Dictionary of New Zealand English*. Auckland: Oxford University Press.

Peters, P. (1998). The survival of the subjunctive: evidence of its use in Australia and elsewhere. *English World-Wide*, 19 (1), 87–103.

Peters, P. (2000). Corpus evidence on Australian style and usage. In D. Blair & P. Collins (eds.), *English in Australia* (pp. 163–78). Amsterdam: John Benjamins.

Peters, P. (2001). Varietal effects: the influence of American English on British and Australian English. In B. Moore (ed.), *Who's Centric Now? The Present State of Post-Colonial Englishes* (pp. 297–309). Melbourne: Oxford University Press.

Peters, P. (2004) *The Cambridge Guide to English Usage*. Cambridge: Cambridge University Press.

Peters, P. (2006). English usage: prescription and description. In B. Aarts & A. McMahon (eds.), *The Handbook of English Linguistics*. Oxford: Blackwell.

Peters, P. (forthcoming). Style and politeness in English pronouns. In S. Yamazaki & R.Sigley (eds.), *Approaching Variation Through Corpora*. Amsterdam: Rodopi.

Ramson, W. S. (ed.) (1988). *Australian National Dictionary*. Melbourne: Oxford University Press.

Schneider, E. W. (2003). The dynamics of new Englishes: from identity construction to dialect birth. *Language*, 79 (2), 233–81.

Simpson, J. (2000). Hypocoristics of placenames. In D. Blair & P. Collins (eds.), *English in Australia* (pp. 89–112). Amsterdam: John Benjamins.

Simpson, J. (2004). Hypocoristics in Australian English. In B. Kortmann et al. (eds.), *A Handbook of Varieties of English*. 2 vols. (pp. 643–56). Berlin: Mouton de Gruyter.

Trudgill, P. (ed.) (1984). *Language in the British Isles*. Cambridge: Cambridge University Press.

Section 3
Colonial and
Post-Colonial English

Introduction

By one reckoning, all English outside England should be called "colonial," whether defined as geographic, cultural, or economic colonialism. But as the previous sections have shown, distinguishing among kinds of colonialism is valuable in tracing the history of the English language. The essays in this section consider the ongoing legacy of English's use as a colonial tool in the so-called "exploitation colonies" of South Asia (Kamal Sridhar), Africa (Alamin M. Mazrui), and the Caribbean (Donald Winford). The former colonies in these geographic areas share an ambivalent attitude towards English, seeing it simultaneously as a reminder of past exploitation and subjugation and as a critical tool for future entry into the corridors of global influence and economic prosperity.

The global spread of English beyond the British Isles and the settlement colonies began as early as the sixteenth century, but as an instrument of trade, not of territorial expansion. Direct British rule of Asian and African peoples would develop incrementally. Later, English would move across the oceans not only as the language of white British (and later American) colonials, but as the language of slaves, former slaves, and others who had learned English either as a second language or, as in the case of later-generation slaves and British domestics, their only language. As both Mazrui and Winford point out, the continuous relocation of non-white English speakers was particularly instrumental in the spread of English in its many forms through West Africa and the Caribbean islands.

While the many varieties of English throughout the "exploitation colonies" were brought there mainly by people with no governmental authority, almost without exception a centralized governing body would eventually instill English as the language of bureaucratic and legal administration, as well as the language of the schools (cf. THE TRANSPLANTATION OF AMERICAN ENGLISH IN PHILIPPINE SOIL). But while such language policies were designed to control the manner in which English was learned and used, language always resists such attempts at constraint. The results are the endlessly creative and innovative uses of English we find currently throughout the world.

Because English spread within the exploitation colonies through the agency of both white and non-white speakers, and because both colonial and post-colonial timeframes are involved, it would be too simple to condemn English as a tool of imperialism. One legacy of British and American colonialism is the feeling throughout the world that English no longer belongs to the English, but to the world, leading many post-colonial peoples to adopt willingly the local variety of English as their national, or in the case of many African nations, pan-continental language (see WORLD ENGLISHES IN WORLD CONTEXTS). As Winford tells us, English speakers from all over the world came together in the Caribbean to create a diversity of Englishes, and they are as distinct from one another as each is from British English (see also CREOLES AND PIDGINS).

This section therefore treats the English languages spoken throughout the former colonies both in their uniquely developing forms (lexicon, syntax, grammar, pronunciation) and in their developing social roles in their home countries.

Michael Matto

39
South Asian English

Kamal K. Sridhar

Linguistically and culturally, South Asian English is a very interesting and dynamic phenomenon: interesting, because English has become one of the languages of communication for South Asians, and a distinctive form of South Asian English has emerged; and dynamic, because the English language is constantly evolving and changing in South Asia, as it is constantly being used to express nuances of South Asian cultures and sensibilities. As Kachru and Nelson (2006) point out, "South Asia is a linguistic area with one of the longest histories of contact, influence, use, and teaching and learning of English-in-diaspora in the world" (p. 153). Kachru (1986) further elaborates, the "use of the term *South Asian English* is not to be understood as indicative of linguistic homogeneity in this variety nor of a uniform linguistic competence. It refers to several broad regional varieties such as Indian English, Lankan English and Pakistani English" (p. 36).

This chapter will focus on the history of English in the countries in the South Asian subcontinent, the users and uses of English, the emergence of South Asian English, and the future of English in South Asia.

In order to do justice to this topic, one has to start with defining the term *South Asia*. In current literature, South Asia is said to comprise the countries of Bangladesh, India, Pakistan, Nepal, Bhutan, Maldives, and Sri Lanka (Kachru 2005: 30).

Historical Background

How and why did the British come to India? Briefly, the end of the year 1600 saw the beginnings of officially sanctioned economic expansion out of Britain to India. By the end of the seventeenth century, the British East India Company controlled virtually all international trade with India. In 1689, with the establishment of the three presidencies or administrative districts in Bengal, Bombay (now Mumbai), and Madras (now Chennai), British rule was established in the subcontinent. In 1773, the British

government established a Governor Generalship in India, and with the India Act of 1784, a department to manage Indian Affairs under British rule was established in the subcontinent by the East India Company. Following the so-called "Mutiny" of 1857, the Act for the Better Government of India in 1858 resulted in the British government assuming the responsibility of governing India (Kachru and Nelson 2006: 154).

The British also brought their language. Kachru (2005) notes, "The formal introduction of English in South Asia has passed through several stages. What started as an educational debate in the seventeenth and early eighteenth centuries culminated in Lord Macaulay's much maligned Minute of 2 February 1835, which initiated planned activity for introducing the English language into South Asian education" (p. 30). During this phase, the role of the missionaries was vital in the spread of English. At the beginning, the educational efforts of the Europeans

> had an ulterior purpose, viz. the propagation of the Gospel. Moreover, they were directed purely to religious education – the object being the instillation of Christian doctrines into the minds of the people through their native language which the Europeans tried to master, as also the spread of Western education among the Indians in order to enable them to appreciate better the Christian doctrines. (Law 1915: 6–7)

(For a detailed history of English in Indian education, see Nurullah & Naik 1951; Kanungo 1962; Kachru 1994; Kachru & Nelson 2006; Sridhar 1979.)

The story of Ceylon, renamed Sri Lanka on May 22, 1972, is not much different: the island was declared a Crown Colony in 1902. A century before this declaration, in 1799, the Rev. James Cordiner went as a chaplain to the garrison in Colombo. He took over as principal of all schools in the settlement. Initial efforts to introduce English in Sri Lanka were again made by the missionaries. The government did not start installing English education until 1831, and by this time, Sri Lanka already had 235 Protestant mission schools, only 90 of which were under the direct control of the government.

A prominent missionary endeavor was the Christian Institution, whose foundation was laid in 1827 by Sir Edward Barnes. The aim of the institution was "to give a superior education to a number of young persons who from their ability, piety and good conduct were likely to prove fit persons in communicating a knowledge of Christianity to their countrymen" (Barnes 1932: 43, quoted in Kachru 2005: 35). (For more details on English in Sri Lanka, see Kandiah 1991; Law 1915; Mendis 1952.)

Independence

South Asia during this period included the following geographical units: India, Pakistan, Burma, Bhutan, Bangladesh, and Nepal. Indian independence in 1947 resulted in the division of India into the following political units: India, with its

Hindu majority, Pakistan, with its Muslim majority, and Bangladesh, which, because of its Muslim majority, was politically a part of Pakistan and was named East Pakistan. Tensions started after Pakistan tried to impose its language, Urdu, as the national language of East Pakistan, even though the majority of the East Pakistanis spoke Bengali. This was resented by the people of East Pakistan, and after a prolonged and bloody war for independence, East Pakistan won its independence from Pakistan in 1971, and thus was born Bangladesh.

Since Independence, the policy regarding the use of English differs in each of these countries. Unlike those living in Pakistan and Bangladesh, Indians in India have continuously used and promoted English, creating a distinctive variety of Indian English. For ease of discussion, I will now present the status of English in India and Pakistan since independence in 1947, followed by the role played by English in each of these countries.

English in India since 1947

English has an exalted position in India; it has permeated all spheres of life in this part of the subcontinent. Its uses are widespread in several domains, including education, social life, politics, music, and the film industry, and sometimes even religion (rituals and religious services are in Sanskrit, but to accommodate the younger generation, sometimes the explanations are given in English). There are more speakers of English in South Asia than in the USA or UK. Estimates of the number of speakers of English in India alone vary from 200 to 330 million (*Encyclopedia Britannica* (2002: 796) estimates 20 percent; Kachru (1986: 54) estimates 35 percent).

After independence in 1947, the question of what role English should play in the educational, political, economic, and cultural life of India was much debated. Driven by nationalism, several leaders called for the removal of English, as it was the language of the rulers, and demanded that Hindi be the national language of India. Hindi was opposed by the speakers of Bengali and South Indian languages (Dravidian languages), who viewed Hindi-speakers as having distinct advantages under this scheme over speakers of their own languages. Others leaders, viewing English as a resource language, saw its immense potential as a language of science and technology, and more so as a language that could act as a "bridge" or "link" language. In the newly drafted Constitution of India, English was given the place of Associate Official Language, until a time Hindi could become the sole national language of India.

During the British period, English had become the medium of instruction, following Macaulay's famous Minute of 1835 and Woods Despatch of 1864. Post-independence, several education commissions were appointed by the government of India and discussed the role of English in Indian education at great length (see Sridhar 1979). The passage of the Official Languages Act in 1967 made English co-equal with Hindi "for all official purposes of the union, for Parliament, and for communication between the union and the states" (Ferguson 1996: 31). As Ferguson points out, of the seven major uses of superposed languages in South Asia, English is a significant

participant in six; namely, as a *lingua franca*, in government, education, literature, influence, and development (p. 32).

Today, English continues to maintain its stronghold in India, even more than before.

English in Pakistan

With the partition in 1947, the fate of English in Pakistan has been described by Mahboob and Ahmar (2004) as "a roller coaster ride." "While it was initially maintained by the Pakistani leadership, it soon became a symbol of resentment amongst the religious parties, who felt that maintaining the status of English symbolized a new form of colonization" (p. 1003). English continued in Pakistan for more or less the same reasons it continued in India: (a) lack of teachers and materials in regional languages to be used for instructional purposes; (b) lack of any other politically neutral language that would be acceptable to all factions of the society; and (c) lack of political clout among religious parties (in the Indian context, the equivalence would be the nationalists who opposed English).

In 1977, when Zia-ul-Haq came to power through a military coup, he justified his actions by implementing rapid Islamization and Urduization, thereby appeasing the religious factions. Urdu was now introduced as the medium of instruction in all schools, except the English-medium schools patronized by the wealthy and politically powerful. By 1987, Zia's administration decided that getting rid of English may have been a mistake. Today, the government realizes the value of English in a global economy and is implementing policies to teach it at the primary level in all schools. This change in policy is supported by most of the people, who prefer learning English to other languages and see it as a means of economic development (Mahboob & Ahmar 2004: 1004). (For more details on English in Pakistan, see Rahman 1990; Baumgardner 1993; Mahboob & Ahmar 2004.)

The position of English is quite similar across almost all countries of South Asia. As Gargesh (2004) surmizes, "It appears that in the age of increasing industrialization, higher science and technical education is available almost solely via English. The educational system reveals a pyramid structure, with the mother tongues forming base, the regional standards occurring in the middle, and English emerging as the sole language on the top" (p. 996).

South Asian Englishes

The major features which contribute to the distinctiveness of South Asian English are varied and complex. First, as Kachru (2005) points out, English is an additional language in South Asia. It may be the first, second, or later language in the linguistic repertoire of a South Asian. Second, English is acquired in the typical sociolinguistic,

educational, and pragmatic contexts of South Asia. Usage depends on the way English has been taught and the functional domains in which it is used. Third, the English language in South Asia has always been taught in the manner of a classical language – that is, as a written language and not a spoken language. Most South Asians can write complex essays in English, but would be hesitant to speak English (p. 43).

Given these features of South Asian English education, there is a cline of bilingualism where one finds a whole range of speakers. At the top are the very proficient users of English (those whose English is like Received Pronunciation), in the middle are the speakers of an educated variety of South Asian English, and below are varieties of pidgin English, used mostly by uneducated speakers. Since most South Asians learn English from their South Asian teachers (rather than native-speakers of English), one finds a wide range of accents, from Punjabi English in the North to Kerala English in the South. This wide range does not affect intelligibility, however, as most South Asians share more or less similar cultural norms.

The languages of South Asia have affected South Asian Englishes in many ways. Since South Asian languages are mostly syllable-timed, it is not surprising that South Asian English has its own syllable-timed rhythm, which is perceived by native speakers of English as a sing-song rhythm. I will now give a few illustrations of the distinctive lexical, grammatical, and pragmatic features of South Asian English.

Lexical

South Asian English is rich and colorful, borrowing extensively from the regional languages spoken. There is no area of experience where words from the local languages have not come into the English language in South Asia. Words from the local languages express local sensibilities, and are perceived as enhancing the expressive resources of the English language. By the same token, English lexical items are appropriate for use in a range of domains and embedded in other South Asian languages. In politics, administration, law and order, legal and court systems, education, entertainment, mass media, food, raw goods and materials . . . everywhere, English words are preferred and used by all South Asians. A friend's son came to the United States in 1972, as a seven year old. He wanted to know the English equivalents for words like car, bus, school, pen, pencil, restaurant, park, etc. When told that these were English words, he declared that these were Kannada words and he only spoke Kannada. He was quite convinced that these words were from his Kannada language, and that we were kidding him! English words are so much part of the Indian languages, and are used in everyday speech all over South Asia, it is hard to explain to a seven-year-old child that these words are borrowed from English.

I conclude the section with a few examples from Pakistani English, as discussed by Baumgardner et al. (1993), quoted in Mahboob and Ahmar (2004: 1053):

I may be a devout believer of the *Purdah* ("segregation") system but . . .

Jewelers observe *hartal* ("strike") . . .

Why can't our *shaadis* (wedding) be something like, "OK bring in the *dulha* (groom) and the *dulhan* (bride), their close friends and relatives: dance, eat, have fun," and that's it?

Among Urdu speakers in India and Bangladesh, the above examples constitute normal mixing of indigenous cultural terms into English, and these sentences can be found in newspapers and heard in conversations all over India as well. (For a detailed discussion of the South Asian English lexicon, see Kachru 1965, 1983 for Indian English; Baumgardner 1993; Mahboob & Ahmar 2004; Rahman 1990 for Pakistani English; Kandiah 1991; Fernando 1976 for Sri Lankan English.)

Grammar

A few grammatical characteristics are shared by all South Asian users of English. For example:

Question formation: There is a tendency to form information questions without changing the position of the subject and auxiliary items: *What you would like to eat? Where you would like to go?*

Reduplication: This is a characteristic feature in many languages of South Asia and is used in both spoken and written educated varieties, and includes various classes of words, as in *hot hot coffee, small small things, to give crying crying* ("incessantly crying") (Kachru 2005: 49).

Verb aspect: The use of present progressive with stative verbs is quite common, as in *I am having an aunt in Chicago, I am loving it, I am having a cold* (Kachru 1983: 497, 510).

Pragmatics

Politeness in Asian society is a conventionalized phenomenon, which is part of the conversational style of South Asian Englishes. In the area of hospitality, it is not sincere enough to say, "Won't you have some more?" One has to say "Take only this much, just this much" (i.e., "just this much more") (Kachru 2003). Kinship terms such as "sister," "auntie," "uncle" are also used, as "Mr." or "Mrs." would be considered uppity (Sridhar 1991: 311). The use appears, for example, when requesting services, such as asking a friend's mother for a glass of water with the words "Auntie, could I have a glass of water, please?" In an earlier study on politeness strategies used by undergraduates in three selected colleges in the metropolitan city of Bangalore, I concluded that the non-native speakers have partial linguistic/communicative competence in English in particular domains, for they do not need English to perform a

great many speech functions for which the mother tongue is typically used (Sridhar 1991: 317).

We can see the English language being molded to meet the cultural demands of Indian thought in the following example: ". . . take seven steps with him, that will make him my ally" (Gauri Deshpande, cited in Gargesh 2004: 1007). The reference here is to a Hindu wedding, where the marriage is finalized when the bride and the groom take seven steps in front of the sacred fire.

Literary creativity among South Asian writers writing in English has been extensive, and is on the increase. There have, however, been discussions about whether Indian writers should write in "proper" British or American English, or in their own variety of Indian English. On this point, an often-quoted statement by the well-known philosopher and creative writer Raja Rao expresses the position clearly:

> We cannot write like the English. We should not. We cannot write only as Indians. We have grown to look at the large world around us as part of us. Our method of expression therefore has to be a dialect which will some day prove to be a distinctive and colorful as the Irish and the American. (Rao 1938, cited in Sridhar 1982: 294)

(For a more detailed discussion, see Kachru 1999; Sridhar 1982, 1992; Sridhar & Sridhar 1980, 1992.)

Conclusion

English occupies a very special position in the lives of South Asians. As has been often said, English is one of the languages South Asians speak in. As used in South Asia, English has been nativized to such an extent that it is not considered a foreign or alien language. Creative writing in English is at its peak, and, as discussed by Braj Kachru (2005), has undergone a process of decolonization. One should not be left with the impression, however, that the position of English has been accepted unequivocally by all in South Asia. Periodically, there is strong opposition to the continuation of English as the Associate Official Language. But in this age of globalization, realizing India's leadership position in the areas of science and technology (made possible by Indians' proficiency in the English language), other South Asian countries now introduce English language instruction in the grade schools, where earlier they introduced English at the junior high or high school level. English has certainly been instrumental in raising the economic profile of India. Arguments opposing English have almost become moot; English is clearly here to stay. And Raja Rao's statement has proved to be prophetic: more and more South Asian writers are emerging as great writers, winning coveted prizes such as the Pulitzer Prize (Jhumpa Lahiri) and the Booker Prize (Arundhati Roy). Novelist V. S. Naipaul, whose characters speak a distinct variety of Caribbean Indian English, was awarded the high honor of the Nobel Prize in Literature.

REFERENCES AND FURTHER READING

Baumgardner, R. J. (1993). *The English Language in Pakistan*. Karachi: Oxford University Press.

Baumgardner, R. J., Kennedy, A. E. H., & Shamim, F. (1993). The Urduization of English in Pakistan. In R. J. Baumgardner (ed.), *The English Language in Pakistan* (pp. 83–203). Karachi: Oxford University Press.

Ferguson, C. A. (1996). English in South Asia: imperialist legacy and regional asset. In R. J. Baumgardner (ed.), *South Asian English: Structure, Use, and Users* (pp. 29–39). Urbana: University of Illinois Press.

Fernando, C. (1976). English and Sinhala bilingualism in Sri Lanka. *Language in Society*, 6, 341–60.

Gargesh, R. (2004). South Asian Englishes. In B. Kortmann & E. W. Schneider (eds.), *A Handbook of Varieties of English, Vol. 1* (pp. 992–1002). Berlin: Mouton de Gruyter.

Kachru, B. B. (1965). The Indianness in Indian English. *Word*, 21 (3), 391–410.

Kachru, B. B. (1983). *The Indianization of English: The English Language in India*. New Delhi: Oxford University Press.

Kachru, B. B. (1986). *The Alchemy of English: The Spread, Functions and Models of Non-native Englishes*. Oxford: Pergamon Press.

Kachru, B. B. (1994). English in South Asia. In R. Burchfield (ed.), *The Cambridge History of the English Language* (pp. 497–553). Cambridge: Cambridge University Press.

Kachru, B. B. (2002). New Englishes. In R. Mesthrie (ed.), *Concise Encyclopedia of Sociolinguistics* (pp. 519–23). Oxford: Elsevier.

Kachru, B. B. (2005). *Asian Englishes: Beyond the Canon*. Hong Kong: Hong Kong University Press.

Kachru, Y. (1999). Culture, context, and writing. In E. Hinkel (ed.), *Culture in Second Language Teaching and Learning* (pp. 75–89). Cambridge: Cambridge University Press.

Kachru, Y. (2003). Conventions of politeness in plural societies. In R. Ahrens, D. Parker, K. Stiersorfer, & K.-K. Tam (eds.), *Anglophone Cultures in South East Asia: Appropriations, Continuities, Contexts* (pp. 39–53). Heidelberg: Universitatsverlag Winter.

Kachru, Y. & Nelson, C. (2006). *World Englishes in Asian Contexts*. Hong Kong: Hong Kong University Press.

Kandiah, T. (1991). Sociolinguistic perspectives in English in South Asia. In J. Cheshire (ed.), *English Around the World: Sociolinguistic Perspectives* (pp. 271–87). Cambridge: Cambridge University Press.

Kanungo, G. B. (1962). *The Language Controversy in Indian Education: Historical Study*. Chicago: Comparative Education Center, University of Chicago.

Law, N. N. (1915). *Promotion of Learning in India by Early European Settlers*. London: Longman.

Mahboob, A. & Ahmar, N. H. (2004). Pakistani English: phonology. In B. Kortmann & E. W. Schneider (eds.), *A Handbook of Varieties of English, Vol. 1* (pp. 1003–116). Berlin: Mouton de Gruyter.

Mendis, G. C. (1952). *Ceylon Under the British*. Colombo: Colombo Apothecarien.

Nurullah, S. & Naik, J. P. (1951). *A History of Education in India*. Bombay: Macmillan.

Rahman, T. (1990). *Pakistani English: The Linguistic Description of a Non-Native Variety of English*. Islamabad: National Institute of Pakistan Studies, Quaid-i-Azam University.

Shahed, F. H. (2001). English in Bangladesh: a study of urban educated public attitudes. PhD dissertation. Jawaharlal University, New Delhi.

Sridhar, K. K. (1979). *English in Indian Bilingualism*. New Delhi: Manohar.

Sridhar, K. K. (1991). Speech acts in an indigenized variety: sociocultural values and language variation. In J. Cheshire (ed.), *English Around the World: Sociolinguistic Perspectives* (pp. 308–18). Cambridge: Cambridge University Press.

Sridhar, K. K. & Sridhar, S. N. (1992). Bridging the paradigm gap: second language acquisition theory and indigenized varieties of English. In B. B. Kachru (ed.), *The Other Tongue: English Across Cultures* (pp. 91–107). Urbana: University of Illinois Press.

Sridhar, S. N. (1982). Non-native English literatures: context and relevance. In B. B. Kachru

(ed.), *The Other Tongue: English Across Cultures* (pp. 291–306). Urbana: University of Illinois Press.

Sridhar, S. N. (1992). The ecology of bilingual competence: language interaction in indigenized varieties of English. *World Englishes*, 11 (2/3), 141–50.

Sridhar, S. N. & Sridhar, K. K. (1980). The syntax and semantics of bilingual code-mixing. *Canadian Journal of Psychology*, 34 (4), 407–16.

40
English in the Caribbean

Donald Winford

The countries that make up the English-official (Anglophone) Caribbean are all former (in some cases current) colonies of England. They include most of the Leeward and Windward Islands, Jamaica, the Bahamas and other islands in the west, and two mainland nations, Belize and Guyana. In most of these, English, as the official language, coexists with a lexically related creole vernacular used as the popular everyday language. Such communities make up the so-called creole continua of the Caribbean. In Dominica and St. Lucia, English coexists with both an English-lexicon vernacular and a French-lexicon creole, while Belize boasts several ethnic languages.

English was introduced to the Caribbean colonies at various times between the seventeenth and nineteenth centuries – a fact that accounts in part for the differences in the contemporary varieties found in these communities. Among the colonies that were settled earliest were Bermuda (1607), St. Kitts (1624), Barbados (1627), and Antigua (1632). English later spread from Bermuda to the Bahamas (1648), to Jamaica (1655), the Cayman Islands and areas of Central America such as the Mosquito Shore, Belize, and the Bay Islands of Honduras. It was not until the eighteenth century that it spread to Windward islands like Dominica, Grenada, St. Lucia and St. Vincent (all previously French), and Trinidad (previously Spanish).

From the seventeenth to the nineteenth century, large numbers of West African slaves were brought to the Caribbean to serve as labor on the plantations that were the mainstay of the economy. The languages of these slaves included those of the New Kwa family (especially Gbe and Akan languages) as well as Kikongo, along with other minor languages. In addition, many indentured servants were brought from all parts of the British Isles to serve as extra labor. Hence the forms of English that were brought to the Caribbean differed significantly, and were restructured in different ways depending on the prevailing social context. In Barbados, for instance, the indentured servants brought from southwest England and Ireland worked alongside African slaves, whom they at first outnumbered. As a result, Barbadian Creole (Bajan) preserves many phonological and morphological features of these dialects. Such creoles

can be referred to as "intermediate" varieties. On the other hand, in places like Antigua and Jamaica, higher ratios of African slaves to Europeans, as well as differences in community settings and codes of interaction between the groups, all conspired to produce highly divergent forms of English-lexicon creoles, even though the English input to these colonies was much the same as in Barbados. These more divergent creoles are usually referred to as "basilectal" varieties.

As a result of the checkered history of its colonization, the Anglophone Caribbean is anything but a linguistically homogeneous area. In addition to the bi- or multilingualism of places like Belize, Dominica, and St. Lucia, the creole continuum situations differ significantly in the degree of linguistic distance between the creole and English. In one group (e.g., Antigua, Belize, Guyana, Jamaica, St. Kitts, and others), the basilect is quite different in its linguistic structure from Standard English, to the point of mutual unintelligibility. These situations are characterized by a wide spectrum of variation, with the local standard (or acrolect) at one end, the creole vernacular (or basilect) on the other, and various types of mixture (the mesolects) in the middle.

Linguistic Aspects of Basilectal Creole Varieties

The basilectal varieties of creole spoken in these communities are often referred to as more "radical" creoles because they show the strongest evidence of influence from West African languages in lexicon, phonology, and syntax. While the bulk of the lexicon of these creoles is of English origin, we find many words that are derived from West African languages. Some of these are shared across the Caribbean, e.g., *bakra* "white man," *nyam* "eat," *kalalu* "(soup made with) okra," *suku(n)ya* "witch, sorcerer," and *pupu* "excrement, defecate." Other words of West African origin tend to be associated more with particular communities, for example, Jamaican *ackee* "type of cashew tree and its fruit," *chaka-chaka* "disorder(ly)," and so on. In most cases too, the English varieties have borrowed words from indigenous languages, as well as other European languages such as Spanish and French, with which they were in contact. In the Central American varieties, for instance, we find words such as *bolero* (a dance), *fiesta* "party," and *komadre* "close female friend" from Spanish; and words like *dowri* "dugout canoe," *ishwili* "lizard" from Miskito (Holm 1983: 13–14). In addition, many English-origin words have changed somewhat in their semantics, a fact that can lead to confusion and miscommunication in attempts by creole speakers to learn and use Standard English. In Trinidad, for instance, *miserable* means "mischievous," while, in all varieties, *foot* includes the leg. Word formation strategies also differ from those of English. All of these creoles employ strategies of reduplication that create new words (e.g., *ripe-ripe* "very ripe") patterned after West African derivational processes. Various dictionaries have been compiled for Caribbean creoles, including Cassidy and LePage (1980) for Jamaica, Holm and Shilling (1982) for the Bahamas, and Winer (forthcoming) for Trinidad.

In phonology, the differences are greatest in the structure of the vowel systems and in prosody. In neither case, however, can we claim a general homogeneity for Caribbean English-lexicon creoles. A Bajan accent is as distinct from a Trinidadian or Jamaican accent, as Welsh and Scottish accents are from Received Pronunciation. With regard to prosody, most attention has been paid to the basilectal varieties of the creoles, especially Jamaican and Guyanese, which use quite different stress/pitch systems and patterns of intonation from those of the standard varieties. But even here, relatively little work has been done, and there is very little agreement as to the analysis of supra-segmental features such as pitch, stress, and intonation. For instance, scholars have described the Jamaican word-level prosodic system alternatively as a stress system, a tonal system, and a system that incorporates both stress and tone. Despite the differences in point of view, it is generally agreed that prosodic differences play a key role in distinguishing the meanings of segmentically identical reduplicated words. Thus, Gooden (2004) shows that words like *red-red* may mean "very red" or "reddish" depending on their prosodic patterns.

The basilectal varieties also employ a smaller inventory of vowels and vowel phoneme oppositions than those in Standard English (SE) because they display mergers of SE vowels. For example, /ɔ, ʊ, æ, ə/ all become /a/, as in /pat/ "pot," /dans/ "dance," /fat/ "fat," /afta/ "after." Vowel oppositions tend to be based primarily on length, thus /sit/ "sit" versus /siit/ "seat," /kat/ "cot" versus /kaat/ "caught," /pul/ "pull" versus /puul/ "pool," etc. English diphthongs are also realized quite differently; for instance, /ei/ and /əu/ become /ie/ and /uo/ respectively in Jamaican (cf. /giem/ "game," /guot/ "goat," but /ee/ and /oo/ in other basilects).

Among consonants, there is somewhat greater similarity between radical creoles and SE. For example, they share the same inventory of stops (/p, t, k/ and /b, d, g/), non-dental fricatives (/s, z, š, ž/), affricates (/č, ǰ/), and nasals (/m, n, ŋ/). But here again there are differences. Like other non-standard English-lexicon vernaculars, Caribbean English Creoles (CECs) lack the dental fricatives (the "th" sounds in *thin* and *that*), for which they substitute /t/ and /d/ respectively. In phonotactics (sound combinations), all these creoles lack final consonant clusters in "-t, -d," hence words like *mist* and *cold* are pronounced /mis/ and /kool/. Some basilectal varieties (e.g., Jamaican Creole) lack certain initial consonant clusters such as those consisting of /s/ plus a stop consonant. Hence words like *spin* and *skin* are pronounced /pin/ and /kin/. Some features are in fact survivals of earlier English pronunciations. For instance, in varieties like Jamaican, initial /b/ is often followed by a /w/ glide, so that *boy* and *boil* are pronounced /bway/ and /bwail/ respectively. In most if not all varieties, initial /k, g/ are followed by a /y/ glide, so that *cat* and *garden* become /kyat/ and /gyaadn/ respectively. We also find metathesis in words like *aks* "ask" and *huks* "husk." Those varieties of CEC most influenced by non-rhotic English dialects lack "r'" after vowels, for instance in words like *car*, *hard*, etc. Varieties more heavily influenced by rhotic dialects such as those of southwest England and Scotland preserve this "r."

Many of these aspects of CEC phonology (particularly those involving vowel articulation and prosody) often cause serious difficulty for speakers of English dialects who

try to communicate with creole speakers. Also, the phonologies of the creoles depart in different degrees from that of English, so that some varieties (e.g, Jamaican) pose a bigger problem for communication than others. Even varieties whose grammar is closer to English (e.g., Bajan) can pose such problems because of their very different phonology. Such differences from SE phonology also constitute a serious obstacle to the successful acquisition of literacy in the early education of creole speakers.

At the levels of morpho-syntax and syntax, the grammars of basilectal CECs differ in many respects from that of SE. Morpho-syntactic differences can be found in the copula system (structures in which the verb "to be" appears in SE). The equative copula is generally *(d)a*, and the locative copula *de*, while adjectival predicates require no copula since they have more verbal properties. The tense/aspect system is character-ized by an aspect-rich system of free pre-verbal markers, as illustrated in the following example sentences from Belize Creole.

(1) i   mi   gat   plees   op   ya   we   mi   an   hi   mi   liv.
    It   PAST have   place   up   here   where 1sg   and 3sg   PAST live.
    "There was a place up here where he and I lived."

(2) a   wã   giv   yu   wan   jook   wid   J.   an   M
    1sg FUT   give   2sg   DET   joke   with   J.   and M
    "I'll tell you a joke about J. and M."

(3) a   tel   ã   a   di   get   ool   nou
    1sg tell   3sg   1sg   PROG   get   old   now
    "I told her I'm getting old now."

(4) a   don   gat   evriting   redi,   inoo,   mis B.
    1sg COMPL have   everything   ready   y'know   miss B.
    "I already have everything ready, you know, Miss B."

The creoles also lack inflections on nouns, verbs, and adjectives. They mark plurality with the suffix *-dem* (di buk dem "the books"), and mark possession through juxtaposi-tion (*di man waif* "the man's wife"), respectively. In their pronominal systems, they display fewer contrasts of case and gender than SE. Thus, Jamaican Creole *im < him* may mean nominative "he, she, it," accusative "him, her, it," or possessive "his, her, its." Finally, in syntax, the creoles employ a wide variety of syntactic constructions that differ from those of SE, and in general have models in West African languages. Among these are directional serial verb constructions (e.g., *Jan ron go a maakit* "John ran to the market"), dative/benefactive serial verb constructions (e.g., *Jan kyari di pikni go a maakit* "John carried the child to the market"), and passivization strategies (e.g., *Di hous peent aredi* "The house has already been painted").

The following sample of Belize creole, rendered in an orthography based on English conventions, exemplifies some of these features.

A narrative in Belize Creole. Bermudian Landing, Belize, 1994
De mi have wa man da Landing whe de mi used to call ole John Arnold. I used to heng wid a eno. He used to retarded. But i does go and come. i never used to trouble nobody.

He no worry wid nobody. But I used to like de wid a fi hear how i discourse and talk and different a thing. But da man whe study high eno teacha. I say da that mussi trip a up to. Because da man whe talk big word. aha, talk big word. And you woulda see a got wa book eena i hand de you woulda say da man da wa business man because i have pen all eena i two pocket. Pen sa and book. He never do without book and always di write. All like how we de right ya now, he di write de di write. You no know whe i di write eeno sa. That's all you see a di write.

Linguistic Aspects of Intermediate Creole Varieties

In places such as the Bahamas, Barbados, and Trinidad, the creole vernaculars are much closer to the local standard, and might be referred to as "intermediate creoles." They are usually considered to be simply dialects of English, since they derive many of their linguistic features from earlier regional dialects of British English. In phonology, for example, Bajan is strongly rhotic due no doubt to stronger influence from southwest English dialects. This is also true of (especially urban) Guyanese creole, which was heavily influenced by Bajan. Trinidadian, which is in many ways an off-shoot of Bajan, is non-rhotic, however. The vowel systems are somewhat closer to that of SE, though their consonantal systems are closer to those of the basilects.

In their tense/aspect systems, these varieties preserve pre-verbal markers such as unstressed *does* (marking habituality) and *did* (relative past), as well as suffix *–ing* (progressive), all of which have close counterparts in British regional dialects. Their copula systems are more similar to that of English, though copula absence is the norm, except with nominal predicates. Like the basilects, they lack inflections on nouns, and with some exceptions, verbs. Their pronominal systems are closer to that of SE, displaying more distinctions of case and gender than the basilects. In syntax, they share only a few features with the basilectal varieties, such as passivization and (rarely) serial verb constructions. The following sample of Trinidadian Creole illustrates some of these features.

A narrative by Ralph Adams. Mayo Trinidad, 1970
A night I los' with Francis. Well I walk, I walk, I walk. I had twelve manicou (a wild animal) toting, you know. All I tell Francis, I say "Francis let us go home nah boy, let us go nah." Francis ain't want to go. Francis don't want to go. But is lost the man lost and I ain't know Francis lost. Eh eh! (Well) I stop by a fig (banana) tree – it had ripe fig on it . . . in the cocoa. Well I eat some ripe fig an' drop the skin right there. (Well) I had the cutlass in my hand . . . (well) you know, curiosity, I just chop the fig-tree, you know? He say, "Let us go." I say "right." Well we rev (circled), we rev, we come back right there. I say "Francis," I say "We ain't heading nowhere, you know, look we was right here just now." He say "No man!" I say "Look where I eat the ripe fig. Look where I cut the fig-tree." He say "Yes boy." I say "You know what it is, le' we go just so, on the right so." And we ain't even walk a . . . a good hundred yards, we meet pitch road. I say "You di(d) real lost, boy!"

Local Standard Varieties

As the sole official language, (Standard) English is used as the medium of communication in such areas as the state bureaucracy, the legal system, the mass media, education, and other areas normally associated with official languages. Hence it enjoys considerable prestige, and is the avenue to educational achievement and social advancement. Yet few West Indians learn it as a native language. In its written form, the official English of the Caribbean differs little from International Standard English – the non-localized variety characterized by a fixed set of grammatical and lexical features accepted by the public worldwide as a suitable model of usage. In its spoken form, however, Caribbean Standard English consists of a variety of localized varieties, characterized by combinations of their own peculiar lexical, phonological, and to some extent syntactic features. In the colonial era, the model for such spoken varieties was generally the speech of English expatriates, but since independence, the speech of highly educated and prestigious West Indians has increasingly become the new model for formal spoken usage. Hence these local varieties have acquired a certain degree of semi-autonomy or shared autonomy vis-à-vis British varieties. Work by Craig (1982) and others discusses some of the phonological and lexical features shared by the new local standard varieties, most of which are due to interference from the creole vernaculars. For example, Irvine (2004) discusses several creole features that characterize the phonology of the local form of Standard English in Jamaica, noting that these are widely used and accepted.

Also of interest is the work done by Allsopp and his associates in compiling the *Dictionary of Caribbean English Usage*, which has demonstrated that there are many lexical features shared by the local standard varieties. One of the aims of the dictionary was in fact to define a Standard Caribbean English as a variety in its own right, distinct from other forms of Standard English.

The Autonomy of Creole Varieties

In the Anglophone Caribbean, the question of the autonomy of the creole vernaculars has long been fraught with controversy, concerning both their linguistic structure and their socio-political status as national vernaculars. DeCamp (1971) was among the first to point to the problem of defining the boundaries of the language varieties in such situations, where there is a continuous spectrum of speech varieties ranging from the creole to the standard. Caribbean linguists, however, have argued that there are sound linguistic grounds for treating the more "radical" creole varieties as autonomous. A large part of the debate over the socio-political status of the creoles has focused on situations such as those in Belize, Guyana, and Jamaica, where the creole is quite distant from the standard. There is a growing trend, among both the

public and the political establishment, to view the creoles in these communities as languages distinct from English. For instance, Beckford-Wassink (1999:66) found that 90 percent of informants in a language attitude survey regarded Jamaican Creole as a distinct language, basing their judgments primarily on lexicon and accent.

In intermediate creole situations such as in the Bahamas, Barbados, and Trinidad, there is a greater tendency to see the creole vernaculars as deviant dialects of English rather than separate varieties. Even here, though, there is a trend toward tolerating the use of these varieties for purposes of teaching the standard. So far, however, support for this comes primarily from linguists or other academics, and is not generally matched by popular opinion.

Changing Attitudes to Creole

The uncertainty over what status and functions to assign to the creoles reflects an ambivalence in attitudes that has long characterized Caribbean communities. While overt recognition is withheld from the creoles, they are positively evaluated as vehicles of the culture and badges of local identity. There is therefore a continuing tension between "public" or "standard" attitudes that extol English while denigrating creole, and more "private" or covert attitudes that bear testimony to a sense of pride in creole. This tension is slowly being resolved – more so in some communities than in others – in favor of a more tolerant and even accepting view of creole and its place in Caribbean society. The changes in attitude have been due to several factors: the growing sense of nationalism in these communities since independence; the emergence of a substantial body of scholarship that demonstrates the validity of the creoles as languages in their own right; the growing tendency to use creole in literary works; and the readiness of the powers-that-be to allow use of creole in contexts such as education.

Creole in Literature

Two decades ago, Rickford and Traugott (1985) pointed out that "more and more writers have been using pidgins and creoles as a vehicle for the presentation of the cultures and rich communities in which these languages flourish." Since then, the use of creole in literature and other written media has expanded greatly. Well-known literary figures such as Naipaul and Lovelace in Trinidad, Louise Bennett in Jamaica and others have exploited the resources of the creoles to evoke the distinctively Caribbean voice of their characters. In addition, translation of other literature such as the Bible into creole has contributed to the lexical and stylistic elaboration of these languages. As Mühleisen (2005) points out, literature and creative writing in

creole have played an important role in the negotiation of creoles as "legitimate" varieties, not the least by contributing to the establishment of orthographic conventions.

Creole in Education

The continuing reappraisal of the place of creole in Caribbean culture is also having a significant impact on language policy and language planning in the Caribbean, particularly in the area of education. Governments have become more supportive of the idea of using creole as a medium of instruction in the schools, and indeed in public education as a whole. Both in Trinidad and Jamaica, for example, educational policy calls for maintaining English as the official language, while promoting the oral use of the creole at school in the early years of primary education. Eventually, such policies may be extended to include the use of creole as both the medium of instruction, and the language in which literacy is first taught, as is happening in bilingual creole situations such as that in the Dutch Antilles.

In order for these policies to work, language planners must address problems of status planning (code selection and the assignment of new functions to the vernaculars), corpus planning (codification and elaboration), and implementation of the new policy. Deciding which variety to codify and what orthography to use continues to pose the greatest problems. While orthographies have been proposed by linguists for varieties such as Jamaican and Belize Creole, they have not been generally accepted by the public. Both in the mass media and in literature, writers continue to use what one described as "chaka-chaka" (mixed up) spelling based on English. Resolution of the problem of the orthography will go a long way toward establishing the autonomy of the creoles.

Most scholars now see the language problems of Caribbean schools as only a part of the language problems facing the society at large. In many communities, there is a large proportion of the population who have little or no literacy skills, and therefore lie beyond the reach of the existing educational system. Hence, as Devonish (1986) points out, "a reform in language education policy cannot take place outside of a more general reform in the roles and functions of the various languages used within the society as a whole" (p. 119). Devonish's attempt to create a uniform variety of Guyanese creole to be codified for use in official functions has not been supported by authorities in that country. But there have been significant developments in other countries regarding the instrumentalization of creole for public purposes. In Jamaica, for instance, posters issued by government agencies are often written in creole. There has even been a proposal made by a government official to amend the Constitution so as to introduce language as a ground for protection against discrimination. It seems to be only a matter of time before at least some Caribbean English-lexicon creoles finally assert themselves as distinctive languages with their own history, and achieve the prestige and recognition they deserve.

REFERENCES AND FURTHER READING

Aceto, M. & Williams J. P. (eds.) (2003). *Contact Englishes of the Eastern Caribbean*. Amsterdam: John Benjamins.

Allsopp, R. (2003). *Dictionary of Caribbean English Usage*. Jamaica: University of the West Indies Press.

Beckford-Wassink, A. (1999). Historic low prestige and seeds of change: attitudes toward Jamaican Creole. *Language in Society*, 28, 57–92.

Bennett, L. (1966). *Jamaica Labrish: Jamaica Dialect Poems*. Kingston: Sangsters.

Blake, C. (2007). The right to linguistic non-discrimination and creole language situations: The case of Jamaica. *Journal of Pidgin and Creole Languages* 23, 1, 32–74.

Cassidy, F. (1961). *Jamaica Talk: Three Hundred Years of the English Language in Jamaica*. London: Macmillan.

Cassidy, F. G. & LePage, R. B. (1980). *Dictionary of Jamaican English*. Cambridge: Cambridge University Press.

Christie, P. (ed.) (1996). *Caribbean Language Issues, Old and New*. Jamaica: University of the West Indies Press.

Christie, P. (2003). *Language in Jamaica*. Kingston: Arawak Publishers.

Craig, D. (1976). Bidialectal education: creole and standard in the West Indies. *Linguistics*, 175, 93–134.

Craig, D. (1982). Toward a description of Caribbean English. In B. Kachru (ed.), *The Other Tongue: English Across Cultures* (pp. 198–209). Urbana: University of Illinois Press.

DeCamp, D. (1971). Toward a generative analysis of a post-creole continuum. In D. Hymes (ed.), *Pidginization and Creolization of Languages*. Cambridge: Cambridge University Press.

Devonish, H. (1986). *Language and Liberation: Creole Language Politics in the Caribbean*. London: Karia Press.

Devonish, H. (1998). On the existence of autonomous language varieties in "creole continuum situations." In P. Christie, B. Lalla, V. Pollard, & L. Carrington (eds.), *Studies in Caribbean Language II* (pp. 1–12). Trinidad: Society for Caribbean Linguistics.

Edwards, W. (1983). Code selection and code switching in Guyana. *Language in Society*, 12 (3), 295–311.

Glinton-Meicholas, P. (1994). *Talkin' Bahamian*. Nassau: Guanima Press.

Gooden, S. (2004). Prosodic contrast in Jamaican Creole reduplication. In I. Plag (ed.), *Phonology and Morphology of Creole Languages*. Linguistische Arbeiten, Vol. 478. Tübingen: Max Niemeyer.

Hackert, S. (2004). *Urban Bahamian Creole: System and Variation*. Varieties of English Around the World, G 32. Amsterdam: John Benjamins.

Holm, J. (ed.) (1983). *Central American English*. Varieties of English Around the World, T 2. Heidelberg: Julius Groos.

Holm, J. & Shilling, A. (1982). *Dictionary of Bahamian English*. Cold Spring, NY: Lexik House.

Irvine, A. (2004). A good command of the English language: phonological variation in the Jamaican acrolect. *Journal of Pidgin and Creole Languages*, 19 (1), 41–76.

LePage, R. B. & Tabouret-Keller, A. (1985). *Acts of Identity: Creole-Based Approaches to Language and Ethnicity*. Cambridge: Cambridge University Press.

Muehleisen, S. (2002). *Creole Discourse: Exploring Prestige Formation and Change Across Caribbean English-Lexicon Creoles*. Amsterdam: John Benjamins.

Mühleisen, S. (2005). Introduction: creole languages in creole literatures: status and standardization. *Journal of Pidgin and Creole Languages*, 20 (1), Special Issue edited by S. Mühleisen, 1–14.

Patrick, P. (1999). *Urban Jamaican Creole: Variation in the Mesolect*. Amsterdam: John Benjamins.

Pollard, V. (2000). *Dread Talk: The Language of Rastafari*. Barbados: Canoe Press; Montreal: McGill-Queen's University Press.

Rickford, J. (1987). *Dimensions of a Creole Continuum*. Stanford, CA: Stanford University Press.

Rickford, J. & Traugott, E. (1985). Symbol of powerlessness and degeneracy, or symbol of solidarity and truth? Paradoxical attitudes toward pidgins and creoles. In S. Greenbaum (ed.), *The English Language Today* (pp. 252–61). Oxford: Pergamon Press.

Roberts, P. A. (1988). *West Indians and Their Language*. Cambridge: Cambridge University Press.

Sand, A. (1999). *Linguistic Variation in Jamaica: A Corpus-Based Study of Radio and Newspaper Usage*. Tübingen: Narr.

Winer, L. (1993). *Trinidad and Tobago*. Varieties of English Around the World, T 6. Amsterdam: John Benjamins.

Winer, L. (forthcoming). *Dictionary of the English/Creole of Trinidad & Tobago*. Montreal/Kingston: McGill-Queens University Press.

Winford, D. (1993). *Predication in Caribbean English Creoles*. Amsterdam: John Benjamins.

41
English in Africa

Alamin M. Mazrui

Africa has the richest and most complex linguistic tapestry of any continent in the world. To this diversity were added the languages of European colonizers of Africa – English, French, Italian, Portuguese – with English showing the greatest promise of becoming a continental language. As early as the 1880s, the pioneer pan-Africanist, Edward W. Blyden, regarded the multiplicity of African languages in Africa as divisive and believed that this linguistic gulf could best be bridged by English partly because English itself was a product of a multicultural heritage, "made up of contributions by Celts, Danes, Normans, Saxons, Greeks, Romans . . . gathering to itself elements from the Ganges to the Atlantic" (Blyden 1994: 243–4). Over a century later, Blyden's vision of English in Africa is getting closer and closer to fulfillment.

Early Contacts

Africa's earliest contacts with the English language go back to the sixteenth century when sailors of British merchant companies traveled to West Africa to trade in ivory, slaves, and spices. At this stage, English seems to have been an important trade language. Though these initial encounters did not lead to local acquisition of the language, they may have stimulated the emergence of varieties of what came to be known as West African Pidgin English.

A more established presence of English in Africa started with settler communities of native speakers of different varieties of the language. These had three different origins. First, there were the people of African origin who were repatriated to Africa and settled in Freetown in the West African country of Sierra Leone, beginning from about 1787. These included emancipated slaves from England, British ex-soldiers in the American War of Independence who had settled in Nova Scotia (Canada), and the Maroons from Jamaica. Africans rescued by the British from slave ships en-route to America were also resettled in Sierra Leone. These repatriates eventually developed a

distinctive Krio culture and community, and after the establishment of Fourah Bay College that admitted students from the entire West African region, they became quite influential in the initial spread of English in the region. Their own English creole (Krio) also impacted on other varieties of English and English-based pidgins of West Africa.

Secondly, there was the establishment of the colony of Americo-Liberians. These were emancipated Blacks from the USA who were resettled in the newly created independent West African nation of Liberia from the 1820s, through the efforts and funds of the American Colonization Society. For a long time to come, Liberia remained the only African country which owed its English to America. Believing that "the English language is the enshrinement of those great charters of liberty which are essential elements of free governments and the main guarantees of personal liberty," Alexander Crummell, the pioneer pan-Africanist, regarded Americo-Liberians as a people with a divine mission to spread English to Africans on the continent (Crummell 1969: 25). In spite of Crummell's vision, however, Liberia's influence on the spread of English in Africa did not extend beyond its own borders.

Finally, colonies of native-speakers of English from England found their way to Southern Africa from the late eighteenth century in search of gold and diamonds, inspired by the vision of the British investor Cecil Rhodes. These followed Dutch-speaking settlers (Afrikaners) whose language evolved into what is today called Afrikaans. Rather than develop its own variety of English, as happened in Sierra Leone and Liberia, however, the English-speaking community in Southern Africa continued to aspire to England's Received Pronunciation as the standard norm in their schools and the media. Numerically more modest waves of English populations later settled in East Africa (Kenya).

The Era of British Colonialism

After the inception of formal European colonialism in Africa, the British linguistic ideology was in conformity with the paternalistic notion of the "dual mandate." The dual mandate advocated, in part, that the British had a duty to facilitate the "civilization" of Africans while, at the same time, safeguarding the integrity of their cultures and identities. In the linguistic realm, this meant providing the Africans access to the English language in such a regulated manner as not to undermine the development of indigenous tongues.

This linguistic dimension of the dual mandate came to find its most explicit expression in the 1925 colonial report of the Phelps-Stokes Commission. The report argued that while "natives" should not be denied the opportunity to acquire English, they have an inalienable right to their language. This was the linguistic philosophy that held sway in virtually all African countries colonized by the British until the end of World War II. In the words of Lord Lugard himself, the architect of the dual mandate policy, "the premature teaching of English . . . inevitably leads to utter disrespect for

British and native ideals alike and to a denationalized and disorganized population" (cited by Coleman 1958: 136–7).

Until about 1945, then, the situation in "Anglophone" Africa was one in which English as well as local African languages maintained a certain degree of complementarity in official institutions of the state. If the English language dominated the higher levels of colonial administration, the high courts, and the legislative council, it was African languages which prevailed in the lower administrative echelons, the lower and "native" courts, as well as in the armed forces. In education too the linguistic implications of the dual mandate came to prevail: the language of early primary education was often a local language; English was introduced later in the educational ladder.

In the period after World War II, a shift in British colonial policy with regard to language and education began to take place. As the national resistance to British colonial rule kept growing in this postwar period, and independence appeared imminent in a number of British-ruled African countries, the British became concerned about creating a new African élite. In the cultural domain, increase in the knowledge of the English language became a crucial step in that direction. Efforts to consolidate the position of English kept mounting, and by 1953 it had been made a compulsory subject in national examinations in elementary schools throughout Anglophone Africa. Indeed the only factor that seemed to deter the colonial education authorities from moving any faster in the establishment of English education was the lack of sufficient teachers of the language.

Ironically, British interest in spreading their language, especially in East Africa, found tremendous support in African nationalist demands for "more English." The colonial education office found itself pressured by African nationalists to move faster than it was prepared to do (because of the shortage of teachers) in the introduction of English. Already the emerging African élite were regarding English as a gateway to a new world of the independent, modern nation-state. Capitalizing on this nationalist mood, the colonial government continued to create conditions favorable for the promotion of English in education and in government business.

The Post-Colonial Period

Ironically, the end of colonialism generated not the decline of English in former British colonies, but its expansion and consolidation. African nations that are described as Anglophone include Botswana, Cameroon (bilingual with French), Gambia, Ghana, Kenya, Lesotho, Liberia, Malawi, Namibia, Nigeria, Seychelles, Sierra Leone, South Africa, Swaziland, Tanzania, Uganda, Zambia, and Zimbabwe. But the frontiers of the language have begun to expand beyond this traditionally Anglophone zone.

The term "Anglophone Africa" became even more appropriate in the post-colonial period. While it is true that Africans who can speak English fluently are still in the minority, the countries themselves betray a high degree of political dependence on

English. With the exception of Tanzania, which launched a Swahilization program in 1967, business in government offices, in legislatures and judiciaries in Anglophone Africa is primarily conducted in English. Not only is the fundamental law based on English principles, but the laws are expressed entirely in English. And in countries like Nigeria, Ghana, Zambia, Zimbabwe, and Uganda, all speeches addressed to the nation have to be given in English. This is apart from the educational system, almost all of which is predicated on the supremacy of English as a medium of instruction. Indeed, some African countries have introduced English at an earlier stage in the educational pyramid than the British themselves did.

The factors that have worked in favor of English in the post-colonial period are many and include the following. First is Africa's relatively weak linguistic nationalism. By linguistic nationalism we mean that version of nationalism that is concerned about the value of its own language, seeks to defend it against other languages, and encourages its use and enrichment. One of the factors underlying relative difference in linguistic nationalism may have to do with the distinction between the oral tradition and the written. The overwhelming majority of sub-Saharan African countries belonged to the oral tradition until the late nineteenth and twentieth centuries. There is no ancient written literature or sacred literature outside Ethiopia, North Africa, and the Islamized city-states of East and West Africa. Without a substantial written tradition, perhaps, linguistic nationalism is slow to emerge, although there are exceptions. As a result of the weak linguistic nationalism, Africans in Anglophone parts of the continent have not been sufficiently resentful of their massive linguistic dependency on English to check the spread of the language.

Then there has been the association of English and the Western cultural legacy at large with modernity. Many policy makers in Anglophone Africa have a tendency to assume that being Anglicized in language and culture improved the chances of "development." There is the assumption that English is necessary for modernization and economic transformation. The experiences of countries like Japan, Korea, and Malaysia, where indigenous languages play a large role in economic transaction and educational policies, have yet to attract the attention of African governments.

The consolidation of English in post-colonial Africa has also been aided by forces of ethnic nationalism. Nationalism usually involves a possessive attitude towards one's own culture and seeks to protect it against "external" encroachments. But, in the context of power politics of the African nation-state, the "out-groups" are often perceived to be not the non-African Other, but members of other African ethnic constituencies. Under the circumstances, the quest for a national language has often tended to favor English because giving the language of any other ethnic group some official status over the others is seen as potentially hegemonic.

The seeming ethnic neutrality of English has made it a popular medium of inter-ethnic communication. The majority of Africans in the lower classes communicate easily across the ethnic divide using multiple languages or an African *lingua franca*. But at the upper horizontal level of the educated élite, inter-ethnic communication is mediated primarily by the English language.

The growing space and frequency of inter-ethnic interaction among the African élite has often led to inter-ethnic marriages. From these unions there has emerged a new "tribe" of Afro-Saxons. These are, in Ali Mazrui's definition, Africans who speak English as a first language. "As the father and mother come from different linguistic groups, they resort to English as the language of the home. English thus becomes the mother tongue of their children, with a clear ascendancy over the indigenous languages of both the father and the mother" (Mazrui 1975: 11). It is conceivable that this English-speaking offspring of mixed ethnic unions will one day develop a consciousness of itself as a group independent of the ethnic affiliations of their parents.

English after Apartheid

The ethnic dynamics of the English language have a different manifestation altogether in the Republic of South Africa, partly because of the character of the country's white constituency. Until the 1990s, the great divide between Black and White in South Africa was indeed racial. But the great cultural divide between White and White was, in fact, linguistic. The White "tribes" of South Africa were the Afrikaans-speaking Afrikaners (of Dutch descent), on the one side, and English-speaking Europeans, on the other.

In time, however, this linguistic division between the White "tribes" of South Africa came to have its own impact on the Black population of the country. More and more Black South Africans felt that if they had to choose between English and Afrikaans, the former was of greater pan-African value since virtually all the surrounding African countries had English as the official language. The two Germanic languages had widely differing implications: Afrikaans was a language of racial claustrophobia; English was a language of pan-African communication. The Soweto riots of 1976, precipitated in part by the forced use of Afrikaans as a medium of education in African schools, were part of this linguistic dialectic.

With the end of political apartheid in South Africa, the English language has made the clearest gains. Although South Africa has declared eleven official languages (theoretically reducing English to one-eleventh of the official status), in reality the new policy only demotes Afrikaans, the historical rival to English in the country. English has continued to enjoy the allegiance of most Black people as the primary medium of official communication.

By a strange twist of destiny English has now also become the language of desegregation in South Africa. Set in the conservative, rural heartland of South Africa, the University of Orange Free State, for example, had always been a proudly Afrikaans and exclusively White institution. In the post-Apartheid period the university came under increasing pressure to be more racially integrated. It was not until the university began offering courses in English in 1993, however, that it was able to attract and increase its enrolment of Black students. Ironically, therefore, democratization in South Africa has accorded the imperial language, English, a new legitimacy as an

instrument for the reconfiguration of the racial landscape in South African education.

Developments after the Cold War

In the period after the Cold War several developments have contributed to the momentum of English expansion. First has been the emergence of the USA as the only super-power and the increasing Americanization of the face of globalization. As the single largest English-speaking country in terms of number of native speakers, and with its economic, political, and technological pre-eminence, the USA is expanding the frontiers of the English language at an unprecedented scale. But because of this American dominance in world affairs, the emergent global English may increasingly be assuming an American articulation. If American-derived English was once limited to the West African country of Liberia, it is fast gaining currency in many other African countries, especially among members of the younger generation.

Secondly, the post-Cold War period has witnessed rising competition within the NATO alliance, especially between the USA, on the one hand, and the European Union, on the other. Throughout the Cold War period, Francophonie – a movement constructed on the ideal of shared cultural experience through the French language – continued to hold sway in former French and Belgian colonies in Africa partly because of the lack of any serious challenge to France from fellow NATO allies in the stadium of African politics and economics. With the end of the Cold War, however, America has felt less constrained from being a player in the French domain of influence, in the process forging its own independent relationships with Francophone countries. New economic possibilities fostered by this new relationship with the USA are now increasing the demand for English in the Francophone African region.

Then there has been the post-Cold War decline of state-nationalism, reducing ideological competition between capitalism and socialism that was once common in African politics. Under the banner of *Ujamaa* (Socialism) and *Kujitegemea* (Self-Reliance), for example, Tanzania launched an ambitious program to recenter its *lingua franca*, Swahili, in education and in the affairs of the state. English was losing to Swahili, and Tanzania became a beacon of hope for those African nationalists eager to see the end of the colonial linguistic legacy. More recently, however, with mounting pressure from the IMF and the World Bank to liberalize the economy, and Tanzania's eventual abandonment of the socialist system, English is rapidly getting rehabilitated. A number of private elementary schools, for example, have now been permitted to operate with English as the medium of instruction.

There have been other post-Cold War developments, of course, that have the potential of slowing down the linguistic anglicization of Africa. These include the rise of dissident Islam which has led to the Arabization efforts in education in the Sudan, and the tide of political pluralism which has given fresh impetus to ethnic-

based languages in the mass media. But these counter-dynamics are so far too modest to really challenge the march of English on the continent.

Between African Languages and African Englishes?

English is also becoming Africanized linguistically in the mill of African social experiences. In the process, there have emerged regional and, in some cases, national varieties of the language, even though there has been no official recognition of these linguistic formations. West Africa may have gone farther in the domestication of the English language than East Africa and Southern Africa — especially in the form of Pidgin English, which is showing evidence of creolization, becoming a native tongue to a number of Nigerians.

Africans have sometimes been nationalistic about these emerging African Englishes, especially when they sense that White native-speakers of the language are monopolistic about setting its standards of propriety and correctness. When a certain Englishman complained about the degeneration of English in Kenya, for example, back came the reply from a certain Meghani, challenging the right of "a tiny English population" to "decide on the form and style of a universal language." Meghani then concluded that "Strictly speaking, English cannot be called English at all, since it is a universal language belonging to all" (cited by Mazrui 2004: 74–5). Meghani thus sought legitimacy for particularistic varieties of English by appealing to its universality.

These developments in the position and character of English in Africa have given rise to two contending schools of thought. The first advocates a change of balance between English and African languages in favor of the latter, a policy shift that would move African languages from the margins to the center of African life. The shift, it is presumed, will be crucial not only for African liberation from Western hegemonic control but also for African renewal in the cultural and intellectual domains. Led by one of the giants of African literature, Ngugi wa Thiong'o (1986), this school insists, for example, that to be African, literature must be composed in African languages. Literature written in English by Africans can at best be described as Afro-Saxon literature.

The second school of thought is the one that seeks to come to terms with English as part of the post-colonial African reality, appropriate it, reconfigure it materially to acquire an African identity and transform it to create a counter- (i.e., anti-imperialist) discourse. In the words of Chinua Achebe, another giant in African literature, the African writer "should aim at fashioning out an English which is at once universal and able to carry his own experiences . . . But it will have to be a new English, still in full communion with its ancestral home but altered to suit its new African surroundings" (Achebe 1965: 29–30). For Achebe and several other writers, Africa cannot extricate itself from the heritage of the English language.

In a poem on the meaning of Africa, Davidson Nicol once defined Africa in the following manner:

> You are not a country, Africa
> You are a concept
> Fashioned in our minds, each to each,
> To hide our separate fears
> To dream our separate dreams
> (Nicol 1968: 59)

What some African writers – like Saro-Wiwa (1992) and Senghor (1975) – have suggested is that the English language was an indispensable stimulus to the very birth of that concept and consciousness of Africa, painful as the birth process itself was. Even as the struggle continues to redefine Africa's linguistic destiny, English therefore continues to exercise its formidable hold on the African imagination, for better or for worse.

References and Further Reading

Achebe, C. (1965). English and the African writer. *Transition* (Kampala), 4 (18), 26–30.

Blyden, E. (1994 [1888]). *Christianity, Islam and the Negro Race*. Baltimore: Black Classic Press.

Coleman, J. S. (1958). *Nigeria: Background to Nationalism*. Berkeley: University of California Press.

Crummell, A. (1969). *Future of Africa*. New York: Negro Universities Press.

Mazrui, A. (2004). *English in Africa After the Cold War*. Clevedon: Multilingual Matters.

Mazrui, A. A. (1975). *The Political Sociology of the English Language: An African Perspective*. The Hague: Mouton.

Mazrui, A. A. & Mazrui, A. (1998). *The Power of Babel: Language and Governance in the African Experience*. Chicago: University of Chicago Press.

Ngugi wa Thiong'o (1986). *Decolonizing the Mind: The Politics of Language in African Literature*. London: Heinemann.

Nicol, D. A. (1968). The continent that lies within us. In A. J. Shelton (ed.), *The African Assertion: A Critical Anthology of African Literature* (pp. 55–9). New York: Odyssey Press.

Saro-Wiwa, K. (1992). The language of African literature: a writer's testimony. *Research in African Literatures*, 23 (1), 153–7.

Senghor, L. S. (1975). The essence of language: English and French. *Culture* 2 (2), 75–98.

Shmied, J. (1991). *English in Africa: An Introduction*. London: Longman.

Part VII
Literary Languages

Introduction

Literature is, among many other things, a record of language use at a moment in history. As the previous parts of this collection have shown, "language in history" involves not only linguistic history but also language as part of political, cultural, economic, and even scientific history. As literary criticism in recent decades has concerned itself with the cultural functions of literature, so does this part of the book look to literature as a cultural agent, with an individual writer's work representing one language user's struggle to press the language into service and address a perceived need.

The first three essays take up what are considered foundational English works and writers through three historical periods: the Old English tradition of *Beowulf*, Chaucer's Middle English literary development, and the Early Modern English rhetoric of Shakespeare. As all three essays demonstrate, each part of the quintessentially English literary tradition is in fact remarkably multivalent. The Anglo-Saxon poetic tradition shares its prosodic roots with other languages of the Germanic family (see ENGLISH AS A GERMANIC LANGUAGE), while also adopting Christian themes and Latin poetic devices. Chaucer's style, lauded by later English writers as "ennobling" their language, develops from the classical translation exercises of his early rhetorical education as well as from exposure to the new French and Italian literary forms encountered during travels required by his profession. And Shakespeare, by writing dramatic characters who respond to the humanists' renewed interest in Classical Latin, helps establish an English poetic tradition in many registers (see also VARIETIES OF EARLY MODERN ENGLISH), in effect codifying a language of Western self-consciousness we still recognize and respond to.

The essays on Jane Austen and William Faulkner stress those writers' interest in the phenomenon of experiencing language in print, reflecting ideologies of reading in their respective times (see EARLY MODERN ENGLISH PRINT CULTURE). Austen, located at a critical moment in the development of the very idea of the novel, engages the changing norms of eighteenth- and nineteenth-century print culture through her narration of scenes of reading, in essence teaching her audience how correctly to read her works. Faulkner also foregrounds scenes of reading, writing, and interpretation, but his aim is to illustrate the fragmentary dislocation created by language, employing an array of typographic devices to disorient the reader.

We find in the work of Joyce, Rushdie, and Morrison the effects of modern language contact, migration, and innovation. Joyce rejects the colonial English of Ireland (see ENGLISH IN IRELAND) as a stepping stone to a larger rejection of the universalizing ideals of such programs as BASIC English, which was an attempt to forge a *lingua franca* by creating a stripped down, functional English for global use. In his essay, Laurent Milesi follows Joyce's linguistic experiments in *Finnegans Wake*, demonstrating that nineteenth-century advances in comparative historical linguistics helped Joyce forge not a functional universal language, but an abundant and prolific

mythopoetic language. Rushdie is also a post-colonial writer, putting in the mouths of characters and narrators alike an Indian English replete with dual-language compounds and reduplications. But as Tabish Khair points out, Rushdie's language is not a record of actual Indian English as spoken "in the streets," but rather functions as an artifice of the post-colonial relationship between English and Indian languages (see also SOUTH ASIAN ENGLISH). Toni Morrison, in contrast, attempts overtly to capture and celebrate in her prose the language of African Americans (see MIGRATION AND MOTIVATION IN THE DEVELOPMENT OF AFRICAN AMERICAN VERNACULAR ENGLISH). Justine Tally contextualizes Morrison's project historically by tracing her connections to the poststructural theories that have dominated discussions of language in Morrison's time.

The authors and works discussed here represent only a handful of those that might have been chosen – these essays should therefore not be read as arguing for a canon of the eight writers most important to HEL. Instead, they exemplify the many kinds of literary analyses that can be performed within the framework of HEL. As both producers and products of their culture, the authors and works discussed are important as examples of language use, in every possible sense of that phrase.

Michael Matto

42
The Anglo-Saxon
Poetic Tradition

Fred C. Robinson

While on his mission to convert pagan Germanic tribes on the Continent, the Anglo-Saxon Bishop Boniface wrote home to his fellow Englishmen imploring them to pray for the conversion of the Germanic pagans, adding, "Take pity upon them; for they themselves are saying, 'We are of one blood and one bone with you'" (Emerton 1976: 75). The Germanic pagans' awareness of their common ancestry with the Anglo-Saxons was shared by the English themselves, who from the time of Bede and Aldhelm (who identifies himself as "nourished in the cradles of a Germanic people") (Lapidge & Herren 1979: 45) through Alcuin and as late as Wulfstan in the eleventh century constantly acknowledged their Germanic derivation. Individual Germanic groups' awareness of their common ancestry finds expression as early as Tacitus, who says, "The Treviri and Nervii even take pride in the German [i.e., Germanic] descent to which they lay claim. Such a glorious origin, they feel, should prevent their being thought to resemble the unwarlike Gauls" (Mattingly 1970: 125). In Old English (OE) literature this sense of intertribal kinship among Germanic peoples is most clearly expressed, perhaps, in the poem about the wandering *scop* (i.e., minstrel) named Widsith, whose "interest in the Germanic heroic age was that of an antiquary and a historian" (Malone 1962: 112), although this sense of kinship is equally clear in *Beowulf* and other OE poems.

The cultural homogeneity of the Germanic peoples is nowhere more apparent than in the form and style of their poetry. If one compares passages from *Beowulf*, the Old High German *Hildebrandslied*, and the Old Saxon *Heliand*, one immediately recognizes that the three poems not only use the same metrical system but also share the same poetic diction and syntax and even the same poetic formulae. (A glance at the Old Icelandic poetic corpus will confirm the presence of a pan-Germanic heritage here too, although the chronologically later Scandinavian poets had begun to evolve newer metrical forms as well.) In view of the close similarity of poetic language revealed in the common formulae, it is not surprising that some scholars have come to believe that the various Germanic languages were in fact mutually intelligible dialects (Moulton 1988).

By way of example, the poetic formula for expressing the idea "to kill someone" in Germanic verse was a periphrasis with the literal meaning "to become as a slayer to someone." In *Beowulf* more than once it is said of a character that he

[him] <u>tō banan wurde</u> "became as a slayer [to him]"

In Old Icelandic the same idea is often expressed identically:

[honum] <u>at bana verða</u>

Notice in the following two verses from, respectively, the Old High German *Hildebrandslied* and the Old Saxon *Heliand* the same expression:

eddo ih imto <u>ti banin werdan</u>
Than hogda he im <u>te banon uuerðan</u>

Not only do these verses all follow the same metrical type, but they are all used exclusively in off-verses (that is the second of two alliterating half-lines), a remarkable example of common practice persisting in diverging Germanic languages. Again, the OE *Andreas* and Old Saxon *Heliand* express the idea "He commanded me to go on this journey" in notably similar ways:

þā hēt hē mē on þysne sīð faran.
Nu hiet he me an thesan sīð faran.

A common way of expressing the idea that news of some event has spread was to say that "seafarers have said that . . ." Note the two following lines, the first from *Beowulf*, the second from the Old High German *Hildebrandslied*:

Ðonne sægdon þæt   sǣlīþende
dat sagetun mī   sęolīdante

From this kind of evidence it becomes clear that the Old English, Old Saxon, Old High German, and Old Icelandic poets were not only adhering to a common metrical form but were also drawing on the same Germanic thesaurus of poetic formulae. In describing the Anglo-Saxon poetic tradition, then, we are in fact describing the Old Germanic poetic tradition.

The Germanic metrical system is found in its most perfect form in the OE *Beowulf*. Each line of verse falls into two half-lines, each of which contains two accented syllables normally long in quantity accompanied by two or more unaccented syllables. The two half-lines are bound together by alliteration. Either or both of the accented syllables in the first half-line must alliterate with the first accented syllable in the second half-line. The second accented syllable in the second half-line must not alliterate.

```
 /        /          /    /
Brūc ðisses bēages    Bēowulf lēofa (1216)
 /   /              /  /
īren ǣrgōd þæt    ðæs āhlǣcan (989)
   /   /    \          /        /
forbarn brōdenmǣl;    wæs þæt blōd tō þæs hāt (1616)
```

The second of these lines illustrates vowel alliteration, in which any vowel alliterates with any other vowel. The first half-line of the third example displays in its final syllable secondary stress. Secondary stress plays a part in certain types of verse. The variety in the patterning of stressed and unstressed syllables in these lines and the fact that unaccented syllables may number anywhere from two to five or six may seem to suggest that as long as there are at least four syllables in a verse the accented and unaccented syllables may be arranged in any given order. This is not the case. Strict rules govern the placement of syllables. There are five different patterns of accented and unaccented syllables that are permitted, and deviation from these patterns renders any sequence of words unmetrical. It will not be necessary to catalogue each of the five types with their manifold variations, but consideration of one or two examples may be useful. The first type (called "type A") is basically two accented syllables, each followed by an unaccented syllable:

```
 /      /
gār tō gūþe
```

This would seem to be simply trochaic meter, but in fact A-lines are more flexible than that. It is permissible to increase the number of unaccented syllables following the first accented syllable, thus introducing considerable variety in the forms this verse-type can take:

```
 /       /           /        /
rīce æfter ōðrum    brūc þenden þū mōte
```

Following the first accented syllable as many as five unaccented syllables are permissible. But one and only one unaccented syllable is permitted after the second accented syllable.

Another verse-type (called "C") has two accented syllables together in the middle of the verse with unaccented syllables at the beginning and end of the verse:

```
      /   /
fram cnēomāgum
```

Variety within this verse-type is attained once more by increasing the number of unaccented syllables at the beginning of the verse; at the end of the verse, however, no more than one unaccented syllable is permitted:

$$\overset{/}{\text{ic eom}} \overset{/}{\text{fr\bar{o}d}} \text{f\bar{e}ores} \qquad\qquad \overset{/}{\text{þonne hit \bar{æ}nig}} \overset{/}{\text{m\bar{æð}}} \text{w\bar{æ}re}$$

It is important to note that the OE verse patterns are a selection of *natural speech patterns*. They involve no distortion of normal pronunciation as do the meters adopted in English after the OE period. Thus to make Shakespeare's line

    Absent thee from felicity a while

a perfect iambic pentameter, a little more than normal accent must fall on *from* and the *-y* of *felicity*. In OE the verses are accented as they would be in normal speech. The metrical status of these verse-types comes simply from the fact that from the multitude of possible speech patterns in OE they and they alone constitute verse. It has been suggested that C-verses, for example, preserve "a rhythm of daily occurrence in our speech (e.g., 'I can't stand him') which has been allowed no *metrical* recognition for centuries" (Lewis 1939: 123). (See HISTORY OF ENGLISH PROSODY.)

Besides its metrical form OE verse is marked by a distinctive poetic vocabulary. Many words occur frequently in verse and never in prose. (Conversely there is a sizable prose vocabulary – words that occur exclusively in prose texts.) Some words have one meaning when they occur in poetry and another meaning when in prose. Thus *swǣtan* means "bleed" in poetry but "sweat" in prose (see A HISTORY OF THE ENGLISH LEXICON).

The poetic vocabulary contains a large number of compounds. Partly this is because the stress patterns in many verse-types favor the sequences of stressed or half-stressed syllables that are peculiar to compounds. But the poets also seem to regard compounding as an inherently poetic manner of expression. Just as Shakespeare occasionally uses compounds in striking ways, as when he has King Lear describe bolts of lightning as "vaunt-couriers of oak-cleaving thunderbolts," the OE poets constantly use compounds to create the stately, emphatic cadence of their verse and to evoke specific moods ranging from martial vigor to melancholy. Typical poetic compounds are *bealocwealm* "painful death," *brēostcearu* "heart's grief," *geōmorfrōd* "wise through sadness," *sceadugenga* "walker in darkness," *sigedryhten* "lord of victory." Some compounds have a metaphorical component, as in *brimhengest* "stallion of the sea" (i.e., a ship), *hildelēoma* "battle-lightning" (i.e., a sword), *hildescūr* "rain-shower of battle" (i.e., a volley of arrows), *merehrægl* "garment of the sea" (i.e., a sail), *sāwolhūs* "house of the soul" (i.e., the human body). These metaphorical compounds are called *kennings*. Kennings can also take the form of a genitive phrase: *bānhūses weard* "ruler of the house of bone" (i.e., reason, intellect,) *brēosta hord* "bosom's treasure-hoard" (i.e., the soul), *swegles tapor* "heaven's taper" (i.e., the sun).

It has been noted since the beginning of Anglo-Saxon studies that poetic words tend to fall into fixed patterns that recur with some frequency in various poems. For example:

> Elene maþelode   him on ondsware
> Hrōðgār maþelode him on ondsware
> "Elene/Hrothgar spoke in answer to him"

Often there is some variation among these fixed patterns of words, and yet it remains clear that all occurrences are related: in *Beowulf*, for example, we find *wēox under wolcnum* and *wōd under wolcnum* while other poems have *wēox þā under wolcnum*, *wǣre under wolcnum*, *wrīdaþ under wolcnum*, and so on. These fixed expressions or formulae are, as was pointed out earlier, shared in common by various Germanic languages. Formulae constitute arrangements of words in metrical units that provide a convenient store of metered phrases available for use by any poet versifying in OE (or in other Germanic languages). Their frequent recurrence throughout Germanic poetry is one of the things that make poetic language different from the language of prose. Fifty years ago it was proposed that the presence of formulae in OE poetry proved that this body of verse was all orally composed since "oral poetry . . . is composed entirely of formulas, . . . while lettered poetry is never formulaic" (Magoun 1953: 446), and it was further suggested that the formula holds the key to understanding how OE verse is constructed and how we should read it. Work on this subject in the intervening years has shown these assumptions to be somewhat simplistic, and while the importance of formulae as a component of OE poetic style is acknowledged, far-reaching conclusions about their implications as to the origin and nature of OE verse have been widely rejected (Benson 1966; Acker 1998).

In deploying their poetic vocabulary, poets often made artful use of repetition and apposition. Repetition could be used anaphorically, as in the *Wanderer* poet's expression of the *ubi sunt* theme:

> Hwǣr cwōm mearg? Hwǣr cwōm mago? Hwǣr cwōm māþþumgifa?
>
> Hwǣr cwōm symbla gesetu? Hwǣr sindon seledrēamas? (92–3)
> "Whither has gone the stallion? Whither has gone the kinsman? Whither has gone
> the bestower of treasure?
> Where are the banquet-seats? Where are the joys of the hall?"

or to create a refrain, as in the *Dēor* poet's *þæs oferēode; þisses swā mæg* (7) "It [i.e., past misfortune] passed away as regards that, so can it as regards this [present misfortune]." More subtly, the *Beowulf* poet uses echoing repetition to mark the arrival of the hero's monstrous adversaries at the beginning of his years of prowess and at their end:

>   oð ðæt ān ongan
> fyrene fremman (100b-101a)
> ". . . until a certain one began to commit crimes"
>   oð ðæt ān ongan
>   . . .   draca rīcsian (2210b-11)
> ". . . until a certain one, a dragon, began
> to tyrannize"

Apposition is pervasive in OE poetry. In part this could be because the metrical system required so many heavily accented syllables within a short space. Instead of saying in *Beowulf* 4–5, "Scyld often terrorized his numerous enemies," the poet of *Beowulf* therefore says, "Scyld, the son of Scef, often terrorized throngs of his foes, multitudes of enemies, seized their royal seats." But if the device was born of metrical exigency, the poets soon made it a major expressive device, using it skillfully to build from an accumulation of details a graphic scene or to suggest syntactically the processes of ruminative thought or of mournful reminiscence. Modern scholars have given the Germanic poets' use of apposition the technical term *variation*, which aptly suggests the poets' use of the device to present a scene or an action or an idea in different successive forms of expression. This in turn gives to Germanic poetry its characteristic narrative mode, a poetry that proceeds not by direct predication (as do most narrative traditions) but by progressive statements and restatements.

Most variations appose nouns with nouns. Thus the Danish shore-guard is made to use nominal variation in a way that reflects his respect for his king:

>   Ic þæs <u>wine Deniga</u>
> <u>frēan Scildinga</u>,   frīnan wille,
> <u>bēaga bryttan</u>,   swā þū bēna eart,
> <u>þēoden mǣrne</u>   ymb þīnne sīð (350b–53)
> "I shall ask the lord of the Danes, the master
> of the Scyldings, the bestower of treasure,
> our famous king about your project, since
> you have requested it." [The components
> of variations are underlined here and below.]

Adjective variation depicts a grieving father's perpetual sadness:

> Swā <u>giōmormōd</u>   giohðo mǣnde
> ān æfter eallum,   <u>unblīðe</u> hwearf
> dæges ond nihtes   oððæt dēaðes wylm
> hrān æt heortan. (2267–70a)
> "Thus sad at heart, joyless, he lamented
> his sorrow alone after them all, roamed
> day and night until surging death touched
> at his heart"

Verbal variation occurs, the second element of the variation usually adding a new detail to the action expressed in the first element:

>   fēond <u>treddode</u>,
> <u>ēode</u> yrremōd (725b–26a)
> "the foe trod, advanced in angry mood"
> Hwīlum heaþorōfe   <u>hlēopan</u> lēton

<u>on geflit faran</u>   fealwe mēaras (864–5)
"At times the famous warriors let their
tawny horses gallop, run in competition"
                    Hī sīð <u>drugon</u>
<u>elne geēodon</u>   (1966b–67a)
"They went their way, pressed on
eagerly"

We even find variation of entire clauses:

                    metod hīe ne cūþon,
dæda dēmend   <u>ne wiston hīe dryten god</u> (180b–81)
"they did not know the Lord, the judge
of deeds, they did not know the Lord God"
<u>Līxte se lēoma,</u>   <u>lēoht inne stōd</u> (1570)
"A radiance shone forth, light shone
within"
<u>se yldesta</u>   <u>andswarode,</u>
<u>werodes wīsa</u>   <u>wordhord onlēac</u> (259–60)
"the leader answered, the chief of the
army spoke"

It is little wonder that variation has been described as "the very soul of the Old English poetic style" (Klaeber 1905–6: 237).

Variation is the most prominent syntactical device in OE poetry, but it is by no means the only one. Intricate and pervasive constraints on word-order in verse (as contrasted with prose) constitute a distinctive "prosodical syntax," which has been shown convincingly to be the working principle of OE verse, a principle that subsumes and organizes the formulaic units, which earlier scholars had thought were the key element in the production of OE verse (Momma 1997). The massive thirty-thousand-line corpus of OE poetry embodies overlapping, interactive metrical, syntactic, lexical systems, and these in turn mirror and interact with larger literary elements such as structure and narrative method (Mitchell & Robinson 1998: 18–31).

Prosodical syntax, poetic diction, traditional formulas, compounds and kennings – all organized under a single complex metrical system – would seem to generate a poetic corpus of monolithic sameness in which the various individual poems all speak in one unvarying voice no matter how diverse their subject matter and styles. But this is not the case. Just as Alexander Pope's heroic couplets have a timbre quite different from that heard in John Dryden's heroic couplets and just as Shakespeare's sonnets and those of John Milton project totally different speaking voices, so too OE poems differ in tone and style one from the other. Moreover, Anglo-Saxon poets contrived to introduce original stylistic embellishments into the traditional poetic form, even while retaining the essential features of that form. By adding an extra metrical

foot to the normal Germanic half-line, poets produced what are called hypermetric verses. These almost always appear in groups or clusters in a poem and must have produced an arresting shift in the poem's metrical movement. Thus when the *Beowulf* poet depicts Queen Wealhtheow entering the royal hall, he marks her entrance with a shift from normal to hypermetric lines:

> . . . glēomannes gyd.   Gamen eft āstāh,
> beorhtode bencswēg,   byrelas sealdon
> wīn of wunderfatum.   þā cwōm Wealhþēow forð
> gān under gyldnum bēage   þǣr þā gōdan twēgen
> sǣton suhtergefæderan;   þā gȳt wæs hiera sib ætgædere, . . . (1160–4)
> ". . . the minstrel's song. Revelry started up again,
> conversation sparkled through the hall, cup-bearers
> poured wine from handsome chalices. Then Wealhtheow
> with her golden crown strode forth, proceeding to
> where the two good kinsmen sat; as yet there was still
> peace between them . . ."

Other poets introduced single half-lines or otherwise shortened verses. The poet of *Wulf and Eadwacer* uses the single half-line *ungelīc is ūs* "it is different for us" as a refrain segmenting his narrative, and the poet of *Deor* does the same thing with his recurring mantra *þæs oferēode; þisses swā mæg*. The single most dramatic verse in *Wulf and Eadwacer* is the metrically shortened *Wulf, mīn Wulf!* and the poem closes with one lone half-line *uncer giedd geador* "our song together." The refrains in *Wulf and Eadwacer* and *Deor* mark off stanzaic units in those poems, while in the poem *Precepts* ten stanzaic units are marked by introductory phrases such as *Ðriddan sȳþe* "A third time," *Feorþan sīð* "A fourth time," *Fiftan sīþe* "A fifth time." In the poem *Instructions for Christians* (Rosier 1966) stanzas are marked off by capital letters in the unique manuscript.

Another formal innovation is macaronic verse. While maintaining the traditional Germanic metrical patterns, the poets of *Aldhelm*, *The Phoenix*, and *The Rewards of Piety* (Robinson 1994: 180–95) all complicate the traditional OE diction by introducing Latin verses alternating with the vernacular. Equally startling is the imposition of an intricate rhyme-scheme on top of the traditional metrical system in *The Rhyming Poem* and here and there in other poems. Again, poets sometimes link successive long-lines by having the final accented syllable of one line alliterate with the alliterative stave of the following line, as in *Exodus* 47b–49:

> Dæg wæs <u>m</u>ǣre
> ofer <u>m</u>iddangeard   þā se <u>m</u>engeo fōr
> swā þæs <u>f</u>æsten drēah   <u>f</u>ela mīssera
> "It was a day famed throughout the
> world when the multitude set out,
> having endured captivity many a year"

This device is used forty times in the poem.

All these embellishments of the basic Germanic poetic form, in addition to such devices as the envelope pattern (Bartlett 1935) and various structural techniques (Mitchell & Robinson 1998: 18–31), illustrate how Anglo-Saxon poets found room within the inherited Germanic forms for experimentation and diversification. The poets' flexibility and inventiveness in using the Germanic poetic tradition is illustrated most dramatically, perhaps, in their adaptation of the formulae passed down from a pre-Christian tradition to accommodate Christian subjects brought to them by missionaries. The epithet *mǣre dryhten* "famous lord" was modified to *ēce Dryhten* "eternal Lord" or *hālig Dryhten* "holy Lord"; *weroda dryhten* "lord of armies" and *sigora dryhten* "lord of victories" yielded to *heofona Dryhten* "Lord of the heavens"; *Gotena rice* "realm of the Goths" and *Wala rice* "realm of foreigners" easily became *heofona rice* "realm of the heavens." Among the Anglo-Saxons the inherited Germanic tradition was stable and enduring but also adaptable.

The OE poetic tradition stands in marked contrast with the post-Anglo-Saxon English tradition primarily because in OE we find an intimate relationship between the language and the poetic forms that are native to that language. All the features of the OE poetic tradition grow organically from the language itself. The pounding accents of OE speech that have been disciplined naturally into meter through the five types of verses, the close interdependence of OE syntax and OE meter, the role that compounding and apposition play in facilitating Germanic metrical patterns – all bind OE poetic expression closely together with the language. The very principle of alliteration, which is such a prominent element in the poetry, came into being because the Germanic accent on the first syllable of words required that the functional ornament of verse should occur at the beginnings of words rather than at the end (as in rhyme). The poetic tradition shared by Chaucer, Shakespeare, and Hardy is totally different. In their verse, foreign forms (classical meters, French rhyme) are imposed upon an alien English speech. The resulting tension can be a source of aesthetic pleasure, but it is a pleasure radically different from that which we experience in OE verse, where the relationship between poetic form and natural speech is not one of tension but rather one of harmony.

REFERENCES AND FURTHER READING

Acker, P. (1998). *Revising Oral Theory: Formulaic Composition in Old English and Old Icelandic Verse.* New York: Garland.

Aertsen, H. & Bremmer, R. H., Jr. (1994). *Companion to Old English Poetry.* Amsterdam: VU University Press.

Bartlett, A. C. (1935). *The Larger Rhetorical Patterns in Anglo-Saxon Poetry.* New York: Columbia University Press.

Benson, L. D. (1966). The literary character of Anglo-Saxon formulaic poetry. *PMLA*, 81, 334–41.

Donoghue, D. (1987). *Style in Old English Poetry.* New Haven, CT: Yale University Press.

Emerton, E. (trans.) (1976). *The Letters of Saint Boniface.* New York: W. W. Norton.

Klaeber, F. (1905–6). Studies in the textual

interpretation of *Beowulf. Modern Philology*, 3, 235–65.

Krapp, G. P. & Dobbie, E. V. K. (eds.) (1932–53). *The Anglo-Saxon Poetic Records*. 6 vols. New York: Columbia University Press.

Lapidge, M. & Herren, M. (trans.) (1979). *Aldhelm: The Prose Works*. Cambridge: Brewer.

Lewis, C. S. (1939). The alliterative metre. In C. S. Lewis, *Rehabilitations and Other Essays* (pp. 119–32). Oxford: Oxford University Press.

Liuzza, R. M. (ed.) (2002). *Old English Literature*. New Haven, CT: Yale University Press.

Magoun, F. P. (1953). The oral-formulaic character of Anglo-Saxon narrative poetry. *Speculum*, 28, 446–67.

Malone, K. (ed.) (1962). *Widsith*. Copenhagen: Rosenkilde and Bagger.

Mattingly, H. (trans.) (1970). *Tacitus: The Agricola and the Germania*. London: Penguin.

Mitchell, B. & Robinson, F. C. (ed.) (1998). *Beowulf: An Edition with Relevant Shorter Texts*. Oxford: Blackwell.

Momma, H. (1997). *The Composition of Old English Poetry*. Cambridge: Cambridge University Press.

Moulton, W. G. (1988). Mutual intelligibility among speakers of early Germanic dialects. In D. G. Calder and T. C. Christy (eds.), *Germania: Comparative Studies in the Old Germanic Languages and Literatures* (pp. 9–28). Cambridge: Brewer.

O'Keeffe, K. O. (1997). Diction, variation, the formula. In R. E. Bjork & J. D. Niles (eds.), *A Beowulf Handbook* (pp. 85–104). Lincoln: University of Nebraska Press.

Orchard, A. (2003). Style and structure. In A. Orchard, *A Critical Companion to Beowulf* (pp. 57–97). Cambridge: Brewer.

Robinson, F. (1985). *Beowulf and the Appositive Style*. Knoxville: University of Tennessee Press.

Robinson, F. (1994). *The Editing of Old English*. Oxford: Blackwell.

Rosier, J. L. (1966). 'Instructions for Christians': a poem in Old English. *Anglia*, 84, 4–22.

43

"In swich englissh as he kan": Chaucer's Literary Language

John F. Plummer

The first point to be made about Chaucer's literary language is that it might not have been English. As Chaucer began writing in the second half of the fourteenth century, two prestigious literary languages, French and Latin, had dominated England for centuries. It seems likely in fact that Chaucer wrote French lyrics early in his career, and his friend and fellow poet John Gower wrote in French and Latin as well as English. But the status of English was rising; English became the language of the law courts in 1362, the chancellor opened parliament in English in 1363, and the king addressed parliament in English in 1367.

The generation of writers that followed Chaucer regarded him as having in effect invented English as a literary language; they spoke particularly of his role in "ennobling" English with rhetorical effects. In "The Life of Our Lady" (ca. 1410), the monk John Lydgate wrote this of him:

> And eke my maister Chauser is ygrave
> The noble Rethor, poete of Brytayne
>
> . . . .
>
> That *made firste, to distille and rayne*
> *The golde dewe dropes of speche and eloquence*
> *Into our tunge, thurgh his excellence*
>   *And fonde the floures, firste of Retoryke*
> *Our Rude speche, only to enlumyne*
> That in our tunge, was neuere noon hym like . . .
> (emphasis added, 1628–37)

Likewise in his *Pilgrimage of the Life of Man* (ca. 1426–8), Lydgate refers to Chaucer as ". . . that poete, / Wyth al hys rethorykes swete / That *was the ffyrste in any age* / *That amendede our langage*" (emphasis added, 19773–6). In his *Regement of Princes* (1412), Thomas Hoccleve praises Chaucer as ". . . flour of eloquence / Mirour of fructuous entendement / O vniuersal fadir in science." About 1450, John Shirley, a

compiler and probably merchant in books, wrote that Chaucer "in oure wolgare [i.e., language] / hade neuer his pere / of eloquencyale retorryke / In Englisshe / was neuer noon him lyke." In an epilogue to his 1478 edition of Chaucer's translation of Boethius' *Consolation of Philosophy*, William Caxton called him "the worshipful *fader & first foundeur & enbelissher* of ornate eloquence in our englissh."

From our perspective, such characterizations of Chaucer's language seem, if not entirely mistaken, certainly misleading. Chaucer's vocabulary shows more romance and Latinate forms than English poets of the thirteenth century, but little of the polysyllabic "aureate" diction (e.g., "eloquencyale," "fructuous entendement") so admired by his fifteenth-century successors. It may be that their high regard for Chaucer led them to attribute to him, to "hear" in him the diction and rhetorical embellishments they themselves valued, to project their stylistic habits onto his work. In terms of romance vocabulary itself, Ralph Hanna (2002: 314) has remarked that "Chaucer may have a gross vocabulary close to half French in terms of items, but his actual poetic usage is (necessarily) a great deal more Anglo-Saxon than that (usually, I would guess, 85 to 90 percent in any protracted passage)."

It is not at all clear what "amending" or "embellishing" the English language would consist of, though it would presumably include the use of rhetorical figures, which Chaucer does; indeed he probably does engage in more troping than his thirteenth-century predecessors and more than many of his contemporaries. But the native English alliterative tradition also used rhetorical devices abundantly. It may be that the rhetoric that "counted" for Chaucer's first readers was the recognizable tropes catalogued by the Latin rhetorical tradition represented by such writers as Geoffrey of Vinsauf. It is instructive, then, to hear Chaucer as he openly acknowledges Geoffrey in the *Nun's Priest's Tale* (VII, 3347–54; all Chaucerian citations will be to Benson 1987):

> O Gaufred, deere maister soverayn,
> That whan thy worthy kyng Richard was slayn
> With shot, compleynedest his deeth so soore,
> Why ne hadde I now thy sentence and thy loore,
> The Friday for to chide, as diden ye?
> For on a Friday, soothly, slayn was he.
> Thanne wolde I shewe yow how that I koude pleyne
> For Chauntecleres drede and for his peyne.

The master rhetorician is invoked here, however, not to lament the death of a king but of a chicken. Another moment in which we hear Chaucer calling upon the learned rhetorical tradition with something less than high seriousness is his invocation of Apollo at the beginning of Book III of the *House of Fame* (1091–108):

> O God of science and of lyght,
> Appollo, thurgh thy grete myght,
> This lytel laste bok thou gye!

> Nat that I wilne, for maistrye,
> Here art poetical be shewed,
> But for the rym ys lyght and lewed,
> Yit make hyt sumwhat agreable,
> Though som vers fayle in a sillable;
> And that I do no diligence
> To shewe craft, but o sentence.
> And yif, devyne vertu, thow
> Wilt helpe me to shewe now
> That in myn hed ymarked ys –
> Loo, that is for to menen this,
> The Hous of Fame for to descryve –
> Thou shalt se me go as blyve
> Unto the nexte laure y see,
> And kysse yt, for hyt is thy tree.

Disclaiming any desire to show "art poetical," and admitting that his versification is "lightweight," even sometimes defective, and claiming more interest in "sentence" than "craft," he nonetheless begs for Apollo's help in voicing what is in his head, promising to kiss the nearest laurel tree in thanks. It is a passage that takes rhetoric as its subject while claiming disinterest in it, decorously invoking classical antiquity while keeping it at arms length with its comic concluding gesture. Which is not to say that Chaucer does not engage in rhetorical devices, because he does, and well, but much more important to Chaucer than the "embellishing" ornament is the fundamental idea of rhetoric as craft, an idea he shared with his fifteenth-century admirers. Chaucer's style is something he took for granted needed to be worked at and mastered, rather than the "natural" or "spontaneous" expression of "genius," and in that he would be more aligned with Hoccleve than with Wordsworth.

Chaucer's literary language in English developed in large part through his many exercises in translation, from Latin (Boethius, Ovid), French (*Roman de la Rose*, Machaut), and Italian (Dante, Petrarch and Boccaccio). Materials, literary *topoi* and forms, rhetorical techniques, narrative styles and metaphors were available in abundance in these other literary traditions, and Chaucer's language, early and late, shows evidence of his absorption of them. Indeed standard educational practice called on schoolboys to transcribe passages from Latin classics and to translate them, so though the French poet Otton de Grandson praised Chaucer as "Grant translateur," he was unique not in the practice of translation so much as in the skill he demonstrated and the scope of his production.

Vocabulary too could come from Chaucer's translation: Bennett (1983: 97, 99) notes that *Knight's Tale* (I, 1494), "That al the orient laugheth of the light," is the first use of "orient" in English to signify the eastern sky, and that Chaucer apparently found it in descriptions of dawn in Dante (*Purgatorio*, XXVII, 94–6), while *Troilus*, v. 1541–3, "Fortune, which that *permutacioun* / Of things hath, as it is hire committed / Through *purveyaunce* and disposicioun / Of heigh Jove as regnes shal be flitted / Fro

folk in folk, or whan they shal ben smitted . . ." is language Chaucer found in Dante's *Inferno*, VII, 78–90: "Ordinó general ministra e duce / che *permutasse* a tempo li ben vani / Di gente in gente" ("ordained a general minister and guide / to *shift*, from time to time, those empty goods / from nation to nation") (Mandelbaum 1992).

Chaucer shows a keen awareness of his relation to other writers and their styles. He enjoys a joke at the expense of the alliterative tradition as he has his Parson say in his *Prologue* (X, 42–3) ". . . I am a Southren man, / I kan nat geest 'rum, ram, ruf,' by lettre," and at the expense of the tail-rhyme romance tradition in his brilliant parody *Sir Thopas*. His self-consciousness about style can be heard in Harry Bailey asking the Clerk to tell a tale, a "murie thyng of aventures"; Harry warns the Clerk not to unleash his rhetorical skills upon the pilgrims: "Youre termes, youre colours, and youre figures / Keepe hem in stoor til so be that ye endite / Heigh style, as whan that men to kynges write" (IV, 16–18).

Chaucer has a long reputation as a bawdy poet, and there is an entire book (Ross 1972) devoted to his risqué innuendo. Recently Larry Benson (1988) has argued that on the contrary, Chaucer, as befit his association with courtly society, is prudish in his language. Benson may be correct in arguing that Chaucer infrequently uses blunt "Anglo-Saxon" words to refer to body parts and functions, preferring to use euphemism, but a striking passage in the *General Prologue* portrait of the Parson reminds us that it is difficult to be certain, from our twenty-first-century perspective, what particular words might have been considered offensive:

> This noble ensample to his sheep he yaf,
> That first he wroghte, and afterward he taughte.
> Out of the gospel he tho wordes caughte,
> And this figure he added eek therto,
> That if gold ruste, what shal iren do?
> For if a preest be foul, on whom we truste,
> No wonder is a lewed man to ruste;
> And shame it is, if a prest take keep,
> A shiten shepherde and a clene sheep.
> (I, 496–504)

Chaucer makes it clear enough that the "shiten shepherde" ("dirty" or even "shitty shepherd") figure is the Parson's own language; the passage is marked as indirect speech by "he tho wordes caughte." Among the virtues Chaucer ascribes to the Parson is plain speaking – his language neither "daungerous ne digne" – and his willingness to speak bluntly even to those in power – "Hym wold he snybben sharply for the nonys" – but given the idealized nature of the Parson's portrait, it seems very unlikely that Chaucer would have allowed him to use language likely to cause offense.

But bawdiness is not primarily a matter of vocabulary. Chaucer often exploits the potential impact of ordinary words used euphemistically, and, as the Wife of Bath's *Prologue* demonstrates, euphemism does not necessarily conceal, and may instead emphasize, the sexual nature of its referent, as in her "bele chose," "quoniam," and

"Chambre of Venus." The *Miller's Tale* by contrast names body parts with what appear to have been common names: "haunchbones," "queynt," "neked ers," but signifies sexual activity quite decorously:

> Withouten wordes mo they goon to bedde,
> Ther as the Carpenter is wont to lye.
> Ther was the revel and the melodye;
> And thus lith Alison and Nicholas,
> In bisynesse of myrth and of solas.
> (I, 3650–4)

Chaucer shows an awareness of the possible effects of euphemism versus coarse language on an audience in the *Merchant's Tale*'s denouement in which the Merchant-Narrator calls attention to his "bluntness" in pointing to May and Damien's arboreal sexual activity:

> Ladyes, I prey yow that ye be nat wrooth;
> *I kan nat glose, I am a rude man* –
> And sodeynly anon this Damyan
> Gan pullen up the smok, and in he throng.
> (IV, 2350–3, emphasis added)

In *Troilus and Criseyde* Book III, 1310–13, the narrator likewise calls attention to the manner in which he indicates that the couple makes love, though here the effect is quite the opposite of the Merchant's studied bluntness: "Of hire delit, or joies oon the leeste, / Were impossible to my wit to seye; / But juggeth ye that han ben at the feste / Of swich gladness, if that hem liste pleye!"

The *Manciple's Tale* shows great awareness of diction and its class implications, as the Manciple grumbles that while things ought to be called by their names, class and power compel polite euphemism. An aristocratic woman having an affair is a "lady, as in love" while a poor woman doing the same thing will be a "lemman," a "knavish" word (though it is understood as courtly by the love-struck Absolon in the *Miller's Tale*), or "wench." Because he has such a keen ear for diction and register, Chaucer can offer us the comic portrait of the impolitic crow who says to Phoebus not simply that his wife is having an affair but that "on thy bed thy wyf I saugh hym swyve" (IX, 256). The Manciple warns us not to make the mistake ourselves of telling a powerful person such bad news, but the words he uses to do so betray his failure to distinguish between truthful words and hurtful words that make the truth hurt even more: "Ne telleth never no man in your life / How that another man hath *dyght* his wife" (IX, 312), he says, which goes well beyond the facts into insult. Though *Riverside* glosses the phrase as "to have intercourse with," it means of course simply "to do," and that is what makes it so coarse and hostile in comparison to a straightforward expression like "had sex with."

Chaucer frequently will establish a contrast between two or more registers of language. In the *Parliament of Fowels* 414–23, Chaucer's tercel eagle, royal bird that he is, speaks in stately, rhetorical, courtly style:

> With hed enclyned and with ful humble chere
> This royal tercel spak and taried nought:
> "Unto my sovereyn lady, and noght my fere,
> I chese, and chese with wil and herte, and thought,
> The formel on your hond so wel iwrought,
> Whos I am al and ever wol hir serve,
> Do what hir lest, to do me lyve or sterve.
> Besecking hire of merci and of grace,
> As she that is my lady sovereyne;
> Or let me deye present in this place."

By way of contrast, the goose speaks in blunt terms, quick and to the point; if the female eagle refuses the tercel's proposal, he should simply find another (561–7):

> And for these water-foules tho began
> The goos to speke, and in hir kakelynge
> She seyde, "Pes! Now tak kep every man,
> And herkeneth which a resoun I shal forth brynge;
> My wit is sharp; I love no taryinge;
> I seye I rede him, though he were my brother,
> But she wol love hym, lat hym love another!"

One finds a wonderful juxtaposition of courtly and colloquial in Troilus III, 106–26. The passage contains four voices: those of Troilus, Criseyde, Pandarus, and the Narrator. It is a complex moment, as each character seeks to influence the will and actions of another without quite saying what is being asked for. The scene is extremely self-conscious linguistically.

> "Thus muche as now, O wommanliche wif,
> I may out brynge, and if this yow displese,
> That shal I wreke upon myn owen lif
> Right soone, I trowe, and do youre herte an ese,   *Troilus' earnest, even naïve*
> If with my deth youre wreththe may apese.   *courtly stylization*
> But syn that ye han herd me somwhat seye
> Now recche I nevere how soone that I deye."
> Ther-with his manly sorwe to biholde,   *A shift to the Narrator*
> It myghte han made an herte of stoon to rewe,   *and his homely metaphor*
> And Pandare wep as he to water wolde,   *A shift to comic exaggeration*
> And poked evere his nece new and newe,   *and comic action*
> And seyde, "Wo bygon ben hertes trewe!   *A shift to Pandarus, who attempts*
> For love of God, make of this thinge an ende,   *to establish rhetorical elevation*
> Or sle us both at ones, er ye wende."   *and seriousness*

"I, what? quod she, "by God and by my trouthe,	*Shift to colloquial speech (Criseyde)*
I not nat what ye wilne that I seye."	
"I, what?" quod he, "That ye han on hym routhe,	*Echoed sarcastically and impatiently*
For Goddes love, and doth him nought to deye!"	*by Pandarus*
"Now thanne thus," quod she, "I wolde hym preye	*Resolution into Criseyde's*
To telle me the fyn of his entente.	*response, in subjunctive: "He should*
Yet wist I neuere wel what that he mente."	*say what he means"*

In *The House of Fame*, the windy pedantic eagle, in contrast to his monosyllabic passenger, is made to sound like a garrulous school master who, comically, draws our attention to his prolixity by claiming – at length – to speak with brief clarity:

> "Telle me this now feythfully,
> Have y not preved thus symply,
> Withoute any subtiltee
> Of speche, or gret prolixitee
> Of termes of philosophie,
> Of figures of poetrie,
> Or colours of rethorike?
> Pardee, hit oghte the to lyke;
> For hard langage and hard matere
> Ys encombrous for to here
> Attones; wost thou not wel this?"
> And I answerde, and seyde, "Yis."
> "A ha" quod he, "lo, *so I can,*
> *Lewedly to a lewed man*
> Speke, and shewe him swyche skiles,
> That he may shake hem by the biles,
> So palpable they shulden be."
> (*House of Fame* 853–69)

Chaucer's dialect, London English, was moving during the fourteenth century from being a southern dialect to something unique, becoming a form of East Midland dialect, based upon different melded dialects of those who migrated there from other parts of the country (e.g., Chaucer's own family). We are of course dependent upon scribes to pass on Chaucer's English and not to overlay it with their own habits. Simon Horobin has concluded that fifteenth-century scribes took care to preserve Type III (late fourteenth-century London) forms in their production of literary manuscripts even when Type IV (post-1430 London) forms were available and presumably the forms they would use personally in other contexts. "This seems to represent a collective response to aspects of the language which were regarded as 'Chaucerian,' and therefore integral to a text of Chaucer's work" (Horobin 2003: 34). "Thus the spellings of AGAIN(ST) using the form <ay-> display a consistency among the earliest and most authoritative *Canterbury Tales* manuscripts. As we move further from the archetype the <ay-> spellings are completely removed across different textual

traditions" (Horobin 2003: 44). I.e., we can speculatively conclude that the <ay-> spelling is Chaucerian, not scribal.

Reflexes of Old English *y* in words such as 'kisse" / "kesse," "mille" / "melle," and "thynne" / "thenne" in Chaucer's work can be used to suggest that he normally preferred the East Midland forms, but sometimes availed himself of the Southeastern form in order to complete a difficult rhyme (Horobin 2003: 46–50). Similarly, David Burnley (2000: 238–40) has shown that Chaucer made good use of dialectal variants for metrical and rhyming purposes. Mustanoja (1968: 64) notes some ways Chaucer seeks metrical regularity by choosing or not to include "to" with an infinitive, apaphetic forms, and the inclusion or not of articles. Chaucer also used final –e for metrical purposes, as Burnley (2000: 239) has shown.

Differences (often minute) between the Hengwrt and Ellesmere manuscripts can lead to difficulties in deciding Chaucerian usage. For example, the use of a preterit verb in a passage otherwise cast in the historical present has been taken (Benson 1961, as cited in Horobin 2003: 55–6) to be a deliberate stylistic choice aimed at particular narrative effect, but the evidence varies considerably in consistency if one takes it from Hengwrt rather than Ellesmere, and it may be that the Ellesmere scribe had adopted – consciously or not – a more regular practice in the time between his work on Hengwrt and Ellesmere (Horobin 2003: 55–6). Similarly, in the philological joke in the *Reeve's Tale*, the number of "northernisms" (Northern –es endings for Southern/London –eth endings) in Ellesmere is greater than in Hengwrt. The Ellesmere scribe or editor might have been hyper-correcting at this point, making Alyn and John sound more Northern than Chaucer, as represented by Hengwrt, had (Horobin 2003: 56–7).

Chaucer began his career writing in four-stress couplets (*Book of the Duchess*) but then moved on to a five-stress line in rhymed couplets and rhyme-royal stanzas, being among the first to do so. He also wrote in prose (*Melibee, Parson's Tale, Boece*). But what is remarkable is that he can make his rhyming pentameter couplets or stanzas sound so "natural," so like the language of everyday speech, as any of the passages quoted earlier demonstrate.

Chaucer's language does not expect punctuation, and as Brown (1986), Beidler (2005), and Chickering (1990) argue, modern editorial habits and conventions can obscure meaning by, for example, disambiguating deliberately ambiguous moments with punctuation. To take an example from the *Summoner's Tale*, the Summoner begins his tale about a hypocritical friar who writes the names of those who give him gifts, presumably to remember them in his prayers, and then erases the names from the tablet as soon as he is out of sight. This detail provokes the pilgrim Friar to burst in with an objection. The Host quiets him down and orders the Summoner to continue, which he does. Modern editions use quite a bit of punctuation, including an indentation with each shift in speaker, to keep straight who is speaking to whom. None of this is found in the manuscripts and nor is it necessary; as this unpunctuated passage shows, the shifts in speaker are clearly indicated by Chaucer's language itself:

And whan that he was out at dore anon
He planed awey the names everichon
That he biforn had writen in his tables
He served hem with nyfles and with fables
Nay ther thou lixt thou Somonour *quod the Frere*
Pees *quod oure Hoost* for Cristes mooder deere
Tel forth thy tale and spare it nat at al
So thryve I *quod this Somonour* so I shal
(III, 1757–64)

Finally, Chaucer appears to have been fond of proverbs, usually using them to lend a homely colloquialism to his text. He seems to have been the first to record a number, e.g., "Nothing ventured, nothing gained" (*Troilus*, II, 807), "Let sleeping dogs lie" (*Troilus*, 764), and "Strike while the iron is hot" (*Melibee*, 1035).

REFERENCES AND FURTHER READING

Baum, P. F. (1961). *Chaucer's Verse*. Durham, NC: Duke University Press.

Beidler, P. G. (2005). Where's the point? In T. L. Burton & J. F. Plummer (eds.), *Seyde in forme and reverence: Essays on Chaucer and Chaucerians in Memory of Emerson Brown, Jr.* (pp. 193–203). Provo: Chaucer Studio Press.

Bennett, J. A. W. (1983). Chaucer, Dante, and Boccaccio. In P. Boitani (ed.), *Chaucer and the Italian Trecento* (pp. 89–113). Cambridge: Cambridge University Press.

Benson, L. D. (1961). Chaucer's historical present: its meaning and uses. *English Studies*, 42, 65–77.

Benson, L. D. (general editor) (1987). *The Riverside Chaucer*. 3rd edn. Boston: Houghton Mifflin.

Benson, L. D. (1988). Chaucer and courtly speech. In P. Boitani & A. Torti (eds.), *Genres, Themes and Images in English Literature* (pp. 16–38). Tübingen: Narr.

Benson, L. D. (1993). *A Glossarial Concordance to the Riverside Chaucer*. New York: Garland.

Brink, B. A. K., ten. (1969 [1901]). *The Language and Metre of Chaucer*. 2nd edn. Revd. F. Kluge. Trans. M. B. Smith. New York: Greenwood Press.

Brown, E. B., Jr. (1986). *The Knight's Tale*, 2639: guilt by punctuation. *Chaucer Review*, 21, 133–41.

Burnley, J. D. (1979). *Chaucer's Language and the Philosophers' Tradition*. Totowa, NJ: Rowman & Littlefield.

Burnley, J. D. (1983). *A Guide to Chaucer's Language*. Norman: University of Oklahoma Press.

Burnley, J. D. (1989). *The Language of Chaucer*. Basingstoke: Macmillan.

Burnley, J. D. (2000). Language. In P. Brown (ed.), *A Companion to Chaucer* (pp. 235–50). Oxford: Blackwell.

Cannon, C. (1998). *The Making of Chaucer's English: A Study of Words*. Cambridge: Cambridge University Press.

Chickering, H. (1990). Unpunctuating Chaucer. *Chaucer Review*, 25, 95–109.

Colloquium: Chaucer and the future of language study. (2002). *Studies in the Age of Chaucer*, 24, 301–54.

Curran, T. (2002). *English from Caedmon to Chaucer: The Literary Development of English*. Prospect Heights, IL: Waveland Press.

Davis, N. (1974). Chaucer and fourteenth-century English. In D. Brewer (ed.), *Geoffrey Chaucer* (pp. 58–84). Athens: Ohio University Press.

Davis, N. (1979). *A Chaucer Glossary*. Oxford: Clarendon Press.

Elliott, R. W. V. (1974). *Chaucer's English*. London: Deutsch.

Hanna, R. (2002). Chaucer and the future of language study. *Studies in the Age of Chaucer*, 24, 309–15.

Horobin, S. (2003). *The Language of the Chaucer Tradition*. Cambridge: D. S. Brewer.

Kerkhof, J. (1966). *Studies in the Language of Geoffrey Chaucer*. Leiden: Universitaire Pers Leiden.

Mandelbaum, A. (trans.) (1992). *Dante Alighieri, Inferno*. New York: Bantam Classics.

Masui, M. (1964). *The Structure of Chaucer's Rime Words: An Exploration into the Poetic Language of Chaucer*. Tokyo: Kenkyusha.

Mersand, J. (1968 [1939]). *Chaucer's Romance Vocabulary*. Port Washington, NY: Kennikat Press.

Mustanoja, T. F. (1968). Chaucer's prosody. In B. Rowland (ed.), *Companion to Chaucer Studies* (pp. 58–84). Oxford: Oxford University Press.

Roscow, G. H. (1981). *Syntax and Style in Chaucer's Poetry*. Cambridge, MA: D. S. Brewer.

Ross, T. W. (1972). *Chaucer's Bawdy*. New York: E. P. Dutton

Sandved, A. O. (1985). *Introduction to Chaucerian English*. Cambridge, MA: D. S. Brewer.

Schlauch, M. (1952). Chaucer's colloquial English: its structural traits. *PMLA*, 67, 1103–16.

Spearing, A. C. (1965). Chaucer's language. In M. Hussey, A. C. Spearing, & J. Winny (eds.), *An Intoduction to Chaucer* (pp. 89–114). Cambridge: Cambridge University Press.

44
Shakespeare's Literary Language

Adam N. McKeown

These days, a discussion of "literary language" is almost obliged to begin with some mention of the difficulties modern literary critics have found with the very notion of separating "literature" from other kinds of writing. Happily, we are to some extent disburdened of this obligation when dealing with the English Renaissance. Shakespeare and his contemporaries would have used the term "poetry" to refer not just to verse but also to drama and prose fiction, and they very much viewed poetry as different from philosophy, historiography, and many other kinds of writing that might now show up in a literary anthology. The great Elizabethan poet and theorist Philip Sidney explains this distinction very clearly in *A Defence of Poetry*. Poetry differs from other forms of learned discourse on the grounds that the poet is not just an observer or reporter of reality but a "maker" – a creator of

> things either better than nature bringeth forth, or, quite anew, forms such as never were in nature, as the heroes, demi-gods, cyclops, chimeras, furies, and such like; so as he goeth hand in hand with nature, not enclosed within the narrow warrant of her gifts, but freely ranging within the zodiac of his own wit. (1971: 23–4)

Shakespeare employs very similar language in a description of poetry in his late tragedy *Timon of Athens*. The Poet, discussing something he wrote in Timon's honor, says that his imagination – his "free drift" (1.1.45) – is not bound to the particulars of nature "but moves itself / In a wide sea of wax" (1.1.46–7). By "wide sea of wax," the Poet means that his poetic imagination is limitless, like the sea, and can, like wax, be shaped into anything. For Sidney, the capacity of poetry to soar beyond "the narrow warrant" of nature separates it from historiography, which is bound "not to what should be but to what is, to the particular truth of things" (1971: 32). And yet poetry is not abstract. Like forms made of wax it is sensuous and vivid, qualities that distinguish it for Sidney from philosophy, which is full of "thorny arguments" that are "hard of utterance and so misty to be conceived" (1971: 31). Poetry is, Sidney

says, "a representing, counterfeiting, or figuring forth; to speak metaphorically, a speaking picture, with this end, – to teach and delight" (1971: 25).

Neither Sidney nor Shakespeare would have proposed, however, that poetic language is a less formal or less scholarly language than the language employed by philosophers or historiographers. As William Webbe suggests in *A Discourse of English Poetry* (1586), poetry is "learnedly compiled" for the purpose of "delighting the readers or hearers as well by the apt and decent framing of words . . . as by the skillful handling of the matter whereof it is intreated" (quoted in Kalas 2007: 57). Of course, if the "skillful handling" of language and subject matter by the writer is a definitive quality of poetry, then any piece of writing that pleases and edifies the reader can be said to have been well composed, and so the logic is frustratingly circular. But as with the question of what constitutes literary language, the particular conditions of early modern England make this problem somewhat less frustrating. The educational system that produced most every author of Shakespeare's time provided rather prescriptive rules about how to write effectively. These rules – which involved not only structure and tone but also choices of phrases and words – comprised the art of rhetoric.

While the Renaissance did not revive the ancient art of rhetoric – it had been very important to medieval education as well – it rose to new prominence thanks to *humanism*. Humanism, which developed in fourteenth- and fifteenth-century Italy, was an academic practice that stressed the mastery of classical rather than ecclesiastic Latin (the Latin of the Roman poets and orators rather than the Latin of the medieval church). The early Italian humanists considered themselves first and foremost *orators*, like the Romans (e.g., Cicero and Quintilian) on whom they modeled themselves and their habits with language (Baxandall 1971: 1). The literary training they developed included reading and translating Latin literature as well as composing original Latin works based on classical models, and by the sixteenth century humanism dominated most secondary and university curricula across western Europe.

Although we do not know for sure when and where Shakespeare received his education, we find traces of humanistic habits with language throughout his work – most notably in the Latin tags that appear frequently in early works like *Titus Andronicus* and *Love's Labor's Lost*. In the latter we also find a parody of humanistic education figured in the high-minded young lords who intend to cloister themselves away for three years to study. The pedant Holofernes in that play, with his florid phrases peppered gratuitously with Latin, recalls the sort of mendicant humanists who made their livings waiting at the courts of the wealthy, often serving as tutors. In *The Taming of the Shrew*, Lucentio assumes such a guise to woo Bianca. He will even reveal his amorous intentions through a mock lesson in Latin translation:

> '*Hic ibat*,' as I told you before, '*Simois*,' I am
> Lucentio, '*hic est*,' son unto Vincentio of Pisa,
> '*Sigeia tellus*,' disguised thus to get your love;
> '*Hic steterat*,' and that Lucentio that comes
> a-wooing, '*Priami*,' is my man Tranio, '*regia*,'

> bearing my port, *'celsa senis,'* that we might
> beguile the old pantaloon.
> (3.2.31–6)

Another such pedant is Sir Hugh Evans from *The Merry Wives of Windsor*, who leads a young boy (named William) through an exercise in double translation. In the exercise, prescribed by the Elizabethan humanist and pedagogue Roger Ascham in *The Schoolmaster* (1570), the student was asked to translate a passage of Latin into English and then, some time later, back into Latin, with the goal of arriving as closely as possible to the original Latin (Ascham 1815: 196–7). William is not a quick study:

> Evans: What is 'lapis,' William?
> William: A stone.
> Evans: And what is 'a stone,' William?
> William: A pebble.
> Evans: No, it is 'lapis:' I pray you, remember in your prain.
> (4.1.28–32)

Perhaps the most trenchant comment Shakespeare makes on the humanistic tradition comes from *Hamlet*, in which Horatio, identified as a "scholar" (1.1.40), is characterized by an unsettling aloofness from the weighty affairs that consume his country and the life of his best friend – an aloofness reminiscent of the King of Navarre from *Love's Labor's Lost* and his dubious idea that study is best undertaken in a "three years' term" (1.1.16) in isolation from the social and political commotion of everyday life.

These examples would seem to depict a Shakespeare who was no devotee of a humanistic education but rather a critic of it – a depiction that squares with Ben Jonson's famous comment that Shakespeare "knew small Latin and less Greek." (Although, to be sure, even though Shakespeare wrote no Latin poetry that we know of and included less Latin in his work than many other Elizabethan poets, his "small Latin" was likely much greater than most anyone's today.) The influence of Shakespeare's rhetorical training on his literary language goes further than allusions to the educational system of which that training was part and parcel, however. We can see the influence of this training in the way he structures his writing. The rhetorical tradition divides oratory into three types: forensic, used to establish truth or falsity (as in a court of law); deliberative, which aims at exhortation; and epideictic, which praises or blames. Obvious instances of these types of rhetorical exercises are everywhere present in Shakespeare's work. The ghost's long initial speech in the last scene of the first act of *Hamlet* is an example of deliberative rhetoric as it is designed to exhort the young prince to take action against Claudius. In *The Winter's Tale*, Leontes and Hermione engage in a lengthy forensic competition in a courtroom in the second scene of the third act. Famously, in the third act climax of *Julius Caesar*, Brutus and Marc Antony square off in a contest of epideictic rhetoric before the Roman mobs, whom the two orators wish to convince of Caesar's culpability or honor, respectively.

As central as rhetorical training was to the Elizabethan literary milieu, early modern poetry was not merely a subspecies of oratory. Shakespeare and his contemporaries would have inherited from their ancient and medieval forebears a distinction between rhetoric and another art they knew as *grammar*, and early modern poetics relates as much to the latter as to the former. For Quintilian, grammar consists not only of the "science of speaking correctly," which it shares with rhetoric, but also of the more elusive practice of "interpreting the poets" (1.4.2). James J. Murphy notes a tendency among early modern theorists of language to differentiate the figures of rhetoric from those of grammar on the basis of whether or not their purpose is to persuade (1974: 190). Persuasion (*movere*), along with teaching (*docere*) and delighting (*delectare*), is one of the three purposes of oratory well known to the rhetorical tradition, but importantly, Sidney omits persuasion from his definition of poetry above, which merely delights and teaches. George Puttenham implies a similar omission in his story of Orpheus from *The Art of English Poesy* (1589). For Puttenham, Orpheus certainly moves his hearers but indirectly, by "discreet and wholesome lessons uttered in harmony and with melodious instruments" (1971: 22). By contrast, Thomas Wilson describes Orpheus in his *Art of Rhetoric* (1560) as having "brought" savage people under "law" and having "forced Pluto himself" to release him from the underworld (1994: 87). Wilson will also say in defense of the value of rhetoric, "[Such] is the power of eloquence and reason, that most men are forced even to yield in that which most standeth against their will" (1994: 42). Henry Peacham describes the coercive strategies of rhetoric even more ominously in *The Garden of Eloquence* (1593), saying that the orator is "the emperor of men's minds and affections" (from "The Epistle Dedicatorie," unnumbered).

This distinction between poetry and rhetoric, while it makes sense in theory, is difficult to identify in practice. What does a poem teach – how does it teach – without persuading? And if oratory is delightful and appealing to our senses, does it not impart more to us than the idea the orator wishes to get across? Will everyone hear a poem or oration the same way? What really is the difference? I do not think we can answer these questions easily – nor am I sure that modern literary theory would recognize these distinctions between rhetoric and poetic as entirely valid ones – but Shakespeare and his contemporaries learned to read and write in a tradition that did recognize these distinctions, at least to some extent, and their habits with language reflect this influence. Shakespeare's writings reveal an understanding of poetry as a "speaking picture" rather than an object lesson or philosophical musing. Poetry is a picture of the world (often an idealized or exaggerated version of it) that allows readers and hearers to think about the world in new and edifying ways.

Shakespeare explores this function of poetic language in the second scene of act two of *Hamlet*, when Hamlet asks the player to recite a speech describing Pyrrhus' assault on Priam and Hecuba's grief at witnessing her husband's death. Hamlet, as well as the player, are moved by the description – the player to the point of tears – even though both have heard the description before. Alone and confused, Hamlet asks with reference to the player, "What's Hecuba to him, or he to Hecuba, / That he should

weep for her?" (2.2.561–2). He is posing a very complicated question about the function and effect of the "speaking picture" of poetry. What are these "speaking pictures" doing to us? How do we relate to the images they describe? Why do they move us (for certainly they do)? Significantly, the player's speech is not so different from the ghost's. Both describe a murder Hamlet has not seen, and both result, ultimately, in Hamlet vowing to take action against Claudius. But the poem, unlike the ghost's speech, is not asking Hamlet to do anything other than form an image in his mind. What he does with that image is up to his own judgment (whereas the ghost leaves him with specific instructions to "Revenge his foul and most unnatural murder"; 1.5.25). Just as significantly, the connection Hamlet makes to the poem is not with its content (which is what captivates him in the ghost's rhetorical performance) but with its emotional effect on the audience. The player's tears, more than the words of the poem, lead Hamlet to revise his emotional relation to his father's death – indeed, a "discreet and wholesome [lesson]," as Puttenham might have called it, that the player could not have intended and that relates only indirectly to the poem itself.

The pictures poetry creates invite us to contemplate the world we think we know and, in so doing, "teach" us how we ourselves understand our own realities. Unlike rhetoric that is designed to impart a particular lesson to a particular audience, the speaking picture of poetry creates circumstances in which individuals must derive their own lessons through imagining a picture in the mind's eyes. What the poem does not say or merely implies becomes, in a way, the most crucial part, since it is this part that the reader must look inward to "see" – the blank that cannot be filled unless the reader or hearer supplies his or her own assumptions of what is true about the world. Shakespeare gives us a working demonstration of this function of the speaking picture of poetry in *The Rape of Lucrece*, when the narrator offers a poetic description of a painting Lucrece is contemplating:

> For much imaginary work was there;
> Conceit deceitful, so compact, so kind,
> That for Achilles' image stood his spear,
> Griped in an armed hand; himself behind,
> Was left unseen, save to the eye of mind:
> A hand, a foot, a face, a leg, a head,
> Stood for the whole to be imagined.
> (1422–8)

Very literally a "speaking picture," the painting is represented for us through the words of the narrator, a painting that leaves out crucial details and trusts the "eye of mind" to fill them in. For Lucrece, ravished and distraught, the missing details are images of violence and misery – "a thousand lamentable objects" (1373).

Shakespeare provides another demonstration of this function of poetry in *Hamlet*, when Claudius and Gertrude react differently to a play that enacts "something like" the circumstances surrounding Old Hamlet's death and the accession of his murderous

brother to the throne of Denmark. Gertrude sees in the play the folly of a lady who "protests too much" (3.2.219) – an apt criticism from a woman who might have protested just a little before consenting to marry her deceased husband's brother less than a month after the funeral. For Claudius – wracked with guilt for having killed his own brother – the play is an indictment. For both, the play becomes a reflection of their own personal and moral preoccupations. Both see a different play in their minds' eyes even though the words they hear are the same.

Perhaps the best way to connect the different ideas about the poetic language Shakespeare not only inherited but also questioned and revised is to consider the writers who most influenced his work. There are many candidates, both ancient and modern. Cicero no doubt influenced Shakespeare as much as anyone, but, as I have suggested, Shakespeare registers misgivings about the humanist tradition that lionized Cicero – and when Shakespeare includes Cicero in *Julius Caesar* he gives the greatest orator of the ancient world only a few perfunctory lines and has Casca dismiss his speeches with the famous words, "it was Greek to me" (1.2.284). The Roman dramatic poets Plautus and Terrence are, in some ways, more compelling candidates. Plautus' *Menaechmi* supplies the story for Shakespeare's first comedy, *A Comedy of Errors*, and the figure of the braggart soldier derived from the *Miles Gloriosus* of Plautus and the *Eunechus* of Terrence is one Shakespeare developed throughout his career, notably in the much beloved Sir John Falstaff. And yet about halfway through Shakespeare's career, while many of his contemporaries were developing "city comedies" influenced by these Roman playwrights and their cutting representations of urban manners, Shakespeare seems to have lost interest in the genre. Raphael Holinshed's *Chronicles* (1580) supplies the plot for many of Shakespeare's history plays, as the classical historians Plutarch and Livy do for many of his plays set in the ancient world. He finds other plotlines in the prolific and underappreciated Elizabethan popular poet Barnaby Riche and even in Robert Greene, the erudite London writer who accused Shakespeare of plagiarism (Barkan 2001: 41). In his sonnets, Shakespeare was also influenced by the Italian poet Petrarch as well as by his own countrymen Thomas Wyatt and Henry Howard, Earl of Surrey (who introduced to English iambic pentameter blank verse, the form which has become synonymous with Shakespeare's dramatic poetry). The most famous sonneteer of Shakespeare's lifetime was Sidney, with whom Shakespeare engaged not only in his own sonnets but also (and somewhat antagonistically) in the late experimental comedies we now call "romances," which take a certain delight in employing the very examples of bad stagecraft mentioned by Sidney in the *Defence* (1971: 65–6).

The one poet to whom Shakespeare returns most often throughout his career and who provides not only storylines but also images, themes, and deeper aesthetic sensibilities is Ovid. The Elizabethan fascination with Ovid has much to do with the Dutch humanist Erasmus, whose influential treatise *De copia* held up Ovid as a model for a lavish and sensuous manner of writing called the "copious style" (1978: 299). The copious style encouraged Elizabethan students to develop their characteristic affection for new words, foreign phrases, and strange ways of saying ordinary things. At the

center of Ovid's opus stands the *Metamorphoses*, a meandering epic-length narrative about humans and gods pursuing dangerous passions and about bodies changing form. It is certainly the most sensuous and sensual work Shakespeare or anyone else of his age was likely to encounter in their formal studies, and, not surprisingly, it is the only specific classical work to do a cameo in any of Shakespeare's writings. In *Titus Andronicus*, Lavinia drags a copy of Ovid's *Metamorphoses* on stage and "quotes the leaves" – pointing to specific passages with the stumps of her arms to explain why her hands and tongue had been cut from her.

It would be easy enough to cite Ovidian moments in Shakespeare: the rape and physical transformation of Lavinia in *Titus Andronicus*, the momentary and perverse affair between Titania and her "translated" half-donkey lover Nick Bottom in *A Midsummer Night's Dream*, *The Rape of Lucrece* and *Venus and Adonis*, the statue of Hermione coming to life in *The Winter's Tale*, just to name the more obvious ones. It may be more useful, in the context of Shakespeare's literary language, to consider instead how Ovid informs the "speaking pictures" Shakespeare creates in his poems.

Throughout the *Metamorphoses*, Ovid's voice is agonizingly aloof, especially in its relentless creation of poetic images in the face of human tragedy – as if the responsibility of the poet, like a naturalist witnessing the behavior of animals, is to keep reporting, to keep reflecting the world back to the hearer in ways that make the world meaningful regardless of how erotic or sad or painful the events taking place may be. The pictures that emerge in Ovid are thus vivid and sensuous but also distant and alien, as if – like those of the actor telling the story of Hecuba's grief in *Hamlet* – they issue from a mind that is at once utterly consumed by the events taking place and utterly separated intellectually and emotionally from them.

In *Titus Andronicus*, for example, when Marcus finds his niece raped and mutilated he delivers a painfully incongruous speech before her ruin:

> Alas, a crimson river of warm blood,
> Like to a bubbling fountain stirr'd with wind,
> Doth rise and fall between thy rosed lips,
> Coming and going with thy honey breath.
> But, sure, some Tereus hath deflowered thee,
> And, lest thou shouldst detect him, cut thy tongue.
> Ah, now thou turn'st away thy face for shame!
> And, notwithstanding all this loss of blood,
> As from a conduit with three issuing spouts,
> Yet do thy cheeks look red as Titan's face
> Blushing to be encountered with a cloud.
> (3.1.22–32)

Compare these lines to Ovid's description of the mutilation of Philomela from book six of *The Metamorphoses* (I use Arthur Golding's 1567 translation, as it sheds some light on how Shakespeare might have read the Latin – if, indeed, he did not draw his Ovid primarily from Golding's translation):

> But as she yearned and called aye upon her father's name
> And strived to have spoken still, he cruel tyrant came
> And with a pair of pinions fast did catch her by the tongue
> And with his sword did cut it off. The stump whereon it hung
> Did patter still. The tip fell down and, quivering on the ground,
> As though that it had murmured it made a certain sound.
> And as the adder's tail cut off doth skip a while, even so
> The tip of Philomela's tongue did wriggle to and fro
> And nearer to her mistressward in dying still did go.
> (6.707–15)

In both Shakespeare and Ovid, the copiousness and the "decent framing" of the language goes inexorably on, even while the subject matter is utterly repellent.

From Ovid I suggest Shakespeare develops this copious infusion of sensuous imagery into the speeches of his characters at the most intense dramatic moments, giving those characters a haunting sense of detachment from their own circumstances and, in turn, an interiority that mimics our own self-consciousness. After murdering Duncan, for example, Macbeth is at once horrified by the blood on his hands and yet capable of pausing to transform the horrific sight into poetry:

> Whence is that knocking?
> How is't with me, when every noise appals me?
> What hands are here? ha! they pluck out mine eyes.
> Will all great Neptune's ocean wash this blood
> Clean from my hand? No, this my hand will rather
> The multitudinous seas in incarnadine,
> Making the green one red.
> (2.3.55–61)

Had we just committed a murder, we probably would not pause to utter strange new words like "multitudinous" and "incarnadine" or emphasize their rich novelty by contrasting them with the simple words "green" and "red." This is a conspicuous instance of the copiousness of which Erasmus would have approved and which Ovid – given that the speech turns a disgusting subject into art through the sumptuousness of the language – would have particularly admired. And yet this most artificial and inflated language paradoxically gives Macbeth a humanity because, in contrast with the blunt emotion of the preceding lines, the copiousness seems detached – the product of intellectual reflection in the most unlikely of circumstances. In the contrast we see something that reminds us of the way we ourselves are both actors in the ongoing drama that is our lives and detached observers of those dramas and ourselves as actors – and we also must recognize the way these two personae are demarcated in the languages we speak, not only to others but also to ourselves.

It is not by accident that this discussion of Shakespeare's literary language concludes with the suggestion that Shakespeare's abiding interest in Ovid helps us recognize how one of his greatest characters' most famous soliloquies works as poetry.

There is much more to Shakespeare the poet than the soliloquy or the monologue but there is nothing *more* Shakespeare than this poetic mode. If we recognize that it derives from a tradition that regards poetry as a "speaking picture" that teaches and delights, we can give some critical substance to the oft made suggestion that Shakespeare, more than anyone else, teaches us what it means to be human. For what is definitive about human beings if not self-consciousness, and what is self-consciousness if not the capacity to act as witnesses to our own lives, to separate ourselves from our experiences, however blissful or devastating, and give them voice?

REFERENCES AND FURTHER READING

Adamson S. et al. (eds.) (2001). *Reading Shakespeare's Dramatic Language: A Guide*. London: Arden Shakespeare.

Alexander, C. M. S. (ed.) (2004) *Shakespeare and Language*. Cambridge: Cambridge University Press.

Aristotle (1995). *Poetics. Aristotle's Poetics, Longinus' On the Sublime, and Demetrius' On Style*. 2nd edn. Ed. S. Halliwell. Trans. S. Halliwell and W. H. Fyfe. Cambridge, MA: Harvard University Press.

Ascham, J. (1815). *The English Works*. London: White and Cochrane.

Barkan, L. (2001). What did Shakespeare read? In M. de Grazia and S. Wells (eds.), *The Cambridge Companion to Shakespeare* (pp. 31–48). Cambridge: Cambridge University Press.

Baxandall, M. (1971). *Giotto and the Orators: Humanist Observers of Painting in Italy and the Discovery of Pictorial Composition, 1350–1450*. Oxford: Oxford University Press.

Blake, N. F. (1983). *Shakespeare's Language: An Introduction*. New York: St. Martin's Press.

Blake, N. F. (2002). *A Grammar of Shakespeare's Language*. New York: Palgrave.

Bolton, W. F. (1992). *Shakespeare's English: Language in the History Plays*. Oxford: Blackwell.

Bradshaw, G. (1993). *Misrepresentations: Shakespeare and the Materialists*. Ithaca, NY: Cornell University Press.

Brook, G. L. (1976). *The Language of Shakespeare*. London: Andre Deutsch.

Crane, M. T. (2001). *Shakespeare's Brain: Reading with Cognitive Theory*. Princeton: Princeton University Press.

Erasmus, D. (1978). *The Collected Works of Erasmus*.

86 vols. Vol. 24. Ed. C. A. Thompson. Toronto: University of Toronto Press.

Hope, J. (2003). *Shakespeare's Grammar*. London: Thomson.

Hussey, S. S. (1992). *The Literary Language of Shakespeare*. 2nd edn. New York: Longman.

Kalas, R. (2007). *Frame, Glass, Verse: The Technology of Poetic Invention in the English Renaissance*. Ithaca, NY: Cornell University Press.

Magnusson, L. (1999). *Shakespeare and Social Dialogue: Dramatic Language and Elizabethan Letters*. Cambridge: Cambridge University Press.

Murphy, J. J. (1974). *Rhetoric in the Middle Ages: A History of Rhetorical Theory from Saint Augustine to the Renaissance*. Berkeley: University of California Press.

Ovid (2002). *Ovid's Metamorphoses*. Trans. A. Golding. Ed. M. Forey. Baltimore: Johns Hopkins University Press.

Peacham, H. (1954). The Epistle Dedicatorie. *The Garden of Eloquence*. Gainesville, FL: Scholars' Facsimiles and Reprints (unnumbered).

Puttenham, G. (1971). *The Arte of English Poesie*. Ed. B. Hathaway. Kent, OH: Kent State University Press.

Quintilian (1920). *Institutio Oratoria*. 4 vols. Trans. H. E. Butler. Cambridge, MA: Harvard University Press.

Shakespeare, W. (2005). *The Oxford Shakespeare: The Complete Works*. 2nd edn. Ed. J. Jowett, W. Montgomery, G. Taylor, and S. Wells. Oxford: Oxford University Press.

Sidney, P. (1971). *A Defence of Poetry*. Ed. J. A. Van Dorsten. Oxford: Oxford University Press.

Wilson, T. (1994). *The Art of Rhetoric*. Ed. P. E. Medine. University Park: Pennsylvania State University Press.

45
Jane Austen's Literary English

Mary Poovey

For a language like English to be "literary," two conditions must obtain. The first is historical: the connotations of *literature* must be delimited in such a way as to liberate this term from both its traditional association with the classical languages and its less restricted sense of "polite learning through reading" (Williams 1976: 151). The second condition is formal: stylistic features must be able to create a mode of writing that does not simply replicate speech but requires (typically silent) reading to actualize semantic possibilities not generated by oral communication. While these conditions have been realized only gradually, through a long history of technological innovation and authorial experimentation, Jane Austen played an important part in normalizing a version of vernacular writing that inextricably links what counts as literary English to a particular mode of reading. In this essay, I briefly examine the delimitation of the concept of literature before turning to the stylistic innovations by which Austen helped place this kind of reading at the heart of the literary experience.

Delimiting "Literature"

Since at least the seventeenth century, *literature* and *literary* had been linked to print, but until the eighteenth century, both words invoked the ability to read and the condition of being well-read rather than a kind of writing. (See EARLY MODEREN ENGLISH PRINT CULTURE.) When Samuel Johnson used the term "literary reputation" in 1773 and when, in his *Life of Cowley*, he referred to "an author whose pregnancy of imagination and elegance of language have deservedly set him high in the ranks of literature," he was hinting at a new differentiation within the more capacious concept of "polite learning" (Williams 1976: 152). This differentiation both established a hierarchy of kinds of writing and began to identify the characteristics that would be used to distinguish more worthy members of this hierarchy from less: works considered "higher" kinds of literature were characterized by a particular style – the "elegant" use of language; and reliance on imagination or creativity.

As John Guillory has pointed out, naturalizing this hierarchy entailed not only the gradual accumulation and loss of the meanings of words, but also the migration of literary practice through sets of social institutions (Guillory, forthcoming). While we need to remember that these were overlapping and geographically uneven, we can identify three large phases in the British version of this institutional history. As "polite learning through reading," literature was associated during the late seventeenth and early eighteenth centuries with the lower level of schools, where it served as a vehicle for promoting vernacular literacy; during the last two decades of the eighteenth century and most of the nineteenth century, literature – now understood in Johnson's more restricted and internally differentiated sense – was simultaneously disseminated beyond the schools through print culture and redefined, in the school setting, as a repository of texts that signaled the (ideal) "standard" of the language and, collectively, a "national literature"; and, beginning in the late nineteenth century and accelerating rapidly after the 1920s, a now even more restricted sense of literature returned to the school in the forms of a canon of "great works" and the analytic practice of "literary criticism."

In its second, arguably most transformative, phase, literature was linked through print culture to the development of new genres and forms of publication: the periodical essay, the novel, newspapers and other kinds of periodicals, encyclopedias, and so on. Critical to this phase was the period between 1780 and 1840, for these years witnessed both the proliferation of kinds of print and, partly in response, an intensification of the process of delimitation that eventually made Johnson's early attempt to discriminate among kinds of literature seem self-evident. At least four characteristics distinguish this phase of delimitation. The first was a by-product of the British government's crackdown on the proliferation of radical publications in the wake of the French Revolution (Keen 1999; Haywood 2004). Paradoxically, while it failed to abolish the radical press, this crackdown, which was epitomized by the seditious libel trials of 1794 and the passage of the Six Acts (1819), helped more conservative writers rank publications according to both content and format: some publications were identified as "vulgar" both because they espoused radical politics in a less-than-"refined" style and because they were published in an affordable ("cheap") format. The second characteristic was a by-product of the professionalization of authorship and the commodification of all kinds of print (Keen 1999; Raven 1992). The demise of patronage during the second half of the eighteenth century meant that authors had to rely on the market for economic support, and the increase in the number of presses, the proliferation of circulating libraries, and the rise in annual numbers of new issues meant that reading materials were increasingly subject to the dynamics of market society. While this enabled many writers (and booksellers) to capitalize on consumer desire, of course, it also led some to intensify efforts to discriminate even among kinds of non-political print – to designate some efforts as merely entertaining or morally pernicious so as to identify others as "serious" or "improving."

The third characteristic followed from the historical developments I have just named: the rise of radical writing, the take-off of print culture, and the resulting

increase of competition among writers. This belonged to an effort on the part of some would-be "serious" British writers to create a progressive history for "refined" literature by identifying (or manufacturing) an "authentic" oral tradition that constituted the roots of the genuine "national literature"; this, in turn, entailed denigrating as "vulgar" modes of print that remained linked to orality – such as the cheap publications associated with mass rallies (McDowell, forthcoming). Finally, the fourth characteristic was confined to what was becoming identified as the highest – or, increasingly, the most imaginative – kind of writing. This entailed, on the one hand, the aggressive self-promotion of a few writers (most prominently, William Wordsworth and Samuel Coleridge), who systematically campaigned for the superiority of writing distinguished by simple language and imaginative intensity; on the other, it entailed the voluntary adoption by other writers of the role of ancillary workers in the great campaign to improve literature. Some of these self-proclaimed "minor" writers, like Thomas De Quincey (Russett 1997), devoted themselves to promoting the work of their superiors and to refining the terms in which this superiority could be recognized; others, like Francis Jeffrey, used critical reviews published in magazines and quarterlies to police the standards of English literature.

Jane Austen's Formal Innovations

Jane Austen (1775–1817) was perfectly placed to take advantage of the take-off of print culture that began in the 1780s, and we know that Austen read widely in almost all of the available genres, including periodical reviews of new literature (Doody 1986). Because of her gender and her family situation – her father was an Anglican rector and two brothers entered the navy – Austen was also particularly vulnerable to the other world historical events that dominated the years between 1789 and 1815: the French Revolution, the ensuing rise of English radicalism, and England's fierce military and legal campaigns against France and social equality (Butler 1975). It is thus not surprising that Austen contributed to the campaign to delimit the category of literature. Although her contribution was probably informed by the theoretical pronouncements of Wordsworth and Coleridge (Deresiewicz 2005), Austen pursued an agenda that differed in significant ways from the plan laid out in *Lyrical Ballads*. Because her chosen genre was the novel, Austen had to distinguish her works not only from "vulgar" writing and "cheap" political propaganda, but also from the racy gothic fiction pouring from the Minerva Press, and, after 1810, from the saccharin didacticism loosed upon the reading public by Hannah More's *Coelebs in Search of a Wife*. Thus Austen's role in establishing a hierarchy within literature did not resemble those of Wordsworth, Coleridge, De Quincey, Jeffrey, or any of the other self-proclaimed guardians of English culture, for Austen had to contend with the much more sweeping charge that simply reading the kind of writing she had chosen to produce tended to "mislead the understanding and corrupt the heart" (Knox 1786, in Keen 2004: 108).

To neutralize such charges against the novel, Austen developed a style that encouraged her audience to read in a manner different from the way they consumed Minerva Press books. While it was (and, to a lesser extent, still is) possible to race through an Austen novel simply to discover what happens, her novels contain gentle rebukes to the naïveté of indiscriminate consumption (*Northanger Abbey*) as well as explicit models of readers who, chastened by the misunderstanding their greedy first perusal generates, go back, reread, and think about what they have read (*Pride and Prejudice*). These thematic hints about proper reading supplement Austen's less explicit – but more pervasive – stylistic cues about reading. Central to her characteristic style is her much-commented-upon use of free indirect discourse, a formal device by which the narrative system (which is sometimes, but not always, centered in a narrator) simultaneously conveys a character's thoughts and, implicitly, comments upon those thoughts. Free indirect discourse provides the reader with two points of view at the same time, one naïve and the other wise; the reader's ability to recognize the narrative's presence in the background of the character's thoughts signals her own level of sophistication, just as the shrinking of the distance between the naïveté of the character and the narrative's judiciousness signals the gradual maturation of the heroine. A typical example of free indirect discourse can be found in *Emma*, when the arrogant but well-meaning heroine recognizes the love she has long harbored, but not known, for Mr. Knightley. Here, Emma displays simultaneously her self-recognition and the limitations of that insight, for only the narrative (and the attentive reader) can register the arrogance implied by Austen's phrasing. "It darted through her with the speed of an arrow, that Mr. Knightley must marry no one but herself" (Austen 1993: 263).

Free indirect discourse is a form of communication that can only exist in writing. It exceeds the medium of speech, just as it exceeds a single point of view. While Austen's use of free indirect discourse has often been noted, however, only a few literary scholars have commented upon a related stylistic device, which is also limited to the print text: the layering of tenses created by Austen's joining the epistolary form to the single-point perspective associated with realism. The vantage point provided by this perspective is located outside and in the future of the novel's action; it organizes the text's narrative system and announces itself by the presence of past tense verbs (Ermarth 1998: 1074). The temporal layering Austen's style creates is especially complex in scenes that contain embedded letters: when she prints a letter, then describes a character reading and reacting to it, Austen layers the present tense of the letter's writing onto another present tense – the moment at which a character reads – then layers both of these presents onto the implicit retrospective vantage point provided by the narrative's past tense verbs. The effect of such layering is both to make the reader conscious of her own reading and to hold out as a reward for careful reading the experience of already-having-read that past tense verbs (and the narrative system) signal. Before discussing further the effects of this stylistic device, it might be helpful to provide an example.

Darcy's letter to Elizabeth Bennet appears in chapter 35 of *Pride and Prejudice*, and, in chapter 36, the narrative describes the way Elizabeth reads, rereads, and,

as a consequence of rereading, revises her first impressions of Darcy and Wickham.

> She read, with an eagerness which hardly left her power of comprehension, and from impatience of knowing what the next sentence might bring, was incapable of attending to the sense of the one before her eyes. His belief of her sister's insensibility, she instantly resolved to be false, and his account of the real, the worst objections to the match, made her too angry to have any wish of doing him justice. . . . But when this subject was succeeded by his account of Mr. Wickham, when she read with somewhat clearer attention, a relation of events, which, if true, must overthrow every cherished opinion of his worth, and which bore so alarming an affinity to his own history of himself, her feelings were yet more acutely painful and more difficult of definition. Astonishment, apprehension, and even horror, oppressed her. . . . In this perturbed state of mind, with thoughts that could rest on nothing, she walked on; but it would not do; in half a minute the letter was unfolded again, and collecting herself as well as she could, she again began the mortifying perusal of all that related to Wickham, and commanded herself so far as to examine the meaning of every sentence. . . . What Wickham had said of the living was fresh in her memory, and as she recalled his very words, it was impossible not to feel that there was gross duplicity on one side or the other; and, for a few moments, she flattered herself that her wishes did not err. But when she read, and re-read with the closest attention, the particulars immediately following of Wickham's resigning all pretensions to the living, of his receiving in lieu, so considerable a sum as three thousand pounds, again was she forced to hesitate. . . . Again she read on. But every line proved more clearly that the affair, which she had believed it impossible that any contrivance could so represent, as to render Mr. Darcy's conduct in it less than infamous, was capable of a turn which must make him entirely blameless through the whole. . . . She grew absolutely ashamed of herself. – Of neither Darcy nor Wickham could she think, without feeling that she had been blind, partial, prejudiced, absurd. "How despicably have I acted!" she cried. – "I, who have prided myself on my discernment! – . . . Had I been in love, I could not have been more wretchedly blind." (Austen 1996: 198–202)

In this description, Austen not only models bad reading and good; she also allows the reader to participate in the transformation of Elizabeth's understanding of events that have already been narrated. These events – the story of Wickham's youth – have in fact been narrated twice, once by Wickham himself, and once by Darcy, in the letter Elizabeth (and the reader) has just read. Juxtaposing the implicit present tense of Darcy writing with the explicit present tense of Elizabeth reading *and* with the equally explicit past tense of the narration helps convert the present tense of the reader's experience into the apparently past tense of retrospection. This past tense position is actually articulated by the narrative system, of course; it is only apparent, or virtual, for the reader, who understands that Elizabeth's new understanding is only partial (especially where it concerns herself) because the narrative's past tense verbs identify this as merely one stage in a process of maturation.

Austen's juxtaposition of past and present tenses was not, strictly speaking, a stylistic innovation. Poetic examples abound, from Chaucer's "The Shipman's Tale"

(Carruthers 2001) to Wordsworth's *Prelude* (Siskin 1988). Importing this device into the novel, however, helped elevate the status of this genre by making careful reading a critical component of understanding. Like Wordsworth's use of double negatives and his repeated, but varied, descriptive returns to a single episode or place, Austen's layering of tenses, along with her reliance on other semantically ambiguous devices – like free indirect discourse and irony – encouraged the reader to read carefully – even to reread – so as to approach the level of wisdom embodied in the narrative system as a whole. The kind of novel epitomized by the Minerva gothics did not require such careful reading, nor did such novels produce the level of interpretive sophistication Austen's novels promised. Even Hannah More and her imitators could not boast of being instructive in this way, for their explicit didacticism encouraged passive obedience, not active discrimination.

Austen's stylistic complexity can be linked to two further developments in the history of literary English, each of which is as important, in its own way, as was the elevation of the novel in the hierarchy of literary genres. The first, once more, is primarily an effect of the layering of tenses I have already described. By producing, alongside the present tense of the characters' and readers' reading experiences, a virtual past tense for the reader – the impression that one will soon know the outcome of the scene or novel one is currently reading because it is contained in a narrative system – Austen's novels help the reader imaginatively convert the temporal experience of reading into an apparently spatialized object: what Percy Lubbock called the "book," which we now call a text (Lubbock 1921). In the early twentieth century, long after Austen's stylistic complexity became the norm for serious fiction, this view of a text as a (imaginary) spatial object made it possible for readers schooled by this kind of style – that is, literary critics – to treat the product of the reading experience as an organic whole whose internal complexities could be resolved into a single, definitive paradox (Warren 1943). In the form of New Criticism, this critical practice, which was initially associated with the extra-mural little magazines, helped usher the study of serious literature – including the novel – into the US university classroom, where it is now firmly ensconced.

The second historical development with which Austen's stylistic complexity is associated involves one of the challenges print culture posed to the social relation among readers. As long as reading aloud dominated the consumption of print, members of an audience initially experienced the contents of a book or newspaper all at the same time and as a social experience. As silent, solitary reading gradually began to replace communal reading during the eighteenth century, however, the reading community became increasingly virtual. Even as the mass production and extensive circulation of books and periodicals made it possible for more readers to read the same thing at the same time, that is, the fact that they did so in different places, at different speeds, and with different levels of attention made whatever sense of social reading an individual might have had an act of faith rather than an immediate experience. When Austen replaced the epistolary form that had dominated eighteenth-century British novels with a guiding, but not controlling, narrative system, she helped make

the isolated reader part of such a virtual community. By simultaneously refining her readers' ability to discriminate among possible interpretations of an event or character and providing an implicit norm for such judgments, Austen's narrative systems solicit the kind of consensus that could (ideally) draw every reader into a single (if still imaginary) community (Ermarth 1998). This, in turn, helped make it possible for readers to discuss the "same" book, even if their initial experiences of the text in question differed in setting, quality, or meaning. Along with periodical reviews, then, which, during the nineteenth century, began to combine long excerpts from the books under review with evaluative judgments, Austen's novels helped replace an actual community of readers and listeners with a virtual community of readers and critics. The latter, of course, is still the social context in which most interpretation, criticism, and, arguably, understanding of a now-delimited version of literature occurs. Fully a product of print culture, this virtual community is the environment in which most of the people reading this essay experience the version of English we think of as literary.

References and Further Reading

Austen, J. (1993). *Emma*. 2nd edn. Ed. S. M. Parrish. New York: Norton.

Austen, J. (1996). *Pride and Prejudice*. Ed. V. Jones. London: Penguin.

Butler, M. (1975). *Jane Austen and the War of Ideas*. Oxford: Clarendon Press.

Carruthers, M. (2001). Meditations on the 'historical present' and 'collective memory' in Chaucer and *Sir Gawain and the Green Knight*. In C. Humphrey & W. M. Ormrod (eds.), *Time in the Medieval World* (pp. 137–56). York: York Medieval Press.

Deresiewicz, W. (2005). *Jane Austen and the Romantic Poets*. New York: Columbia University Press.

Doody, M. A. (1986). Jane Austen's reading. In J. D. Grey (ed.), *The Jane Austen Companion* (pp. 347–63). New York: Macmillan.

Ermarth, E. (1998). Realism. In P. Schellinger (ed.), *Encyclopedia of the Novel*. Vol. 2 (pp. 1071–8). Chicago: Fitzroy Dearborn.

Guillory, J. (forthcoming). The location of literary culture. In *Literary Study in the Age of Professionalism*. Chicago: University of Chicago Press.

Haywood, I. (2004). *The Revolution in Popular Literature: Print, Politics and the People, 1790–1860*. Cambridge: Cambridge University Press.

Keen, P. (1999). *The Crisis of Literature in the 1790s*. Cambridge: Cambridge University Press.

Keen, P. (ed.). (2004). *Revolutions in Romantic Literature: An Anthology of Print Culture, 1780–1832*. Ontario: Broadview Press.

Knox, V. (1786). On reading novels and trifling books without discrimination. In P. Keen (ed.) (2004), *Revolutions in Romantic Literature: An Anthology of Print Culture, 1780–1832* (pp. 107–8). Ontario: Broadview Press.

Lubbock, P. (1921). *The Craft of Fiction*. London: Jonathan Cape.

McDowell, P. (forthcoming). *Fugitive Voices: Print Culture, Popular Oralities, and the Idea of Oral Tradition*.

Raven, J. (1992). *Judging New Wealth: Popular Publishing and Responses to Commerce in England 1750–1800*. Oxford: Clarendon Press.

Russett, M. (1997). *De Quincey's Romanticism: Canonical Minority and the Forms of Transmission*. Cambridge: Cambridge University Press.

Siskin, C. (1988). *The Historicity of Romantic Discourse*. New York: Oxford University Press.

Warren, R. P. (1943). *Understanding Fiction*. New York: Appleton-Century-Crofts.

Williams, R. (1976). *Keywords: A Vocabulary of Culture and Society*. New York: Oxford University Press.

46

Joyce's English

Laurent Milesi

Joyce's momentous contribution to renewing previously held conceptions of literature and literariness cannot be envisaged without a consideration of his reshaping of the very notion of what literary language or literature as an experiment in language meant. Indeed the various stages of his ongoing reappraisal of the novelist's medium of expression may be selected as the feature of his writing which most conditioned its technical transformations, such as the rewriting of the verbose, "classical" novel *Stephen Hero* into the more concise modernist *Portrait of the Artist as a Young Man*, and the readoption of an aesthetics of expansion from the halfway mark in the development of *Ulysses* onwards to supersede the earlier aesthetics of economy, when Joyce's modern Odyssey turned from a sequel to *A Portrait*, mixing stream of consciousness with third-person narration, into an increasingly self-reflexive work in which the narrative technique ascribed to each chapter is foregrounded as subject. Whereas in *A Portrait* the narrator's language, which becomes gradually more articulate and analytic in order to reflect the development of Stephen's intellect, still serves as a focal point giving the reader a retrospective side-glance into the artistic alter ego's maturation at choice moments, Joyce's abandonment of the "initial style" of *Ulysses* for a versatile style more capable of rendering the circuitous wanderings of the protagonist away from home shifted the literary emphasis from storytelling proper to style as narrative. With time, fiction writing acquired an increasingly metafictional dimension, exploring new forms for their own sake, and such elements as the mnemonic flashbacks of the interior monologue came to operate as the self-reflexive linguistic traces of a work consciously recycling its past utterances. One of the earliest seeds of creation for what will become *Finnegans Wake*, known during the seventeen years of its gestation as *Work in Progress*, was in fact a thorough parodic reshaping of Joyce's most salient stylistic poses to date, especially several passages from *Ulysses* complete with adverse critical reactions, as is evidenced by the *Scribbledehobble* workbook, compiled over many years but started soon after the completion of *Ulysses*.

This constant privileging of the linguistic in the literary is recorded in now-famous pronouncements often suggestive of an attritional war against the materiality and

semantic oppressiveness of an inherited language of tradition from which a new beauty aspired to be created (Ellmann 1982: 397, 546, 702). As with other fellow modernists (Pound, T. S. Eliot), rejecting tradition and often delving back into the distant past for inspirational models also meant challenging the new orthodoxies for not suiting the medium to an expressive end. In a letter to his brother Stanislaus, after providing wittily reductive summaries of some of the short stories in Hardy's *Life's Little Ironies*, Joyce castigates the latter's lack of realism: "Is this as near as T. H. can get to life, I wonder? . . . What is wrong with these English writers is that they always keep beating about the bush" (Ellmann 1975: 136–7). Similarly, two other letters see him question Gissing as a "realist" and ask, after dismissing *Demos*: "Why are English novels so terribly boring?" (Ellmann 1975: 77, 123). Throughout his career Joyce will feel the need to challenge insular, monolithic modes of literary expression by subjecting them to cosmopolitan influences, not only to break beyond the confines of literary English as he inherited it at the dawn of the twentieth century, but also, paradoxically, to purify and re-energize it through hybridization and defamiliarization (cf. the famous "tundish scene" in chapter 5 of *A Portrait*).

From an early age Joyce's ear was attuned to the pronunciations and turns of phrase of different idioms and sociolects. History had given Ireland and its inhabitants a keen taste for witticisms (the well-famed Irish bull) coupled with a legendary garrulity epitomized by the Citizen in "Cyclops," the Hiberno-English – or, in Joyce's days, Anglo-Irish – dialect with its many local and provincial inflections which he will tap in his fiction on numerous occasions, an archaic tongue (Irish Gaelic) which, in his own opinion, nationalists were artificially striving to revive (and which is the object of a subtle linguistic satire in *Finnegans Wake*) (Milesi 1993), and various obscure cants like Shelta (tinkers' slang), Béarlagair Na Sáer ("vernacular of masons") or Bog Latin, which were later to join the list of linguistic curios for Joyce's last book (see ENGLISH IN IRELAND). The English language itself provided a ready enough model of historico-linguistic versatility, with the alliterative rhythms of old Anglo-Saxon verse, the Norman influence in its early shaping, its longstanding tradition of conceits, wordplay, and linguistic innovations of all kinds easily absorbed into the "onomato-poetic" fabric of its structure, long before school and university (where he learnt Latin, Italian, French, a modicum of Gaelic – and Dano-Norwegian and German by himself in order to read Ibsen and Hauptmann in the original) and his exiled life in Switzerland, Italy, Istria, and France were to equip Joyce with the unprecedented polyglottism which will irradiate his more mature fiction (Ellmann 1975: 153, 284). The composition of *Finnegans Wake* will also provide the occasion for researching new languages, often by compiling indexes of lexical entries and grammatical features from the relevant articles of the eleventh edition of the *Encyclopaedia Britannica*, while several trips or periods of forced inactivity due to his eye problems also allowed him to teach himself some Flemish (while he was in Ostend in September 1926) and, in 1928, Spanish and Russian.

Joyce's linguistic bent can be "officially" traced back to his matriculation paper on "The Study of Languages" (1898/99); this juvenile essay advocates the scholarly

acquaintance with ancient tongues, which allows for a better understanding of the history and etymology of one's own, and already manifests a keen awareness of the uniqueness of each of the world's interrelated idioms, the importance of translation and of the pivotal role of the writer as a custodian of a nation's language. To his brother Stanislaus he also declared his intention of studying grammar, which "would be a better whetstone for youth than geometry" (Ellmann 1975: 62), a discipline which one should understand according to its etymological signification of "art or technique of the letter." Joyce's extensive pre-draft notes for *Ulysses* and *Finnegans Wake* will later fully reflect this enduring fascination for the etymological and structural lineaments of any language as ballast for literary use. "Oxen of the Sun" in particular, with its compendium of styles culled from the most representative moments in the history of English literature and counterpointed with the gestation and final delivery of a baby boy, from Anglo-Saxon alliterative verse to broken doggerel and modern-day slang, will mark the first full-blown attempt at depleting all the literary styles available to the Irish writer by the turn of the century. But the virtuoso chapter offers a "mere" linguistic, diachronic condensation of the "odyssey of style(s)" (cf. Lawrence) which makes most of the chapters of *Ulysses* such a literary tour de force: the philologico-philosophizing of "Proteus," the newspaper-style presentation, complete with headings, of "Aeolus," the musical fugue of "Sirens," the mock-romantic reverie of "Nausicaa" mimicking young girls' mawkish magazines, the theatricalization of the hallucinatory phantasmagoria of "Circe," the jaded style of "Eumaeus" with its deliberately maladjusted, circumlocutionary prose, the catechis-tic-scientific flavor of "Ithaca," and the unpunctuated female flow of Molly Bloom in "Penelope," to name but a few. Writing himself into the night of *Ulysses*, then the dream of *Finnegans Wake*, Joyce could only contemplate as his next logical move a widening of his linguistic palette to an ever-increasing number of foreign idioms and idiolects, some seventy to eighty in the final work, depending on classifications (cf. *FW* 54.05–19, especially "at sixes and seventies," and *FW* 20.13–16: "So you need hardly spell me how every word will be bound over to carry three score and ten toptypsical readings throughout the book of Doublends Jined") (Milesi, in Rabaté (2004: 153).

Steeped in nineteenth-century historical linguistics and the "popular philology" already prevalent in his days of formation (Kenner 1974; Downing 1998; Downing, in Van Hulle 2002: 121–66) – like his fictional counterpart Stephen Dedalus, who "read Skeat's *Etymological Dictionary* by the hour" (*Stephen Hero* 26) – Joyce often allowed his narrative to acquire deeper symbolic resonance through a condensation of the etymological aura of a word. Especially in *Finnegans Wake*, a lexical element which strikes the reader as a foreignized coinage or nonce-word turns out, on closer scrutiny, to be an old forgotten English form recorded in the *OED* and excavated from the palimpsestic fabric of the language, such as *FW* 18.06: "rede" for "read" in the obsolete sense of "To guess, to make out or tell by conjecture" (in the proto-historical exchange between Mutt and Jute); *FW* 475.18: "clomb," archaic for "climbed;" *FW* 531.19: "gause," i.e., gauze + gas but equally a variant spelling of the former, etc.

But Joyce's wide-ranging interest did not stop at the diachronic studies, inventories, and taxonomies of linguistic systems and families of the Humboldtian era. From the combination of the scant surviving evidence of his Paris library and, more reliably, his copious notetaking during the gestation of *Work in Progress*, we know that he kept up to date with the proliferation of contemporary trends and theories in what was becoming modern linguistics: the work by Danish linguist Otto Jespersen on the nature of (the English) language and on an international idiom (Rosiers & Van Mierlo, in Van Hulle 2002: 55–70); German linguist Fritz Mauthner's and I. A. Richards's on metaphor (Van Hulle 2002: 91–118); Meillet and Cohen's timely publication of an encyclopedic survey of the world's languages. Towards the late 1920s, Joyce enthusiastically attended lectures on comparative phonetics and linguistics by the Jesuit Father Marcel Jousse, who also staged performances of the Gospel to demonstrate the gestural origin of language. These linguistic pantomimes found their way especially into the riddle of the "Mime of Mick, Nick, and the Maggies" in *Finnegans Wake*, with the gestural-phonetic description of the word "heliotrope." Based on the archetypal game of Angels and Devils or colors, and first called the "Twilight games," the riddle, central to the whole chapter (*Finnegans Wake* II.1), gives Shem (the Devil) three guesses at the color of the underwear of 28 or 29 girls (Maggies, a plural version of Issy his sister), guarded by his twin brother Shaun (the righteous Angel), in a pantomime or "twintomime" (*FW* 223.09). Used to strengthen the Vichian framework already in place, Jousse's rather eccentric teachings were soon bolstered up by Sir Richard Paget's two 1930 book publications: *Human Speech* and especially *Babel, or The Past, Present, and Future of Human Speech*, which expound a more scientific view of the gestural articulation of sound as an "etymological" basis for the constitution of oral language, and a "Gesture Theory of human speech" consonant with Jousse's (Milesi, in Van Hulle 2002: 75–89). Working away from his juvenile enthusiasm for the rhythmic epiphany and view of art as gesture in *Stephen Hero* or in his early musings on rhythm and dance (*The Workshop of Deadlus*), Joyce took into uncharted territory the post-symbolist elevation of music as the paragon any art should aspire to, as he probed into language for its many rhythmical inflections, the play between phonemes and graphemes, or even its dysfunctioning as entropic noise, culminating in the *Wake*'s ability to "tune in" to idioms and languages as one would to frequencies of radio stations in a polyphonic babel (e.g., *FW* pp. 500–1). Also during these years of theoretical ferment, Joyce became acquainted with the work of C. K. Ogden – for whom he recorded the closing pages of the "Anna Livia Plurabelle" chapter in August 1929 – in pragmatic linguistics and especially his contemporary project of a Basic English, short for British American Scientific International Commercial (English), yet another internationalist medium of communication and artificial construction comprising a select vocabulary of 850 words capable of turning English into an easily graspable second language and *lingua franca*, and which was to gain political support especially after World War II as a tool for peace. These interests testify to Joyce's underlying dream of a literary language providing an aestheticized universal language, as in "Circe" where Stephen Dedalus exclaims: "gesture, not music not odour, would

be a universal language, the gift of tongues rendering visible not the lay sense but the first entelechy, the structural rhythm" (*Ulysses* 15: 105–7).

Faced with this vast array of sometimes conflicting linguistic theories, the critic may well wonder how Joyce related to them from a literary or even ideological point of view. It is worth noting that, although Joyce's keen awareness of the literary potential of language's materiality stretches as far back as the very first lines of "The Sisters," with the uncanny signifiers of paralysis, gnomon, and simony distilling their substance throughout the story and, more generally, the whole collection, his more intensive forays into etymology, structure, meaning, and individual idioms, as well as artificial universal constructs, correspond with the ironic turn taken by his more mature novelistic production, from the "second half" of *Ulysses* onwards (1918–19). Joyce showed a lasting interest in the philosophy of Giambattista Vico, with its conception of a linguistic, more specifically poetic and imaginative, consciousness at the root of culture and mental activity, and his emphasis on the insights etymology can offer into historical processes. But his no-nonsense approach even to such a longstanding structural influence as the eighteenth-century Neapolitan philosopher, captured in the famous statement "I use his cycles as a trellis" (Ellmann 1982: 554), may be generalized as the key to the relativizing mixture of irony, detachment, and pragmatism to which this variegated material was increasingly subjected. One salient instance of his leveling off of all such competing doctrines can be seen in *Finnegans Wake*, p. 378, where, kicked off by "-mock Gramm's [Grimm's] laws," such silly-sounding names as the "pooh-pooh" and "bow-wow" theories of the origin of speech (culled from Jespersen's *Language*) provide the facile trigger for humorous dismissal as "outer nocense" (i.e., utter nonsense), alongside a recall of the Vichian-Joussean tripartite scheme for the evolution of language: "In the buginning is the wuid, in the muddle is the sounddance and thereinofter you're in the unbewised again, vund vulsyvolsy" (*FW* 378.29–31). The ultimate test of the linguistic as well as literary material he generously ransacked for reprocessing into *Ulysses* and *Finnegans Wake* was not its ideological soundness or even its aesthetic value, as with the cosmopolitan flair and cultural pantheon of Pound's *Cantos*, but its thematic recyclability within the crucible of Joyce's literary art, its true usefulness as opposed to its useful truth founding a truly Joycean poetics of the letter.

Among the palette of the world's idioms which Joyce amassed for inclusion in what will become *Finnegans Wake*, the so-called "artificial languages" form a specific category. Alongside Japanese, Esperanto (the "language of hope") is one of the first languages of non-competence to have found its way into the drafts of *Work in Progress* – appropriately enough, in chapter III.4, heralding a new dawn – thus confirming how relevant such still fashionable ideals were to his own work, if only as a counterpoint. For although Joyce's "artificial tongue with a natural curl" (*FW* 169.15–16) seemingly shares with attempts at an international language a similar extraction of mainly west-European idioms as the basis for its creation and viability, the ideological aims of "Wakese" and artificial universal constructions are ultimately radically different. Whereas Basic English and suchlike operate through forceful reduction, minimalism,

and simplification in order to survive as an instrumental communicational tool, Joyce's Wakean language evinced ever-increasing expansiveness and jubilatory excess as it grew in fluency and scope. Besides, "however basically English" (*FW* 116.25) Joyce's last work may inevitably be, thus reminding us indirectly that its polyglottal web remained rooted in a recognizably English morpholexical substratum, the "cosmopolitics" at work in Wakese is at variance with the imperialist nature of a universalist "Basic English," and Joyce's ideal desire to let every fragment of the *Wake* speak to any citizen of the world should not be misconstrued as the triumph of the communicative, let alone commercial, proselytizing function of literature, a literary globalization *avant la lettre*, but as that of the imaginative force of poetry in bridging the post-babelian linguistic gap, if only in a dream. What Joyce's own imagination of a universal language makes clear is that global communication is not achieved through the reduction of difference and meaning to a mythically common denominator but by multiplying and cross-fertilizing localisms in a cosmopolitics of linguistic hybridity rather than national purity. More artistic than artificial, Joyce's ultimate literary brew of multilingual portmanteau words might best be called "synthetic" and aims to eschew both the excesses of the naturalization of the national and the depoeticized, "basic" aridity of universalist creations. In calling into question the (inter)nationalist ideology and politics at work in any linguistic identification and foregrounding the drama of representation and kinship, it ultimately forces the reader to rethink the relationship between "natural" and "artificial," national, international, and local idioms.

No doubt developing some of the lines Joyce himself had thrown to him, Samuel Beckett had already stressed the parallel between the *Wake*'s international synthetic language and "Father Dante's" interregional construct exhumed after ruthlessly vivisecting municipal idioms and parlances in *De Vulgari eloquentia* (Beckett 1972). If Dante's sifting of the pure Italian language from the multiplicity of coarse Italic dialects led him to a synthetic, utopian creation through a kind of "linguistic alchemy," its aim went beyond mere communication – language as vehicular for political and economic purposes – into the realm of literature (the later fashioning of the *Divine Comedy*) but also "religious politics": turning the universalizing of the *vulgare* into an illustrious redemption of Babel. It is quite fitting therefore that Joyce's ultimate artistic alter ego, Shem the Penman, mainly in the chapter devoted to his scathing portrait by his twin brother Shaun (*Finnegans Wake* I.7), will concentrate the references to Dante's project of a synthetic linguistic composition and verbal echoes of *De Vulgari eloquentia*, after the significant mention of his "synthetic ink" (*FW* 185.7; see Boldrini 2001: esp. 117–21; Boldrini, in Milesi 2003: 180–94). Through his intimate knowledge of Dante, Joyce grasped the thematic continuity between the problematic of linguistic universality and the myth of Babel, which enabled him to avoid the ideological strictures seen above and take his literary-linguistic creations into the sphere of mythopoetics.

Deployed along a trajectory from Babel (the division of language into several languages) to Pentecost (their reconciliation), *Finnegans Wake* incessantly replays the drama of the evolution, corruption, multiplication, and redemption of language as a

creative *felix culpa* (happy fault) whose dynamic unit is the miscegenated portmanteau word, which aptly reconciles, as it were through a process of *at-one-ment*, estranged languages and the cultures they represent into a localized, transcultural synthesis, just as the whole encyclopedic universe is subsumed into the microcosmic Dublin family of the Earwickers. From the quaint blend of popular beliefs and scientificity that presided over the nineteenth-century philological tradition, Joyce also derived the notions of a language "character" and "family" and made them his own for fictional purposes in his last work. This thematization or even "characterization" of languages freely complies with or by-passes and betrays the stricter laws of historical kinship to fully exploit the range of imaginary valencies offered by cultural, geographical, etc., coincidences. This recreative process known within the text itself as *"{t}he abnihilisation of the etym"* (*FW* 353.22), i.e., at once the annihilation of the atom or, in linguistics, the etymon and also creation *ab nihilo* from both, is also reminiscent of the Vichian equivalence between the history of families and institutions and the history of language(s), a topos that one may trace back to the alignment of idioms with the genealogies of peoples in the Bible and its exegetical traditions.

As the pinnacle of Modernism's revolutionary aesthetics, *Ulysses* and especially *Finnegans Wake* soon became the epitome of elitist impenetrability in the eyes of their detractors. Yet recent reappraisals of Joyce's Wakean idiom, once held to be the acme of linguisticism, have concluded in favor of its generous anti-nationalist geopolitics, and in spite of Joyce's fictional redeployment of Vico's somewhat antimodernist philosophy and philology, his poetics is salvaged by the more progressive framework of ethics and humanity in his Dublin microcosm. Similarly, Joyce's notorious relativism – seen for instance in his exposure, in several sections of *Ulysses* and *Finnegans Wake*, of the theoretical naivety of unqualified adherence to explanatory, analogical systems, etymologism as a foundation of linguistic truth, the lure of taxonomies, and of a belief in the organicity of language as a system – should not be interpreted as a radical disengagement of the language of literature from issues of ethico-political responsibility lying beyond aesthetic representation, but on the contrary as an affirmation of difference, yet equality within a linguistic melting pot (here one can also think of Bloom's humble, yet touching reflections on love and humanity under pressure from the bellicose nationalist Citizen in "Cyclops"). Against contemporary radical etymologism *à la* Heidegger, monolingual simplification or "debabelization" (Basic English) but also selective synthetic universalism (e.g., for Esperanto), and any steadfastly observed theory at all, Joyce's pliable Wakean narrative, "told . . . in universal, in polygluttural, in each auxiliary neutral idiom . . . and anythongue athall" (*FW* 117.12–16), promotes the commonality of roots through the intercultural "pollylogue" (*FW* 470.09) of its portmanteau idiom. Unlike his fellow modernists, especially Pound, who parted literary allegiance with the Irish writer at some point near the end of *Ulysses* and was entirely dismissive of the *Wake* – "nothing short of divine vision or a new cure for the clapp [*sic*] can possibly be worth all the circumambient peripherization" (Ellmann 1982: 584) – Joyce succeeded in developing a viable mixture of poetics and cosmopolitics in a radically revamped practice of "literary language."

REFERENCES AND FURTHER READING

Atherton, J. S. (1974). *The Books at the Wake: A Study of Literary Allusions in James Joyce's "Finnegans Wake."* Mamaroneck, NY: Paul P. Appel.

Beckett, S. (1972 [1929]). Dante . . . Bruno. Vico . . . Joyce. In S. Beckett et al. (eds.), *Our Exagmination Round His Factification for Incamination of Work in Progress* (pp. 3–22). London: Faber.

Boldrini, L. (2001). *Joyce, Dante, and the Poetics of Literary Relations: Language and Meaning in "Finnegans Wake."* Cambridge: Cambridge University Press.

Downing, G. M. (1998). Richard Chenevix Trench and Joyce's historical study of words. *Joyce Studies Annual*, 9, 37–68.

Ellmann, R. (ed.) (1975). *Selected Letters of James Joyce.* New York: Viking.

Ellmann, R. (1982). *James Joyce.* New and revd. edn. Oxford: Oxford University Press.

Joyce, J. (1955). *Stephen Hero.* Ed. J. J. Slocum & H. Cahoon. New York: New Directions.

Joyce, J. (1969 [1914]). *Dubliners: Text, Criticism, and Notes.* Ed. R. Scholes & A. W. Litz. New York: Viking.

Joyce, J. (1975 [1939]). *Finnegans Wake.* London: Faber.

Joyce, J. (1977 [1944]). *A Portrait of the Artist as a Young Man: Text, Criticism, and Notes.* Ed. C. G. Anderson. London: Penguin.

Joyce, J. (1986 [1922]). *Ulysses: A Critical and Synoptic Edition.* 3 vols. Ed. H. W. Gabler, with W. Steppe & C. Melchior. New York: Garland.

Kenner, H. (1974). Joyce and the 19th-century linguistics explosion. *Atti del Third International James Joyce Symposium, Trieste 14–18 giugno 1971* (pp. 45–60). Trieste: Università degli Studi.

Lawrence, K. (1981). *The Odyssey of Style in "Ulysses."* Princeton, NJ: Princeton University Press.

Mason, E. & Ellmann, R. (eds.) (1989 [1959]). *The Critical Writings of James Joyce.* Ithaca, NY: Cornell University Press.

Milesi, L. (1993). The perversions of 'Aerse' and the Anglo-Irish middle voice in *Finnegans Wake.* *Joyce Studies Annual*, 4, 98–118.

Milesi, L. (ed.) (2003). *James Joyce and the Difference of Language.* Cambridge: Cambridge University Press.

Rabaté, J.-M. (2004). *Palgrave Advances in James Joyce Studies.* London: Palgrave.

Scholes, R. & Kain, R. M. (eds.) (1965). *The Workshop of Dedalus: James Joyce and the Raw Materials for "A Portrait of the Artist as a Young Man."* Evanston, IL: Northwestern University Press.

Van Hulle, D. (ed.) (2002). *James Joyce: The Study of Languages.* Brussels: Peter Lang.

47

Faulkner's Language

Noel Polk

– words are no good; . . . words dont ever fit *even what they are trying to say at.*
Addie Bundren, in *As I Lay Dying*

The extent to which William Faulkner endorsed Addie Bundren's well-known formulation about words is not completely clear, though there is some reason to doubt that he was in complete agreement with her. He, after all, made of himself – with *As I Lay Dying* and *The Sound and the Fury* and *Absalom, Absalom!* – one of the twentieth century's foremost experimenters with language and the way words work, and he set about as a fiction writer to try to find ways to make words "say." Clearly he understood words' power to appall and excite, to persuade to love and hate. But he was also supremely aware of words' slipperiness, of how they floated around and toward meaning as a moth flirts with a flame. He was from the beginning of his career very interested in the gap between any word and its meaning: to use de Saussure's terms, though Faulkner wouldn't necessarily have known them, he constantly played in the gap between the signifier and the signified, in the abyss that can fall between any word and what it is trying to say at.

Like e. e. cummings, Faulkner saw language as a field of play, a vast field of constantly evolving and crisscrossing contingencies that made it inherently unstable: it was for Faulkner, then, an apt analogue to life, probably in all centuries but certainly in the twentieth, whose customs and mores and histories he undertook to describe. His novels and stories are fairly consistent in their investigation of language, of words' slipperinesses and their confusions; of their sounds and their incredibly complicated written representations. Most of his books contain a scene of writing, reading, or interpretation, and at least two of his novels turn on such scenes. At top dead center of *Go Down, Moses*, for example, are Isaac McCaslin's attempts to read the business ledgers of his family's plantation in order to understand his family history: the ledgers, written over the course of several decades to record the expenses connected with

running the plantation, also record the lives and deaths and births of the McCaslin slaves and other information about the farm's daily business over the years. The authors of the ledgers are his father and his uncle, who write a minimally literate written English based in idiosyncratic and inconsistent misspellings, abbreviations, symbols, and fragmentary sentence structures; there are many gaps in the information these ledgers provide such that to the extent that Isaac insists upon constructing a unified, coherent family history from them, he must fill in many of those gaps. The entire novel turns upon his gap-filling, and it remains a central question in the study of *Go Down, Moses* whether Isaac's gap-filling produces a true history or a false one suited to his own needs.

Doomed by his craft to deal with inadequate words, Faulkner resorted to an inventive array of other visual devices – italics; double and single quotation marks; flush-left paragraph margins; dialogue separated by dashes; uncapitalized and unpunctuated and ungrammatical passages in characters' speeches and thoughts and written expressions; extremely long compound-complex sentences (which always parse, except when they are not supposed to); literal blank spaces and gaps in the text; and line drawings of a coffin and of an eyeball as part of the text – to supplement what words by themselves could not communicate.

He understood that we construct our language, as we do life itself, from multiple and interminable series of contingencies generated out of a constantly expanding and altering frame of reference for each speech utterance, frames that create the gaps in language where ambiguities and double meanings occur. Faulkner found it useful to his fictional intentions to foreground these contingencies, to treat them as part of the language rather than as adjuncts to it, and in his best work he exploited those gaps and contingencies to challenge our sense of what and how language signifies. Indeed, the title *The Sound and the Fury* comes from the passage in *Macbeth* which defines life as "a tale told by an idiot . . . *Signifying nothing.*" That is, the novels do not produce a conventional, reductive, interpretable "meaning," in any real sense. They are all about the problematics of meaning, its elusiveness; they do not generally "solve" issues or mysteries but merely explore them: *Absalom, Absalom!* is constructed by its various narrators almost completely of language and narrative – the narrators have precious little, almost nothing in fact, of evidence upon which to base their conjectures about Thomas Sutpen's family. The novel leaves us with the uncomfortable feeling that none of the narrators' explanations of why Henry Sutpen kills Charles Bon really explain the killing or are true in any sense at all except the narrative one – they are "true enough," as Mr. Compson says.

I can best illustrate Faulkner's language by a brief look at some examples from *The Sound and the Fury.* In the opening sequence, the narrator, Benjy Compson, stands at the fence that separates him from the old pasture which his family has sold in order to fund his brother Quentin's education at Harvard; the purchasers have converted the pasture into a golf course. Benjy watches the golfers without knowing what they are doing, while Luster, his black caretaker, looks for a quarter he has lost. Benjy hears one of the golfers call "caddie," and begins moaning in agony for his beloved lost

sister "Caddy." Neither readers nor Luster understand why he moans. Faulkner may seem here to play a bit false with us, in writing the word that the golfer says rather than the word that Benjy hears, but it may not be false to his larger intentions of forcing a collision between oral, aural, and written words, so that they exist in a quadrangulation of significations among narrator, reader, golfers, and author that emanate from a single speech act, which is also at the same time a single written act. Not incidentally, this collision also works to decenter our narrator, to challenge traditional notions of how writers and speakers generate narrative and to make readers uncertain where the narration comes from.

Benjy's response to the golfer's command is not a matter of misunderstanding the sounds the golfer makes; he does not misunderstand what he hears, though he does misunderstand what the golfer says. Inscribing the scene on paper, Faulkner had to decide how to represent that sound, [kædɪ], visually. He chose a deliberate misdirection, a miscommunication, or perhaps *dys*communication, with his reader *and* with his narrator. If he had written that the golfer says "Here, Caddy," he would have misrepresented the unambiguous intent of the golfer's oral communication, though of course he would have more accurately represented the meaning that Benjy ascribes to those phonemes. He chose to misrepresent what Benjy hears rather than what the golfer says. Just as he plays with Benjy's hearing of the phonemes [kædɪ], so does he play with the way we read, with the mechanical signs of punctuation and spelling that harness and control, that give rhythm and shape and weight and expressive meaning to, the silent words that appear on the paper.

He uses the visual representation of language as a direct objective correlative to the states of each of the narrators' minds. Frequently they work against the words themselves, revealing things other than what the characters are actually saying, and often revealing things that the narrators are incapable of saying or are specifically trying to keep from saying, things that have caused them pain and shame. Words are, for Quentin and Jason, lids they use to seal that pain in the unconscious, though it constantly insists upon verbalizing itself. We have access to their pain largely through what they *don't* say.

Benjy's section prepares us powerfully for the much more complex linguistic situations in the next three sections. Benjy tries to say and can't; his brothers try not to say, and can't keep from it. He keeps helplessly recycling his past, slipping from one time level to another through verbal or visual associations. Quentin's relationship with his past is quite different. Episodes, telling moments from that past, exist in degrees of intensity, of psychic pain, which his consciousness has dwelled upon, worked through and over, in ways that continue to torture him. All of Quentin's past tries to crowd in on him at once, every painful episode tries to elbow its way past all the others into consciousness simultaneously. But whereas Benjy's memory is flat and two-dimensional, like the language of his section, Quentin's is like a large fluid-filled balloon that he is trying to flatten out, to control; but every time he steps on one spot, on one painful memory, the balloon erupts upward and outward at another point, constantly reshaping itself to its own pernicious energy.

Quentin cannot control the chaos of his amoeba-like memory and he finally suc-
cumbs to it. The protective walls he builds with his formal eloquence are constantly
breached by visual intrusions from his past, italicized fragments of phrases and images
that emerge briefly, even flickeringly, in no apparent order or relation, through the
barriers of his language before he is able to stamp them down again, in his futile effort
to keep them from full verbalization. His memories evolve out of scenes of trauma,
all centered in his loss of Caddy: her wedding; his conversation with Herbert Head,
the husband his parents trapped for Caddy; her love affair with Dalton Ames and his
humiliating inability to defend her honor; his long conversation with his father,
whether real or imagined, whether a single conversation or an amalgam of several
similar ones, about the meaning – or the meaninglessness – of life; and, perhaps, his
fear that he might be a homosexual. The substance of his monologue is his effort to
sort out, analyze, and come to terms with those scenes of pain that he can handle, and
to evade, to repress, those that he cannot.

Faulkner records Quentin's efforts to control his thoughts through the representation of his syntax, grammar, and punctuation. The more in control he is, the more
intricate and sophisticated the structure of his sentences, the cohesion of his paragraphs; the less lucid his mind, the less formal or "normal" Faulkner's representation
of his language on paper becomes. The most painful scenes are the farthest removed
from representational normalcy (Ross 1989: 173–4). One can thus trace Quentin's
psychic disintegration, his movements into and out of lucidity, in the degree of normality of his language's representation, from the intricately structured sentences of
some passages to the almost complete disintegration of traditional language representation in others; this disintegration occurs especially in two scenes close to the end of
his section that abandon punctuation and paragraph indentation, and in the penulti-
mate paragraph of his section in which he finally also yields up the capital "I," the
orthographical symbol of the fragile ego he has managed to cling to, to the lower case
"i," which represents graphemically his disintegrated self. Each of these three scenes
springs into consciousness at moments when his psychic censors are completely
relaxed; the crucial one, that recounting Caddy's love affair with Dalton Ames and
his ineffectual efforts to stop it, occurs when Quentin is literally unconscious, or at
least floating in some twilight zone between consciousness and unconsciousness,
having been knocked out by Gerald Bland. Language's grammatical formality, then,
is for Quentin a conscious way to keep away from those things he does not want to
think, those things he does not want to say.

Quentin is capable of poetic analogies, similes, and metaphors, of complicated but
perfectly balanced parallel structures:

> I quit moving around and went to the window and drew the curtains aside and
> watched them running for chapel, the same ones fighting the same heaving coat-sleeves,
> the same books and flapping collars flushing past like debris on a flood, and Spoade.
> (p. 78)

This sentence contains and controls all the moiling activity of the Harvard yard below his window, the running and fighting and heaving and flapping and flushing, within its intricately parallel and rhythmic poetic structures, until Spoade intrudes upon his ordering language. Grammatically, "Spoade" is the second element of a compound direct object of the verb "watched" – I watched them and Spoade – but its placement at the end of the sentence, following the comma, has the effect of alienating Spoade from the controlled rhythms of the rest of the sentence. Spoade disrupts the order of Quentin's mind and of his syntax because he reminds Quentin of discomfiting conversations about homoeroticism and about virginity, a train of thought he passively follows back home to Jefferson to yet another version of his all consuming conversation with his father. As he moves backward toward that conversation he loses control of syntax and of cohesion:

> Calling Shreve my husband. Ah let him alone, Shreve said, if he's got better sense than to chase after the little dirty sluts, whose business. In the South you are ashamed of being a virgin. Boys. Men. They lie about it. Because it means less to women, Father said. He said it was men invented virginity not women. Father said it's like death: only a state in which the others are left and I said, But to believe it doesn't matter and he said, That's what's so sad about anything: not only virginity and I said, Why couldn't it have been me and not her who is unvirgin and he said, That's why that's sad too; nothing is even worth the changing of it, and Shreve said if he's got better sense than to chase after the little dirty sluts and I said Did you ever have a sister? Did you? Did you?

Fragments of conversations at Jefferson and at Cambridge crowd confusingly together in a near-complete breakdown of cohesion in the desperation of the paragraph's final sentences, which breakdown signals the loss of the carefully controlled observation of the world outside his window that began the passage. Reaching the juxtaposition of "little dirty sluts" and "sister," however, Quentin realizes he is on dangerous ground and quickly jerks himself back, away from this direction, and into a new paragraph, an ordered and detailed description of Spoade that moves him safely back into the midst of the crowd, again contains and controls him both poetically and syntactically by making him over into a turtle, the very model of static non-aggression: "Spoade was in the middle of them like a terrapin in a street full of scuttering dead leaves" (p. 78).

If Benjy is non-verbal and trying to say, and if Quentin is extremely verbal and trying not to say, trying to maintain order by keeping his words inside his head, Jason is intensely, loudly, desperately, gloriously oral. He keeps himself talking loudly so that he won't have to listen to the voices that threaten him: he drowns out one horrendous noise with an even more horrendous one.

One of the reasons Jason has been taken as "saner" than his brothers is the relative normality of Faulkner's representation of his speech. His monologue almost completely lacks the visual markers, italics the most noticeable, of his brothers'

incoherencies and psychic instabilities. It moves as much by associative logic as his brothers' do, but because his psychic censor is much stronger than Quentin's, he is always able to stop himself just short of speaking that which he most fears, and so he does manage to maintain a kind of control over his syntax – and so over his psyche – that his brothers utterly fail at. But Jason cannot hide his diversionary tactics, and although Faulkner uses no italics in Jason's section, he still plays with the conventions of punctuation and representation in ways that reveal Jason's unconscious to us.

In certain ways Faulkner plays with the artifices of representation more daringly here than in the first two monologues. Some of them can be demonstrated by noting one difference between the 1929 Cape & Smith first edition text and the 1984 Random House New Corrected Text, which relies heavily on Faulkner's carbon type-script of the novel. It occurs toward the end of a long funny diatribe that begins "Well, Jason likes work," and moves immediately to a predictable litany into which Jason compresses all of the objects of his anxieties by the same sort of fluid association characteristic of Quentin's and Benjy's monologues; the association, though, is very revealing. From his savagely ironic acceptance of his need to work, he jumps imme-diately to the reasons he has to work and like it, all of which revolve around the complex of circumstances that he consciously sees as a betrayal of his chances to "get ahead" in life: Quentin's suicide, his father's death, Caddy's defalcation, Benjy's cas-tration, and his mother's whining domination, all of which he jokes about in order to keep them at a distance. Clearly, Jason is in pain. Though he here mostly maintains control over his syntax, the energy of the passage suggests that that pain is about to spill over into associations that he cannot control. He doesn't, for example, name Caddy, his brother Quentin, or Father, although he does name his niece and Ben, who are the tangible, daily reminders of his abandonment by the others. But the passage continues, a few lines later:

> It's your grandchild, which is more than any other grandparents it's got can say for certain. Only I says it's only a question of time. If you believe she'll do what she says and not try to see it, you fool yourself because the first time that was the Mother kept on saying thank God you are not a Compson except in name, because you are all I have left now, you and Maury and I says well I could spare Uncle Maury myself and then they came and said they were ready to start. Mother stopped crying then. She pulled her veil down and we went down stairs. (p. 196)

Jason's narrative here runs directly into, and then backs away from, a syntactical breakdown, as he realizes that he is approaching dangerously near one of his scenes of pain, his father's funeral. He still will not name Caddy, though clearly he is about to try to convince his mother that his sister will not keep her word not to see Miss Quentin. He starts to tell her how he knows Caddy won't keep her word by recalling her return to Jefferson to their father's funeral, but as he approaches the words "father's funeral," he realizes that he has entered dangerous territory, and he stumbles:

> because the first time that was the Mother kept on saying.

The Cape & Smith editors of the first edition, believing that something was amiss, rendered this passage this way:

> because the first time that was that Mother kept on saying. (SF 1929: 244)

But this editorial intervention neither corrects nor clarifies what is happening in these few words (Polk 1985: 63). Jason catches himself back, just in time, from stumbling rhetorically into his father's grave. He starts to tell his mother that she can't trust Caddy because Caddy lied "the first time" she promised never to try to see her daughter again; Jason is on the verge of putting into words the scene of his and Caddy's confrontation over his father's grave, which has been triggered in his memory by his conversation with his mother about why he has to work, why he "likes" work. But he stalls. Faulkner's carbon typescript and his holograph manuscript render this passage as it appears in the 1984 New Corrected Text, and the passage is perfectly understandable as Faulkner wrote it if we try to hear Jason stumbling over his words. A more traditional novelist, using more traditional syntactical signs, might have rendered the passage as

> because the first time – that was – the – Mother kept on saying

a formulation which would have visually approximated the rhythms of Jason's stumbling uncertainty at how to avoid what he is afraid he is about to say. Faulkner denies us the written punctuation that tells us how to hear Jason as he speaks, as he rushes blindly into a danger zone, halts, backs up, tries a couple of times to start over, and then finds a safer direction to pursue, in which he talks not to but rather about his mother.

Faulkner's concern with language was not merely an intellectual exercise, but is rather directly rated to his treatment of his characters, his understanding of their completely human predicaments in the twentieth century. He made it part of his fictional enterprise to re-energize the American language by constantly forcing newness on it, because he knew that language had to be new to be sufficient to express the newness of the new century that had already been defined by Freud, Einstein, revolution, and world war. He understood that the new century demanded a language that Wallace Stevens knew needed to be "living," it must "learn the speech of the place. / It has to face the men of the time and to meet / The women of the time. It has to think about war / And it has to find what will suffice. / It has to construct a new stage" (Stevens 1997: 218–19).

NOTE

For this essay I've borrowed from and recontextualized portions of my essay "Trying Not to Say," which appears in my *Children of the Dark House*.

REFERENCES AND FURTHER READING

Bleikasten, A. (1976). *The Most Splendid Failure: Faulkner's The Sound and the Fury*. Bloomington: Indiana University Press.

Faulkner, W. (1984 [1929]). *The Sound and the Fury*. New, corrected edn. New York: Random House.

Godden, R. (1993). Tyrrhenian vase or crucible of race? In N. Polk (ed.), *New Essays on The Sound and the Fury* (pp. 71–97). Cambridge: Cambridge University Press.

Lockyer, J. (1991). *Ordered by Words: Language and Narration in the Novels of William Faulkner*. Carbondale: Southern Illinois University Press.

Matthews, J. T. (1982). *The Play of Faulkner's Language*. Ithaca, NY: Cornell University Press.

Polk, N. (1985). *An Editorial Handbook for William Faulkner's The Sound and the Fury*. New York: Garland.

Polk, N. (1996). Trying not to say. In N. Polk (ed.), *Children of the Dark House: Text and Context in Faulkner* (pp. 99–136). Jackson: University Press of Mississippi.

Ross, S. (1989). *Fiction's Inexhaustible Voice: Speech and Writing in Faulkner*. Athens: University of Georgia Press.

Stevens, W. (1997). Of modern poetry. In *Collected Poetry and Prose*. New York: Library of America.

48

Twixt the Twain: East-West in Rushdie's Zubaan-Tongue

Tabish Khair

It has become common critical practice to insert a reference to Rudyard Kipling in every other paper on Salman Rushdie. However, the "twain" in the title of this essay is as much a reference to Mark Twain, perhaps the only major novelist whose textual presence has not been traced by critics in Rushdie's highly intertextual novels, as it is a dusty colonial memento from Kipling, whose East and West, despite the "twixt," could actually undergo a same-sex bonding on muscular horseback.

The Ghost of Mark Twain

If Rushdie has tried to leap the steed of his creativity over the much-muddied, junk-filled ditch between East and West *à la* Kipling's horsemen, he has also been haunted by the shade of Mark Twain, the first *major non-British* novelist who came to be celebrated for his ability to copy certain *post-colonial* speech patterns and rhythms in English. Rushdie has been praised, and not without reason, for a similar ability. As Anita Desai, herself a stylishly correct writer of the language, puts it, it was Rushdie who "finally brought the *spoken* language off the streets onto the printed page . . . Suddenly it was made apparent that the Indian writer had as distinctive and authentic a voice as the American or the Caribbean" (my emphasis; quoted in Lal 1995: 130). Salman Rushdie has also been criticized, and again not altogether without reason, for his English. Bruce King has accused Rushdie of "loud braying" in his later novels (King 1997: 212) and Harish Trivedi has cast nuanced doubt on its relationship to Indian English:

It could be argued that the single most remarkable novum that Rushdie introduced in his use of English here was his incorporation of some Indian, i.e. Hindi-Urdu/Hindustani, words, phrases and collocations. He did not subvert English from within, in the trendy radical catch-phrase of his youth; rather, he changed it from without. He did

not alter the basic ingredients; he only added some new spices. (Trivedi, in Mukherjee 1999: 73)

Some – though not all – of this controversy is a consequence of certain myths about literature in general and about English in India in particular. To take the general myth first, from the time of Mark Twain downwards, critics writing about literary languages in English have often been guilty of what Jacques Derrida termed "logocentrism." One does not need to buy the entire Derridaean package to recognize the dominant logocentrism of criticism that establishes a binary opposition between "a pure, inner core or origin (in language, voice), and the externalized mediation of this core or origin (writing)" (Johnson 1997: 40). This opposition also privileges the originary or inner core over the externalized mediation; that is, voice or speech over writing. A conservative critic talks about the purity of some version of standard English and how it remains true to the "real rhythms" of the language; a radical critic finds some working-class dialect or Caribbean Creole to celebrate. But even though these two kinds of critics are liable to come to blows over the language that "matters," their basic assumption is the same: literary language is the work of a tape-recorder.

This is a misleading assumption. Literary languages do not simply imitate or mimic spoken language. However, they can, in some cases and under certain circumstances, give the impression of doing so. This impression is art and being art it is artificial; it is not simple verisimilitude or mimicry. This was as true of Mark Twain as it is of Salman Rushdie. However, even critics – and where is the brave critic that doesn't these days? – who disdain any discussion of art (or literature) as imitation of "reality," talk of some kinds of literary languages in terms of a similar imitation of audio "reality." It is in this sense that the "twain" in the title of this essay is not Rudyard but Samuel: the genuine achievement of Rushdie is haunted by the shades of Mark Twain, just as Twain's own achievement tends to be underplayed if his vital literary language is attributed to a mind not very different from the insides of a Sony ghetto-blaster.

But Mark Twain is also connected, if tangentially, to the other set of assumptions that plague and often retard any real discussion of Rushdie's fiction. In the year 1835, when Samuel Langhorne Clemens, later to become Mark Twain, was born in Florida, USA, then the first Anglophone post-colonial nation, a descent as significant, if not more, was seeing the light of day in colonized India. Roughly around the time when Baby Samuel sucked air into his lungs and set about bawling, Thomas Babington (later Lord) Macaulay dipped his pen in ink and put the final touches to his *Minute on Education*. Both the acts, in two different halves of the globe, had to do with language, but their legacies would be very different. In the USA, Baby Samuel's no doubt lusty bawling would lead in due course to the literary language of Mark Twain, a language that tricked the reader into believing that he was reading a dialect and thus helped "the spoken language of the streets" of America obtain a better balance with Standard English. In India, Macaulay's edict would lead to creativity of a different

sort: creativity in a language that has a very different relationship to the spoken language of the Indian streets than Twain's literary language had with the "spoken language" of America. Hence, the "history of defamiliarizing English," as Lock puts it, has a different trajectory and significance in India than in the USA (or, for that matter, Ireland or Wales).

The Ghost of Lord Macaulay

It is faulty to see Macaulay's *Minute* in isolation: Indians like Raja Rammohan Roy had been pressing for education in English for some time. However, when Macaulay resolved the ongoing debate between "Orientalists" (who wanted Indians to be educated in their own languages) and "Anglicists" (who wanted Indians to be educated in English), he – and his followers – introduced an essentialist and evaluative binarism into the choice that was largely missing from the thought of Indian reformers like Rammohan Roy. Roy, who had started his reformist career in Farsi (not English, as is widely assumed), saw English as a window to modern and scientific education. His assumption was that English would be adopted by Indians in the public sphere (as Farsi had been in the past), while other Indian languages would continue to operate in the private sphere. This, actually, is how it has turned out in much of urban middle-class India.

Macaulay, however, saw English as an instrument of control – it would create a buffer zone of colonial subjects – and a symbol of superiority: "a single shelf of a good European library was worth the whole native literature of India and Arabia" (Macaulay, in Allen & Trivedi 2000: 198). The end result was a gradual divorce of education in English and education in other Indian languages. When the schools of theology in Europe were finally turning into modern and secular universities, Indian madrassas and ashrams were receding into traditional and time-warped branches of learning, while modern education at the highest level was largely imparted to a small urban class in "English-medium" institutions. The prestige and the advantages of a cosmopolitan and up-to-date education drove some of the most progressive and ambitious Indians, provided they could afford it, to these English-medium institutions, which continue to be prestigious (and for good reasons) in independent India. But it also created a strange situation in which some Indians started writing creatively in English, either from choice or necessity, about an India in which most people did not speak English. This matter was complicated by the sudden introduction of English, its relatively short history in India and its comparative distance from other Indian languages. Sanskrit had once been the language of the élite too, but it was also related to many of the languages spoken by ordinary people. Farsi was a language of the élite that had come from outside India, but it too had left deep traces in a variety of Indian languages. English was much more of a newcomer, and it had come from too far away and was too differently dressed to be able to squat in easy camaraderie with other Indian languages for at least a century or two. As Aijaz Ahmad has noted, English is

still the language most removed in its cultural ambience from other Indian languages (1992: 249–51).

In short, Rushdie cannot write "the spoken language" of the Indian streets, simply because English is not really spoken in the streets of India. It is spoken, at times, in its drawing-rooms and offices, its clubs and shopping arcades, its airports and privileged schools. To reduce Rushdie to a tape-recorder is not only to get lost in this set of myths about India and English in India, it is also to lose sight of Rushdie's real achievement: for the body of Rushdie's literary language, haunted as it is by various ghosts, is remarkable both as a work of art and as an index of socio-historical changes.

The Ghostly Body of Rushdie's Literary Language

Rushdie's literary language is partly an index of the socio-historical changes that India has undergone since 1835. English still has a special (though embattled) relationship of privilege to other Indian languages, but it is also an Indian language to the extent that it is spoken, read, and written by many Indians. Recent census figures suggest that about 4 percent of India speaks English, though many of these English-speakers presumably also speak other languages. Four percent of India is 40 million people, which is larger than the population of most European nations. Moreover, a smattering of English will be familiar – legible or audible – to a number of urban Indians who might not be able to speak or write it with any degree of fluency. Here again, it is necessary to quote figures to indicate the extent of urban India. As Ashis Nandy puts it, "If urban India, which is roughly one-fourth of India, declares independence, rural India would still remain the world's second largest country but urban India would be, by itself, the world's fifth largest country" (2000: 196). (See WORLD ENGLISHES IN WORLD CONTEXTS.)

In other words, since the days of Macaulay, English has come to permeate the rich linguistic matrix of India even as it has also been, to some extent, nativized. All Indian languages contain hundreds of English (and European) words today, some so deeply camouflaged that they can only be distinguished by the scholarly eye, just as English contains hundreds of Indian words. Rushdie's use of Hindustani words in his fiction is an index of this change. So is his post-independence and diasporic bravado with the English language. Such bravado would be difficult, if not impossible, to imagine in a fully colonial subject striving to mimic the "correct" language of the colonizer.

"Eat, na, food is spoiling," says Padma, the much-ignored listener-lover of Saleem-the-narrator-protagonist, in Rushdie's *Midnight's Children*. Padma is the kind of semi-literate, working-class urban Indian who would speak, at best, broken English, replete with non-English idiomatic flourishes. As such, the fact that she is made to speak broken English in *Midnight's Children* is neither surprising nor brave. Indians had for long been accused of assaulting English. It was an accusation that had provoked the

Bombay journalist Malabari to such a degree even in the nineteenth century that he had felt the need to answer back:

> "Me comb mit him!" Talk of "Babu English" after this. A Babu schoolboy would blush at it. But why blame the poor German maid? There are thousands of English *ladies* and *gentlemen* who can not speak German or any Indian dialect any better. Is it not curious that the average Englishman, who scorns to pick up foreign languages while travelling, insists upon foreigners speaking to him in English? . . . How many are the English scholars who handle the [English] language more effectively than, for instance, Sambhu Chunder Mookerji, or Rajendralal Mitra, Kristodas Pal, or Keshub Chunder Sen? (*The Indian Eye on English Life, or Rambles of a Pilgrim Reformer*, first published in 1893, quoted from extracts reprinted in Khair et al. 2005: 366–81)

Rushdie's bravery then lies in exorcising this viciously scoffing ghost of monolingual colonialism, and he does so not by making Padma speak as she does but by making his narrators in *Midnight's Children, Shame* (1983), *The Satanic Verses* (1988), *The Moor's Last Sigh* (1995), the exceptional and often overlooked *Haroun and the Sea of Stories* (1990), and some of the stories in *East, West* (1994) speak as they sometimes do. In this, at his best, Rushdie tries to avoid the relationship of colonial power that the narrator has with some of his characters in, say, V. S. Naipaul's early works in which the narrator speaks Standard English and the characters speak broken English.

Rushdie's bravery has a past. It is informed by various literary ghosts, not just those that are visible, such as the ghosts of Kipling's literary language and of G. V. Desani's experiments in *All About H. Hatterr* (1948), from which Rushdie has obviously learnt much, but also those that cannot be seen by Rushdie or his critics. These include the many Indians who in different ways struggled with a problem that Raja Rao conceptualized in the foreword to his *Kanthapura* (1938), a major experiment with English in the Indian context:

> One has to convey in a language that is not one's own the spirit that is one's own. One has to convey the various shades and omissions of a certain thought-movement that looks maltreated in an alien language. I use the word 'alien', yet English is not really an alien language to us. It is the language of our intellectual make-up – like Sanskrit or Persian [Farsi] was before – but not of our emotional make-up. We are all instinctively bilingual, many of us writing in our own language and in English. We cannot write like the English. We should not. We cannot write only as Indians. (Rao 1984: v)

But Rushdie's bravery also had a present. It was something that could have happened only in a certain phase of the relationship of English with India and Indians. While Rao's injunction to write neither as the English nor "only as Indians" still held, a number of Indians in the big cities and abroad had grown into adulthood capable of "thought-movements" only or largely in English. English – and a less self-conscious, more exuberant version of it, as evident in the film columns of Shobha Dé around

that time – had pervaded the fabric of professional middle-class life in the bigger cities, and particularly the circuit of "diasporic Indians" that Rushdie inhabited.

As such when Rushdie created his literary language, he had various rich usages to draw upon. Indians had brought their words into English, as various editions of the *Oxford Dictionary* continue to witness, and they had also started losing their self-consciousness about speaking "correct" English, which was partly the consequence of the birth of the midnight generation, of people who had been born after Independence and did not associate English solely with the British. Even major English newspapers in India had given in to the flood and started using Indian-English compounds like "lathi-charge" (baton charge). Moreover, English had already been fractured in various literary works elsewhere. Approximations of Creoles were being celebrated as literary languages: Mark Twain had spawned – even without any direct literary inheritance in most cases – a brilliant brood of illegitimate children in "post-colonial" societies, ranging from Derek Walcott to Ken Saro-Wiwa.

But, to return to the central thesis of this essay, Rushdie did not simply replace the keys of his typewriter with the mike of a tape-recorder. There was much he could work with, but it did not add up to a coherent literary language: partly because literary languages are, by definition, crafted and not copied, and partly because, as illustrated above, English is not spoken in the streets of India. The latter is a problem any serious writer of English in India, or actually any serious writer who wishes to narrate India and Indians in English, has to confront. Rushdie's option – though perhaps the flashiest – is only one of various possible solutions.

Rushdie's option moves in two directions. At its most complex, his language contains references, insights, puns, and jokes – such as the "Rani of Cooch Nahin" (which subtly plays on an actual Indian place and ex-monarchy, "Cooch Behar," and the fact that "Cooch Nahin" [kuch nahin] means "nothing") in *Midnight's Children* – which are fully accessible only to readers who know the many dialects and offspring-languages of Hindustani spoken mostly in North India (and Pakistan). But Rushdie also writes for a non-North Indian readership and, hence, his language also turns to face another direction and conveys an atmosphere of "Indianness" to the reader who can access India only in English. This can suggest post-modernist or magic realist playfulness. It can also lead to problems.

For instance, some Indian reviewers have pointed out that "cultivated, highly anglicized, upper-class Indians" like Aurora (*The Moor's Last Sigh*) would not speak the (supposedly) "mongrel English" that Rushdie makes them speak. More problematically, some of Rushdie's language use – especially in and after *The Moor's Last Sigh* – appears gratuitous at first glance. Consider the acronym of Mynah's (the Moor's sister) feminist group. This is given as "WWSTP," which is then glossed as "We Will Smash This Prison (Is Jailko Todkar Rahenge)." This gloss reverses what appears to be the logical order of explanations – Hindustani followed by English. The Hindustani version appears particularly superfluous when one realizes that it does not tally with the acronym. It is *not* needed to explain the acronym. The only reason it is there is to confer a degree of vernacular "authenticity" on Rushdie's description – not

because it is needed (as the full version of a Hindustani acronym) or because it is meant to convey a mite extra to Hindustani speakers.

There is, no doubt, some truth in this interpretation of Rushdie's "slips." But, given the heavily associative nature of Rushdie's oeuvre, one has to note that Is Jailko Todkar Rahenge was the slogan on a poster put out by the Women's Liberation Group to mark International Women's Day in Bombay in 1982. (The poster was reproduced on page 107 of Kumar's illustrated history of women's movements in India, published in 1993.) Rushdie's slips, unlike the errors of lesser writers, carry interesting echoes.

One feature of Rushdie's language is his use of Hindustani-English compound neologisms: such as "dia-lamp" in *The Moor's Last Sigh*. This is something he appears to have adapted from G. V. Desani and certain Indian English usages. For instance, Indian English newspapers often write about something called a "lathi-charge": a baton-charge, but for the fact that Indian policemen do not use sleek, short batons. They use long bamboo sticks – lathis. Hence, "lathi-charge" describes a reality with a difference.

Rushdie's neologism, *dia-lamp*, is not the same as actual Indian English neologisms (like *lathi-charge*). *Lathi-charge* unites two different words, each carrying a particular semantic charge, to convey a third meaning. But "dia" is itself a lamp, at best a clay lamp. A "dia-lamp" is a "lamp-lamp": such redundant compounds are not found in actual Indian English usage, except in ironic post-Rushdie mimicry (and in the "staged English" of Desani's 1948 novel from which Rushdie might have taken it). But again, before one makes this an argument against Rushdie, it has to be noted that such compound words – combining an English word with a Hindustani equivalent – are not uncommon in Urdu and Hindustani. And Rushdie, at his best, can combine or superimpose Indian and English words with devastating effectiveness: for example, the "mainduck" ("menduk" or "frog" in Hindustani) of *The Moor's Last Sigh* is not only explained within the text but is also meant to be read in English (Main Duck = Big Boss) with an added load of significance.

Rushdie's literary language can be accessed in its full complexity only when it is seen as the (at times brilliant) art of an original talent impacting on given socio-historical factors. It is not a tape-recording of Indian English, partly because of the class-cultural dimension highlighted above and partly because, as Braj Kachru points out, there are "several varieties within [the] variety" of Indian English. Rushdie often manages to combine many of the oral and chirographic registers that can be found in some of these varieties – at his best focusing on some prominent aspects and at his worst ignoring social subtleties in favor of something like staged English. Above all, he uses that hybrid language in novels that champion – in style, plot, and theme – a particularly appropriate worldview of playful hybridity, of palimpsest cultures. In spite of the occasional limitations of Rushdie's experiment, his literary language cannot be dismissed as West-facing gimmickry: it is part of a larger philosophical and historical point being made about life and India. And it is in the way the nature of this point fits in with the art of his language that Rushdie achieves his acknowledged stature as one of the major novelists of his generation.

REFERENCES AND FURTHER READING

Ahmad, A. (1992). *In Theory*. Delhi: Oxford University Press.

Allen, R. & Trivedi, H. (eds.) (2000). *Literature and Nation: Britain and India 1800–1990*. London: Routledge, in association with the Open University.

Brennan, T. (1989). *Salman Rushdie and the Third World: Myths of the Nation*. London: Macmillan.

Cundy, C. (1998). *Salman Rushdie*. Manchester: Manchester University Press.

Fletcher, M. D. (ed.) (1994). *Reading Rushdie: Perspectives of the Fiction of Salman Rushdie*. Amsterdam: Rodopi.

Gorra, M. (1997). *After Empire: Scott, Naipaul, Rushdie*. Chicago: University of Chicago Press.

Johnson, C. (1997). *Derrida*. New York: Routledge.

Kachru, B. B. (1994). English in South Asia. In R. Burchfield (ed.), *The Cambridge History of the English Language*. Vol. 5 (pp. 497–553). Cambridge: Cambridge University Press.

Khair, T. (2001). *Babu Fictions: Alienation in Contemporary Indian English Novels*. Delhi: Oxford University Press.

Khair, T., Leer, M., Edwards, J., & Ziadeh, H. (eds.) (2005). *Other Routes: 1500 Years of African and Asian Travel Writing*. London: Signal Books, in association with Indiana University Press.

King, B. (1997). Colonial wounds. *London Magazine: India*, 37, 5 & 6.

Lal, M. (1995). *The Law of the Threshold: Women Writers in Indian English*. Simla: Indian Institute of Advanced Study.

Lock, C. (2004). The writing of elsewhere: Nigerian echoes and reflections. *Literary Research/ Recherche littéraire*, 21.41–2: 177–93.

Mehrotra, A. K. (ed.) (2003). *A History of Indian Literature in English*. London: Hurst.

Mukherjee, A. P. (1990). Characterization in Salman Rushdie's *Midnight's Children*: breaking out of the hold of realism and seeking the alienation effect. In V. Kirpal (ed.), *The New Indian Novel in English: A Study of the 1980s* (pp. 109–20). New Delhi: Allied Publishers.

Mukherjee, M. (ed.) (1999). *Rushdie's Midnight's Children: A Book of Readings*. Delhi: Pencraft International.

Nandy, A. (2000 [1995]). *The Savage Freud, and Other Essays on Possible and Retrievable Selves*. New Delhi: Oxford University Press.

Rao, R. (1984 [1938]). *Kanthapura*. Oxford: Oxford University Press.

49

Toni Morrison: The Struggle for the Word

Justine Tally

What makes a work "black"? The most valuable point of entry into the question of cultural (or racial) distinction, the one most fraught, is its language – its unpoliced seditious, confrontational, manipulative, inventive, disruptive, masked and unmasking language.

Morrison (1989b: 110)

How to be both free and situated; how to convert a racist house into a race-specific yet non-racist home. How to enunciate race while depriving it of its lethal cling? They are questions of concept, of language, of trajectory, of habitation, of occupation, and, although my engagement has been fierce, fitful, and (I think) constantly evolving, they remain in my thoughts as aesthetically and politically unresolved.

Morrison (1999: 5)

In so many interdisciplinary debates of contemporary academia, the formal and forma-tive role of language in defining, expanding, and undermining the individual and collective identity has repeatedly trumped discussions of content. A present-day reader no longer simply consumes the "surface structure" of a narrative, but becomes an implicit interpreter and, indeed, producer of meanings not always apparent on the first encounter with the text. Possibly no other contemporary writer has been so deeply engaged in exploring the powder-keg hidden in the heteroglossia of the written word as Toni Morrison. The explosions she has set off have often rocked the complacency of the academic and literary world. Struggling to find a language that would com-municate "race-specificity without race prerogative" (Morrison 1999: 5) has consti-tuted one of the major concerns of her career. Reading Toni Morrison is a joy not just because of the intricate human stories she weaves about her own black community, but because the author clearly revels in the *jouisance* of the English language even as she uses her narration to tackle problems posed by major philosophers and theorists, all without ever losing her total dedication to the aesthetic beauty of the text.

Multiplicity of Meaning

So intent has Morrison been on the primacy of language that the opening *Dick and Jane* primer text of her very first novel graphically illustrates the descent into chaos of Pecola Breedlove, *The Bluest Eye* (1970) as the transcendentally marked "saddest I." Ostensibly intending to divulge the plot of the novel immediately so that the reader can concentrate on the "how" rather than the difficult "why" of Pecola's destruction, Claudia's lyrical opening implicitly lays out the themes of the novel in one extraordinarily beautiful sentence: "Quiet as it's kept, there were no marigolds in the fall of nineteen forty-one" (p. 3). A quiet repetition of this sentence will echo the phonetic significance of each of its three phrases: the insistence on the plosives /k/, /p/, /t/ together with the fricative /s/ suggest the whispered taboo of illicit sexuality; the marked use of /o/ and /r/ in the second phrase recalls Poe's designation of these sounds as the most *mournful* in the English language; and the repetition of /f/ calls attention to the duplicity in meaning of the word "fall." As to meaning, the gossipy implications of "quiet as it's kept" hold within them what cannot be repeated openly, i.e., the incestuous abuse of Pecola by her father, whereas the absence of marigolds simultaneously establishes the parallels of the major metaphors of the novel – the earth, seeds, flowers, and growing things – and signals the irreparable harm caused by an ideal of beauty that is based on external physical characteristics: not only does the marigold bloom in the fall, it also has medicinal properties for curing wounds of the skin; there were none available. The introduction of the seasons (the novel will represent an inversion of their usual cyclical succession by beginning with the fall) is accompanied by the explicit mention of the timeframe in which the story unfolds. There is certain irony in citing the date of the United States' entry into a world war fought against an empire that violently advocated an Aryan ideal of a blonde, blue-eyed super-race, while the same ideology continued to be propagated on their own home front through racial discrimination and the omnipresence of whiteness as a socially defining construct.

Throughout her writing career Morrison has progressively extended this exploration of the multiple relationships between signifieds and signifiers to include more complex and more "meaning-full" techniques in her later novels, an effort that Henry Louis Gates, Jr., has located securely within the "black" tradition:

> Black people have always been masters of the figurative: saying one thing to mean something quite other has been basic to black survival in oppressive Western cultures. Misreading signs could be, and indeed often was, fatal. "Reading," in this sense, was not play; it was an essential aspect of the "literacy" training of a child. This sort of metaphorical literacy, the learning to decipher codes, is just about the blackest aspect of the black tradition. (Cited in Pérez-Torres 1997: 96)

Indeed, Morrison herself notes that her own special use of irony is deeply indebted to the African American oral tradition:

I can't really explain what makes the irony of Black people different from anybody else's, and maybe there isn't any, but in trying to write what I call Black literature . . . there seems to be something distinctive about it and I can't put it into critical terms. I can simply recognize it as authentic. And irony is the mainstay. Other people call it humor. It's not really that . . . And taking that which is peripheral, or violent or doomed or something that nobody else can see any value in and making value out of it or having a psychological attitude about duress is part of what made us stay alive and fairly coherent, and irony is a part of that – being able to see the underside of something, as well. (Jones & Vinson 1994: 175)

Irony is often the protective buffer of Morrisonian characters, through which tragedy is admitted into the discourse, but kept at arm's length through understated, unemotional language:

He fell for an eighteen-year-old girl with one of those deepdown spooky loves that made him so sad and happy he shot her just to keep the feeling going. (Morrison 1992: 3)

Slowly but steadily, for about four years, True Belle got things organized. And then Rose Dear jumped in the well and missed all the fun. (Morrison 1992: 102)

Yet while attributing her own love of language to her black heritage and acknowledging the incorporation into her writing of rhetorical strategies typical of the black community, Morrison has nonetheless worked to develop her own specific techniques and personal style, searching for what she calls the "identifiable qualities" (Morrison 1989a) in her fiction that would function as artistic properties similar to those that differentiate, say, the great jazz musicians. Among these, some of the most prominent are (1) the "fabrication" of composite adjectives that are more that just the sum of their components; (2) an economy of language which powerfully conveys meaning with a minimum of linguistic terms; (3) a duplicity of meaning in which language simultaneously sustains two equally weighted interpretations, (4) the use of "silence" or omission to convey meaning; and (5) a difficulty of interpretation which demands a high degree of reader participation in the expansion of the meaning of the text.

Morrison's best-known creation is her description in *Beloved* (1987) of Sethe's third child as the "crawling already? baby," conveying not only the motor skills of the child, but more importantly Sethe's own amazement, amusement, and affection for her first daughter. This strategy is even more pronounced in the following novel, *Jazz* (1992), in which allusions to social context and intertext are sparked. A description of Dorcas – "Cream-at-the-top-of-the-milkpail face of someone who will never work for anything" (p. 12) – contains the envy and disdain of privileged light-skinned mulattos who benefited socially and economically from their closer proximity to "whiteness"; while on the train the "green-as-poison curtain separating the colored people eating from the rest of the diners" (p. 31) conjures up the ill-feeling between "races" signified in the small, external but constantly irritating signs of racial superiority. The

"ready-for-bed-in-the-street clothes" (p. 55), the "dirty, get-on-down music the women sang and the men played" (p. 58), and "that life-below-the-sash" (p. 60) all attest to the association between the new music and a libertine sexuality fixed in the minds of the black middle class in the 1920s, a preoccupation with sexual morality also manifest in the fury Alice feels for Joe's "snake-in-the-grass stealing of the girl in her charge" (p. 76) with its Old Testament reference.

A second narrative strategy that Morrison perfects is the distillation of meaning into a minimum of poignant words that spark the imagination to complete a much larger narrative. Also in *Jazz*, a novel which focuses on stories and the process of storytelling, a tragic episode of horror, pain, and loss is related in only two sentences:

> Or had it been the news of the young tenor in the choir mutilated and tied to a log, his grandmother refusing to give up his waste-filled trousers, washing them over and over although the stain had disappeared at the third rinse. They buried him in his brother's pants and the old woman pumped another bucket of clear water. (Morrison 1992: 101)

The event itself calls up the sexual mutilation and lynching of black males during the post-Reconstruction era, often on trumped-up accusations of rape, as a means to keep blacks confined within an economically restricted social stratum. The empathy generated becomes all the more powerful because expressed in emotionless, almost Hemingwayesque language.

Thirdly, simultaneous duplicity in meaning also offers Morrison a strategy for maintaining two ontological levels in her narratives. In *Beloved* Denver interprets the eponymous character's answer to her question "What's it like over there, where you were before? Can you tell me?" as a description of her perceptions as a "dead child" in the underworld of spirits, while it is equally if not more possible that she is, in fact, speaking of her experience in the hold of the ship during the Middle Passage:

> "Dark," said Beloved. "I'm small in that place. I'm like this here." She raised her head off the bed, lay down on her side and curled up. . . .
> "Were you cold?" . . .
> "Hot. Nothing to breathe down there and no room to move in." (Morrison 1987: 75)

Indeed, the very epigraph in *Beloved* taken from Romans 9:25 signals the deceptive duplicity of the eponymous protagonist – "I will call them my people, which were not my people; and her beloved, which was not beloved" – which, apart from its biblical import, lends itself linguistically to two more, distinctly different interpretations. If "beloved" is used as a noun, then we have a case of mistaken identity, which some critics argue is indeed the case; Beloved therefore may be a young woman, not a ghost. If, however, the term is used as an adjective, then this *revenant* may in fact be evil itself, and not beloved at all.

In *Paradise* (1998) the emphasis on "twins" and "twinning" reinforces this idea of ontological duplicity. Pat Best, a schoolteacher intent on chronicling the history of the "8-rock" community of Ruby, struggles for clarity as she tries to make sense of events:

> She wiped her eyes and lifted the cup from its saucer. Tea leaves clustered in its well. More boiling water, a little steeping, and the black leaves would yield more. Even more. Ever more. Until. Well, now. What do you know? It was clear as water. (Morrison 1998: 217)

In addition to the previous three linguistic strategies, Morrison uses "silence" to highlight questions of loaded racial/racist discourse: what is not said or explained has as much meaning as what is included. In her short story entitled "Recitatif" (1983) the author experiments with the "raceless" description of two young girls who meet in a shelter at a very early age and then coincidentally four more times as they grow up. One of them is black and the other is white, but their respective "racial identity" is never marked through language. If the reader makes a choice, s/he must come face to face with personal prejudice, *not* because of any stereotypical linguistic expressions in the text.

In a similar vein of experimentation *Paradise* opens with a powerful "They shoot the white girl first." By beginning the novel with no antecedent for the pronoun, Morrison immediately calls attention to the impersonal nature of stereotyping based on "race and gender." Because there is no explicit mention of exactly *which* of the four women who find their way to the convent is the white girl, the reader is left in uncertainty and even consternation. The author's studious omission, however, is a device to make the reader aware of just how useless racial category is in conveying any real understanding of the individual. For Morrison, racial designation conveys information, but it is an empty category, and racialized language is always loaded.

Readers of Morrison's literature must, therefore, fill in the "gaps" of the text that she intentionally leaves open: "My writing expects, demands participatory reading . . . It's not just about telling the story, it's about involving the reader" (Tate 1983: 125). The end of *Jazz*, for example, makes this participation explicit in the final "address" of the book to the reader. But at times this exigency makes for difficult reading, a complaint often filed by Morrison readers, particularly with respect to her later works. It usually concerns, however, scenes of serious import, and I believe that in these cases Morrison intentionally makes the reader strive for meaning in order to personally and imaginatively reconstruct the outrage. Once that construction is complete, the scene will no longer be so easily dismissed, indeed haunting the reader thereafter. In Morrison's novel *Love* (2003), the reader is unceremoniously thrown without warning into a scene with no lead-up, not even an antecedent for the personal pronoun until fully five sentences into the section:

Maybe his girlish tears were worse than the reason he shed them. Maybe they were a weakness the others recognized and pinpointed even before he punked out. Even before the melt had flooded his chest when he saw her hands, curving down from the snow white shoelaces that bound them. They might have been mittens pinned crookedly on a clothesline, hung there by some slut who didn't care what the neighbors said. And the plum polish on nails bitten to the quick gave the mitten-tiny hands a womanly look and made Romen think she herself was the slut – the one with no regard for what people might think. (Morrison 2003: 52)

The subtleties of this description means that the reader must pay close attention to the cues: shoelaces that bind the hands, the repetition of "slut" and the reflexive "herself" that projects shame away from the protagonists and onto the victim. It is the search for those clues that sears the scene into the reader's mind, the horror that will not be so easily discarded and ignored.

John Duval states that Morrison's fiction "contains numerous scenes in which the main thing that is not represented is the main thing" (2000: 106). Such subtlety has its problems, however, as Duval claims that "missing" or glossing over Son's rape of Jadine in *Tar Baby*, for example, distorts the implications of Jadine's problematic flight from her "ancient properties." It certainly means that Morrison demands a sophisticated audience, one who will make the effort to construe the story with her, and while this may alienate a reading public who prefer an easier read, the multiple layers of meaning that surface in the text make the extra effort well worth the while for readers ready to take up the challenge.

Narration and Theories of Language

The referentiality of language works on several simultaneous planes such that Morrison's words speak on various levels. One of the most interesting is the almost ludic experimentation in her novels with the theories of language propagated in the last three or four decades. Even in her earliest work she seems to manifest an explicit interest in theory, as seen, for example, in the Derridean "hauntology" of signs, narratively expressed in *Sula* (1973) through the presence of Eva's absent leg, or "the something newly missing" over the water where Chicken Little disappears and drowns.

Yet nowhere does Morrison more explicitly examine contemporary theories of language than in her trilogy *Beloved*, *Jazz*, and *Paradise*, in which Foucault, Bakhtin, and the so-called French Feminists (Julia Kristeva, Luce Irigaray, and Hèléne Cixous), respectively, take center stage. Indeed, one of the most valid arguments for considering these three novels *as a trilogy* is precisely this "narrative discussion" of theoretical concepts of discourse. Having elsewhere set out the importance of Bakhtin to *Jazz*, and of feminist theory to *Paradise* (Tally 2001, 2006), I wish to specifically focus here on the narrativization of Foucaultian theory in *Beloved*.

In spite of the fact that *Beloved* actually begins with a number, the "Word" and who controls it makes up an integral part of the text. From the moment in which Sethe overhears schoolteacher (and it is important to note that this character will only be known by a name associated with control of knowledge and discourse) instructing his nephews to write down her animal characteristics on one side of the page and line them up with her human features, Sethe bolts, and decides to run to protect her children from an insidious inscription by dominant white ideology. But Michel Foucault's equation of power + discourse = truth is everywhere manifest in the silencing of the subservient characters: when the nephews pin Sethe down and take her milk, she tries to tell an impotent Mrs. Garner, whose own goitrous affliction renders her speechless; Paul D has been harnessed with the "bit" and cannot speak; Halle goes mad and is consequently inarticulate, slathering his face with butter. Sixo's "comic" attempt to modify the terms of his oppression with schoolteacher reinforces a Foucaultian imposition of "truth" through his argument over the meaning of the shoat:

> "You stole that shoat, didn't you?"
> "No. Sir," said Sixo, but he had the decency to keep his eyes on the meat.
> "You telling me you didn't steal it, and I'm looking right at you?"
> "No, sir. I didn't steal it."
> Schoolteacher smiled. "Did you kill it?"
> "Yes, sir. I killed it."
> "Did you butcher it?"
> "Yes, sir."
> "Did you cook it?"
> "Yes, sir."
> "Well, then. Did you eat it?"
> "Yes, sir. I sure did."
> "And you telling me that's not stealing?"
> "No, sir. It ain't."
> "What is it then?"
> "Improving your property, sir."
> "What?"
> "Sixo plant rye to give the high piece a better chance. Sixo take and feed the soil, give you more crop. Sixo take and feed Sixo give you more work."
>
> Clever, but schoolteacher beat him anyway to show him that definitions belonged to the definers – not the defined. (Morrison 1987: 190)

Later when Stamp Paid tries to explain to Paul D the circumstances of Sethe's murdering her own daughter, the illiterate Paul D refuses to acknowledge the newspaper account because the picture there drawn of Sethe may look a little like her, but "That ain't her mouth," mentioning her *mouth* in some form at least twelve times over five pages (pp. 154–8); that is to say, this isn't her story.

In spite of Baby Suggs' dedication to her people, she herself finally acknowledges white control of the discourse. Loved for her preaching of bodily and spiritual

wholeness to the ex-slaves, Baby refuses to return to the clearing after Sethe's murder of the child. Stamp Paid pleads with her:

> "Say the Word!" . . . Bending low he whispered into her ear, "The Word. The Word."
> "That's one other thing took away from me," she said. (Morrison 1987: 178)

For Foucault, while the truth of any discourse is governed by power, at the micro-level this control is imposed on the individual body. So startled is Sethe over the inscription of her "animal characteristics" that she backs away from the scene in horror –

> I commenced to walk backward, didn't even look behind me to find out where I was headed . . . When I bumped into a *tree* my scalp was prickly. . . . My head itched like the devil. Like somebody was *sticking fine needles* in my scalp. (Morrison 1987: 193, emphasis added)

– a sensation that is repeated when schoolteacher and his posse come to reclaim his property, and then again in her frustrated (but more appropriate) attempt to stab Mr. Bodwin, mistaking him for schoolteacher: "Little hummingbirds *stick needle* beaks right through her headcloth into her hair and beat their wings" (pp. 163, 262 [though verb tense changes]; emphasis added). More dramatically, in retribution for Sethe's having told Mrs. Garner of the nephews' abuse, Schoolteacher has her whipped. Amy, the young woman who later assists her in childbirth, describes the awful scarring as a "chokecherry," a tree Sethe will carry on her back until the end of her days. Crucially, John Irving reminds us that the original word for (beech) tree in Old English was *bec*, the origin of our modern-day word for *book*, possibly because writing was first done on bark (Irving 1980: 32–3). It is Sethe's resistance to inscription by the powerful that prompts her to act – run away, kill her child, and later attack Bodwin – a passionate refusal of the dominant discourse that literally "needles" her.

Sethe's truth is not Foucaultian, but "simple, not a long drawn-out record of flowered shifts, *tree cages*, selfishness, ankle ropes and wells" (Morrison 1987: 163; emphasis added). Failing in her attempt to explain her actions to Paul D, Sethe feels the inadequacy of verbal communication, described as a "forest" springing up between them. Sethe says goodbye to him "from the far side of the trees" (p. 165).

Morrison's mastery of and attention to language means that recognition of her specific choices is integral to any interpretation of her texts, and though some critics emphasize Sethe's psychic destruction in the novel, I would argue that the author's narrative belies that interpretation. After all, Foucault himself will eventually include individual resistance to these dominant *epistemes* of truth as part of his philosophical theory. In *Beloved*, though Sethe is *bodily* inscribed with the discourse of the powerful, it is also true that by the end of her story, Paul D attempts to empower her and return her subjectivity to her. It is noteworthy that the last word of this section, before the final coda, is "Me?"

REFERENCES AND FURTHER READING

Duval, J. N. (2000). *The Identifying Fictions of Toni Morrison: Modernist Authenticity and Postmodern Blackness*. New York: Palgrave.

Irving, J. (1980). *American Hieroglyphics*. New Haven, CT: Yale University Press.

Jones, B. W. & Vinson, A. (1994 [1985]). An interview with Toni Morrison. Rpt. in D. K. Taylor-Guthrie (ed.), *Conversations with Toni Morrison* (pp. 171–87). Jackson: University Press of Mississippi.

Morrison, T. (1970). *The Bluest Eye*. New York: Alfred A. Knopf.

Morrison, T. (1973). *Sula*. New York: Alfred A. Knopf.

Morrison, T. (1981). *Tarbaby*. New York: Alfred A. Knopf.

Morrison, T. (1983). Recitatif. In I. A. Baraka & A. Baraka (eds.), *Confirmation: An Anthology of African American Women*. New York: Morrow.

Morrison, T. (1987). *Beloved*. New York: Alfred A. Knopf.

Morrison, T. (1989a). Identifiable qualities. Interview with Margaret Busby. Producer/Director Sindamani Bridglal. Corentyne Productions.

Morrison, T. (1989b). Unspeakable things unspoken: the Afro-American presence in American literature. *Michigan Quarterly Review*, 28, 1, 1–34.

Morrison, T. (1992). *Jazz*. London: Chatto and Windus.

Morrison, T. (1998). *Paradise*. New York: Alfred A. Knopf.

Morrison, T. (1999). Home. In W. Lubiano (ed.), *The House that Race Built*. New York: Random House.

Morrison, T. (2003). *Love*. London: Vintage.

Pérez-Torres, R. (1997). Knitting and knotting the narrative thread – *Beloved* as postmodern novel. In N. J. Peterson (ed.), *Toni Morrison: Critical and Theoretical Approaches* (pp. 91–109). Baltimore: Johns Hopkins University Press.

Tally, J. (1999). *Paradise Reconsidered: Toni Morrison's (Hi)stories and Truths*. Hamburg: Lit.

Tally, J. (2001). *The Story of Jazz: Toni Morrison's Dialogic Imagination*. Hamburg: Lit.

Tally, J. (2003). The politics of discourse in Toni Morrison's trilogy. In M. Sweney & M. Peprnik (eds.), *{Mis}understanding Postmodernism and Fiction of Politics, Politics of Fiction* (pp. 303–22). Olomouc: Palacky University Press.

Tally, J. (2006). The nature of erotica in Morrison's *Paradise* and the em-body-ment of feminist thought. In F. Gysin & C. S. Hamilton (eds.), *Complexions of Race: The African Atlantic* (pp. 83–95). Hamburg: Lit.

Tate, C. (ed.) (1983). *Black Women Writers at Work*. New York: Continuum.

Taylor-Guthrie, D. K. (ed.) (1994). *Conversations with Toni Morrison*. Jackson: University Press of Mississippi.

Part VIII
Issues in Present-Day English

Introduction

The six essays included in this section consider issues surrounding English in today's world: ethnic varieties of English in America; English education for students with non-traditional backgrounds; and postcolonial Englishes. As these essays demonstrate, an effective way to approach contemporary issues is often to place them in their historical contexts first. African American Vernacular English (AAVE), for instance, has its origin in the migration of slaves and indentured servants from Africa in the seventeenth through the nineteenth centuries. The subsequent development of AAVE cannot, however, be separated from the history of internal migration, human rights, and labor issues within the United States. In this sense, AAVE may best be considered an ethnic language rooted in the culture of its communities. (See MIGRATION AND MOTIVATION IN THE DEVELOPMENT OF AFRICAN AMERICAN VERNACULAR ENGLISH.) Compared to AAVE, Latino English has a relatively short history. Yet this subject can shed light on the study of ethnic Englishes in America, because the recent growth in American Latino populations has enabled us to investigate important topics like the acquisition of English as an interlanguage by adult immigrants and the practice of bilingualism among second- and third-generation Latinas and Latinos. (See LATINO VARIETIES OF ENGLSH.)

Because of changes in demography and society at large, English education at the university level must be concerned, now more than ever, with ethnic minorities and first-generation college students from the working- or lower-middle class. These "new students" must negotiate their position between their own language (whether a non-English first language or a non-standard social dialect of English) and the power dialect of English endorsed, covertly or overtly, by the university and other institutions. (See TEACHING ENGLISH TO NATIVE SPEAKERS.) The rift becomes even greater for students who learn English as a foreign language in a non-English-speaking environment. These students also face a gap between the "standard English" taught in the classroom and the "broken English" which in their reality dominates global communication in practical spheres like business. (See EARNING AS WELL AS LEARNING A LANGUAGE.) Instructors of English in either setting must be aware of the social situation of their students and encourage them to approach English not as a body of knowledge or a set of skills but, instead, as a space where they can experience the process of thinking, writing, or simply doing things with the language.

During the Early Modern period, when England expanded its political influences to the rest of Britain and to Ireland, English became an attractive option for the proto-colonial subjects who recognized a promise of success in the sovereign language. The allure of English has remained strong in the postcolonies where the language is often associated with political and economic power. Very few today would entirely reject the idea that English is the *lingua franca* of the twenty-first century, the hegemonic language having an unprecedented sway over the entire globe. But expansion means modification, too. Currently, some of the largest English-speaking populations are located in Anglophone colonized countries like India and, somewhat paradoxically,

in non-English-speaking countries like China. With its spread to Asia, Africa, and Latin America, English has been indigenized to these particular geographies and hybridized through the creativity of local speakers. Now that world Englishes have multiple centers, the concept of singular standard English may well be on its way to becoming obsolete. (See WORLD ENGLISHES IN WORLD CONTEXTS.) It is, therefore, important for us to revisit the creolization and pidginization of English in the early phases of the modern period, especially since the development of English-based colonial languages may serve as a pointer for the future of English(es). Recent studies have modified some of the long-held beliefs. For example, pidgins and creoles are not two stages in a linear evolution of colonial languages. Rather, they had parallel development in different parts of the world under different circumstances. (See CREOLES AND PIDGINS.) Creoles, pidgins, and AAVE did not derive from baby talk employed by colonizers to communicate with slaves and indigenous people. Instead, each of these languages constitutes a unique case reflecting the complexity of its colonial history and hence requiring a detailed study and a nuanced interpretation. No single discourse of modernity can paint the picture of linguistic colonization and decolonization with its broad brush.

Haruko Momma

Migration and Motivation in the Development of African American Vernacular English

Mary B. Zeigler

African American Vernacular English (AAVE, also Black English, Ebonics) is the language system employed within African American speech communities to communicate that society's thoughts, feelings, and experiences in their daily interactions. A speech community is a sociolinguistic concept that describes a group of speakers, whether socially or geographically located, who share unique and mutually accepted linguistic norms for communicating understanding, values, and attitudes. A vernacular speech community conveys cultural heritage and maintains linguistic legacy, employing unmonitored everyday speech acquired from family and community networks. The term *vernacular* differentiates an ethnic designation from a racial one, thereby allowing for some African Americans who do not use the language and some non-African Americans who do (DeBose 2005; Labov et al. 1968; Rickford 1999; Smitherman 2000; Wolfram et al. 1999).

AAVE has a speech population with the most widespread usage of all the vernaculars native to American English, with speech communities established in the South and in urban centers throughout the South, East, North, West, and Midwest. Even before the 1996–7 Ebonics debates awakened new discussions of its systematic patterning, AAVE received more scholarly attention than any other social or socio-ethnic variety of American English. Most studies examined its typological aspects, attempting to determine whether its pronunciation and grammatical features were systematic and how those features compared with standard varieties of English. Since the 1960s advent of sociolinguistics, the sociological applications within the study of dialect difference and language variation have made a significant impact on AAVE research and scholarship. This chapter discusses the typological and sociological issues concerning the development of AAVE from a diachronic (historical) and a synchronic (comparative) perspective: (1) the question of origins; (2) the influence of African American migration; (3) the present-day features of AAVE; (4) the conflict between AAVE and Standard English in education; and (5) the motivation for its affluent development.

Origin(s)

Studies questioning the origins of AAVE argue four hypothetical points of view: (1) the Pre-Linguistic Deficit perspective; (2) the Anglicist; (3) the Africanist; and (4) the Creolist.

The first hypothesis, the Pre-Linguistic Deficit perspective, developing during the late nineteenth and early twentieth centuries, presented the earliest perception of the origin of African American Vernacular English, one that still influences public perceptions today: Black English is the ungrammatical result of an unsuccessful attempt to speak American English. The essence of these early estimates of AAVE language origins can be summed up in the words of Ambrose E. Gonzales (1924):

> Slovenly and careless of speech, these Gullahs seized upon the peasant English used by some of the early settlers . . . , wrapped their clumsy tongues about it as well as they could, and, enriched with certain expressive African words, it issued through their flat noses and thick lips as so workable a form of speech that it was gradually adopted by other slaves and became in time the accepted negro speech of the lower district of South Carolina and Georgia . . . (as found in Rickford & Rickford 2000)

This assumption postulates that African Americans were incapable of producing a "good" English.

Closely akin to the Pre-Linguistic Deficit theories, the early Anglicist Hypothesis of the early twentieth century does not recognize the African linguistic features as significant to the origins of AAVE either. It argues that slavery wiped out most, if not all, African linguistic and cultural traditions, and that the apparently distinctive features of AAVE come from English dialects spoken by the early British colonists (Krapp 1924; Smith 1967; Mencken 1979).

After mid-century, the regional dialectology studies, initiated by the Linguistic Atlas project, modified this Anglicist perception. Dialectologists recognized the African American Gullah as a legitimate language system, but as a dialect derived from old style English (Kurath 1949; Williamson & Burke 1971; McDavid 1979). Later studies by present-day Neo-Anglicists examine creoles and contemporary African American diaspora languages, such as Nova Scotian English and Samaná English, to affirm their origins as varieties of the language spoken in English colonies or places of African American migration (Poplack & Sankoff 1987; Poplack 2000; Poplack & Tagliamonte 2001).

Although the hypotheses of the Deficit Theorists and the Early Anglicists were well accepted, they were countered by a third hypothesis, the Africanist perspective. Scholars taking an Africanist stand contend that the African American vernacular bears the vivid imprint of the African languages spoken by slaves who came to this country in waves from the seventeenth to the mid-nineteenth centuries. Melville J. Herskovits, in his 1941 study *The Myth of the Negro Past*, introduced the field of Africanisms in North America and placed it on sound anthropological footing.

Herskovits's work built a case for African influence to dispel the dualistic myth about the origins of Negro English:

- that black Africa, the homeland of American Negroes, was a cultural desert that had contributed nothing to the rest of the world and, therefore, that the slaves who came here were primitive savages without even the vestiges of a viable culture;
- that whatever culture Africans might have had in the Old World was lost, except, perhaps, for some "savage" survivals in music and dance. (Daniels 2002: 56)

According to Montgomery (1994), Herskovits used the tools of linguistic science to "[focus] on evidence of deeper, more indirect relationships between Old World and New World phenomena that reflect cultural transmissions" (p. 23).

Equally compelling and far-reaching into the diaspora, Lorenzo Dow Turner, after researching for more than two decades in West Africa, Europe, and North America, published his seminal work in 1949, *Africanisms in the Gullah Dialects*. His work is credited with having led the effort to identify the African heritage in North America. Montgomery cites David DeCamp (1973: xi) as saying that "Turner almost single-handedly convince[d] his academic peers that at least in Gullah, and perhaps also in black English generally, the black American has a genuine continuous linguistic history leading back to Africa" (Montgomery 1994: 3).

The most recent and most complex of the four perspectives on AAVE origins is the Creolist Hypothesis. The central question is whether AAVE origins can be compared to that of the "creole" varieties spoken today in the Caribbean, and whether it was ever influenced by them. Both the Creolists and Africanists believe that since the Gullah language of coastal South Carolina and Georgia is a confirmed creole, and since Africans settled in these sites in great numbers before moving inland, then this serves as proof that the resulting AAVE must have creole origins (Rickford & Rickford 2000).

These perspectives on AAVE origins have two characteristics in common. First, they all speculate on what the language must have been like, since they lack original documents to provide the evidence for what it was really like. And secondly, they all admit that African Americans were not taught any English, but acquired and nurtured their own variety within their own communities. In fact, African Americans were prohibited by law from being taught English literacy skills; learning them and having better access to them eventually became a motivating factor for migration.

Migration

The development of African American varieties of English parallels directly with a history of migration for people of African descent into and throughout America from the seventeenth century into the present century.

In the early social history of African American speech communities, Africans migrated by force of enslavement and by will of indenture from the West African Atlantic coast into the East Atlantic coast of America. The first groups of Africans migrating into the Atlantic coast, from Virginia to South Carolina, to work tobacco and rice plantations in the seventeenth and eighteenth centuries, established the foundation for an African English in America (Walvin 2006: 83). During the American colonial period more than 300,000 Africans migrated into linguistically mixed coastal and island settlements, establishing the first African American communities along the Atlantic coast and the first African American varieties of English, pidgin and creole Englishes (the Schomburg Center). By the end of the colonial period, according to the 1790 American Census, the black population had grown to 750,000, two and a half times its immigrant population; 91 percent lived in the South (Sernett 1997: 17). Of the major stream of immigrants until ca. 1820, approximately 600,000 were European, but almost 400,000 were African (Daniels 2002: 6), a steadily increasing influence of African American settlement on "the distinct culture of the Old South" (Daniels 2002: 30), with large numbers in compact spaces forming physical, cultural, and linguistic communities.

During the nineteenth century, migration and settlement patterns continued to deepen within the core of enslavement with blacks developing and maintaining speech communities in the urban as well as the rural South. In the rural South, the migratory route for enslavement moved blacks from the Atlantic coast plantations further westward toward the Mississippi River and along the Gulf coast from Louisiana to St. Louis. New settlements of blacks developed with increasing numbers due to natural reproduction, the in-migration from the Caribbean, and the continued importation of West Africans. Their variety of English was influenced by contact with local languages and new cultural and language infusions from contact with newly arriving West Africans (Walvin 2006). Life in the rural South was inherently tied to a growing population of enslaved African Americans. The demand for enslaved blacks was equally high, if not higher, in the most populous cities (with populations of at least 10,000) which formed an "urban perimeter" around the rural South (Wade 1964; Goldin 1976). In the urban South from 1820 to 1860, enslaved and free blacks were subject to much the same legislation – except free blacks could own property – and both were employed in mostly commercial occupations, many with skills specific to urban areas. On the Atlantic coast side of the perimeter (in Savannah, Charleston, Norfolk, Richmond, Washington, and Baltimore), on the Gulf coast side (in Mobile and New Orleans), and on the northern perimeter at the Mason-Dixon Line (in St. Louis and Louisville), black communities worked at major ocean ports for shipping to the North or abroad and at inland trading posts processing rural agricultural products (Goldin 1976). The migratory route out of the South was made clear to them.

Before the Civil War, most free blacks left the South, motivated by the search for a better life. They clustered in small communities in the larger cities just north of the Mason-Dixon Line, crossing the Ohio River to Cleveland, Cincinnati, and Chicago.

They helped to establish African American speech communities and the foundations for the black urban North that would develop in the twentieth century.

Early nineteenth-century African American movement was primarily by force of enslavement, but in the second half of the century, the movement was by force of will to remain at what was for them home. African Americans remained primarily in Southern settlements and in African American communities. After the Civil War, most freed blacks remained in small agricultural communities, while others moved into larger towns and cities in the urban South. About 90 percent of all African Americans lived in the South (African American Mosaic). It was not until the twentieth century that African Americans moved with massive deliberation away from the South.

African American twentieth-century migratory settlement patterns transferred the African American speech community from the rural South to the urban North, West, and Midwest. Expecting to find a better education and better jobs, African Americans looked toward the North as the Promised Land of freedom and prosperity. Within the period from 1916 until 1970, encompassing the two Great Migrations, more than 6.5 million Southern blacks moved to the urban North. This movement was one of the most significant demographic shifts in the history of the US. By 1970, African American English had become a predominantly Northern variety of English, with more Northern speakers than Southern (Chappell 1998; Sernett 1997).

Then in the early1970s the migratory pattern began to reverse itself. African Americans began their return to the South – the new South Migration – bringing transformed African American speech communities into a new urban South. The rates had actually begun to slow in the 1950s, but it was not until the late 1960s that the number of African Americans moving to the South eclipsed the number leaving. Since 1970, black migration to the South has continued to grow. Many migrants – a majority of them college-educated – seek economic opportunities in a reascending Southern economy; some want to escape deteriorating conditions in Northern cities; others return to be nearer to kin, or to retire in a familiar environment with a better quality of life than that found in the urban North (see Chappell 1998; Schomburg Center 2006). The migratory movement that began in the South in the mid-nineteenth century has made a somewhat circular turn and ended in the South at the start of the twenty-first century. (See AMERICAN ENGLISH SINCE 1865.)

Present-Day Features of AAVE

Did this history of migration cause AAVE to develop differently, in a direction away from Southern AAVE and toward white vernacular English? "Yes," it would, and "No," it didn't. Two conflicting answers to a very contentious question. Yes, AAVE would develop differently in its Northern diaspora due to language contact and social networks. When one language variety migrates into a region of higher density with another language variety, its contact with that dominant language causes it to adopt

new language features. In the case of AAVE in its diaspora regions, it would adopt lexical items and later some pronunciation features from long-term residents of their home communities and from their co-workers in their working communities. The most easily discernible pronunciation differences occur with vowels because they are markers of regional accent (Labov 1994).

No! AAVE didn't develop away from the linguistic and cultural South itself, at least not significantly beyond the surface features already examined. The settlement patterns of the Northward migrants put them into pre-existing AAVE speech communities similar to their Southern home. And the extremely large numbers moving into geographically restricted spaces in the Northern cities encouraged the maintenance of AAVE communication networks, another factor contributing to maintaining similarity rather than fostering difference among AAVE speakers North and South.

And, No! Other than the pronunciation and lexical features indicated, and for the same social and communication network reasons, AAVE did not migrate toward white vernacular Englishes. This is one of the major issues related to the consideration of AAVE as a social dialect: its converging with other varieties of English. Comparison of AAVE to features within surrounding speech communities revealed some similarities. However, the analysis showed that wherever that similarity existed the AAVE speech community used the feature more frequently than did its neighboring community. Studies have uncovered eight unique features (Fasold 1981; Mufwene & Rickford 1998; Wolfram & Schilling-Estes 2006).

Pronunciation features

The pronunciation distinctions occur with consonants:

1. Devoicing of voiced stops in stressed syllables (e.g., [bɪt] for *bid*).
2. Reduction of final consonant clusters when followed by a word beginning with a vowel (e.g., *lif up* for *lift up*); or when followed by a suffix beginning with a vowel (*bussing* for *busting*). When it occurs in verbs, especially ending in t and d (*look* from *looked* and *pass* from *past /passed*) it can cause a shift in verb form, from the inflected form to the base.

Noun features

3. Plural -*s* absence on the general class of noun plurals (e.g., *four girl* for *four girls*).
4. Possessive -*s* absence (e.g., *man hat* for *man's hat*).

Verb features

5. -*s* absence in third person singular, present tense (e.g., *she walk* for *she walks*) and -*ed* absence in past tense (e.g., *she walk* for *she walked*) occur in instances of

word-final consonant cluster simplification. This phonological feature affects a morphological result.

6. Stressed *been* (often represented as *BIN* in modern studies of AAVE) is an AAVE camouflaged form, a structure that closely resembles a standard English form but masks underlying differences. The stressed *been* marks an action or state that took place or began in a long ago remote time and is still relevant (e.g., He *BIN* stop smoking) while *has been/'s been* refers to a recent past.

7. Absence of the present tense copula and auxiliary *BE* (e.g., *She nice*; *She in the house*; *She runnin' in the hallway*).

8. Use of habitual *be* (e.g., *Sometimes my ears be itching*; *She don't usually be here*).

These morphological and syntactic features are systematic occurrences in AAVE. When a language consists of a systematic rendering of its word structures (morphology) and its phrase and clause structures (syntax), the language is grammatical. English, for instance, as a word-ordered language, does not rely on inflections to mark word function, except in the case of pronouns. Therefore, this systematic absence of inflectional features in AAVE, urban or rural, is not unusual and makes it comparable to the standard. Because AAVE is structured and systematic, it is a grammatical variety of English, not random or careless speech as many mistakenly assume it to be (Martin & Wolfram 1998; Mufwene & Rickford 1998; Green 2002).

AAVE in Education

During the 1960s, when blacks began a migratory return to the South, the controversial issues of AAVE origins and grammaticality directly influenced the linguistic issue relating to the conflict between AAVE and Standard English in education.

Language scholars began to address the complexity of the linguistic system of blacks in urban speech communities and to assert its linguistic validity, especially in matters of education. In the mid 1960s, publications exploring the relation between social dialects and language learning (Shuy 1964) and between non-standard speech and the teaching of English (Stewart 1964) began a decade of linguistics research on AAVE (1964–74) that was strongly oriented to educational concerns. Labov et al. (1968) and Wolfram (1969) provided the first large-scale quantitative sociolinguistic surveys of AAVE. And Baratz and Shuy (1969) and Fasold and Shuy (1970) dealt with the ways in which the systematic nature of AAVE could be implemented to improve the methods used to teach inner city African American children to read. According to Rickford and Rickford (1995), Labov's (1970) review of non-standard English became "a standard textbook in a number of institutions concerned with teacher training," and Burling's (1973) text on AAVE examined "the problem" of African American inner city children not learning to read as well as their white suburban peers and explored possible solutions to this problem.

By the 1970s, when the numbers of African Americans moving to the South began to swell to migratory proportions, AAVE was no longer just "Black talk." In 1975, anthropologist Paul Stoller intended to summarize current linguistic research; instead, he encouraged educators to reconsider their knowledge and attitudes:

> Regardless of whether black speech has been classified erroneously, it is clear that its structure is affected by social forces. Thus the nature of black speech, like the nature of any other American dialect, depends upon sociocultural and linguistic forces. (Stoller 1975: 9–10)

Stoller could very well have been testifying at the 1977–9 King/Ann Arbor case. Parents of fifteen African American students attending the Martin Luther King Jr. Elementary School filed a lawsuit charging that the school, the Ann Arbor school district, and the state of Michigan had "failed to properly educate the children, who were thus in danger of becoming functionally illiterate." In 1979, federal court judge Charles W. Joiner ruled in favor of the students, stating that "the unconscious but evident attitude of teachers toward the home language causes a psychological barrier to learning by the student" (Rickford & Rickford 2000; Smitherman 1981).

The Ebonics debate of 1996–7 revived the 1960s deficit-or-difference arguments and the ever-present Pre-Linguistic Deficit hypothesis that linguists thought had been resolved. Although initiated in Southern California, it was merely the second chapter of the Ann Arbor story, a continuation of the same issue. Proponents of the deficit theory maintained that not only was the vernacular grammatically insufficient to communicate adequately, but also that its use inhibited the effective thought and communication processes of its speakers. Sociolinguistic studies proved that these varieties have differences that are consistent with language systems, and that social and ethnic dialects persist because they contain means by which a community can maintain its cultural connections. The Oakland School Board resolution recognized that the distinctive language of African American children was a valid linguistic system by which to communicate and to educate (see Perry & Delpit 1998).

AAVE did not disappear, did not converge with other English vernaculars after its migration out of the South. The records of the 1977–9 Ann Arbor trial indicate its continuation in the North; the Oakland School Board resolution denotes its continued existence in the West. Sociolinguists have come to realize that social variations do not depend on the geographical region for development. Wolfram and Schilling-Estes (2006) contend that "ethnic groups tend to form subcultures within the larger culture, and part of the distinctiveness of these subcultures may derive from linguistic difference." Therefore, "the greater the isolation of an ethnic group from the mainstream of society, the greater its linguistic distinctiveness will be" (p. 166). Had AAVE really changed, its basic features of difference would not have persisted in these various urban settings throughout America.

Motivation

AAVE has developed into, essentially, a unified language throughout the US despite time and the migrations, despite regional variations in accent and lexical choice. The number of AAVE speech communities has increased rather than declined. How could AAVE, Black English, have developed to become so distinctively and linguistically consistent throughout a history of contention and dispersion?

The answer to this query lies not within the origins of Black English, nor within the structure of the speech variety, but rests instead within the motivation of the African American Vernacular speech community. Within a community, kinship factors – such as common roots, common social circumstances, and common political encounters – contribute to a sense of belonging that is manifested in that society's everyday linguistic interactions. Speakers within that community are motivated to maintain their linguistic kinship through heritage, identity, and language politics.

Heritage

The linguistic heritage of AAVE comes through an oral tradition that has served as a fundamental vehicle for survival. The oral tradition preserves the heritage of African Americans and its use reflects a collective spirit that has been kept alive and reinvigorated by word-of-mouth secular and religious discourse. The songs, stories, folk sayings, verbal interplay, lessons, and precepts about life and survival are passed down from one generation to the next. The tradition is practiced in verbal interplay, such as the game of insults – snappin, playin the Dozens, and the "yo' mama" jokes – or in the proverbs that use figurative language and rhetorical strategies for indirect confrontation and socializing children. The tradition of struggle is also exemplified in "sounding Black," a speaking style beyond grammar and pronunciation, as used in Black Womanist language, and in rap music. For African American speech communities, this linguistic heritage of oral tradition and word-of-mouth discourse began with their importation from Africa, the origins of an interlocking cultural and philosophical network (Smitherman 2000). It developed as African American through their colonization in pre-Civil War America, adjusting to new realities. And it provided the core of communication networks in their post-colonial diasporation from the South, and then in their return to their revitalized Southern home.

Identity

Along with cultural heritage, community identity is also a motivation in the development of AAVE. The Civil Rights activities of the 1960s motivated blacks to return to reconsider life in the South. African Americans mounted public protests asserting not only their public rights but also their community identities. Their strongest

discursive assertion was their calling themselves "Black" – as James Brown acclaimed, "Say It Loud – I'm Black and I'm Proud" (1968) – and referring to their speech as "Black English." Formerly terms of denigration and negative stereotype, these now became labels of community pride and self-assertiveness. Having been called *Coloured/ Colored* and *negro*, blacks began to assert that they were *Negro*, then *Afro-American*, they were now *Black* and *African American* (Smitherman 1994).

Ultimately, African Americans maintained their usage of AAVE despite the negative attitudes expressed toward it and toward its speakers. "The primary answer is its role as a symbol of identity" (Rickford & Rickford 2000: 222). This is the driving force – the motivation – of low-prestige languages and dialects around the world, including Schwyzendeutsch in Switzerland, Canadian French in Canada, Appalachian English in America, and Catalan Spanish in Spain. They are noted as markers of solidarity. It is a way of reclaiming their cultural identity through a deliberate choice of nomenclature that reconnected them to their heritage and claimed a space within the culture of America (see Zeigler & Osinubi 2002).

Language politics

Language politics or linguistic pride? In response to the ever-present Deficit Hypothesis, which seeks to marginalize a group by condemning its language, many African American vernacular speakers deliberately go against the mainstream; others simply do so by conditioning from their surrounding speech community. Thereby the present-day hip-hop discourse and rap-genre have become linguistic rebels. Their rebellion has furthered the distinctive linguistic difference of AAVE. If viewed through a post-colonial perspective, it is evident that AAVE may well have been the colonized Africans' means of restructuring a language that had been imposed on them by the colonizer. As the African American community developed, members increasingly utilized their own version of that language to assert their community "as the central, generating force of power, language, and self-identification" (Zeigler & Osinubi 2002: 593). African Americans "flipped the script" on the intentional bias exerted toward them through their language and used it as a motivator rather than a terminator. Speakers within that community are motivated to maintain that linguistic kinship through heritage, identity, and language politics.

Conclusion

Ultimately, despite the arguments concerning its origin, the questions about its grammaticality, and controversies regarding its use in education, African American Vernacular English has developed as a native American variety. Due to its history of migration and because of its internal community motivators of heritage, identity, and linguistic pride, it has maintained a distinctive speech community unified by cultural difference. That stability of difference has preserved an African American speech community and asserted a cultural and linguistic self.

REFERENCES AND FURTHER READING

African American Mosaic: A Library of Congress Resource Guide for the Study of Black History and Culture. (2006). Library of Congress. www. loc.gov/exhibits/african/afam008.html.

Baratz, J. & Shuy, R. (eds.) (1969). *Teaching Black Children to Read*. Washington, DC: Center for Applied Linguistics.

Baugh, J. (1999). *Out of the Mouths of Slaves: African American Language and Education Malpractice*. Austin: University of Texas Press.

Burling, R. (1973). *English in Black and White*. New York: Holt-Rinehart.

Chappell, K. (1998). The New Great Migration to the South. *Ebony*, 53 (11), 58–60, 62, 142.

Daniels, R. (2002). *Coming to America: A History of Immigration and Ethnicity in American Life*. 2nd edn. New York: Perennial.

DeBose, C. E. (2005). *Sociology of African American Language: A Language Planning Perspective*. New York: Palgrave/Macmillan.

DeCamp, D. (1973). Foreword to L. D. Turner, *Africanisms in the Gullah Dialect* (pp. v–xi). Ann Arbor: University of Michigan Press.

Fasold, R. (1981). The relationship between black and white English in the South. *American Speech*, 56, 153–89.

Fasold, R. & Shuy, R. (eds.) (1970). *Teaching Standard English in the Inner City*. Washington, DC: Center for Applied Linguistics.

Goldin, C. D. (1976). *Urban Slavery in the American South: 1820–1860, A Quantitative History*. Chicago: University of Chicago Press.

Gonzales, A. E. (1924). *Black Border: Gullah Stories of the Carolina Coast*. Columbia, SC: State Company.

Green, L. J. (2002). *African American English: A Linguistic Introduction*. Cambridge: Cambridge University Press.

Herskovits, M. (1941). *The Myth of the Negro Past*. Boston: Beacon Press.

Krapp, G. P. (1924). The English of the Negro. *American Mercury*, 2, 190–5.

Kurath, H. (1949). *Handbook of the Linguistic Geography of New England*. Ann Arbor: University of Michigan Press.

Labov, W. (1970). The study of language in its social context. *Studium Generale*, 23, 30–87.

Labov, W. (1994). *Principles of Linguistic Change: Internal Factors*. Oxford: Blackwell.

Labov, W., Cohen, P., Robins, C., & Lewis, J. (1968). A study of the non-standard English of Negro and Puerto Rican speakers in New York City. *Cooperative Research Report* 3288. Vols. 1 & 2. Philadelphia: US Regional Survey (Linguistics Laboratory, University of Pennsylvania).

Lanehart, S. L. (ed.) (2001). *Sociocultural and Historical Contexts of African American English*. Philadelphia: John Benjamins.

McDavid, R. I. (1979). *Dialects in Culture: Essays in General Dialectology*. Ed. W. A. Kretzschmar, Jr. Tuscaloosa: University of Alabama Press.

Majors, C. (1994). *From Juba to Jive: A Dictionary of African American Slang*. New York: Penguin.

Martin, S. & Wolfram, W. (1998). The sentence in African-American Vernacular English. In S. S. Mufwene, J. R. Rickford, G. Bailey, & J. Baugh (eds.), *African-American English: Structure, History, and Use* (pp. 11–36). New York: Routledge.

Mencken, H. L. (1979 [1949]). *The American Language*. With annotations and new material by R. I. McDavid, Jr. assisted by D. W. Maurer. New York: Alfred Knopf.

Montgomery, M. (ed.) (1994). *Crucible of Carolina*. Athens: University of Georgia Press.

Montgomery, M. & Mille, K. W. (2002). Introduction. In L. D. Turner, *Africanisms in the Gullah Dialect*. Columbia: University of South Carolina Press.

Mufwene, S. S. & Rickford, J. (1998). Introduction. In S. S. Mufwene, J. R. Rickford, G. Bailey, & J. Baugh (eds.), *African-American English: Structure, History and Use*. New York: Routledge.

Perry, T. & Delpit, L. (eds.) (1998). *The Real Ebonics Debate: Power, Language and the Education of African American Children*. Boston: Beacon Press.

Poplack, S. (ed.) (2000). *The English History of African American English*. Oxford: Blackwell.

Poplack, S. & Sankoff, D. (1987). The Philadelphia Story in the Spanish Caribbean. *American Speech*, 62 (4), 291–314.

Poplack, S. & Tagliamonte, S. (2001). *African American English in the Diaspora.* Oxford: Blackwell.

Rickford, J. R. (1999). *African American Vernacular English.* Oxford: Blackwell.

Rickford, J. R. & Rickford, A. E. (1995). Dialect readers revisited. *Linguistics and Education,* 7, 107–28.

Rickford, J. R. & Rickford, R. J. (2000). *Spoken Soul: The Story of Black English.* New York: John Wiley and Sons.

Schomburg Center (2006). *In Motion: The African American Migration Experience.* New York Public Library. www.inmotionaame.org.

Sernett, M. C. (1997). *Bound for the Promised Land: African American Religion and the Great Migration.* Durham, NC: Duke University Press.

Shuy, R. (1964). *Social Dialects and Language Learning.* Urbana, IL: National Council on Teacher Education.

Smith, R. (1967 [1926]). Gullah. *Bulletin of the University of South Carolina,* 190, 14–21.

Smitherman, G. (ed.) (1981). *Black English and the Education of Black Children and Youth: Proceedings of the National Invitational Symposium on the King Decision.* Detroit: Center for Black Studies, Wayne State University.

Smitherman, G. (1994). *Black Talk: Words and Phrases from the Hood to the Amen Corner.* Boston: Houghton-Mifflin.

Smitherman, G. (2000). *Talkin that Talk: Language, Culture and Education in African America.* New York: Routledge.

Stewart, W. A. (1964). *Non-Standard Speech and the Teaching of English.* Washington, DC: Center for Applied Linguistics.

Stoller, P. (ed.) (1975). *Black American English: Its Background and Its Usage in the Schools and in Literature.* New York: Dell.

Turner, L. D. (1949). *Africanisms in the Gullah Dialects.* Chicago: University of Chicago Press.

Wade, R. D. (1964). *Slavery in the Cities.* New York: Oxford University Press.

Walvin, J. (2006). *The Atlas of Slavery.* New York: Pearson, Longman.

Williamson, J. & Burke, V. M. (eds.) (1971). *A Various Language: Perspectives on American Dialects.* New York: Holt, Rinehart, and Winston.

Wolfram, W. (1969). *A Sociolinguistic Description of Detroit.* Washington, DC: Center for Applied Linguistics.

Wolfram, W., Adger, C. T., & Christian, D. (1999). *Dialects in Schools and Communities.* Mahwah, NJ: Lawrence Erlbaum.

Wolfram, W. & Schillings-Estes, N. (2006 [1998]). *American English: Dialects and Variation.* 2nd edn. Oxford: Blackwell.

Zeigler, M. B. & Osinubi, V. (2002). Theorizing the postcoloniality of African American English. *Journal of Black Studies,* 32 (5) (May), 588–609.

51

Latino Varieties of English

Robert Bayley

Introduction

In 2004, Latinos in the United States numbered 40,424,000, or approximately 14 percent of the total population (Pew Hispanic Center 2005). While the majority of Latinos continue to speak Spanish at home, data from the 2000 Census show that an increasing number of Latinos from all national groups reported speaking only English at home. In 1980, for example, approximately 3.3 million Latinos reported speaking only English at home, compared to 10.2 million who reported speaking Spanish. In 2000, 6.8 million Latinos reported speaking only English at home, compared to 24.6 million who reported speaking Spanish (Pew Hispanic Center 2005). Large-scale studies also indicate that English plays an increasingly important role in the lives of second and third generation US-born Latinos. For example, a recent survey of a well-stratified sample of the US Latino population reported data for language use across immigrant generations that appear remarkably similar to the pattern of language shift found in earlier groups of immigrants from other parts of the world (Brodie et al. 2002). Figure 51.1 shows reported language dominance by first, second, and third and higher Latino immigrant generations.

The results of Brodie et al.'s (2002) study show that most Latino immigrants (72 percent) are Spanish-dominant. Not surprisingly, a very substantial portion of second generation speakers, i.e., the first US-born generation, is bilingual (47 percent), although an almost equal number of second generation speakers consider themselves English-dominant (46 percent). By the third generation and beyond, 78 percent of the Latino adults surveyed reported that they were English-dominant and only 22 percent considered themselves to be bilingual. None claimed Spanish dominance. Surveys such as Brodie et al. (2002), as well as data from the US Census Bureau, serve to counteract the widespread myth that Latino immigrants resist learning English. On the contrary, they confirm the findings of scholars such as Wong Fillmore (1991) and Hakuta and Pease-Alvarez (1994) that suggest that Latinos, like other immigrants and their descendants, are in greater danger of losing their heritage language than

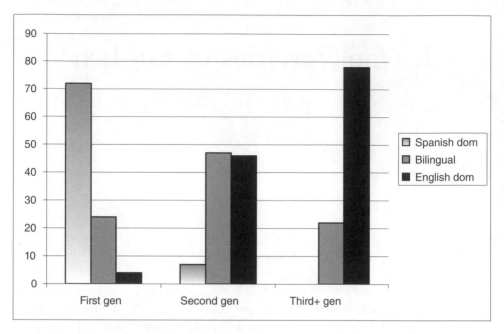

Figure 51.1   Language dominance among Latino adults across immigrant generations (data source: Brodie et al. 2002)

they are of failing to learn English. Such surveys, however, tell us nothing about the varieties of English used in Latino communities. People do not merely shift from language X to language Y. Rather, they shift from a particular variety of language X to a particular variety of language Y, and sometimes they create a new variety of language Y in the process. This chapter outlines some of the major features of the English varieties spoken in US Latino communities. Given the diversity of the US Latino population, it is impossible to explore fully all of the many communities. Therefore, the chapter focuses on the English of people of Mexican and Puerto Rican descent. The chapter is organized as follows. First, I distinguish between the learner varieties of English, or interlanguages, usually spoken by Latinos who moved to the US as adults, and the varieties of English spoken by Latinos who were born in the US or who immigrated at a very early age. Second, I briefly review some of the major distinctive features of Mexican American, or Chicano, English and Puerto Rican English. Finally, I offer several suggestions for work that needs to be done to understand more fully both the linguistic features of these dialects, as well as other English varieties spoken by US Latinos, and the roles they play in speakers' lives.

Defining Latino Varieties: Interlanguages or Ethnic Dialects

In comparison to many varieties of English, Latino varieties have been relatively neglected. The relative neglect of Latino English varieties, which Peñalosa commented

on as early as 1980, may be a consequence of the difficulty of defining the limits of the dialects, as well as other questions that do not figure in accounts of non-contact varieties of English. Among these questions are the extent and nature of the influence of the Spanish substrate, the distinctions between the learner varieties spoken by immigrants and the native varieties spoken by US-born Latinos and by those who immigrated as young children, and the relationships among the varieties of English spoken by Latinos and other vernacular dialects.

This chapter focuses on these ethnic dialects, particularly Chicano English (ChE) and Puerto Rican English (PRE), spoken by people who acquired English as their first language, who acquired English and Spanish simultaneously, or who began to acquire English when they enrolled in elementary school, usually around the age of five, well before the end of the critical period for second language acquisition. Speakers of ChE tend to be concentrated in the urban *barrios* of California and the southwestern United States, while speakers of PRE tend to be concentrated in the East Coast, particularly in the New York area. However, given the spread of the Latino population in recent years, speakers of Latino varieties of English may also be found in many other areas, particularly in cities such as Chicago that have long drawn large numbers of Mexican immigrants as well as migrants from Puerto Rico (Farr 2005), and beginning in the 1990s, in states such as Georgia and North Carolina, which have experienced a very rapid growth in their Latino populations (see, for example, Bayley 2007; Wolfram et al. 2004). Speakers of Latino English varieties may or may not speak Spanish in addition to English. Nearly all, however, live in communities where Spanish is widely spoken and most have at least some passive knowledge of Spanish. Indeed, many Latino English speakers come from families where Spanish is used to varying degrees in the home. Excluded from the definition are people of Latino ancestry who have fully assimilated into the dominant culture and who speak English varieties that are indistinguishable from those of middle and upper-middle-class Anglos in the same regions.

This definition of Latino English distinguishes these native-speaker dialects from interlanguages, or the varieties of learner language spoken by native-speakers of Spanish who immigrated to the United States as adolescents or adults. Although the widespread use of Spanish in Latino communities may well influence the English spoken by native English-speaking Latinos, features of Latino English varieties that diverge from the regional standard cannot be explained simply as a result of interference from Spanish. In second language acquisition, interference is a psycholinguistic construct that attempts to explain how features of a learner's first language inhibit the acquisition of features of a second language. Such a construct has no relevance for describing a language variety that is the sole or dominant variety of a group of speakers. Since there are many Latino English speakers who do not speak any Spanish, Spanish cannot be the proximate source of their native English dialect. Nevertheless, because Latino English speakers are often in daily contact with fluent speakers of Spanish and because many Latinos live in communities where they have only minimal

contact with speakers of Anglo varieties, it would be surprising indeed if there were no Spanish influence on their English phonology and grammar.

The following sections summarize basic features of Chicano and Puerto Rican English, some of which are unique to the particular ethnic dialects and others of which are shared with other vernacular varieties of English.

Chicano English

Phonology

Chicano English shares the general catalogue of vowel phonemes and most of the associated phonological features of the US English dialects of the regions in which Chicanos reside (Fought 2003; Mendoza-Denton 1997; Penfield & Ornstein-Galicia 1985; Santa Ana & Bayley 2004; Thomas 2001). ChE phonology does, however, exhibit a number of systematic differences from other US dialects. In the most recent full-length treatment of the dialect, Fought (2003) summarizes the distinctive features of the ChE vowel system, at least as spoken in Los Angeles:

1. Less frequent vowel reduction. For example, in contrast to speakers of most Anglo varieties, ChE speakers often produce an unreduced vowel in the preposition *to*, i.e., [tʰu] instead of [tʰə].
2. Frequent lack of glides in many areas where they would be present in Anglo speech, particularly the high vowels, usually realized as [ij] and [uw] in Anglo speech. Fought (2003: 64) also notes that, among the Los Angeles Chicano adolescents she studied, the diphthongs [ej] and [ow] were variably realized without a glide, although the absence of a glide was not as frequent as in the case of the high vowels. She provides the following examples of vowels without glides: *least* realized as [lis]; *ago* realized as [əgo]; *LA zoo* realized as [əlezu]
3. Variable neutralization of /i/ and /ɪ/, particularly in the *-ing* morpheme, where it often co-occurs with an alveolar nasal, e.g., [in]. Among some groups of younger Chicanos, raising and tensing of /ɪ/ is particularly common in what Mendoza-Denton (1997: 100) has referred to as the Th-Pro set, i.e., *anything*, *something*, *nothing*, and *thing*. In fact, Mendoza-Denton (1997: 103) reports that the northern California gang girls she studied used the raised variant at rates above 90 percent.

ChE also shares a number of phonological processes with other vernacular dialects. For example, variable consonant cluster reduction, or *-t,d* deletion (e.g., [mɪst] may be realized as [mɪs]) is a widely studied feature of many English dialects. Bayley (1994) and Santa Ana (1992, 1996) report that *-t,d* deletion is extremely common in the informal speech of Chicanos in Texas and California, respectively. They also report that for the most part, Chicanos exhibit an overall pattern that is similar to speakers

of other vernacular dialects. For example, ChE speakers are more likely to delete a /t/ or /d/ that is part of a monomorpheme like *mist* than they are to delete a /t/ or /d/ that forms a past tense ending in a word such as *missed* [mɪst]. Like speakers of other dialects, ChE speakers are also more likely to delete a /t/ or /d/ from a cluster that precedes a consonant, e.g., *missed my bus*, than from a cluster that precedes a vowel, e.g., *missed Anna*.

Among the consonantal features common to ChE and other vernacular dialects is the variable substitution of the stops [t] and [d] for the interdental fricatives [θ] and [ð] as in *tink* for *think* and *den* for *then*. In addition, Fought (2003: 69) observes that there is a strong tendency for ChE speakers to glottalize the final voiceless stops [p, t, k].

Morphology and syntax

The majority of ChE morphological and syntactic features that diverge from prescriptive norms are found in many other vernacular dialects, including those spoken in non-contact situations. For example, ChE exhibits both regularization of irregular verbs (1) and variable absence of 3rd sg. -*s* (2):

(1)   When I was little and that teacher hit my hand on my- my upper side of the hand that when she *striked* me with that, that just blew my mind. (San Antonio, f, 30)
(2)   If somebody *come* up and *push* me then I'll just probably have to push em back or something. (San Antonio, f, 12)

ChE also exhibits variable absence of past-tense marking, as in (3), variable copula absence, as in (4), and generalization of past-tense forms to the past participle, as in (5).

(3)   I saw some girl, she, she *look* pretty. (San Antonio, f, 12)
(4)   . . . they Ø like, "you speak a little bit weird." (San Antonio, f, 12)
(5)   It was in the apple that the witch had *gave* Snow White that wasn't poisonous (San Antonio, f, 11)

In addition, like nearly all English vernaculars, ChE exhibits variable multiple negation, or negative concord, as in (6), *don't* as a singular form as in (7), and *ain't* as a negative, as in (8):

(6)   I *didn't* have that dream *no more*. (Los Angeles, m, 19)
(7)   She *don't* like it here in the courts and my dad . . . he *don't* live with us. (San Antonio, f, 15)
(8)   You fight back because you know they touched you and they *ain't* supposed to do that. (San Antonio, f, 12)

In fact, negative concord is one of the very few non-phonological variables that has been systematically investigated in ChE. Fought (2003) examined 328 tokens drawn from sociolinguistic interviews with 28 young Chicanos and Chicanas in southern California. Fought analyzed the data with VARBRUL, a specialized application of the statistical procedure known as logistic regression that has long been used in sociolinguistics (for an overview, see Bayley 2002). This statistical method allows the researcher to consider simultaneously all of the factors that may potentially influence the use of a specific linguistic form.

Fought's results provide evidence that negative concord in ChE is subject to systematic linguistic conditioning. The syntactic environments considered differ greatly in their effect on speakers' use of negative concord. For example, negative concord was present only 22 percent of the time when the clause contained a negative subject and a pronoun, adverb, or determiner (*Nobody said nothing*), compared to 74 percent for a negative auxiliary plus adverb (*I won't do it no more*) (Fought 2003: 147).

Relative pronoun choice, e.g., *the guy who/that/Ø I saw*, has also been the object of systematic study in ChE. Bayley (1999) examined the alternation of *wh-* words, *that*, and zero in the speech of middle- and working-class Mexican Americans in Texas and California. Results of multivariate analysis indicated that relative pronoun choice is constrained by a complex array of linguistic and social factors including the grammatical category of the subject of the relative clause (noun, pronoun, or relative pronoun), features of the antecedent, social class, and age. Perhaps the most striking result of this study was the very high rate of use of *that* as a relativizer, including its use with human antecedents at a rate of 80 percent, where prescriptive norms would favor *wh-*.

Features specific to ChE include patterns of reported speech and use of modals, both of which have been studied by Wald (1987, 1996) among speakers in East Los Angeles. With respect to reported speech, Wald (1987) observed three main features. First, the East LA speakers used *tell* to introduce questions:

(9)   I *told* Elsinore: "Is that your brother?" (f, 52)

Second, the East LA speakers, in contrast to most other vernacular dialect speakers, sometimes extended complementizer *that* to direct speech following *tell*:

(10)   I told him *that* "I can't go out with you no more . . ." (Wald 1987: 58)

Third, the East LA speakers Wald studied used inversion only with *wh-*questions and never with *yes/no* questions:

(11)   a. He asked me where did I live.
       b. He asked did I live there. (Wald 1987: 60)

More recently, Wald (1996) examined the use of *would* in *if*-clauses with both stative and non-stative verbs, as in (12):

(12) If he'*d* be here right now, he'*d* make me laugh. (Wald 1996: 520)

Wald found that *would* was used much more frequently with non-stative than with stative verbs and suggested that the use of *would* in hypothetical clauses might be more common in ChE than in other vernacular varieties as a result of substrate influence (Wald 1996: 521–2).

Finally, with respect to modals, Fought (2003) discusses the extension of *could* rather than *can* to refer to competence:

(13) Nobody believes that you *could* fix anything. (Fought 2003: 100)

As Fought observes, this usage has not been found in African American Vernacular English (AAVE) data or in the speech of the Anglos she interviewed. Nor does it have any relationship to Spanish syntactic patterns. She suggests that this is an independent innovation in ChE.

Puerto Rican English

Puerto Rican English as spoken in the Eastern United States, particularly in New York City, shares a number of features with Chicano English and other vernacular dialects, including variable consonant cluster reduction and negative concord. It differs from ChE, however, in showing considerable influence from AAVE. Wolfram (1974), for example, found numerous instances of AAVE influence in the speech of adolescents with extensive contacts with the African American community. Examples include habitual *be*, copula absence (*He Ø ugly*), and absence of third person singular *-s* (*She like to act*). Wolfram also reported that other features that are found in the speech of Latino groups with and without extensive contacts with the African American community, such as consonant cluster reduction, were more frequent in the English of Puerto Ricans with intense contact with AAVE speakers than in the speech of those without such contacts.

Although there are relatively few studies of PRE, recent work by Zentella (1997) and Slomanson and Newman (2004), along with earlier work by Wolfram (1974), does allow us to identify many of the main characteristics of the dialect. Zentella, for example, provides an extensive inventory of grammatical features shared by AAVE and PRE, with examples drawn from "Isabel," one of the focal participants in her 14-year ethnographic study of a single block in New York City. In addition to those mentioned above, features include: overgeneralization of the possessive pronoun /s/ (*a friend of mines*); absence of concord with 'be' (*There is things she can't do*); double subjects, or left dislocation (*Her boyfriend, he's from Guatemala . . .*); hypercorrection of irregular past tense (*Before we spoked about that*) (Zentella 1997: 172). However, as Zentella illustrates with further examples from Isabel's written English, these and other vernacular features are variable. That is, although Isabel uses non-standard forms, she

also uses standard ones. For example, Zentella provides examples of Isabel's English without negative concord or lack of subject-verb agreement:

(14)   Unfortunately, my son doesn't have a baby sitter any longer. (Zentella 1997: 173)

Finally, although Zentella did not find standard variants of every non-standard form in Isabel's data, she does note that in some cases, the standard forms outnumbered the non-standard forms. For example, in the written corpus that provided many of the examples, 85 percent of the verbs were used with appropriate tense-mood-aspect-morphemes and 84 percent of the copulas were supplied (Zentella 1997: 173–4).

Slomanson and Newman (2004) forms part of a larger ongoing project on New York Latino English. Based on recent developments in sociolinguistics that examine group affiliations as well as traditional demographic categories such as ethnicity, age, and gender (Eckert 2000; Mendoza-Denton 1997), they studied several New York high school peer cultures: hip-hop, skater, geek (computer-oriented), and family oriented. In their initial work, they examined contact-sensitive vowels in the speech of New York Latino adolescents. Variables were selected to assess the degree of contact with the Spanish, AAVE, and New York Euro-American Vernacular English (NYEAVE). Slomanson and Newman found that the particular peer culture was associated with "targets for assimilation." For example, Latinos who identified with the hip-hop culture tended to use more monophthongal (ay), as in [tam], a variable associated with AAVE, than members of other groups, even though they had little contact with African Americans. The skaters, a Euro-American oriented peer group, used the fewest monophthongal (ay) vowels. Members of both groups also used some features associated with NYEAVE. Finally, somewhat surprisingly, the family oriented group, the only balanced Spanish-English bilinguals among the youth Slomanson and Newman studied, used very few of the variants identified as a possible result of Spanish contact.

Slomanson and Newman (2004) also examined the relationship between peer group identification and the pronunciation of laterals. In both NYEAVE and AAVE, /l/ onsets tend to be relatively dark, while in both non-Caribbean and Caribbean Spanish /l/ onsets are lighter. In contrast to the findings for their vocalic variables, Slomanson and Newman found that family oriented youth used significantly more light /l/ onsets, which they identified as a Spanish-contact feature, than members of groups that identified with African or Euro-Americans. With respect to codas, they found that the hip-hop and family oriented peer group speakers showed a significant tendency to vocalize (l), e.g., *Paul* is pronounced with a final back upglide, when compared to members of the skater and geek groups. They attribute the vocalized coda /l/s to convergence with AAVE and the dark /l/ variants to convergence with NYEAVE.

Slomanson and Newman (2004) have only examined a few variables so far. Nevertheless, their study does demonstrate the kind of careful work that needs to be done

if we are to have a full understanding of the Latino varieties of English spoken in the Eastern US at the beginning of the twenty-first century.

Conclusion

This chapter has outlined some of the basic features of two Latino English varieties: Chicano English and Puerto Rican English. Given the complexity and the geographic dispersion of those two communities, it has not been possible to provide a full inventory of the relevant features. For example, ChE is distinguished from the Euro-American English varieties with which it coexists by distinct intonation patterns (Santa Ana & Bayley 2004). Space limitations (along with the relative paucity of research), however, precluded a treatment of that important topic. Other topics remain equally open for exploration. The literature on the linguistic features of PRE is particularly sparse, for example, despite the fact that many Puerto Ricans have shifted to English as their dominant language and express their identity through a distinct variety of English. The new Latino diaspora, particularly the movement of Latinos into the South, presents other opportunities for research. Slomanson and Newman (2004) have shown that at least some Puerto Rican and other Latino youth in New York are adopting features of the local Euro-American vernacular. To what extent is that process occurring in new areas of Latino settlement such as Georgia and the Carolinas? Finally, in cities such as Los Angeles, New York, and Chicago, which are home to Latinos of many different national origins, are pan-Latino English varieties developing? For example, do Mexican immigrants in New York City, many of whom have settled in East Harlem, a traditional area of Puerto Rican settlement, adopt features of PRE or is New York Euro-American Vernacular the target language for those relatively recent immigrants? Mendoza-Denton (1999), in a review of research on the sociolinguistics of US Latinos, showed that considerable progress has been achieved since Peñalosa (1980) wrote about the neglect of Chicano English. However, as suggested by the questions posed above, a great deal remains to be done. Moreover, studies of US Latino English varieties have the potential not only to inform us about language use in the largest US minority community. Such studies also have the potential to provide important insights into language maintenance and shift, identity formation, and dialect contact, among many other topics of vital interest to students of language.

REFERENCES AND FURTHER READING

Bayley, R. (1994). Consonant cluster reduction in Tejano English. *Language Variation and Change*, 6, 303–26.

Bayley, R. (1999). Relativization strategies in Mexican-American English. *American Speech*, 74, 115–39.

Bayley, R. (2002). The quantitative paradigm. In J. K. Chambers, P. Trudgill, & N. Schilling-Estes (eds.), *The Handbook of Language Variation and Change* (pp. 117–41). Oxford: Blackwell.

Bayley, R. (2007). Spanish. In C. R. Wilson, M. Montgomery, & E. Johnson (eds.), *The New*

Encyclopedia of Southern Culture. Chapel Hill: University of North Carolina Press.

Bayley, R. & Santa Ana, O. (2004). Chicano English: morphology and syntax. In B. Kortmann & E. Schneider (eds.), *A Handbook of Varieties of English*. Vol. 2 (pp. 374–90). Berlin: Mouton de Gruyter.

Brodie, M., Steffenson, A., Valdez, J., Levin, R., & Suro, R. (2002). *2002 National Survey of Latinos*. Menlo Park, CA and Washington, DC: Henry J. Kaiser Family Foundation and the Pew Hispanic Center.

Eckert, P. (2000). *Linguistic Variation as Social Practice*. Oxford: Blackwell.

Farr, M. (ed.). (2005). *Latino Language and Literacy in Ethnolinguistic Chicago*. Mahwah, NJ: Lawrence Erlbaum.

Fought, C. (2003). *Chicano English in Context*. Basingstoke: Palgrave Macmillan.

Hakuta, K. & Pease-Alvarez, L. (1994). Proficiency, choice, and attitudes in bilingual Mexican American children. In G. Extra & L. Verhoeven (eds.), *The Cross-linguistic Study of Bilingual Development* (pp. 145–64). Amsterdam: Netherlands Academy of Arts and Sciences.

Mendoza-Denton, N. (1997). Chicana/Mexicana identity and linguistic variation: an ethnographic and sociolinguistic study of gang affiliation in an urban high school. PhD dissertation, Stanford University.

Mendoza-Denton, N. (1999). Sociolinguistics and linguistic anthropology of US Latinos. *Annual Review of Anthropology*, 28, 375–95.

Peñalosa, F. (1980). *Chicano Sociolinguistics*. Rowley, MA: Newbury House.

Penfield, J. & Ornstein-Galicia, J. L. (1985). *Chicano English: An Ethnic Contact Dialect*. Amsterdam: John Benjamins.

Pew Hispanic Center. (2005). *Hispanics: A People in Motion*. Washington, DC: Pew Hispanic Center.

Santa Ana, O. (1992). Chicano English evidence for the exponential hypothesis: a variable rule pervades lexical phonology. *Language Variation and Change*, 4 (3), 275–88.

Santa Ana, O. (1996). Sonority and syllable structure in Chicano English. *Language Variation and Change*, 8 (1), 63–89.

Santa Ana, O. & Bayley, R. (2004). Chicano English: phonology. In B. Kortmann & E. Schneider (eds.), *A Handbook of Varieties of English*. Vol. 1 (pp. 417–34). Berlin: Mouton de Gruyter.

Slomanson, P. & Newman, M. (2004). Peer group identification and variation in New York Latino English laterals. *English World-Wide*, 25, 119–216.

Thomas, E. R. (2001). *An Acoustic Analysis of Vowel Variation in New World English*. Durham, NC: Duke University Press.

Wald, B. (1987). Spanish-English grammatical contact in Los Angeles: the grammar of reported speech in the East Los Angeles contact vernacular. *Linguistics*, 25, 53–80.

Wald, B. (1996). Substratal effects on the evolution of modals in East LA English. In J. Arnold, R. Blake, B. Davidson, S. Schwenter, & J. Solomon (eds.), *Sociolinguistic Variation: Data, Theory and Analysis* (pp. 515–30). Stanford, CA: CSLI.

Wolfram, W. (1974). *Sociolinguistic Aspects of Assimilation: Puerto Rican English in New York City*. Washington, DC: Center for Applied Linguistics.

Wolfram, W., Carter, P., & Moriello, B. (2004). Emerging Hispanic English: new dialect formation in the American South. *Journal of Sociolinguistics*, 8, 339–58.

Wong Fillmore, L. (1991). When learning a second language means losing the first. *Early Childhood Research Quarterly*, 6 (3), 323–46.

Zentella, A. C. (1997). *Growing Up Bilingual: Puerto Rican Children in New York*. Oxford: Blackwell.

52

Teaching English to Native Speakers: The Subject Matter of Composition (1970–2005)

Mary Soliday

For well over a century now, most direct instruction in English to native speakers has occurred in remedial and/or freshman courses housed within English departments. And also for much of that period, teaching English to native speakers meant teaching grammar, expository prose writing, or literature to new college students. But, soon after the new English course was established (in 1873, at Harvard; see ENGLISH, LATIN, AND THE TEACHING OF RHETORIC), debates over its status emerged, and have continued to the present day. Unlike its counterparts in other fields, English composition is uniquely tied to teaching students, rather than to teaching a subject. For this reason, present-day issues in teaching English often turn on an old question: What, after all, is the proper subject matter for English composition?

The subject matter for English teaching derives, in part, from what we perceive the needs of new students to be. Indeed, the professional study of composition responded directly to the pressure to welcome large numbers of "new students" to the academy – ethnic minorities, and first generation college, working- or lower-middle-class students who, by the early 1970s, seemed to need more direct writing instruction than ever before. A central issue for composition teachers originates from this historic concern to help socially diverse groups assimilate to the academy. Writing teachers work through, and with, the dynamic tension that exists between a writer's language and that of the institution.

Today, one thread that continues to weave through disparate discussions concerns the relationship between the writer's intentions and the institution's demands. Should the subject matter of a writing course concern the writer's work or should it concern academic writing? This tension has, Joseph Harris (1997) points out, driven debates about the teaching of writing since 1966, when educators from Great Britain and America gathered at Dartmouth College for a famous, and highly influential, three-week Seminar on the Teaching and Learning of English. Some of the field's richest debates have examined the authority that we grant to students and their language as

opposed to the privileged position we grant to teachers and to the powerful dialect academics use. What do we do when students bring ways of thinking or languages to school that conflict, sometimes dramatically, with our own? In this context, the politics of language can become an important content for a writing class.

The subject matter of English composition derives also from institutional change. By the late 1990s, many four-year schools had abolished remedial English – thereby downsizing their freshman English programs. At the same time, along with the steady growth of professional education, writing across the curriculum (WAC) was gaining momentum and influence in many institutions. In this context, teachers began to wonder whether it is even possible to offer general skills instruction in a writing course: perhaps all writing instruction had to occur in some type of disciplinary framework. Today, then, the writing course may be changing shape as WAC perspectives change its traditional role in the university and thus its subject matter.

The Writer and the Academy

In the 1970s, when composition became a serious field for graduate study, teachers argued that the proper subject for English composition was the student writer him or herself. There was a growing consensus, sustained by the era's social movements, that student writers always had to struggle to write "up" to teachers who were experts in the subject matter they wrote about (usually literary). Composition came of age during the Open Admissions movements of the 1960s, so there was a further sense that students who have been historically underrepresented in the academy were especially overwhelmed by the institution's judgments of the individual's attempts to write. In this period, teachers developed pedagogies that honored the intentions of the novice writer and placed the teacher's expertise in a less authoritative role. They focused on the process of writing rather than on evaluating a final product, while reading, long the center of the literature classroom, now enjoyed a much less significant role. From its inception, then, composition studies drew strength from the tension between the individual student writer and the (possibly oppressive) academy.

Robert Brooke's *Writing and Sense of Self* (1991) empirically documents how he and another teacher made the student writer the subject matter of the writing classroom. Brooke argues that students learn to write when they learn to become writers, or to adopt a writer's role. This is difficult to do in college, he notes, because the roles of being a good student and that of being a writer are often in conflict. To teach students to become writers, Brooke says, he abandoned a traditional syllabus and began to organize his class around a writers' workshop. The writers' workshop helps to resolve the conflict between student and writer's roles because it organizes learning around the writer's, not the reader's, intentions. In Brooke's new syllabus, students choose their topics – often reflective and narrative genres – and help to set their own deadlines. Familiar rhythms of the class include brainstorming and planning, drafting and peer reading; and students create portfolios of their work for the teacher to evaluate.

"It was," Brooke writes, "a shift from a focus on my authority in the classroom to a focus on their authority in their worlds" (p. 1).

In Brooke's workshop, students write for a community of readers they know – a peer, commenting on a draft, or a teacher, holding an impromptu conference in her office after class. Moreover, if the essay is about a student's life experience, then this reader is not an expert in the subject matter. It is the writer's authority, not the reader's, which takes center stage. Peter Elbow, one of the original architects of the writers' workshop, explains in a debate about its efficacy that he wants his students "to care about their intentions and to insist that readers respect them" (1995: 77).

This pedagogy has been quite influential in college classrooms, and elsewhere – the writers' workshop is now the basis for the mandated literacy curriculum in the New York City public elementary schools. But for many teachers, the situation that constrains a student's writing to begin with – the academy itself – cannot be ignored. What role, they asked, does reading play in a writers' workshop? How, they wondered, can students really achieve authority if they don't contend with the power dialects spoken in schools and related institutions? Perhaps most importantly, however, for this group of teachers, academic writing is an appropriate subject matter for a writing course because it is not necessarily oppressive, but offers to students a way of thinking critically and reflectively about the world.

For instance, though they are equally concerned to help student writers acquire more authority, David Bartholomae and Anthony Petrosky's *Facts, Artifacts, and Counterfacts* (1986) argues that students cannot write fluently in the institution without speaking its language. Indeed, from their perspective, any writing students do, whether it's about their experiences or not, will be shaped to some degree by the rhetorical situation in which they find themselves; one cannot write beyond the institution of which one is a part. The question of institutional authority assumed salience for these teachers also because the curriculum Bartholomae and Petrosky helped to construct at the University of Pittsburgh served remedial writers, often working-class, first-generation college students. To help them move into the regular life of the college, *Facts, Artifacts and Counterfacts* invites students to act like their professors from the start – to try out the language of intellectual inquiry.

In one of the courses that Bartholomae and Petrosky describe, remedial writers joined a seminar focused on adolescent development where they read books like Margaret Mead's *Coming of Age in Samoa*. The course started by teaching students that academic readers don't derive their understanding of texts just by mining its "facts"; instead, they learn to "compose" interpretations of what they read – for reading, like writing, is itself a recursive, often messy, process. Gradually, through a careful sequence of assignments, students in this seminar used a variety of texts – their peers' autobiographies, as well as books like Mead's – to develop their own theory of adolescent growth. To do that, they had to understand how intellectuals develop and conceptualize their categories or how they decide what counts as good evidence, and why. In this and a later text for more advanced writing courses (*Ways of Reading* 2004), Bartholomae and Petrosky offer academic reading and writing as a powerful subject

matter for teachers, and for scholarship. As Bartholomae argues in a debate with Peter Elbow, "academic writing is the real work of the academy," and a "key term in the study of writing and the practice of instruction" (Bartholomae 1995: 63).

The Politics of Academic Writing

As I mentioned above, composition studies professionalized in an era whose rhetoric, at least, tried to give maximum authority to students, who were often seen in some conflict with repressive institutions. After all, that era saw a tidal wave of protest movements such as civil rights or women's liberation that had multiple effects on academic life. One such effect was the effort to redress social injustice through higher education, most notably through affirmative action or open admissions policies. No writing teacher addressed these issues more eloquently than Mina Shaughnessy (1977), who directed the writing program during the first phase of Open Admissions at the City College of New York, where I teach. Shaughnessy preferred to make grammar and academic writing the subject matter of a writing course, but she also maintained that the new students changed how teachers thought about their subjects and their academic roles. "From these students," she wrote, "we are learning to look at ourselves and at the academic culture we are helping them to assimilate with more critical eyes" (p. 292).

Shaughnessy also identified a core tension in composition studies: the conflict between the student's language and that of the institution. For the new students, Shaughnessy thought, college "both beckons and threatens," promising new ways of thinking but also asking them to surrender their values in favor of those of the academy (p. 292). Other teachers elaborated Shaughnessy's assessment, and by 1991, Patricia Bizzell identified "the tension between the individual student, with his or her own cultural identity and creative potential, and the conventional requirements of standardized writing instruction" (p. 129) as central to composition teaching.

Because writing teachers act as linguistic gatekeepers for their institutions, they perhaps confront this tension more keenly than anybody else. Often, writing teachers in this position work with remedial students who must pass entrance or exit tests and courses if they are to proceed through college. Just as often, these students bring with them to college other languages or dialects that are socially quite distant from the language typically preferred by faculty. In a trenchant historical critique, Bruce Horner and Min-Zhan Lu (1999) argue that writing teachers should not ignore the political dimensions of teaching remedial students when they seek primarily to teach them to mimic conventional forms. In their view, non-traditional college students cannot be expected to quickly shed their own languages in favor of adopting academic ways with words. If we do expect such an easy assimilation, these scholars warn, we bury the conflicts that many students do experience. It is possible, however, to bring these conflicts to light in a writing class by making its content the study of the politics of language.

Shifts in student populations and admissions policies provided the context for this and the related work of many writing teachers in the 1970s and 1980s (the growth of remedial writing programs surged during this period). But towards the century's end, another context for these conversations was provided by a general interest across the humanities and social sciences in textual politics, and the politics of education. For instance, many English departments were rocked by intense debates over the politics of representation, which included critiquing the status of traditional authors and the makeup of the literary canon itself. In composition, many teachers critiqued the status of conventional academic writing and the traditional effort to assimilate students to a seemingly neutral dialect. For these teachers, the appropriate subject for English composition is critical literacy – where students learn to make social change by studying how cultures perpetuate social inequality. Not unsurprisingly, critical literacy as a subject matter provoked as much heated debate among writing teachers as revisions to the traditional canon did among teachers of literature.

As one example, William Thelin (2005) documents how he makes critical literacy the central subject matter of his composition class at the University of Akron. In this account, Thelin describes how he adapted Ira Shor's (1996) widely influential theory for democratic education, itself the product of decades of teaching at the City University of New York, to a class attended by writers who must pass an exit exam to continue to freshman English. Thelin argues that critical literacy must begin by equalizing hierarchical relationships that the institution has already established, which means that students have to learn to take direct responsibility for what, as well as how much, they will learn. So in Thelin's class, students and teacher vote on the texts they will read; co-construct the syllabus and course policies; and develop and then sign contracts specifying how much work will be done for grades that the students wish to earn. In these ways, the teacher does not merely "give" or transfer his knowledge to his students, but together, they actively co-construct what will be learned and how it will be learned.

The content of a class like Thelin's is also likely to include readings from cultural studies, and, indeed, for their class text, Thelin and his students did choose an anthology of essays, *Rereading America* (Colombo et al. 1998), which asks undergraduates to consider the historical and cultural makeup of the American family, gender roles, or the American Dream. When the writing program at the University of Cincinnati recommended *Rereading America* for its second required writing course, the director of the program, Russel Durst (1999), decided to conduct an empirical study of how students and teachers responded to the goals established by advocates of critical literacy. In Durst's view, his program's version of critical literacy asks "students to examine their relationships to language and other cultural tools in an attempt to understand their role as actors in history and to realize their potential to create change on both a small and large scale" (p. 3).

In their focus on how teachers and students actually experience the abstract goals for achieving critical literacy, Thelin and Durst also respond to a longstanding debate in the field about the role of cultural studies content in a writing course and, more

generally, the aims of political teaching. With so many fields taking a political turn, several writing teachers ask whether it is appropriate to foist the teacher's (usually leftist) views upon young writers, and they worry about the problem of indoctrination (Hairston 1992). Certainly, while debates over the politics of teaching have played out more vocally in composition than perhaps elsewhere, this conflict in values will not disappear, as even science teachers, long immunized as objective, are encountering resistance from parents and students to the traditional cornerstone role that evolution plays in biology. As writing teachers have long understood, since we do not always claim the same values that our students do, newcomers may experience acute conflicts when they must assimilate an institution's language, values, or ways of thinking in order to succeed.

Finally, many writing teachers object to a focus on cultural studies in freshman English because they are concerned that a fidelity to the subject will trump our historic fidelity to our students' authority. Faculty who are dedicated to their subjects will not focus on the student whose work, these teachers feel, should furnish the content of the course. In a recent review essay, Richard Fulkerson (2005) objects to books like Colombo's *Rereading America* on two grounds: there is always the specter of indoctrination, but also, he suspects, these books reflect "content envy on the part of writing teachers" (p. 663). The proper subject matter for a writing course is, Fulkerson contends, the student him or herself:

> Reading, analyzing, and discussing the texts upon which the course rests are unlikely to leave room for any actual teaching of writing. So we get a "writing" course in which writing is required and evaluated, but not taught. I agree with Gary Tate, who remarked, "if we are serious about teaching *writing* rather than literature or politics or religion, we can – should – make the writing of our students the focus (content) of the course." (p. 665)

In the twenty-first century, the struggle over what should constitute the proper subject matter of composition continues to be waged around which text we prefer: a discipline's, or the student's. Traditionally, the discipline's text was a literary one, as the teaching of literature has long been synonymous in some institutions with the teaching of writing. Today, however, writing across the curriculum (WAC) provides us with fresh, and complicating, perspectives for thinking further about which kind of text should hold sway in freshman writing classes.

General Skills Instruction vs. Situated Learning

While WAC also grew out of the ferment of the 1970s, in recent years it has gained momentum as academics increasingly expressed their sense that university life is fragmented. In many cases, WAC programs were started with the hope that they could create some dialogue between liberal arts programs, now declining in prestige

on many campuses, and well-funded professional programs, now rapidly increasing their status. By the late 1990s, the remedial programs associated with composition's early phase had been legislated out of many four-year colleges and shifted to two-year schools; at institutions like the City University of New York, this left WAC with a growing institutional presence. Today, when we consider the subject matter of teaching English, we do it only within this changing institutional context.

This context highlights for us a conflict centering around whether we can separate the teaching of writing from the learning of a specific subject matter. Earlier, I mentioned Russel Durst's study of the writing program at the University of Cincinnati, which recorded how teachers and students actually respond to the aims of critical literacy teaching. Many of the Cincinnati students objected to the course content, arguing that required writing courses needed to launch them into another discipline or profession by giving them a set of useful general skills. Here, the students articulated a longstanding belief that learning to write happens once: this is why freshman writing courses have been for so long firmly parked in English departments. It is also why, in many institutions, a course in general skills instruction is assumed to prepare (for instance) young engineers to write – and why technical literacy instruction does not, generally speaking, occur within schools of engineering. According to David Russell (1991), the belief in the efficacy of general skills instruction extends at least back to the late nineteenth century, when the disciplines professionalized but scholars neglected to develop rhetorics for their own fields. Today, we often assume, along with the Cincinnati students, that "good writing" floats above these specific contexts: once we learn to write, the thinking seems to go, we can write anywhere for anyone.

However, an explosion of research focusing on writing in university, workplace, and community contexts argues that we nearly always have to learn to write again when we enter new social situations (e.g., Dias & Paré 2000). In the strongest version of this claim, Aviva Freedman (1995) argues that we learn to use language tacitly because we need to accomplish specific goals: a student will learn to write competently in a biology class because, for instance, she is learning how to do biology. For evidence, Freedman cites student writing from discipline-specific and composition classes that she and a research team compared; they found that students wrote better arguments in the first than in the latter type of class. To paraphrase, Freedman concludes that the students produced better papers in the discipline-specific classes because we learn to write competently (or well enough) by being immersed in particular social situations, tacitly absorbing the unspoken rules for writing (such as genre) by learning to speak as those around us are speaking.

The rapid growth of WAC testifies to a growing conviction among faculty in higher education that they, too, can participate in the teaching of writing. At City College, faculty can teach writing classes in their disciplines – to fulfill a second semester writing requirement. At Cornell and Duke Universities, students can choose from a roster of theme-based writing courses taught by faculty from across the disciplines (Monroe 2003). At the University of Calgary, Doug Brent (2005) describes

research seminars for freshmen taught by faculty in a communications program. And many schools are examining how Princeton University has created an autonomous writing program offering students a choice of theme-based writing seminars taught by faculty from English but also, when they are available, from other departments.

These configurations put pressure on the traditional writing course, while also raising interesting questions about the relationship between language and subject matter. Freedman's claim that students will learn to write without special instruction if they receive practice over the years has long predated WAC programs. However, scholarship sounds a cautionary note, suggesting that the issue is hardly resolved, for it is not clear whether students in writing intensive courses improve their writing by doing, for instance, history, or whether, as in a traditional writing course, they can reflect on what they have learned about language use in general (Greene 2001; Beaufort 2004). Perhaps as important, students in content courses do benefit from explicit instruction; not all students will learn to write confidently or competently in a biology class by absorbing the course material (Soliday 2005). Especially helpful in this regard is longitudinal research, which focuses on how students write across courses and semesters. Some of the best studies conducted so far (Sternglass 1997; Carroll 2002) show that explicit writing instruction plays a significant role in students' learning.

To provide explicit instruction in writing means, of course, that teachers have to split their allegiance between covering a subject and teaching the rhetoric of the subject. If we believe that learning to write will happen as Freedman argues that it does, as a result of being drenched in the language of a situation, then faculty won't have to divide their attention. But interesting research on how faculty talk about their assignments (e.g., Giltrow 2000; Wilner 2003) alerts us to the truth of David Russell's assertion that historically the disciplines neglected to develop a self-consciousness about the role that language plays in constructing knowledge. In short, faculty have difficulty making the rhetoric of their fields visible for their students; though expert writers themselves, they have not practiced how to help students try on the academic languages that they speak every day, but that may be alien to their students. Expertise in a subject matter does not always translate easily into expertise in the teaching of writing.

Where, finally, does all of this leave the teaching of English to native speakers? The newly professionalized composition teacher of the 1970s who identified the student writer as the proper subject matter would today share, at least in some quarters, that focus with many others: literature, of course, but also academic reading and writing; the politics of language; critical literacy and cultural studies; and, increasingly, particular themes from all disciplines. I have not done justice to the complexity of the debates over what constitutes the proper subject matter for English teaching, but have sketched the general contours of change in order to link these, again very generally, to broader institutional change. For it bears repeating that few courses of instruction in the university are so closely tied to institutional shifts in policy, program, and student population. With new subjects entering the writing classroom all the time, writing teachers continue to ask whether it is possible – or desirable – to

surrender the focus on the student's authority that grew out of composition's origins in the social protest movements of the 1960s.

Similarly, as teachers explore instruction beyond the traditional general skills framework, they are responding to institutional changes that we are beginning to grapple with in earnest in the new century. With the decline of remedial writing programs and the growing clout of professional schools, teachers must also ask what role a traditional writing course plays in undergraduate education. For, beyond teaching general language skills or rhetoric, the traditional writing course can also introduce students to a broadly critical way of thinking we usually associate with the liberal arts. Working out the relationship between writing for specific professional programs and writing more generally for college (and beyond) remains a core challenge for writing teachers today.

No wonder freshmen writing programs provoke so much disagreement; no wonder their content has been debated ever since, in the last third of the nineteenth century, Harvard developed the first full-fledged program for instruction in the mother tongue. As even my brief overview suggests, the teaching of English is uniquely involved with students and demographic shifts, but also with changes in institutional policy and mission. For this reason, as our institutions and student populations change over the next century, we can expect our debates about composition's subject matter to evolve accordingly.

REFERENCES AND FURTHER READING

Bartholomae, D. (1995). Writing with teachers: a conversation with Peter Elbow. *College Composition and Communication*, 46 (1), 62–71.

Bartholomae, D. & Petrosky, A. (1986). *Facts, Artifacts, and Counterfacts: Theory and Method for a Reading and Writing Course*. Upper Montclair, NJ: Boynton/Cook.

Bartholomae, D. & Petrosky, A. (2004). *Ways of Reading: An Anthology for Writers*. 7th edn. Boston: Bedford.

Beaufort, A. (2004). Developmental gains of a history major: a case for building a theory of disciplinary writing expertise. *Research in the Teaching of English*, 39 (2), 136–78.

Bizzell, P. (1991). *Academic Discourse and Critical Consciousness*. Pittsburgh: University of Pittsburgh Press.

Brent, D. (2005). Reinventing WAC (again): the first-year seminar and academic literacy. *College Composition and Communication*, 57 (2), 253–76.

Brooke, R. (1991). *Writing and Sense of Self: Identity Negotiation in Writing Workshops*. Urbana, IL: National Council of Teachers of English.

Carroll, L. A. (2002). *Rehearsing New Roles: How College Students Develop as Writers*. Carbondale: Southern Illinois University Press.

Colombo, G., Cullen, R., & Lisle, B. (eds.) (1998). *Rereading America: Cultural Contexts for Critical Thinking and Writing*. 4th edn. Boston: Bedford.

Dias, P. & Paré, A. (eds.) (2000). *Transitions: Writing in Academic and Workplace Settings*. Cresskill, NJ: Hampton Press.

Durst, R. (1999). *Collision Course: Conflict, Negotiation, and Learning in College Composition*. Urbana, IL: National Council of Teachers of English.

Elbow, P. (1995). Being a writer vs. being an academic: a conflict in goals. *College Composition and Communication*, 46 (1), 72–87.

Freedman, A. (1995). The what, where, when, why and how of classroom genres. In J. Petraglia (ed.), *Reconceiving Writing, Rethinking Writing Instruction* (pp. 121–44). Mahwah, NJ: Lawrence Erlbaum.

Fulkerson, R. (2005). Composition at the turn of the twenty-first century. *College Composition and Communication*, 56 (4), 654–87.

Giltrow, J. (2000). "Argument" as a term to talk about in student writing. In S. Mitchell & R. Andrews (eds.), *Learning to Argue in Higher Education* (pp. 129–45). Portsmouth, NH: Boyton/Cook.

Greene, S. (2001). The question of authenticity: teaching writing in a first-year college history of science class. *Research in the Teaching Of English*, 35 (4), 525–69.

Hairston, M. (1992). Diversity, ideology, and teaching writing. *College Composition and Communication*, 43 (2), 179–93.

Harris, J. (1997). *A Teaching Subject: Composition Since 1966*. Upper Saddle River, NJ: Prentice-Hall.

Horner, B. & Lu, M.-Z. (1999). *Representing the "Other": Basic Writers and the Teaching of Basic Writing*. Urbana, IL: National Council of Teachers of English.

Monroe, J. (ed.) (2003). *Local Knowledges, Local Practices: Writing in the Disciplines at Cornell*. Pittsburgh: University of Pittsburgh Press.

Russell, D. (1991). *Writing in the Academic Disciplines, 1870–1990: A Curricular History*. Carbondale: Southern Illinois University Press.

Shaughnessy, M. (1977). *Errors and Expectations: A Guide for the Teacher of Basic Writing*. New York: Oxford University Press.

Shor, I. (1996). *When Students Have Power: Negotiating Authority in a Critical Pedagogy*. Chicago: University of Chicago Press.

Soliday, M. (2005). Mapping genres in a science of society class. In A. Herrington & C. Moran (eds.), *Genres Across the Curriculum* (pp. 65–82). Logan: Utah State University Press.

Sternglass, M. (1997). *Time to Know Them: A Longitudinal Study of Writing and Learning at the College Level*. Mahwah, NJ: Lawrence Erlbaum.

Thelin, W. (2005). Understanding problems in critical classrooms. *College Composition and Communication*, 57 (1), 114–41.

Wilner, A. (2003). The challenges of assignment design in discipline-based freshman writing classes. *Composition Forum*, 14 (2), 65–98.

53

Earning as well as Learning a Language: English and the Post-colonial Teacher

Eugene Chen Eoyang

Introduction

The title of this essay reflects my conviction that "language" is a subject different from other subjects that are "taught." "Deep" analysis (assuming that learning a grammar is learning a language), mere imitation (verbal mimicry), memorization (rote learning) – all these have been tried, often in combination. They have been, if we compare the amount of time spent with the amount of mastery achieved, largely unsuccessful. I believe the root of the problem is a fundamental error in our perception of language as a subject to be learned. In order to explain what I mean, one must first dispel some false presumptions that thwart our efforts in language instruction.

The first false presumption is virtually unchallenged: to learn a language, one must live in the country where it is spoken. The presumption is misleading because it doesn't specify the length of time or the degree of immersion. Surely no one would claim that one year's continuous residence in a foreign country is sufficient for acquiring that language, much less a summer. Yet, this is precisely what many educational programs in all countries promise. Even extended residence in a country is no guarantee that one will learn the language spoken in that country. This can be attested to by the thousands of expatriates who manage to live for many years in a foreign country, situated if not immersed in the local culture, without acquiring even a nodding familiarity with the native tongue. Conversely, there are numerous examples of individuals whose command of a foreign language is remarkable, even without extended residence in the second language venue. I have personally encountered, for example, individuals whose English was extremely proficient despite the fact that they never set foot in an English-speaking country. The "osmosis" theory of language learning is widely held – alas, among professionals as well as the general public – but it has no validity.

The question to be asked first is whether a language is a body of knowledge, a set of skills, or a fund of experiences. If it is a body of knowledge, then mere transfer of information from source to target is what is required; if it is a set of skills, then repeated exercise and reinforced training will be the appropriate learning strategy; but if it is a fund of experiences, then neither information transfer nor the inculcation of skills will be sufficient. It is my impression that language instruction – including English language instruction – has focused too much on the transfer of knowledge and the acquisition of skills. What has been neglected is the concern with language as a fund of experiences: the process of transferring knowledge might be characterized as *acquisition*, where the content remains unchanged in the transmission and the behavior of the learner is unaffected; the process of inculcating skills is subsumed in *training*, where repeated and habitual actions establish an individual level of control. The process of undergoing a fund of experiences I characterize as *earning*, which involves will as well as ability. Learning a second language constitutes all three processes, of acquisition, of training, and of earning. The literature on acquisition dominated the first phase of studies on language learning, and comprised mostly descriptive grammars, glossaries, and corpuses; the literature on training has emerged in the second phase, and constitutes a good part of the research on second language instruction. The third phase, what I call earning, has been touched on, if at all, in anecdotal accounts of the way we learn a second language. It is the aspect which has attracted the least systematic attention.

What's Being Taught

The voluminous literature on how to teach a language rarely asks what it is that's being taught: if it's mere subject matter, then language is like old-fashioned history – dates and facts; if it's verbal skills, then language is like an activity, like swimming or riding a bicycle, where actions are internalized; but if it's a human experience to which one must adapt, and by which one is shaped, then what is required is a mode of instruction different from that employed in teaching an academic subject or imparting a particular skill. Before we proceed to the part of instruction that involves "earning," perhaps we might analyze the intellectual and mental faculties involved in information transfer as well as in imparting specific skills. In the first instance, the necessary tools are an accurate memory and diligent understanding. The learning process does not necessarily involve any individual adaptation to the material transmitted: facts are neutral, concepts are theoretical, processes and methodologies are, or should be, objective and not subjective. (I'm distinguishing the impersonal reception of information and facts from the very idiosyncratic interpretation of what one learns.) The imparting of skills, on the other hand, requires personal adaptation to the skills being taught: one learns to swim, or to ride a bicycle, by imprinting the skills on one's own motor, mental, or somatic reflexes: mastery involves being personally and specifically imbued with a particular sets of skills: there is no abstract acquisition, no

impersonal understanding. Each challenge must be met individually and idiosyncratically. The third phase of learning, "earning," goes beyond both the relatively straightforward reception of information as well as the reinforced, implicitly imprinted set of skills, and must be adapted to individual strengths and limitations. What it requires is the development of what I shall call – borrowing from John Dewey – "funded experience." Funded experience differs from ordinary experience insofar as it is experience that serves as an investment for future learning. It is not merely reflective experience, but rather experience that prompts changed behavior, which in language learning becomes verbal and mental adaptation.

The trouble with concepts like "acquisition," "competence," and "performance" in the discourse on language learning is that they presuppose certain premises which are far from appropriate to the phenomenon of language. For example, "acquisition" posits language as a content to be possessed; "competence" suggests a task to be carried out; and "performance" presupposes a pre-existing script that must be enacted. But language is not content nor task nor text. It is not a code to be deciphered, nor a body of knowledge to be transmitted, nor a play to be enacted. Language is a semantic experience to be shared. It cannot be learned with just the cool logic of analytical reason (scientists with extremely analytical minds often make the worst language learners), or else every descriptive linguist would be a fluent speaker of the language he or she studies. It cannot be taught by mere imitation or else every unoriginal person would be an adept in the learning of languages. The trouble with language instruction is the very inauthenticity of its mode of delivery. No one learned his or her native language in a classroom. When one proceeds to teach language, particularly as an academic subject, one adopts the analytical sequences inherent in the attempt to provide systematic approaches to teaching a subject. The haphazard, intuitive way most children learn their first language can't be replicated in the classroom. This misleads many into thinking that there is a finite course in which a language can be learned, much as one can acquire a computer language, like COBOL, PASCAL, or LISP. Children do not learn their first languages with a user's manual – whether in the form of grammars or guides.

The fundamental flaw in most ESL approaches is that they assume that because we learned our first language a certain way, we can learn a second language in the same way. Even if we could reconstruct the incredibly absorptive brain of an infant at a period when the learning curve is higher than it will ever be again, we cannot replicate the psychological condition of being a virgin learner. In approaching a second language, the adult learner has a formidable disadvantage – which is that he already knows his first language. Imitating from a clean slate, as a child does, is psychologically as well as ontologically different from imitating as an adult. In the first instance, it is unprejudiced learning, non-evaluative and non-judgmental: it is totally trusting. No child queries the logic in the (first) language; but the same child as an adult will always compare subsequent languages against the first language, however relevant or irrelevant the differences or similarities may be. (Recent research on the brain indicates a physiological warrant in early and late acquisition of the second language. Joy Hirsch

and Karl Kim (1997), using MRI techniques, suggest that when acquired early, native and second languages tend to be represented in common frontal cortical areas; but when acquired later, second languages are spatially separated from native languages.)

The first issue, of conceiving the project of English being taught as a foreign language (EFL) or as a second language (ESL), significantly misprises the situation, since English, with its global reach, is often not an entirely closed book to its learners, and students are not being taught English as either a foreign or as a second language. Another category needs to be recognized, to which I give the acronym TUE, which stands for "Teaching Unbroken English." As I have indicated in an earlier essay (Eoyang 1999), I agree with the Japanese businessman who rejected the claim that English was the global language: "English is not the global language," he said. "Broken English is the global language."

"Native" Proficiency

We may examine the necessary but not sufficient elements of what should be taught when we teach English: phonetics; grammar; communicative competence. While the proper pronunciation of any language is promoted by the users of that language, communicative competence is not crucially impaired by deviations in pronunciation, whether by "foreign-accented" speech or by regional variants. The British speaker of English can hardly be blamed for initially misunderstanding the Australian, when he takes the remark "I just came TO-DIE" as a wish to end one's life rather than an observation as to when someone arrived. Correct pronunciation is a social concern, and there are those whose incorrect pronunciation have enhanced their image. Teachers of mathematics or science are, for example, not discommoded when they speak with a thick German accent; nor are diplomats or engineers disadvantaged when they speak with a French accent.

Grammar is also not a warrant of native proficiency. Indeed, "correct" pronunciation and grammar are only reflections of the norms of usage, the standard in the sense of most widespread, not necessarily the most superior. And errors of subject-verb agreement are sometimes complex. Faculty have been known to argue about whether the word "faculty" is singular or plural. One hears both "The faculty is displeased with the president" and "the faculty are displeased with the president" – and it isn't always obvious that the first refers to an academic body and the second to congeries of individuals. Indeed, one can argue the exact opposite about the relationship between grammar and pronunciation to native fluency. Native speakers of English have often observed that someone's English is too "correct" to be native. English that does not have the rough-hewn characteristics of personal adaptation seems unnatural, inauthentic, a "hothouse" English rather than a routine mode of expression.

If "correct" grammar and exact pronunciation are not the reliable hallmarks of native fluency, what is? From the viewpoint of discourse analysis, one would have to

say "functional effectiveness," i.e., the ability to *do* something with language. That ability, to express, to direct, to query, to muse, to scold, to charm, to persuade, even to philosophize – that is the warrant of proficiency. To be able to negotiate in the language, to use the conventions as well as the perversities of the language comfortably, this is a far more practical watermark of proficiency than any comparison with an elusive – and variable – "native speaker" (compare Paikeday 1985). "Functional effectiveness" involves more than pragmatics, more than even what Ruquiya Hasan and Gillian Perrett (1994: 181ff.) call "systemic functional" (which emphasizes a social theoretical basis): it subsumes the ability not merely to behave in a language, but to think and imagine in that language. In many ways, this definition of proficiency is both more and less exigent that the total imitation of a native.

The modern teacher of English faces a dilemma which did not trouble his or her predecessor. In the past, teaching English meant teaching the King's (or the Queen's) English; it meant teaching the literature written in English by English authors; and it meant indoctrinating the student to being, in fact, English. Now, one has to take notice of the English of the American dialects, whether in the rustic colloquialisms of Mark Twain's Missouri, the southern cadences of William Faulkner's Yoknapatawpha County, the Caribbean accents of a Derek Walcott, the urban Chicago patois of Saul Bellow's *Augie March*, the Harlem locutions of Ralph Ellison's *Invisible Man*, and the lilting cadences of Raja Rao's *Kanthapura*. Nor can we confine ourselves exclusively to the literature of Great Britain and the United States, since English now includes the plays of the Nigerian Wole Soyinka, the novels of his compatriot, Chinua Achebe, and the drama of the white South African Athol Fugard as well as of the Black African Ngugi Wa Thiongo, whose early work was written in English under the name of James Ngugi. Then there are the exiles who write in English, including V. S. Naipaul, Salman Rushdie, and Kazuo Ishiguro. Nor should we overlook the expatriate writers who adopted English after producing distinguished work in their original languages: they would include Vladimir Nabokov (Russian), Czelaw Milosz (Polish), Isaac Bashevis Singer (Hebrew), and Joseph Brodsky (Russian) – the last three Nobel laureates. To put it paronomastically, English, nowadays, is no longer as English as the English.

In other words, "native proficiency" is a chimera not worth pursuing: it sets up a false – perhaps, as Paikeday reminds us, a non-existent – model. The purpose of learning any language is, of course, to negotiate meaning in a particular linguistic culture, it is not to perform a flawless impersonation of a native.

Making a language one's own involves immersing oneself in the culture, defined as linguistically related artifacts, constructions, and situations; culture becomes the context which must inform the lessons of the language learner attempting to master the grammatical structure of the language. Locutions have no validity absent of a real life relevance and force, which is why "textbook" instruction will always fail, especially those "textbook" lessons which inauthentically try to imitate life situations.

Every language has its idiosyncrasies, just as every speaker of any language has his or her idiolect. Psycholinguistically, the non-native speaker must not aspire to perfect

imitation, because mimicry only implies inauthenticity, both to the self-conscious producer of the language and to the native interlocutor. Mimicry can easily turn into mockery. Native speakers do not apologize for departing from the norm: indeed, they relish inventing their own variations on the common theme. Yet, languages are not neutral conveyors of meaning: they embody their own history, their own point of view, their specific perspective. It has been observed that speaking a different language manifests a different personality, or at least a different aspect of the same personality. I am not here trying to typecast languages – any language can accommodate any number of temperaments and personal styles. But to assume that all languages are equally bland and colorless – like a perfectly transparent pane of glass – is to miss what is interesting and undeniably unique about each language.

The "Dues" and Don't's of Language Learning

I want to return to the comparison made earlier of language learning to learning a skill, like swimming or riding a bicycle. In only a superficial way can the two kinds of imprinting, whether on the mind or in the muscles, or on some combined form of somatic and mental training, be likened to one another. Of such motor and physical skills like swimming and riding a bicycle, the skill, once imprinted, is never lost. No one ever hears of someone drowning because somehow the swimmer had *forgotten* how to swim once he found himself in the water. One can ride a bicycle even after having no practice for many years. But language is different: even a short hiatus in the use of the language, and one's proficiency atrophies markedly, as expatriates have often remarked. This occurs for two reasons. The first is that language is constantly changing, whereas the moments of forces in riding a bicycle and the laws of buoyancy in swimming never change. Language skills need to adapt constantly to changing conditions. Physical skills also appear to be imprinted more indelibly than language skills. Without regular use of a language, no matter what language, even one's first language, but especially with an arduously acquired second language, one cannot simply absorb the lessons abstractly in a textbook or in a classroom. Without actual use, there can be no language progress. That use constitutes the "dues" one must pay to the language. Without paying these dues, learning a language is a waste of time, as with the thousands of adults who have forgotten whatever "high school French" they were taught.

To conceptualize languages in a way that captures both their transparency and their unique character, I like to think of different languages as different prisms through which one can view the world. Each speaker can see the light refracted in this prism, but what is refracted may be different from prism to prism. Each prism offers a different perspective: different realities will be viewed in different ways through different prisms. At the cognitive level, this point has already been established in English by the work of George Lakoff, Mark Johnson, and Mark Turner which focuses on how basic metaphors and paradigms of thought in English subsume a particular mindset.

The prism model suggests that the object is not to find semantic equivalents in negotiating a foreign language; it is rather to adopt a different cultural mindset, to make another language virtually second nature. The mechanical acquisition of rules (rules which native speakers are scarcely aware of) is likely to make the student more rather than less self-conscious, more rather than less ill at ease in a foreign language. (The intuitive and tacit inculcation of these rules is, of course, another matter.) Above all, teaching students to see through the English prism (or the French, or the Chinese), is a way to avoid the bane of language acquisition: which is translation, either into or out of one's native language. And the bane in the reading of foreign texts is the annoying and interminable need to look up words in a bilingual dictionary, sometimes repeatedly for the same word. This annoying incompetence is the result of translating for meaning, for the word to be referenced is a cipher, and the definition is what rewards the search; the student, upon finding the meaning, forgets the original word, which is now as indecipherable as it was before. That is why single language dictionaries are pedagogically more sound; they not only wean the student from his native language, they also enrich and reinforce his vocabulary in the language he is acquiring.

The view of the world through a language prism reminds the language learner that the enterprise does not involve translating foreign concepts into native vocabulary, but of understanding foreign concepts natively, or as the Russian formalists would put it, "to see the strange as familiar." Therefore, the task of the teacher is not merely teaching students how to speak differently but also of explaining how they might, to a real extent, *think* differently. The successful language teacher effects a kind of metempsychosis, where the student is transformed into another version of him/herself.

Teaching English as Something "Foreign"

Different students require different pedagogical approaches. In teaching English composition in Hong Kong, I have specifically avoided citing in class any published samples of text models to follow: this would have been counterproductive for a number of reasons. Given the proclivity among Hong Kong students to copy rather than emulate, offering models to copy would only encourage their copyist habits, and further undermine any attempts at self-development. I have also tried to motivate the students by using embarrassment as a means of reminding them to concentrate on eliminating the same errors from their writing. At the start of a semester, I excerpt examples of composition mistakes on an overhead transparency, with the name deleted; later on, if the same error is made repeatedly, I threaten to leave the name exposed. Finally, I try to instill confidence in the students by selecting from their work potentially excellent samples which I edit and correct and show on the overhead screen. Displaying examples of creditable prose, and reminding them that one of them was the original author (my role being limited merely to that of an editor), I try to convey the point that each of them has the capacity to write well.

My strategy is to get my students to pay regular "dues" to the English language, to make it part of their lives, and to develop an aspect of their personality in English. Only in this way can students be impelled to "earn" their English rather than merely to learn their English. For the best instruction is an ephemeral thing if one doesn't "keep up" with the language. Regular involvement in a language is a kind of "verbal citizenship" that one takes out, without which language study is an empty show, an exercise in pointless and forgettable mimicry. The best instructor of ESL in the world will have ultimately failed if he or she has not by the end of the period of instruction instilled in the students the will to pay their dues, to earn their English even after the class has concluded. We are not like swimming instructors, where it's a question of "once taught, forever learned." What we engage in is an exercise in futility if the student fails to continue his or her involvement with the language.

Pedagogical Challenges

In a post-colonial and post-modern era, the use of English poses perhaps as many advantages as difficulties. To its advent as a global *lingua franca*, there is as much to deplore as to celebrate. There is a tendency, particularly among native English speakers, and not a few benighted stalwarts of business, who think that the pervasive use of English obviates the need to learn other languages or to understand other cultures. The more enlightened business executives, however, realize that multilinguality is a must for world-class executives. Indeed, a significant portion of the CEOs of top Fortune 500 companies command more than one language as well as substantial experience in more than one culture. The accounting firm of Deloitte, Touche, and Tohmatsu has a standing policy to promote international experiences among their employees, particularly those with executive potential. (Of course, the East-West combination of the company's title already bespeaks an international perspective at the very core of leadership, not merely a Western corporation that is adding "token" Asian representation at the highest levels.)

There is the danger that the widespread use of English may be confused with the tendency toward globalization. The "triumphalist" rhetoric of some commentators (usually Anglocentric) does not help to reassure "second" and "third world" cultures that the use of English is not merely a twenty-first century version of the hegemonic practices of British imperialism of the nineteenth century, with the only difference being that English is now predominantly American English, and that the hegemons in the twenty-first century are the Americans rather than the British. It would indeed be unfortunate if English as a *lingua franca*, far from being merely a facilitator of communication between peoples, were to become a factor in the erasure of all cultures other than Anglo-American.

But if the "triumphalist" view of English as a global language is misleading and unhelpful, so is the imputation that English is a reflection of the evils of globalization. Such a view would overlook the salient fact that the very authors of post-colonial

theory – whether Antonio Gramsci or Michel Foucault or Edward Said – were first written, published, and read in so-called "hegemonic" European languages (Italian, French, and English). Indeed, without these languages, it is questionable that the world would be as alert as it is of the evils of cultural imperialism. Nor would the ethnicities of various non-hegemonic cultures – whether those of the Indian subcontinent (*vide* Raja Rao, Rabindranath Tagore), the Caribbean (Derek Walcott, V. S. Naipaul), Africa (Wole Soyinka, Chinua Achebe, James Ngugi, if not Ngugi Wa Thiongo) – be as well known in the world as they are.

These empirical complexities and confusions and inequalities are not without pedagogical consequences. There is no theoretical adjudication that will survive classroom experience, and one must resort to circumstantial exigencies. To insist on Oxbridge English in Australia, or to require American pronunciation in India, would be a pedagogical impropriety that is sure to stir resentment in the local student. Yet, on the global scene, it may be necessary to train the ear to accept a wide latitude of phonetic variation if English is to be truly a *lingua franca*. The last thing one needs is a *lingua franca* which is variously incomprehensible to different speakers.

The post-colonial teacher of English, to avoid ethnocentrically favoring one standard of pronunciation over another, has to acknowledge that "Received Pronunciation" is a great deal more variegated than it was in the past. Not only regional accents, but regional expressions seep into the language – whether it's "Bollywood" from south India, "billabong" or "fair dinkum" or "bushranger" from Australia (all are listed in the *Encarta Concise World Dictionary* and the *Oxford English Dictionary*). And, as so-called "foreign" cultures become "ethnic" in the United States and the United Kingdom, the world's culture becomes part of the English language: the vocabulary of diplomacy reflects the French influence in international statesmanship, with words like *détente, attaché, aide-de-camp, coup d'état, communiqué, espionage, sabotage*, etc. And the multitude of ethnic cuisines available in the United States and the United Kingdom, in more or less authentic forms, include the familiar *pizza* and *lasagna* from Italy, but also *dim sum* from China, *kimchi* from Korea, *sushi* and *sashimi* from Japan, *fajitas* and *tacos* from Mexico, *nan, poppadom* (var. *popadum, popadam*), and *samosas* from India, and, of course, *baguette* and *croissant* from France.

The teaching of English in a post-colonial and post-modern age is fraught with pitfalls, not only with respect to the populations being taught, but also with respect to the presumed notion of "Received Pronunciation," which is much more chimerical than before. We are faced not with one English language, but with "World Englishes." Ironies abound: English is at once demonized as the language of the imperialist, yet it is also the preferred language for anti-imperialist, post-colonial theory; English lays claim to be the world's language, yet more of the world is reflected in English than in any other language; citizens of the United States and United Kingdom are uncomfortable with "triumphalist" claims for English, but the enthusiasm for English in other parts of the world seems boundless. For instance, some years ago, Korea considered making English a national language: "English is no longer a secondary language and has already become a primary language," Lee Nam-ki, chairman of

the Korean Fair Trade Commission, has declared (*Korea Times* 2001). China has recently mandated that English be adopted as the medium of instruction in all technical courses at universities and colleges (*South China Morning Post* 2001).

Conclusion

There are several myths about language which have, in my opinion, bedeviled language learning and language teaching theory. The first is that language is a tool, a functional instrument. English is often viewed as a means for upward mobility, either in securing better employment opportunities or a higher social class. Certainly this is one of the effects, possibly some of the benefits of acquiring English. But if English is seen only as a tool, then learning English should be much easier than it is: tools should not be difficult to master – their function is, after all, to facilitate use. The misconception lies in the character of a tool, which is mute and material, whereas language is expressive and intangible; a tool has no personality, whereas speakers of a language, any language, are inescapably idiosyncratic; a tool is not organic and does not change: it can only be replaced, whereas a language is in constant flux and adapts to new realities, new situations, and is constantly evolving. Languages die only when their speakers become extinct.

The second myth that muddles theories of language learning is to conceive of language as a code. But the definition of codes is that they yield disambiguated messages and are invariant in their meaning, whereas language, even when it involves only one word with one meaning, let alone words with multiple meanings, carries different weights in different contexts. Even the notion of correctness is often contraverted with natural languages. For example, an illogicality uttered by a non-native speaker is a solecism, whereas an illogicality uttered by a native, and repeated by other natives, becomes an idiom. A deviation in pronunciation by a non-native is undecipherable, but deviations produced by natives are called "accents." Surely real codes do not behave so perversely; real codes do not depend on deictic relationships, they do not embody personal styles, and are not subject to situational inflections. Language, on the other hand, is vital and not so much indeterminate as multidimensional: it operates on more than one level, semantically, psycholinguistically, sociolinguistically, sometimes even psychosomatically.

The third myth about language, and about English, is that one can speak meaningfully about standards, confusing inflexible rules and regulations with "best practices": British English, according to some, is superior to any other, including Irish English, which has produced some of the finest writers of English – Swift, Shaw, Wilde, Yeats, Joyce, and Beckett – but who are hypocritically tolerated by their inclusion in the canon of "British" or English Literature. We cannot continue to muddle up "English" when it refers to a world language with "English" when it refers to the language of the United Kingdom. It is time we define "English" as a transnational phenomenon, as in Tom MacArthur's and Braj Kachru's reference to "World Englishes": we use

"British English" to designate specifically the literature of Albion, restricted to the language of the British Isles. Even that would not be sufficient to extirpate "foreign" elements from the strictly British canon. Language purists seem unaware that the nationhood they invoke is not what it used to be: the "our" is a different "our" from what it was generations ago. As Lam (1999) says, "A prominent feature of today's global cultural landscape is the intermingling of customs and lifeways and the presence of multiculturalism within national borders" (p. 389).

The post-colonial teacher of English must abandon the rigidities of textbook rules and regulations and the dogmas of grammar. Their prospect is both more daunting and more inviting: they must learn to share with the student English as a culture, in all its complexity, its untidiness, its multifariousness – and its fascination.

It is important to learn English because so much of the modern world is English – in mindset, in logic, in style, in organization, in character. Understanding this world involves nothing less than implanting the template of the English language in our own minds, for only when there is a verbal simulacrum of the world outside – contiguous and unmediated by the inevitable translation into another language – can one be said to truly understand. For those whose ignorance engenders fear and apprehension, not to say prejudice, it is the teacher's job to assuage, to persuade, to reassure, to encourage even before he or she can instruct. Hasan's injunction about teachers, both humbling and inspiring, is that "in the mundane line of learning, very often, unlike the teacher in the classroom, no one is consciously teaching us." I confess to teaching people unconsciously. Indeed, I might say that some of my best teaching has been unconscious. For as with every good teacher, we teach the student, not the subject. English is, in one sense, merely a means by which, we, along with our students, "make sense of our life experience" (Hasan & Perrett 1994). Teaching is not a transitive activity, what one person does to another. It is an intransitive process, where learning takes place, not because of an agent (and sometimes in spite of the teacher). Teaching English is a pretext for exploration, not a doctrine to be promulgated; an intuition to be lived, not a text to be recited. We cannot truly learn English without investing the time and the effort to earn it first.

NOTE

Portions of this essay have been reproduced or adapted from Eoyang (2003), reprinted by permission.

REFERENCES AND FURTHER READING

Bennet, M. J. (1997). How not to be a fluent fool: understanding the cultural dimension of language. In A. E. Fantini (ed.), *New Ways in Teaching Culture* (pp. 16–21). Alexandria, VI: TESOL.

Eoyang, E. (1999). English as the world's language. *Hong Kong Linguist*, 19–20, 16–22.

Eoyang, E. (2003). Teaching English as culture: paradigm shifts in postcolonial discourse.

Diogenes, 50 (2), 3–16; originally published in French as "L'enseignement de l'anglais comme langue de culture," *Diogène*, 198 (April-June 2002), 1–19.

Halliday, M. & Hasan, R. (1985). *Language, Context, and Text: Aspects of Language in a Social-Semiotic Perspective*. Oxford: Oxford University Press.

Hasan, R. & Perrett, G. (1994). Learning to function with the other tongue. In T. Odlin (ed.), *Perspectives on Pedagogical Grammar* (pp. 179–226). Cambridge: Cambridge University Press.

Hirsch, J. & Kim, K. (1997). *Nature*, 388 (10 July), 171–4.

Holborow, M. (1999). *The Politics of English*. London: Sage.

Kramsch, C. (1993). *Context and Culture in Language Teaching*. Oxford: Oxford University Press.

Lakoff, G. & Johnson, M. (1980). *Metaphors We Live By*. Chicago: University of Chicago Press.

Lam, W. S. E. (1999). The question of culture in global English-language teaching: a postcolonial perspective. In L. Liu (ed.), *Tokens of Exchange: The Problem of Translation in Global Circulations* (pp. 375–97). Durham, NC: Duke University Press.

Paikeday, T. M. (1985). *The Native Speaker is Dead!* New York: Paikeday.

Soyinka, W. (1976). *Myth, Literature and the African World*. Cambridge: Cambridge University Press.

Yallop, C. (1999). English around the world. In E. Ronowicz & C. Yallop (eds.), *English: One Language, Different Cultures* (pp. 26–45). New York: Cassell.

54

Creoles and Pidgins

Salikoko S. Mufwene

Introduction

The title of this chapter is a deliberate subversive reversal of the traditional phrase *pidgins and creoles*, which is consistent with the mistaken assumption that creole vernaculars have evolved from antecedent pidgin *lingua francas*. I show below that there is no documentary evidence that supports this position. The socio-economic history of the colonization of the world by Europe since the fifteenth century speaks against it. If anything, that history suggests that creoles and pidgins developed concurrently, by gradual divergence from closer approximations of European colonial languages spoken initially by Creole populations and interpreters, respectively. Their development is a concomitant of gradual changes in the socio-economic ecologies of the transmission of European colonial languages, a process in which less and less competent speakers served as models to new learners, thus favoring more and more divergence from the original targets. As argued in Mufwene (2001, 2005), the restructuring of the systems into the new varieties proceeded, in kind, in the same way as it has in other languages. Creoles and pidgins just highlight the role that contact has always played in those other cases.

Thus, neither creoles nor pidgins can be singled out as a structural type of languages with a particular combination of features or evolutionary processes that set them apart from other languages. Creoles vary as much among themselves as indigenized Englishes do, taken as a group, and certainly no less than the "native Englishes" of the United Kingdom, North America, and Australia, if only there were a reliable yardstick to use. Within each socio-historical grouping, the language varieties both resemble, and differ from, each other by the Wittgensteinian family resemblance principle as much by their structural features as by the ecological peculiarities of their emergence.

Moreover, creoles and pidgins are not all genetically related either, except to the extent that the languages they have evolved from, misnamed *lexifiers* in creolistics, are Indo-European. In this respect, it is also plausible to argue that creoles (those that have evolved from European languages, the focus of this chapter) are new Indo-European language varieties, but this position challenges the received doctrine in creolistics. In order for this essay to be both informative and manageable within the space limits, I focus on what kinds of language varieties creoles and pidgins are, how they evolved, and some of what is entailed by the position I defend.

What are Creoles and Pidgins?

Strictly speaking, creoles and pidgins are new language varieties which developed out of contacts between colonial non-standard varieties of a European language and several non-European languages around the Atlantic and in the Indian and Pacific Oceans during the sixteenth to nineteenth centuries. *Pidgins* typically emerged in trade colonies which developed around trade forts or along trade routes, such as on the coast of West Africa. They are reduced in structures and specialized in functions (typically, trade), and initially they served as non-native *lingua francas* to users who preserved their native vernaculars for their day-to-day interactions. Some pidgins have expanded into regular vernaculars, especially in urban settings, and are called *expanded pidgins*. Examples include Bislama and Tok Pisin (in Melanesia) and Nigerian and Cameroon Pidgin Englishes, which are structurally as complex as *creoles* (based on, for instance, Féral 1989; Jourdan 1991). One can certainly argue that the structural complexity of a language variety is ethnographically a function of the communicative functions into which it is put, even as a *lingua franca*, although from a typological perspective it is difficult to say whether a language is structurally more complex than another, especially whether a language that has complex morphosyntax is also more complex semantically or phonologically.

Creoles are vernaculars that developed in settlement colonies whose primary industry consisted of sugarcane, coffee, or rice cultivation and whose majority populations were non-European slaves, in the case of the Atlantic and Indian Oceans, or contract laborers, in the case of Hawaii. The latter was colonized by Americans in the nineteenth century, when slavery was being abolished, and did not experience extensive ethnolinguistic mixing, which raises questions about using Hawaiian Creole English as an exemplar of how creoles developed everywhere. Examples of other creoles include Cape Verdian Crioulo (from Portuguese) and Papiamentu in the Netherlands Antilles (apparently Portuguese-based but influenced by Spanish); Haitian, Mauritian, and Seychellois (from French); Gullah in the United States, Jamaican, and Guyanese (all from English); as well as Saramaccan and Sranan in Surinam (both from English, with the former heavily influenced by Portuguese and the latter by Dutch).

To be sure, the traditional inclusion of Cape Verdian Crioulo and Papiamentu in this category also suggests that it may not be fully justified to associate the

development of creoles (exclusively) with the colonial plantation industry. Both vernaculars developed in territories where this particular industry did not succeed and was given up quite early in their histories. Since, in this particular case, Cape Verde and Curaçao functioned primarily as slave depots with only a tiny minority population of non-European permanent residents and very few European colonists with them, the rapid population replacement of people forced by the contact conditions to communicate in the colonial language may be a more critical factor, along with population structure and pattern of population growth (Mufwene 2001, 2005), for the identification of such contact-based varieties as creoles, rather than the drastic disproportion of European and non-European populations traditionally invoked in the literature.

The terms *creole* and *pidgin* have also been extended to some other varieties that developed during the same colonial period, out of contacts among primarily non-European languages. Examples include Delaware Pidgin, Chinook Jargon, and Mobilian in North America; Sango, (Kikongo-)Kituba, and Lingala in Central Africa; Kinubi in Southern Sudan and in Uganda; and Hiri Motu in Papua New Guinea (Holm 1989; Smith 1995). Many of these varieties have historically been designated with the name *jargon*, which is much older in French and English and simply means "a variety unintelligible to the speaker or writer." The term *pidgin* did not arise until the early nineteenth century (Baker & Mühlhäusler 1990) or perhaps the late eighteenth century (Bolton 2002). Although it has usually been traced etymologically to the word *business* (as in *business English*), the Cantonese phrase *bei chin* (lit. "pay" or "give money") seems to be its more probable etymon (Comrie et al. 1996: 146). Aside from the ecology of its emergence, it is phonologically more plausible to derive the word from the proposed Cantonese etymon than from the English alternative. Convergence, of course, need not be excluded here as an explanation. In the original, lay people's naming practice, the term *jargon* was an alternate to *pidgin*, and no specific structural features were associated with their identification.

It is very likely from Canton that the term *pidgin* was spread by sailors and traders to the rest of the Pacific, including Melanesia, where it was indigenized to *pisin* (as in *Tok Pisin*). Linguists subsequently generalized its usage, unfortunately without providing steadfast operational criteria for its extension, to other colonial trade *lingua francas*. Hall (1966) and Mühlhäusler (1986) went as far as to stipulate that pidgins are more stable than jargons, which are an earlier stage in the *Jargon > Pidgin > Creole > Post-Creole* "life-cycle." This putatively evolves by progressive structural expansion, stabilization, and closer approximations of the acrolectal variety of the base language.

The fact that the term *pidgin* emerged in Canton, thousands of miles away from the American Iberian colonies where the term *creole* originated in the sixteenth century, should have cast doubt on the scenario that derives creoles from pidgins by a putative process of *nativization* interpreted as (structural expansion through the) acquisition of native speakers. So should the fact that expanded pidgins have equally complex structures developed largely through the agency of adult L2-speakers using

it increasingly as a vernacular. The socio-economic histories of the territories where creoles developed speak against the Hall-Mühlhäusler position, to which I return below.

Chaudenson (1992) and Mufwene (1997) argue that creoles developed by *basilectal-izing* away from the base language, i.e., by developing a *basilect* – the variety the most different from the *acrolect*, the variety of the upper class. Mufwene (2001, 2005) emphasizes that creoles and pidgins developed in separate places, in which Europeans and non-Europeans interacted differently – sporadically in trade colonies but regularly in the initial stages of settlement colonies. The main justification for this position is that plantation settlement colonies typically developed from homestead societies, in which the non-Europeans were minorities and well-integrated and their children spoke the same colonial koinés as the children of European descent. It is only during the later stage of the plantation phase that the basilects, typically identified as creoles, developed by the regular process of gradual divergence from earlier forms of the colonial language.

The term *creole* was originally coined in Iberian colonies, apparently in the sixteenth century, in reference to non-indigenous people born in the American colonies (for references, see Mufwene 1997). It was adopted in metropolitan Spanish, then in French, and later in English by the early seventeenth century. By the second half of the same century, it was generalized to descendants of Africans or Europeans born in Romance colonies. Usage varied from one colony to another. The term was also used as an adjective to characterize plants, animals, and customs typical of the same colonies (Valkhoff 1966).

Creole may not have applied widely to language varieties until the late eighteenth century, though Arveiller (1963) cites La Courbe's *Premier voyage* of 1685 (1913: 192), in which it is used for "corrupted Portuguese spoken in Senegal." Such usage may have been initiated by metropolitan Europeans to disfranchise particular colonial varieties of their languages. It is not clear how the term became associated only with vernaculars spoken primarily by descendants of non-Europeans. Nonetheless, several speakers of creoles (or pidgins) actually believe they speak dialects of their lexifiers (Mühlhäusler 1985; Mufwene 1988).

Among the earliest claims that creoles developed from pidgins is the following statement in Bloomfield (1933: 474): "when the jargon [i.e., pidgin] has become the only language of the subject group, it is a *creolized language*." Hall (1962, 1966) reinterpreted this, associating the vernacular function of creoles with nativization. Since then, creoles have been defined inaccurately as "nativized pidgins," i.e., pidgins that have acquired native speakers and have therefore expanded both their structures and functions and have stabilized. Hall then also introduced the pidgin-creole "life-cycle" to which DeCamp (1971) added a "post-creole" stage (see below).

Among the creolists who dispute the above connection is Alleyne (1971), who argues that fossilized inflectional morphology in Haitian Creole (HC) and the like proves that Europeans did not communicate with the Africans in foreigner or baby talk (see below). As noted above, Chaudenson (1992, 2001, 2003) argues that

plantation communities were preceded by homesteads, on which mesolectal approximations of European koinés, rather than pidgins, were spoken by earlier slaves. Like some economic historians, Berlin (1998) observes that in North American colonies Creole Blacks spoke the European language fluently. In ads on runaway slaves in British North American colonies, "bad" or "poor English" is typically associated with slaves imported as adults from Africa. Diachronic textual evidence also suggests that the basilects developed during the peak growth of plantations (in the eighteenth century for most colonies!), when infant mortality was high, life expectancy short, the plantation populations increased primarily by massive importation of labor, and the proportion of fluent speakers of the earlier colonial varieties kept decreasing (Chaudenson 1992, 2001; Mufwene 2001).

According to the life-cycle model, as a creole continues to coexist with its base language, the latter exerts pressure on it to shed some of its "creole features." This developmental hypothesis may be traced back to Schuchardt's (1914) explanation of why African-American English (AAE) is structurally closer to North American English than Saramaccan is to English in its region, viz., coexistence with the base language in North America and absence of such continued contact in Suriname. Jespersen (1921) and Bloomfield (1933) anticipated DeCamp (1971), Bickerton (1973), and Rickford (1987) in invoking *decreolization* as "loss of 'creole' features" to account for speech continua in creole communities.

It is in the above context that DeCamp (1971) coined the term *post-creole continuum*, which must be interpreted charitably. If a variety is creole because of the particular socio-historical ecology of its development (see below), rather than because of its structural peculiarities, it cannot stop being a creole even after some of the features have changed. Besides, basilectal and mesolectal features continue to coexist in these communities, suggesting that creole has not died yet. Lalla & D'Costa (1990) present copious data against decreolization in Caribbean English creoles, just as Mufwene (1994) adduces linguistic and non-linguistic arguments against the same process for Gullah. On the other hand, Rickford & Handler (1994) show that in the late eighteenth century, Barbados had a basilect similar to those of other Caribbean islands. It now seems to have vanished. How and why it was lost here but not elsewhere in the Caribbean calls for an explanation.

Closely related to the above issue is the common assumption that creoles are separate languages from their base languages whereas related non-creole colonial offspring of the same European languages are considered as their dialects. Such is the case for the non-standard French varieties spoken in Quebec and Louisiana, as well as on the Caribbean islands of St. Barths and St. Thomas. Likewise New World non-standard varieties of Spanish and Portuguese are not considered creoles, despite structural similarities which they display with Portuguese creoles. Has the fact that similar varieties are spoken by descendants of both Europeans and Africans in territories where there has been more race hybridization influenced the naming practice? Although not officially acknowledged by creolists, the one obvious criterion behind the naming practice has been to identify as creoles those varieties of European languages which

have been appropriated as vernaculars by non-European majorities (Mufwene 2001; DeGraff 2003). There is otherwise no yardstick for measuring structural divergence from the base language, especially since the feature composition of the latter was not the same in every relevant contact setting. Besides, contact was a factor in all colonial settings, including those not associated with creoles.

It has also been claimed that creoles have more or less the same structural design (Bickerton 1981, 1984; Markey 1982). This position is as disputable as the other, more recent claim that there are creole prototypes from which others deviate in various ways (Thomason 1997; McWhorter 1998). The very fact of resorting to a handful of prototypes for the would-be essentialist creole structural category suggests that the vast majority of them do not share the putative set of defining features, hence that the combination of features proposed by McWhorter (1998) cannot be used to single them out as a unique type of language. On the other hand, structural variation among creoles that have evolved from the same base language can be correlated with variation in the socio-historical ecologies of their developments (Mufwene 1997, 2001, 2005). The notion of "ecology" includes, among other things, the structural features of the base and substrate languages, the ethnolinguistic makeups of the populations that came in contact, how regularly they interacted across class and ethnic boundaries, and the rates and modes of population growth.

To date the best-known creoles have evolved from English and French. Those of the Atlantic and Indian Oceans are, along with Hawaiian Creole, those that have informed most theorizing on the development of creoles. While the terms *creole* and *creolization* have been applied often uncritically to various contact-induced language varieties, several distinctions, which are not clearly articulated, have also been proposed in addition to those discussed above, for instance, *koiné, semi-creole, intertwined varieties, foreign workers' varieties* of European languages (e.g., Gastarbeiter Deutsch), and *indigenized varieties* of European languages (e.g., Nigerian and Singaporean Englishes). The denotations and importance of these terms deserve re-examining (Mufwene 1997, 2001, 2005).

The Development of Creoles

The central question here is: How did creoles develop? The following hypotheses are the major ones competing today: the substrate, the superstrate, and the universalist hypotheses.

Substratist positions are historically related to the *baby talk hypothesis*, which I have traced back to nineteenth-century French creolists. Putatively, the languages previously spoken by the Africans enslaved on New World and Indian Ocean plantations were the primary reason why the European languages which they appropriated were restructured into creoles. These French creolists assumed African languages to be "primitive," "instinctive," in a "natural" state, and simpler than the relevant "cultivated" European languages. Creoles' systems were considered to be reflections of those

non-European languages. The baby talk connection is that, in order to be understood, the Europeans supposedly had to speak to the Africans like to babies, their interpretation of foreigner talk.

The revival of the substrate hypothesis (without its racist component) has been attributed to Sylvain (1936). Although she recognizes influence from French dialects, she argues that African linguistic influence, especially from the Ewe group of languages, is very significant in Haitian Creole. Unfortunately, she states in the last sentence of her conclusions that this creole is Ewe spoken with a French vocabulary. Over two decades later, Turner (1949) disputed American dialectologists' claim that there was virtually no trace of African languages in AAE. He showed phonological and morphosyntactic similarities between Gullah and some West-African (especially Kwa) languages, concluding that "Gullah is indebted to African sources" (p. 254). It is not clear why this cautious statement has been misinterpreted to say that Gullah's grammatical structures originate in African languages. That African languages must have influenced the structures of languages that evolved from the appropriation of the European colonial languages by their speakers is an obvious phenomenon that does not exclude the origination of the features themselves from the original target, or base, languages. As I have argued in various publications, the influence may have lain in the selection from among the variants available in the target, favoring those variants that were congruent with features of some African languages (Mufwene 2001, 2002a, 2005; see also Corne 1999; Chaudenson 2003).

Mufwene (1990) identifies three main schools of the substrate hypothesis today. The first, led by Alleyne (1980, 1996) and Holm (1988), is closer to Turner's approach and is marked by what is also its main weakness: invocation of influence from diverse African languages without explaining what kinds of selection principles account for this seemingly random invocation of sources. This criticism is not *ipso facto* an invalidation of substrate influence; it is both a call for a more principled account and a reminder that the nature of such influence must be reassessed (Mufwene 2001, 2002a).

The second school has been identified as the *relexification hypothesis*. The proponents of its latest version, Lefebvre (1998) and Lumsden (1999), argue that Haitian is a French relexification of languages of the Ewe-Fon (or Fongbe) group. This account of the development of creoles has been criticized for several basic shortcomings, including the following: (1) its "comparative" approach has not taken into account several features that Haitian (also) shares with non-standard varieties of French; (2) it downplays features which Haitian shares also with several other African languages which were represented in Haiti during the critical stages of its development; (3) it has not shown that the language appropriation strategies associated with relexification are typically used in naturalistic second language acquisition; and (4) it does not account for those cases where structural options not consistent with those of Ewe-Fon have been selected into Haitian. Moreover, relexificationists assume, disputably, that languages of the Ewe-Fon group are structurally identical and that no competition of influence was involved among them.

The least disputed version of the substrate hypothesis is Keesing's (1988), which shows that substrate languages may impose their structural features on the new, contact-induced varieties if they are typologically relatively homogeneous, with most of them sharing the relevant features. Thus Melanesian pidgins are like (most of) their substrates in having DUAL/PLURAL and INCLUSIVE/EXCLUSIVE distinctions and in having a transitive marker on the verb. Sankoff and Brown (1976) had shown similar influence with the bracketing of relative clauses with *ia*. However, the pidgins have not inherited all the peculiarities of Melanesian languages. For instance, they do not have their VSO major constituent order, nor do they have much of a numeral classifying system in the combination of *pela* with quantifiers. (For an extensive discussion of substrate influence in Atlantic and Indian Ocean creoles, see Muysken & Smith 1986; Mufwene 1993).

Competing with the above genetic views has been the *dialectologist*, or superstrate, hypothesis, according to which the primary, if not the exclusive, sources of creoles' structural features are the non-standard varieties of their base languages. Speaking of AAE, Krapp (1924) and Kurath (1928), for example, claimed that this variety was an archaic retention of the non-standard speech of low-class whites with whom the African slaves had been in contact. According to them, African substrate contributions to the African American vernacular were limited to a few isolated lexical items such as *goober* "peanut," *gumbo*, and *okra*. It would take until McDavid (1950) and McDavid & McDavid (1951) before the possibility of some limited African grammatical influence on AAE was recognized. This change of heart did not discourage D'Eloia (1973) and Schneider (1989) from correctly invoking several dialectal English models to rebut Dillard's (1972) thesis that AAE developed from an erstwhile West-African Pidgin English brought over by slaves. Since the late 1980s, Shana Poplack and her associates have strengthened this position by showing that AAE shares many features with white non-standard vernaculars in North America and England, thus it has not developed from an erstwhile creole. (See especially Poplack 1999; and Poplack & Tagliamonte 2001 for a synthesis.) Because some of the same features are also attested in creoles (Rickford 1998), we come back to the question of whether, in the first place, most features of creoles did not originate in their base languages, which in no way implies that they have been integrated intact in the new systems.

The *universalist hypotheses*, which stood as strong contenders in the 1980s and 1990s, have forerunners in the nineteenth century. For instance, Adolfo Coelho (1880–6) partly anticipated Bickerton's (1981) *language bioprogram hypothesis* in stating that creoles "owe their origin to the operation of psychological or physiological laws that are everywhere the same, and not to the influence of the former languages of the people among whom these dialects are found." Bickerton pushed things further in claiming that children made creoles by fixing the parameters of these new language varieties in their unmarked, or default, settings as specified in Universal Grammar (see also Bickerton 1999). To account for cross-creole structural differences, Bickerton (1984: 176–7) invokes a "Pidginization Index" (PI) that includes the following factors: the

proportion of the native to non-native speakers during the initial stages of colonization, the duration of the early stage, the rate of increase of the slave population after that initial stage, the kind of social contacts between the native speakers of the base language and the learners, and whether or not the contact between the two groups continued after the formation of the new language variety. (Most of these factors have been rearticulated in the ecological model synthesized in Mufwene (2001, 2005), except that children are not accorded a privileged role in the development of creole and no stage is posited in the development of the colony during which communication was based on a pidgin.)

Some nagging questions with Bickerton's position include the following: Is his intuitively sound PI consistent with his creolization *qua* abrupt pidgin-nativization hypothesis? Is the abrupt creolization hypothesis consistent with the social histories of the territories where classic creoles developed (Mufwene 1999, 2001, 2005)? How can we explain similarities of structures and in complexity between abrupt creoles and expanded pidgins when the stabilization and structural expansion of the latter is not necessarily associated with restructuring by children? Is there convincing evidence for assuming that adult speech is less controlled by Universal Grammar than child language is? How can we account for similarities between "abrupt creolization" and naturalistic second-language acquisition? However, not all creolists who have invoked universalist explanations have made children critical to the emergence of creoles. For instance, Sankoff (1979) and Mühlhäusler (1981) make allowance for Universal Grammar to operate in adults too.

Few creolists subscribe nowadays to one exclusive genetic account, as evidenced by the contributions to Mufwene (1993). The *complementary hypothesis* (Hancock 1986, 1993; Mufwene 1986, 2001, 2005) seems to be an adequate alternative, provided we can articulate the ecological conditions under which the competing influences (between the substrate and superstrate languages, and within each group) may converge or prevail upon each other. This position was well anticipated by Schuchardt (1909, 1914) in his accounts of the geneses of Lingua Franca and of Saramaccan. More and more research is now underway uncovering the socio-historical conditions under which different creoles have developed, for instance, Chaudenson (1979), Baker (1982), Arends (1989, 1995), Corne (1999), and Mufwene (2001).

Still, the future of research on the development of creoles has some problems to overcome. So far, knowledge of the colonial non-standard varieties of the European languages remains limited. There are few comprehensive descriptions of creoles' structures – which makes it difficult to determine globally how the competing influences interacted among them and how the features selected from diverse sources became integrated into new systems. Few structural facts have been correlated with the conclusions suggested by the socio-historical backgrounds of individual creoles. Other issues remain up in the air; for instance, what are the most adequate principles that should help us account for the selection of features into creoles' systems? (See AFRICAN AMERICAN VERNACULAR ENGLISH; WORLD ENGLISHES IN WORLD CONTEXTS.)

Conclusion: Creolistics and General Linguistics

For developmental issues on creoles and pidgins, the following edited collections are good starting points: Hymes (1971), Valdman (1977), Hill (1979), Muysken and Smith (1986), Mufwene (1993), Arends et al. (1995), and Kouwenberg and Singler (2008). More specific issues may be checked in volumes of the Creole Language Library (John Benjamins) and of Amsterdam Creole Studies, in the *Journal of Pidgin and Creole Languages*, and in *Etudes Créoles*. Several issues of *Pacific Linguistics* also include publications on Melanesian creoles, by which research on the development of creoles remains minimally informed.

Studies of structural aspects of creoles have yet to inform general linguistics beyond the subject matters of time reference and serial verb constructions. For instance, studies of lectal continua (e.g., Escure 1997) have had this potential, but little has been done by creolists to show how their findings may apply to other languages. The mixed nature of *mesolects*, those intermediate varieties combining features associated both with the *acrolect* and the *basilect*, should have informed general linguistics against the fallacy of assuming monolithic grammatical systems (Mufwene 1992; Labov 1998). The notion of "acrolect" deserves rethinking (Irvine 2004). Creolistics has been bridging with research on grammaticalization, an area that promises to be productive, as evidenced by Kriegel (2003). Andersen (1983) was an important step to consolidate common interests between second-language acquisition and the development of creoles. DeGraff (1999) bridges research on the latter topic with research (child) language development and on the emergence of sign language. Creolistics can also contribute fruitfully to research on language vitality, including language loss (Mufwene 2002b, 2004, 2005, 2008).

There is much more literature on the genesis, sociology, and morphosyntax of creoles and pidgins than on their phonologies, semantics, and pragmatics. With the exception of time reference (e.g., Singler, 1990; Michaelis, 1993; Schlupp, 1997) and nominal number (for references, see Tagliamonte & Poplack 1993), studies in semantics and pragmatics are scant. On the other hand, the development of quantitative sociolinguistics owes a lot to research on AAE since the mid-1960s (see, for example, Labov 1972) and Caribbean English creoles (e.g., Rickford 1987). Numerous publications in *American Speech*, *Language in Society*, and *Language Variation and Change* reflect this. There are also several surveys of creolistics today, including the following: Romaine (1988), Holm (1988), Manessy (1994), Arends et al. (1995), and Mühlhäusler (1986). They vary in geographical areas of focus and adequacy. Kouwenberg and Singler (2008) is likely to become a standard reference for several years, with which Chaudenson (2003) and Mufwene (2001, 2005, 2008) will have to compete in regard to their divergence from the received doctrine. DeGraff (2003) will be a forceful deterrent from treating creoles as being the outcomes of an exceptional evolution and a good wakeup call for uniformitarianism. Efforts to bridge research on the development of creoles with that on other contact-based varieties and phenomena (e.g.,

Thomason & Kaufman 1988; Mufwene 2001, 2005, 2008; Myers-Scotton 2002; Thomason 2001; and Winford 2003) are noteworthy.

REFERENCES AND FURTHER READING

Alleyne, M. C. (1971). Acculturation and the cultural matrix of creolization. In D. Hymes (ed.), *Pidginization and Creolization of Languages* (pp. 169–86). Cambridge: Cambridge University Press.

Alleyne, M. C. (1980). *Comparative Afro-American: An Historical-comparative Study of English-based Afro-American Dialects of the New World*. Ann Arbor: Karoma.

Alleyne, M. C. (1996). *Syntaxe Historique Créole*. Paris: Karthala.

Andersen, R. (ed.) (1983). *Pidginization and Creolization as Language Acquisition*. Rowley, MA: Newbury House.

Arends, J. (1989). *Syntactic Developments in Sranan: Creolization as a Gradual Process*. Unpublished PhD dissertation, University of Nijmegen.

Arends, J. (ed.) (1995). *The Early Stages of Creolization*. Amsterdam: John Benjamins.

Arends, J., Muysken, P., & Smith, N. (eds.) (1995). *Pidgins and Creoles: An Introduction*. Amsterdam: John Benjamins.

Arveiller, R. (1963). *Contribution à l'étude des termes de voyage en français (1505–1722)*. Paris: D'Artrey.

Baker, P. (1982). *The Contribution of Non-Francophone Immigrants to the Lexicon of Mauritian Creole*. Unpublished PhD dissertation, School of Oriental and African Studies, University of London.

Baker, P. & Mühlhäusler, P. (1990). From business to pidgin. *Journal of Asian Pacific Communication*, 1 (1), 87–115.

Berlin, I. (1998). *Many Thousands Gone: The First Two Centuries of Slavery in North America*. Cambridge, MA: Harvard University Press.

Bickerton, D. (1973). The nature of a creole continuum. *Language*, 49 (4), 640–69.

Bickerton, D. (1981). *Roots of Language*. Ann Arbor: Karoma.

Bickerton, D. (1984). The language bioprogram hypothesis. *Behavioral and Brain Sciences*, 7, 173–221.

Bickerton, D. (1999). How to acquire language without positive evidence: what acquisitionists can learn from creoles. In M. Degraff (ed.), *Language Creation and Language Change: Creolization, Diachrony, and Development* (pp. 49–74). Cambridge, MA: MIT Press.

Bloomfield, L. (1933). *Language*. New York: Holt, Rinehart and Winston.

Bolton, K. (2002). Chinese Englishes: from Canton jargon to global English. *World Englishes*, 21 (2), 181–99.

Chaudenson, R. (1979). *Les Créoles français*. Paris: Fernand Nathan.

Chaudenson, R. (1989). *Créoles et enseignement du français*. Paris: L'Harmattan.

Chaudenson, R. (1992). *Des Îles, des hommes, des langues: essais sur la créolisation linguistique et culturelle*. Paris: L'Harmattan.

Chaudenson, R. (2001). *Creolization of Language and Culture*. London: Routledge.

Chaudenson, R. (2003). *La Créolisation: théorie, applications, implications*. Paris: L'Harmattan.

Coelho, F. A. (1880–6). Os dialectos românicos ou neolatinos na Africa, Asia, ae America. *Bolletim da Sociedade de Geografia de Lisboa*, 2, 129–96 (1880–1); 3, 451–78 (1882); 6, 705–55 (1886).

Comrie, B., Matthews, S., & Polinsky, M. (1996). *The Atlas of Languages: The Origin and Development of Languages throughout the World*. New York: Facts on File.

Corne, C. (1999). *From French to Creole: The Development of New Vernaculars in the French Colonial World*. London: University of Westminster Press.

DeCamp, D. (1971). Toward a generative analysis of a post-creole speech continuum. In D. Hymes (ed.), *Pidginization and Creolization of Languages* (pp. 349–70). Cambridge: Cambridge University Press.

D'Eloia, S. G. (1973). Issues in the analysis of Negro nonstandard English. Review of Dillard (1972). *Journal of English Linguistics*, 7, 87–106.

DeGraff, M. (ed.) (1999). *Language Creation and Language Change: Creolization, Diachrony, and Development*. Cambridge, MA: MIT Press.

DeGraff, M. (2003). Against creole exceptionalism. *Language*, 79 (2), 391–410.

Dillard, J. L. (1972). *Black English: Its History and Usage in the United States*. New York: Random House.

Escure, G. (1997). *Creole and Dialect Continua*. Amsterdam: John Benjamins.

Faine, J. (1937). *Philologie créole: études historiques et étymologiques sur la langue créole d'haïti*. Port-au-Prince: Imprimerie de l'Etat.

Féral, C. de. (1989). *Pidgin-English du cameroun*. Paris: Peters/SELAF.

Hall, R. A., Jr. (1958). Creole languages and genetic relationships. *Word*, 14, 367–73.

Hall, R. A., Jr. (1962). The life-cycle of pidgin languages. *Lingua*, 11, 151–6.

Hall, R. A., Jr. (1966). *Pidgin and Creole Languages*. Ithaca, NY: Cornell University Press.

Hancock, I. (1986). The domestic hypothesis, diffusion and componentiality: an account of Atlantic Anglophone creole origins. In P. Muysken & N. Smith, *Substrata versus Universals in Creole Genesis* (pp. 71–102). Amsterdam: John Benjamins.

Hancock, I. (1993). Creole language provenance and the African component. In S. S. Mufwene (ed.), *Africanisms in Afro-American Language Varieties* (pp. 182–91). Athens: University of Georgia Press.

Hill, K. C. (ed.) (1979). *The Genesis of Language*. Ann Arbor: Karoma.

Holm, J. (1988). *Pidgins and Creoles, Vol. 1: Theory and Structure*. Cambridge: Cambridge University Press.

Holm, J. (1989). *Pidgins and Creoles, Vol. 2: Reference Survey*. Cambridge: Cambridge University Press.

Hymes, D. (ed.) (1971). *Pidginization and Creolization of Languages*. Cambridge: Cambridge University Press.

Irvine, A. G. (2004). A good command of the English language: phonological variation in the Jamaican acrolect. *Journal of Pidgin and Creole Languages*, 19 (1), 41–76.

Jespersen, O. (1921). *Language: Its Nature, Development and Origin*. New York: W. W. Norton.

Jourdan, C. (1991). Pidgins and creoles: the blurring of categories. *Annual Review of Anthropology*, 20, 187–209.

Keesing, R. M. (1988). *Melanesian Pidgin and the Oceanic Substrate*. Stanford: Stanford University Press.

Kouwenberg, S. & Singler, J. V. (eds.) (2008). *Handbook of Pidgin and Creole Linguistics*. Oxford: Blackwell.

Krapp, G. P. (1924). The English of the Negro. *American Mercury*, 2, 190–5.

Kriegel, S. (ed.) (2003). *Grammaticalisation et réanalyse: approches de la variation créole et française*. Paris: CNRS Editions.

Kurath, H. (1928). The origin of dialectal differences in spoken American English. *Modern Philology*, 25, 385–95.

La Courbe, M. L. de (1913). *Premier voyage du sieur de la Courbe fait a la coste d'Afrique en 1685, publié avec une carte de Delisle et une introduction par P. Cultru*. Paris: Champion.

Labov, W. (1972). *Language in the Inner City: Studies in Black English Vernacular*. Philadelphia: University of Pennsylvania Press.

Labov, W. (1998). Co-existent systems in African-American vernacular English. In S. S. Mufwene, J. R. Rickford, G. Bailey, & J. Baugh (eds.), *African-American English: Structure, History, and Use* (pp. 110–53). London: Routledge.

Lalla, B. & D'Costa, J. (1990). *Language in Exile: Three Hundred Years of Jamaican Creole*. Tuscaloosa: University of Alabama Press.

Lefebvre, C. (1998). *Creole Genesis and the Acquisition of Grammar: The Case of Haitian Creole*. Cambridge: Cambridge University Press.

Lumsden, J. (1999). Language acquisition and creolization. In M. DeGraff (ed.), *Language Creation and Language Change: Creolization, Diachrony, and Development* (pp. 129–57). Cambridge, MA: MIT Press.

McDavid, R., Jr. (1950). Review of Lorenzo Dow Turner's Africanisms in the Gullah dialect. *Language*, 26, 323–33.

McDavid, R., Jr. & McDavid, V. (1951). The relationship of the speech of the American Negroes to the speech of whites. *American Speech*, 26, 3–17.

McWhorter, J. H. (1998). Identifying the creole prototype: vindicating a typological class. *Language*, 74, 788–818.

Manessy, G. (1994). *Créoles, pidgins, variétés véhiculaires: procès et genèse*. Paris: CNRS Editions.

Markey, T. L. (1982). Afrikaans: Creole or non-creole? *Zeitschrift fur Dialektologie und Linguistik*, 49, 169–207.

Michaelis, S. (1993). *Temps et aspect en créole seychellois: valeurs et interférences*. Hamburg: Helmut Buske.

Mufwene, S. S. (1986). The universalist and substrate hypotheses complement one another. In P. Muysken & N. Smith, *Substrata versus Universals in Creole Genesis* (pp. 129–62). Amsterdam: John Benjamins.

Mufwene, S. S. (1988). Why study pidgins and creoles? Column. *Journal of Pidgin and Creole Languages*, 3, 265–76.

Mufwene, S. S. (1990). Transfer and the substrate hypothesis in creolistics. *Studies in Second Language Acquisition*, 12, 1–23.

Mufwene, S. S. (1992). Why grammars are not monolithic. In D. Brentari, G. Larson, & L. MacLeod (eds.), *The Joy of Grammar: A Festschrift in Honor of James D. McCawley* (pp. 225–50). Amsterdam: John Benjamins.

Mufwene, S. S. (ed.) (1993). *Africanisms in Afro-American Language Varieties*. Athens: University of Georgia Press.

Mufwene, S. S. (1994). On decreolization: the case of Gullah. In M. Morgan (ed.), *Language, Loyalty, and Identity in Creole Situations* (pp. 63–99). Los Angeles: Center for Afro American Studies.

Mufwene, S. S. (1997). Jargons, pidgins, creoles, and koinés: what are they? In A. Spears & D. Winford (eds.), *Pidgins and Creoles: Structure and Status* (pp. 35–70). Amsterdam: John Benjamins.

Mufwene, S. S. (1999). The language bioprogram hypothesis: hints from Tazie. In M. DeGraff (ed.), *Language Creation and Language Change: Creolization, Diachrony, and Development* (pp. 95–127). Cambridge, MA: MIT Press.

Mufwene, S. S. (2001). *The Ecology of Language Evolution*. Cambridge: Cambridge University Press.

Mufwene, S. S. (2002a). Competition and selection in language evolution. *Selection*, 3 (1), 45–56.

Mufwene, S. S. (2002b). Colonization, globalization, and the future of languages in the twenty-first century. *MOST Journal on Multicultural Societies*, 4 (2), 162–93.

Mufwene, S. S. (2004). Language birth and death. *Annual Review of Anthropology*, 33, 201–22.

Mufwene, S. S. (2005). *Créoles, écologie sociale, évolution linguistique*. Paris: L'Harmattan.

Mufwene, S. S. (2008). *Language Evolution: Contact, Competition, and Change*. London: Continuum Press.

Mühlhäusler, P. (1981). The development of the category of number in Tok Pisin. In P. Muysken (ed.), *Generative Studies on Creole Languages* (pp. 35–84). Dordrecht: Foris.

Mühlhäusler, P. (1985). The number of pidgin Englishes in the Pacific. *Papers in Pidgin and Creole Linguistics* No.1, *Pacific Linguistics*, A72, 25–51.

Mühlhäusler, P. (1986). *Pidgin and Creole Linguistics*. Oxford: Blackwell. Revd. edn. (1997) London: University of Westminster Press.

Muysken, P. & Smith, N. (eds.) (1986). *Substrata versus Universals in Creole Genesis*. Amsterdam: John Benjamins.

Myers-Scotton, C. (2002). *Contact Linguistics: Bilingual Encounters and Grammatical Outcomes*. Oxford: Blackwell.

Poplack, S. (ed.) (1999). *The English History of African-American English*. Oxford: Blackwell.

Poplack, S. & Tagliamonte, S. (2001). *African American English in the Diaspora*. Oxford: Blackwell.

Rickford, J. R. (1987). *Dimensions of a Creole Continuum: History, Texts, and Linguistic Analysis of Guyanese Creole*. Stanford: Stanford University Press.

Rickford, J. R. (1998). The creole origins of African-American vernacular English: evidence from copula absence. In S. S. Mufwene, J. R. Rickford, G. Bailey, & J. Baugh, *African-American English: Structure, Theory, and Use* (pp. 154–200). London: Routledge.

Rickford, J. R. & Handler, J. S. (1994). Textual evidence on the nature of early Barbadian speech, 1676–1835. *Journal of Pidgin and Creole Languages*, 9, 221–55.

Romaine, S. (1988). *Pidgin and Creole Languages*. London: Longman.

Sankoff, G. (1979). The genesis of a language. In K. C. Hill (ed.), *The genesis of language* (pp. 23–47). Ann Arbor: Karoma.

Sankoff, G. & Brown, P. (1976). The origins of syntax in discourse: a case study of Tok Pisin relatives. *Language*, 52, 631–66.

Schlupp, D. (1997). *Modalités prédicatives, modalités aspectuelles, et auxiliaires en créole*. Tübingen: Max Niemeyer.

Schneider, E. W. (1989). *American Earlier Black English: Morphological and Syntactic Variables*. Tuscaloosa: University of Alabama Press.

Schuchardt, H. (1909). Die Lingua Franca. *Zeitschrift fur Romanische Philologie*, 33, 441–61.

Schuchardt, H. (1914). *Die Sprache der Saramakkaneger in Surinam*. Amsterdam: Johannes Muller.

Singler, J. V. (ed.) (1990). *Pidgin and Creole Tense-mood-aspect Systems*. Amsterdam: John Benjamins.

Smith, N. (1995). An annotated list of pidgins, creoles, and mixed languages. In J. Arends, P. Muysken, & N. Smith, *Pidgins and Creoles: An Introduction* (pp. 331–74). Amsterdam: John Benjamins.

Sylvain, S. (1936). *Le Créole haïtien: morphologie et syntaxe*. Wettern, Belgium: Imprimerie De Meester.

Tagliamonte, S. & Poplack, S. (1993). The zero-marked verb: testing the creole hypothesis. *Journal of Pidgin and Creole Languages*, 8 (2), 171–206.

Thomason, S. G. (1997). A typology of contact languages. In A. K. Spears & D. Winford, *The Structure and Status of Pidgins and Creoles* (pp. 71–88). Amsterdam: John Benjamins.

Thomason, S. G. (2001). *Language Contact: An Introduction*. Washington, DC: Georgetown University Press.

Thomason, S. G. & Kaufman, T. (1988). *Language Contact, Creolization, and Genetic Linguistics*. Berkeley: University of California Press.

Turner, L. D. (1949). *Africanisms in the Gullah Dialect*. Chicago: University of Chicago Press.

Valdman, A. (ed.) (1977). *Pidgin and Creole Linguistics*. Bloomington: Indiana University Press.

Valkhoff, M. F. (1966). *Studies in Portuguese and Creole – With Special Reference to South Africa*. Johannesburg: Witwatersrand University Press.

Winford, D. (2003). *An Introduction to Contact Linguistics*. Oxford: Blackwell.

55

World Englishes in
World Contexts

Braj B. Kachru

Introduction

The concept "world Englishes," and the spread of the English language as a global phenomenon, is better contextualized if the diasporic locations of the language are related to the colonial expansion of the British empire. The first phase of diaspora was initiated with the Act of Union that annexed Wales to England in 1535. The Act specified:

> no personne or personnes that use the Welsshe speche or langage shall have or enjoy any manner of office or fees within the Realme of Onglonde Wales or other the Kinges dominions upon peyn of forfeiting the same offices or fees onles he or they use and exercise the speche or language of Englische.

Edwards (1993:108) considers this as "The most damaging section of the Act of Union, as far as the Welsh language was concerned and thus a significant element in its collective consciousness, was its emphasis on English as the language of preferment." The result was, as Edwards emphasizes, "English became essential for success." (See ENGLISH IN WALES.)

It is this luring construct of "success" that the medium has represented since 1535, and continues in the present century. In 1603 – just 68 years after Wales – Scottish monarchies lost their independence and King James VI acquired the status of King James I of England and Scotland. The march of the Empire continued into Ireland – yet another non-English speaking region. In 1707 the state of Great Britain was established, and the English language further expanded its territory – it was no longer only the language of England.

The second phase of diaspora implanted the language across the continents: on the one side in North America including Canada, on the other side in Australia and New Zealand. It was during the third phase, the glorious period of the British Raj, that

the sun never set on the Empire, and now never sets on the English language. The English-speaking members of the Raj came into direct contact with structurally, and culturally, unrelated languages, e.g., African, East Asian, and South Asian. These distinctly different contexts of linguistic ecology opened up, theoretically and methodologically, challenging research areas in language contact and convergence and multilingual interactions.

In later years, when English became a part of the educational systems in these far flung colonies, the linguistic, cultural, and ideational challenges raised issues about the norms, standards, and content of the methodology and models for the teaching and learning of English. A variety of conceptual frameworks have been suggested for characterization of the unprecedented cross-cultural global spread of the English language (e.g., McArthur 1993; Kachru 1985; Bolton 2006a). These issues continue to be discussed, debated, and constructed in various ideological and theoretical frameworks with increasing vehemence and aggressiveness.

I shall discuss below one such model, the Concentric Circles model, which has been used in several conceptual and pedagogical studies since the 1980s.

Concentric Circles Model

The Concentric Circles model (see figure 55.1) is not just a heuristic metaphor for schematizing the diffusion of the English language. The model presents a schema for historical, educational, political, social, and literary contextualization of the English language with reference to its gradual – and unprecedented – expansion with the ascendancy of the British Raj and later in the post-colonial period. This representation of the spread of English is not in terms of any hierarchical priority, or any preferential ranking. The Inner Circle is *inner* with reference to the origin and spread of the language, and the Outer is *outer* with reference to geographical expansion of the language – the historical stages in the initiatives to locate the English language beyond the traditional English-speaking Britain; the motivations, strategies, and agencies involved in the spread of English; the methodologies involved in the acquisition of the language; and the *depth* in terms of social penetration of the English language to expand its functional range in various domains, including those of administration, education, political discourses, literary creativity, and media.

As these regional styles and registers evolved and developed, the linguistic creativity in a variety of functional contexts gradually manifested itself in, what is termed, *acculturation* and *nativization* (indigenization) of these languages (see Kachru 1983). The medium of a transplanted imperial language was hybridized in the local – African, Asian, and Latin American – socio-cultural, ideological, and discoursal contexts. The language acquired yet other meaning systems and ways of representing them. It is through these linguistic processes that the *Africanization* and *Asianization* of the English language began. The same regular linguistic processes had earlier worked in the case of the Americanization of American English, or Englishes in Canada, Aus-

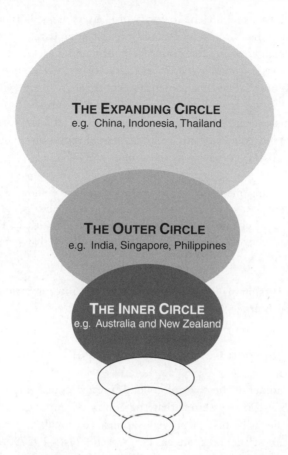

Figure 55.1   Three concentric circles of Asian Englishes

tralia, and New Zealand. These conceptual terms, "nativization" and "acculturation," refer to the changes a language – or its varieties – undergo at one or more linguistic levels, e.g., phonetic, lexical, syntactic, stylistic, and discoursal.

What happened to diasporic Englishes is not different from what has happened to other such diasporic languages in other parts of the world: Francophone varieties of French, Swahili in parts of Africa, Spanish in Latin America, and languages such as Arabic, Sanskrit, and Hindi. In the case of English, the colonized territories of the Empire had their distinct geographies, their traditional – and longstanding – social, cultural, religious, and administrative realities. There were also long and rich oral and literary traditions. The English language may not necessarily have been their "native" language, as language specialists define it. However, as time passed, in many Outer Circle regions English acquired "functional nativeness" in terms of its social penetration, and expanded its "range" in terms of local domains of function (see Kachru 2005: 9–28).

The English-speaking regions in each Circle are indeed dynamic and not static – or unchanging. In historical terms, then, the Inner Circle comprises L_1 speakers of

varieties of English that include the majority of L_1 users of the language (e.g., Britain, USA, Canada, Australia, and New Zealand). The Outer Circle includes the Anglophone colonized countries in, for example, South and East Asia, and Africa. The Expanding Circle has a different historical narrative with reference to acquisition of English than the Outer Circle. The constituents of this Circle, e.g., China, Europe (inc. Germany, Russia), Iran, Iraq, Korea, Saudi Arabia, Taiwan, Thailand, provide yet another story of history and acquisition of English (see, for example, Berns 2005).

In McArthur's view this Concentric Circles model represents "the democratization of attitudes to English everywhere in the globe" (1993: 334):

> This is a more dynamic model than the standard version, and allows for all manners of shadings and overlaps among the circles. Although "inner" and "outer" still suggest – inevitably – a historical priority and the attitudes that go with it, the metaphor of ripples in a pond suggests mobility and flux and implies that a history is in the making.

(For a detailed discussion of "a range of meanings and interpretations" of the concept *world Englishes*, see Bolton 2006a: 240.)

Speech Communities and Fellowships

In 1957, the first holder of the chair of general linguistics at London University, John Rupert Firth (1890–1960), asserted that the "unity of language is the most fugitive of all unities whether it be historical, geographical, national, or personal. There is no such thing as *une langue une* and there has never been" (Firth 1957: 29). If any evidence is needed to support Firth's assertion, world Englishes provide it in abundance. The range of speech communities of Englishes includes, for example, monolinguals, bidialectals, bilinguals, and multilinguals. In many regions of the English-using world, the traditional dichotomies of *native* vs. *non-native* or L_1 and L_2 users are not necessarily applicable or insightful. An unparalleled feature of world Englishes is that among the languages of wider communication, Englishes comprise more users who have acquired a variety of language as an L_2, L_3 or nth language in their language repertoires.

It is evident in table 55.1 that the two major English-using countries in the world are India and China, both in the Outer and Expanding Circles of English.

Linguistic Centers and Canonical Shift

There are now multiple centers of linguistic canons and canonicity of world Englishes. In a prescient observation in 1975, George Steiner stated, "It does look as if the principal energies of the English language, as if its genius for acquisition, for innovation, for metaphoric response, has also moved away from England" (p. 5). And, Steiner rightly points out that

Table 55.1 The statistics of world Englishes (guesstimates based on various published resources)

Society	Approximate population (million)	Percentage of L_1/L_2 English users	Approximate totals (million)
INNER CIRCLE			
United States	293		
United Kingdom	59		
Canada	32		
Australia	20		
New Zealand	4		
OUTER CIRCLE			
India	1,000	33	330
Philippines	86	56	48
Pakistan	159	11	17
Malaysia	24	32	8
Bangladesh	141	5	7
Hong Kong	7	35	2
Singapore	4	50	2
Sri Lanka	20	10	2
EXPANDING CIRCLE			
China	1,300	18	234
Japan	127	33	42
Indonesia	238	5	12
Thailand	60	10	6
South Korea	49	9	4
Vietnam	83	5	4
Myanmar	43	5	2
Taiwan	22	10	2
Cambodia	13	5	0.6
Laos	6	5	0.3

any map of "world-English" today, even without being either exhaustive or minutely detailed, would have to include the forms of the language as spoken in many areas of east, west and South Africa, in India, Ceylon [now Sri Lanka], and United States possessions or spheres of presence in the Pacific. (p. 4)

The map suggested by Steiner has changed in terms of the spread of the language, its multiple canonicities, the identities of Englishes, and the formal and functional implications of such identity constructions. We see that ongoing process active in East and South Asia, several other parts of Africa, and other regions. The debate still continues particularly about methodological questions and more pragmatic issues concerning intelligibility in the varieties of Englishes and cross-cultural communication among the various users.

Models and Standards

Who determines the models and standards for varieties of world Englishes? An answer to this question has been debated, discussed, and vehemently argued not only with reference to Outer and Expanding Circles: there is a long history of debates for an appropriate model(s) for Inner Circle countries. What is *standard* English? American linguist Leonard Bloomfield (1933: 48) provides an insightful answer:

> Children who are born into homes of privilege, in the way of wealth, tradition, or educa-
> tion, become native speakers of what is popularly known as "good" English; the linguist
> prefers to give it the non-committal name of *standard* English. Less fortunate children
> become native speakers of "bad" or "vulgar" or, as the linguist prefers to call it, non-
> standard English.

In the post-colonial period the appropriateness of a model has passionately been argued within theoretical, ideational, and pragmatic contexts. The speech communities of world Englishes have traditionally been divided thus: those who are considered privileged – norm-providing – native speakers, primarily from the Inner Circle; those Anglophone countries who use *institutionalized* varieties of English in their local socio-linguistic contexts in, for example, Africa and Asia, are considered *non-native* speakers – speakers from the Outer Circle; and those who have assigned restricted roles to English in their educational and administrative policies and have no extended history of the use of English, comprise the Expanding Circle (e.g., China, Japan, Korea, the Middle East, Thailand). The Expanding Circle has traditionally been dependent on external "educated" models, primarily from the Inner Circle (see Berns 2005).

One controversial, privileged, and socially highly restricted model, termed Received Pronunciation (RP), was presented by the arbiters of "standard" English in the Outer and Inner Circles. The British phonetician Abercrombie considers RP "a bad thing rather than a good thing. It is an anachronism in present day democratic society" (1951: 14). In his view, RP provides an "accent bar," which does not represent the social reality of England. In psychological terms "the accent bar is a little like colour-bar – to many people, on the right side of the bar, it appears eminently reasonable" (p. 15). And finally, Abercrombie has a pragmatic concern about RP when he says that it is not the only variety that represents "educated English," since "those who talk RP can justly consider themselves educated, they are outnumbered these days by the undoubtedly educated people who do not talk RP" (p. 15).

The question of models and standards ultimately is a social, and attitudinal, question, and applies to RP the same way as it does to "standard" (or "General") American, Australian, or Canadian Englishes. Thus the position of Abercrombie, over half a century later, is now articulated under different theoretical, ideational, and pedagogical constructs. What it shows is that the framework of the Circles is indeed dynamic and fluid. The changes in the Inner Circle have their implications for the other Circles, too. (See Bolton 2006a, 2006b; THE RISE OF RECEIVED PRONUNCIATION; CLASS, ETHNICITY, AND THE FORMATION OF "STANDARD ENGLISH".)

Paradigms of Marginalization and Mythology

The issues of the paradigms of marginalization, specifically with reference to Englishes around the world, have been discussed in detail in several studies (e.g., Kachru 1987, 1988, 1991). The result of these paradigms, and resultant mythology, is that it suppresses the major pragmatic – and functional – realities. The reality of world Englishes actually is that of pluracentricism, multiculturalism, and multicanonicity – that of hybridity and fusion. The mythology, however, continues to emphasize the following four myths which may be characterized as follows:

1. The *interlocutor myth* that most of the interaction in Englishes takes place between L_1 speakers and L_2 speakers of the language. In the real world of Englishes, the language is a medium of communication among and between those who use it as an additional language: Singaporeans with Indians, Japanese with Chinese and Taiwanese, Germans with Pakistanis and Nigerians. The interlocutors cover a large spectrum of cultures, nationalities, mix of languages, regions, and identities. The medium of communication – spoken and/or written – is from a wide varieties of world Englishes.
2. The *monoculture myth* that English represents primarily – if not essentially – the Judeo-Christian traditions and dominant ideologies of the Inner Circle. In the real world of Englishes, the medium is used to impart local and native religions, cultural and social traditions – Asian, African, and Latin American. There is abundant evidence of this in nativized, culture-specific acculturation in creative writing, media, popular culture, and discourses of social interaction (e.g. Kachru & Nelson 2006).
3. The *mode-dependence myth* that the *exocentric models* (of the Inner Circle), in spoken or written mediums, have become codes of communication in Anglophone Asian and African countries. In the real world of African and Asian communicative contexts, it is the *endocentric* (local/regional) varieties that have currency. In spite of language policing in favor of exocentric models of English, the prevalent varieties are that of endocentric Englishes (e.g., in Hong Kong, Singapore, Taiwan; see Kachru 2005: 239–50). This conflict about the choice between *localized* and *external* models has resulted in much discussed *linguistic schizophrenia*.
4. The *Cassandra myth* that the impending linguistic disasters and doom of canonical standards of the English language are inevitable, if variations and linguistic diversification and creativity are not curtailed. In the real world of Englishes, it is through the processes of acculturation and innovations that, contextually and culturally, Asian and African identities of world Englishes and literatures have been constructed, thus enriching the Englishes.

The discourse of marginality has evolved into a genre of its own with many ideological, political, economic, and psychological constructs (e.g., Bolton 2006a, 2006b; Kachru 1986; Pennycook 1994; Phillipson 1992; for a review of earlier literature, see

Trömel-Plötz 1981). In these constructs generally three strategies are prevalent. First, the strategy to *depower* and *derationalize* each other's arguments. One example is Selinker's arguments for "fossilization and simplicity," and his wonder at "why colleagues appear *emotional* about the topic" (1993: 22, emphasis added). The word "emotional" here has a marginalizing effect in which contrast is provided between objectivity and rationality on the one hand and "emotion" on the other. The emphasis is shifted from the validity of the argument to the psychological state of the person who critiques Selinker's hypothesis. Then there is the often displayed strategy of the *sociolinguistic ostrich*. This strategy, as has been discussed in the literature, entails negation of the distinctions between the contexts of English as an *additional* (or *second*) language, or English as a *foreign* language, as presented by, for example, Richard Bailey and Randolph Quirk.

In all three strategies an attempt is made to negate the distinction between the Outer and Expanding Circles. The bilingual's creativity and socio-culturally motivated innovations – and variations – are characterized as a "managed . . . revolutionary shift" (Bailey 1990: 86), and as "liberation linguistics" (Quirk 1985). In the past decades it has been well argued that such hypotheses and generalizations are questionable from sociolinguistic, pragmatic, and empirical perspectives (see Kachru 1985, 1986).

Bilinguals' Creativity and Contact Literatures

The global pressure of Englishes – primarily in diasporic contexts – has evolved into multiple institutionalized varieties of world Englishes. It is now questionable whether traditional theoretical, analytical, and methodological constructs can account for the cross-cultural creativity in what are termed contact literatures in world Englishes in South, Southeast and East Asia, and West and South African varieties of Englishes. It is well demonstrated now that bilinguals' creativity has resulted in a variety of linguistic processes and cultural transference that include, for example, stylistic, lexical, and discoursal innovations. These processes are well illustrated in, for example, the Sanskritization and Kannadaization in Raja Rao's *Kanthapura* (1938), *The Serpent and the Rope* (1960), and *The Chessmaster and His Moves* (1988), and the Yorubaization and Igboization of Amos Tutuola and Chinua Achebe. What is characteristic of these creative writers is that, in Rao's case, he has transcreated the South Asian linguistic resources into English, as have Tutuola and Achebe in the African contexts and styles.

In contextualization of these texts such creativity does not have to be consistent with the canon of what are termed the "Platonic-Aristotelian sequence" and Anglo-Saxon thought patterns. In such literary creativity, Asian and African patterns of communication and speech acts have evolved. The African and Asian "contact literatures" adopt all the linguistic and cultural processes – and transfers – that are present in languages in contact. The linguistic strategies and processes used in contact

literatures in English are not different from those used, for example, in French (e.g., Francophone Africa), in Persian (e.g., in India and Pakistan), or in Hindi (e.g., in Fiji, Trinidad, and South India).

The hybridization, blending, and fusion of languages, and "mixing" of subvarieties of an institutionalized variety of English, is effectively used in, for example, Singlish in Singapore English, Bazaar or Babu varieties in South Asian Englishes, and pidgins in Nigerian English. The medium of English is appropriately adapted and localized to the contexts of local interactions and discourses (see Bolton 2006b). In their monumental grammar, Quirk et al. (1985: 27–8) have termed such varieties of English "interference varieties." This is yet another attitudinally loaded term that conceptualizes bilinguals' creative strategies as

> so widespread in a community and of such long standing that they may be thought stable and adequate enough to be institutionalized and hence to be regarded as varieties of English in their own right rather than stages on the way to more native-like English.

The institutionalized varieties have acquired the "right" by demonstrating the relationship between discourse structure and thought patterns, and by their distinct architecture of language. An often-quoted and well-crafted example is provided by Nigerian writer Chinua Achebe. In his *Things Fall Apart* (1966: 20) Achebe insightfully illustrates how one text – nativized and Africanized – is contextually more effective and true to African interactional patterns as compared with an Englishized text. In presenting the two texts, Achebe provides the reader "some idea of how I approach the use of English." In the nativized – or Africanized – text the Priest tells one of his sons why it is essential to send him to church. The Africanized version reads:

> I want one of my sons to join these people and be my eyes there. If there is nothing in it you will come back. But if there is something then you will bring back my share. The world is like a mask, dancing. If you want to see it well, you do not stand in one place. My spirit tells me that those who do not befriend the white man today will be saying "had he known," tomorrow.

And regarding the second text, Achebe asks, "supposing I had put it another way. Like this for instance":

> I am sending you as my representative among these people – just to be on the safe side in case the new religion develops. One has to move with the times or else one is left behind. I have a hunch that those who fail to come to terms with the white man may well regret their lack of foresight.

And Achebe's pragmatically and contextually appropriate answer is: "The material is the same. But the form of the one is in character and the other is not. It is largely a matter of instinct but judgment comes into it too."

It is, then, creative *instinct* and *judgment* concerning appropriate *form* that determines the construction of text – it is the constraints of the medium (in this case, English) that determine structuring of the *mantras* (messages). The *mantras* are intended to represent the socio-cultural meaning of the African (in this case, Yoruba) messages. Almost four decades earlier, in 1938, India's philosophical novelist, Raja Rao (1908–2006), in his first novel, *Kanthapura*, referring to the *sthala-purana* (the legendary history) of India, and the use of such legends in Indian English, says:

> The *Puranas* are endless and innumerable. We have neither punctuation nor the treacherous "ats" and "ons" to bother us – we tell one interminable tale. Episode follows episode, and when our thoughts stop our breath stops, and we move on to another thought. This was and still is the ordinary style of our storytelling. I have tried to follow it myself in this story. (Rao 1963: vii–viii)

The linguistic and stylistic processes Rao used for Indianization of Indian English "exhibit" themselves in the "uniquely Nigerian" English of Nigeria's Amos Tutuola and Chinua Achebe. Taiwo observes that Tutuola "has carried Yoruba speech habits into English and writes in English as he would speak in Yoruba . . . He is basically speaking Yoruba but using English words . . . the peculiar rhythms of his English are the rhythms of Yoruba speech" (1976: 85).

The functional and sociological realities of world Englishes are now significantly altered. In contextualizing this unprecedented linguistic phenomenon the monolithic, and pragmatically unrealistic, terms such as *world English*, *global English*, or *international English* misrepresent the real world of world *Englishes*.

Toward a Socially and Functionally Realistic Paradigm

A socially and functionally realistic conceptualization of world Englishes, specifically in the Outer Circle, was outlined in the 1960s, with reference to India (Kachru 1961). However, in 1978 two independently planned conferences were organized in the United States, first at the East-West Center in Honolulu, Hawaii (April 1–15), second at the University of Illinois at Urbana-Champaign (June 30–July 2). The Honolulu conference statement recognized that "English used as an international or auxiliary language has led to the emergence of sharp and important issues that are in urgent need of investigation and action" (Smith 1981: xvii). This distinction represents "the use of English for international (i.e., external) and intranational (i. e., internal) purposes." A further distinction was made between "those countries (e.g., Japan) whose requirements focus upon international comprehensibility and those countries (e.g., India) which in addition must take account of English as it is used for their own national purposes." The participants emphasized that this "fundamental distinction" was yet not recognized by professional organizations (Smith 1981: xvii).

The conference at the University of Illinois primarily focused on "English in non-native contexts." The interaction between the scholars and the conference agenda "broke the traditional pattern of such deliberations: no inconvenient question was swept under the rug. The professionals, both linguists and literary scholars, and native and non-native users of English, had frank and stimulating discussions" (Kachru 1997: 210).

The emphasis at the two conferences, then, gradually developed sociolinguistic profiles of world Englishes, discussed and illustrated cultural and interactional motivations for concepts such as *nativization* and *acculturation* and their implication for a theoretical, methodological, and pedagogical shifts. These deliberations continued scholarly interactions in both the Inner Circle and Outer Circle countries. The debate that was initiated then continues unabated in all the Circles. It was McArthur (1993: 334), who, referring to the logo-acronym *WE* of the journal *World Englishes* (launched in 1984), appropriately observed that it "serves to indicate that there is a club of equals here," and "the democratization of attitudes to English everywhere on the globe." The result of this "democratization" dissolves, as McArthur suggests, the trinity of ENL, ESL, and EFL nations.

Conclusion

There is now increasing realization that the identities and multiple functions of world Englishes are better conceptualized if the traditional "owners" and "ownership" of English – and its linguistic and cultural norms of creativity – are viewed from contextually relevant perspectives. Those perspectives entail a shift in theoretical, methodological, and socio-cultural constructs of the language and its users. In its varied functions, across cultures and languages, the current profile of the English language includes the following characteristics:

1. The models for creativity in the language are provided by *multi-norms* of literary and oral styles and strategies.
2. The processes of nativization and acculturation in Asian, African, and other varieties are determined by distinctly different linguistic contexts and cultures, and "contexts of situation."
3. The interaction in the language is not necessary between two or more monolingual "speakers-hearers," but often includes two or more multilingual users of the language.
4. The bilingual's or multilingual's creativity and linguistic strategies are not identical to the interactional strategies of two monolinguals.
5. Bilinguals' creativity is not merely the interaction of and mixing of two or more languages, but also a fusion of multiple cultural, aesthetic, social, and literary backgrounds.

In other words, the readers and hearers who are not part of the speech-fellowship of the variety of English, who do not share, or recreate, the "meaning system," have to familiarize themselves with linguistic processes and discoursal strategies. What we find inhibiting, limiting, unintelligible, or *non*-English in one variety of world Englishes may actually be the result of linguistically, culturally, and contextually appropriate use of the language.

There continues to be a paucity of research, in theory and application, concerning the design and linguistic constructs of multilinguals' hybridized creativity and communication. The focus of research must include what multilinguals "can say" and "can mean," and the range in *saying* and *meaning*, in a variety of English, as Halliday (1973: 43) discusses, though not specifically in the context of world Englishes. This then entails, to use J. R. Firth's concept, "renewal of connection" between the text (written and oral) with the "context of situation." In his recent studies, Bolton (2006a: 264) emphasizes this conceptualization of world Englishes – and the ongoing debate – when he reminds us that

> the sociolinguistically complex sites of English-using African and Asian societies are no more exotic side-shows, but important sites of contact, negotiation, and linguistic and literary creativity . . . perhaps the major challenge from world Englishes is how the center-periphery balance might be best redressed, or "recentered" and "pluricentered."

Bolton aptly warns us:

> This however is likely to be no easy task, given the apparent commodification and homogenization of the work in this field, both theoretical and pedagogical.

Of the following resources for study and research on world Englishes, see especially Bolton & Kachru (2006); Burchfield (1994); Crystal (1995); Kachru (1997); Kachru et al. (2006); McArthur (1992, 1993); Quirk & Widdowson (1985); Schneider et al. (2004).

REFERENCES AND FURTHER READING

Abercrombie, D. (1951). R.P. and local accent. *The Listener*, September 6. Rptd. in D. Abercrombie (1965). *Studies in Phonetics and Linguistics*. Oxford: Oxford University Press.

Achebe, C. (1966). *Things Fall Apart*. London: Heinemann.

Bailey, R. W. (1990). English at its twilight. In C. Ricks & L. Michaels (eds.), *The State of the*

Language (pp. 83–94). Berkeley: University of California Press.

Berns, M. (2005). Expanding on the Expanding Circle: where do we go from here? *World Englishes*, 24 (1), 85–93.

Bloomfield, L. (1933). *Language*. New York: Holt, Rinehart and Winston.

Bolton, K. (2006a). World Englishes today. In B. Kachru, Y. Kachru, & C. Nelson (eds.), *The*

Handbook of World Englishes (pp. 240–70). Oxford: Blackwell.

Bolton, K. (2006b). Varieties of Englishes. In B. Kachru, Y. Kachru, & C. Nelson (eds.), *The Handbook of World Englishes* (pp. 289–312). Oxford: Blackwell.

Bolton, K. & Kachru, B. B. (eds.) (2006). *World Englishes: Critical Concepts in Linguistics*. 6 vols. New York: Routledge.

Burchfield, R. (ed.) (1994). *The Cambridge History of the English Language*. Cambridge: Cambridge University Press.

Crystal, D. (1995). *The Cambridge Encyclopedia of the English Language*. Cambridge: Cambridge University Press.

Edwards, G. D. (1993). The response of education to the native language of Wales. In R. Khoo, U. Kreher, & R. Wong (eds.), *Languages in Contact in a Multilingual Society: Implications for Language Teaching and Learning* (pp. 107–28). Singapore: SEAMEO Regional Language Centre.

Firth, J. R. (1957). *Papers in Linguistics 1934–51*. Oxford: Oxford University Press.

Halliday, M. A. K. (1973). *Explorations in the Functions of Language*. London: Edward Arnold.

Kachru, B. B. (1962 [1961]). An analysis of some features of Indian English: a study in linguistic method. PhD dissertation, University of Edinburgh.

Kachru, B. B. (1983). *The Indianization of English: The English Language in India*. Delhi: Oxford University Press.

Kachru, B. B. (1985). Standards, codification and sociolinguistic realism: the English language in the Outer Circle. In R. Quirk & H. G. Widdowson (eds.), *English in the World: Teaching and Learning the Language and Literatures* (pp. 11–30). Cambridge: Cambridge University Press.

Kachru, B. B. (1986). *The Alchemy of English: The Spread, Function and Models of Non-native Englishes*. Oxford: Pergamon Press. Rptd. (1990). Urbana, University of Illinois Press.

Kachru, B. B. (1987). The power of English. *World Englishes*, 5 (2–3), 121–40.

Kachru, B. B. (1988). The spread of English and sacred linguistic cows. In P. H. Lowenberg (ed.), *Language Spread and Language Policy: Issues, Implications and Case Studies. Georgetown Round Table on Language and Linguistics 1987* (pp. 207–

28). Washington DC: Georgetown University Press.

Kachru, B. B. (1991). Liberation linguistics and the Quirk concern. *English Today*, 7 (1), 1–13.

Kachru, B. B. (1997). World Englishes 2000: resources for research and teaching. In L. E. Smith & M. L. Forman (eds.), *World Englishes 2000* (pp. 209–51). Honolulu: University of Hawaii Press.

Kachru, B. B. (2005). *Asian Englishes Beyond the Canon*. Hong Kong: Hong Kong University Press.

Kachru, B. B., Kachru, Y., & Nelson, C. L. (eds.) (2006). *The Handbook of World Englishes*. Oxford: Blackwell.

Kachru, Y. & Nelson, C. (2006). *World Englishes in Asian Contexts*. Hong Kong: Hong Kong University Press.

McArthur, T. (ed.) (1992). *The Oxford Companion to the English Language*. Oxford: Oxford University Press.

McArthur, T. (1993). The English language or the English languages? In W. F. Bolton & D. Crystal (eds.), *The Penguin History of Literature. 10: The English Language* (pp. 323–41). London: Penguin.

Pennycook, A. (1994). *The Cultural Politics of English as an International Language*. London: Longman.

Phillipson, R. (1992). *Linguistic Imperialism*. Oxford: Oxford University Press.

Quirk, R. (1989). Language varieties and standard language. *JALT Journal*, 11 (1), 14–25.

Quirk, R. & Widdowson, H. G. (eds.) (1985). *English in the World: Teaching and Learning the Language and Literatures*. Cambridge: Cambridge University Press.

Quirk, R. et al. (1985). *A Comprehensive Grammar of the English Language*. 2nd edn. London: Longman.

Rao, R. (1963 [1938]). *Kanthapura*. New York: New Directions.

Schneider, E. W., Burridge, K., Kortmann, B., Mesthrie, R., & Upton, C. (2004). *A Handbook of Varieties of English*. 2 vols. Berlin: Mouton de Gruyter.

Selinker, L. (1993). Fossilization as simplification. In M. L. Tickoo (ed.), *Simplification: Theory and Application. Anthology Series 31* (pp. 14–28). Singapore: SEAMEO Regional Language Centre.

Smith, L. E. (ed.) (1981). *English for Cross-Cultural Communication*. London: Macmillan.

Steiner, G. (1975). *'Why English?' Presidential Address*. London: English Association.

Taiwo, O. (1976). *Culture and the Nigerian Novel*. New York: St. Martin's Press.

Trömel-Plötz, S. (1981). Language of oppression. *Journal of Pragmatics*, 5, 67–80.

Part IX
Further Approaches to Language Study

Introduction

The methodologies and the resources available for language study are constantly evolving. New technologies facilitate new methods of data collection and analysis, while cultural changes demand that new questions be asked about the role of language in human affairs. The essays in this section outline four approaches to the study of language that have recently been or are currently being developed, and that have much to tell us about the history of English: statistical stylistics (stylometry), corpus linguistics, sociolinguistics, and cognitive linguistics.

Within the study of the history of English, it is well accepted that semantic and syntactic changes in the language will impede the modern reader's precise understanding of an earlier writer's meaning. But we must also consider whether *stylistic* conventions of the past can mislead us. David Hoover in his essay "Style and Stylistics" observes that "stylistics necessarily rests upon a distinction between 'what' is said (content) and 'how' it is said (form)," suggesting that we must accept a level of meaning not contingent on form if we are to talk about changing style in writing. Acknowledging the difficulties in this formulation, the essay goes on to offer an overview of the many ways in which the "how" of language is explored today through both traditional and new methods of stylistic analysis.

Hoover's piece concludes with an example of "stylometry," one new approach to literary stylistics which uses computer-driven lexical analysis to find statistically significant features of a given author's writing style, which can be useful both for authorial attribution and for textual dating. Computers are also central to the development of "Corpus Linguistics," introduced here by Anne Curzan. This field of research uses wide-ranging databases of historical texts as the basis for intricate statistical analyses. Computer databases, by making manageable exponentially larger bodies of textual evidence, promise to open avenues of historical language study impossible to fathom before computers made handling the data possible.

Advances in technology are only one way changes in the culture affect language study. Our understanding of language and its history is always framed by the questions deemed worth asking. Since the 1960s, some linguists, following the pioneering work of William Labov, have foregrounded questions of race, class, and gender in their studies of language, a focus not much found in earlier philological programs nor in Chomsky's generative grammar (see also ISSUES OF GENDER IN MODERN ENGLISH; CLASS, ETHNICITY, AND THE FORMATION OF "STANDARD ENGLISH"). Robin Tolmach Lakoff uses a recent public incident of apparent gender insensitivity to demonstrate how the sociolinguist might analyze a historical moment defined by language use. Lakoff "illustrates the way American society uses literate narrative to understand itself" by employing her "Undue Attention Test" – a set of parameters that measure when a story of public language use gets more media attention than expected, signaling that the language itself is in the midst of a critical formative moment.

Another break from the dominant Chomskian mode of linguistic analysis can be found in more semantic-based analyses. Dirk Geeraerts illustrates how the methods of "Cognitive Linguistics" can aid the scholar of HEL in diachronic semantic studies. Focusing on the ideas of "prototypicality" and "conceptual metaphors," Geeraerts demonstrates why "language is not considered to be an autonomous system, but rather an aspect of human life that is integrated into cognition and culture at large." Language, in creating meaning, interacts with other cultural agents which are, ultimately, the products of human cognition themselves.

Michael Matto

56
Style and Stylistics

David L. Hoover

Style can be simply defined as a distinctive way of doing anything, from ballroom dancing to computer programming. Here, however, the focus will be on literary style, a distinctive way of writing literary texts (for simplicity, ignoring spoken texts). This definition emphasizes the centrality of the linguistic and rhetorical characteristics of texts. Stylistics, then, is the study of style. Both style and stylistics are notoriously difficult to define (for multiple definitions, see Wales 2001). "Style" is often applied to literary periods, genres, and national or international movements and more centrally to single authors, texts, or parts of texts. Stylistics, with many different forms and emphases, has a long and often illustrious history, and forms parts of some of the most important monuments of literary studies, dating back at least to Aristotle's *Poetics*.

In spite of its long tradition of importance, stylistics has been relegated to a minor role over the past few decades, especially in the United States, for reasons that are complex, but most saliently include the rise of critical theory and the hegemony of Chomskyan linguistics. Many strands of recent critical theory turn their attention away from the text to the role of the reader, to the effects of race, gender, or politics, or to the cultural and institutional contexts of literary texts. The very category of the literary even threatens to disappear, as texts not traditionally considered literary increasingly become the focus of attention. These approaches have competed very successfully for the attention of students of literature over the past few decades.

Some approaches that are deeply influenced by ideas about the instability of the sign and the tendency of texts to disintegrate under critical pressure (especially deconstruction), however, go further, questioning the stability of textual meaning and the legitimacy of stylistics. Fish (1981), for example, famously attacked stylistics as a pseudo-scientific attempt to specify universal connections between textual features and textual styles and meanings. McGann (2001) argues for a performative and deformative criticism that seems to reject the meaning of the text as a valid subject of

research, and urges changing the text to liberate criticism from textual tyranny. (For a rather different use of text alteration, see Pope 1995; Hoover 1999, 2004c, 2006b.)

At the same time that these critical approaches gained ascendancy, Chomsky's introspective, sentence-oriented, formalist, and anti-textual program came to dominate linguistics. His mentalist approach emphasizes the formal nature of grammar, downplays semantics, focuses on competence/deep structure rather than performance/ surface structure, ignores literature, and restricts itself to the scope of the sentence. These orthodoxies tend to deny the legitimacy of stylistics, which is centrally concerned with meaning, surface differences, and patterns of style that typically require a whole text or passage for expression. Even in the face of an inhospitable climate within literary and linguistic studies, however, stylistics has responded with increasingly sophisticated methods and approaches, producing new insights into literary texts that seem certain to endure.

If a style is a distinctive way of writing, stylistics necessarily rests upon a distinction between "what" is said (content) and "how" it is said (form). Without some version of this distinction, paraphrase and translation would be impossible, for both imply a content that survives the alteration of form. Without the distinction, successful parodies would be impossible, and the fact that some readers can recognize the authors of texts they have never read would be inexplicable, for both imply that authorial style is at least partly independent of content. As reasonable as the distinction is, it is also problematic. If language is meaningful, how can different language fail to have different meaning? And the idea that the content of a text has no stylistic implications also seems difficult to accept. Those who reject the form/content distinction cite the extreme difficulty of translating poetry and the differences among translations of the same poem into the same language as evidence that all style is (also) content and that even the choice of subject matter is a stylistic one (see Halliday 1981).

A pluralistic approach to style that rejects any absolute distinction between form and content but accepts different *kinds* of meaning seems more defensible than either extreme (see Leech & Short 1981: 29–40). This approach assumes a continuum from language differences that clearly signal different states of affairs, different contents, and those that signal different ways of expressing the "same" content, different styles. For example, replacing "summer's" with "winter's" in "Shall I compare thee to a summer's day?" (the opening line of Shakespeare's Sonnet XVIII) seems quintessentially a change in content, but replacing "to" with "with" seems more stylistic. Calling one end of this continuum *content* and the other *style* will cause no harm, so long as no claim is made that the two labels name completely disparate aspects of a literary text.

This brief overview provides some sense of the variety and nature of stylistics, but studying the style of texts from earlier periods of the language presents special problems, the most significant of which is that we lack the native speaker's feel for earlier periods of the language. Reading and studying Middle English texts is very different

from growing up speaking Middle English. Twenty-first-century readers of Chaucer are typically struck by just how modern his ideas often seem, but his language is sometimes quite foreign, and matters are much worse for Middle English texts in dialects more distant from the line that leads to Modern English.

Our lack of intimate familiarity with the language, coupled with an incomplete understanding of medieval culture, makes understanding the subtleties of humor and irony especially tenuous. These problems are often extreme for Anglo-Saxon literature, and are not inconsiderable for texts written even within the last century, especially if they are in a dialect different from the reader's. For example, when a British writer uses "er" to mark a hesitation in speech, as in "I, er, haven't decided," many American readers (mentally) pronounce "er" just as they would in a word like "over." They may not realize that most British speakers do not pronounce the "r" in "er" or "over" and that "er" suggests to a British reader a pronunciation quite similar to the one that "uh" suggests to an American reader in "I, uh, haven't decided."

Because stylistics concentrates on patterns and differences, the change from manuscript to print culture and the related changes in spelling and punctuation over the history of English also present challenges for studies of earlier literature. It is difficult to know, for example, whether a difference between two Middle English forms has a stylistic basis or simply varies freely. The rise of Standard English and the changing roles of editors and publishers must also be kept in mind. These problems decrease in importance with more recent texts, but editorial regularization can sometimes affect even texts of the relatively recent past. For example, Henry James (1843–1916), like some of his contemporaries, sometimes treats contractions like "doesn't" as if the two syllables were separate words, but the space between "does" and "n't" is usually removed, sometimes silently, in modern editions. All of these special difficulties must be kept in mind in any investigation of literary style in earlier periods of the language.

Far too many varieties of stylistics exist for a brief discussion like this one to describe them all. Rather, I will select some of the most distinctive and central approaches for discussion. A general linguistic approach to style is perhaps best exemplified by *Style in Fiction* (Leech & Short 1981; 2nd edn. 2007), the winner of the 2005 Poetics and Linguistics Association prize for the most influential book in stylistics in the past 25 years (PALA 2006). I have already indicated my debt to this book in my discussion of style and content, but its broad coverage of linguistic and stylistic categories and its functionalist analysis of the semantic, syntactic, graphological, and phonological levels at which style resides are all important. Leech and Short also provide seminal discussions of the creation of the fictional world, mind style (following Fowler), the rhetoric of text, the broader category of discourse and discourse situation, and conversation. Finally, they present a careful framework for the description of speech and thought presentation in fiction that continues to be refined and expanded (see Semino & Short 2004). This book is perhaps the best single introduction to stylistics (see also Fowler 1996), but there are three collections of articles (Freeman 1970, 1981; Weber 1996) that provide a good sense of the development of

the field over the past 35 years. Browsing journals like *Language and Literature*, *Style*, *Journal of Literary Semantics*, *Poetics*, and *Poetics Today* will give a fairly clear picture of the current state of research. PALA runs an annual international conference, as does IGEL (Internationale Gesellschaft für Empirische Literaturwissenschaft/International Society for the Empirical Study of Literature and Media).

Text world theory is an active area of research in current stylistics that owes much to the notion of "possible worlds" in philosophy. Perhaps the most important early work is that of Ryan (1991), who provides a careful and detailed examination of how authors create fictional worlds. Ryan's "principle of minimal departure," the idea that the fictional world of a text is assumed to be the same as the real world except where otherwise indicated, seems profoundly important to the way fictional texts work. Complications occur when the fictional and real worlds occupy different times in history, but the principle of minimal departure helps to explain both how authors evoke much of the real world within a fictional context and how that world can be altered – subtly or radically. Very accessible discussions of text worlds are those of Werth (1999), Semino (1997), and New (1999); in addition, Stockwell (2000) discusses the special problems facing creators of science fiction text worlds that are extremely different from the real world (see also Hoover 2004c).

In the context of the history of the English language, text world theory helps to explain some of the difficulties modern readers have in approaching pre-contemporary literary texts. Consider the beginning of Edith Wharton's *The Age of Innocence* (1920):

> On a January evening of the early seventies, Christine Nilsson was singing in Faust at the Academy of Music in New York. Though there was already talk of the erection, in remote metropolitan distances "above the Forties," of a new Opera House which should compete in costliness and splendour with those of the great European capitals, the world of fashion was still content to reassemble every winter in the shabby red and gold boxes of the sociable old Academy.

The first sentence carries a huge weight of associations and evocations of the cultured, upper-class New York city of the late nineteenth century. Step back about 200 years, to Jonathan Swift's *Gulliver's Travels* (1726), and the task of the reader becomes much more difficult:

> MY FATHER had a small Estate in Nottinghamshire; I was the Third of five Sons. He sent me to Emanuel-College in Cambridge, at Fourteen Years old, where I resided three Years, and applied my self close to my Studies: But the Charge of maintaining me (although I had a very scanty Allowance) being too great for a narrow Fortune; I was bound Apprentice to Mr. James Bates, an eminent Surgeon in London, with whom I continued four Years; and my Father now and then sending me small Sums of Money, I laid them out in learning Navigation, and other parts of the Mathematicks, useful to those who intend to travel, as I always believed it would be some time or other my Fortune to do.

Another important, varied, and active area of research is cognitive stylistics (or cognitive poetics), an approach that grows out of cognitive linguistics. The seminal work in this area is *Metaphors We Live By* (Lakoff & Johnson 1980), with its insistence on the centrality of metaphor to ordinary language. Simply put, language is as it is because of the characteristics of our bodies and the physical world, and we use simple, physical metaphors to help us understand and organize our ways of thinking about abstractions (see Johnson 1987). For example, the metaphor "life is a journey" has been extremely prevalent both in English and in other languages (famously at the beginning of Dante's *Divine Comedy*). Because movement through space is so basic and universal an activity, we use our experience of it to understand the more difficult and abstract idea of living through time. And the metaphor is complex, with many mappings between the physical and the abstract. If life is a journey, living through time is moving through space, and lives, like journeys, have beginnings, ends, stages, goals, and obstacles; they also involve diverging paths on which one could lose one's way (see Lakoff 1987; Lakoff & Turner 1989; also COGNITIVE LINGUSITICS).

Also central to the cognitive approach is the notion of mental spaces, conceptual configurations in the mind of various elements of experience or imagination; these can be combined or blended to form new constructs (Fauconnier & Turner 2002). Frames, structured conventional situations, are used to understand ordinary life as well as narrative fiction; for example, if we are told that a friend or a character has gone to the supermarket, we can call upon our knowledge of this ordinary activity to help us fill in details we are not given (see Emmott 1997). Schemas are a related notion, though more strongly implying activities: we construct narratives or scripts for repeated activities. In real life, for example, we do not have to work very hard to cope with going into a new store to buy a new product because we have a stored schema or script that already specifies the general shape of a store transaction. In fiction, schemas help us to build up a richly textured fictional world without requiring the author to present each detail explicitly. Conversely, in a fantasy text the author must avoid activating or accessing the reader's frames and schemas, which would evoke too much of the ordinary world and threaten the fantastic world of the text (see Werth 1999; Semino 1997; Stockwell 2000). Good selections of essays with cognitive approaches to specific literary texts are available (Semino & Culpeper 2002; Gavins & Steen 2003).

Although many areas of stylistics have responded to criticism like that of Fish by giving up the claim of objectivity and attempting to integrate themselves into mainstream critical theory, empirical approaches have moved in the opposite direction. Most work in this area uses reader surveys as the primary source of information about literary response. The classic study is that of van Peer (1986), who shows convincingly that extreme claims about the instability of textual meaning cannot be correct. For example, judgments about whether literary language is striking are not purely subjective; foregrounding is a phenomenon readers can agree upon. When asked to underline the most striking parts of poems, readers underline the same parts that preliminary literary analysis shows to be deviant or foregrounded. Even more remarkably, both

students who have studied stylistic analysis and those without any literary background agree in their judgments. The REDES (Research and Development in Empirical Studies) project and Miall and Kuiken (2006) have websites providing links and resources in this area. A very recent development in empirical approaches to literature is research into the connections between brain activity and literary experience and response. This approach uses brain scans in an attempt to locate and characterize various kinds of aesthetic experiences (Quartz & Starr 2006). Given the extremely intense research into brain function, this area seems ripe for future growth.

Corpus stylistics is another area in which there has recently been a burst of activity. Borrowing techniques and ideas from corpus linguistics, this approach uses giant natural language corpora (Louw 1993), or specially created corpora (Semino & Short 2004; Hoover et al. forthcoming; Stubbs 1996) to study literary style. Partly a response to the difficulty of defining a norm against which stylistic judgments can be measured, corpus stylistics is also driven by a desire to base stylistic judgments and analysis on very large amounts of information. Semino and Short (2004) study how speech, writing, and thought are presented in a corpus of 250,000 words of fiction, news, and biography/autobiography. Their careful annotation of such a large corpus of texts provides a solid basis for generalizations about the representation of speech, writing, and thought in texts, and paves the way for more work on literary texts using the same framework. Both Louw (1993) and Sinclair (2004) demonstrate the importance of "semantic prosodies" (roughly, meanings spread over words and their context). For example, the verb "happen" typically occurs in a negative context; bad things quintessentially happen. But this negative meaning would not normally be considered part of the meaning of the word. The verb "budge" may be defined as "to move slightly," but it nearly always occurs with a negative (Sinclair 2004), and no movement actually occurs. This kind of contextual meaning is especially important for second language learners, who might be tempted to use words in inappropriate contexts, but literary texts also exploit semantic prosodies for special effects. In *Howards End*, Forster first matches and then reverses the semantic prosody of "budge" for humorous effect:

> "One bit of advice: fix your district, then fix your price, and then don't budge. That's how I got both Ducie Street and Oniton. I said to myself, 'I mean to be exactly here,' and I was, and Oniton's a place in a thousand."
>
> "But I do budge. Gentlemen seem to mesmerize houses – cow them with an eye, and up they come, trembling. Ladies can't. It's the houses that are mesmerizing me. I've no control over the saucy things. Houses are alive. No?"

I have used two created corpora to investigate William Golding's style (Hoover 1999). Hoover et al. (forthcoming) use both created and natural language corpora and a variety of techniques to investigate fiction, poetry, and drama. The existence of huge numbers of electronic texts and increasingly sophisticated kinds of analysis should assure the rapid growth of corpus stylistics. (See CORPUS-BASED LINGUISTIC APPROACHES.)

Finally, statistical stylistics (stylometry), sometimes considered a branch of humanities computing, is also a very active area of research. Like corpus stylistics, this approach benefits greatly by having electronic texts available, and typically proceeds by examining a corpus of texts. Stylometry, however, is more centrally statistical and computational, using methods first developed for authorship attribution. Burrows's classic (1987) study of Jane Austen (1775–1817) shows that the dialogue of various characters in Austen's novels can be distinguished by using principal components analysis of the frequencies of the most frequent words in the novels (for a technical explanation, see Binongo & Smith 1999). Authorship studies have assumed that the use of very frequent words (almost exclusively function words) is so routinized as to be unconscious, so that their frequencies constitute an authorial "word print." Austen was presumably not controlling these words consciously; rather, she had such a discriminating ear for dialogue that she intuitively differentiated her characters' voices on the basis of their fictional psychologies.

Many studies by Burrows and others use this methodology (I can mention only a few). Burrows (1992b) shows that the frequencies of the 75 most frequent words of 40 first-person narratives by authors from Defoe to Doctorow strikingly divide them into groups based on their dates of birth, marking a historical evolution in English style in this genre. In one of several careful and important studies, Craig (1999a) investigates Ben Jonson's *A Tale of a Tub* for evidence of an early composition date with late revisions by using discriminant analysis. Segmenting the play into many 2,000-word segments with different starting points reveals that some parts of the play are consistent with Jonson's earliest writings, and some with his latest, and that the changes in style are often very abrupt. This pattern supports the idea that the play may be a late revision of earlier work (see also Craig 1999b). McKenna and Antonia (2001) probe the differences among interior monologue, dialogue, and narrative in Joyce's *Ulysses*, arguing that multivariate analysis of Gerty McDowell's language can contribute to the interpretation of form, meaning, and ideology in the novel. Stewart (2003) shows that Charles Brockden Brown (1771–1810) created a consistent narrative voice for Carwin, a character who narrates one chapter of *Wieland* and the unfinished novel *Carwin*. He then shows how two chapters of *Wieland* narrated by two other characters also cluster with Carwin's and discusses how these quantitatively anomalous results can be integrated into the larger critical debate surrounding the interpretation of this early American novel. I use a modification of Burrows's technique to examine intratextual style variation in Orwell, Golding, and Wilde (Hoover 2003); in addition, Rybicki (2006) presents a fascinating study of a trilogy of nineteenth-century Polish novels and two translations separated by 100 years in which some aspects of characterization in the original remain surprisingly constant in the very different translations.

More recently, Burrows has created three new statistical methods for authorship attribution and stylistic analysis, both again based on the frequencies of frequent words. The first method, Delta, is especially effective in picking the correct author out of a large field of claimants (Burrows 2002a, 2003; Hoover 2004a, 2004b, 2008,

in press), but Burrows (2002b) also uses it to examine the intersection between authorship and translation. I show that it can also be used to study how authors differentiate narrators or letter writers and to investigate the changes in Henry James's style over time (Hoover et al. forthcoming). The other two methods are based on words of moderate frequency and relatively rare words, in both cases examining the consistency of the use of the words in different authors (Burrows 2005, 2006). It is safe to assume that these and other methods of statistical analysis will continue to be productive and innovative ways of studying style.

I conclude this brief discussion of style and stylistics with a small demonstration. In *The Moonstone* (1868), Wilkie Collins experiments in an innovative way with point of view, dividing the narration among a succession of disparate characters. Franklin Blake's engagement to Rachel Verinder is broken off when the moonstone, her huge yellow diamond, mysteriously vanishes. Once the mystery is solved, Blake insists that the person who has the most direct and complete knowledge of each part of the story write it. The seven main narrators include Blake; Betteredge, an old family servant; Miss Clack, a hypocritical friend of the family; Mr. Bruff, the family lawyer; Mr. Cuff, a famous detective; Ezra Jennings, a disgraced and mysterious doctor; and Rosanna Spearman, a female servant secretly in love with Blake. These narrators, like Austen's characters, seem so distinct that the fictional division of the novel into narratives by different "authors" can be taken literally to test whether stylometric methods can tell them apart (for more detail, see Hoover et al. forthcoming). Testing 46 Victorian novels shows that Collins's style is very distinct, binding his ten novels closely together and clearly distinguishing them from 36 novels by five of his contemporaries, Charlotte Brontë, Charles Dickens, George Eliot, William Thackery, and Anthony Trollope. Will the various narrators of *The Moonstone* be distinctive within this consistent Collins style?

Figure 56.1 shows that principal component analysis succeeds in separating all of the narrators but Jennings, and his two sections, though widely separated from each other, do not clearly cluster with any other character (long narrations are divided into roughly equal sections). This result is interesting both because it shows that Collins was able to distinguish the narrative voices of his characters distinctly throughout this long novel, and because it suggests that a closer examination of Jennings's style should be worthwhile. By way of contrast, consider figure 56.2, which shows the results of a similar study of the dialogue of the main characters of Henry James's *The Ambassadors* (large speaking parts are again divided into roughly equal sections). Unlike Collins, James does not consistently distinguish the voices of his characters. Only the eccentric Miss Barrash and Madame de Vionet are clearly distinct here, and Chad and Little Bilham are not clearly grouped with any other characters (this is the best character separation I was able to achieve). Sections of dialogue by Maria Gostrey and especially Strether are spread very widely, showing that James's chief interest is not in developing strongly distinct characters but in creating a subtle and complex set of interrelationships. One interesting point in both these figures is a tendency for the structure of the novels to show through the character differentiation or lack of it.

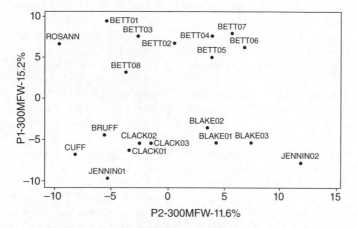

Figure 56.1   The seven major narrators of *The Moonstone*

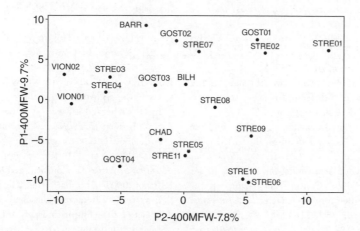

Figure 56.2   The dialogue of the six main characters of *The Ambassadors*

Except for BETT08, Betteredge's sections are roughly in order of presentation from left to right, and the same tendency can be seen in Clack, Jennings, and Blake. The pattern is weaker in James, but the earlier sections of Strether and Gostry tend to appear near the top of the graph. Further analysis of the narrative location of the sections would reveal whether or not the context and content of the sections is driving these similarities.

REFERENCES AND FURTHER READING

Binongo, J. N. G. & Smith, M. W. A. (1999). The application of principal component analysis to stylometry. *Literary and Linguistic Computing*, 14, 445–65.

Burrows, J. F. (1987). *Computation into Criticism.* Oxford: Clarendon Press.

Burrows, J. F. (1992a). Not unless you ask nicely: the interpretative nexus between analysis and information. *Literary and Linguistic Computing*, 7, 91–109.

Burrows, J. F. (1992b). Computers and the study of literature. In C. S. Butler (ed.), *Computers and Written Texts* (pp. 167–204). Oxford: Blackwell.

Burrows, J. F. (2002a). 'Delta': a measure of stylistic difference and a guide to likely authorship. *Literary and Linguistic Computing*, 17, 267–87.

Burrows, J. F. (2002b). The Englishing of Juvenal: computational stylistics and translated texts. *Style*, 36, 677–99.

Burrows, J. F. (2003). Questions of authorship: attribution and beyond. *Computers and the Humanities*, 37, 5–32.

Burrows, J. F. (2005). Who wrote *Shamela*? Verifying the authorship of a parodic text. *Literary and Linguistic Computing*, 20, 437–50.

Burrows, J. F. (2006). All the way through: testing for authorship in different frequency strata. *Literary and Linguistic Computing*, 22, 24–7.

Craig, H. (1999a). Jonsonian chronology and the styles of *A Tale of a Tub*. In M. Butler (ed.), *Re-Presenting Ben Jonson: Text, History, Performance* (pp. 210–32). Basingstoke: Macmillan.

Craig, H. (1999b). Contrast and change in the idiolects of Ben Jonson characters. *Computers and the Humanities*, 33, 221–40.

Emmott, C. (1997). *Narrative Comprehension: A Discourse Perspective*. Oxford: Oxford University Press.

Fauconnier, G. & Turner, M. (2002). *The Way We Think: Conceptual Blending and the Mind's Hidden Complexities*. New York: Basic Books.

Fish, S. E. (1981). What is stylistics and why are they saying such terrible things about it? In D. C. Freeman (ed.), *Essays in Modern Stylistics* (pp. 53–78). London: Methuen.

Fowler, R. (1996). *Linguistic Criticism*. 2nd edn. Oxford: Oxford University Press.

Freeman, D. C. (ed.) (1970). *Linguistics and Literary Style*. New York: Holt.

Freeman, D. C. (ed.) (1981). *Essays in Modern Stylistics*. London: Methuen.

Gavins, J. & Steen G. (eds.) (2003). *Cognitive Poetics in Practice*. London: Routledge.

Halliday, M. A. K. (1981). Linguistic function and literary style: an inquiry into the language of William Golding's *The Inheritors*. In D. C. Freeman (ed.), *Essays in Modern Stylistics* (pp. 325–60). London: Methuen. Also in J. J. Weber (1996), *The Stylistics Reader* (pp. 56–86). New York: Arnold.

Hoover, D. L. (1999). *Language and Style in The Inheritors*. Lanham, MD: University Press of America.

Hoover, D. L. (2003). Multivariate analysis and the study of style variation. *Literary and Linguistic Computing*, 18, 341–60.

Hoover, D. L. (2004a). Testing Burrows's Delta. *Literary and Linguistic Computing*, 19, 453–75.

Hoover, D. L. (2004b). Delta prime? *Literary and Linguistic Computing*, 19, 477–95.

Hoover, D. L. (2004c). Altered texts, altered worlds, altered styles. *Language and Literature*, 13, 99–118.

Hoover, D. L. (2006). Hot-air textuality: literature after Jerome McGann. *Text Technology*, 15, 75–107.

Hoover, D. L. (2008 in press). Word frequency, statistical stylistics, and authorship attribution. In D. Archer (ed.), *What's in a Word-List? Investigating Word Frequency and Keyword Extraction*. Aldershot (U.K.): Ashgate.

Hoover, D. L., et al. (forthcoming). *Approaches to Corpus Stylistics*. London: Routledge.

IGEL (2006). Internationale Gesellschaft für Empirische Literaturwissenschaft (International Society for the Empirical Study of Literature and Media). Online. www.arts.ualberta.ca/igel/.

Johnson, M. (1987). *The Body in the Mind: The Bodily Basis of Meaning, Imagination, and Reason*. Chicago: University of Chicago Press.

Lakoff, G. (1987). *Women, Fire, and Dangerous Things*. Chicago: University of Chicago Press.

Lakoff, G. & Johnson, M. (1980). *Metaphors We Live By*. Chicago: University of Chicago Press.

Lakoff, G. & Turner, M. (1989). *More than Cool Reason: A Field Guide to Poetic Metaphor*. Chicago: University of Chicago Press.

Leech, G. N. & Short, M. ([1981] 2007). *Style in Fiction: A Linguistic Introduction to English Fictional Prose*. 2nd edn. Harlow: Pearson Education.

Louw, W. (1993). Irony in the text or insincerity in the writer: the diagnostic potential of semantic prosodies. In M. Baker et al. (eds.), *Text and Technology* (pp. 152–76). London: Collins.

McGann, J. J. (2001). *Radiant Textuality: Literature After the World Wide Web*. New York: Palgrave.

McKenna, C. W. F. & Antonia, A. (2001). The statistical analysis of style: reflections on form, meaning, and ideology in the 'Nausicaa' episode of *Ulysses*. *Literary and Linguistic Computing*, 16, 353–73.

Miall, D. S. & Kuiken, D. (2006). *Reader Response: Empirical Research on Literary Reading*. Online. www.ualberta.ca/%7Edmiall/reading/index.htm.

New, C. (1999). *Philosophy of Literature: An Introduction*. London: Routledge.

PALA (Poetics and Linguistics Association) (2006). *Style in Fiction* Symposium. Online. www.lancs.ac.uk/fass/events/styleinfiction/. PALA website: www.pala.ac.uk/.

Pope, R. (1995). *Textual Intervention: Critical and Creative Strategies for Literary Studies*. London: Routledge.

Quartz, S. & Starr, G. (2006). Probing the humanistic brain. Online. www.hss.caltech.edu/humanities/research/brain-imaging.

REDES (2006). *Research and Development in Empirical Studies*. Online. www.redes.de/.

Ryan, M. L. (1991). *Possible Worlds, Artificial Intelligence and Narrative Theory*. Bloomington: Indiana University Press.

Rybicki, J. (2006). Burrowing into translation: character idiolects in Henryk Sienkiewicz's trilogy and its two English translations. *Literary and Linguistic Computing*, 21, 91–103.

Semino, E. (1997). *Language and World Creation in Poems and Other Texts*. London: Longman.

Semino, E. & Culpeper, J. (eds.) (2002). *Cognitive Stylistics: Language and Cognition in Text Analysis*. Amsterdam: Benjamins.

Semino, E. & Short, M. (2004). *Corpus Stylistics: Speech, Writing, and Thought Presentation in a Corpus of English Writing*. London: Routledge.

Sinclair, J. (2004). *Trust the Text*. London: Routledge.

Stewart, L. (2003). Charles Brockden Brown: quantitative analysis and literary interpretation. *Literary and Linguistic Computing*, 18, 129–38.

Stockwell, P. (2000). *The Poetics of Science Fiction*. London: Pearson Education.

Stubbs, M. (1996). *Text and Corpus Analysis: Computer-Assisted Studies of Language and Culture*. Oxford: Blackwell.

van Peer, W. (1986). *Stylistics and Psychology: Investigations of Foregrounding*. London: Croom Helm.

Wales, K. (2001). *A Dictionary of Stylistics*. London: Pearson Education.

Weber, J. J. (ed.) (1996). *The Stylistics Reader*. New York: Arnold.

Werth, P. (1999). *Text Worlds: Representing Conceptual Space in Discourse*. London: Longman.

57

Corpus-Based Linguistic Approaches to the History of English

Anne Curzan

The invention of the computer and the world of electronic communication it has generated may well provide historians of English with a pivotal historical moment to divide (artificially) the period of Modern English from whatever we call the period that follows it, much like the printing press has served as the historical break between Middle English and Early Modern English. Computer technology has also given historians of English an entirely new methodology for approaching historical linguistic questions: (historical) corpus linguistics. Today some of the most exciting and innovative scholarship on the history of the English language is corpus-based.

Corpus linguistics involves the systematic study of language based on computerized, systematically compiled, searchable, and in various ways "representative" collections of texts (written or spoken). While some scholars view corpus linguistics as a subfield of linguistics, it is most usefully viewed as a methodology – a way to approach the linguistic questions that scholars have been asking about the development of English for decades if not for centuries. Corpus linguistics has significantly advanced scholars' ability to gather extensive quantitative evidence and to systematically analyze linguistic relationships, between linguistic forms, between linguistic forms and frequency, and between linguistic forms and extralinguistic factors. It has also often prompted scholars to ask different research questions.

Histories of English often describe developments within the language without describing the research processes that allow us, as scholars in the field, to make the assertions we make about specific linguistic changes in English. What are the sources of data in history of English scholarship, and how do historians of English move from these sources to generalizations about developments in the English language? This essay, focused on corpus-based studies, addresses electronic corpora as one new, critical source of data and shows how students, not just established scholars, can design searches that allow them to collect and analyze historical linguistic data about English – amounts of data that would have been inconceivable even just a few decades ago. A computer can read through one million words of text and list all examples of a particular construction in a matter of seconds – a search that might defeat even the

most diligent human reader. As a result, computerized corpora allow researchers to analyze and interpret comparatively large amounts of systematically compiled data and thereby enrich our understanding of language change generally and of how specific languages have changed over their histories.

Definition of a Linguistic Corpus

In modern corpus linguistics, the term *corpus* is generally understood to refer specifically to an electronic collection of texts designed for linguistic research. Key design features include the corpus's sampling and representativeness, its finite size, its machine-readability, and its status as a standard reference (McEnery & Wilson 1996: 21–4). Corpora can include written and (transcribed) spoken texts; the included texts can be representative excerpts of longer works or full texts (often of shorter works). Corpora can encompass multiple genres of texts to be more comprehensive and allow comparisons across genres (e.g., *A Representative Corpus of Historical English Registers*, known as the *ARCHER* corpus), or they can target a specific genre to allow more detailed description of that genre (e.g., the *Lampeter Corpus of Early Modern English Tracts*). Corpora can be synchronic, including texts from a period shorter than about thirty years (or one generation); or corpora can be diachronic, designed to capture language use over multiple generations of speakers/writers. One million running words is often taken as a reasonable size for examining a relatively common linguistic feature; however, for rarer linguistic features, a one-million word corpus will probably produce an insufficient number of hits for analysis. A few corpora provide syntactic tagging, allowing researchers to search a grammatical feature (e.g., modal verbs) rather than just given lexical strings (e.g., *might*, *can*); most corpora to date, however, tag only textual information.

In terms of textual tagging, most corpora designed for linguistic research take into consideration sociolinguistic features of the included texts, such as the gender, age, race/ethnicity, regional origin, and socio-economic status of the speaker/writer. Corpus-based historical linguistics has developed over the past twenty-five years roughly simultaneously with historical sociolinguistics; the fundamental premise that linguistic change is affected by social factors in addition to linguistic constraints has shaped the design of many historical corpora. The *Helsinki Corpus*, for example, tags every text for the author's age, gender, and rank (where known), as well as for the text's regional origins (where known) and genre. With these tags, scholars can examine the effects of these sociolinguistic factors as well as those of genre on linguistic change. While all historical corpora must rely on written texts, a corpus like the *Corpus of Early English Correspondence* (CEEC) is designed to provide access to written language that is presumed to be closer to the vernacular than most written genres, and the letters provide evidence of genuine communication between people of different genders, ages, and social ranks. Unfortunately, much of this sociolinguistic information is often unknown for earlier periods of English. Historical linguists try to account

for all the available sociolinguistic variables, recognizing the limits of what is available, and scholars strive to determine which social variables might have been most relevant in a given period (e.g., Nevalainen and Raumolin-Brunberg (2003) argue for rank and/or social and regional mobility as more appropriate classifications for the Early Modern English period than the modern sociolinguistic category "class").

Historical corpora are typically defined as corpora that include language earlier than the current generation's language. Almost all historical corpora include exclusively written texts. Historians of English must accept the lack of access to actual spoken English before the modern period and work instead with a range of written texts, from more colloquial to more formal. While linguistics privileges the spoken language as the primary object of inquiry, the history of written English is part of the "history of English," and scholars intuit what they can about the spoken language from a range of written language (for further discussion of corpus-based evidence of language change, see Curzan, forthcoming). Historians of English also emphasize that the history of English continues around us every day; in that way, examining the linguistic variation in contemporary corpora, which more often include spoken data, is research on the ongoing history of English. And as Claridge (forthcoming) points out, all contemporary corpora will technically become historical corpora if we just wait thirty years.

While corpus designers aim to be reasonably representative across multiple variables, a historical corpus can only be as comprehensive as the available texts. For the history of English, there are significant gaps in the evidence available, particularly the further back in time one goes. The entire corpus of Old English texts is only about 3.5 million running words, and most of these texts are in formal genres: religious texts, historical chronicles, literature, etc. This dearth of texts that might capture more colloquial English continues through at least the Early Modern English period, although the CEEC provides invaluable material for the fifteenth through nineteenth centuries. At the same time, historical corpora often include some less canonical texts, making these texts part of the readily available evidence for studying a language's development. There are also large "unprincipled" historical collections of texts available which can be used for historical research, as discussed below.

Survey of Historical Corpora of English

The *Helsinki Corpus*, which contains about 1.5 million words of text from ca. 750–1710 and was completed in 1991, remains a central resource for historians of the English language. It allows scholars to explore systematically changes from Old English through Early Modern English (for details on the corpus, see Kytö 1991). The *Helsinki Corpus* continues to be a source for "benchmark" general results about overall historical trends that can be tested and supplemented by studies based on specialized corpora that provide more extensive coverage of a specific genre, of a historical period, of a dialect, etc.

Since 1991, many historical corpora have supplemented the *Helsinki Corpus*. ARCHER adopts a similar approach in terms of covering multiple genres and it extends the historical coverage forward: 1650–1990. *ARCHER* has allowed very interesting research on the historical development of English genres. Biber and Finegan (1997), for example, describe the increasing differentiation of fiction and news texts from medical, science, and legal prose, both in terms of style and intended audience, from the seventeenth century through the present. As fiction and news have become more popular registers, they have reversed an early trend toward more "literate" styles and have adopted many more "oral" characteristics. In contrast, medical, scientific, and legal texts, which have become highly specialized registers, have followed a steady development toward more "literate" styles with little to no narrative.

Other historical corpora focus on particular genres: for example, correspondence/ letters (e.g., the CEEC, 1417–1681), dialogues (e.g., *The Corpus of English Dialogues*, 1560–1760), newspapers (e.g., *Zurich English Newspapers Corpus*, 1661–1791), medical texts (e.g., the *Corpus of Early English Medical Writing*, 1375–1750), and pamphlets (e.g., the *Lampeter Corpus*, 1640–1740). Others have included language from only one regional variety, such as the *Helsinki Corpus of Older Scots* (1450–1700). All these corpora have narrowed the historical range of coverage from the scope of the *Helsinki Corpus*, anywhere from a few decades to a few centuries. (Claridge (forthcoming) provides a more detailed survey of currently available historical corpora.)

As mentioned above, some of the largest electronic collections of historical texts available right now are not systematically compiled for linguistic research. For example, the *English Poetry Database* contains works by more than 1,300 poets, from 600–1900. It includes only poetry, no prose, and it was not designed to provide balanced coverage by author, region, or historical period; but with these caveats, researchers can mine the data for historical linguistic evidence, be that the phonological information that rhyming pairs provide or the morphosyntactic or semantic uses of lexical items. The *Dictionary of Old English Corpus* makes available electronically the entire collection of Old English texts used for that project; given how little Old English material has survived, it is immensely valuable to have all this text available electronically. The Middle English Compendium offers access to over sixty full-text electronic versions of Middle English works (in the *Middle English Prose and Verse Corpus*), as well as all of the material currently available electronically in the *Middle English Dictionary*. The entire *Oxford English Dictionary* (OED), including revisions for the new edition as they are completed, is online, making it a fully searchable collection not only of quotations but also of, for example, etymological information. Again, it is important to note that the *OED* was not created with this kind of linguistic searching in mind; the selection of quotations favors particular authors and historical periods, a search can pull up the same quotation multiple times from different headwords, and the quotations come with no textual context and limited sociolinguistic information. That said, given their relatively large size, these electronic text collections still offer a rich and valuable resource to historical

linguists gathering evidence of language change, particularly of less frequent linguistic phenomena, and they can complement more traditional corpus-based studies (see Curzan & Palmer 2006).

For examining more recent developments in Modern English or even change in progress, there are several linguistic corpora, including *Lancaster-Oslo/Bergen* (LOB), *Freiburg-LOB*, *Brown*, *Freiburg-Brown*, *London-Lund*, and the *Corpus of London Teenage Talk* (COLT) – all available on CD-ROM – and the *Michigan Corpus of Academic Spoken English* (MICASE), available free online. The largest and clearly pre-eminent corpus of both written and spoken English (100 million words total), the *British National Corpus* (BNC), is now available outside the European Union; the second release of the *American National Corpus* (ANC), with over 20 million words, is available through the Linguistic Data Consortium. Some instructors and scholars in the United States and elsewhere have been exploring the possibilities offered by text collections such as the *Michigan Modern English Collection*, the *American Verse Project*, and the *African-American Verse Database*, as well as newspaper databases (e.g., *The New York Times Online*, *Lexis-Nexis*), for studying the written language of the present day and over the modern period.

Corpus-Based Historical Research Methodologies in Action

Histories of English can sometimes frame linguistic developments as a process of the language moving from one feature to another (e.g., the earlier third-person singular verb ending *–eth* as in *speaketh* being replaced by *–s* as in *speaks*) rather than as a process of speakers, over time, shifting their language use such that they favor one linguistic feature or variant over another. These concise statements about changes in English provide us critical information about the endpoints of a given linguistic change, but they tell us little or nothing about *how* the change happened; in other words, they do not give us a sense of a change's transmission or implementation across time and speech communities. For example, were there patterns to which speakers used the innovative form *speaks* and which speakers maintained the more conservative *speaketh*, while this linguistic shift was in progress? In fact, corpus-based studies suggest there were; for instance, women generally seem to have led in the adoption of the innovative *–s* forms (cf. Nevalainen & Raumolin-Brunberg 2003).

The endpoints of specific language changes are clearly important, but they are not the whole story. Language change is much messier and always involves language variation. We know from observing language change in real time in current varieties of English that "language change" occurs when some speakers – often younger speakers – in some speech communities – be those based on region, ethnicity, socioe-conomic status, or other factors – gradually come to favor a different language variant than other speakers. For example, many speakers in northern cities in the Midwestern United States are coming to favor a pronunciation with /e/ rather than with /æ/ in words such as *bag*; or younger speakers across the United States show an increasing tendency to use *like* rather than *say* or *go*, as in *I'm like that was a great movie*

and he's like whatever. Two hundred years from now, histories of English will be able to look back and say that /æ/ "became" /e/ in particular regions and that *go* and *say* were replaced in certain registers by *like*, but the process on the ground, with real speakers, is both more subtle and more untidy. In short, corpora provide historical linguists with one key tool for drawing a more detailed picture of the sociolinguistic as well as grammatical and textual factors involved in the implementation of a given language change.

Most corpus-based research on the history of English has focused on morphosyntactic developments; these linguistic features are readily and reliably searchable, require large data sets to return a sufficient number of examples, and are of continuing historical and theoretical interest. For example, the rise and fall of different roles of periphrastic *do*, one of the most discussed developments of the Early Modern English period, have been charted using corpus-based methodologies (cf. Rissanen 1991; Nurmi 1999). In the Early Modern English period, auxiliary *do* gradually becomes the preferred form for negative constructions (e.g., *I do not know* vs. *I know not*), for yes-no questions (e.g., *Do you say?* vs. *Say you?*), and for negative imperatives (e.g., *Do not go* vs. *Go not*). As Raumolin-Brunberg and Nurmi (1997) demonstrate, while the endpoint is clear (the rise of auxiliary *do* to become the standard in these constructions), more data (perhaps especially from more vernacular sources) can disrupt the linearity suggested by such generalizations; they show how, for example, the "decline" of affirmative *do* includes both rises and falls in its frequency as it competes with other variants. Recent corpus-based work has examined the rise in use of quotative *like*, some of it debunking the myth that women are necessarily leading this change, examining the construction in varieties other than American and British English (see D'Arcy 2004, among others), and showing the expansion of *like*'s discourse functions (see Barbieri 2005, among others).

Corpora can also help scholars track semantic shifts. Heikkinen and Tissari (2002) examine the semantics of the Old English noun *bliss*, which appears almost entirely in religious contexts in Old English, alongside the semantics of the adjective *happy* in Early Modern and Modern English, which undergoes secularization to take on more personal and material meanings. McEnery (2006) employs a range of corpora to trace the history of "bad language" and speakers' attitudes toward it. A more current example would be the very recent shift of *peruse* from meaning "to read carefully, to pore over" to "to skim, to scan." Contemporary corpora of spoken American English show the change well underway if not complete for many younger speakers; corpora of contemporary written American English will then capture the spread of this change across written genres.

Of particular theoretical interest are the studies of lexical items that seem to have undergone grammaticalization, including the pronominalization of *one* (Rissanen 1997); the grammaticalization of emerging modals such as *gotta*, *gonna*, and *wanna* (Krug 2000); the grammaticalization of a written phrase such as *videlicet* in court texts (Moore 2004); and the formation of complex prepositions such as *in view of* (Hoffmann 2005). Corpora allow scholars to analyze the role of frequency and collocational

patterns in the grammaticalization of these constructions. (See HISTORY OF ENGLISH SYNTAX.)

More recently, as corpora with written dialogue (from drama to court depositions) have become available, scholars have exploited corpora to examine discourse features. For example, Jucker (2002) provides a historical look at five discourse markers, drawing on data from plays, fiction, and trial records in the *Helsinki Corpus*, describing the process of pragmaticalization as well as the relative frequency of each discourse marker. As mentioned above, taking text types rather than linguistic constructions as the focus, studies of the development of specific registers have also enhanced our understanding of the history of English and the changing relationship of spoken and written language. To date, historical phonology has generally relied on more traditionally compiled evidence.

The rest of this section provides an extended example of the types of questions electronic corpora can help scholars pursue and how one could approach the research. Many histories of English include multiple versions of the Lord's Prayer, written in different historical periods, to capture some of the changes that the English language has undergone. If we take just the first two phrases, we already see many differences, including shifts in the relative pronoun (in Modern English, *that*, *which*, or *who/whom/whose*), here in reference to "our Father" (all texts except the Modern English are taken from Horobin & Smith 2002: 7).

Old English (West Saxon dialect, late ninth century)
þū ūre fæder, þe eart on heofonum, sīe þīn nama gehālgod.
Middle English (Central Midlands, ca. 1380)
Oure fadir, þat art in heuenys, halewid be þi name.
Early Modern English (Book of Common Prayer, 1549)
Our Father, which are in heaven, Hallowed be thy Name.
Modern English (Book of Common Prayer, 1928)
Our Father, who art in heaven, Hallowed be thy Name.

As standard grammars of Old English describe, *þe* functions as a relative pronoun or marker, referring to both animate and inanimate antecedents. Throughout the Middle English period, *þat* (*that*) and later also *which* are used consistently instead of the fairly rare *who* to refer to persons; at the same time, *whose* and *whom* are both used as relatives (*whose* for both people and things – a notable asymmetry in the pronoun system; Mustanoja 1960: 199–201). It seems to be in the sixteenth century that *who* becomes established as a relative pronoun for human antecedents but even then it is less frequent than *that* or *which* with human antecedents (as exemplified by *Our Father which* in the 1549 text).

Corpus-based methodologies allow us not only to test these assertions, but also to examine whether there are patterns to the historical variation. If we were working with a syntactically tagged corpus, we could begin by searching for all relative pronouns in given periods; however, as noted above, very few corpora are so tagged. If

we were working with a small corpus, we could search all instances of *which*, *that*, *þe*, *who*, etc., but we would obtain a lot of extra or erroneous hits (e.g., demonstrative uses of *that*). Another possibility is to search selected strings such as *a/the person that/which/who*, *a/the woman that/which/who*, etc. In searches of texts from earlier periods, we would also have to handle all the spelling variants of the relevant forms (e.g., *þe*, *ðe*, *the*), unless the corpus were lemmatized.

Clearly by Modern English, the shift to *who* as the primary relative pronoun for human antecedents has happened. A search of the electronic *Modern English Collection*, which spans literature from the late eighteenth century through the twentieth century, shows very few uses of *that* in reference to some selected personal antecedents; but importantly, it does show these uses, particularly in spoken text such as the Clarence Thomas hearings (see table 57.1.) The numbers for nominative versus objective occurrences of *that* in reference to a personal antecedent are intriguing, and they suggest the benefits of corpus-based work: the data can reveal patterns we do not expect. These numbers raise the possibility that *that* is functioning in some ways as a substitute for *whom* – a form with which speakers are becoming less comfortable – when an object form is required. This is the kind of usage that prescriptive grammars tend to ignore and yet speakers often exploit – and that surfaces in corpus-based research, which examines a range of language in use. (For a corpus-based study of the relatively rare contemporary uses of *which* with human antecedents, see Mair 1998.)

Prescription on the correct use of the relative pronouns *who/whom/whose* with human antecedents seems to be fairly recent, and I address it briefly here because it highlights the fact that researchers must always bring to bear historical information and critical analytic tools to develop the implications of the data that corpora help us compile. Grossman puts the prescriptive rule succinctly in her highly prescriptive book *The Grammatically Correct Handbook* (1997: 136): "Who comes after anyone who breathes . . . Things that don't breathe (and animals you're not crazy about) are followed by 'that' . . ." Two centuries earlier, however, Lindley Murray, in his influential grammar

Table 57.1   Search results from the *Modern English Collection*

Search String	Frequency	Search String	Frequency
a/the person who	266	*a/the woman who*	365
a/the person whom	21	*a/the woman whom*	59
a/the person whose	12	*a/the woman whose*	25
a/the person that	29	*a/the woman that*	25
	16 nominative		14 nominative
	13 objective		11 objective
a/the person which	1 (dated 1582)	*a/the woman which*	0

of 1795, himself used phrases such as *the Lord that* and *he that* in his section on relative pronouns. Chronologically, it appears that prescription on the use of *who* forms for persons follows usage: it increases as the *who* forms become the most frequently used. At the same time, Sidney Greenbaum's observation in his modern descriptive grammar that both *who* forms and *that* can be used for persons does not capture the overwhelming use of *who* forms. In his 1921 book *Language*, Edward Sapir notes, in a footnote, that *that* is often used instead of *whom*, but he sees this as the drift away from *who/whom* as a relative pronoun. Instead, it appears that *that* may be serving as a stop-gap measure in the face of the demise of *whom* (perhaps because some prescriptive grammarians are too worried about the demise of *whom*!).

How might the shift from *that* to *who/whom* with personal antecedents have happened? As described above, corpora can help linguists view the details of a change's spread, from speaker to speaker, community to community, generation to generation. To answer this question, a corpus such as the CEEC, with its more colloquial letters and extensive sociolinguistic information about the authors, could be very valuable. Scholars have used this corpus to test hypotheses such as the role of gender in language change – which might well be relevant here if the case of the relative pronoun *which* replacing *the which* in the Early Modern English period is any indication, as it was a change apparently led by women.

Modern sociolinguistic research has developed two general principles about the role of women in language change: (1) women tend to favor incoming prestige forms more than men in change from above, given their higher sensitivity to language standards; (2) women tend to be innovators in change from below. Historical corpus-based studies of gender have both confirmed and challenged these modern findings, and more empirical studies of earlier changes in English will continue to enrich and complicate sociolinguistic theory on these questions. Nevalainen and Raumolin-Brunberg (2003) list the following as changes led by women: the rise of *you*, *my/thy*, and *its*; the use of singular third-person *–s* instead of *–th*; the use of *do* in negative statements; and the use of *which* instead of *the which*. All this historical evidence supports the hypothesis that women lead in changes from below. However, other historical corpus-based findings challenge the principle that women favor prestige forms in change from above. As Nevalainen (2002) demonstrates, in the early sixteenth century, when multiple negation was gradually being replaced by single negation in Standard English, men promoted the change. (See ISSUES OF GENDER IN MODERN ENGLISH.)

Corpus data can often challenge linguists' intuitions about language change, observed larger historical trends, and modern hypotheses about the effects of sociolinguistic factors. For example, given the overall shift in the history of English from a more synthetic to a more analytic syntax, one would expect the periphrastic forms of comparative and superlative adjectives (e.g., *more gentle, most stupid*) to come to dominate the inflected forms (e.g., *gentler, stupidest*). However, Kytö and Romaine (2000) demonstrate that the inflected forms have been reasserting themselves since the Early Modern English period – with British English leading American English; according to this study, inflected forms now constitute the majority in current forms

of both varieties. Kytö and Romaine (1997) also exploit corpora to examine which adjectives tend to favor uninflected forms (e.g., adjectives ending with *-ful*, *-ous*) and which favor inflected forms (e.g., adjectives ending with *-y/-ly*, *-le*). Interested scholars of the history of English could follow up on this research by pursuing, for example, other factors potentially involved in the distribution of inflected versus uninflected forms, such as clipping (is it *comfier* or *more comfy?*) or the proliferation of *-y* forms in current English in innovative constructions (e.g., *spendy*, *textbooky*).

Conclusion

Corpora allow historians of English to test generalizations about developments in the language and create more detailed, nuanced descriptions of the implementation of these linguistic developments. Corpora have the power to surprise us, leading us to new insights and to questions we did not realize we needed or wanted to ask. As the descriptions above also make clear, corpora can only be as smart as their designers and users, who must create searches that exploit the corpora intelligently and carefully and who must provide the critical, qualitative analysis that gives meaning to and complements more quantitative results. And while corpora open up entirely new possibilities because they enhance the speed and scope of research, they also introduce new sources of error, from a reliance on edited works to the foibles of a computer trying to read human language, which in the end will always have idiosyncrasies. Historians of English should see corpora as one more tool – and an extremely valuable one – in the toolbox available for furthering our understanding of the history of English, used best when used with other critical tools such as close reading of single texts, work with original manuscripts, careful analysis of patterns unique to individual speakers or speech communities, and a healthy dose of linguistic knowledge and scholarly intuition.

Further Work with Corpora

For good introductory textbooks on corpus linguistics, see Biber et al. (1998), McEnery and Wilson (1996), and Meyer (2002). For a discussion of ways to incorporate historical corpora into teaching, see Curzan (2000).

Availability is an issue for some of the corpora discussed in this chapter. The *Helsinki Corpus of English Texts*, the *Lampeter Corpus of Early Modern English Tracts*, the *Helsinki Corpus of Older Scots*, and several other corpora are available publicly on CD-ROM; many other historical corpora (including the *Corpus of Early English Correspondence* and the *Corpus of Early English Medical Writing*) are still in the development phase, available for pilot research projects but not for public consumption; and the distribution of other historical corpora such as *ARCHER* and *ICAMET* has so far been hindered by copyright restrictions.

References and Further Reading

Barbieri, F. (2005). Quotative use in American English. *Journal of English Linguistics*, 33 (3), 222–56.

Biber, D., Conrad, S., & Reppen, R. (1998). *Corpus Linguistics: Investigating Language: Structure and Use*. Cambridge: Cambridge University Press.

Biber, D. & Finegan, E. (1997). Diachronic relations among speech-based and written registers in English. In T. Nevalainen & L. Kahlas-Tarkka. (eds.), *To Explain the Present: Studies in the Changing English Language in Honour of Matti Rissanen* (pp. 253–75). Helsinki: Société Néophilologique.

Claridge, C. (forthcoming). Historical corpora. In A. Lüdeling, M. Kytö, & T. McEnery (eds.), *Handbook of Corpus Linguistics*. New York: Mouton de Gruyter.

Curzan, A. (2000). English historical corpora in the classroom. *Journal of English Linguistics*, 28 (1), 77–89.

Curzan, A. (forthcoming). Historical corpus linguistics and evidence of language change. In A. Lüdeling, M. Kytö, & T. McEnery (eds.), *Handbook of Corpus Linguistics*. New York: Mouton de Gruyter.

Curzan, A. & Palmer, C. C. (2006). The importance of historical corpora, reliability, and reading. In R. Facchinetti & M. Rissanen (eds.), *Corpus-Based Studies in Diachronic English* (pp. 17–34). Bern: Peter Lang.

D'Arcy, A. (2004). Contextualizing St. John's youth English within the Canadian quotative system. *Journal of English Linguistics*, 32 (4), 323–45.

Grossman, E. (1997). *The Grammatically Correct Handbook: A Lively and Unorthodox Review of Common English, for the Linguistically Challenged*. New York: Hyperion.

Heikkinen, K. & Tissari, H. (2002). *Gefeoh* and *Geblissa* or Happy Birthday! On Old English *bliss* and Modern English *happy*. In H. Raumolin-Brunberg, M. Nevala, A. Nurmi, & M. Rissanen (eds.), *Variation Past and Present: VARIENG Studies on English for Terttu Nevalainen* (pp. 59–76). Helsinki: Société Néophilologique.

Hoffmann, S. (2005). *Grammaticalization and English Complex Prepositions: A Corpus-Based Study*. New York: Routledge.

Horobin, S. & Smith, J. (2002). *An Introduction to Middle English*. Edinburgh: Edinburgh University Press.

Jucker, A. H. (2002). Discourse markers in Early Modern English. In R. Watts & P. Trudgill (eds.), *Alternative Histories of English* (pp. 210–30). New York: Routledge.

Krug, M. (2000). *Emerging English Modals: A Corpus-Based Study of Grammaticalization*. New York: Mouton de Gruyter.

Kytö, M. (compiler). (1991). *Manual to the Diachronic Part of the Helsinki Corpus of English Texts: Coding Conventions and Lists of Source Texts*. Helsinki: Department of English, University of Helsinki.

Kytö, M. & Romaine, S. (1997). Competing forms of adjective comparison in Modern English: What could be more quicker and easier and more effective? In T. Nevalainen & L. Kahlas-Tarkka (eds.), *To Explain the Present: Studies in the Changing English Language in Honour of Matti Rissanen* (pp. 329–52). Helsinki: Société Néophilologique.

Kytö, M. & Romaine, S. (2000). Adjective comparison and standardization processes in American and British English from 1620 to the present. In L. Wright (ed.), *The Development of Standard English, 1300–1800* (pp. 171–94). Cambridge: Cambridge University Press.

McEnery, T. (2006). *Swearing in English: Bad Language, Purity and Power from 1586 to the Present*. New York: Routledge.

McEnery, T. & Wilson, A. (1996). *Corpus Linguistics*. Edinburgh: Edinburgh University Press.

Mair, C. (1998). *Man/woman which* . . . – Last of the old, or first of the new? In A. Renouf (ed.), *Explorations in Corpus Linguistics* (pp. 123–33). Amsterdam: Rodopi.

Meyer, C. F. (2002). *English Corpus Linguistics: An Introduction*. Cambridge: Cambridge University Press.

Michigan Corpus of Academic Spoken English. www.micase.umdl.umich.edu/m/micase/.

Modern English Collection. www.hti.umich.edu/p/pd-modeng/.

Moore, C. (2004). Representing speech in early English. PhD dissertation, University of Michigan.

Murray, L. (1968 [1795]). *English Grammar*. Menston: Scolar.

Mustanoja, T. (1960). *A Middle English Syntax*. Helsinki: Société Néophilologique.

Nevalainen, T. (2002). Women's writing as evidence for linguistic continuity and change in Early Modern English. In R. Watts & P. Trudgill (eds.), *Alternative Histories of English* (pp. 191–209). New York: Routledge.

Nevalainen, T. & Raumolin-Brunberg, H. (2003). *Historical Sociolinguistics*. London: Longman.

Nurmi, A. (1999). *A Social History of Periphrastic Do*. Mémoires de la Société Néophilologique 56. Helsinki: Société Néophilologique.

Raumolin-Brunberg, H. & Nurmi, A. (1997). Dummies on the move: prop-ONE and affirmative DO in the 17th century. In T. Nevalainen & L. Kahlas-Tarkka (eds.), *To Explain the Present: Studies in the Changing English Language in Honour of Matti Rissanen* (pp. 395–417). Helsinki: Société Néophilologique.

Rissanen, M. (1991). Spoken language and the history of DO-periphrasis. In D. Kastovsky (ed.), *Historical English Syntax*. Topics in English Language 2 (pp. 321–42). New York: Mouton de Gruyter.

Rissanen, M. (1997). The pronominalization of *one*. In M. Rissanen, M. Kytö, & K. Heikkonen (eds.), *Grammaticalization at Work: Studies of Long-Term Developments in English* (pp. 87–143). New York: Mouton de Grutyer.

58

Sociolinguistics

Robin Tolmach Lakoff

What is Sociolinguistics?

Sociolinguistics is the study of language in its social context. That definition includes both the way in which humans use differences in linguistic form to determine the social positions of themselves and others, and the way in which speakers tailor their linguistic behaviors to the social context in which they are speaking. Examples of the first include dialect differences, gender differences, and other encodings of social position and status, and the ways in which we as hearers use these differences to determine: Is the other *like* or *unlike* me (do we, in some sense, "speak the same language")? Is my interlocutor more powerful or less powerful than I am, or just as powerful? Examples of the second include our ability to arrange our discourse on a scale of formality: we talk one way (in terms of vocabulary and grammar) with intimates, another with more distant acquaintances and strangers.

Sociolinguistics is the most socially relevant of all aspects of linguistics, since it talks about how people use (and abuse) language socially and politically. Sociolinguistics uses "core" linguistics (phonology, morphology, syntax, semantics, and pragmatics) to explain how the forms of language, as analyzed in these areas, are given social meanings.

Sociolinguistics has only recently separated itself from core linguistics, although (as has been argued by Labov 1972a) it can reasonably be seen as the true basic or core linguistic area, since it deals with the intersection of language form and social construction, a connection that is at the root of our humanness. The term itself was not much used before the late 1960s, when Labov and his co-workers began to use it to differentiate between the work they were doing and the autonomous linguistics of the Chomskyan school (transformational generative grammar). Prior to the Chomskyan domination of the field and during the ascendancy of American Structuralism, as first defined by Bloomfield (1933) and the major linguistic theory in America from the 1920s through the early 1960s, a lot of what was considered, simply, as

"linguistics" included what today would be categorized as "sociolinguistics": dialectology, cross-cultural comparisons, English usage, and so on. But once core linguistics was defined as "linguistics" proper, what was left became, by default, marginalized as, for instance, psycholinguistics and sociolinguistics.

Sociolinguistics is inherently interdisciplinary. It draws from and contributes to the knowledge base of many other disciplines: most obviously, cultural anthropology, psychology, and education; less obviously, literary theory, political science, and sociology. The same kinds of work may be assigned to one field rather than another purely on the basis of the departmental affiliation of its author.

In *Language* (1933), Bloomfield defined the subject of linguistics as oral, spontaneous, and decontextualized forms of language, studied in an antimentalistic (non-interpretive) way. But this definition, useful and productive as it was, excludes many of the most important and fascinating aspects of language. Much of what is most significant about language lies in its social uses: the distinction it makes between public and private, oral and written, ephemeral and eternal, spontaneous and non-spontaneous. A complete explanatory theory of language would need to discuss all of these, and would therefore have to include in its database examples of each, analyzed as situated in their social and psychological contexts.

Besides the constraint against the non-spontaneous, including the written, traditionally American linguists (both Bloomfieldian and Chomskyan) have shared another taboo, avoiding the study of "structure above (or beyond) the sentence level." There are reasonable justifications for this. Within Bloomfieldian antimentalism, the recognition of discursive structures as rule-governed entails interpretation. An analyst must discuss what makes a narrative "good"– satisfying to its creators and hearers. Within transformational grammar, the study of units consisting of combinations of sentences is simply not possible; analysis begins and ends at the sentence level. Moreover, syntactic rules are formal, involving the presence and ordering of concrete units: noun phrase, main verb, relative clause and so on; the more amorphous "idea units" of narrative and other kinds of connected discourse are not accessible to such analysis. Hence, until quite recently, the study of connected text "above the sentence level" has rarely been attempted within linguistics, socio- or otherwise (as exceptions, see Labov & Waletzky 1967; Labov 1972b).

I mention the foregoing because the rest of this essay violates conventional linguistic theory and practice. Many of my colleagues would not consider what follows (socio)linguistics. But definitions and fields must change, if they are to progress, and extending the domain of (socio)linguistics to include larger and more abstract units and non-spontaneous forms of utterance is essential: in complex and literate societies such as ours, these kinds of discourse are the principal means by which we make sense, create cohesion, and define ourselves as group members or non-members. The example I am using studies the construction, deconstruction, and possible reconstruction of gender roles through a story that made its way through various American media during the winter and spring of the year 2005, and thereby illustrates the way American society uses literate narrative to understand itself.

Methods of Data Collection

The aim of sociolinguistic data collection is to find spontaneous language used naturally. This turns out to be a difficult task. Labov (e.g. 1972a) talks about the "Observer's Paradox" as a hindrance to that ideal. The Observer's Paradox states that the investigator needs to get spontaneous and natural data, but all possible (and ethical) methods of data collection interpose an element of unnaturalness or non-spontaneity. The most successful work minimizes that element, but it is always there. There are two major methods of data collection, as follows.

The interview or questionnaire. Suppose the investigator wishes to study the ways in which speakers of Standard American English can respond to compliments. A simple way to get this kind of data is through a questionnaire: volunteers are asked to provide a list (orally and face to face, or in writing on a form) of the ways they (or people in general) might appropriately respond to an utterance intended and understood as a compliment. The subject might be asked to produce a list, or be asked to evaluate (perhaps on a numerical scale) a set of possible responses. Often the subject is offered a brief scenario within which the compliment-response pair occurs. After a suitable number of interviews, the investigator tallies up the percentages for each response and draws conclusions based on them.

The interview method has some advantages. The interview itself is short, making it relatively easy to get subjects to cooperate and to tabulate the responses. It is possible to get a great deal of data from many subjects. But the method necessarily creates the Observer's Paradox: speakers are asked to judge or produce examples without contextualization or at best in artificial contexts. Hence these responses do not represent what speakers actually do, but rather only what speakers think they do, or think other people do, or think they should do (because it's polite, normal, elegant, etc.) or think the investigator wants them to say they do. The more interesting (and, often, touchy) the topic (e.g., gender differences in linguistic behavior), the more probable it is that the subject's responses will be inaccurate. For these reasons, many sociolinguists avoid this method, and the principal journal of the field, *Language in Society*, will not accept for publication articles based on interview-generated data.

The recording of spontaneous discourse. Conversation analysis makes great use of this method, usually through the use of a tape recorder. In this method, an investigator places a tape recorder in the midst of a group of people who are having, or are about to have, a "natural" conversation, e.g., at a dinner party. The investigator later transcribes the tapes, and the transcripts are analyzed. Patterns emerge representing the forms of typical conversation: turn-taking rules, gaps and overlaps, the structure of adjacency pairs (like question-answer or conversational openings).

Ethically participants must be asked in advance whether they are willing to participate, and the tape recorder must be kept in plain sight throughout the conversation. Investigators claim that after about ten minutes subjects forget about the tape

and start speaking completely "naturally," but since it is (ethically) impossible to do a contrastive study with a concealed tape recorder, we can't know this for sure.

Taping of spontaneous utterance has a clear advantage over interview elicitation because data are naturally produced and therefore much closer to people's real behavior. It is an excellent method for collecting examples of patterns that recur frequently (e.g., those of conversational interaction). It is useful, too, because it avoids introspection: investigators need not deal with the meanings of contributions, only with their structures. But for a study of possible responses to compliments, this method is impracticable. Compliments are relatively rare: one would have to collect reams of tapes of conversations in order to get a usably large amount of data. Too many important linguistic behaviors are off-limits for this kind of study.

Interpretation and the Role of the Investigator's Mind

Bloomfield's antimentalist stance required that the investigator discover a corpus, not make sense of it. Therefore making generalizations and providing explanations for the data are outside the realm of structuralists and their sociolinguistic descendants. There were good reasons for Bloomfield's position: trained as an anthropologist, he was wary of pre-scientific anthropological tradition, which permitted a western observer to see his subjects through western eyes, as "strange," "inexplicable," and, inevitably, "inferior." Not only did this perspective produce intellectually untenable understandings of non-western cultures, it offered excuses for socially and politically disastrous actions by individuals and governments throughout the colonial period. The interpretation of cultures sharply different from one's own was also apt to produce false results because of incorrect contextualization. Western investigators did not share the cultural background of their subjects, and therefore could not understand the meanings of their utterances. Structuralists felt that only by taking themselves completely out of the picture could investigators avoid the perils of mentalism.

That was the accepted assumption of American linguistics until the late 1950s. It meant that linguists could not effactually study syntax, semantics, or pragmatics, all of which – to be done intelligently – require some kinds of interpretation by someone, subjects or investigators, or both.

Transformational generative grammar offered an alternative, but provided no corrective to the corruptibility and unreliability inherent in introspective methods. The two sides of the argument exist within sociolinguistics: should sociolinguistic research be purely empirical and non-interpretive? Or are there types of research and specific circumstances in which introspective methods, carefully controlled, have a place and in fact are essential? Without being able to say *why* speaker A said utterance B in context C, or what B was apt to mean, in that context, to hearer D, a great deal of what is interesting about language use and its consequences is inaccessible to study. For instance:

- Everything that involves interpretive ideas: "power," "stereotype," and "identity."
- Understanding and misunderstanding the inexplicit (e.g., contextualization cues (Gumperz 1982), politeness (Brown & Levinson 1987)).
- The creation of social connections (and disconnections) via discursive choices (e.g., "speaking for another" (Schiffrin 1994), discourse markers (Schiffrin 1987)).
- How we communicate by not communicating (e.g., metacommunication and conversational style (Tannen 1984); conversational implicature (Grice 1975)).

Without theory and methodology allowing an investigator to say things like, "the speaker, in saying Y, meant to communicate X," or "the speaker meant to communicate X, but the addressee understood Y," none of these crucial concepts are available for investigation. While several important areas are still open to sociolinguistic research, for instance dialectology and variation (e.g., Labov 1972c), and conversation analysis (e.g., Sacks et al. 1974), it would impoverish the field to discard the former topics. Labov's methods remain the gold standard for pure empiricism, but even he is edgy about his important work on narrative structure (e.g., Labov 1972b), since it violates his own caveats.

In determining how to go about their work, sociolinguists must find the best compromise between the need to make use of rigorous methods of discovery and analysis, and the desire to study everything that is of interest in language use. I am aware of no generally agreed upon resolution to this conflict.

Sociolinguistics, again as initiated by Labov (1972c), has had significant things to say about another area of linguistics often considered totally unrelated: historical linguistics. Labov's work addresses a paradox: language always changes over time, but at any moment a language (e.g., Standard American English) seems invariant and homogeneous. How does homogeneous synchronic structure turn into diachronic change?

Labov's answer was that language is always in flux; there are always variations across or within seemingly invariant speech communities. Most of these variations are tiny and imperceptible to speakers (hence the appearance of invariance). Over time, these tiny differences aggregate into the large shifts that are recognized as diachronic change. Labov doesn't say exactly how this occurs.

The Changing Role of Gender in Public Discourse

Over the last thirty to forty years, questions about gender differences have been raised in academia (across many fields), the sciences, religion, and politics. Many answers given by experts violate conventional wisdom and question comforting age-old stereotypes. During the 1990s many of these controversies receded in favor of new understandings of gender and gender roles, as women showed that they could succeed

in areas previously reserved for men, and as everyone showed that rigid gender roles and expectations could change.

Those conclusions may have been premature. Gender is the oldest and psychologically most salient distinction among human beings. Even stereotypical differences between races (and classes, much less so) prove extraordinarily hard to overcome. So it should not be surprising that the old ideas never died, but merely were in hibernation.

The moment of reversal was September 11, 2001. The horrific events of that day profoundly shook Americans' group identity: the sense of America's invulnerability and supremacy over all other nations. The events of 9/11 occurred, moreover, during a conservative turn already under way, politically and culturally.

If we see the changes in the American perception of gender roles between the 1970s and 2000 as a profound shift in personal identity, add to that the upheaval in group identity caused by 9/11, and superimpose a conservative mood, then the apparently quiescent question of gender differences would naturally re-emerge. So, for instance, a seemingly minor comment by Harvard President Lawrence H. Summers was all that was needed to arouse an impassioned dialogue on gender. Summers' offhand remarks, in the socio-political context in which they were delivered, attracted an inordinate amount of both public and private attention, and therfore passed what I have called (Lakoff 2000) the Undue Attention Test (UAT).

The Summers Case as a Study in Sociolinguistics

On January 14, 2005, Harvard President Lawrence H. Summers delivered what were later characterized as "off the cuff" remarks at a conference at the National Bureau of Economic Research in Cambridge, Massachusetts, convened on the topic "Diversifying the Science and Engineering Workforce: Women, Underrepresented Minorities, and their S. & E. Careers." In his remarks, Summers suggested some reasons women might be underrepresented in university science, mathematics, and engineering faculties. Such positions, he suggested, "require extraordinary commitments of time and energy [including] 80-hour weeks. . . . Few married women are willing to accept such sacrifices" (Dillon 2005). Secondly, he cited research showing that more high school boys than girls score very high and very low on standardized math tests, differences that "possibly" arose from biological differences between the sexes.

Immediately, the storm broke.

We can read the controversy as a continuing story, or narrative, running through the popular media between January 17 (the Dillon article just cited) and late spring 2005. I am basing my discussion principally on articles that appeared in the *New York Times* over that period, with a few from other print media. But the argument went far beyond these sources, not only in print but on television and radio news, magazine, and talk shows. I am concentrating on the *Times* as the US paper of record, but a great many similar stories occurred in all these formats.

To know how to "read" the story, that is, interpret both the explicit content and the profusion and direction of the reportage, the reader must be aware of the social, psychological, and political context within which the events took place. Otherwise, the story is bewildering. Why should anyone – let alone everyone – care what a university president, speaking well outside his own field of expertise (economics), hypothesizes about the scarcity of women in science? During the period January 17 to May 31, 2005, Lexis-Nexis lists 258 stories in major papers containing the name "Lawrence H. Summers." By comparison, for the same period in 2004, only 30 such documents are listed. From this perspective, the case passes the UAT: an inordinate amount of public discourse about a topic that would seem to be lacking in general interest.

But stories that pass the UAT do so because, when their context is fully understood, the interest is far from "undue": the topic represents something that participants in the culture find, at that point in time, to be highly salient and problematic. The "problem" in this case is the recurrent question of differences between the sexes. Do differences in men's and women's success in highly prestigious fields like the sciences still exist – despite attempts to equalize the playing field – because of the innate differences Summers alluded to, in which case nothing much can or should be done to rectify the situation; or because of social differences, including prejudice against women within the scientific community, and unequal distribution of child care and housework between members of couples?

The questions Summers raised had been dealt with in various disciplines, in many ways, again and again over thirty-five years. But in 2005 they could still provoke passionate back-and-forth response for several reasons.

First, the topic itself is inflammatory and unresolved. If the differences should turn out to be biologically based, that might lead many to conclude that women are inherently inferior in other ways as well, and some would take that conclusion as an invitation to undo legislatively the accomplishments of the last thirty years. If, on the other hand, Summers' assertion proved incorrect, changes would have to be made in hiring and promotion practices by departments and universities that wanted to seem equitable, and by couples who wanted egalitarian relationships.

Secondly, the source of the statement was no ordinary guy, but a man with a great deal of intellectual clout. Not only had Summers been President Clinton's Secretary of the Treasury, but he was currently the head of the most ancient and prestigious of American universities. Among the non-academic public, Harvard is Harvard and everyone else is not. So if the same statements had been made by (say) the president of Yale or of the University of California, my guess is that they would not have created a similar firestorm.

Lastly, and to my mind most importantly, the issue of gender equity had recently become embroiled in controversy after a long period of relative calm. At the moment Summers made his remarks, America was ready to re-fight gender issues because the country was controlled by a religiously conservative Republican administration and Congress; because we were fighting two wars (on "terrorism" and in Iraq), and war always tends to polarize gender roles; and because the confounding of our American

group identity by the events of 9/11 had created, for many Americans, a crisis in our individual identities as gendered persons. So the story had stamina because of the context in which the remarks were made.

In fact, the Summers story was not the first harbinger of new concern over gender issues. Over the previous few years there had been some media attention to gender roles. An article by Lisa Belkin in the *New York Times Magazine* (Belkin 2003) talks at length and with approval about women who have abandoned prestigious careers to become "stay-at-home moms." An article in the *New York Times'* Sunday *Week in Review* (Warner 2004) quoted men whose wives were working at high-salaried jobs as resentful and complaining. Alessandra Stanley (2004), commenting on the season's new television shows, argued that they were re-creating and reinforcing old gender stereotypes (including in her attribution *Desperate Housewives*, soon to become a major hit).

The Narrative

I frame the Summers case as a story, or "narrative," using Labov's (1972b) definition: a minimal narrative consists of two "narrative clauses," temporal statements whose order cannot be rearranged without changing their meaning or creating nonsense. In this case there are four main "narrative clauses," that is, major story developments:

1. The original event and its immediate fallout (Dillon 2005; Traub 2005).
2. Analysis of the validity of Summers' claims, including a pair of Op-Ed articles (Judson 2005; Murray 2005) arguing for and against the existence of biological differences, citing scientific studies that came to opposite conclusions. Appearing nine days after the Summers statement, these articles occupy, extraordinarily, almost a full Op-Ed page. The argument continues with Angier and Chang (2005), the day after the Op-Ed pieces; Pinker (2005), writing in *New Republic*; Healy and Rimer (2005a); Cox and Alm (2005); and Dean (2005b). Each side claims to have "science" on its side – but different science with different underlying assumptions about what constitutes a valid scientific approach. There was also discussion of environmental barriers to women's achievement (Dean 2005a); Shulevitz (2005); Warner (2005) in *Newsweek*; and Rimer (2005c), whether collegial prejudice or the unfair distribution of domestic duties.
3. While the arguments of (2) were playing out, a related topic surfaced: an examination, often negative, of Summers' performance as Harvard president (Rimer 2005a, b; Healy & Rimer 2005b; Atlas 2005; McGinn 2005, in *Newsweek*'s business section, showing how far the story had spread; Cohen 2005; and Donadio 2005, in the *Times* Sunday *Book Review*, also illustrating spread beyond the science and education pages). These stories focused on Summers' confrontational and belittling style in dealing with his faculty, often arguing that the style was counterproductive. Indeed, during this period the Harvard faculty voted twice

to give Summers a vote of no confidence, necessitating several apologies on his part.

4.   Finally, there were discussions of the role of gender elsewhere than in science and university governance. Dowd (2005) in a *Times* Op-Ed column, muses on why so few other women are willing or able to serve as political commentators (she suggests, because women speaking critically are viewed much more unfavorably than are men, and because women are much more strongly affected than men by negative response). Tierney (2005), in the same place, argues that women are simply less competitive than men, as demonstrated by the fact that men virtually always are the winners of Scrabble tournaments. An article in the *Times'* Sunday *Arts and Leisure* section (Allen 2005) points out that, at auction, the works of modern female artists fetch lower prices than those of their male counterparts. While none of these directly addresses the Summers controversy, it seems probable that they would not have been written except within the penumbra of that dispute. (See ISSUES OF GENDER IN MODERN ENGLISH.)

Conclusions

First, language and the world it represents are interconnected. It is impossible to make sense of the discourse around the Summers case without understanding the social and political settings within which it was situated.

Secondly, all levels of language are grist for the sociolinguist's interpretive mill. All are predictable and rule governed, and we use all – spontaneous and planned; oral and written; formal and informal; verbal and non-verbal – to make sense of the world around us and present ourselves and our identities to one another.

Third, the domain of sociolinguistics, as of linguistics more generally, is everything that we as human beings use language to achieve, intentionally or otherwise.

REFERENCES AND FURTHER READING

Allen, G. (2005). The X factor. *New York Times*, May 1.

Angier, N. & Chang, K. (2005). Gray matter and the sexes: still a scientific gray area. *New York Times*, January 24.

Atlas, J. (2005). The battle behind the battle at Harvard. *New York Times*, February 27.

Belkin, L. (2003). The opt-out revolution. *New York Times Magazine*, October 26.

Bloomfield, L. (1933). *Language*. New York: Henry Holt.

Brown, P. & Levinson, S. (1987). *Politeness*. Cambridge: Cambridge University Press.

Cohen, A. (2005). The Lawrence Summers mess: Harvard enters the internet age. *New York Times*, February 28.

Cox, W. M. & Alm, R. (2005). Scientists are made, not born. *New York Times*, February 28.

Dean, C. (2005a). For some girls, the problem with math is that they're good at it. *New York Times*, February 1.

Dean, C. (2005b). Scientist at work: Evelyn Fox Keller. Theorist drawn into debate 'that will not go away.' *New York Times*, April 12.

Dillon, S. (2005). Harvard chief defends his talk on women. *New York Times*, January 18.

Donadio, R. (2005). The tempest in the ivory tower. *New York Times Book Review*, March 27.

Dowd, M. (2005). Dish it out, ladies. *New York Times*, March 31.

Grice, H. P. (1975). Logic and conversation. In P. Cole & J. Morgan (eds.), *Speech Acts: Syntax and Semantics 3* (pp. 41–58). New York: Academic Press.

Gumperz, J. (1982). *Discourse Strategies*. Cambridge: Cambridge University Press.

Healy, P. & Rimer, S. (2005a). Furor lingers as Harvard chief gives details of talk on women. *New York Times,* February 18.

Healy, P. & Rimer. S. (2005b). Amid uproar, Harvard head lists his goals. *New York Times*, February 26.

Judson, O. (2005). Different but (probably) equal. *New York Times*, January 23.

Labov, W. (1972a). The study of language in its social context. In W. Labov, *Sociolinguistic Patterns* (pp. 183–259). Philadelphia: University of Pennsylvania Press.

Labov, W. (1972b). The transformation of experience in narrative syntax. In W. Labov, *Language in the Inner City* (pp. 354–96). Philadelphia: University of Pennsylvania Press.

Labov, W. (1972c). On the mechanism of linguistic change. In W. Labov, *Sociolinguistic Patterns* (pp. 160–82). Philadelphia: University of Pennsylvania Press.

Labov, W. & Waletzky, J. (1967). Narrative analysis. In J. Helm (ed.), *Essays in the Verbal and Visual Arts* (pp. 12–44). Seattle: University of Washington Press.

Lakoff, R. (2000). *The Language War*. Berkeley: University of California Press.

McGinn, D. (2005). Bully in the pulpit. *Newsweek*, February 28.

Murray, C. (2005). Sex ed at Harvard. *New York Times*, January 23.

Pinker, S. (2005). Sex ed. *New Republic*, February 14.

Rimer, S. (2005a). At Harvard, the bigger concern of the faculty is the president's management style. *New York Times*, January 26.

Rimer, S. (2005b). Some of Harvard's leading professors confront its president. *New York Times*, February 16.

Rimer. S. (2005c). For women in science, the pace of progress in academia is slow. *New York Times*, April 15.

Sacks, H., Schegloff, E., & Jefferson, G. (1974). A simplest systematics for the organization of turn-taking in conversation. *Language*, 50, 696–735.

Schiffrin, D. (1987). *Discourse Markers*. Cambridge: Cambridge University Press.

Schiffrin, D. (1994). *Approaches to Discourse*. Oxford: Blackwell.

Shulevitz, J. (2005). The mommy trap. (Review of Judith Warner, *Perfect Madness*). *New York Times Book Review*, February 20.

Stanley, A. (2004). Old-time sexism suffuses new season. *New York Times*, October 1.

Tannen, D. (1984). *Conversational Style*. Norwood: Ablex.

Tierney, J. (2005). The way to win. *New York Times,* May 31.

Traub, J. (2005). Lawrence Summers, provocateur. *New York Times*, January 23.

Warner, J. (2004). Guess who's left holding the briefcase? (It's not mom). *New York Times,* June 20.

Warner, J. (2005). Mommy madness. *Newsweek,* February 21.

59

Cognitive Linguistics

Dirk Geeraerts

Cognitive linguistics is an approach to the analysis of natural language that focuses on language as an instrument for organizing, processing, and conveying information. This implies that the analysis of meaning is of primary importance for linguistic description: in cognitive linguistics, the formal structures of language are studied not as if they were autonomous, but as reflections of general conceptual organization, categorization principles, processing mechanisms, and experiential and cultural influences. Cognitive linguistics originated with a number of Californian linguists in the late 1970s and early 1980s, basically as an attempt to carry further the interest in meaning phenomena that was typical of the so-called "generative semantics" movement within generative linguistics. In contrast with generative semantics, however, cognitive linguistics is situated entirely outside the generative tradition. Leading figures within cognitive linguistics are George Lakoff, Ronald W. Langacker, Len Talmy, Charles Fillmore, and Gilles Fauconnier.

The renewed interest in semantics that drives the development of cognitive linguistics opens up exciting perspectives for historical linguistics, specifically because it is an integrated approach, i.e., an approach in which language is not considered to be an autonomous system, but rather an aspect of human life that is integrated into cognition and culture at large. Such an integrated approach is particularly congenial to historical studies: when you look at language from a historical perspective, you naturally tend to see it as part of a more or less familiar, more or less exotic, culture, one in which the thoughts and experiences of people are partly recognizable, partly mysterious – and you would be interested in how the language reveals those thoughts and experiences.

To illustrate (and note that it is an illustration, not an exhaustive overview) how productive the cognitive linguistic approach may be, let us have a look at two specific ideas from the rich inventory of descriptive and analytic tools produced by cognitive linguistics. The first idea is that of *prototypicality* as a model for the internal semantic structure of words: if we look at the relationship between the different readings of a

word, what kind of structure can we expect? The second idea is that of *conceptual metaphors* as one of the models that connect different words and lexical expressions: If we look at the vocabulary of a language as a whole, rather than individual words, what kind of conceptual structures do we detect? These two ideas will first be introduced in their own right. Afterwards, two succinctly presented case studies will demonstrate how exciting an application of these models to historical materials may be. The first case study is based on Molina (2000, 2005); the second on Geeraerts and Grondelaers (1995).

Prototypicality

The prototype model specifically highlights two structural characteristics of the semantic structure of words: differences of structural weight on the one hand, and fuzziness and flexibility on the other. To illustrate, consider the word *fruit*. This is a polysemous word: next to its basic, everyday reading ("sweet and soft edible part of a plant, containing seeds"), there are various other readings conventionally associated with the word. In a technical sense, for instance ("the seed-bearing part of a plant or tree"), the word also refers to things that lie outside the range of application of the basic reading, such as acorns and pea pods. In an expression like *the fruits of nature*, the meaning is even more general, as the word refers to everything that grows and that can be eaten by people (including, for instance, grains and vegetables). Further, there is a range of figurative readings, including the abstract sense "the result or outcome of an action" (as in *the fruits of his labour* or *his work bore fruit*), or the somewhat archaic reading "offspring, progeny" (as in the biblical expressions *the fruit of the womb*, *the fruit of his loins*).

Each of these readings constitutes a separate sense of *fruit*, but in turn, each sense may be thought of as a set of things in the outside world. The basic sense of *fruit*, for instance, corresponds with a set including apples, oranges, and bananas (and many other types of fruit). If you think of *fruit* in this central sense as a category, the set consists of the members of the category. These members are "things" only in a broad sense. In the *fruit* example, they happen to be material objects, but in the case of verbs, they could be actions, or situations, or events; in the case of adjectives, they could be properties; and so on. Given this example, we can now describe the two structural characteristics that receive special attention within a prototype-theoretical framework.

Differences of structural weight

Differences in salience involve the fact that not all the elements at a specific level of semantic analysis carry the same structural weight. For instance, the everyday reading of *fruit* occupies a more central position than the archaic reading "offspring" or the technical reading. Various indications may be adduced for this central position. For

one thing, the central reading more readily springs to mind when people think of the category: on being asked what *fruit* means, you are more likely to mention the edible parts of plants than a person's offspring. For another, the "edible part" reading is more frequent in actual language use.

In addition, the "edible part" reading is a good starting point for describing the other readings. It would probably be easier to understand the expression *fruit of the womb* (if it were new to you) when you understood the "edible part" reading than the other way round. The basic reading, in other words, is the center of semantic cohesion in the category; it holds the category together by making the other readings accessible. Three features, in short (psychological salience, relative frequency of use, interpretive advantageousness), may be mentioned as indications for the central position of a particular reading.

Centrality effects are not restricted to the level of senses and readings, however, but may also be invoked at the referential level, i.e., the level where we talk about the members of a category. When prompted, Europeans will more readily name apples and oranges as types of fruit than avocados or pomegranates, and references to apples and oranges are likely to be more frequent in a European context than references to mangos. This does not exclude, moreover, cultural differences among distinct parts of Europe.

The terminology used to describe these differences of structural weight is quite diverse, and the description in the foregoing paragraphs has featured such (intuitively transparent) terms as *salience*, *typicality*, and *centrality*. The most technical term however is *prototypicality*: the central reading of an item or the central subset within the range of a specific reading is the prototype.

Fuzziness and flexibility

How clearly distinguishable are the elements of a semantic description? Consider the question whether the central sense of *fruit* can be delimited in a straightforward fashion. Such a delimitation will take the form of a definition that is general and distinctive: it is general in the sense of naming characteristics that are common to all fruits, and it is distinctive in the sense of being sufficient to distinguish the category "fruit" (in the relevant sense) from any other category. (If a definition is not distinctive, it is too general: it will cover cases that do not belong in the category to be defined.)

Now, many of the characteristics that one might be inclined to include in a definition of the central reading of *fruit* do not have the required generality: they are not necessarily sweet (lemons), they do not necessarily contain parts that are immediately recognizable as seeds (bananas), they are not necessarily soft (avocados). There are, to be sure, a number of features that do have the required generality: all fruits grow above the ground on plants or trees (rather than in the ground); they have to ripen before you can eat them, and if you want to prepare them (rather than eat them raw), you would primarily use sugar, or at least use them in dishes that have a

predominantly sweet taste. Taken together, however, these features do not suffice to prevent almonds (and other nuts), or a vegetable like rhubarb (which is usually cooked with sugar), from being wrongly included in the category that is to be defined.

We have to conclude, then, that the central sense of *fruit* cannot receive a definition that is both general and distinctive. If we shift the attention to the members of a category, similar effects may be observed: the borderline of categories is not always clearly delineated. For instance, is a coconut or an olive a fruit?

Observations such as these lead prototype theory to the conclusion that semantic structures need not necessarily consist of neatly delineated, rigidly defined entities, but that they may rather be characterized by a certain amount of fuzziness and vagueness – a fuzziness and vagueness that entails flexibility: if the criteria for using a word are less stringent than a naive conception of meaning would suggest, there is likely to be a lot of plasticity in meaning.

Conceptual Metaphors

Suppose that you talk about relationships in the following way.

(1)   He is known for his many rapid *conquests*. She *fought* for him, but his mistress *won* out. He *fled* from her *advances*. She *pursued* him relentlessly. He is slowly *gaining ground* with her. He *won* her hand in marriage. He *overpowered* her. She is *besieged* by suitors. He has to *fend* them off. He *enlisted* the aid of her friends. He made an *ally* of her mother. Theirs is a *misalliance* if I've ever seen one.

All these expressions are related by a common theme: love is war. A source domain (war) is more or less systematically mapped onto a target domain (love). The target domain is understood in terms of the source domain; the conceptual structure that we associate with the source domain (like the recognition that a war involves specific actions like fighting and spying and fleeing and finding allies) is invoked to bring structure to the target domain.

Crucially, this mapping involves not just a single word, but a whole set of lexical items, an entire subfield of the vocabulary. In such cases, cognitive linguistics speaks of *conceptual metaphors*: metaphorical mappings that are not restricted to a single item but that overarch an entire subset of the vocabulary. From a cognitive point of view, such conceptual (rather than lexical) metaphors are extremely interesting, because they may well reveal underlying patterns of thought, basic models that we use to reason about a given topic (like love).

Case Study 1: The Word *Sore*

In contemporary English, *sore* essentially refers to a specific type of wound or physical injury, viz. a bruise, a raw place on the body as caused by pressure or friction. In Old

English, however, the range of application is much broader. The following set of quotations shows that, next to the "wound" reading as represented by (2), we find references to bodily suffering (3), to sickness (4), and to emotional suffering (5).

(2) Wið wunda & wið cancor genim þas ilcan wyrte, lege to þam sare. Ne geþafað heo
     þæt sar furður wexe (ca. 1000: Sax.Leechd. I.134)
     'For wounds and cancer take the same herb, put it on to the sore. Do not allow
     the sore to increase'

(3) þisse sylfan wyrte syde to þa sar geliðigað (ca. 1000: Sax.Leechd. I.280)
     'With this same herb, the sore [of the teeth] calms widely'

(4) þa þe on sare seoce lagun (ca. 900: Cynewulf Crist 1356)
     'Those who lay sick in sore'

(5) Mið ðæm mæstam sare his modes (ca. 888: K.Ælfred Boeth. vii §2)
     'With the greatest sore of his spirit'

Given that Old English *sore* (in the form *sar*) has a wider range of application than contemporary *sore*, what could have happened? How can we describe the semantic shift from Old English to contemporary English? Let us first have a closer look at the Old English situation. Two features that link up directly with the prototype-theoretical model as described above need to be mentioned.

First, the different meanings in Old English have a different status and a different weight within the cluster of applications. This becomes clear when we have a look at the frequencies of the *sore* quotations that may be found in the *OED* (simplified from Molina 2000: 99) in the successive centuries (see figure 59.1).

While the "bodily suffering" reading appears first and occupies the central position in the initial semantic structure of *sore*, the "injury, wound" reading takes up a dominant position only much later. What we see, in other words, is an illustration of the first feature of prototypicality as defined: in the semantic structure of words, we have to distinguish central from peripheral instances. In the case of *sore*, the core meaning shifts over time from "bodily suffering" to "wound."

But *sore* illustrates the second feature of prototypicality as well. *Sore* and *sorrow* are etymologically unrelated, but the "emotional suffering" reading of *sore* overlaps with *sorrow*, which exhibits only that meaning. In fact, the frequent co-occurrence of *sore*

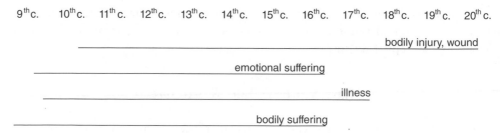

Figure 59.1   Distribution of *sore* meanings over time

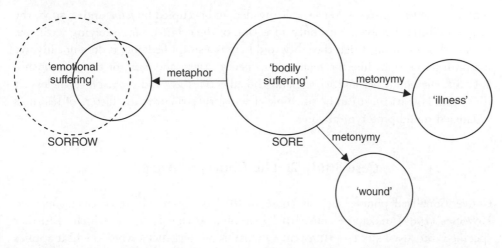

Figure 59.2 The *sore* cluster in Old English

and *sorrow* in alliterating binominals, as in examples (6) and (7), indicates that both words were readily recognized as (near-)synonyms: in Old English, the formal close-ness and the semantic overlap between the two words seem to converge towards an incipient merger. From the prototype point of view, this specific configuration of *sore* and *sorrow* illustrates the absence of rigid borderlines between words.

(6)   Ant te unseli swalen sunken to helle, to forswelten i sar & i sorhe eaure (1150–
      1250: St Juliana)
      'And the unhappy souls sink to hell, to die in sore and sorrow ever'
(7)   On heorte he hafde sorge & sar (ca. 1205: Lay. 7998)
      'In the heart he had sorrow and sore'

Summarizing, the initial situation in the semantic history of *sore* is one in which the concept of "bodily suffering" occupies the center of the word, with metonymical extensions towards "illness" and "wound" on the one hand, and on the other with a metaphorical extension towards "emotional suffering" that constitutes an overlap, possibly even an incipient merger, with *sorrow*. Figure 59.2 graphically represents the situation. Solid circles represent meanings of *sore*, the dotted circle that of *sorrow*. The size of the circles identifies the centrality of the meaning: "bodily suffering" is the core of the *sore* structure. The links with the secondary readings are identified as being metonymical or metaphorical.

The major force in the transition towards the present-day situation may now be identified: the French loan *pain*, first attested in 1297, takes over the meaning of *sore*. But typically (and this is where the fruitfulness of a prototype-theoretical approach shows up most clearly), it does not substitute *sore* in a wholesale manner, but rather occupies the central area of the meaning of *sore*, leaving only the specialized "wound" reading with *sore* itself. In terms of the graphical representation of figure 59.2, the

center of the *sore* cluster is so to speak invaded and occupied by *pain*, and as such, the original cluster dissolves, with only a fraction of the original range staying with *sore*. It should be mentioned that the story told here is a simplified one: it does not involve intriguing questions like the relationship between *pine* and *pain*, or the relationship between the nouns *sore* and *sorrow*, and the adjectives *sore* and *sorry*. Nevertheless, it illustrates how useful it can be to think of semantic structures as clusters of readings organized round prototypical cores.

Case Study 2: The Concept "Anger"

Conventionalized phrases such as those in (8) have been subsumed by Lakoff and Kövecses (1987) under the conceptual metaphor ANGER IS HEAT, which is further specified into ANGER IS THE HEAT OF A FLUID IN A CONTAINER when the heat applies to fluids, and into ANGER IS FIRE when the heat is applied to solids.

(8)   I had reached the *boiling point*. She was *seething* with rage. He lost his *cool*. You make my blood *boil*. He was *foaming* at the mouth. He's just *letting off steam*. Don't get *hot* under the collar. Billy's a *hot*head. They were having a *heated* argument. When I found out, I almost *burst* a blood vessel. He got *red* with anger. She was *scarlet* with rage. I was *fuming*. When I told him, he just *exploded*. *Smoke* was pouring out of his ears. He was breathing *fire*. Those are *inflammatory* remarks. That *kindled* my ire. He was *consumed* by his anger.

At a lower level of analysis, these and many similar expressions are grouped together under labels such as when the intensity of anger increases, the fluid rises (his pent-up anger *welled up* inside him), intense anger produces steam (I was *fuming*), and when anger becomes too intense, the person explodes (when I told him, he just *exploded*). Next to the basic conceptual metaphor ANGER IS HEAT, less elaborate metaphorical patterns such as ANGER IS INSANITY, ANGER IS AN OPPONENT, ANGER IS A DANGER-OUS ANIMAL, and CAUSING ANGER IS TRESPASSING are identified. Lakoff and Kövecses tend to interpret these findings in terms of physiological effects: increased body heat is taken to be a physiological effect of being in a state of anger, and anger is met-onymically conceptualized in terms of its physiological effects.

If we now have a look at the following Shakespeare quotations from *Taming of the Shrew*, we may easily come to the conclusion that these examples too illustrate the conceptual metaphor ANGER IS HEAT.

(9)   Now were not I a little pot and soon hot (4.1.5–6)
(10)   Is she so hot a shrew (4.1.21)
(11)   I tell thee, Kate, 'twas burnt and dried away,
       And I expressly am forbid to touch it;
       For it engenders choler, planteth anger,
       And better 'twere that both of us did fast,

Since of ourselves, ourselves are choleric. (4.1.170–4)

(12) *Gru.* What say you to a neat's foot?

  Kath. 'Tis passing good, I prithee let me have it.

  Gru. I fear it is too choleric a meat.

    How say you to a fat tripe finely broil'd?

  Kath. I like it well, good Grumio, fetch it me.

  Gru. I cannot tell, I fear 'tis choleric.

    What say you to a piece of beef and mustard?

  Kath. A dish that I do love to feed upon.

  Gru. Ay, but the mustard is too hot a little. (4.3.17–25)

But would these older images have the same, allegedly universal physiological basis as the contemporary expressions described by Lakoff and Kövecses? It has been described by various authors (among them Schäfer 1966; Pope 1985) how the psychology of Shakespeare's dramatic characters unmistakenly refers to the theory of humors. The humoral theory, to be precise, is the highly influential doctrine that dominated medical thinking in Western Europe for several centuries.

The foundations of the humoral doctrine were laid by Hippocrates of Kos. Physiologically, the four humoral fluids regulate the vital processes within the human body; the secretion of the humors underlies the dynamical operation of our anatomy. Psychologically, on the other hand, they define four prototypical temperaments, i.e., a person's character is thought to be determined by the preponderance of one of the four vital fluids in his body. Thus, the *choleric* temperament (given to anger and irascibility) is determined by a preponderance of the yellow bile, while the *melancholic*, gloomy and fearful, suffers from a constitutional excess of black bile. The *phlegmatic* personality is typically placid and unmoved, while the *sanguine* temperament (defined in correlation with blood, the fourth humor) is passionate, optimistic, and brave. The singular combination of physiological and psychological concepts that characterizes the theory of humors also shows up in the fact that a disequilibrium of the fluids does not only characterize constitutional temperaments, but also causes temporary diseases – which are then typically described in bodily, biological terms as well as in psychic terms. For instance, an overproduction of yellow bile may be signaled by the patient's vomiting bile, but also by his dreaming of fire. In the same line, an excess of blood shows up in the redness of the skin and swollen veins, but also in carelessness and a certain degree of recalcitrance. In this sense, the humoral theory is a medical doctrine: it identifies diseases and their symptoms, and defines a therapy. Obviously, the basic therapeutic rule will be to restore the balance of the humors, given that a disturbance of their well-balanced proportion is the basic cause of the pathological situation. The long-lasting popularity of blood-letting, for instance (a standard medical practice that continued well into the nineteenth century), has its historical origins in the theory of humors.

The connection between yellow bile and fire that was mentioned a moment ago is not accidental. It is part of a systematic correlation between the human, anatomical microcosm and the macrocosm, thought to be built up from four basic elements.

Thus, yellow bile, black bile, phlegm, and blood corresponded with fire, earth, water, and air, respectively. In the Aristotelian elaboration of the Hippocratic doctrine, these correlating sets of microcosmical and macrocosmical basic elements were defined as combinations of four basic features: cold, warm, wet, and dry. Blood was thought to be warm and wet, phlegm cold and wet, yellow bile warm and dry, and black bile cold and dry.

The classical humoral doctrine received the form in which it was to dominate the Middle Ages in the work of Galen (129–99 CE). He added a dietary pharmacology to the humoral edifice. All plants (and foodstuffs in general) could be characterized by one of four degrees of warmth, cold, wetness, and dryness. Given that diseases are caused by an excess of one of the four humors, and given that these are themselves characterized by the four features just mentioned, the basic therapeutic rule is to put the patient on a diet that will ensure a decrease of the superfluous humor.

In the course of the Middle Ages, the Galenic framework was further developed into a large-scale system of signs and symbols. In a typically medieval analogical way of thinking, widely divergent phenomena (ranging from the ages of man to astrological notions such as the system of the planets and the signs of the zodiac) were fitted into the fourfold schema presented by the medical theory. In table 59.1, an overview is given of a number of those correlations.

The humoral edifice began to be undermined as soon as the Renaissance introduced renewed empirical medical investigations, like Harvey's discovery of the circulation of the blood. However, the disappearance of the theory from the medical scene was only very gradual, and it took approximately another three centuries before the last

Table 59.1   A system of humoral correspondences

	Phlegm	Black bile	Yellow bile	Blood
Characteristic	cold and moist	cold and dry	warm and dry	warm and moist
Element	water	earth	fire	air
Temperament	phlegmatic	melancholic	choleric	sanguine
Organ	brain/bladder	spleen	liver/stomach	heart
Color	white	black	yellow	red
Taste	salty	sour	bitter	sweet
Season	winter	autumn	summer	spring
Wind	North	West	South	East
Planet	moon	Saturn	Mars	Jupiter
Animal	turtle	sparrow	lion	goat

vestiges of the humoral framework were finally removed. The standard view of the historians of medicine is, in fact, that only in the middle of the nineteenth century did the humoral pathological conception receive its final blow.

It will be clear by now that the conceptualization of anger in the Shakespeare quotations conforms to the model furnished by the theory of humors: anger is caused by choler (12), the production of which may be stimulated by certain kinds of food (12)(13); while a choleric temperament is a permanent personality trait (12), the main attribute of the choleric personality is hotness (10)(11). The fact that passages such as the ones quoted above can be multiplied from the work of Webster, Marlowe, or Jonson, leads Schäfer (1966) to the conclusion that the humoral conception of physiology and psychology is something of a true fashion in Elizabethan drama. He attributes this to the fact that it is only in the middle of the sixteenth century that the doctrine became known to a wider audience than that of learned men who could read the medical authorities in their Latin and Greek originals. It is only, in other words, after the invention of printing that works such as Thomas Elyot's *Castel of Helthe* (1539), Andrew Boorde's *A Breuyary of Helth* (ca. 1542) and *A Compendyous Regyment or A Dyetary of Helth* (ca. 1542), or Thomas Vicary's *A Profitable Treatise of the Anatomie of Mans Body* (1548) could be widely distributed, and that they could contribute to the spreading of the humoral doctrine to the community at large. But if this dissemination of the doctrine of humors from the realm of learned knowledge to that of popular belief implies that it is technically a piece of *gesunkenes Kulturgut*, the question arises how far it actually sank. In particular, how deep did it become entrenched in the language itself?

In table 59.2 we have systematically brought together a number of items and expressions in three European languages (English, French, and Dutch) that can be considered a part of the legacy of the theory of humors.

Table 59.2   Lexical relics of the humoral doctrine

	English	French	Dutch
PHLEGM	*phlegmatic* 'calm, cool, apathetic'	*avoir un flegme imperturbable* 'to be imperturbable'	*valling* (dialectal) 'cold'
BLACK BILE	*spleen* 'organ filtering the blood; sadness'	*mélancolie* 'sadness, moroseness'	*zwartgallig* 'sad, depressed' (literally 'black-bilious')
YELLOW BILE	*bilious* 'angry, irascible'	*colère* 'anger'	*z'n gal spuwen* 'to vent (literally 'to spit out') one's gall'
BLOOD	*full-blooded* 'vigorous, hearty, sensual'	*avoir du sang dans les veines* 'to have spirit, luck'	*warmbloedig* 'passionate' (literally 'warm-blooded')

If we zoom in on one of the cells of table 59.2, still further examples may be found. According to Roget's *Thesaurus*, the items listed under (13) all refer to anger or related concepts.

(13)   *choler* 'anger', *gall* 'anger', *rouse one's choler* 'to elicit anger', *stir one's bile* 'to elicit anger', *galling* 'vexing, causing anger', *choleric* 'irascible', *liverish* 'irascible', *splenetic* 'irascible', *hot-blooded* 'irascible', *fiery* 'irascible', *hot-headed* 'irascible'

Given these lexical relics of the humoral doctrine, it will be obvious that the conceptual metaphor ANGER IS THE HEAT OF A FLUID IN A CONTAINER neatly fits into the humoral views: the body is the container of the four cardinal fluids, and anger involves the heating up of specific fluids (either yellow bile as the direct source of ire, or blood as the mixture of the four humors). This means, in other words, that the purely physiological interpretation put forward by Lakoff and Kövecses needs to be interpreted along cultural and historical lines. When we recognize that the medieval physiological-psychological theory of the four humors and the four temperaments has left its traces on our emotional vocabulary, we learn to see the ANGER IS THE HEAT OF A FLUID IN A CONTAINER metaphor as one of those traces. It is then not motivated directly by the physiological effects of anger, as Lakoff and Kövecses suggest, but it is part of the historical (but reinterpreted) legacy of the humoral theory.

More generally, an adequate analysis of the motivation behind cultural phenomena in general and language in particular has to take into account the diachronic dimension. Cultural models, i.e., the more or less coherent sets of concepts that cultures use to structure experience and make sense of the world, are not reinvented afresh with every new period in the culture's development. Rather, it is by definition part of their cultural nature that they have a historical dimension. It is only by investigating their historical origins and their gradual transformation that their contemporary form can be properly understood.

And Next?

The *sore* and "anger" case studies illustrate how rewarding it can be to apply the descriptive apparatus of cognitive linguistics to the semantic history of the language. On the level of individual words and on the level of the broad cultural models that cut across the vocabulary respectively, *prototype theory* and *conceptual metaphor theory* help us to get a better insight into the life of the language. At the same time, the case studies reveal numerous open questions: questions about the mechanisms of lexical substitutions and the interaction of cognition and cultures – questions that call for further research. Readers wishing to engage in such questions may profit from the following publications. General introductions to cognitive linguistics include Lakoff (1987), Ungerer and Schmid (1996), Dirven and Verspoor (2004), Croft and Cruse (2004), Geeraerts and Cuyckens (2007). Specifically for prototype theory, see Taylor

(2003); for metaphor, Kövecses (2002). For the application of cognitive linguistics to historical semantics, see Geeraerts (1997) Blank and Koch (1999), Koivisto-Alanko (2000), Fabiszak (2001), Soares da Silva (2003), Tissari (2003), Allan (2007), and Gevaert (2007).

References and Further Reading

Allan, Kathryn (2007). *Metaphor from Old English to Present Day English*. Oxford: Basil Blackwell.

Blank, A. & Koch, P. (eds.) (1999). *Historical Semantics and Cognition*. Berlin: Mouton de Gruyter.

Croft, W. & Cruse, D. A. (2004). *Cognitive Linguistics*. Cambridge: Cambridge University Press.

Dirven, R. & Verspoor, M. (2004). *Cognitive Exploration of Language and Linguistics*. 2nd revd. edn. Amsterdam: Benjamins.

Fabiszak, M. (2001). *The Concept of 'Joy' in Old and Middle English: A Semantic Analysis*. Piła: Wyższa Szkoła Biznesu.

Geeraerts, D. (1997). *Diachronic Prototype Semantics*. Oxford: Clarendon Press.

Geeraerts, D. & Cuyckens, H. (eds.) (2007). *The Oxford Handbook of Cognitive Linguistics*. New York: Oxford University Press.

Geeraerts, D. & Grondelaers, S. (1995). Looking back at anger: cultural traditions and metaphorical patterns. In J. R. Taylor & R. E. MacLaury (eds.), *Language and the Cognitive Construal of the World* (pp. 153–79). Berlin: Mouton de Gruyter.

Gevaert, C. (2007). *The History of Anger. The Lexical Field of Anger from Old to Early Modern English*. PhD thesis. University of Leuven, Leuven.

Kövecses, Z. (2002). *Metaphor*. Oxford: Oxford University Press.

Koivisto-Alanko, P. (2000). *Abstract Words in Abstract Worlds: Directionality and Prototypical Structure in the Semantic Change in English Nouns of Cognition*. Helsinki: Sociéte Néophilologique.

Lakoff, G. (1987). *Women, Fire and Dangerous Things*. Chicago: University of Chicago Press.

Lakoff, G. & Kövecses, Z. (1987). The cognitive model of anger inherent in American English. In D. Holland & N. Quinn (eds.), *Cultural Models in Language and Thought* (pp. 195–221). Cambridge: Cambridge University Press.

Molina, C. (2000). Give sorrow words. PhD thesis. Universidad Complutense, Madrid.

Molina, C. (2005). On the role of onomasiological profiles in merger discontinuations. In N. Delbecque, J. Van der Auwera, & D. Geeraerts (eds.), *Perspectives on Variation* (pp. 177–94). Berlin: Mouton de Gruyter.

Pope, M. (1985). Shakespeare's medical imagination. In S. Wells (ed.), *Shakespeare Survey 38* (pp. 175–86). Cambridge: Cambridge University Press.

Schäfer, J. (1966). *Wort und Begriff 'Humour' in der elisabethanischen Komödie*. Münster: Aschendorff.

Shakespeare, W. (1997). *The Taming of the Shrew*. In G. B. Evans (ed.), *The Riverside Shakespeare*. 2nd edn. Boston: Houghton-Mifflin.

Soares da Silva, A. (2003). Image schemas and category coherence: the case of the Portuguese verb 'deixar'. In H. Cuyckens, R. Dirven, & J. Taylor (eds.), *Cognitive Approaches to Lexical Semantics* (pp. 281–322). Berlin: Mouton de Gruyter.

Taylor, J. R. (2003). *Linguistic Categorization*. 3rd edn. Oxford: Oxford University Press.

Tissari, H. (2003). *LOVEscapes: Changes in Prototypical Senses and Cognitive Metaphors since 1500*. Helsinki: Sociéte Néophilologique.

Ungerer, F. & Schmid, H. J. (1996). *An Introduction to Cognitive Linguistics*. London: Longman.

Glossary of Linguistic Terms

Haruko Momma

The following glossary includes some of the linguistic terms occurring in two or more essays in this volume. The definitions provided here reflect the way the terms are used by the authors. For more general or detailed definitions, consult dictionaries of linguistic terms or the glossaries appended to textbooks of the history of the English language. For terms related to speech sounds, see the "Note on Phonetic Symbols and Orthography" on pp. xxiv–xxviii.

accusative *See* case.

acrolect *See* dialect, social.

active *See* voice, grammatical.

adverbial clause *See* clause type.

affix A morpheme, or word element, that can be attached to a word to form another word. An affix is a **prefix** when added to the beginning of a word (e.g., *mis-* in *misdeed*) and a **suffix** when added to the end of a word (e.g., *– er* in *grinder*). **Affixation** is a productive way to coin new words in PDE.

affricate A consonant in which a stop is released by a fricative articulated in the same position. PDE has two affricates: /č/ or /ʧ/ as in *char*; /ǰ/ or /ʤ/ as in *jar*. *See further* "Note on Phonetic Symbols and Orthography."

agreement Matching of grammatical forms within a phrase (e.g., *this book*, *these books*) or a sentence (e.g., *there is a way*, *there are ways*). Also called **concord**.

allo- Indicates a variant form of a unit. For **allophone**, *see* **phoneme**.

alveolar A consonant produced by the tip of the tongue against the ridge behind the upper teeth: e.g., /t, d, s, z, n, l/. *See further* "Note on Phonetic Symbols and Orthography."

analytic language *See* synthetic language.

Anglo-Norman French spoken by the Normans in England after the Norman Conquest. A geographical variety of Norman French.

Anglophone English-speaking, usu. pertaining to a person or a region in a colonial or post-colonial setting. An **Anglophone** is an English-speaking person typically in Canada.

Anglo-Saxon *See* periodization.

animate Pertains to nouns that refer to living beings: e.g., *child*, *lawyer*, *cat*. Opposite of **inanimate**.

antecedent A constituent, or a part of a clause, that is referred back to usu. by a pronoun: e.g., in the sentence *this is the man whom I mentioned*, the noun phrase *the man* is the antecedent of the relative pronoun *whom*.

article There are two kinds in English: the **definite article** *the* and the **indefinite article** *a(n)*. The former has derived from OE demonstrative forms like *þæm, þa* ('the'), and the latter from the OE numeral *an* ('one').

aspect Refers to a category of the verb pertaining to time. A sentence like "they are traveling" (i.e., *be* + Present Participle) is **progressive** in aspect, as it expresses an action in progress. A sentence like "they have traveled" (i.e., Auxiliary + Past Participle) is **perfect** in aspect, as it expresses a completed action. In some Indo-European languages, perfect is considered a tense category.

aspirate A sound articulated with a puff of breath: e.g., the *t* sound in *top*. *See further* "Note on Phonetic Symbols and Orthography."

auxiliary A verb functions as an auxiliary when occurring with a participle or an infinitive without *to*: e.g., *have* is an auxiliary verb in *we have met* (but a main verb in *I have the book*); *be* is an auxiliary verb in *you are chosen* (but a main verb in *I am happy*). The use of *do* as auxiliary (e.g., *we do not know; did you meet them?*) was established in the Early Modern English period. **Modal auxiliaries** are verbs like *must, can, shall,* and *may*. They were originally main verbs but came to be used exclusively as auxiliaries through grammaticalization.

back vowel A vowel articulated with the highest point of the tongue placed at the back of the mouth. Back vowels in PDE include /u, ʊ, o, ɔ, ɑ/. *See further* "Note on Phonetic Symbols and Orthography."

basilect *See* dialect, social.

borrowing *See* loan word.

C May stand for "consonant" as in CVC (consonant–verb–consonant, for words like *cat*), or for "complement" as in SVC (subject–verb–complement, for a clause like *they are students*).

case Refers to inflections, or grammatical forms, of pronouns, nouns, and adjectives to denote their syntactic functions within the clause. Old English had at least four cases. **Nominative** and **accusative** are cases for the subject and direct object of a clause, respectively: e.g., in *se cyning greteþ þone biscop* ('the king greets the bishop'), *se cyning* is in the nominative case, and *þone biscop* is accusative. The **dative** case is most typically used for indirect objects: e.g., *þæm bioscope* in *he hit geaf þæm bioscope* ('he gave it to the bishop'). **Genitive** is typically a case to denote possession: e.g., *þæs bioscopes* in *þæs bioscopes boc* ('the bishop's book'). The Old English case distinction, such as *se, þone, þæm, þæs* became obscured in the Middle English period and was mostly lost by Early Modern English. PDE has retained case distinction in personal pronouns: e.g., *they* (subjective), *them* (objective), *their* (possessive).

clause A syntactic unit that contains at least a subject and a verb: e.g., *I ran*. In certain clauses, the subject or the verb (or both) may be omitted though understood: e.g., *don't (you) run!*; *(it is) done*.

clause element The **subject** is a clause element that determines verb agreement and refers to the thing that is being talked about in the clause: e.g., *the cat* in the clause *the cat is sleeping*. The **object** is a clause element being affected by the action taken by the subject, either directly or indirectly: e.g., in the clause *we sent her flowers*, *flowers* is a **direct object**, and *her* is an **indirect object**. The **complement** completes a clause by describing another element: e.g., the word *happy* is a complement in both *I am happy* (complementing the subject *I*) and *it made me happy* (complementing the object *me*). A **predicate** is the portion of a clause excluding the subject: e.g., *is sleeping* in the clause *the cat is sleeping*.

clause type A clause that may stand alone as a sentence is a **main clause** (also called an **independent clause**): e.g., *the children went away*. A **subordinate clause** cannot stand alone as a sentence. A subordinate clause is an **adverbial clause** when introduced by an adverbial conjunction like *when* or *although* (e.g., *the children went away*

when it started to rain); a **relative clause** when introduced by a **relative pronoun** like *who* or *which* (e.g., *the children **who were playing there** went away*).

clear *l* *See* dark *l*.

cognate Having a common linguistic ancestor. **Cognate languages** have derived from a shared parent language: e.g., English and German from proto-Germanic. **Cognate words** derive from an earlier single word or word element: e.g., the English *eight* and the Latin *octo* from PIE **oktō(u)*.

complement (C) *See* clause element.

compound A word consisting of two or more independently existing words: e.g., *tablespoon, gentlewoman*. In English, **compounding** has been a productive method of word formation.

concord *See* agreement.

conjugation The inflection of verbs. A **finite verb** is conjugated or inflected in correspondence with the subject of the clause: e.g., *he **likes** to read/they **like** to read*. Of the non-finite forms, the **infinitive** may occur after auxiliary verbs (e.g., *we **will come***) or verbs like *want, like* (*I **like** to read*); the **present participle** has the *–ing* ending and may occur in the progressive construction (e.g., *they were **running***); the **past participle** may have an ending like   *ed, –en* and occur in the passive or perfect construction (e.g., *books were **selected**; they have **traveled***).

consonant Refers to speech sounds other than vowels: e.g., [k, m, v, s]. A consonant is produced by restricting the flow of air at a specific point in the mouth, nose, or both. *See further* "Note on Phonetic Symbols and Orthography."

consonant cluster Two or more consonants occurring together: e.g., [cl] in *clean* or [str] in *string*. **Consonant cluster reduction** or **simplification** is observed in many varieties of English: e.g., *mist* may be pronounced as [mɪs] in AAVE, Chicano English, and Carribean creoles; *kn-* as in *knee* was a cluster in medieval English and was pronounced as [kn].

constituent A word or word group that forms a distinct grammatical unit within the clause: e.g., the clause *in this year King Charles passed away* consists of three constituents, namely, an adverbial phrase (*in this year*), a noun phrase (*King Charles*), and a verb phrase (*passed away*).

copula A verb that links a subject and its compliment: e.g., *is* in *she **is** nice*. **Copula absence** (e.g., *she Ø nice*) is observed in, for example, AAVE and Chicano English.

creole Refers to languages developed typically through contacts between European languages and non-European languages in plantation colonies, and spoken by local populations for generations: e.g., Caribbean creoles and Gullah. *See also* pidgin.

dark *l* The *l* sound in *ale* (except for the varieties in certain regions of Wales and Ireland), as opposed to the **clear *l***, the sound found in words like *light*.

dative *See* case.

declarative A type of sentence that makes statements (e.g., *it rained yesterday*). To be contrasted with the interrogative, which poses questions (e.g., *did it rain yesterday?*).

declension Refers to inflections of nouns (e.g., *book*/*books, man*/*men*), pronouns (e.g., ***they***/***them***), and, in case of OE and Early ME, adjectives (e.g., *eald cyning* 'old king'/ *ealdes cyninges* 'old king's').

determiner A word that occurs with a noun to restrict its meaning: e.g., *the, this, that*.

diachronic Pertaining to historical dimensions of language: e.g., linguistic change over the course of time. Cf. synchronic.

dialect, historical Old English dialects include **Anglian** (which consists of **Northumbrian** and **Mercian**), **Kentish**, and **West Saxon**. From the late tenth century onwards, **late West Saxon** was widely used as a written standard. Middle English dialects are conventionally identified by the regions like Northern, Midlands, and Southern, although they comprised a continuum with many more varieties. The dialect of London, which evolved in stages during the late Middle English period, became a privilege dialect on which the standard form for ModE was based.

dialect, social In a society where two or more non-standard linguistic varieties are used, the one whose prestige is lower than the other(s) is the **basilect**, while the one with prestige is the **acrolect** (often serving as local standard); any variety that falls in between is a **mesolect**. Any variety of a language used by a specific individual is considered an **idiolect**.

dialectology The study of dialects.

digraph A combination of two letters to signify one phoneme or sound: e.g., *th* in *three, sh* in *shine*.

diphthong Vowels produced by having one sound gliding into another: e.g., /ɔɪ/ in *boy*; /aɪ/ in *buy*. *See further* "Note on Phonetic Symbols and Orthography."

direct object (DO) *See* clause element.

discourse A linguistic unit larger than a sentence. Discourse may comprise a statement, a dialogue, a debate, etc.

disyllabic Consisting of two syllables: e.g., *e·cho* and *be·lieve* are disyllabic words. A word is **monosyllabic** when having only one syllable (e.g., *bid*, *stretch*), **trisyllabic** when having three syllables (e.g., *un·der·stand*, *com·pa·ny*).

do **as auxiliary** *See* auxiliary.

dual *See* number.

–*(e)th* ending *See* third person present singular.

etymology The historical study of words, in relation to their earlier forms and meanings and also to the forms and meanings of their cognates.

feminine *See* gender.

finite verb *See* conjugation.

fricative A consonant having audible friction produced by forcing air through a constricted part in the mouth: e.g., /f, v, s, z, θ, ð/. *See further* "Note on Phonetic Symbols and Orthography."

fronting 1. Movement usually of back vowels to the front of the mouth: e.g., *good* sounding like *gid* in America's West Coast speech. 2. Movement of a syntactic element from its unmarked, or regular, position to the beginning of a sentence: e.g., *coming home he was*, a construction found in parts of Wales.

front vowel A vowel articulated with the highest point of the tongue placed at the front of the month. Front vowels in PDE include /i, ɪ, e, ɛ, æ/. *See further* "Note on Phonetic Symbols and Orthography."

function word Refers to words belonging to parts of speech that convey grammatical or logical relationship rather than lexical contents: e.g., prepositions (*on*, *from*), conjunctions (*but*, *or*).

future *See* tense.

gender In Old English, each noun has a gender: namely, **masculine**, **feminine**, or **neuter**. These **grammatical genders** are not directly related to natural genders:

e.g., *wif* ('woman') is neuter. This grammatical category has been lost in ModE, except for the personal pronouns *he*, *she*, and *it*.

genitive *See* case.

Germanic A branch of the Indo-European family to which English belongs. English is a member of the **West Germanic** division, together with German, Dutch, etc. The other two divisions are **North Germanic** (e.g., Danish, Norwegian) and **East Germanic** (Gothic).

glide A sound transition from one vowel to another (e.g., a diphthong as in *toy* or *eight*) or from one consonant to another (e.g., *cat* pronounced as /kyat/ and *boy* as /bway/ in some Caribbean varieties).

grammar The structure of a language esp. in contrast with vocabulary and pronunciation. A grammatical account is prescriptive or normative when given as correct usage, and descriptive when presented as a reflection of actual usage.

grammaticalization A historical process in which lexical words or phrases take on grammatical functions usu. from repeated usage: e.g., the auxiliary *wanna* from *want to*; the adverbial/adjectival ending *–ly* from OE *lic* ('body'); the prepositional phrase *in view of*.

grapheme A unit or character in a writing system: e.g., <i>, <t>. See further "Note on Phonetic Symbols and Orthography."

Great Vowel Shift Traditionally refers to a series of sound changes, beginning in the ME period and ending in ca. 1600, through which long vowels were raised and/or diphthongized: e.g., *food* from [foːd] to [fuːd], *house* from [huːs] to [haʊs].

Gullah English-based creole language spoken in coastal South Carolina and Georgia.

***h*-dropping** Non-realization of [h-] in the initial position of a word: e.g., *heir* (with *h*-dropping) as opposed to *hereditary* (without *h*-dropping). *H*-dropping is a common feature both historically and dialectally.

headword Refers to items listed at the beginning of dictionary entries.

high vowel A vowel articulated with the highest point of the tongue close to the top of the mouth: e.g., /i, u/. *See further* "Note on Phonetic Symbols and Orthography."

idiolect *See* dialect, social.

IE = Indo-European.

imperative *See* mood.

***i*-mutation** An OE sound change (sixth to seventh centuries) that resulted in the fronting and/or raising of vowels occurring near the sound [i] or [j]: e.g., ModE *man/ men*, *full/fill*.

inanimate *See* animate.

independent clause *See* clause type.

indicative *See* mood.

indirect object (IO) *See* clause element.

Indo-European (IE) The language family to which English belongs. It consists of divisions such as Germanic, Italic, Celtic, Indo-Iranian, among many others.

infinitive *See* conjugation.

inflection A change in the form of a word to provide grammatical information: e.g., *-s* as in *books* for plural; *-ed* as in *played* for past tense. Applies to both conjugation and declension.

interrogative *See* question.

intonation Articulation of speech pertaining to pitch, tone, and contour. Varieties of English can often be distinguished from each other by the intonation.

intransitive *See* transitive.

lengthening Sound change usu. involving the turning of a short vowel into a long vowel: e.g., a set of quantitative changes in ME known as the Open Syllable Lengthening. Sound change from long to short vowels is called **shortening.**

lexeme A word seen as a semantic unit in abstraction: e.g., items like *goes*, *going*, and *went* are forms of the lexeme *go*.

lexical Pertaining to words, vocabulary, or the lexicon.

lexicography Writing of a dictionary or dictionaries; done by **lexicographers.**

lexicon Vocabulary of a given language, esp. as opposed to grammar or speech sound. Also called **lexis**. The study of the structure of a lexicon is called **lexicology**.

lingua franca A language of communication used among people with different first languages.

linguistics An academic discipline or a scholarly field that concerns the study of language as science. The subfields of linguistics may be defined by their formal categories (e.g., phonology for the pattern of speech sounds, syntax for sentence structure), methods (e.g., **corpus linguistics** for electronic-based quantitative analysis), perspectives (e.g., **historical linguistics**), or intersections with non-formalistic factors (e.g., **cognitive linguistics** concerning information, **sociolinguistics** concerning social issues).

loan word A word borrowed from another language: e.g., *castle* (French), *inflammation* (Latin), *koala* (Australian aboriginal). In English, **borrowing** was a particularly productive method of word formation in the early modern period.

low vowel A vowel articulated with the tongue towards the low point of the mouth: e.g., /æ, ɑ/. *See further* "Note on Phonetic Symbols and Orthography."

main clause *See* clause type.

marker Any unit that indicates a specific feature: e.g., *–ed* as a tense marker for preterit; *-'s* as a case marker for the possessive; conjunctions like *when* and *although* as subordinate markers; a phonological or intonational pattern as a marker for the speaker's regional or social background.

masculine *See* gender.

mesolect *See* dialect, social.

meter Specific patterning of stress or rhythm employed in the composition of verse. The traditional meter of English was based on alliteration and stress. Later, syllable-based meters, such as iambic and trochaic, were adopted.

Middle English (ME) *See* periodization.

modal auxiliary *See* auxiliary.

Modern English (ModE) *See* periodization.

monophthong A vowel that is not a diphthong, that is, produced without any noticeable change in its quality: e.g., /ɪ/ in *bid* and /ʌ/ in *bug*. See further "Note on Phonetic Symbols and Orthography."

monosyllabic *See* disyllabic.

mood A verb form indicating the speaker's viewpoint on his or her utterance. PDE has three moods. **Indicative** is used for stating fact: e.g., *stopped* in *we stopped arguing*. **Subjunctive** expresses suggestion, hypothesis, etc.: e.g., *stop* in *I suggest that we stop arguing*. **Imperative** is used for command: e.g., *stop* in *stop arguing!*

morpheme The smallest meaningful unit in a language: e.g., the word *meaningful* consists of three morphemes, *mean* and the two affixes *-ing*, and *-ful*.

morphology The study of the inner structure of words including inflections and affixes.

morphosyntax Interaction between morphology and syntax: e.g., function of inflections on the sentence level; grammaticalization.

multiple negation Use of two or more negative elements in one sentence to denote negation: e.g., *I cannot go no further* (Shakespere); *I didn't say nothing* (colloquialism). It came to be considered non-standard in the prescriptive grammar of the eighteenth century.

nasal A speech sound produced by letting much of the air go through the nose. All of the three PDE nasals are consonants: /n, m, ŋ/. *See further* "Note on Phonetic Symbols and Orthography."

neuter *See* gender.

nominative *See* case.

number A grammatical category for counting. PDE has two numbers: **singular** and **plural**. The distinction is usually made by the inflectional ending *–s*: e.g., *one book*, *two books*. OE had an additional number, **dual**, for the personal pronouns *wit* ('we two') and *git* ('you two').

object (O) *See* clause element.

OE = Old English. *See* periodization.

Old English (OE) *See* periodization.

onomasiology The study of words approached from the topical viewpoint. Concerned with questions like "what is the name of this thing or concept?"

onset One or more consonants placed before the vowel of a syllable: e.g., *p-* in *pen*; *st-* in *star*.

orthoepy The study of correct pronunciation mostly in conformity with established speech patterns.

orthography Practice of writing, esp. in a conventional system of spelling. ModE orthography became established mostly by 1650, due to the rapidly growing print culture. OE orthography was developed in the monastic reform during the late tenth century.

palatalization Sound change involving consonants adjacent to [y/j] or a front vowel: e.g., OE [g] became [y/j] in *geard* ('yard'); ModE [z] has become [ž/ʒ] in *occasion*; in PDE [t] in the collocation *without you* may be pronounced as [č/ʧ].

participle *See* conjugation.

part of speech *See* word class.

passive *See* voice, grammatical.

past *See* tense.

PDE = Present-Day English. *See* periodization.

perfect *See* aspect.

periodization The history of English is conventionally divided into three periods. **Old English (OE)** spans beginnings through the Norman Conquest and the few subsequent decades. The term **Anglo-Saxon** may be used for Old English to underline its connection with the Germanic languages of the Continent. The second period is **Middle English (ME)**, which ends in the late fifteenth century. ME is often divided into Early and Late Middle English, though without a clear dividing point. The third period is **Modern English (ModE)**. Early Modern English corresponds roughly with the Renaissance period. Contemporary English may be called **Present-Day English (PDE)**, although there is no consensus as to when it begins.

periphrasis The use of one or more additional words rather than inflections to express grammatical information: e.g., *more gentle* as opposed to *gentler*. Some periphrastic constructions include auxiliaries: e.g., progressive (*they **are** running*), perfect (*we **have** moved*), and the auxiliary *do* (***do** not ask* as opposed to the older construction *ask not*).

person A grammatical category which subdivides into three parts: **first person** (*I* and *we*) referring to the speaker(s); **second person** (*you*) referring to the addressee(s); and **third person** (*he, she, it*, and *they*) referring to one or more individuals who are neither the speaker(s) nor the addressee(s).

philology The study of language in its cultural and social contexts. May refer specifically to the study of historical languages before the rise of modern linguistics in the early twentieth century.

phoneme The smallest unit of sound to make a semantic distinction in a given language: e.g., the words *top* and *tap* are distinguished by the phonemes /ɑ/ and /æ/. *See further* "Note on Phonetic Symbols and Orthography." An **allophone** is a variant of a phoneme: e.g., the sound [v] was an allophone of /f/ in Old English; hence [væt] would have been a variant pronunciation of *fæt* ('vessel'). The **phonemicization** of [v] and several other consonants took place in Middle English.

phonetics The study of speech sounds. *See further* "Note on Phonetic Symbols and Orthography."

phonology The study of phonemes and other characteristics of the systems of speech sounds in individual languages.

pidgin A language variety developed usu. in a trade colony as a language of communication for European traders and the local populations. Pidgins typically have a reduced linguistic structure at first but may gain complexity both in grammar and vocabulary as they are used by generations of speakers as vernaculars: e.g., Tok Pisin, Nigerian Pidgin English.

plosive *See* stop.

plural *See* number.

possessive A grammatical form for indicating possession: <'s> is a possessive ending for nouns (e.g., *cat's paw*); **possessive adjectives** include *my, their*, etc. and **possessive pronouns** include *mine, theirs*, etc. *See also* genitive *under* case.

pragmatic Pertains to meaning yielded at various levels of usage or in the context of utterances. **Pragmatics** is the study of such meaning.

predicate *See* clause element.

prefix *See* affix.

present *See* tense.

Present-Day English (PDE) *See* periodization.

prestige Pertaining to a language, dialect, or form that is considered to have greater social value than others: e.g., in much of the ME period, French was a prestige language in England; in the late ME period, the London variety of English became a prestige dialect.

preterit *See* tense.

progressive *See* aspect.

prosody 1. In the study of poetry, it concerns meter and other techniques of versification. 2. In the study of spoken sounds, it concerns intonation, pitch, stress, rhythm, etc.

protolanguage An unrecorded or unattested language from which a group of historically attested languages have presumably derived. Hence all Indo-European languages are supposed to share **Proto-Indo-European** as parent language. Likewise, **Proto-Germanic** is the presumed ancestor of all Germanic languages.

question A sentence that asks for information or response. Also called **interrogative**. In a **yes-no question**, the expected answer is either "yes" or "no": e.g., *did you see them?* A **wh-question** is formed with a *wh-* word like *when, where, who*: e.g., *when did you see them?*

raising Movement of the pronunciation of a vowel to a higher point in the mouth: e.g., English in New Zealand is characterized by the raising of the short /æ/ to /ɛ/, and the short /ɛ/ to /ɪ/.

Received Pronunciation (RP) Prestige accent in Present-Day British English. Originally based on English in London and southern England, RP has come to be spoken as a geographically non-localized variety among the educated class.

register A style or variety of language used for a specific occasion or purpose (e.g., liturgy, courting), or adopted by a particular social group or genre of writing (e.g., polite speech, legal document).

relative clause, relative pronoun *See* clause type.

rhotic May refer to varieties of English that articulate /r/ in all positions of a word. **Non-rhotic** varieties pronounce /r/ before vowels (e.g., *red*) but not after vowels (e.g., *car, third*).

RP = Received Pronunciation.

S = subject. *See* clause element.

schwa A vowel pronounced in the central part of the mouth: e.g., *u* in *bud*, *a* in *trial*. Its phonetic symbol is [ə]. *See further* "Note on Phonetic Symbols and Orthography."

Second person singular and plural (*you, thou,* etc.) In Old and Early Middle English, second person singular and plural were morphologically distinguished (e.g., *þu* and *ge*). In the thirteenth century, English adopted the French custom of using the plural form for the singular to register respect or politeness. This dual usage of *thou/ye* for second-person singular lasted until early Modern English when the plural form (*you*) became the norm for the singular. Some varieties of English employ distinct forms for second-person plural: e.g., *y'all, yous*.

semantics The linguistic study of meaning.

shortening *See* lengthening.

singular *See* number.

sociolinguistics The study of language in its social context.

standardization Establishment of a system of spelling, grammar, or pronunciation as a prestige variety.

stop Refers to consonants such as /p, t, k, b, d, g/. Produced by blocking the flow of air before articulating. Also called **plosive**. See further "Note on Phonetic Symbols and Orthography."

stress Auditory prominence (loudness, duration, etc.) given to a syllable in the articulation of a word or sentence: e.g., in the word *suc·cess*, the syllable *–cess* is **stressed**. In poetry, each line has a metrical pattern created by stressed and unstressed syllables.

subject (S) *See* clause element.

subjunctive *See* mood.

subordinate clause *See* clause type.

substrate, substratum (*pl.* **substrata**) A non-dominant language or variety of language that has nonetheless influenced the dominant language or variety of language in a given community: e.g., Irish influences on the English language in Ireland; African influences on Gullah.

suffix *See* affix.

synchronic Pertaining to language at a specific historical point (and at least within a generation): e.g., analysis of syntax, phonology, etc. in PDE. *Cf.* diachronic.

syntax The study of the grammatical arrangement of words within sentences, clauses, or phrases.

synthetic language A language that uses inflections to convey grammatical information: *gentler, gentlest*. An **analytical language** tends to use separate words to convey grammatical information: e.g., *more gentle, most gentle*. OE is more synthetic than ModE, whereas some English-based creoles are more analytical than PDE.

tense A grammatical category for the indication of time through the forms of verbs. Historically, Proto-Indo-European had five to six formal tenses, but the number was reduced to two in Germanic. Hence English has two formal tenses: **present** (e.g., *it works*) and **past** or **preterit** (e.g., *it worked*). In addition, English has developed **future** indications through auxiliaries (e.g., *it will work, I am going to rest*).

third person present singular *–(e)th* and *–(e)s* The OE and ME form for this verb conjugation was *–(e)þ/–(e)th*: e.g., *he drincþ win* ('he drinks wine'). This historical form was gradually replaced by the dialectal variant *–(e)s* until the latter became the norm by 1600. Some varieties of PDE demonstrate *-s* absence: e.g., *she walk* for *she walks*.

transitive Pertains to verbs occurring with a direct object: e.g., *she has a car*. Verbs are **intransitive** when they take no direct object: e.g., *she walks to school*. Some verbs may be used either as transitive or intransitive: e.g., *God divided the Red Sea; the Red Sea divided*.

trisyllabic *See* disyllabic.

typology Classification of languages according to general features of their design, such as synthetic/analytic spectrum or element order. Typologically, English became more analytic (and less synthetic) as it passed from OE to ME to ModE. Like many other Germanic languages, OE had a tendency towards **verb-second (V-2)** order, that is, a tendency to place the finite verb immediately after the first constituent, or element, of an independent clause (cf. *never did I know the fact*); subsequently, English became an SVO language, that is, a language characterized by Subject–Verb–Object element order (e.g., *I never knew the fact*).

variant An alternative form for a given linguistic unit, such as spelling, inflection, intonation, phoneme. A variant usu. refers to a less common or non-standard form.

velar A consonant produced by the back of the tongue against the velum or the soft palate: e.g., /k, g, ŋ/. *See further* "Note on Phonetic Symbols and Orthography."

verb second (V-2) *See* typology.

vernacular 1. A native tongue spoken by members of a community where a different language carries prestige: e.g., in medieval England, English was a vernacular in relation to Latin, the language of the Church; in colonies or post-colonies where English was or is the official language, local varieties – whether non-European aboriginal languages or English-based creoles – may be considered vernaculars. 2. A non-standard variety native to some members of the community: e.g., AAVE or Latino varieties of English as opposed to standard American English.

vocalic Pertaining to a vowel or vowels. Hence **postvocalic** means occurring after a vowel (e.g., *r* in *car*); **prevocalic** means occurring before a vowel (e.g., *the* in the phrase *the apple*); and **intervocalic** means between vowels (e.g., *f* in the OE *hlaford* 'lord', pronounced as [v]).

voice, grammatical The way in which the relationship between a verb and a subject is expressed. The **active** voice indicates that the subject is the agent of the action stated in the verb: e.g., *they **wrote the report***. The **passive** voice indicates that the subject is the recipient of the action stated in the verb: e.g., *the report **was written** by them*. PIE and Gothic had the medio-passive voice.

voice, phonetic Refers to speech sounds produced with vibration of the vocal cords. Includes all vowels and many consonants. In PDE, **voiced** consonants include /b, d, g, v, z, ð/. **Voiceless** consonants included /p, t, k, f, s, θ/. *See further* "Note on Phonetic Symbols and Orthography."

vowel Refers to speech sounds other than consonants: e.g., [ɪ, u, æ, ɑ]. A vowel is produced without major restriction on the flow of air in the mouth and can comprise the center of a syllable. *See further* "Note on Phonetic Symbols and Orthography."

word class A category referring to a group of words that share syntactic and morphological characteristics. Also called **part of speech**. Word classes in traditional English grammar include **noun** (e.g., *tree, imagination*), **adjective** (e.g., *thin, indispensable*), **adverb** (*slowly, therefore, very*), **verb** (*to tell, to concentrate*), **pronoun** (*you, everyone, many*), **preposition** (*from, upon*), **conjunction** (*and, although, when*).

Index